D0080461

An Introduction to ANSI C on UNIX

Wes Given

Paul S. Wang
Kent State University

PWS Publishing Company
Boston

PWS
Publishing Company

20 Park Plaza
Boston, Massachusetts 02116

Computer Science Editor: *Frank Ruggirello*
Editorial Assistant: *Rhonda Gray*
Production: *Ruth Cottrell*
Print Buyer: *Martha Branch*
Designer: *John Edeen*
Copy Editor: *Betty Duncan*
Cover painting: Between *by Dina Herrmann*
Cover Design: *Paula Goldstein*
Signing Representative: *Art Minsberg*
Compositor: *Ocean View Technical Publications*

UNIX is a registered trademark of American Telephone and Telegraph
Company (AT&T).

*This book is printed on acid-free paper that meets Environmental Protection
Agency standards for recycled paper.*

© 1993 by PWS Publishing Company. © 1992 by Wadsworth, Inc.
All rights reserved. No part of this book may be reproduced, stored in a retrieval
system, or transcribed, in any form or by any means -- electronic, mechanical,
photocopying, recording, or otherwise -- without the prior written permission
of the publisher, PWS Publishing Company, 20 Park Plaza, Boston MA.

PWS Publishing Company is a division of Wadsworth, Inc.

4 5 6 7 8 9 10—96 95 94

Library of Congress Cataloging-in-Publication Data

Wang, Paul S.
    An introduction to ANSI C on UNIX / Paul S. Wang.
      p.   cm.
    Includes index.
    ISBN 0-534-14232-X (alk. paper)
     1. C (Computer program language) 2. UNIX (Computer file)
  I. Title.
QA76.73.C15W355 1992
005. 13'3—ac20
                                     91-24324
                                         CIP

Contents

8   Performing Input and Output   251

9   Error Handling and Debugging   273

10   Unix System I/O Facilities   301

11   Program Maintenance   329

12   Multiprogramming   353

Appendices

Index

Preface

C is one of the most popular programming languages in both academia and industry. With the new ANSI standard, C becomes uniform across different computer systems, further fueling its rapid growth. However, because of their historical relationships, UNIX remains the best environment for teaching, learning, and applying C. Evolved from *traditional* C, ANSI standard C offers new and improved constructs making the language even better. Many systems offer both traditional and ANSI C compilers, and some compilers can process either style of program. Converting a program written in one to the other is also easy.

The book is for learning C as a second language and assumes access to a UNIX system. The coverage follows the ANSI standard and takes full advantage of the environment and utilities on UNIX. The presentation is straightforward and easy to follow. The early chapters are quite gentle, but the pace quickens as you make progress. The material contains much information, advice, and good examples. Features of this text are described in detail next.

Introduction to UNIX

One strength of this textbook is anticipating the needs of students. It begins with a good introduction to UNIX, covering features related to C programming: use of the Shell, the **vi** text editor, compiling and running C programs, dealing with files, controlling multiple jobs, and so on. Other related topics of UNIX are covered as the need arises. The popular **emacs** editor is also explained in Appendix 1.

Hands-On Approach

The best way to learn programming is to write programs. A primer collects basic information on C so that you can begin to write complete and nontrivial programs early. Simple input/output, decision making, iteration, command-line arguments, and error handling are covered so you can write useful programs and run them as commands on UNIX. Advice on thinking effectively in C and developing a consistent formatting style is also given.

Comprehensive Coverage

The book goes on to cover many subjects in depth. Besides the basic topics, the C preprocessor, separate compilation, recursive programming, dynamic-storage management, use of standard library functions, input/output functions and system calls, error handling, and debugging are also covered. Examples help illustrate C constructs and how they are applied together rather than in isolation. Modern software concepts such as data abstraction, program encapsulation, and generic functions are introduced and practiced.

Arrays and Pointers Made Easy

The single, most crucial and difficult topic in C programming is pointers. This text uses an intuitive approach to treating pointers that makes this important concept clear and straightforward. The approach leads naturally into an understanding of pointers from the viewpoint of arrays, which is easier to grasp. Multiple dimensional arrays are also presented clearly. The use of pointers in conjunction with other constructs is explained explicitly with examples. Many practical applications show the power and efficiency afforded by arrays and pointers.

Writing Good Programs

An Introduction to ANSI C on UNIX is more than a book on the syntax and semantics of the C language. It teaches how to write good programs to solve problems. Program structures, file organization, breaking down a large problem into manageable pieces, and methods to handle errors and exceptions are discussed throughout the book. Rules of thumb are given for writing programs that are less likely to contain errors and easier to test and debug.

Testing and Debugging

Unless and until a program can be rigorously proven correct, thorough testing and debugging is still necessary to improve program reliability. Techniques for testing programs and locating bugs are discussed. The interactive debugger **dbx** of UNIX is presented and applied to several programs. The **dbx** utility makes the difficult task of debugging much easier.

Use of Library Functions

The standard library functions are an integral part of C. Familiarity with their use and application provides an important advantage because using well-written and well-tested library functions is better than "reinventing the wheel." Two chapters are devoted to library functions covering input/output, characters, strings, storage allocation, and numeric standard library functions. Ample examples show how these functions are used in practical applications.

Basic and Advanced Materials

The book contains enough material for a second programming course (two to three credit hours) at the sophomore or junior level in college. Such a course would begin with careful coverage of Chapters 1 and 2. Many small and medium-size programs can be worked on by the time Chapter 3 is covered. Parts of Chapter 4 on the C preprocessor can be saved for later. The topics of arrays, pointers, library functions, and structuring of data are the main focus and the materials are interesting and challenging for the best of students. Chapters 10–12 are optional.

The text can also be used for a more advanced course on C (or C and UNIX) at the senior college or beginning graduate level. The first two chapters can be covered quickly, leaving more time to concentrate on the rest of the book. The main focus should be covered carefully. Larger programming projects can be assigned. Finer points in formatted input/output, I/O system calls of UNIX, the *curses* library, program profiling, the *make* facility, and multiprogramming can be included. Material in Chapter 12 will keep even the most advanced students happy.

It is also possible to use the book in conjunction with a text on UNIX for a comprehensive UNIX operating system course.

Easy Reference

As an instructional guide, this text reads smoothly and presents subjects in a bottom-up approach, building new materials on old ones that have been covered already. However, this book is also a valuable reference tool. Information has been organized for easy reference with in-line explanations for commands, tables, figures, and summaries to help collect information together. There are also twelve appendices and a comprehensive index for locating answers to specific topics.

ANSI Standard C Versus Traditional C

Although the text is based on ANSI C, it can also be used effectively as a traditional C book. Many examples run under both versions. Others require simple changes to compile by a traditional C compiler. However, teaching ANSI C is advisable because it is the standard for the future.

C compilers that conform to the ANSI standard are widely available from computer vendors. Also, the Free Software Foundation offers a very good implementation of ANSI C that runs on most UNIX systems. It can be obtained free of charge from

> The Free Software Foundation
> 675 Massachusetts Avenue
> Cambridge, MA 02139
> (617) 876–3296

Machine-Readable Examples

Throughout the text, concepts and programming constructs are amply illustrated with examples of practical importance. There are over 120 files containing source codes in ANSI C. The machine-readable examples are available together with the **vi** macros in Appendix 3 in either 5¼ inch or 3½ inch format for $14.75 from

SOFPOWER
3766 Fishcreek Road, Suite 177
Stow, OH 44224

An order form appears at the back of this book.

Acknowledgments

The actual writing of this book began in 1989 when the suggestion was made in our department to upgrade our C course into a three-credit required course. The course is now a formal part of our computer science curriculum. In the beginning, John G. Michalakes considered being a coauthor but was unable to do so because of his busy schedule. However, I still enjoyed our debates about how to make the book better and the many suggestions he shared with me. Later, John also served as a reviewer of the final draft and made additional comments and observations. I am grateful to him. Deep appreciation also goes to Scott Rhine, a computer science student with an interest in writing, who helped review early drafts, corrected errors, and suggested improvements. Many thanks, too, go to Frank Ruggirello, computer science editor at Wadsworth, whose expert guidance has been very important. I also wish to express my thanks to the following reviewers for their suggestions and comments: David Bozak, SUNY Oswego; John Connely, California Polytechnic State University–San Luis Obispo; John Cross, Indiana University of Pennsylvania; Nerain Gehani, Bell Laboratories; John Michalalakes, Argonne National Laboratory; Charles Miller, Shippensburg University; John Remmers, Eastern Michigan University; and Dan Stubbs, California Polytechnic State University–San Luis Obispo.

Last, but not least, I want to thank my wife, Jennifer, and children, Laura and Deborah, for their support and encouragement.

Introduction

The C language and the UNIX operating system are well-established standards in the computer industry. Together, they lead the trend toward portability and open-system architecture. UNIX is the best and most widely available environment to learn and use C. Furthermore, C and UNIX share one common programming philosophy: "small is beautiful." This principle contributes greatly to their success and ever-increasing popularity.

A programming language is a medium with which you communicate with the computer. As a general-purpose programming language, C is compact, efficient, and portable. With the establishment of the ANSI standard, C becomes uniform across different computer systems. Your knowledge of C will always be useful, and the same C program will run on a wide variety of computer systems.

The C language, with just over 30 reserved words, is easy to learn, but its power and conciseness make mastering C a real challenge. After you become familiar with the language, you will find C an efficient medium to convey your programming ideas.

Evolution of C

In 1970, Ken Thompson, of AT&T Bell Laboratories, wrote an early version of the UNIX system in B, a language derived from the earlier BCPL language developed by Martin Richards. At about the same time, Thompson and Dennis Ritchie were working on an early version of C, which they improved and expanded, enabling UNIX to be rewritten in C in 1973.

Both BCPL and B influenced the design of C. However, unlike the two *typeless* languages, C provides a variety of data types. The original definition of the C language was set forth in the C reference manual contained in *The C Programming Language* published in 1978. Since then, the C language and the UNIX system have evolved together and become very popular. In 1983, the American National Standards Institute (ANSI) formed a committee to establish a modern, complete definition of C. The result, after more than five years of standardization work, is the ANSI standard C or ANSI C. The ANSI standard incorporates the traditional C language together with many popular extensions. This book follows the ANSI standard.

Features of C

C is a language that is general enough for all types of programming but also efficient enough for writing system programs. The language supports several built-in data types. Basic types are characters, integers, and floating-point numbers of several sizes. The array groups a number of elements of the same basic type for easy access and manipulation. From these, you can create data types of your own design.

Constants, variables, and function calls are simple expressions; each expression has a value. Expressions are combined with operators to form larger ones. Operations on a few bits or even a single bit are possible. This allows you to have low-level control over data and operations when necessary for added efficiency.

In C, functions can be recursive. Arguments for functions are always passed by copying their values (*pass by value*). Local variables are normally *automatic*, or created and destroyed with each function invocation. Global variables can span just a single file or the entire program. A function can return a value of any basic or derived type.

A C program consists of one or more *source-code files* containing data and function definitions. Each source-code file is regarded as a *compilation unit* by the C compiler and can be compiled independently. Compiled files, called *object files*, are used to build the executable version of the C program.

ANSI Standard C

The ANSI standard for the C language is based on traditional C and contains relatively little change. Because many traditional C programs have been written through the years, one should be aware of the main differences between traditional and ANSI C. Most traditional C programs, however, should work in ANSI C without modification. Also, modifying ANSI C programs to work as traditional C programs is simple.

The most important ANSI C feature is the syntax for declaring and defining functions. The parameter types are declared inside, instead of after, the function parameter list. This is a welcome change and allows compilers to easily detect errors caused by mismatched function call arguments. Other ANSI C additions include assignment of user-defined structures, enumerations, and single-precision floating-point arithmetic (traditional C supports only double-precision arithmetic). The ANSI standard also bans the interchange of pointers and integers without explicit type conversions.

In addition, ANSI C now defines a *standard library* to accompany the language. The library contains functions to perform input/output, manipulate strings, calculate mathematical functions, access the operating system, and so on. Also included is a set of standard *header files* to provide the necessary declarations for any program to use the library. A program must include the correct header files for the particular library functions employed. Special header files also record system-dependent quantities such as the size of the largest integer and floating-point number. The library and the headers closely model the standard I/O library and other libraries already available on UNIX systems.

C compilers that conform to the ANSI standard are becoming widely available. For instance, the **gcc** (Gnu C compiler) is a very good implementation of ANSI C and is available from the Free Software Foundation at no cost (see "Preface"). This compiler runs on UNIX and can be obtained via computer networks.

C and UNIX

You can write system-level programs in C for UNIX. Therefore, UNIX remains the ideal system and predominant environment for learning and using C. The popularity of UNIX makes both traditional and ANSI C widely available. The richness of C-related tools on UNIX makes programming convenient and productive. Among the utilities are

- Efficient text editors
- Well-tested and full-featured C compiler
- Command shells with control of multiple jobs
- Hierarchical file structure with access control
- Interactive source-level debugging
- Direct system calls from C
- Additional program libraries
- Uniform file, device, and interprocess input and output
- Tools for creating and maintaining program libraries
- Performance-measuring and analysis utilities
- Automation of program maintenance
- Multiprogramming
- Interprocess communication

This is only a partial list of helpful features and facilities covered in this book. The goal is not to teach UNIX but to explain those UNIX features as they relate to C. Familiarity with these features will make C programming much easier and you much more productive as a programmer.

The establishment of ANSI C will help the language become available on more non-UNIX systems. Even then, these "foreign" systems will most likely try to emulate what UNIX already offers.

UNIX Systems

UNIX is a multiuser time-sharing system. You interact with the system by issuing commands and receiving results on a terminal or workstation. Within the overall file system, you have your personal file directory known as your *home directory*. A text editor, such as **vi** or **emacs**, creates text files and prepares programs. Normally, you create a C source-code file and put it in a file, often in your own home directory. You can then compile your program with a UNIX command to produce an *executable file* that will execute your program. It is also possible to invoke your own program in exactly the same manner as any other UNIX command.

Many versions of UNIX exist, but they are all basically the same system adapted to run on different computers. In fact, major computer makers now offer and support UNIX systems with their own enhancements: SUN-OS from Sun Micro Systems, ULTRIX from Digital Equipment Corporation (DEC), Hewlett-Packard's HP-UX, and AIX from IBM. Parallel computer vendors such as Encore and Sequent have adopted UNIX to control multi-processors. But the two most widely used versions continue to be the AT&T-supported UNIX System V and Berkeley UNIX, from the University of California at Berkeley (UCB). Our presentation of the C language will assume the general UNIX environment. If a particular usage is different under Berkeley or System V UNIX, it will be specifically noted.

Organization of Materials

This book is intended for someone who is learning a second programming language. Access to a UNIX system and an ANSI C compiler[1] is assumed. No familiarity with UNIX is necessary, and enough introductory material for UNIX usage is included to make learning C on UNIX a pleasant experience.

Care has been taken to make the material straightforward and easy to understand. The best way to learn programming is to write programs. Thus, you will begin writing whole programs early. Interesting examples and challenging exercises encourage this hands-on approach. The early chapters are quite gentle. There are many basic examples, a guide on program style, and suggestions on effective thinking in C. The pace, however, does pick up. When you are through, you will have gained a level of unusual proficiency.

One of the most difficult topics in C for a beginner is *pointers*. Our presentation leads into the pointer concept from the more well-understood array construct. Many practical examples are given with illustrations on how pointers are used either by themselves or in combination with other features of C. The result should prove to be a very clear explanation of this key topic.

Materials here are presented with a modern point of view. Concepts from structured programming, functional programming, data abstraction, and program encapsulation are employed in the framework of C programming. Many topics, normally left out by lower-level books, are covered in depth.

Chapter 1 provides a brief introduction to the UNIX system to familiarize you with the operating and programming environment. Enough basic information is given on files, shell commands, the C compiler, I/O redirection, and UNIX processes, to get you started in the right direction.

Chapter 2 follows with a C primer covering enough basics to get you started writing whole programs: program structure, constants, variables, function definitions, expressions, control flow, and decision-making statements. Also discussed are character arrays, command-line arguments, and error handling.

Chapter 3 deals with key constructs in C, such as iteration, multiple branching (`switch`), internal and external variables (scoping), recursion, type definitions (`typedef`), and type conversions. Emphasis is on recursive programming techniques and problem solving with recursion. Many examples illustrate the power of recursion.

Chapter 4 presents the C preprocessor, which constitutes the first stage of the C compiler. Header file inclusion, symbolic constant definition, and macro expansion are explained.

---

[1] Available from the Free Software Foundation at no cost (see "Preface").

Chapter 5 introduces important standard library functions for string manipulation, variable argument lists, dynamic storage allocation, and mathematical calculations. Applications show how these functions are used in practice. When writing a program, it is important to avoid "reinventing the wheel" and to use existing library functions as much as possible.

The critical subject of arrays and pointers is the only focus of Chapter 6. Because pointer concepts tend to be hard to grasp, special attention has been paid to making the descriptions clear and easy to follow. The method used is to lead into a full discussion of pointers from the viewpoint of an array, a subject much easier to master. The use of arrays and pointers in applications is demonstrated extensively. Through pointers, you can also pass function names as arguments and manipulate data of arbitrary types.

A large part of programming lies in the representation and structuring of data. Chapter 7 covers the subject of establishing user-defined data types. For a program, the data structure used will affect the way procedures are written as well as the run-time performance. Thus, well-structured data are every bit as crucial to a program as efficient procedures. Many commonly used data structures are given as examples. Many practical applications are shown.

Input and output supported by the standard library is the subject of Chapter 8. These library functions allow you to use buffered I/O streams, control I/O formats, open new streams, close streams, delete/rename files, and read/write text or binary files. We also show how arrays and structures can be handled in I/O operations.

Chapter 9 describes ways to handle errors from library and system calls, treatment of signals, and debugging. The interactive debugger **dbx** and its application are explained in detail. Rules of thumb on writing good programs and techniques for program testing are also presented.

Chapter 10 covers I/O facilities supplied by UNIX. These include directory and file status access, low-level I/O system calls, I/O to the terminal, and the *curses package*. Relations between the low-level I/O routines and the I/O stream supported by the C library are explained. A full window-oriented menu program to illustrate the use of the curses package is included.

Chapter 11 describes a set of useful UNIX tools for organizing, managing, and maintaining your C programs. These include the compiler, linker/loader, performance profiler, indexing tagger, the library maintenance tool **ar**, and the maintenance automation facility **make**.

Multiprogramming is the subject of Chapter 12. Here you'll learn how to create and control concurrent processes, coordinate their activities, and send and receive messages between processes. The material is very interesting but more advanced. The instructor may include or exclude the material depending on the level of the course.

There are 12 appendices to complement the material presented and to collect related information in one place. Beginners will find summaries on **vi**, **emacs**, the ASCII character set, UNIX commands, and C constructs useful. The completeness of the appendices will make the book a handy reference.

A Programmer's Introduction to UNIX

The use of UNIX is ever-increasing in academic institutions, industry, and government organizations. Powerful but low-cost UNIX workstations are available from almost all major computer vendors including SUN, DEC, HP, IBM, and UNISYS, to name a few. UNIX also runs on personal computers.

This chapter contains introductory materials to UNIX for the purpose of using and learning C. The interactive use of the UNIX system shell, a user interface and command interpreter, is described. Other topics include editing text (**vi**), compiling programs (**cc**), managing on-line files, redirecting input and output, and controlling multiple-running programs.

UNIX and C derive some of their power and efficiency from the terse notations used. Many beginners may find the commands cryptic and hard to remember. But once you are familiar with the notations, you will enjoy their brevity and power.

We will concentrate on features of UNIX most directly related to the immediate needs of writing C programs. As a result, some topics are excluded on purpose. More advanced relationships and interactions between C and UNIX will be discussed as needed in later parts of the book.

If you have little prior exposure to UNIX, this chapter will get you started. If you have some experience, skip over the parts that you know.

1.1 The UNIX System Shell

After login, you interact with UNIX through a user-interface program called the *shell*; the shell program invoked upon login is called the *login shell*. You issue commands to the shell to initiate all computations, including invoking the C programs you will write. The shell displays a prompt signaling that it is ready and waiting for your next command, which it then interprets and executes. On completion, the shell again signals readiness by displaying another prompt.

There are several popular shells:

- *sh* shell: The original shell written by S. R. Bourne, also known as the *Bourne shell*
- *ksh* shell: The Korn shell, an enhanced *sh*
- *csh* shell: The C-shell developed at UCB

All these shells are programmed in C. The primary function of a shell is to serve as a *command interpreter* that reads your command and tells the system what to do. Each defines a specific syntax for giving these commands. The *csh* uses a command syntax similar to that of the C language, hence the name C-shell. For *sh* and *ksh*, the prompt is usually the dollar sign ($) at the beginning of a line. For *csh*, the prompt is usually the percent sign (%). We shall refer to any of these as "the shell" and make a distinction only when necessary.

Shell Commands

As already mentioned, virtually anything you do on a UNIX system is done by issuing a command at the shell level. Some commands are contained inside the shell itself (*shell built-in commands*), but most are independent programs automatically located and executed through the shell (*nonbuilt-in commands*). Invoking the C compiler and executing your own C program are examples of the latter.

A command consists of one or more words separated by blanks. A *blank* consists of one or more SPACE and/or TAB characters. The first word is the *command name* (from here on, the name of a command will appear in **bold-face**), while the remaining words of a command line are *arguments* to the command. When typing a command line, terminate it by pressing the RETURN key. This key generates a NEWLINE character, the actual character that terminates a command line. Multiple commands can be typed on the same line if they are separated by a semicolon (;).

The simple form for a command looks like this:

command *arg* ...

Figure 1.1: Command Interpretation Cycle

The arguments are usually filenames, and the number of arguments depends on the particular command. The ellipses (. . .) indicate possible additional arguments. Some commands may take no argument. For instance,

   ls

lists the names of files in a directory.

Sometimes an *option* is given on the command line to specify a particular *command option* to make the command behave in a modified way. For example, if **ls** is followed by a space and then −a, the "all" option is activated and

   ls −a

lists all files rather than leaving out certain files (those whose names begin with a period). Another form

   ls −l *filename*

tells **ls** to list information just for one file and to use the "long" option, thus requesting a more detailed report on the given file.

After receiving a command, the shell goes through the command interpretation cycle (Figure 1.1). Having read in the command as typed on the keyboard, the shell transforms the command string through a series of well-defined substitutions. The substitution mechanism lets you reuse a previous command (history), type a different name (alias) for a command, use wildcard characters in filenames, and reference values of shell-level variables. Only the latter two substitutions are supported uniformly by the three shells *sh*, *ksh*, and *csh*. These features will be explained when the need arises.

The transformed command is then executed. A shell built-in command is executed directly by calling the shell subroutine supporting the command. The execution of a nonbuilt-in command is more complicated. The shell executes the given nonbuilt-in command as a *child process*, the shell being the *parent process*. The child process *inherits* the *running environment* of its parent (see Section 1.8).

After a command is executed, the shell will display the next prompt. For example, if you enter the nonbuilt-in command

    who

it is run as a child process that displays a summary of users currently on the system. Here is a typical output of **who**:

```
rsmith    ttyp0    May 12 12:10
pwang     ttyp1    May 10 17:37
jdoe      ttyp2    May 12 13:13
```

The output shows the login name, terminal identification, and time of login for each user on-line. The above output is followed by a prompt displayed by your shell.

Concise documentation for all the available commands is kept on the system as files. On-line access to the manual descriptions of any nonbuilt-in command is obtained by simply entering

    man *command-name*

Built-in commands are described as part of the particular shell whose description is accessed the same way:

    man csh
    man sh

Aborting a Command

It is possible to abort a command before it is finished. For instance, you may issue a command and then realize that you have made a mistake. Perhaps you give a command, and nothing happens. Or you are testing your C program and it gets into an infinite loop or misbehaves in some other way. These are occasions when you want to abort execution of the command. To abort, simply type the *interrupt character*, which is usually the DELETE key or ^C, where ^C is control-C. This interrupts (forcefully terminates) execution and returns you to the shell level. (In this book we use the symbol ^X to stand for control-X for any letter X.)

It is important for you to first identify what is your interrupt character. You then can interrupt any computation that is not going right. This is especially handy when you are experimenting with C programs that are yet to be debugged. Try the following:

1. Type part of a command.
2. Before you press RETURN, press DELETE or ^C.
3. The character that cancels the command and gives you a prompt is your interrupt character.

1.1.1 Output Control

You can also control the output that you receive on the terminal. If the information is screening by too fast for you to read, entering

will halt output until you type

to resume output. If there is too much output and you don't want to see it any more, type

and the rest of the output from the command being executed will be discarded.

1.2 Source-Code Editing: The Visual Editor vi

You need to use a text editor to create and modify C programs. Several editors are available under UNIX, but **vi** (pronounced vee-eye) is the standard full-screen editor. Actually, **vi** is the only screen editor officially supplied with System V and Berkeley UNIX. This section introduces enough of **vi** for editing C programs. Readers who are familiar with **vi** or choose to use another editor may skip this section. Another popular editor is **emacs**, which is summarized in Appendix 1.

Full-screen editors such as **vi** make use of special protocols for addressing and moving the cursor—protocols available on most modern CRT terminals. Because these protocols differ from terminal to terminal, the operating system needs to know the type of terminal you are using. This won't be a problem on the terminals connected directly to your system; it already knows their type. Informing the system to accommodate a different terminal type is possible. Do this by setting the shell environment variable TERM

```
setenv  TERM vt200
```

in *csh*. In *sh* or *ksh*, you need to set the variable and use the **export** command to put that variable in the environment:

```
TERM = vt200
export TERM
```

Of course, you need to know what terminal you are using. It is recommended that you use a direct-connect terminal for the time being.

Normally, the setting of the terminal type is included in a system file (`.login` for *csh* and `.profile` for *sh* and *ksh*) in your home directory. Your login shell reads this file every time you log in. You can edit these standard files to add any commands you need for every login session.

To invoke the editor **vi** from the shell level, type

> **vi** *file*

to edit the file named *file*. If the file exists, your screen will display the beginning of the file. Otherwise, you will create a new file by that name. A C source-code file usually uses the file name suffix `.c`. Once inside **vi**, you are working in an environment different from the shell. In **vi** you can create text, make changes, move text about, and so on. To exit from **vi** and save the file with the changes, type the **vi** command

> **zz**   (save *file* and exit **vi**)

which makes the changes permanent on the disk, terminates **vi**, and returns to the shell level. If you want to quit **vi** without saving the changes, type the **vi** command

> **:q!**   (exit **vi**, no save)

followed by a RETURN.

Let's go through a quick editing session. Type

> **vi** myfile

to call **vi** on a file named `myfile`. Because `myfile` does not yet exist, it will be created. The screen will clear except for a column of tilde (~) characters, a cursor, and perhaps a brief message on the last line. The **vi** editor has two modes: the command mode and the insert mode. The *command mode* is used for moving the cursor, deleting text, moving text, and other functions; the *insert mode* is used for entering and changing text. The **vi** editor always begins in the command mode. Let's enter insert mode by typing `i` (you do not need to press RETURN) and input the following three lines of text:

```
It is time for all
good men to come to
the aid of their planet.
```

We are done inserting text, so exit the insert mode by pressing the ESC key. Because beginners tend to forget to leave the insert mode before they type another **vi** command, the command ends up being inserted into their text.

We decide we've made a mistake; we want the text to read *Now is the time* instead of *It is time*. To make this change is simple. Recall that we are in the command mode after pressing ESC; therefore, we use the arrow keys to move the cursor to the *I* of *It*, the beginning of the first word we want to change. Now press the **d** key then the **w** key and the entire word *It* is deleted. Notice how the word disappears and the rest of the line slides over so that the *i* in *is* is now at the cursor. Next, press **i** to return to the insert mode. Type the word *Now*, add a space, and then press ESC to return to the command mode. We also want to insert the word *the* before the word *time*, so position the cursor at the *t* in *time*. Now, press **i** (for insert mode) and type *the*, add a space, and press ESC. The corrections are done.

New users of **vi** sometimes find it difficult to remember which mode they are using. You can find out quickly by tapping the SPACE BAR a couple of times. If the cursor moves to the right without changing the text, you are in the command mode. If, on the other hand, the text after the cursor is pushed farther right (or if characters disappear), then you are inserting spaces and you must be in the insert mode. Backspace a couple of times to delete the spaces, and you're back where you started. There is another method: Whenever you are unsure of which mode you are in, press ESC a couple of times and you will hear your terminal "beep" when you are safely back in command mode.

As you use **vi**, any changes you make are only made to a buffer. To leave the editor and save the buffer to disk, type **ZZ** (without pressing RETURN). The editor will report that it has saved the buffer in a new file named myfile and then return you to the shell.

You have just created and edited a file named myfile containing the three lines

```
Now is the time for all
good men to come to
the aid of their planet.
```

The **vi** editor is very powerful, and many different commands are available to handle all sorts of editing chores, many of which you will probably never use. The following list of essential **vi** commands serves most practical purposes.

Cursor Movement

h   (or LEFT ARROW) Moves the cursor one position to the left (see Figure 1.2).

j   (or DOWN ARROW) Moves the cursor down one position.

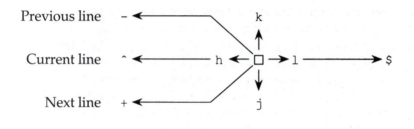

Figure 1.2 Cursor Movement

k   (or UP ARROW) Moves the cursor up one position.

l   (or RIGHT ARROW) Moves the cursor one position to the right.

+   Moves the cursor to the first nonblank character on the next line (same as RETURN).

–   (minus sign) Moves the cursor to the first nonblank character on the previous line.

^   Moves the cursor to the first nonblank character on the current line.

0   (zero) Moves the cursor to the first column on the current line.

$ Moves the cursor to the end of the current line.

G   Moves the cursor to the end of the file.

*n*G   Moves the cursor to the beginning of the *n*th line of the file. This is handy for correcting syntax problems in C source files because the C compiler will give the line number on which it first detects a syntax problem.

Deletion

*n*x   Erases *n* characters starting from the cursor, one character if *n* is omitted. The positive integer *n* is called a repeat number. If *n* is 1, it can be omitted. Many of the commands given here can take a repeat number.

*n*dw   Deletes *n* words.

*n*dd   Deletes *n* lines, **dd** for deleting one line. Where a line is deleted, an @ is sometimes shown in its place just to indicate its absence.

Insertion

i   Enters the insert mode. Subsequent key strokes will be inserted immediately to the left of the cursor. When the insertion is completed, press ESC to mark the end of the insertion and to return to command mode. Insertions may be more than one line.

a   Enters insert mode. This is identical to **i** above, except that the insertion occurs to the immediate right of the cursor.

A   Goes to the end of the line and begins inserting there.

o   Opens a blank line after the current line and enters the insert mode.

O   Opens a blank line before the current line and enters the insert mode.

Other Useful Commands

:w   Writes the buffer to disk and continues editing. Do this after a certain amount of editing to avoid losing your work if the system crashes.

ZZ   Writes out the file being edited and exits from **vi** (same as **:wq**).

:q!   Quits; exits **vi** without saving the file.

/patternESC   Searches from the current cursor position down to the first occurrence of *pattern*. For example, **/whileESC** searches for the text pattern while. The cursor will be left at the beginning of the pattern found. Some special characters can be used to specify patterns. A RETURN can be used instead of the ESC for this search command.

?patternESC   Searches, as before, but in the opposite direction.

n   Jumps to the next occurrence of the last search pattern.

N   Jumps to the previous occurrence of the last search pattern.

.   (a period) Repeats the most recent command that modified the buffer.

This section is only an introduction, but it should provide enough material for you to start editing your files.

1.2.1 Your First C Program

Now we are ready to use **vi** to create a very simple C program. Type

> **vi** myprog.c

and enter the following program:

```
#include <stdio.h>

main()
{       printf("C and UNIX are becoming\n");
        printf("industry standards.\n");
}
```

A C source file must use a name with a suffix `.c`. The program begins with a line

```
#include <stdio.h>
```

to include the standard I/O header file `stdio.h`. This line must be present for any program that uses standard library I/O calls. It is good programming practice to always have this line in your program.

The above program contains one *function* named `main`, which has two statements. Each statement is a call to the library function **printf**, which performs output of data. Save this program and return from **vi** to the UNIX system shell level and issue the command

cc `myprog.c`

to compile it. The executable program now should be in a file named `a.out`. Run it with the command

a.out

which displays on your terminal the message

```
C and UNIX are becoming
industry standards.
```

In C a sequence of characters enclosed in double quotation marks is a *character string constant*. In this example, each **printf** is given a character string to output. The notation `\n` stands for a NEWLINE character. The effect of a NEWLINE is to cause the output to start another line. We'll have more to say about character strings later.

Notice that the statements are indented to make them easier to read. Such formatting is very useful for making complicated coding easier to understand. In this book, we will adopt a consistent formatting style, which will be explained in Section 2.18.

The **vi** editor has an *autoindent* feature in the insert mode that is convenient for formatting programs. Use the **vi** commands

```
:set autoindent
:set noautoindent
```

to activate or deactivate this feature. With `autoindent`, **vi** automatically supplies enough white space to align a new line with the previous line. When the automatically supplied indentation is not needed, type

> `^D`   (cancel indentation)

to cancel one level of supplied indentation while in the insert mode. Use as many **^D**s as needed. This is how you get the closing } on the last line of this program to align with the opening {.

Other features in **vi** that help programming include the automatic *bouncing* of the cursor to the opening bracket— (, [, or {—when a closing bracket is typed. Use

> `:set showmatch`
> `:set noshowmatch`

to activate or deactivate this feature. Also, the **vi** command

> `%`   (move to balancing bracket)

explicitly moves the cursor to the balancing bracket.

It is bothersome to use `:set` to activate the features you want every time you edit a file with **vi**. Avoid this by defining the right value for the environment variable `EXINIT` in your `.login` or `.profile`. To always activate `autoindent` (**ai**) and `showmatch` (**sm**), use

> `setenv EXINIT 'set ai sm'`

for *csh* or

> `EXINIT='set ai sm'`
> `export EXINIT`

for *sh* and *ksh*. Appendix 2 contains a list of all **vi** commands. Appendix 3 contains a definition for `EXINIT` suggested for entering and editing C programs.

1.3 UNIX Files and Directories _____

Like other modern operating systems, UNIX allows users to keep their programs and data on-line in files that are immediately accessible. The structure used to store and manage files on-line is called a *file system*. For managing your own files and for writing C programs that access files, understanding the structure and organization of the file system and how files are accessed is important.

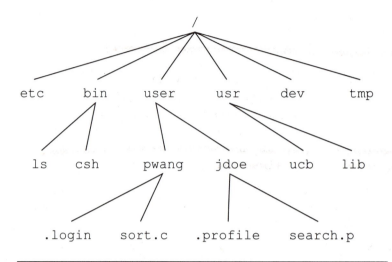

Figure 1.3: A Sample File Tree

The entire file system for UNIX is a big tree structure with a root named by the single character /. If a file contains a program or data, it is known as a *regular file* or simply a *file*. A file called a directory contains the names and addresses of other files stored below it. In turn, the files in a directory can be regular files or other directories. This *hierarchical file structure* can be visualized as a file tree. Internal nodes on the file tree represent directories, and leaf nodes represent files. Figure 1.3 shows a sample UNIX file tree.

Current Working Directory and Filenames

Each user on UNIX has a personal file directory known as the *home directory*. Your home directory will have your user ID as its name, and it will usually be contained in another directory, such as user (Figure 1.3). Besides files, you may also have subdirectories under your home directory. In fact, it is a good idea to have your files organized by category into different subdirectories, especially once your collection of files is too large to be handled conveniently within a single directory. Establishing separate directories for groups of related C programs is also common practice.

To access a file or directory in the file system, it is necessary to call it up by its name, and there are several ways to do this. The most general, and the most cumbersome, way to specify the name of a file is by listing all the nodes leading from the root to the target file. The nodes are separated by the slash / character. This character string is known as the *absolute pathname*, or *full pathname*, of the file. For example, the file sort.c in Figure 1.3 has the absolute pathname

```
/user/pwang/sort.c
```

As you can imagine, the full name is often long. Fortunately, a filename can also be specified relative to the *current working directory* (also known as *working directory* or *current directory*). So if the current working directory is /user, then the name pwang/sort.c suffices. A *relative pathname* gives the path on the file tree leading from the working directory to the desired file.

The third and simplest way to access a file is used when the working directory is the same as the directory in which the file is stored. In this case, simply use the file name. Thus, a UNIX file has three names:

- A full pathname (/user/pwang/sort.c)
- A relative pathname (pwang/sort.c)
- A simple filename (sort.c)

The ability to use relative pathnames and simple filenames depends on the ability to change between working directories. If your working directory is jdoe and you wish to access the file sort.c, either specify the absolute pathname /user/pwang/sort.c or change your working directory to pwang and simply refer to the file by name, sort.c. It is important to keep this in mind when writing C programs that refer to user-specified filenames. *The program should be able to work correctly no matter which of the three forms a filename is given in.*

When you log in, your working directory is automatically set to your home directory. The command

pwd   (print **w**orking **d**irectory)

displays the absolute pathname of your current working directory. You can also enter

ls

to display the filenames in your current directory. The command

cd *directory*   (change working **d**irectory)

will change your working directory to the specified directory (given in any of the three forms). As a C programmer, you may elect to keep your C programs in subdirectories under your home directory and use the above commands to visit different directories as desired.

There are two special directory pointers (. and ..) in every directory: '.' points to its own directory, and '..' points to the parent directory. Thus, if you are currently in /user/pwang and you issue the command

cd ..   (change to parent directory)

you'll end up in the directory /user.

You may name a file with any string of alphanumeric (letter and/or digit) characters except the character /. A simple filename is a sequence of characters up to a maximum length that is system-dependent. On Berkeley UNIX, it can be up to 256 characters. System V may sometimes restrict filename length to 14 characters.

Handling Files and Directories

Writing a C program involves creating one or several files containing the program. Once files are created, they can be copied, renamed, moved, and destroyed using commands at the shell level.

The command to copy a file is **cp** and has the form

> **cp** *filename1 filename2*   (**copy files**)

The first argument is the file to be copied, and the second is the destination. If the destination file does not exist, it will be created; if it already exists, its contents will be overwritten.

The **mv** (move) command renames the file given by the first argument to that specified by the second argument. After the command

> **mv** *filename1 filename2*   (**move files**)

filename1 no longer exists. If *filename2* was there before, it is now replaced.

Once a file or subdirectory has outlived its usefulness, you will want to remove it from your files. UNIX provides the **rm** command for files and **rmdir** for directories:

> **rm** *filename1 filename2 ...*   (**remove files**)
> **rmdir** *directory1 directory2 ...*   (**remove directories**)

The argument of **rm** is a list of one or more filenames to be removed. The command

> **rm** *.o

erases all files with the filename suffix .o. The asterisk * is a wild-card character that matches any character string (except a leading period). Be careful removing files with the wild card. If you accidentally put a space after the * in *.o in the above **rm** command, you will delete all your files!

The **rmdir** command takes as its argument a list of one or more directory names, but note that **rmdir** only deletes a directory if it is empty. Generally, to remove a directory from your files, you must first "sweep it clean" using **rm**.

UNIX provides the **mkdir** command for creating directories.

mkdir *name*   (**make directory**)

creates a directory with the given name. When specifying a filename or directory name as an argument for any command, you can use any of the three filename forms.

File manipulations can also be done from within your C program, as we will see in Section 2.16, and Chapters 8 and 10.

The grep Command

Often you must look for a file whose name you have forgotten. Looking through each and every file to find it is troublesome. Fortunately, there is the command **grep**. If you remember what's in the file you are looking for, give the command

grep *string* *   (string matching in files)

Now **grep** will look through each file for the given *string*. It displays each line containing the string with the name of the file every time there is a match.

This can be handy when you are looking for a C source-code file containing a particular function or construct. (Use **grep** on *.c.)

System Directories

The UNIX System also uses the file system to store its own programs and data. UNIX *system directories* contain executable commands, source code for programs, documentation, system management data, and so on. The concept of files is so universal in UNIX that devices such as terminals, printers, and tape drives are considered special files and are kept under an appropriate system directory. Table 1.1 shows a few of the major system directories.

Try browsing through these system directories. In particular, visit the directory /usr/include.

cd /usr/include
pwd   (just to verify if you wish)
ls -1 *.h   (* is a wild card)

You'll see many files with the .h suffix. These files are *header files* containing standard declarations for C programs. For instance, the file stdio.h is there.

Directory	Contains
/bin and /usr/bin	Executable (binary) files for UNIX commands, the **cc** command is in /bin/cc
/usr/include	Header files for C programs with filename suffix .h
/usr/lib	*Library* files including those for C
/etc	UNIX data files such as the password file and the terminal capability file
/dev	Special files representing I/O devices
/usr/man	On-line manual pages for UNIX commands, system calls, and library functions
/tmp	Temporary scratch files also used by the C compiler for intermediate files

Table 1.1: UNIX System Directories

1.4 Compiling and Running C Programs

Besides C a UNIX system may offer Pascal, FORTRAN 77, LISP, C++, and other languages. Programs are kept in source-code files. UNIX uses a set of conventions for naming files written in different languages. Table 1.2 shows some commonly used suffixes.

We have seen the use of **cc** to compile myprog.c (Section 1.2.1). This section explains how to compile and run a C program under UNIX.

1.4.1 The C Compiler

To program in C, it is important to have a clear idea of what the C compiler does and how to use it. A compiler not only translates programs into machine code to run on a particular computer but also takes care of arranging suitable *run-time support* for the program by providing input and output and other interfaces to the operating system. Therefore, a compiler is not only computer-specific but also operating system–specific. As we have seen, on UNIX systems the **cc** command compiles C programs.

The compilation process of **cc** consists of five phases (Figure 1.4). To provide an overview, the functions of these phases are listed briefly here; many of the aspects will be discussed later.

Suffix	For
.c	C source file
.h	C header file
.f	FORTRAN 77 source file
.p	Pascal source file
.lsp	LISP source file
.s	Assembly-code file
.o	Object-code (compiled) file

Table 1.2: Filename Suffixes

1. *Preprocessing*: The first phase is performed by the **cpp** (C preprocessor) program. It handles constant definition, macro expansion, file inclusion, and conditional compilation.
2. *Compilation*: Taking the output of the previous phase as input, the **ccom** program performs syntax checking, parsing, and assembly-code generation.
3. *Optimization*: This optional phase improves the efficiency of the generated code for speed and compactness.
4. *Assembly*: The assembler program **as** is used to create an object file containing binary code and relocation information to be used by the linker/loader.
5. *Loading*: The **ld** program is the linker/loader, which combines all object files and links in necessary library subroutines to produce an executable program.

The descriptions here give only a rough idea of the process. At this point, it is sufficient to know that **cc** does all five stages automatically.

The cc Command

As we have mentioned, **cc** is used to compile C programs. The suggested form of the **cc** command is

> **cc [** *option* **]** ... *filename* ...   (compile C programs)

Brackets used in the description of a command indicate optional arguments. They are *not* part of the command. A filename ending in .c is taken as a C source file, and a corresponding object file (.o) will also be produced. A filename ending in .o is taken as an object file, which is loaded into the final

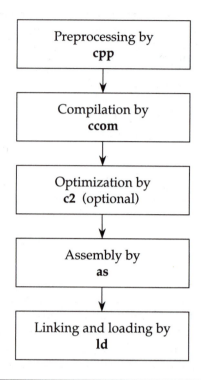

Figure 1.4: Compilation Phases

executable module. When compiling a single .c file into an executable module, the .o file produced is automatically deleted.

A few often-used options for **cc** are listed here. More details can be found in Chapter 11. You can also enter

    man cc

to see all the available options. In doing so, make sure that you access the documentation for the ANSI standard C compiler, which may or may not be represented by the **cc** command. For the Free Software Foundation C compiler, it is likely to be called **gcc**. Whatever the compiler command name may be, the basic usage should be identical to the traditional **cc** on most UNIX systems.

-c   Suppresses the loading phases and produces .o files only.
                No executable module will be produced.

-o *name*   Names the executable module with the specified name
                instead of the default a.out.

-o	Invokes the **c2** code optimizer phase. Used to produce faster running code, it is generally used only when producing final, production versions of a program.
-g	Causes the compiler to produce additional symbol table information for the symbolic debugger **dbx** (Chapter 9).

The command to run a program is simply the name of the executable file. For all practical purposes, an executable file *is* a UNIX command.

Getting Hard-Copy Output

No matter what program you run, you will probably want the results printed on paper (hard copy). The **script** command can help produce hard copy of your computations. Type

    script *file*   (record terminal session)

to begin recording your terminal session into a file named *file* (or to a file named `typescript` if you entered the **script** command without an argument). While **script** is active, all input and output to and from your terminal are also sent to the file. Recording stops when you type **^D** at the beginning of a command line. The file can then be printed.

The **script** command is useful for recording almost anything you wish to keep in a file for analysis later or to produce hard copy. For example, to run a C program with the **script** command, use the following sequence of commands:

```
script hardcopy
cc myprogram.c
a.out
^D
```

The **script** command starts recording in the file `hardcopy`. A lone **^D** on the last line stops the recording and gets you out of **script** and back to the shell level.

Now that you have what you want in the file `hardcopy`, the command

    lpr `hardcopy`   (produce hard-copy printout—Berkeley)

will produce a printout on a line or laser printer. If your system supplies multiple printers, the option -P*printer* can be supplied to **lpr** to send the output to the designated printer. The default printer used is specified by the environment variable `PRINTER`. On System V UNIX, the **lp** command is usually used to produce hard-copy printout, and the option -d*name* is used to send output to the named printer.

Command	Purpose
cc `myprog.c`	Compiles C program
a.out	Executes `a.out`
mv `a.out` *filename*	Renames `a.out`
lpr [`-Pprinter`] *filename*	Produces printout—Berkeley
lp [`-dname`] *filename*	Produces printout—System V
script *file*	Records terminal session in *file*
more *file* or **less** *file*	Displays `file`—Berkeley
pg *file*	Displays `file`—System V

Table 1.3: Command Summary

You should try to avoid unnecessary paper-based output by reviewing a file on your terminal before producing a hard copy. This can be done by

> **more**   hardcopy   (display a file—Berkeley)

The **more** command displays the file on your terminal one screenful at a time, continuing to the next screenful only when you press the SPACE BAR. The command **less** is an improved version of **more**. Among other things, it also goes backward if you type the letter *b*. On System V UNIX, the command **pg** is used, instead of **more**, in a similar way.

Table 1.3 summarizes commands related to compiling and running a C program.

1.5   Protecting Files: Access Control

Once you have written a C program, you may or may not wish to share it with others on the system. A simple mechanism grants or denies access to files by different users on the system. The protection mechanism works by controlling access initiated by any program.

A user usually can browse through the entire file system looking at and using any file that is not specifically protected. Each file has an *owner ID*, a *group ID*, and a 9-bit access control code. These bits, also called *protection bits*, specify access permission to a file for three classes of users: the owner, members in the group, and all others (Table 1.4). The u and o types of users are

User Type	Meaning
u	Owner or creator of the file (user)
g	Members in the group of the file
o	All users other than u and g
root	The superuser

Table 1.4: File-User Types

self-explanatory. The g type of a user is defined by a systemwide "group definition file" (usually /etc/group).

The first three protection bits pertain to u access, the next three to g access, and the final three to o access. Each of the three bits grants (bit is 1) or denies (bit is 0) one specific form of access:

r   *Read* permission (first bit).

w   *Write* permission (second bit).

x   *Execute* permission (third bit).

Thus, the protection-bit pattern

    110100100   (octal 0644)

specifies r, w for u, and r for g and o.

Examining the Permission Settings

The **ls** -l command provides a file listing with a variety of useful information.

```
-rw-rw-rw- 1 smith 129 Jan 20 1:24 myprog.c
drwx------ 1 smith 800 Jan 24 3:04 projects
```

For the file myprog.c, the owner is smith. It contains 129 characters and was last modified on January 20 at 1:24 A.M. The leading character gives the file type: - indicates myprog.c is an ordinary file; d says projects is a directory. The *protection bits* are displayed by nine characters after the file type (Figure 1.5).The protection setting of the file myprog.c

```
-rw-r--r--
```

gives read permission to everyone but write permission to only u.

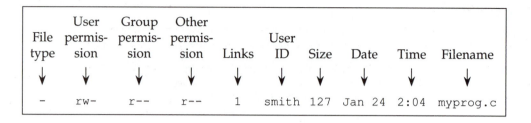

Figure 1.5: File Attributes

Setting Permissions

Depending on the default setting on your system, a file is usually created with either of these default protections

```
-rw-r--r--
-rw-------
```

This may be suitable for some but not all of your files. To change the protection mode on a file, use the command

chmod *mode filename*   (**change** protection **mode**)

where *mode* can be an octal number to set all 9 bits specifically. For example,

chmod 644 myprog.c

sets the access permission of the file myprog.c to rw-r--r--. Alternatively, the *mode* can specify modifications to the existing permissions of the file. In which case, the command is given in the forms

chmod o-w *filename*
chmod a+x *filename*
chmod u-w+x *filename*
chmod a=rw *filename*

The first example denies write permission to others, and the second makes the file executable by all. The third example takes away write and grants execute permission for the owner. The fourth example permits only read and write for all (regardless of what permissions had been assigned before).

These protections will keep out all users except a very special class, the superuser.

The Superuser

The superuser has read, write, and execute permission on all files in the system regardless of the protection bits. In general, file-access control does not restrict any access and actions initiated by a superuser. Typically, only system administrators and a few other selected users ("gurus" as they're sometimes called) have access to the superuser password, which for obvious reasons is considered top-secret.

1.6 Redirecting Input and Output

One of the outstanding features of the UNIX system is its uniform treatment of file and device input and output. This has profound implications both at the shell level and for C programs. Basically, a program can be written without specifying a fixed source of input or output. The terminal keyboard and display are standard I/O channels for each program. We refer to the keyboard as the *standard input* and the display as the *standard output*. There is also a *standard error output*, which is used to send error messages to your terminal.

When you write a program, you normally assume that input is coming from standard input and output is produced on standard output. You would like, however, not to rewrite the program every time it is used for a different input or output source. This is possible on a UNIX system because such a program can also be used, without modification, with other I/O sources. The flexible *I/O redirection mechanism* enables the standard input and standard output to be connected to a target file, I/O device, or another program. Table 1.5 shows the shell-level notations used for I/O redirection. Note the difference between the shells for standard error output redirection.

Notation	Function
> *file*	Sends standard output into *file*
>> *file*	Sends standard output to end of *file*
< *file*	Takes standard input from *file*
>& *file*	Sends standard output and error to *file* (for *csh*)
2> *file*	Sends standard error to *file* (for *sh* or *ksh*)

Table 1.5: Shell-Level I/O Redirection

Let us look at some examples of redirection.

ls > myfiles

sends the standard output of the command **ls** into the file myfiles. This means the normal output of **ls** will not be displayed on the terminal but will be sent to myfiles instead. Similarly, if you run **a.out** after compiling your C program and type

    a.out > myoutput

the results displayed by **a.out** will be stored in myoutput. You can examine the contents with **vi** or **more** as before. Note any error output produced by **a.out** would still come to the standard error output, which is the terminal.

Just as the standard output, the standard input of a program can also be redirected. The command

    cat *file*

takes the given *file* as input and produces it without change to the standard output. The result is to display *file* on your terminal. When **cat** is given no argument, it takes input from the standard input. Now try this on the computer:

1. Type
   cat > notes
2. Without getting a prompt, type a few lines of text (anything that comes to mind), followed by a lone **^D** on the last line.
3. Give the command
   more notes

You'll see that **cat** has sent what you typed on the keyboard (the standard input) to the file notes.

Redirecting output is a powerful operation. For instance, the command

    cat *file1 file2* > *file3*　　　　　(file concatenation)

creates *file3* if it does not already exist, by appending *file2* to the end of *file1*. This file concatenation is where **cat** got its name. Take care, though. If *file3* already exists, its contents will be overwritten. It is also incorrect to use the name of either *file1* or *file2* as *file3*.

The standard output of a command does not have to be redirected to a file; instead, it can be sent to another command as the second command's standard input. This is done by placing a *pipe* between the two commands. A pipe is obtained by using a vertical bar between two commands. For example,

    ls | more　　　　(a pipeline)

redirects the standard output of **ls** as standard input of **more**. The resulting construct is called a *pipeline*. The pipeline here makes lengthy output from **ls** easy to view on a CRT.

Pipes allow you to build new tools by combining existing commands; many of the more advanced UNIX commands are built from primitive ones in precisely this manner. The pipe is an example of a hallmark principle of the UNIX philosophy: "Don't reinvent the wheel." It allows programmers to build programs from pieces that have already been written and tested instead of having to rewrite all pieces again from scratch.

The shell-level redirection is supported by C-level mechanisms. We will return to this remark in Chapter 12.

1.7 Multiple Concurrent Jobs

Beginners on UNIX use the computer in strict accordance with the command interpretation loop described in Figure 1.1, which means one command has to finish before another is started. But this is not necessary because several jobs may be run at the same time, or *concurrently*.

When a job is run in the ordinary fashion, in accordance with the command interpretation loop, it is said to be running in the *foreground*. If, however, you end a command with an & (ampersand) character, the resulting job will instead be run in the *background*. This means the shell is allowed to display a new prompt and run your next command without waiting for the (background) job to finish. It is as if the background job does not even exist, provided it makes no demands for terminal input/output. Long-running jobs that do not need terminal input/output can run in the background. If a background job does generate output, it will appear (often annoyingly) on the terminal unless you redirect the output to a file.

An excellent candidate for the background is the compilation of a lengthy C program. When you issue the **cc** command, redirect output and any error messages to some file and then place the whole job in the background:

```
cc big.c >& somefile &           (for csh)
cc big.c > outfile 2> errorfile &   (for sh or ksh)
```

In the command for *csh*, the first & deals with redirection (Section 1.6) and has nothing to do with putting the job in the background. The trailing & is the significant one from the standpoint of job control. This is an example of an unfortunate UNIX trait, overloaded operators. In the *ksh* version, normal output is sent to outfile, while error messages are sent to errorfile.

The *csh* (also *ksh* but not *sh*) provides another major convenience, the ability to temporarily *suspend* the currently executing job so that another job can be started. The *csh* lets you type a special *suspend character* (usually ^z) while a program is running, which will cause it to "stop in its tracks" until you signal it to resume. When you type ^z to suspend a job, the message

```
Stopped
```

and a new shell prompt will appear on your terminal to provide confirmation that the current job has been stopped.

When testing newly written C programs, it is often convenient to suspend the text editor in order to run, for example, the compiler.

Because it is possible to start and then suspend or put in the background quite a few jobs, this can quickly become unmanageable. Fortunately, the command

jobs   (display existing jobs)

can be used to display a list of all unfinished jobs on the terminal. A typical output from the **jobs** command looks like this:

```
[1]   +      Stopped      vi sort.c
[2]   -      Stopped      mail smith
[3]          Running      a.out
```

In this case, there are two suspended jobs, with job numbers 1 and 2, and one job running in the background, 3.

From this state, the *csh* allows you to restart a stopped job, pull a background job into the foreground, or terminate a job entirely. The *job-ID* specifies the job you wish to change, and it can be typed in a number of ways:

```
%job-number
%name-prefix
%+
%-
```

The percent sign shown here is part of what you type to specify the job (it is *not* the shell prompt). For example, the job-ids %1, %+, and %v all refer to job [1] in the example above. The job %+ is always the most recently suspended (the current job), and %- is always the next most recently suspended (the previous job). The %- is useful when you are going back and forth between two jobs. When using the name-prefix form, you need just enough prefix of the command name to uniquely distinguish it from other jobs. This means %mail, %ma, or %m all refer to job [2]. Note that the name-prefix form is not suitable if there are two jobs with the same command name.

A job can be resumed (brought to the foreground) by the shell-level command

fg *job-id*   (bring job to foreground)

If you wish, you can abbreviate the command to *job-id*. For example, %1 will put job [1] into the foreground. %+ (or simply **fg**) resumes the current job, and %- resumes the previous job.

Suspending a job using ^z is not the same as exiting or terminating it, and if you try to log out while your shell still has suspended jobs, you will get the message There are stopped jobs. A second consecutive logout command will cause logout regardless of stopped jobs, but this is not considered good practice. Some jobs left hanging in this way will save their buffers before they die, a waste of valuable disk space. Jobs should be exited properly, or at the very least killed, before logout.

Sometimes you will need to terminate a program that you are running (in the foreground). Do this by typing the *interrupt character* (Section 1.1), usually the DELETE key or ^c, which aborts the executing job and returns you to the shell level. If the interrupt character does not stop your program, try using ^\ (control-back slash). If that does not abort the job, your last resort is the **kill** command. Use ^z to suspend the job and get to the shell level, then type

kill -9 *job-id*   (forcefully terminate a job)

This will surely terminate the job. The suspension, resumption, and termination with ^c or **kill** of jobs are handled using *signals* in UNIX (Chapter 9).

1.8 More on Processes

We have mentioned that the shell establishes a child process to execute a nonbuilt-in command. This section describes the concept of a UNIX process in more detail.

An independently executing program is a process. In UNIX any existing process (*parent*) can also create a new (*child*) process. When a UNIX system is first started, it has only one process called the *init process*. All other processes are descendants of *init*, including your login shell, text editor, C compiler, and C program.

When a child process is created, it inherits certain attributes of its parent process, notably user and group IDs, open I/O channels, and environment variables and their values. All processes execute concurrently, and they coordinate and communicate with one another through mechanisms provided by UNIX.

Two topics on processes that we discuss here are **input/output** and the environment variables.

1.8.1 Standard Input and Output

When a child process is born, it inherits certain properties from its parent. Inheriting from your login shell, each of your processes is provided with three *buffered I/O streams*:

stdin   The standard input stream reads from the keyboard.

stdout   The standard output stream outputs to the terminal screen.

stderr   The error output stream outputs to the terminal screen.

These standard I/O streams are used in C programs and operations on them are supported by *library functions*, prewritten C routines, contained in the standard C libraries. We have already used the function **printf** to send data to stdout.

The standard I/O is an important mechanism that makes I/O easy to manage and forms an essential part for shaping program components called *filters*, which can be combined to achieve new functionalities.

1.8.2 Filters and Pipelines

In a C program, input is usually *read* from stdin, and output is *written to* stdout. If there are any error or diagnostic messages to display, you also write to stderr. Input from a file and output to a file can be achieved through redirection as described in Section 1.6. The advantage of following this convention is to enable the combination of a program with others in a pipeline, making the program more versatile and useful in many unforeseen situations.

A program designed to fit as a stage in a pipeline is called a *filter*. A filter is distinguished from other programs by the following characteristics:

- A filter takes input from the standard input and does not require an input filename argument.
- A filter does not require an output file argument because it uses standard output.
- A filter performs a well-defined transformation on the input and produces the output with no header, trailer, label, or other formatting.
- A filter does not take any part of its input as instructions or commands to the filter.
- With few exceptions, a filter does not interact with the user for additional parameters other than those supplied on the command line.

- Any error or diagnostic output produced by a filter is sent to the standard error output so that error messages do not disappear or scramble the output from this filter to the next filter down the pipe.

These characteristics help a filter fit into a pipeline. The overall purpose is to make a program produce output that can be fed into another program as input to be processed directly.

Later, when we give C-programming examples, many of them will follow the filter conventions.

1.8.3 Environment Variables

Standard I/O is just one set of attributes that a child process inherits from its parent. It also inherits environment variables and their values.

The exact manner in which a process performs depends on its *execution environment*. A text editor, for example, needs to know the capabilities of the terminal with which it is dealing in order to work correctly. When a process accesses a file, permission may or may not be granted, depending on which user invoked the process, or the *user ID* of the process.

In UNIX, environment parameters that can be assigned values by the user are kept in a set of shell *environment variables*. These environment variables, together with other values (user ID, current working directory, standard I/O file descriptors, etc.), constitute the *environment* in which your shell process executes. This environment is *inherited* by (passed to) each and every child process the shell establishes.

For the terminal type, the environment variable TERM is used to record the name of the terminal you are using. Once a process knows the terminal type, it can deal with the terminal effectively. The environment variable HOME is set to the full pathname of your home directory and HOST to the name of your computer.

The shell built-in command **printenv**, or **env**, displays all environment variables and their values. A sample output is

```
HOME=/user/smith
SHELL=/bin/csh
PATH=/usr/ucb:/bin:/usr/bin:/usr/local/bin:.
TERM=hp2622
USER=smith
```

where SHELL indicates the program used as the user's login shell; PATH, the command search path; TERM, the terminal type; USER, the user ID. As a rule, environment variables use uppercase names.

In Section 1.2, we have seen how to set the variable TERM. To see your TERM setting, enter

echo $TERM

to display the value of the variable TERM. To access the value of a variable, prefix the variable name with a dollar sign ($). The **echo** command is a shell built-in command that displays its arguments.

Here is another example. The command

cd $HOME/C-homework

will return you to your C-homework directory.

Environment inheritance occurs at the time when a child process is established. After separation, a child process can modify its copy of the environment and not affect the copy in the parent, and vice versa. But if the child process starts a child of its own, then the modified environment is passed on.

1.8.4 Exit Status

When a child process terminates, it returns an *exit status* to the parent process. The exit status of a command is captured by the shell in the variable $status (*csh*) or $? (*sh* and *ksh*).

By convention, the value of the exit status is zero for normal termination of a command and nonzero otherwise. A command can use different positive integers to indicate various abnormal termination conditions. Some commands just use the integer 1 for all abnormal terminations.

Consider the **cc** command. If it fails because there is a syntax error (program statements did not follow language rules), an exit status 1 will be given. Immediately after the failure, you can use

echo $status   (use $? for *sh* or *ksh*)

to examine the exit status.

1.9 Summary

UNIX provides the best environment on which to learn and use C. Many useful UNIX features related to C programming were introduced. The UNIX system shell is a user interface through which you initiate and control all your computations. Different shells exist, and the three most popular shells are *csh, ksh,* and *sh.* Shell built-in commands are subroutine calls performed within the shell. Most UNIX commands are nonbuilt-in commands and are executed by establishing a child process. A compiled C program is invoked as a nonbuilt-in command. The file `.login` (`.profile`) is a standard login initialization file for *csh* (*ksh* and *sh*).

The full-screen editor **vi** is standard on UNIX systems and can be used to write C programs. The **vi** editor works in two modes: command mode and insert mode. A number of basic **vi** commands were discussed. The full set of **vi** commands are included in Appendix 2. Another popular editor, **emacs**, is described in Appendix 1.

The UNIX file system is a tree structure of directories and files. A file has such attributes as owner, group, and access permissions. To access a file, an absolute pathname, relative pathname, or simple filename can be used. A C source-code file must use the `.c` suffix. Each user has a home directory for personal files. General utilities such as commands (executable files), data files, and header files are stored in system directories. The C compiler **cc** is such a utility. The command **cc** compiles C programs and automatically carries out five separate stages of the compilation process: the C preprocessor **cpp**, the compiler **ccom**, the optional code optimizer **c2**, the assembler **as**, and the loader **ld**. Among the options for **cc**, **-c** (produces an `.o` file only, no `a.out`) and **-o***name* (uses *name* for an executable file) are frequently used.

On UNIX a C program executes as a child process of your shell. There are three prearranged I/O streams for each process: `stdin`, `stdout`, and `stderr`. By default, the standard I/O streams are connected to your terminal; but they can be redirected at the shell level to files and other executing programs. By connecting several programs with I/O redirection, a pipeline can be formed. A filter is a program that is specially written to fit into a pipeline.

The shells *csh* and *ksh* provide a convenient job-control feature whereby you can control multiple jobs simultaneously. The jobs are child processes created by your shell. A child process inherits the execution environment of its parent process. The attributes inherited by a child process include open I/O streams and environment variables and their values.

Exercises

1. Type the shell-level command

   echo `$TERM`

   This shows you the system's idea of what terminal you are using. Check and see if this is set correctly. If not, find out how to set `TERM` to the correct terminal type.

2. What is the full pathname of your home directory? Enter the command **ls** -a for your home directory. Do you see files you normally do not see?

What is the full name of your `.login` (`.profile`) file? What access permissions do these files have? Who owns these files?

3. Use an editor (**vi** or **emacs**) to examine your `.login` (or `.profile`) to see the settings, if any, of the environment variables TERM and PRINTER. If either is absent, you need to add their correct setting in this file.

4. In **vi** (or **emacs**), how do you move to the beginning of the buffer, to the end of the buffer, to any specific line number, and to the beginning or end of a line?

5. In your favorite editor, find out how to delete a word, a line, and a number of lines? Find out how to "cut and paste."

6. Establish a directory under your home directory for all the C programs you will learn to write. What command is used to remove unwanted files? Directories?

7. (a) How do you see a long directory listing of the file? How do you view the file on the screen and not have it scroll by too quickly? (b) How do you change its access permission? How do you combine two files into one? How do you give a file a new name?

8. How do you display the names of all files in your directory? All files with the ending `.c`? How do you remove all files with the ending `.o`?

9. If a user with user ID bob is in his home directory and types

   cd `../bob`

   what happens? What happens if somebody else types the same command?

10. Type in a simple program in C to display the message:

    ```
    C is a powerful language, especially on a UNIX system.
    ```

    Compile it and run it. Use **script** to get a file containing an execution of the program. Rename this file `myoutput`, and print a hard copy of it.

11. Run the above C program but redirect its output into a file. Compare the content of this file with the file `myoutput` created earlier.

12. After working for a while on the system editing programs and compiling, you are ready to log out. But your **logout** command results in the message

    ```
    There are stopped jobs.
    ```

    How can you log out now? Describe two alternatives.

13. What is an I/O stream? Which three standard I/O streams does each process have?

14. What is the exit status when you do a successful **ls** `filename`? What if the file does not exit? What happens when you interrupt a job?

15. You have seen how a number of shell commands can be put in a file (`.login` or `.profile`). In general, you can put several commands together into a file of your own. Such a file is called a *shell script*. If you add execution permission to a shell script, you can use its filename as a command name at the shell level. The very first character of a *csh* (*sh*) script should be a # (`:`). Try to write a shell script of your own.

A C Primer _____

_____

_____

Having a fundamental understanding of the environment UNIX
provides for C, we are ready to write a few programs. This chapter
introduces many aspects of the C language; examples illustrate the
basics. The purpose is to provide a good overview and to get you
started writing interesting programs quickly.

The approach focuses on basic information: program structure,
constants, variables, expressions, arrays, functions, and simple
input/output. Control-flow constructs `if`, `while`, `for`, and `do-while`
are introduced. The presentation of these topics concentrates on
central concepts and common usage rather than comprehensiveness.
Some examples given in this chapter might be written more
concisely, efficiently, or elegantly using more advanced constructs,
but these are the subjects of later chapters.

Other topics covered here include argument passing, error handling,
and important specifics related to writing a C program to be
executed under UNIX.

The examples and their variations should be tested on your UNIX
system as you go through the chapter.

2.1 Program Structure

A program is a step-by-step procedure, written in a language such as C, to solve a given type of problem or to perform a specific set of tasks. To write a program, we must first know what parts go into it and how the components are organized to build the whole program.

In C the basic building blocks of a program are *functions*. A function receives *arguments*, performs predefined computations on the arguments, and returns results. A *function call* activates (or *invokes*) a function, passes arguments to the function, and produces the values it returns.

A C program, large or small, consists of one or more functions. Each function contains *statements* that specify a sequence of computing actions to be carried out and *variables* that are used to store values needed and produced during the computations. Functions normally have distinct names, and one function must be named main. The function main is the *entry point*, the place where execution of the program begins. Aside from this basic structure, C is flexible. Functions can be given in any order and can be contained in one or several source-code files.

Functions

A function can be viewed as an independent computation unit. The arguments are its input, and the computation results, or *return values*, are its output (Figure 2.1).

A well-organized program contains many small functions that perform well-defined duties. A function can call other functions in the course of its computations. The idea is to write functions to perform simple computations, then to use them in other functions for more complicated tasks. In this way, we can break down any complex problem into a series of steps that are individually straightforward but combine to achieve the given goal, much like workers on an assembly line.

To define a function, we specify a *header* and a *body*. The function header states the function name and the type of the return value. The header also specifies variables, known as *formal parameters*, which receive the incom-

Figure 2.1 A Function as a Computation Unit

ing arguments. These formal parameters are used in the function body to perform computations.

The function body consists of a sequence of *declarations* and *statements* enclosed in braces, {}. A declaration supplies information to the C compiler, and a statement specifies actions for execution. As we progress, you will learn about many different kinds of declarations and statements. The general form of a function is

• general form of a function

```
valuetype name ( type arg1, type arg2, ... )   (header)
{ variable declarations                         (body begin)
       statements
}                                               (body end)
```

(local to fcn), may be init'd.

} Simple (end w/ ;)
  Compound (encl. in {})

The *valuetype* specifies the type of the value returned by the function. If it is omitted the function is presumed to return a value of type integer (int). If the function does not return a value, then its *valuetype* is given as void.

Depending on the number of arguments needed, the header may specify zero or more formal parameters. If there are no formal parameters, the parameter list is given as an empty list, (). Furthermore, the function body may contain zero or more declarations and statements. These and other items will be described presently.

But let's first look at another very simple program that, like the example in Chapter 1 (Section 1.2.1), consists of just one function main:

```
main()
{ int i, j, k;
      i = 10;
      j = 20;
      k = (i + j)/2;
      printf("i is %d,", i);
      printf(" and j is %d\n", j);
      printf("average is %d\n", k);
}
```

For this function, the header is simply the function name main and an empty list of formal parameters (which cannot be omitted). Thus, we know the function takes no arguments.

The function body above contains the declaration

```
int i, j, k;
```

establishing the three variables i, j, and k, each of type int (single-precision integer). A simple declaration consists of a *type name* followed by a list of variable names separated by commas and terminated by a semicolon. A few more examples appear below:

```
int age;
float rate, speed;
char c, d;
```

These declare the variable `age` of type `int`, `rate` and `speed` of type `float` (single-precision floating-point), and `c` and `d` of type `char` (a single character).

Variables, such as `i`, `j`, `k`, declared in a function body are used within the function and will not conflict with any variable with the same name used elsewhere. Therefore, we say such variables are *local* to the function.

After the declaration, there are six statements: three assignments and three calls to **printf**, the standard library function we used before. If you put this program in the file `ave.c` and give the shell commands

cc `ave.c`
a.out

to compile and run it (see Section 1.4), the screen will display the following lines.

```
i is 10, j is 20
average is 15
```

The assignment statement

```
k = (i + j)/2;
```

consists of a variable `k`, the assignment operator =, and an expression on the right-hand side. The right-hand expression is evaluated, and the resultant value is assigned to the variable on the left. There are different kinds of expressions. An *arithmetic expression* involves the arithmetic operators such as +, −, *, /, and so on. Generally, an *expression* is a constant, a variable, or other expression connected by operators. We will return to this remark later.

The `%d` in the **printf** call indicates where the integer is to be spliced into the output string. Again, **\n** is the NEWLINE character. The three **printf** calls can also be combined into one

```
printf("i is %d, and j is %d\n average = %d\n", i, j, k);
```

which produces the same output.

Let's turn our attention to the active parts of a function, the statements.

2.2   Statements

The computational steps in a function are expressed by a sequence of statements that perform in ways predefined by the language. The statements are *executed* one by one in the given order when the program runs.

Generally, two kinds of statements are available:

1. *Simple statement*: One single statement terminated by a semicolon
   (;).
2. *Compound statement*: Zero or more statements grouped together
   by { and }. A compound statement has the same structure as a
   function body. In fact, the function body is itself a compound
   statement. A compound statement can be used anywhere a simple statement can.

For example, each of the six statements in the main function of ave.c is a
simple statement. Together they form the compound body of main. A compound statement is sometimes also referred to as a *block*.

A common programming mistake is to forget the semicolon terminator.
When this happens in a program, because the C compiler cannot easily
determine that a semicolon is missing, it will almost always issue a warning
about some other alleged syntax problem. These erroneous warnings can be
confusing to a beginner. So be sure to use the semicolon where it is needed:

1. A declaration always ends with a ;.
2. A simple statement is terminated by a ;.
3. There is no ; after a compound statement or after the closing } of
   a block.

For an example of item 3, see the while statement used by the factorial
function in the next section.

2.3 A Simple Function

As our first example, which is not a main function, let's write a function that
computes *n* factorial for a nonnegative integer *n*. Recall *n* factorial is

$$n! = n * (n-1) * \ldots 3 * 2 * 1$$

Hence, 1! = 1, 2! = 2, 3! = 6, and so on.

```
/* factorial function computes n! for nonnegative n */
/* version 1 */

int factorial(int n)
{ int ans = 1;
      while ( n > 1 )
      {     ans = ans * n;
            n = n - 1;
      }
      return(ans);
}
```

Notice that the first two lines above the function do nothing but are nonetheless very important. In a program, *comments* are any number of characters or lines enclosed in /* and */. A comment supplies auxiliary information or *documentation* to make a program easy to understand and is ignored by the C compiler.

The function `factorial` is defined with one formal parameter n of type *int*. The return value is of type `int` also. When a function is called, the sequence of execution, or *control flow*, goes to the first statement in the called function. Then the control flow proceeds in order of the statements until either the end of the function or a `return` statement is reached. Either way, control flow then *returns* to the point in the program just after the function call. As in the `factorial` example, if `return` is given an argument, then that is the return value of the function. If control flows off the end of a function or returns through a `return` with no argument, the return value is undefined.

Note again that the definition of `factorial` follows the general structure of a function. The body starts with the variable declaration

```
int ans = 1;
```

declaring `ans` of type `int` and giving it an initial value of 1. It is possible to declare `ans` without the initial value and then use an assignment statement immediately to assign a value to it. But declaration with initialization is more compact and sometimes efficient.

Consider a statement such as a = b + c/d;. The binary representations and operations required are different, depending on the data types of the variables involved. Type declarations are supplied so the compiler can generate the correct codes. Thus, a declaration is an instruction to the compiler and is not executed at run time. The C compiler requires that a variable be declared before it is used.

2.4 The `while` Statement

In the `factorial` function, the `while` statement

```
while ( n > 1 )
{    ans = ans * n;
     n = n - 1;
}
```

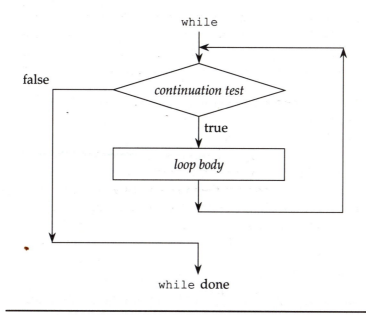

Figure 2.2: The while Loop

specifies repeated execution of two statements forming a *loop*. The *condition* n > 1 (enclosed in parentheses) controls how many times the body of the while loop (enclosed in braces) is executed. Here is the way while works (Figure 2.2):

1. The condition is tested first. If n is greater than 1 (the condition is true), then the body of while is executed once.
2. The condition is tested again. If it is true, then the body is executed again.
3. The repetition continues until the condition is tested false, when the while statement will be finished and control will go to the next statement.

Because the continuation of the loop depends on the condition being true, we refer to such a condition as a *continuation condition*. The variable n in this example is called a *loop-control variable* because its value changes for each repetition of the loop and it determines when the loop stops.

Taking a particular value for n—say, 4—you can follow the actions of this while loop and convince yourself that the variable ans actually becomes *n!* (24 in this case).

A Main Program for `factorial`

To test the `factorial` function, we can write a main program to call it:

```c
#include <stdio.h>

main()
{ int n;
    printf("Please enter value of n =");
    scanf("%d", &n);        /* read user input into variable n */
    if ( n >= 0 )
    {   printf("factorial(%d)=", n);
        printf("%d\n", factorial(n));
    }
    else
        printf("factorial of a negative number is undefined\n");
}
```

The call to the function `factorial` happens inside the second **printf**. When the function call takes place at run time, a copy of the value of the argument `n` is passed to the `factorial` function.

You can put the functions `main` and `factorial` in a file, compile this file with the **cc** command, at the UNIX system shell level, and then run **a.out**. You should first see the message

```
Please enter value of n =
```

Now type in a *small* integer—say, 5—then press RETURN. If it works correctly, the screen should display

```
factorial(5)=120
```

Now let's go through the main program. The line

```c
#include <stdio.h>
```

is a *directive* to the C preprocessor to include the *standard I/O header file* `stdio.h`. A *header file* usually contains declarations to allow functions and variables in one file to be used by functions in other files. The `stdio.h` header file is needed for C standard I/O library functions such as **scanf**.

2.5 Simple I/O Data Formats

Like the **printf** function, **scanf** is also part of the standard I/O library. In the factorial example,

```c
scanf("%d", &n);
```

reads an integer from standard input (the keyboard) and stores it in the variable n. The input data *format* is specified by the first argument in the form of a string constant (`"%d"`). The memory locations where the input data should be stored are supplied as the other arguments to **scanf**. Here, the `%d` specifies an integer (`int`) input format. The second argument `&n` supplies the memory address of the integer variable n. The **scanf** function requires `&n`, rather than n, because it needs to store a value accessible through n in the calling function after **scanf** returns.

In C an address of a memory location is called a *pointer*. The unary operator `&` obtains the memory address of the given variable. Thus, `&n` is a pointer to the value of n.

Like **scanf** the **printf** function also requires data formats to perform output. For example,

```
printf("factorial(%d)=", n);
printf("%d\n", factorial(n));
```

Here `%d` not only specifies an integer output format but also the position where that integer is spliced into the overall output, as given by the first argument to **printf**. The values to be used in the output are given, in order, as the remaining arguments to **printf**. Therefore, the function **printf** may take *any number of arguments* depending on how many values are involved in the output. In each of the above **printf** calls, only one integer is involved, and the second argument supplies that value.

There are fundamental reasons why data formats are necessary in I/O requests. To output the value of a variable, it must first be converted from its internal binary representation to a standard representation suitable for human understanding. Integers are commonly converted to base 10 notation (decimal) for output. A similar conversion in the other direction must take place during data input. The data formats in **printf** and **scanf** indicate specific representation conversions.

Besides the `%d` integer format, many other data formats are available for **scanf** and **printf** and will be discussed when the need arises. A comprehensive coverage of these two functions can be found in Chapter 8.

2.6 Simple Conditional Statements

Let us now look at the `if` statement in the factorial example. The `if...else` statement provides *conditional branching* and can be used in the simple form

```
if  ( condition )
     statement one
else
     statement two
```

The parentheses around the *condition* are mandatory. The condition is first tested to decide which one of the two given statements is executed. If the condition is true, then only statement one is executed; otherwise, only statement two is executed. Because a statement, by definition, can be either simple or compound, then statement one or two here can be compound in the form { st_1; ... st_n; }.

The else part can also be omitted, resulting in the form

```
if   ( condition )
        statement
```

The effect is to execute the given statement only if the condition is true. Failing this, the statement is skipped over, and control flows to the next statement after the if statement.

The following statement

```
if ( n > 0 )
        m = m + n;
else
        m = m - n;
```

adds to m the absolute value of n. The condition

```
n > 0
```

is a *relational expression*. Its value is *true* only if the current value of n is greater than zero; otherwise, its value is *false*. The > is a relational operator. Table 2.1 lists the relational operators for numeric comparisons.

Do *not* confuse the relational operator == with the assignment operator =. If you use one less equal sign, your test condition becomes an assignment, which is perfectly legal in C. The value of the assignment now, mistakenly,

Operator	Meaning
>	Greater than
<	Less than
==	Equal to
!=	Not equal to
>=	Greater than or equal to
<=	Less than or equal to

Table 2.1: Relational Operators

becomes the test result. This mistake will not cause compilation or execution errors, except the answer produced will be wrong.

The logical constants *true* and *false* (also known as Boolean values) are represented by integers: *false* by zero and *true* by nonzero. Because of this, the condition

```
if ( n != 0 )          (n not equal to 0)
```

is the same as the simplified condition

```
if ( n )
```

$0 = false$
$non\text{-}0 = true$

Generating a Factorial Table

By slightly modifying the main program, we can generate a series of factorial values and display them in a table format.

```
#include <stdio.h>

main()
{ int n, i=0;
        printf("Please enter value of n =");
        scanf("%d", &n);
        if ( n >= 0 )
            while ( n >= 0 )                /* output all n factorials */
            {     printf("factorial(%d)=%d\n", i, factorial(i));
                  i = i + 1;
                  n = n - 1;
            }
        else
            printf("factorial of a negative number is undefined\n");
}
```

If you compare this version of main with the previous one, you will see that the only change made was to the `if` statement. Instead of putting out factorial(*n*), we now use a `while` loop to output factorial(0) to factorial(*n*). (Exercise 4 at the end of this chapter suggests a more efficient implementation.) The following table is generated for *n* = 12:

```
factorial(0)=1
factorial(1)=1
factorial(2)=2
factorial(3)=6
factorial(4)=24
factorial(5)=120
factorial(6)=720
```

```
factorial(7)=5040
factorial(8)=40320
factorial(9)=362880
factorial(10)=3628800
factorial(11)=39916800
factorial(12)=479001600
```

As you can see, the factorial grows very rapidly with increasing *n*. In fact, factorial(13) would go over the maximum size of type int on most 32-bit computers. Section 2.9 gives more information on the size of numbers.

2.7 Characters and Character Input and Output

Among the most basic operations in C programming are the input and output of characters. To illustrate these operations, let's write a filter (Section 1.8.2) that does the following:

1. Reads characters from standard input.
2. Converts any uppercase characters into lowercase characters.
3. Writes all characters out to standard output.

We first write a function that converts uppercase characters to lowercase characters. Our lower function is called with a character and returns the lower case of this character:

```
int lower(int c)
{     if ( c >= 'A' && c <= 'Z' )
          return( c + 'a' - 'A' );
      else return(c);
}
```

A character enclosed in single quotes such as 'Z' is a *character constant*. A character is represented by its integer code in the computer's character set, normally ASCII (see Appendix 4).

Again, we use the if construct:

> if (*character is uppercase*)
>   *compute and return lowercase value*
> else
>   *return character unchanged*

The relational expression c >= 'A' tests whether the ASCII value of c is greater than or equal to (>=) the constant character 'A'. The result is 0 if the answer is no (false), and the result is 1, *or any nonzero value*, if the answer is yes (true). The second test c <= 'Z' works similarly.

Logical Operator	Meaning
&&	Logical operator *and*
||	Logical operator *or*
!	Logical operator *not* (unary)

Table 2.2: Logical Operators

The && is the *logical and* operator used in

```
if ( c >= 'A' && c <= 'Z' )
```

to determine if both tests are true. (Table 2.4 lists the logical operators.) Satisfying this logical condition means c is uppercase. To compute the corresponding lowercase character, we add to c a constant shift, 'a' - 'A'. This method works as long as the uppercase (lowercase) characters have consecutive values between 'A' and 'Z' ('a' and 'z').

Now all the main program has to do is to call the function lower on each input character and output what lower returns.

```
#include <stdio.h>

main()
{ int c;
    int lower(int c);            /* function prototype */
        while ( (c = getchar()) != EOF )
        /* read characters until end of file */   while not
            putchar(lower(c));                          eof
}
```

Note that the function lower is declared before it is used in the body of main. Generally, a function should be declared before it is used. The declaration

```
int lower(int c);
```

tells the C compiler that lower is a function that takes one argument of type int and returns a value of type int. In general, such a declaration takes the form of a function header terminated by a semicolon and is called a *function prototype*. Parameter names in a function prototype are optional but can provide valuable indications of the nature of the parameters. These function declarations are *new-style* defined by the ANSI standard. The traditional *old-style* function declaration, given with no parameter types, is also allowed but discouraged.

The standard I/O library functions **getchar** and **putchar** are used to read and write characters. They are usually implemented as *macros* in the stdio.h header file (Chapter 4): **getchar**() returns an int representing a character read from the standard input, and **putchar**(*c*) writes a character represented by *c* out to standard output. When there is no more input, **getchar**() returns a special value EOF (end of file), which is a *symbolic constant* (Section 4.3) whose value is defined in the stdio.h header file. Usually EOF is minus one (–1), which is a value that cannot be confused with any character. This is why the variable c in the main program has to be declared int rather than char.

The while condition

```
( c =  getchar() ) != EOF
```

is standard for reading characters from stdin until end of file is reached. This condition is true if c is *not equal to* EOF and becomes false only when end of file is reached. For keyboard input, a **^D** typed at the beginning of a line signifies end of file.

Note we have used an assignment on the left-hand side of the relational operator !=. In C an assignment statement such as

```
c = getchar()
```

is also an expression, called an *assignment expression*, whose value is that of the left-hand side after the assignment. In the while condition, the parentheses are needed around the assignment because the relational operator != has *higher precedence* than the assignment operator =. Without the parentheses, the result of

```
getchar() != EOF
```

would be assigned to c. When an expression is evaluated, an operator with higher precedence will be carried out before one with lower precedence. (Appendix 6 lists the relative precedence of all operators.) Parentheses can be used to override precedence rules as we have done here.

Put this program into a file—say, lowercase.c—compile, and run it with the following shell-level commands:

```
cc lowercase.c
mv a.out lower
lower
```

You have invoked the program as the command **lower**. Now type a mixture of uppercase and lowercase characters on the keyboard and press RETURN. You should see the same line displayed with all uppercase characters turned into lowercase characters. Type as many input lines as you like. Finish up by typing **^D** at the beginning of a line.

UNIX System Input Processing

When a character is typed, you would expect it to be processed by the program and to show up in the output immediately. Instead, you have to press RETURN before all characters typed on that line are processed. What actually happens is that UNIX holds keyboard input in a *buffer*, a holding area, to allow input editing and sends the input to the receiving program only after receiving a RETURN. The system program that interfaces your terminal and your program is a *terminal driver* known as the `tty`. The `tty` performs a set of complicated tasks and has distinct modes in which it controls your terminal (see Chapter 10).

The **lower** command satisfies the conditions for the filter set in Section 1.8.2. Thus, it can work with files through the use of I/O redirection at the UNIX system shell level. For instance,

> **lower** `< old > new`

will take input from the file `old` and send output to the file `new`. We can also use **lower** in a pipeline.

> **cat** `file1 file2 |` **lower** `> file3`

2.8 More Basic Constructs

Having seen some simple examples and having an idea of the overall structure of a C program, we are ready to look at a few more frequently used expressions and statements.

The `for` Loop

As we have mentioned, C has the usual arithmetic operators +, −, *, and /. In addition, there is the integer remainder operator % (e.g., `15 % 6` is 3). But there is no power or exponentiation operator. Therefore, we will write a power function that can raise integers to an integer power in order to illustrate the `for` statement.

```
int power(int a, int n)
{ int i, ans = 1;
      for ( i = 1 ; i <= n ; i = i+1 )
              ans = ans * a;
      return(ans);
}
```

In the function `power`, the `for` loop is in the general form

```
for ( init expr ; cont condition ; incr expr )        (loop control)
       statement                                       (loop body)
```

The statement for a loop body can be simple or compound. The loop control consists of three expressions separated by two semicolons. In the function `power`, the initialization expression

```
i = 1
```

is executed before the `for` loop starts. Then the continuation condition

```
i <= n
```

is tested. If true, the *statement*, or body, of the `for` loop is executed once. Then the increment expression

```
i = i + 1;
```

is executed, followed by a re-examination of the continuation condition. If it is true, the body is executed once again. If it is false, the `for` statement is finished. Figure 2.3 further illustrates the control flow of `for`.

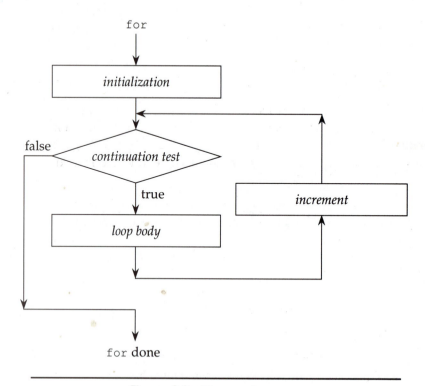

Figure 2.3: The `for` Loop

The `for` is a specialized `while`, and the iteration keeps going only while the test condition remains true. Thus, it is possible for the body of the `for` to be *skipped without ever being executed* if the test condition is false to start with. It is also worth noting that only two semicolons are used in the loop-control part of the `for`. Details on the forms of expressions themselves are discussed in Section 2.10.

It is possible to omit one or more of the three expressions in the `for` loop control. The absence of an expression indicates a *no-op*, an operation that does nothing. Thus, an infinite loop can be written as

```
for(;;) { /* loop body */ ... }        (infinite loop)
```

It is also possible to write a `for` with an empty loop body. In which case, the loop body is a *no-op*, and the effective computations would be contained in the loop control.

The function `power` assumes that the exponent n is nonnegative. It does not work for a negative n. Strictly speaking, there should be a check for the sign of n before the `for` loop is entered. Another concern is the size of the answer. If the answer exceeds the maximum size for the type `int`, `power` will fail. The handling of arithmetic overflow and underflow is implementation-dependent. It could happen that the variable `ans` suddenly becomes zero when overflow occurs. These problems can be solved when you are more familiar with the language.

Increment and Decrement Operators

The unary operators ++ (increment) and -- (decrement) are characteristic of the C language. These special operators are used to increase or decrease the value of an integer variable by 1 (this is especially useful in loops). Applied to a variable i, the special operator performs four separate functions in a single step:

- Accesses the current value of i.
- Adds or subtracts 1 from this value.
- Assigns the new value to i.
- Produces the old or new i as the value of the expression.

Specifically,

`i++`   Increment after: Adds 1 to i, gives old value of i.

`++i`   Increment before: Adds 1 to i; gives new value of i.

`i--`   Decrement after: Subtracts 1 from i, gives old value of i.

`--i`   Decrement before: Subtracts 1 from i; gives new value of i.

The idea is to combine referencing the value of a variable with assigning a new value to the variable to get shorter, more efficient running code. For example,

```
j = 2 * i++;
```

means use the old value of i in the multiplication with 2 and then change the value of i by adding 1 to it. Thus, it is shorthand for

```
j = 2 * i;
i = i + 1;
```

but more efficient. Similarly, the increment before usage in

```
j = 2 * ++i;
```

is short for

```
i = i + 1;
j = 2 * i;
```

which is very different from the increment after operation.

Here is the power function with the increment operator:

```
int power(int a, int n)
{ int i, ans;
      ans = 1;
      for ( i=1 ; i <= n ; i++ ) ans = ans * a;
      return(ans);
}
```

Note here we could have written ++i instead of i++ in the loop control of the for because the value of this increment expression is not used.

A yet more efficient implementation of power combines n-- with while, a construct we explained in Section 2.4.

```
int power(int a, int n)
{ int ans = 1;
      while ( n-- > 0 )
              ans = ans * a;
      return(ans);
}
```

Note the n-- in the while condition here cannot be replaced by --n. However, the relational expression n-- > 0 can be replaced by the simple n-- without changing the meaning of the while loop.

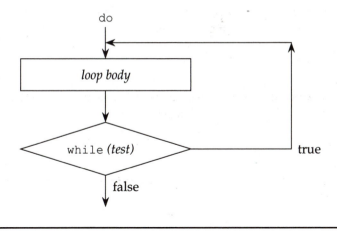

Figure 2.4: The do-while Loop

The do-while loop

The while and the for loops test the continuation condition at the beginning of the loop. If the condition is false to begin with, the while or for loop body is skipped without being executed. The do-while loop is the same as while, except it tests the continuation condition at the end of the loop (Figure 2.4). Therefore, a do-while loop body is executed *at least once*.

The general form of the do statement is

```
do body while ( condition ) ;
```

where the loop body is again a simple or compound statement. An example using the do-while construct is the octal_print function in Section 2.13.

The Multiway if

We have seen the simple if-else statement and how to use it. Let's look at the general form of the if statement:

```
if ( exp1 )
        statement-1
else if ( exp2 )
        statement-2
...
        . . .
else
        statement-i
```

There can be zero or more else if parts, and the else part is also optional.

This pattern specifies a multiway branching: if *exp1* is true, *state-ment-1* is executed; if *epx2* is true, *statement-2* is executed; if nothing is true, the *statement-i* is executed. In other words, the logical expressions are examined in order, and the first true expression triggers the execution of the corresponding statement. At most, one of the statements is executed. Control then goes to the next statement beyond the if.

Applying the if statement, let's write a function int_compare that takes two int quantities, a and b, and returns 1, 0, or –1, depending on whether a is bigger than, equal to, or less than b, respectively.

```
int int_compare(int a,  int b)
{    if ( a > b )
          return(1);
     else if ( a < b )
          return(-1);
     else
          return(0);
}
```

Actually, we don't need to insist on getting 1, 0, and –1 from int_com-pare. Instead, we can require the returned value to be positive, zero, or neg-ative, depending on the relative size of a and b. If we do that, then int_com-pare becomes simply

```
int int_compare(int a,  int b)
{     return( a-b );
}
```

A statement within an if can be another if to form a *nested* if state-ment. The function even_or_odd returns 2, 1, or 0 for n positive even, posi-tive odd, or neither, respectively.

```
int even_or_odd(int n)
{    if ( n > 0 )
          if ( n % 2 == 0 )           /* inner if begin */
               return(2);
          else
               return(1);             /* inner if end   */
     return(0)
}
```

The arithmetic operator % computes the remainder (Section 2.10). A good question here is "To which if does the else belong?". In C, an else or an if else clause automatically goes with the immediately preceding open `if`. An `if` without an `else` can be closed off by enclosing it in { }, making it a compound statement.

2.9 Data Types and Declarations

Unlike many other high-level languages that offer a wide variety of basic data types, C offers only a few, keeping the language simple and compact. The *basic types* are `char`, `int`, `float`, and `double`—a short list indeed considering that even a character string is not a basic type.

Data Type `char`

We have used characters in a limited way without details of the character type. A `char` type is a single byte (typically, 8 bits), enough to hold one character in the character set. A common standard is ASCII (American Standard Code for Information Interchange) shown in Appendix 4. A `char` byte represents a character with an integer encoding defined in the character set. In ASCII each character has a nonnegative integer code. For instance, the letters Z and z are represented by 90 and 122, respectively.

Like `'A'` and `'Z'`, a character constant is specified within single quotation marks. The value of a character constant is merely its integer code. For example, in ASCII `'9'` has numeric value 57. A character constant and its equivalent integer value are interchangeable in usage. However, by using the character constant notation you make your program *character-set-independent* and easier to read.

A few special characters are specified by two-character *escape sequences* such as `'\n'`, the NEWLINE character we discussed before. Table 2.3 contains a list of all such escape sequences.

`\n`	NEWLINE	`\r`	RETURN
`\t`	TAB	`\v`	VERTICAL TAB
`\'`	SINGLE QUOTE	`\"`	DOUBLE QUOTE
`\\`	BACKSLASH	`\b`	BACKSPACE
`\f`	FORMFEED	`\a`	BELL
`\?`	QUESTION MARK	`\0`	null character
`\ooo`	Octal byte	`\xhh`	Hexadecimal byte

Table 2.3: Character Escape Sequences

Character	Constant	Integer Value	Bit Pattern	Octal Notation	Hex Notation
Zero	'0'	48	00111001	060	0x30
NEWLINE	'\n'	10	00001010	012	0xa
Plus sign	'+'	43	00101011	053	0x2b
Cap *A*	'A'	65	01000001	0101	0x41
Small *a*	'a'	97	01100001	0141	0x61
^D	'04'	4	00000100	04	0x4

Table 2.4: Character Representations

Any constant, byte-size, bit pattern can also be specified using a notation with one to three octal (base 8) digits (0-7) or one to two hexadecimal (base 16) digits (0 . . . 9, *a* . . . *f*, *A* . . . *F*). Some byte-size patterns (anything over 128) do not correspond to any character code in ASCII. Table 2.4 shows a sample of characters in various notations.

Data Type `int`

Type `int` holds an integer quantity. The size (number of bits) of type `int` is machine-dependent and normally reflects the machine word size. Besides `int`, there are `short int` and `long int` types. Again, their sizes are machine-dependent. Typically, on a 32-bit computer, you'll have a 16-bit `short int`, a 32-bit `int` and a 32-bit or 64-bit `long int`. Dropping the word `int`, you can specify these types simply as `short` or `long`.

The `signed` and `unsigned` Integers

Integer types such as `int` and `char` normally are interpreted with a leading *sign bit*. This means if the leading bit is zero the quantity is positive; otherwise, it is negative. Thus, if `char` uses 8 bits, then the value ranges from –128 to 127. Hence, about half of the available representations are taken up by negative values.

In cases where the negative values are not needed, a representation with a leading sign bit will waste 50 percent of the possible values. However, this can be avoided. The qualifiers `signed` and `unsigned` can be used on `int`, `char`, and other integer types to enable (default) and disable the use of the sign bit. An `unsigned` number obeys integer arithmetic modulo 2^n where *n* is the number of bits in the type. Therefore, for *n* = 32, `unsigned int` values range between 0 and $2^{32} - 1$. The signed and unsigned representations of a positive integer are the same. The maximum and minimum values of various data types are implementation-dependent and are kept in the standard header files `limits.h` and `float.h`. Symbolic constants such as `INT_MAX` and `INT_MIN` (typically $2^{31} - 1$ and -2^{31} on a 32-bit computer) are defined in `limits.h`. If your C does not have the file `limits.h`, you should look in the file `values.h` to find the maximum integer `MAXINT`.

The short test program

```
#include <limits.h>

main()
{ unsigned int a = INT_MAX + 1;
  int b = INT_MAX + 1;
      printf("%u, %d \n", a, b);
}
```

will show you the value of `INT_MAX` and the meaning of `unsigned` versus `signed` quantities. Note the `%u` format for **printf** is for unsigned integers.

Forms of Constants

An integer constant is composed of an optional sign (+ or −), followed by a sequence of digits. An integer given in octal or hex begins with a 0 (zero) or a 0x prefix, respectively. If an integer constant given in your program is large and does not fit into an `int`, the compiler will take it as a `long`. You can also use trailing characters to explicitly indicate `long`, `unsigned`, and so on, as shown in Table 2.5.

Number	Type	Number	Type
−9876	int	−9876L or −9876l	long
1234U or 1234u	unsigned	1234UL or 1234ul	unsigned long
025	Octal int	0xFFF	Hex int
025L	long octal	0xFFFul	unsigned long hex
3.14159	double	32e-4 or 32E-4	double
3.1416f or 3.1416F	float	314e-4l or 314E-4L	long double

Table 2.5: Integer and Floating-Point Constants

A single-precision floating-point type, `float`, has a size suggested by the machine architecture. A double-precision floating point, `double`, typically uses twice as many bits as `float`. There is also `long double`, which usually supplies yet more precision.

A floating-point constant contains a decimal point (3.1416), an exponent (31416e-4), or both. The type is assumed to be `double` unless the constant has a trailing f or F (`float`), l or L (`long double`) (Table 2.5).

Variables and Identifiers

A variable is an *identifier* referring to a memory location holding a value. There is more to an identifier than just variable names. It can be a function name, a symbolic constant, and so on. An identifier consists of a sequence of letters, digits, and underscores (_) whose first character must not be a digit. Uppercase and lowercase letters are different. An identifier can be of any length, but only the first 31 characters are *significant*. This means two identifiers with the same first 31 characters will be treated as the same. The number of significant characters may be less than 31 for identifiers used across different files.

As mentioned before, the data type of a variable must be declared before it is used in a program. When a variable is declared it can also be initialized. For example,

```
char shift='a' - 'A';
int i = 7;
float x = 1.2f;
long double pi = 3.141592653589793L;
```

With only one exception (Section 3.3), the initialization expression must involve only constants. The different types of expressions you can form is our next subject.

2.10 Operators and Expressions

Constants, variables, and function calls are the simplest sorts of expressions. When combined with operators, they form more involved expressions. Whether an expression is simple or complicated, it always gives a value.

An operator acts on operands. A *binary operator* takes two operands, and a *unary operator* takes only one operand. In an expression involving multiple operators, the order in which the operations are carried out is very important. In the expression,

```
a + b / c
```

the division is carried out before addition. We say that the operator / takes precedence over +. Appendix 6 shows the relative precedence of all operators. When in doubt, you can always use parentheses to override the precedence rules as in

```
(a + b) / c
```

The following sections describe the available operators and expressions. For easy reference, Tables 2.6–2.9 summarize the operators and expressions.

2.10.1 Arithmetic Expressions

Table 2.6 shows the variety of arithmetic expressions. When the divide operator / is used on two integers, the result, or value, produced is an integer quotient. Any fractional part will be discarded. The increment and decrement operators can be used only on actual variables. Therefore, an expression like (a+b)++ is incorrect.

The arithmetic operator % provides the remainder, or *modulo operation*, for integer operands. To compute i modulo j means to divide i by j and take the remainder. If both i and j are nonnegative, then the result is nonnegative and smaller than j. Otherwise, you can only count on the absolute value of the result to be smaller than the absolute value of j. Furthermore, % does not work for floating-point numbers. The modulo operation (mod for short) is useful in many situations.

Expression	Description
a/(3.4+b)-3*c	Usual precedence and type conversions
i/4	Integer division truncates any fractional part
i % j	Integer reminder; denominator j should be positive
x*x*x	No built-in power operator
++i, j++	Pre/postincrement (integer only)
--i, j--	Pre/postdecrement (integer only)

Table 2.6: Arithmetic Expressions

Expression	Description
0	Logical false
1 or nonzero	Logical true
a > b, a < b, a >= b, a <= b	Relational expressions have logical values
a == b, a != b	Equal, not equal
a > 0 && a < 1	True if first *and* second relations are true
a > 1 || a < -1	True if first *or* second relation is true
a || ! b && c	*a* or [(not *b*) and *c*]
a > b ? a : b	Conditional expression; if (*a* > *b*), then value is *a*, else *b*

Table 2.7: Relational and Logical Expressions

Consider computing the next tab position, given any current column position. On a typical terminal, tab stops are set eight columns apart. So the next tab stop is given by

```
c - (c % 8) + 8
```

for any current column position c. The UNIX system command **expand** uses this principle to replace each tab character in a text file by an equivalent number of spaces.

2.10.2 Relational and Logical Expressions

We have seen some relational and logical expressions before. Table 2.1 lists the set of all relational operators. Table 2.7 shows all forms of relational and logical expressions.

The relational operators have higher precedence than the operator &&
(logical and), which takes precedence over || (logical or). *Evaluation of a logical expression stops as soon as the logical value of the whole expression is determined.* This may leave some operands unevaluated. For example, the expression

```
exp1 && exp2
```

is true only if both *exp1* and *exp2* are true. If *exp1* turns out to be false, the value of the whole must be false; therefore, *exp2* is not evaluated. Similarly, in evaluating *exp1 || exp2*

if *exp1* is true, the value of the whole expression is true, and *exp2* will not be evaluated.

The unary operator ! (logical not) *negates* the logical value of its operand. The negation turns true into false, and vice versa. Because it is a unary operator, it has precedence over all relational and other logical operators. For an example of a rather complicated logical expression, see the readline function in Section 2.13.

C also features the *conditional expression* formed with the *ternary operator* ? :, which takes *three* operands:

exp0 ? exp1 : exp2

The expression has value *exp1* if *exp0* is true, and *exp2* otherwise. Thus, the expression

```
c = a > b ? a : b
```

sets c to max(a,b).

2.10.3 Assignment Expressions

An *assignment* is a statement as well as an expression because it produces a value—that of the left-hand side after the assignment is made. Hence, an assignment can be used anywhere an expression can. Furthermore, like the increment and decrement operators, the assignment operator = can combine with other operators to form efficient shorthand expressions. Table 2.8 shows the allowable combinations.

To see assignment expressions in action, let's write a function to compute the sum of the squares of the first n odd integers:

```
int sum_squares(int n)        /* n is assumed positive */
{ int sum, i;
    sum = i = 1;
    n *= 2;                    /* n = n * 2             */
    while ( (i += 2) < n ) sum += (i * i);
    return(sum);
}
```

In sum_squares the assumption is made that the argument n is positive. The while loop is completely bypassed for the case n = 1. The parentheses around i += 2 in the while condition are necessary because assignment operators have lower precedence than almost all other operators. For the same reason, the parentheses around i * i are unnecessary but included for readability.

Expression	Comment
a = b = 1	a = (b = 1)
(c = getchar()) != EOF	Assignment expression used in a relational expression
a += b	Shorthand for a = a + b
a *op*= b	Shorthand for a = a *op* b, allowable *ops*: +, −, *, /, %, <<, >>, &, ^, |

Table 2.8: Assignment Expressions

Some older C compilers still accept such outdated usages as =−. If you happened to enter the code

    x=−y;   (possible old style)

to assign −y to x, you may be in for a surprise. It could be taken to mean x = x − y. It is good practice to always surround your assignment operator = with white space.

2.10.4 Bitwise Operations

Another group of operators let you deal with data at the bit level. These include << (left shift), >> (right shift), as well as bitwise logical operators & (and), | (or), and ~ (not). The bitwise operators take only operands of integer types (Table 2.9).

Unlike the increment and decrement operators, bitwise operations do not alter their operands. Thus, j = i << 4 produces an integer value equal to left-shifting i by 4 bits without damaging the contents of i. If you want to actually modify i, use

    i <<= 4;

A 1-bit leftshift on an integer is normally equivalent to multiplying by 2. Thus, the above operation results in a value 16 times that of i.

Let's apply bitwise operations as an alternative way to compute the next tab stop. By zeroing out the last three bits of the current column position c, we can use

    (c & ~07) + 8

to produce the position of the next tab stop. The bit pattern ~07 (bitwise not applied to octal 7) is all 1's except the lowest 3 bits. It is used as a *mask* by the

Expression	Comment
n & 017	Bitwise and; value is n with all but lower 4 bits masked away
i | j	Bitwise i or j
i ^ j	Bitwise i **exclusive or** j
i << 4	Value is **left shift** i **by 4 bits**
j >> 5	Value is **right shift** j **by 5 bits**
~n	**1's complement of** n

Table 2.9: Integer Bitwise Expressions

bitwise & operation to produce a value same as c but with the last three bits blocked out.

Bitwise operations not only allow manipulations at the bit level but also provide an efficient way to perform certain arithmetic operations involving positive or unsigned integers (Exercise 11). For example, left-shifting the number 3 by 1 bit gives 6. Conversely, right-shifting 6 by 1 bit gives 3.

An example of bitwise operations is the function octal_print in Section 2.13.

2.11 Arrays

Basic Concepts

An array is composed of consecutive memory locations, *array cells*, each of which holds data of the same type. For example,

```
int b[10];
```

declares b an array and defines for it 10 cells, b[0] through b[9], each just large enough to hold a quantity of type int. Unlike some other languages, in C *array index goes from 0 to the dimension –1*. This is important to keep in mind. Here are some typical usages:

```
b[0] = 17;
n = b[i+1] - 13;
for ( i = 0 ; i < 10 ; i++ ) b[i] = 0;
```

b[0]	b[1]	b[2]	b[3]	b[4]	b[5]	b[6]	b[7]	b[8]	b[9]
2	3	5	7	11	13	17	19	23	29

Figure 2.5: The Integer Array b

The array b can be declared and initialized to hold the first 10 prime numbers as follows:

```
int b[]={2,3,5,7,11,13,17,19,23,29};
```

When the array size is left unspecified, the C compiler figures out the dimension of b from the number of data items supplied. Figure 2.5 provides a graphical representation of the array b.

Once an array is created, its cells can be used to store and retrieve data of a given type. Cells are accessed using the index notation b[i] where each array cell can be thought of and treated as a separate variable. Thus, an array can be viewed as a set of subscripted variables.

Character Arrays

In C a character string, or simply *string*, is represented by a character array. The notation

```
"Happy Birthday"
```

specifies a string constant. Figure 2.6 shows the structure of an array containing this string. The special *null character* '\0' (BACKSLASH zero) marks the end of a character string. The null character has an integer value of zero.

To create the array, do the following:

```
char st[15];          (declare st character array length 15)
st[0] = 'H';
st[1] = 'a';
    .                 (and so on)
    .
    .
st[12] = 'a';
st[13] = 'y';
st[14] = '\0';        (string terminator)
```

A much easier but entirely equivalent way is to initialize it using the following shorthand notation:

```
char st[] = "Happy Birthday";
```

| H | a | p | p | y | | B | i | r | t | h | d | a | y | \0 |

Figure 2.6: A String as a Character Array

As before, the compiler figures out how large to make st in order to accommodate the character string and the extra terminator at the end.

To illustrate the usage of character strings, let's write a function strequal(x,y) that returns a one (for true) or zero (for false), depending on whether the character strings x and y are equal.

```
int strequal(char x[], char y[])       /* array formal parameters */
{ int i=0;
        if ( x == y ) return(1);       /* same memory locations   */
        while ( x[i] == y[i] )
        {       if ( x[i] == '\0' )
                    return (1);        /* strings equal           */
                i++;

        }
        return(0);                     /* strings unequal         */
}
```

The header of strequal declares two array formal parameters x and y. In general, the notation

type var[]

as part of the formal parameter list declares *var* an array of the given *type*.

Now let us see how strequal works. If the condition (x == y) is true, then x and y refer to the same memory location. This means that we are actually comparing a string with itself, which should return one immediately. If x and y point to different memory locations, they can still contain the same characters and be equal. So we use a while loop to compare the individual characters to determine if they are equal.

Now we can write a main program to test strequal:

```
main()
{ char a[]= "abcde";
  char b[]= "abcde";
  char c[]= "abcd";
      if ( strequal(a,b) )
          printf("a is equal to b\n");
```

```
        if ( ! strequal(b,c) )        /* ! is logical not */
            printf("b is not equal to c\n");
    }
```

A handy-to-use set of string-manipulation library functions, including one that compares two strings, is available. These will be discussed in Chapter 5. Check these out before you write a string function that already exists.

2.12 Pointers

A *pointer* is the address of the memory location where a piece of data is stored. A pointer variable can be declared by preceding the variable name with an asterisk (`*`). Here are some examples:

```
int *i, *j;
```
(The value of `i` and `j` are pointers to `int`)
```
char *c;
```
(The value of `c` is a pointer to `char`)
```
long *k;
```
(The value of `k` is a pointer to `long int`)
```
float *x;
```
(The value of `x` is a pointer to `float`)
```
double *y;
```
(The value of `y` is a pointer to `double`)

The memory location where a variable stores its value is obtained by the unary `&` operator (the address-of operator). Thus,

```
int i = 512;
int *j;
```
(declare `j` to be an int pointer variable)
```
j = &i;
```
(`j` is assigned the address of `i`)

results in `j` being a pointer to where 512 is stored. To be specific, let's say the value of `i` is stored at memory location 49132. Then the variable `j` has the value 49132. To obtain the value 512 through `j`, use the *unary value-of operator* `*`. For instance, `*j + 2` gives 514. The notation `*j` is equivalent to a variable of type `int`. To illustrate this, consider

```
*j = 0;
```

This puts zero where the value 512 was formerly; so `i` is now zero also. Figure 2.7 further illustrates the pointer concept.

Because memory locations are usually referenced as byte or word counts, a pointer is usually represented by a single-precision integer value. Much more will be said about pointers in Chapter 6.

Array Assignments

When we see an assignment such as u = v, we normally think of the variable u getting a copy of the value of v. In C this is correct except for arrays. In fact, an array name, b for instance, is actually a *constant pointer* to the first cell of

Figure 2.7: The Meaning of a Pointer

the array. Therefore, the array name cannot be used as a variable on the left-hand side of an assignment. Hence, the following is incorrect:

```
int foo[10];
foo = b;        (incorrect; array name foo is not a variable)
```

To make an array assignment, we need a pointer variable of the correct type on the left-hand side of the assignment. To assign b to a variable x, we need

```
int *x;
x = b;          (array assignment is by pointer)
```

Now the elements of b can also be accessed via x. Keep in mind that the cells of the array b are still where they were, only now x can also access them. Thus,

```
x[3] = 96;
```

will result in b[3] containing 96 as well.

Similarly, when an array name is used in a function call, a pointer to the first cell is passed to the called function.

2.13 Examples

We have outlined quite a few constructs, and it is time to combine them in larger examples to further illustrate their use in building programs. We will study two programs: readline for reading input lines and octal_print for displaying an octal number. In the process, we will show how control-flow constructs, arrays, and relational, logical, arithmetic, and bitwise expressions are used in the proper C fashion.

The readline Function

The readline function reads a line from standard input, stores the line in a character array, and returns the length of the line. This function is useful in other programs, to obtain user input.

```
int readline(char s[], int max)
{ int c, i = 0;
      max--;                          /* max is the size of the array s */
      while ( i < max && (c = getchar()) != EOF && c != '\n')
              s[i++] = c;
      if ( c == '\n' ) s[i++] = c;
      s[i] = '\0';                    /* string terminator           */
      return(i);
}
```

The `while` condition in `readline` is the most complicated expression we have encountered so far. It consists of three relational expressions connected by two logical operators. The effect is to read characters into the array s until either a `'\n'` is reached, the end of the file is reached, or the array is full (i == max). After the `while`, the `'\n'`, if any, is deposited into the array, then the string terminator `'\0'` is added at the end. The number of actual characters read is then returned.

On UNIX, a text file or input supplied through the keyboard normally consists of complete lines each terminated by a `'\n'` character. The last line in the file is no exception. The `readline` function makes this assumption. Therefore, the returned value is always the number of characters read even when end of file is reached.

A file `readline.c` can be established as follows:

```
#include <stdio.h>
#define SIZE 100
/* put definition of readline here */

main()
{ char line[SIZE];
  int n;
      while ( (n = readline(line, SIZE)) > 0 )
          printf("n=%d \t line=%s", n, line);
}
```

Here we have used the C-preprocessor directive `#define` (Section 4.3) to establish a symbolic name `SIZE` for the constant `100`. Once defined, a symbolic constant can be used instead of the actual constant in the source code. It is good practice to avoid using numeric constants in programs; use symbolic constants with meaningful names. This approach not only makes programs easier to understand but also lets you modify every occurrence of a constant by simply changing its `#define` line.

After compilation with

cc `readline.c`

you can run the program with

a.out `< testdata`

and get a display of something like

```
n=6      line=ABCDE
n=10     line=123456789
```

Octal Conversion

To illustrate use of the character arrays and some of the other topics we have covered so far, let us now write a function `octal_print` that displays a decimal integer in octal notation. Our strategy is to first compute the octal characters and store them in a character array `s[]`. The characters are then output using **putchar**:

```
#define DIG 20
void octal_print(int x)
{ int i = 0, od;
  char s[DIG];              /* up to DIG octal digits       */
      if ( x < 0 )          /* treat negative x             */
      {    putchar('-');    /* output minus sign            */
           x = -x;
      }
      do
      {    od = x % 8;             /* next higher octal digit        */
           s[i++] = (od + '0');   /* octal digits in char form      */
      } while ( (x = x/8) > 0 );  /* quotient by integer division   */
      putchar('0');               /* octal number prefix            */
      do
      {    putchar(s[--i]);       /* output characters on s         */
      } while ( i > 0 );
      putchar('\n');
}
```

The procedure to convert an integer to octal is to divide by 8 repeatedly until the quotient becomes 0. The remainders become a sequence of octal digits. For the integer 2978, we have

Number	Quotient	Remainder
2978	372	2
372	46	4
46	5	6
5	0	5

giving the octal number 05642.

The function `octal_print` is declared `void` because it does not return a value. The printing procedure first examines the sign of the integer `x`. If `x` is negative, a minus sign is written to standard output, and `x` becomes positive. The first `do-while` loop computes the octal digits for `x` and stores them in the character array `s`.

After the conversion is done, the octal digits are in the array `s` and the index `i-1` points to the leading digit. The octal prefix `0` is sent out before the second `do-while` loop displays the characters in `s`.

You already know that `%` is the remainder, or *mod operator*. Thus, the expression `x % 8` gives the remainder of `x` by 8. Also, if `n` is a digit between 0 and 9, the expression

    `n + '0'`   (value of character `'0'` plus n)

is a machine-independent way to obtain the numeric character of `n`.

Also note that in this function, the `i++` (increment after) and `--i` (decrement before) operations are critical. If `i++` were replaced by `++i`, the array cell `s[0]` would be left unused. Similarly, if `--i` were replaced by `i--`, an unassigned cell of `s` would be accessed.

To test `octal_print`, use a straightforward main function:

```c
#include <stdio.h>

/* put octal_print here */

main()
{   octal_print(0);
    octal_print(-1);
    octal_print(0123456);
    octal_print(-0123456);
    octal_print(999);
    octal_print(-999);
    octal_print(2978);
}
```

After compilation and execution, this program displays the output

```
00
-01
0123456
-0123456
01747
-01747
05642
```

Octal Conversion with Bitwise Operations

A more efficient version of `octal_print` uses bitwise operations to achieve
the modulo 8 and the divide by eight operations:

```
#define LOWDIGIT 07          /* least significant octal digit mask */

void octal_print(register int x)
{ register int i = 0;
  char s[DIG];
      if ( x < 0 )
      {   putchar('-');
          x = -x;
      }
      do {  s[i++] = ((x & LOWDIGIT) + '0');
                                    /* mod performed with &    */
          }  while ( ( x >>= 3) > 0 ); /* divide x by 8 via shift */
      putchar('0');
      do {  putchar(s[--i]);
          }  while ( i > 0 );
      putchar('\n');

}
```

When performance is a concern, like in this example, use the `register` *modifier* to indicate to the compiler quantities that should be kept in machine registers for faster access. Treatment of the `register` *declaration* depends on the
number of registers available on a given computer and the way a particular
compiler works.

2.14 Command-Line Arguments

When a C program is executed, it is possible to supply arguments to the C
program on the command line at the shell level. This section describes the
way *command-line arguments* are passed to a C program on UNIX.

When you invoke a C program at the shell level, any command-line arguments you supply are passed as character strings to the C function `main`. A `main` function expecting arguments is normally declared as follows:

```
int main(int argc, char *argv[])
```

The parameter `argc` is an integer. The notation

```
char *argv[]
```

declares the formal array parameter `argv` as having elements of type `char *` (character pointer). In other words, each of the arguments `argv[0]`, `argv[1]`,..., `argv[argc-1]` is a character pointer. The meanings of the formal arguments `argc` and `argv` are as follows:

`argc`	The number of command-line arguments, including the command name
`argv[n]`	A pointer to the *n*th command-line argument as a character string

If the command name is **cmd** and if it is invoked as

cmd *arg1 arg2*

then

`argc`	Is 3
`argv[0]`	Points to the command name **cmd**
`argv[1]`	Points to the string *arg1*
`argv[2]`	Points to the string *arg2*
`argv[3]`	Is 0 (NULL)

The parameters for the function `main` can be omitted if they are not needed.

Now let's write a program that receives command-line arguments. To keep it simple, all the program does is echo the command-line arguments to standard output.

```
/* the echo command */
#include <stdio.h>

int main(int argc, char *argv[])
{ int i = 1;                          /* begin with 1       */
    while ( i < argc )
    {    printf("%s", argv[i++]); /* output string      */
         printf(" ");                  /* output a space     */
    }
```

```
        printf("\n");                       /* terminate output line */
        return(0);
}
```

The program displays each entry of `argv` except `argv[0]` using the string
format `%s` of **printf.** To separate the strings, the program displays a space
after each `argv[i]`, and the last argument is followed by a NEWLINE.

Note that `main` is declared to return an int and the last statement of
`main` is

```
    return(0);
```

The return value of `main` indicates, to the invoker of the program,
whether the program executed successfully and terminated normally. This
value is referred to as the *exit status* and receives special treatment from
UNIX. A zero exit status is normal, whereas a positive exit status indicates
abnormal termination. At the UNIX system shell level, different actions can
be taken depending on the exit status of a command. Thus, it is advisable to
always use a return statement in the main program, even though it would
work without one.

As another example, let's rewrite a main program for the factorial function (Section 2.3) so that the argument n is supplied directly on the command
line:

```
#include <stdio.h>
#include <stdlib.h>   /* for atoi, not necessary on some systems */

int main(int argc, char *argv[])
{ int j;
        if ( argc != 2 )
        {    printf("factorial takes one integer argument\n");
             return(1);                 /* abnormal termination of main */
        }
        j = atoi(argv[1]);    /* ASCII string to integer conversion */
        printf("factorial(%d)=%d\n", j, factorial(j));
        return(0);
}
```

Now put this main program and the factorial function in a file, say, `facto-
rial.c`. Then compile with

cc `factorial.c -o factorial`

to create the executable file `factorial`. Now enter the command

factorial 5

at the shell level to get the output

```
factorial(5)=120
```

In the function `main`, the number of arguments supplied on the command line is checked first. If the correct number of arguments is not supplied, a message is displayed and the program terminates returning an abnormal exit status 1. It is a good idea for the `main` function to always check for the correctness of the command-line arguments before processing them.

Because command-line arguments are passed to `main` as character strings, the string `"5"` must be converted to an integer 5 before the function `factorial` can be called. The standard library function **atoi** is supplied for just this purpose because it converts an ASCII character string representation of a number to an integer. Other such conversion functions include **atof** (string to float) and **atol** (string to long). On some systems, you need to include the header file `stdlib.h` to use these conversion functions.

2.15 Function Calls and Passing of Arguments

As mentioned before, the definition of a function specifies the number and type of arguments it requires. The parameters given in the function header are called *formal parameters*. When a function is called, it must be supplied with the correct number and type of arguments. The arguments in the function call are known as the *actual arguments*, or, simply, *arguments*. The definition of `factorial` has a formal parameter n. In the function call `factorial(j)`, the variable `j` becomes the actual argument. When a function call is executed, the data objects referenced by the actual arguments are bound to the formal parameters so that they can be referenced in the body of the function. This binding is called *argument passing*.

When a function with more than one argument is called, *there is no restriction on the order in which arguments are evaluated*. Therefore, we cannot write code that depends on any specific order of argument evaluation. Thus, the function call

```
power(i++, i);        (incorrect usage)
```

is wrong because the result depends on which of the two arguments is evaluated first. You should use instead something like

```
power(i, i+1);
```

Parameters in a function header are formal in the sense that any name can be used for them without changing the meaning of the function. This is much like in mathematics—for example, when we say $f(x) = x^2$, we can just as well say $f(y) = y^2$.

Formal parameters are local to a function. When a function call is made, a copy of the value of the actual argument is passed to the formal parameter. In other words, arguments are *passed by value*. With pass by value, a function can work only on copies of the actual arguments, not on the actual arguments themselves. Therefore, the actual arguments will have the same values before and after the function call.

When necessary, modifying data in the calling function is possible. Do this by passing *pointers* as actual arguments. Recall that a pointer is the memory location, or address, of a piece of data. Once the called function gets the address, it can proceed to modify data stored there. As a result, we indirectly alter data in the calling function.

There is no automatic copying of the elements in an array when it is passed as an argument. Instead, the address of its first element is passed. (This is the value of the array name.) Therefore, the formal array parameter becomes another name by which the same array elements can be accessed.

2.16 I/O Streams

In Section 1.8.1, we discussed `stdin`, `stdout`, and `stderr`—three ready-made channels for input and output in each process. These actually are pointers to buffered I/O *streams* defined in the standard I/O library. Streams are defined to be of type `FILE` in the header file `stdio.h`. A stream pointer is therefore of type `FILE *` (pointer to type `FILE`).

We have seen character input and output performed with **getchar()** and **putchar()** in Section 2.7. They, in turn, use the library functions

```
int getc (FILE *stream)
int putc (int c, FILE *stream)
```

The **getc** function returns the next character read from the given *input stream*, and **putc** outputs the character *c* to the specified *output stream*. In fact, **putchar**(*c*) is just **putc** (*c*, stdout);, and **getchar**() is simply **getc** (*c*, stdin);.

Although the standard I/O streams are handy, there are occasions when you want to open your own I/O streams to read or write a file. The standard I/O library function **fopen** is used to open new streams:

```
FILE *fopen (char *filename, char *mode);
```

The function **fopen** takes two character string arguments *filename* and *mode*. Again, *filename* can be a simple, relative, or full pathname. The *mode* is a *string* indicating whether the given `file` is opened for reading (`"r"`) or writing (`"w"`) (see Chapter 8 for other possible modes). For example,

```
FILE *fp;
fp = fopen("mydatafile", "r");
```

gives you the stream `fp` to read the file `mydatafile`. After using a stream that you have opened, you should also close it. A stream is closed with the library function

```
fclose  (FILE *stream);
```

which sends any characters remaining in the buffer to the proper receiver (called *flushing the buffer*) before closing the stream.

The next section gives an example that uses all three standard streams and shows how to perform input and output to a file. Chapter 8 discusses other input/output functions provided by the standard C library.

2.17   Error Handling

A very important aspect of programming concerns the handling of possible errors during the execution of a program. Many kinds of errors can occur at run time. The main program may be invoked with an incorrect number of arguments or unknown options. A function expecting a positive argument may be passed a negative value. Arithmetic operations can overflow or underflow. A well-written program should detect errors and take appropriate actions.

Displaying Error Messages

The main program should first check the arguments supplied on the command line for correctness. If the arguments are unacceptable, then a clear message should be displayed stating the nature of the error and its cause (if known). Use the stream `stderr` for sending error messages to ensure that error messages appear on the terminal, even if normal output through `stdout` is redirected. To send output to a specific output stream, use the library function **fprintf**. This function has a leading f in its name and is not to be confused with **printf**. It is a *file version* of **printf** in the sense that you can specify a file or stream where you want the output to go. A conditional statement such as

```
if ( argc != 3 )
{    fprintf(stderr, "%s: expects 2 arguments but was given %d\n",
                  argv[0], argc-1);
     fprintf(stderr, "Usage %s inputfile outputfile\n", argv[0]);
     exit(1);
}
```

checks the number of command-line arguments supplied. Note that the value of `argc` is by definition the number of command-line arguments *plus* 1. Always identify the program unit or subunit displaying the error message. The command name `argv[0]` identifies which program is announcing the error, in case it is executed in a pipeline or concurrently with other programs. When appropriate, a function name further narrows down the error location. In the above example, the program refers to its own name as `argv[0]`, which is better than assuming a specific filename.

After displaying an error message, a program may continue to execute, return a particular value not produced normally, or elect to abort. The library function **exit** is called to terminate the execution of a program:

```
void exit(int status);
```

When **exit** is called anywhere in a program, the entire program is terminated. For normal termination, `status` should be 0. For abnormal termination such as an error, a *positive* `status`, usually 1, is used. The routine **exit** first calls **fclose** on each open stream before executing the system call **_exit**, which causes immediate termination without buffer flushing.

Another common source of execution errors can be failed *system* and *library calls*. A library call such as **fopen** may fail because the file to be opened is not there or the access permission is denied. Similar failures can result from system calls, direct calls to functions supplied by UNIX. System calls normally return a value −1 to indicate failure instead of aborting. Failed C library functions typically return a −1 or NULL. The symbolic constant NULL is usually defined in `stdio.h` and stands for a pointer with the invalid value 0. In any case, the returned value of a system or library call must be checked for such error indications before a program continues. Here is a typical call to **fopen** with the proper error check:

```
FILE *out;
if ( (out = fopen(argv[2], "w")) == NULL )
{   fprintf(stderr, "%s: cannot open %s for writing\n",
            argv[0], argv[2]);
    exit(1);
}
```

Note that **fopen returns** NULL **if it fails**.

Error-Handling Example

Here we take the `lowercase` example first discussed in Section 2.7 and rewrite it into a full program complete with appropriate input/output and error handling. The intention is to define a **lowercase** command that works either as a filter when given no arguments or as a file transformer when

given an input file and an output file. Of course, the principal function is still
to map all uppercase letters into lowercase letters.

```
/*************    Program lowercase.c ****************************/
#include <stdio.h>

int lower(int c)
{    if ( c >= 'A' && c <= 'Z' )
        return( c +  'a' - 'A' );
    else return(c);
}


main(int argc, char * argv[])
{ int c;
  FILE *in, *out;                /* I/O stream pointers              */
      if (argc == 3)             /* I/O files supplied on command line */
      {   if ( (in = fopen(argv[1], "r")) == NULL )       /* (1)     */
          {   fprintf(stderr, "%s: Cannot open %s for reading\n",
                    argv[0], argv[1]);
              exit(1);
          }
          if ( (out = fopen(argv[2], "w")) == NULL )       /* (2) */
          {   fprintf(stderr, "%s: Cannot open %s for writing\n",
                    argv[0], argv[2]);
              exit(1);
          }
      }
      else if ( argc == 1 )    /* use stdin and stdout              */
      {   in = stdin;
          out = stdout;
      }
      else                                                /* (3) */
      {   fprintf(stderr,
              "%s: takes 0 or 2 arguments but was given %d\n",
                argv[0], argc-1);
          fprintf(stderr, "Usage: %s [ inputfile  outputfile ]\n",
                argv[0]);
          exit(1);
      }
      /*  the actual processing */
```

```
    while ( (c = getc(in)) != EOF )
        putc(lower(c), out);
    return(0);
}
/*************** End of lowercase.c  ****************************/
```

The main program of `lowercase.c` anticipates common errors: failure to open the input file (line 1), inability to open the output file (line 2), and wrong number of arguments (line 3). In the last case, a brief guide of how to use the command is actually displayed.

2.18 Thinking in C

It has often been said that language is the medium for thought. This is also true for a programming language. How well you program in C will depend on how well you think in C. Avoid formulating your ideas in another programming language and then translating the *foreign* thoughts into C. It takes some time for anyone to get used to the terse but efficient, cryptic but concise, statements of C. However, it is not difficult. A little effort on your part will help unleash the power of C and make programming much more fun.

Here are some ideas for improved C programs:

- Include `<stdio.h>` to use standard I/O streams.
- Declare functions and variables before using them.
- Terminate a declaration with a semicolon.
- Terminate a simple statement, but not a compound statement, with a semicolon.
- Increment with ++; decrement with --.
- Use shorthand assignments (x += 5, rather than $x = x + 5$).
- Remember that a character string is an array of characters terminated by `'\0'`.
- Use zero-based indexing for arrays. Thus, `int arr[100]` has its index running from 0 to 99.
- A character is represented by an integer and can be used as such.
- There is no exponentiation operator.
- The address-of operator `&` produces a pointer.
- The value-of operator `*` produces a value through a pointer.
- Arguments of functions are always passed by value.
- Loops in C use continuation conditions. The iteration ends when the condition becomes false.
- Logical false is zero, and logical true is anything else.
- Learn useful idioms such as `for( ;; )` (infinite loop), `for ( i=0 ; i < j ; i++ )`, `while( i-- )`,

while((c = getchar()) != EOF). (Idioms will be pointed out throughout the book.)

- Apply the ternary operator ?: to form conditional expressions; use the % operator to compute the remainder.
- Avoid hard-coded constants and always use ALL CAPS for symbolic constants and macros (Chapter 4).

Developing a consistent formatting style in which to render your C programs also helps. You will avoid syntax errors and make programs readable. The style used in this book is explained here with an example:

```
/* logical function strequal compares strings x and y  */
/* returns 1 if x is equal to y, 0 otherwise           */

int strequal(char x[], char y[])               /* (1) */
{ int i=0;                                      /* (2) */
  /* more declarations if any */
    if ( x == y ) return(1);                    /* (3) */
    while ( x[i] == y[i] )                      /* (4) */
    {   if ( x[i] == '\0' ) return(1);          /* (5) */
        i++;                                    /* (6) */
    }   /* end of while */                      /* (7) */
    return(0);                                  /* (8) */
} /* end of function strequal */
```

Use comments to document the purpose and effects of the function, the meaning of the arguments, and the value returned. Format the function body as follows:

1. Start the function header flush with the left margin.
2. Format the function body as a compound statement. Line up the opening brace with the function name. Indent local variable declarations one level. Use separate lines for readability as needed. If possible, initialize variables.
3. Indent another level all statements in a block. Keep statements on separate lines for readability. For statements such as if, while, for, and so on, some programmers prefer to always use compound blocks, even if they contain only one statement.
4. Format while as a block.
5. Keep a simple statement on one line. Some programmers may prefer using another line for the body of the if statement. That is all right as well.
6. Indent statements inside a block another level.
7. Line up the closing brace for while vertically with the opening brace. A comment can be added to clearly indicate the end of a multiline construct.

8. Always put a `return` at the end of a function.
9. Line up the closing brace of a function vertically with the opening brace. If the function is lengthy, a comment at the end will help as well.
10. Include comments alongside key statements to explain their purposes.

Give functions and variables meaningful names, using the underscore (_) to connect multiple words when appropriate. Be careful with long names. Use at most 31 characters for names internal to a file and less characters for names to be used across different files.

The `autoindent` feature of **vi** is very helpful for formatting C programs. Appendix 3 provides a set of **vi** macros useful for creating C source code. Our program examples will follow the formatting conventions closely. However, because explanations are usually included in the text, our examples tend not to have extensive comments.

2.19 Summary

This chapter presented a careful collection of materials to give the beginner an overall view of C programming and the ability to write interesting programs right away. Many topics were covered, sometimes with a "broad brush." This primer leads the reader through the basics of C in a logical fashion and provides a good foundation for the comprehensive treatment of topics to come in later chapters.

Functions are the basic building blocks of a C program. A program may involve many functions contained in one or more files. A function definition consists of a header and a body. The header specifies the function name, the number and type of formal parameters, and the type of any returned value. A function not returning any value has a value type `void`.

The function body is a block, or compound statement, consisting of zero or more declarations for local variables followed by zero or more statements, all enclosed in `{ }`. Functions must be declared before used. In a function prototype, an empty argument list is specified as `(void)`. Function arguments are always passed by value.

The `main` function is the entry point of a program. Command-line arguments are passed to the main program in the form of character strings. The return value of `main` is a termination status, which is available to the UNIX system shell. A zero status indicates normal termination, and a positive status indicates abnormal termination.

There are only four basic data types: `int`, `char`, `float`, and `double`. Type qualifiers `short`, `long`, and `unsigned` are used to obtain size and sign variations of these basic types. A variable must be declared before it is used and can be initialized when declared.

Constants and variables are combined by operators into expressions. There are arithmetic, relational, logical, increment and decrement, assignment, and bitwise operators. There is no power operator for exponentiation. Additionally, there is a ternary conditional operator (? :).

An array is a sequence of memory locations, which stores data of a given type. A character string is represented by an array of characters terminated by '\0'. Array elements are indexed starting from zero. The array name is a constant pointer to the first element of the array.

A pointer is the memory address where a piece of data is stored. Pointer variables provide a way to access data items through indirection. The address-of operator & produces a pointer. The value-of operator * obtains a value through a pointer.

Frequently used control-flow statements include if, while, for, and do-while.

The standard I/O library facilities **printf**, **scanf**, **putchar**, and **getchar** provide convenient input and ouput using the buffered streams stdout and stdin. Additionally, **putc**, **getc**, and **fprintf** perform input and output with any stream. The **fopen** call opens a new stream, and **fclose** flushes an existing stream before closing it.

A function ought to check the correctness of its arguments. An error message should identify its originator and be sent to stderr. When system or library calls fail, certain predefined values, like –1 and NULL, are returned. A calling function must check for such return values and take appropriate actions.

Advice on thinking in C was given. A recommended program-formatting style was also described. These principles form the *foundation* on which all the elaborate constructs of later chapters will be built. No time spent in their mastery should be considered wasted.

Exercises

1. Write a simple main program to display some strings, integers, and floating-point numbers using the **printf** function.

2. Rewrite the function lower to get a function upper that does just the opposite.

3. To the factorial function, add a check to detect any negative input. If the argument is negative, an error message is displayed, and the value zero is returned.

4. Explain why calling `factorial(j)` repeatedly with `j` being 0, 1, 2, ... , is grossly inefficient. Write a more efficient function to produce a list of factorial values.

5. If `x` is a numeric character (`'0'` through `'9'`), what is the meaning of the expression `(x - '0')`?

6. Write a filter program `expand.c` that replaces all TAB characters in its input by an equivalent number of spaces. (*Hint*: Follow the example lowercase.) You may assume that TAB stops are eight characters apart. Does your program work as well as the UNIX system command **expand**?

7. Consider the function `readline`. What would happen if the line read is longer than the size of the array `s`? Add a check for this condition and insert the appropriate error-handling code for `readline`.

8. Write a reverse-echo program that takes all words on the command line and displays them backward, character-by-character.

9. Take the `octal_print` function and turn it into a `hex_print` to output numbers in hexadecimal notation. (*Hint*: Hexadecimal digits are 0–9 followed by *A–F*.)

10. Consider the `octal_print` function. Is there any integer value within single precision that it may not handle correctly? Why?

11. Consider the bitwise-shift operations of integer quantities. In what exact situations do the left- and right-shift operations actually correspond to multiplication and division by 2?

12. How do you implement "divide by a power of 2 and take remainder" with the bitwise `&` operation? What restrictions apply to the integer being divided in this case?

13. Let's define words in a file to be the tokens separated by one or more white-space characters (SPACE, TAB, NEWLINE). Write a program to count the number of words in the input file (`stdin`). Compare the output of your program to that of the UNIX system command **wc**.

14. Modify the word-count program in Exercise 13 to take an optional argument, which is the name of the input file.

15. Examine the function definition

```
int myabs(int a)
{    if ( a >= 0 )
     {    return(a); };
     else
     {    return(-a); };
}
```

and spot any syntax problems. Try to compile it and see what your compiler does. Explain in detail the source of any error.

16. Write a temperature-conversion program that converts either a Fahrenheit or a Celsius input supplied on the command line to the other.

17. Take any of the above programs and put its source code into more than one file. Then separately compile the individual source files into .o files. Finally, combine the .o files into an executable file.

18. Write a function `string_cmp` to compare two strings x and y. The returned value is 1, 0, or –1 depending on whether x is larger than, equal to, or less than y, using lexicographic (dictionary) ordering.

19. Look at the file `/usr/include/stdio.h` on your system and try to understand it as much as possible.

20. Write a program to display the partial sums of odd positive integers from 1 to 31. (*Note*: Partial sums are 1, 1 + 3, 1 + 3 + 5, etc.)

21. Take the idea in Exercise 20 and write a program to compute the integer square root. For example, the integer square root of 11 is 3.

22. Write a function `is_leap_year` that takes an integer year and returns zero if false and nonzero if true. (*Hint*: Use the `%` operator.)

23. Certain identifiers are reserved by C and cannot be used for other purposes. Name five reserved words in C.

24. Write a program to count the number of decimal digits in any integer given to the program through `stdin`.

25. Write a program `make_change` that will decide the proper number of each coin to give to make up any given amount of change from 1 to 99 cents.

26. NIM is a game in which two players alternate in drawing counters, pennies, or the like, from a set of 12 arranged in three rows of 3, 4, and 5 counters, respectively. With each move, a player is allowed to draw either 1, 2, or 3 counters. The player who draws the last counter loses. Write a program to play NIM with a person.

Key Constructs

Information provided so far represents a cross-sectional view of C programming. The introductory materials allowed you to start writing nontrivial programs. We begin in this chapter to cover many subjects in depth and to show how to take advantage of special features of C.

You will learn about loops, multiway choices, variable scoping, recursive functions and their use, declaring and using local and global variables, enumerations, type definitions, and type casting.

New features introduced in ANSI C are emphasized. The constructs are illustrated by practical examples.

3.1   Iteration Control

Iteration is the repeated execution of a set of statements in a program. Such repetitions make it possible for a short program to perform a very large number of operations. The constructs `while`, `for`, and `do-while` perform iterations. We have seen the syntax of each of these three constructs and some simple examples in Chapter 2. Here we will discuss the full complement of facilities for iteration control and put them to substantial use. For easy reference, Table 3.1 gives a summary of the three constructs.

An iteration is normally specified by the following components:

1. *Control variables*: One or more variables that take on new values for each successive repetition.
2. *Successor statements*: One or more statements that assign new values to the control variables in preparation for the next repetition.
3. *Loop body*: A sequence of zero or more statements that is executed once for each repetition.
4. *Continuation condition*: A logical or relational expression tested before or after each repetition. If the condition is true, then the next repetition is performed; otherwise, control flows to the program statement just after the iteration construct.

Besides normal termination via item 4, the loop body may contain statements that cause *early termination* of the iteration. An example is the function `is_member`, which determines whether a string contains a particular character:

```
int is_member(char c, char *str)
{ int i = 0;
     while ( str[i] != '\0' )
     {   if ( str[i] == c ) return(1);      /* return true  */
         i++;
     }
     return(0);                             /* return false */

}
```

```
while ( continuation condition ) body

for ( init-exp ; cont-cond ; incr-exp ) body

do body while ( continuation condition )
```

Table 3.1: Iteration Constructs

The control variable i, initially 0, is incremented by 1 for each repetition. Normal termination comes when the string s has been completely examined and no match for c has been found. Early termination via the return statement occurs as soon as a match for c is found in s. Here are a couple of calls to this function:

```
is_member('a', "abcdefgh");
is_member('-', argv[1]);
```

A shorter implementation of is_member uses the for construct:

```
int is_member(char c, char *str)
{ int i;
      for ( i = 0 ; str[i] != '\0' ; i++ )
            if ( str[i] == c ) return(1);
      return(0);
}
```

The break and continue Statements

In the is_member example, we used the return mechanism to achieve early termination of an iteration. This technique is restrictive and cannot be used in a situation where you want to break out of an iteration without causing the entire function to return. The break statement is used in such situations. When break is executed, control transfers immediately to the first statement after the iteration. An application of break is found in the monotonic function which examines an integer array and returns 1 or 0 depending on whether the sequence of integers is monotonic. A sequence of values is monotonically increasing if each value is no smaller than the previous one. Similarly, a sequence is monotonically decreasing if each value is no larger than the preceding one:

```
int monotonic(int a[], int n)        /* int array a of dimension n */
{ int i;
      for ( i = 0 ; i < n - 1 ; i++ )
            if ( a[i+1] < a[i] ) break;
      if ( i == n - 1 ) return(1); /* increasing                 */
      for ( i = 0 ; i < n - 1 ; i++ )
            if ( a[i+1] > a[i] ) return(0);
      return(1);                     /* decreasing                 */
}
```

You should try this program with various increasing, decreasing, repeating, length-one, and other sequences of integers.

Now that you know how `break` works, let's turn our attention to the `continue` statement. Similar to `break`, instead of breaking out of the loop, `continue` *goes to the end of the loop body*. Within `while` or `do-while`, this means that control transfers immediately to the test-condition part. Inside `for`, it transfers to the increment step. In other words, `continue` skips the rest of the loop body to reach the loop control of the next repetition. To demonstrate how this can be convenient, let's write a function `string_match` that determines whether a given character string, `str`, is contained in another character string, `line`. The function `string_match` returns 1, 0, or –1 for true, false, or error, respectively.

```
int string_match(char str[], char line[])
{ int i, j, k;
    if ( str[0] == '\0' )              /* str is empty              */
      {   fprintf(stderr,"string_match: empty match string\n");
          return(-1);
      }
    for ( i = 0 ; line[i] != '\0' ; i++ )
    {   if ( line[i] != str[0] )
            continue;                  /* skip rest of loop body    */
        for ( j=i+1, k=1 ; line[j]==str[k] && str[k] != '\0' ;
                    j++, k++ ) { }
        if ( str[k] == '\0' )          /* end of str is reached     */
            return(1);                 /* successful match          */
        else if ( line[j] == '\0' )    /* end of line is reached    */
            return(0);                 /* match no longer possible  */
    }
    return(0);                         /* failed to match           */
}
```

The function `string_match` uses a straightforward strategy. The string `str` is matched, in turn, with a series of substrings starting at `line[0]`, `line[1]`, and so on. A successful match returns the value 1. Otherwise, the next substring is used. The value 0 is returned when there are no more substrings to match with `str`.

In `string_match`, a nested `for` loop is employed. The outer `for` iterates over the substrings `line[0]`, `line[1]`, and so on. If the first character of the substring does not match `str[0]`, we skip the rest of the loop body and continue with the next substring.

The inner `for` is interesting because it has an empty body and two loop-control variables, `j` and `k`. Also, the *comma operator* (`,`) is used in the initialization and increment steps. Two expressions connected by a comma become one expression whose value and type are those of the second expression. A sequence of expressions connected by commas are evaluated sequentially from left to right. Such a sequence of expressions can be used anywhere a single expression can.

The algorithm used in `string_match` is not the most efficient. One simple improvement is to stop matching and return zero as soon as the substring becomes shorter than `str` because no further match is possible. Try to implement this modification.

The goto Statement and Labels

Structured programming advocates avoiding the arbitrary transfer of control provided by the `goto` statement. In fact, it is possible to write code without ever using `goto`. Experts generally agree that `goto` should be used rarely if at all. However, sometimes `goto` can be used to advantage. Mainly, it is useful in breaking out of a deeply nested loop because `break` gets you out of only the immediately enclosing loop.

```
while ( ... )
        while ( ... )
        {
                . . .
                for ( ... )
                {
                    ...
                    if ( /* something wrong */ ) goto error;
                    ...
                }
        }
    . . .
error: /* take care of errors here */
```

The general form of the command is

```
    goto label;
```
          (label must be in the same function)

A *label*, such as `error` above, followed by a colon (`:`) is placed in front of the target statement for control transfer. A `goto` label has the same form as a variable and can be attached to any statement in the same function as the `goto`. A label must be unique, appearing in only one place, although it can have several jumps to it.

Whereas `goto` branches to a fixed location in your program, another construct provides multiple branching depending on the run-time value of an expression. This is the `switch` statement, the subject of the next section.

3.2 Multiple Choice

Whereas the `if . . . else if . . . else` construct remains the general-purpose decision-making mechanism, the `switch` statement provides a very handy way to select among a set of predefined choices. The syntax is

```
switch ( expression )
{       case constant-exp1 :
            statements
        case constant-exp2 :
            statements

        . . .

        default:
            statements

}
```

The `switch` construct is like a structured multiple `goto`. The switching *expression* is evaluated first. The resulting value is matched against each integer-valued constant `case` label. In a `switch`, all `case` labels must be distinct. Control is transferred to the matching `case` or to the `default` if nothing matches. There is no sequential, case-by-case matching at run time; control is transferred directly. If the optional `default` case label is not given and if nothing matches, the execution of `switch` is successfully completed.

Following control transfer to a `case` label, the statements at the selected label and all statements under other `case` labels after it will be executed in sequence. This behavior is called *fall through*, and it makes `switch` very different from a multiple `if`. The `break` statement can also be used to break out of the `switch` statement. It is often the last statement for each `case` in order to prevent fall through. With fall through completely prevented, the order in which the `case` labels are given becomes unimportant. At each `case` label, there can be zero, one, or more statements. This allows several `case` labels to precede one group of statements, making it convenient for certain situations.

To get familiar with these concepts about `switch`, you may want to experiment with the following test program:

```
main()
{ int j = 4;
        printf("1: switch(%d)\n", j);
        switch(j)
        {   case 1:
            case 3:   printf("A: case 1 or 3\n");
            case 5:   printf("B: case 5\n");
```

```
            default:  printf("C: case default\n");    /* deliberate */
            case 2:   printf("D: case 2\n");
        }
        j = 2;
        printf("2: switch(%d)\n", j);
        switch(j)
        {   case 5:   printf("E: case 5\n");
            default:  printf("F: case default\n");
            case 2:   printf("G: case 2\n");

        }

    }
```

The output produced is

```
1: switch(4)
C: case default
D: case 2
2: switch(2)
G: case 2
```

Having a good idea of the syntax and semantics of `switch`, we are now ready to apply it in actual programs. One frequent application of `switch` is in the handling of *command-line options*. Generally speaking, UNIX system commands use the following convention to specify arguments.

command [*options*] [*files*]

An option is usually specified as

-character

a minus sign followed by a single character. A command can take zero or more options. When giving more than one option, the single-letter options can sometimes be combined by juxtaposing (putting into one word) the letters and preceding them with a single -. For example,

ls -l -g

can be given alternatively as

ls -lg

There are exceptions to these conventions. Some commands such as **ps** and **tar** use options but do not require a leading minus sign. Other options may require additional characters or words to complete the specification. For example, the -o option of **cc** takes an output filename.

When implementing a command, the `main` program may contain a `switch` to process all of the options recognized by the command:

```
main(int argc, char *argv[])
{ int i, k;
  char *token;
        /* go through each command-line arg */
        for ( i = 1, token = argv[1] ; i < argc ; token = argv[++i] )
        {   if ( token[0] != '-' ) continue;    /* token not an option */
          for ( k = 1 ; token[k] != '\0' ; k++ )
          /* option processing    */
              switch (token[k])
              {    case 'C':  Cflag = 1;        /* turn on Cflag      */
                          break;
                   case 'd':  dflag = 1;        /* turn on dflag      */
                          break;
                   /*   ...   */
                   case 'R':  Rflag = 1;
                          break;
                   default:   fprintf(stderr, "%s: %c unknown option\n",
                                      argv[0], token[k]);
                              exit(1);
              } /* end of switch */
        } /* end of outer for */
}
```

Each command-line argument (`token`) is checked for a leading `'-'` sign to see if it is an option. Then, each individual character in an option *turns on* an appropriate option flag by setting it to 1 (true) via the `switch` statement. The flags are usually external variables initialized to 0. The assignment

```
token = argv[1];
```

makes `token` a pointer to the string representing the first argument whose characters are accessed by `token[0]`, `token[1]`, and so on. This method of option processing allows options to be given anywhere on the command line. It also permits juxtaposition of options.

In this example, the `default` label catches all undefined options and causes the program to display an error message before terminating. One consequence is that a single mistyped option will cause termination. Alternatively, you can ignore unrecognized options or simply issue a warning without terminating the program.

Another, more subtle consequence is that no filename given to this command can begin with the – character. This may help explain why it is not a good idea to have such a filename on UNIX systems.

Finally, because the `case` label must be an integer-valued constant or constant expression, a string constant such as `"color"` cannot be used as a `case` label. This may help explain why most UNIX system commands use seemingly cryptic single-letter options. Of course, it is possible to process options specified by strings, but not with the `switch` construct.

Having presented the control-flow statements, we now turn our attention to other key constructs with which a good C programmer must be thoroughly familiar. Let's begin with scoping rules for variables.

3.3 Automatic Variables and Variable Scoping

Internal Variables

We already know that a variable must first be declared before it can be used. But the effect of a variable declaration is also regulated by *scoping rules*, governing the extent to which a declared variable is known. The scope of a local variable is its immediate enclosing block (compound statement). Generally, a variable cannot be used outside of its scope. Two variables with the same name in different scopes are two distinct variables. A variable declared inside a function or a block is *internal* to the function or block. Internal variables are local, or private, to the block in which it is declared and cannot be accessed from the outside. For example, the variables i, j, and k in the function `string_match` are internal. Internal variables normally only come into existence when the function or block is entered and are destroyed automatically after the block is exited. Such variables are known as *automatic variables*. The dynamic nature of automatic variables also allows their initialization to involve *any* expression, not just constants.

However, if an internal variable is declared `static` then it is not an automatic variable. Instead, it is created and initialized at compile time and retains its value even after the function or a block is exited. This same value is available when the function or block is entered again. Consider a function that keeps track of how many times it is called. The two lines

```
static int my_count = 0;
my_count++;
```

can be put in the function to do the job. Static variables can only have constant initializers.

External Variables

Not all variables are internal. It is also possible to use *external variables*, which are not local to any function or block. Because an external variable can be shared by many functions, it is sometimes referred to as being *global*. Because its value can be set and used by any function, an external variable provides a way, besides argument passing, for functions to communicate data. Unlike automatic variables, external variables always exist and retain their values until the entire program is terminated.

An external variable must be *defined* by a type declaration outside of all functions in a source-code file. When placed outside of functions, the declarations

```
int overall_maximum;
int global_count = 0;
char name[]= "John Smith";
```

define the external variables `overall_maximum`, `global_count`, and the character array `name`. When an external variable is defined, its data type is fixed and storage allocated. A variable can be defined only once. If the compiler detects an attempt to define a variable more than once, it will fail.

To use an external variable in a function, at least one of the following conditions must be met. The variable has been

- Defined earlier in the file.
- Declared `extern` earlier in the file.
- Declared `extern` in the function.

To use `global_count`, you may include the declaration

```
extern int global_count;
```

in the function. If many functions share an external variable, programming can be tedious. It is easier simply to put the necessary `extern` declarations outside the functions at the beginning of a file.

Consider obtaining the total number of function calls made during a run of your program. Define an external `global_count` and initialize it to zero as shown above. Then just do `global_count++` once in each function.

Let's illustrate the scoping rules further with an example:

```
long x;
float y;
int z;
fn(char c, int x)         /* parameter x hides global x */
{ double y;               /* local y hides global y     */
  extern int z;           /* refer to global z          */
      y = 3.14159;        /* assignment to local y      */
      {    char y;        /* hides first local y        */
          y = c;          /* assign to second local y   */
      }
```

```
    y = y / 3.0;              /* assign to first local y   */
    z++;                      /* increment global z        */
}
```

Here we can see how the global variable `float y` is hidden by the local `double y` in the function `fn`. This local `y` is in turn hidden by the local variable `char y` inside the block. Once you are outside of the block, but still in the function `fn`, the variable `y` of type `double` resurfaces. This further illustrates the scope rules. We will have more to say about variable and declarations in Section 3.5.

It is important to realize that functions are the basic programming unit in C. The scoping of variables is defined relative to functions; and it is just one of many aspects of functions covered in this chapter. Another interesting and important topic is recursive functions, our next subject.

3.4   Recursion

A *recursive function* is a function that either directly or indirectly *calls itself*. We will show how this feature is a powerful problem-solving tool.

Many problems are solvable by a type of algorithm that reduces the original problem into one or several smaller problems of exactly the same nature. The solutions of the smaller problems then combine to form the solution of the original problem. These subproblems can be further reduced by applying the same algorithm *recursively* until they become simple enough to solve. A recursive algorithm can be implemented most naturally by a recursive function.

Here is a recursive version of `factorial`:

```
int factorial(int n)                     /* n must be nonnegative */
{    if ( n == 0 ) return(1);
     return( n * factorial(n-1) );       /* recursive call        */
}
```

To appreciate the power of recursion and to see how it is applied to solve nontrivial problems, we will study several examples.

Greatest Common Divisor

Consider computing the *greatest common divisor* (gcd) of two integers. The gcd of integers a and b is defined as the largest integer that evenly divides both a and b. The gcd is not defined if both a and b are zero. A negative a or b can be replaced by its absolute value without affecting the gcd. Hence, we can assume that a and b are nonnegative and not both zero. The recursive algorithm to compute gcd(a, b) can be described by the pseudocode:

Call Level	a	b
1	2970	1265
2	1265	440
3	440	385
4	385	55
5	55	0

Table 3.2: Recursion of gcd(2970,1265) = 55

1. If b is zero, the answer is a.
2. If b is not zero, the answer is gcd(b, a mod b).

It is interesting to note that the idea for this simple but effective integer gcd algorithm is credited to Euclid, a Greek mathematician (ca. 300 B.C.).

The recursive C function for Euclid's algorithm is straightforward:

```
int gcd(int a, int b)       /* integer greatest common divisor */
{   if ( b == 0 )
         return(a);
    else
         return ( gcd(b, a % b) );
}
```

Note, the function gcd calls itself, and the value of the arguments for each successive call to gcd gets smaller (see Table 3.2). Eventually, the second argument becomes zero and the recursion unwinds: The deepest recursive call returns, then the next level call returns, and so on until the first call to gcd returns.

When a function is called recursively, each new invocation gets its own set of formal parameters and automatic variables, independent of the previous set. This is consistent with how automatic variables and formal parameters are normally treated.

Another good example of recursive programming is the quicksort algorithm.

Quicksort

Sorting means arranging data items into a specified order. When data items are in order, information retrieval is much easier. Among many competing sorting algorithms, the quicksort algorithm remains one of the fastest.

Let us consider arranging an array of integers in increasing order with quicksort. The idea is to pick any element of the array as the *partition element* pe. By exchanging the elements, the array can be arranged so all elements to the right of pe are greater than or equal to pe. Also, all elements to the left of pe are less than or equal to pe. Now the same method is applied to sort each of the smaller arrays on either side of pe. The recursion is terminated when the length of the array becomes less than 2:

```
void quicksort(int a[], int i, int j)
{ /* sort a[i] to a[j] inclusive */
  int k;
  int partition(int a[], int, int);
    if ( i >= j )  return;
    k = partition(a, i, j);      /* k is  position of pe */
    quicksort(a, i, k-1);        /* sort left subarray   */
    quicksort(a, k+1, j);        /* sort right subarray  */
}
```

first call i = 0
j = size of array − 1

The function quicksort is called with i the lower index and j the higher index of the array. If j is bigger than i, the function partition is called to select a pivot element and to split the array into two parts. The returned value of partition is the index of the partition point. The smaller arrays to either side of pe are then sorted by calling quicksort recursively.

The function partition is not recursive, and a simple implementation of it is easy. However, we present a reasonably efficient partition and describe how it works before returning to our discussion of recursion.

The arguments to partition are the array a and two indices low and high. The range of the array from a[low] to a[high] inclusive is to be partitioned. Basically, the middle element is chosen to be the pe. Then, we search simultaneously from both ends of the range toward the middle for elements belonging to the other side, interchanging out-of-place entries in pairs. Finally, the searches in opposite directions end when they meet somewhere in the range, pinpointing the location of the pivot element.

The partition function begins by exchanging the rightmost element with pe. Starting from the two ends, we first search from left to right for an element larger than pe and then from right to left for an element smaller than pe. The two elements located are exchanged. Thereafter, the searches in opposite directions continue. Eventually, no more exchanges are needed, and the searches meet somewhere between low and high inclusive. This is the *partition spot* that contains an element larger than or equal to pe. The pe at the rightmost position is now interchanged with the element at the partition position. Finally, the index of the partition element is returned:

```
int partition(int a[], int low, int high)
{ /* partition a[low] through a[high]   */
  register int pe, i, j;
  void exchange(int b[], int, int);  /* function prototype        */
        i = low;
        j = high;
        /* choose middle element as partition element             */
        exchange(a, (i+j)/2, j);
        pe = a[j];        /* move pivot to right end               */
        while ( i < j )
        {    while ( i < j && a[i] <= pe ) i++;
             while ( i < j && a[j] >= pe ) j--;
             if ( i < j ) exchange(a, i, j );
        }
        if ( i != high )
             exchange(a, i, high);  /* pe to partition location    */
        return(i);        /* return index of partition element     */
}
void exchange(int b[], int i, int j)
{ /*  array b is modified */
  int t;
        t = b[j]; b[j] = b[i]; b[i] = t;
}
```

Another feature of `quicksort` is that the reordering is performed *in place*. No auxiliary array, as required by some other sorting algorithms, is used. The best way to understand how `quicksort` works is to manually try an example with less than 10 entries.

The Recursion Formula

For many people, recursion is a new way of thinking and brings a powerful tool for problem solving. Given a problem, two questions can be asked:

- Do I know a way to solve the problem if it is small?
- For a larger problem, can it be broken down into smaller problems of the same nature whose solutions combine into the solution of the original problem?

If you answered yes to both questions, then you already have a recursive solution.

Recursive programs are concise and easy to write once you recognize its overall structure. All recursive solutions use the following sequence of steps:

1. *Termination conditions:* Always begin a recursive function with tests to catch the simple or trivial cases at the end of the recursion. A terminal case (array size less than two for `quicksort` and remainder zero for `gcd`) is treated directly, and the function call returns.

2. *Subproblems:* Then, break down the given problem into smaller problems of the same kind. Each is solved by a recursive call to the function itself passing arguments of reduced size or complexity.

3. *Recombination of answers:* Finally, take the answers from the subproblems and combine them into the solution of the original bigger problem. The function call now returns. The combination may involve adding, multiplying, or other operations on the results from the recursive calls. For problems like `gcd` and `quicksort`, no recombination is necessary, and this step becomes a trivial return statement.

This *recursion engine* is deceptively simple. The program looks small and innocent, but the logic can be mind-boggling. To illustrate its power, we will consider the Tower of Hanoi puzzle.

Tower of Hanoi

Legend has it that monks in Hanoi spend their free time moving heavy gold disks to and from three poles made of black wood (Figure 3.1). The gold disks, different in size, are numbered from 1 to n according to their sizes. Each disk has a round hole at the center to fit the poles. In the beginning, all n disks are stacked on one pole in sequence with disk 1, the smallest, on top and disk n, the biggest, at the bottom. The task is to move the gold disks one-by-one from the first pole to the third pole, using the middle pole as a resting place if necessary. There are only three rules to follow:

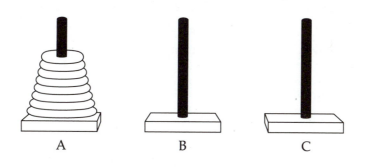

Figure 3.1: Tower of Hanoi Puzzle

1. A disk cannot be moved unless it is the top disk on a given pole, and only one disk can be moved at a time.
2. A disk must be moved from one pole to another pole directly. It cannot be set down someplace else.
3. At any time, a bigger disk cannot be placed on top of a smaller disk.

To simplify our discussion, let us label the first pole A, the second pole B, and the target pole C. If you have not seen the solution before, you might like to try a small example first, say, $n = 3$. It does not take long to figure out the following sequence:

```
move disk 1 from A to C
move disk 2 from A to B
move disk 1 from C to B
move disk 3 from A to C
move disk 1 from B to A
move disk 2 from B to C
move disk 1 from A to C
```

It turns out that you need seven moves for the case $n = 3$. As you get a feel of how to move three disks, you are tempted to do four disks, and so on. But you will soon find that there seems to be no rule to follow, and the problem becomes much harder with each additional disk. Fortunately, the puzzle becomes very easy if you think about it recursively.

Let's apply our recursion engine to this puzzle in order to generate a sequence of correct moves for the problem: Move n disks from pole A to C through B.

1. Termination condition: If $n = 1$, then generate "move disk 1 from A to C" and return.
2. Subproblems: For $n > 1$, we will do three smaller problems:

   a. Move $n - 1$ disks from A to B through C.
   b. Move disk n from A to C.
   c. Move $n - 1$ disks from B to C through A.

   There are two smaller subproblems of the same kind, plus a trivial step.

3. Recombination of answers: This problem is solved after the subproblems are solved. No recombination is necessary.

Two recursive calls and a move of disk n is all that it takes. This looks almost too simple, doesn't it? But it works. Here is an implementation:

```
void hanoi(int n, char *a, char *b, char *c)
{    if ( n == 1 )                                       /* step 1  */
     {   printf("move disk 1 from %s to %s\n, a,c);
         return;
     }
     hanoi(n-1, a, c, b);                                /* step 2a */
     printf("move disk %d from %s to %s\n, n, a, c);/* step 2b */
     hanoi(n-1, b, a, c);                                /* step 2c */
}
```

During the course of the solution, different poles are used as the source, middle, and target poles. This is the reason why the `hanoi` function has the a, b, and c parameters in addition to n, the number of disks to be moved at any stage.

Test the `hanoi` function with

```
main()
{ void hanoi(int, char *, char *, char *);
        hanoi(3, "A", "B", "C");      /* 3 disks */
        hanoi(6, "A", "B", "C");      /* 6 disks */
}
```

Because $2^n - 1$ moves will be needed for n disks, you should test the program only with small values of n. But the monks in Hanoi are not so fortunate, they have 200 heavy gold disks to move, and the sun may burn out before they are finished!

Though elegant and powerful, recursion often does not save storage or execution time. In fact, the nested function calls required by recursion represent additional processing when compared with a nonrecursive implementation of the same algorithm. But the logic behind the recursion engine provides a problem-solving strategy unparalleled by other methods. Many seemingly complicated problems can be solved easily with recursive thinking. Thus, the main advantages of recursion are its problem-solving power and conciseness.

3.5 More on Declarations

Knowing how declarations work and how to use them properly and effectively is just as crucial to programming as familiarity with functions, expressions, and statements.

The C compiler takes expressions and statements in a source-code file and produces corresponding machine codes to run on a particular computer. Unlike an expression or a statement, a declaration does not specify code executed at run time. Instead, declarations provide necessary or supplementary information so the compiler can generate correct code for the statements. In other words, declarations instruct the compiler, whereas statements specify program actions. Some declarations, such as `int` and `float`, provide necessary information without which compilation of a C program cannot succeed. Other declarations, such as the `register` modifier, give auxiliary information to help the compiler produce more efficient code (Section 2.13).

In this and the next several sections, we will present additional topics on declarations: outside declarations, linkage for global identifiers, read-only variables, enumeration, and `typedef`.

When a declaration also causes storage allocation for a variable, it is called a *definition*. Declarations of automatic variables and declarations with initialization are common examples of definitions. However, declarations such as

```
extern int x;                 (external variable declaration)
float cube_root(float);       (function prototype declaration)
```

are not definitions because they do not allocate storage. The storage for `x` should be provided by a unique definition somewhere in the program. In a C program, a variable can be defined only once but may be declared multiple times, usually in different files, provided that all declarations are consistent.

3.5.1 Declarations Outside Functions

We already know when a declaration is given inside a function or block, it is an *internal declaration*. If a declaration is not placed inside any function or block, then it is traditionally called an *external declaration*. But, to avoid possible confusion, we will refer to externally placed declarations as *outside declarations*.

If an outside declaration is a definition, then it creates a global variable. Thus, we must have clear rules about when an outside declaration becomes a definition.

1. An outside declaration with an initializer is a definition:

```
int counter = 0;
extern int max = 0;
int a[] = {1,2,3,4,5};
char name[] = "Wang";
```

2. An outside declaration with `extern,` but without an initializer, is not a definition.

3. An outside declaration without an `extern` or an initializer is taken as a *tentative definition*. All tentative definitions of a variable will be ignored when a definition is encountered. Otherwise, they become one single definition with a compiler-supplied initial value zero. This applies to simple variables as well as arrays.

Internal and External Linkage

A global variable used in multiple files must be declared with the `extern` specifier to establish its *external linkage,* correspondence with the same global variables in other files. Although this mechanism lets you use the same global variables across files, it also presents dangerous global-variable-name conflicts between those files. This is especially true if the files are written at different times or by different programmers. You can protect your per-file global variables by using the `static` specifier with their definitions. A `static` global variable has *internal linkage* and is not accessible from other files.

In C all functions are global (with external linkage) and are accessible from any outside file. This may not be desirable for certain functions. Fortunately, you can declare any function *local to a file* to avoid global-name conflicts and to prevent outside access. This is again done by putting the `static` specifier in front of the function header.

3.5.2 Using Local and Global Identifiers

The following practical rules summarize concepts regarding declarations covered so far:

1. Declare a local or internal variable inside a function or a block. Such variables can be initialized. An internal variable is automatic unless specified `static`.

2. Define a global variable with external linkage exactly once using an outside definition with initialization.

3. Use the `static` specifier to establish global variables with internal likage and avoid global-name conflicts.

4. Place outside declarations with `extern` at the beginning of a file for all global variables defined or used in other files. This is usually done by including the appropriate header files (see Section 4.2).

5. A function declared `static` is local to a file.

6. A function must be declared with a prototype before called. For functions returning `int`, such declarations can, but should not, be omitted. To use a function defined in another file, place the function prototype with `extern` at the beginning of the file.

3.6   Circular Buffer

Global variables are convenient for multiple functions to maintain and manipulate shared data. Let's apply our knowledge of global variable declarations in a nontrivial example, the implementation of a *circular buffer*.

A first-in-first-out (FIFO) character buffer is often useful as a data structure to transfer characters from a producer to a consumer. The *producer* is the provider of characters for the buffer, and the *consumer* is the receiver of characters out of the buffer. In sequential processing, we can think of the producer and consumer as different parts of the same program. In concurrent (or parallel) processing (Chapter 12), they can be independently running programs. The buffer is usually represented as a character array of an appropriate size. In the beginning, the buffer contains nothing and is therefore empty.

Normally, `head` and `tail` indices keep track of the start of characters yet to be consumed and the start of empty spaces available in the buffer, respectively. The `head` advances as characters are consumed, and the `tail` advances as new characters come in. When an index reaches the end of the buffer, it wraps around to the beginning of the buffer. This wrap-around property makes the buffer *circular* (Figure 3.2).

Obviously, consuming from an empty buffer or producing into a full buffer is an error.

Our circular buffer implementation uses a global character array `cb` of `SIZE` elements. The indices `head` and `tail` are also external integer variables initialized to zero. There is one additional external integer variable,

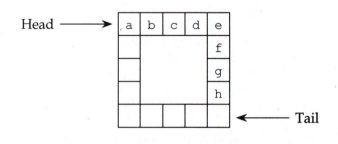

Figure 3.2: Circular Buffer

length, representing the number of unconsumed characters in the buffer. If length is zero, the buffer is empty. On the other hand, if length becomes equal to SIZE, then the buffer is full.

All the external variables are declared static so that they are global only in the file cirbuf.c and cannot be confused with the same names in other files. More important, these quantities cannot be referenced or assigned by functions in any other file.

```
/******* file  cirbuf.c  ***********************************/
#include <stdio.h>
#include "cirbuf.h"      — user defined header file (" ")
#define SIZE 256

static char  cb[SIZE];
static int head = 0;   /* index of first char in buffer    */
static int tail = 0;   /* index of first char after buffer */
static int length = 0;

#define EMPTY() ( length == 0 )
#define FULL() ( length == SIZE )
#define MOD(x) (if ( (x) >= SIZE ) x -= SIZE)

int produce(char c)    /* producer calls this function      */
{     if ( FULL() )
      {   fprintf(stderr, "produce: buffer full\n);
          return(-1);
      }
      cb[tail++] = c;
      length++;
      MOD(tail);
}

int consume()           /* consumer calls this function      */
{ char c;
      if ( EMPTY() )
      {   fprintf(stderr, "consume: buffer empty\n);
          return(-1);
      }
      c = cb[head++];
      length--;
      MOD(head);
      return(c);
}
```

- no main prog.
- file to be compiled Sep. 8 then used w/ other file

```
int full() { return( FULL () ); }
int empty() { return( EMPTY () ); }

/********* end of file cirbuf.c ************************/
```

Note that three macros—FULL, EMPTY, and MOD—are defined (see Section 4.3). MOD is used for index wraparound. FULL and EMPTY cannot be used outside this file, but the functions full and empty can.

Associated with the file cirbuf.c is a header file cirbuf.h.

```
/******** file cirbuf.h  ********************************/
int full(void);      /* test for buffer full        */
int empty(void);     /* test for buffer empty       */
int produce(char c);/* insert c into buffer         */
int consume(void);   /* remove next char from buffer */
/******** end file cirbuf.h ***************************/
```

that is included by any file that wishes to make use of the circular buffer mechanism.

In testing the implementation, SIZE can be reduced so wraparound happens sooner. Another aspect to notice is the way errors are handled. Instead of exiting, a value −1 is returned. It is up to the calling function of consume or produce to detect the error and treat it appropriately.

When you are sure everything is working, enter

cc −c cirbuf.c

to establish the object file cirbuf.o, ready to be combined with any file that uses the circular buffer.

Let's put the circular buffer to use. Our example program counts the number of words, separated by SPACE, TAB, and/or NEWLINE characters, in the standard input. A producer function input obtains input characters and deposits them in the circular buffer until it is full. Then, a consumer function word_count takes characters out of the buffer and counts the number of words until the buffer is empty. These two steps are repeated until the input is finished:

```
/********* file wordcount.c ******************************************/
#include <stdio.h>
#include "cirbuf.h"                 /* use circular buffer           */

int wcnt =0;                        /* global word count             */

int input()                        /* obtain input from stdin       */
{ int c;
```

```
        while ( ! full() )              /* while circular buffer not full */
        {   if ( (c = getchar()) != EOF )
                produce(c);             /* deposit into buffer            */
            else
                return(0);              /* input closed                   */
        }
        return(1);                      /* buffer full                    */
}


int word_count()                        /* count number of words          */
{ int c;
  static int word = 0;                  /* partial word indicator         */
        while ( ! empty() )             /* while buffer not empty         */
            switch( c = consume() )     /* remove one char from buffer    */
            {   case ' ' :
                case '\t':
                case '\n':              /* word delimiters                */
                    if ( word != 0 ) wcnt++;
                                        /* word complete                  */
                    word = 0;           /* partial-word indicator false   */
                    break;
                default:
                    word = 1;           /* partial-word indicator true    */
            }
}


main()
{   for (;;)                            /* loop forever                   */
        if ( input() )                  /* input is producer              */
            word_count();               /* word_count is consumer         */
        else
        {   word_count();
            break;
        }
    printf("total %d words\n", wcnt);
}
/***** end of file wordcount.c ****************************************/
```

Note how the partial-word indicator word is used to avoid counting words
of length zero. Now we can compile the file by

    cc wordcount.c cirbuf.o -o mywc

and test the executable **mywc** with

mywc < *file*

Compare the output of **mywc** with that by the UNIX system command **wc**.

3.7   Enumerations

The *enumeration type* is a user-defined integer type consisting of a number of symbolic names representing constant integer values. Enumeration is a feature, standardized by ANSI C, that provides a convenient way to associate symbolic names to integer constants.

The declaration `enum` is used to establish a new enumeration type:

```
enum name { symbol1[ = val1],
            symbol2[ = val2],
            ...
      };
```

The declaration establishes *name* as a new `enum` *tag*. The integer values val_1, val_2, and so on are optional. For example,

```
enum Days { MON=1, TUE=2, WED=3, THU=4, FRI=5, SAT=6, SUN=7 };
```

establishes the `enum` tag `Days` whose symbols are `MON`, `TUE`, and so on. The integer values of the constant symbols are explicitly specified here. If unspecified, the symbols are given consecutive integer values following the last specified entry or from zero. Thus,

```
enum Days { MON=1, TUE, WED, THU, FRI, SAT, SUN };
```

is an equivalent declaration of `Days`. The values of the enumeration constants do not have to be distinct, allowing declarations such as

```
enum Days { MON=1, TUE, WED, THU, FRI, SAT, SUN,
            mon=1, tue, wed, thu, fri, sat, sun };
```

However, the constant symbols must be distinct among *all* enumeration types. This means that having used `MON` in the enumeration type `Days`, you cannot use `MON` again in another enumeration type, say, `Weekdays`.

Once an enumeration tag is established, you can declare and use *enumeration variables* of that type. An enumeration variable should only take on values defined in the enumeration type:

```
enum Days x;
for ( x = MON ; x <= SUN; x++ )
      printf("day= %d\n", x);
```

Thus, the enumeration variable `x` is an integer variable intended to take on only the values 1 through 7 inclusive. Be warned that a compiler is not required to check for the validity of values assigned to an enumeration variable.

Here are a few more examples of enumeration types:

```
enum Boolean { NO, YES, FALSE=0, TRUE };        /* NO = 0, YES = 1 */
enum White_space
{    SPACE = ' ',
     NEWLINE = '\n',
     TAB = '\t',
     RETURN = '\r' };
```

Boolean values 1 and 0 are used in mathematical logic to represent true and false, respectively. Thus, the function string_match (Section 3.1) that returns 0 or 1 can be declared as

```
enum Boolean string_match(char str[], char line[])
{   ...
    ...
          return(YES);      /* matched  */
    ...
       return(NO);          /* no match */
}
```

Anonymous enumerations are declared by leaving out the name part. An anonymous enumeration is sometimes an alternative to #define constants (Section 4.3).

```
enum { TABLE_SIZE = 256,  TERMINATOR = -1 };
```

There are, however, significant differences between an enumeration constant and a preprocessor-defined symbolic constant. The latter is not restricted to representing integers and is effective in one file only. The former must be an integer and must be unique throughout the entire program.

3.8 Read-Only Variables and Parameters

Also new with the ANSI standard is the type qualifier const. If a type name is preceded by const, it becomes a constant or read-only type. If a variable or array element is declared read-only, the value of the variable will stay constant and cannot be changed after initialization:

```
const float pi =  3.14159f;
const int lower_limit = 32;
const char greeting[] = "Hello:\n"        (array of read-only char)
```

Similarly, the declaration

```
const char *str = "Hello:\n";
```

prevents any assignments through the pointer variable `str`. For instance, `*(++str) = 'A'` is illegal. However, the pointer variable `str` itself can still be set. Thus, `++str` is legal because `const` modifies only `char` here.

The `const` qualifier is often used in function declarations. For example, the function header

```
enum Boolean string_match(const char str[], const char line[])
```

means that the entries of `str` and `line` are read-only in `string_match`. The compiler will check for any illegal attempts to modify read-only data in a function.

3.9   The `typedef` Declaration

The `typedef` declaration is used to create new names for basic and user-defined data types (Chapter 7). The new name should be either more descriptive or more compact to use. Once a new type name has been established, it can be used just like any other type name:

```
typedef int Enrollment;        (Enrollment is int)
typedef short Age;             (Age is short)
typedef char *Cbuffer;        (Cbuffer is char *)
typedef char *String;         (String is char *)
```

Note that we used capitalized identifiers as the new type names. This convention makes it simpler to distinguish `typedef` names from other names. With these new type names, we can use

```
Age x;
String a, b = "hello there", argv[5];
```

to declare `x` short and `a`, `b`, and `argv[0]` through `argv[4]` char *.

Using `typedef` names is also handy in function headers such as

```
main(int argc, String argv[])
```

Having seen some examples, we are ready for the general syntax of `typedef`. To establish a new type name `Abc`, just declare `Abc` as if it were a variable of the desired type, then precede the entire variable declaration with the modifier `typedef`. Hence,

```
typedef char * StringArray[];
```

defines the type name `StringArray` and allows the `main` function header
to be written as

```
main(int argc, StringArray argv)
```

It must be pointed out that `typedef` does not actually create a new
data type; rather, it simply gives a new name to an existing type. The `struct`
declaration, on the other hand, is used to define new types (see Chapter 7).

Besides aesthetics, using `typedef` simplifies complicated declarations
and provides readability and documentation for a program. Clearly, an `Age`
variable is more specific than an arbitrary `int` variable, `Cbuffer` says more
about the intended purpose of a variable than `char *`, and `StringArray` is
more to the point than what it replaces. Later when we deal with complex
data structures (Chapter 7), `typedef` will come in handy.

3.10 Implicit and Explicit Type Conversions

An operator acting on operands of the same type produces a result of the
same type. But if the operands are of different types, then they must be converted to a common type before the operation is performed. For example, an
integer must be converted to floating point before an arithmetic operation
with another floating-point number. Such conversions are made automatically according to a set of rules in the C language and are known as *implicit
type conversions*.

Because a `char` is just a small integer, characters can be used freely in
arithmetic expressions involving integers or other characters. If a `char` is
converted to an `int` and then back to a `char`, no information is lost.

Implicit type conversion also takes place whenever the two sides of an
assignment have different types; the right-hand-side value is converted to
the type of the left-hand side. For instance, if a floating-point number is
assigned to an integer variable, the fractional part is truncated. Therefore, the
function

```
int round(float f)
{ int g;
  float frac;
     g = f;                         /* truncate fractional part */
     frac = f - g;
     return ( (frac < 0.5) ? g : g+1 );

}
```

performs the rounding of a `float` to the nearest integer.

Rule	If One Operand Is	Convert Other Operand to
1	`long double`	`long double`
2	`double`	`double`
3	`float`	`float`
4	`long int`	`long int`
5	Convert all `char` and `short` to `int`	

Table 3.3: Arithmetic Conversions

When a `double` is converted to a `float`, the value is truncated or rounded depending on the C compiler for your specific machine.

For binary arithmetic operations with operands of two different types, the operand of a *lower* type will be automatically converted to the operand of a *higher* type. Appendix 8 gives the precise rules. If there are no `unsigned` operands, the rules given in Table 3.3, applied sequentially, will suffice for most applications.

In a function call, when an argument has a different type than the corresponding formal parameter, type conversion is also performed automatically. However, the argument conversion only takes place if the function call has been declared by a function prototype supplying the necessary type information. It is best to avoid using this feature and use explicit type casting whenever an argument in a function call differs from the declared type of the formal parameter.

Explicit Type Cast

A programmer can also request an explicit *type conversion* to force data of one type to become another. The *type cast*

```
( type-name ) expression
```

converts the given *expression* to the named type. With this type casting, we can rewrite our `round` function as

```
int round(float f)
{    return ( (int) (f + 0.5) );
}
```

3.11 Summary ⎯⎯⎯⎯⎯⎯⎯⎯⎯⎯

The logical structure of an iteration consists of four parts: control variables, loop body, successor steps, and continuation conditions. The `while`, `for`, and `do-while` constructs provide different ways to specify iterations. The `continue` statement finishes the current repetition of a loop. The `break` statement breaks out of the innermost loop or `switch`. Arbitrary `goto` statements are allowed but should be avoided in most situations.

The `switch` statement provides efficient multiway branching to codes marked by constant `case` labels. Once control is transferred to a `case`, execution then proceeds to fall through all cases after that, unless the `break` statement is used. The `switch` statement is often used to process command-line arguments.

Depending on its scope, a variable can be local to a function or block (internal variables), known to all functions throughout one file but not to anything outside the file, or global and accessible by all parts of your program. Automatic variables are created and destroyed as their program block is entered and exited, whereas static variables retain their value independent of control flow.

Recursion is a powerful problem-solving tool. Recursive functions are easy to write if you follow the simple template: (1) Check the trivial case as the end condition of recursion; (2) break down the problem into subproblems solved with recursive calls; (3) combine the solutions of the subproblems to get the overall solution.

Declarations are instructions to the compiler and do not result in executable code. External declarations are given outside of functions and are also referred to as outside declarations. An external variable is initialized to zero by default.

As shown by the circular buffer example, keeping the data structures and their access and manipulation functions together in a single file is always advisable. The data structures and certain private functions should have internal linkage. The functions accessible from other files should be declared in a corresponding header file.

The declaration `enum` establishes an enumeration type of names having integer constant values, whereas the declaration `const` indicates the read-only property of data. The `typedef` declaration can give meaningful names to basic and user-defined data types.

Built-in rules govern conversion of types when an operator is given different data types. Type conversions also take place when passing arguments to a function and when explicitly requested in a program.

Exercises

1. A *bitonic* sequence of integers consists of one monotonic sequence of zero or more elements followed by another. For example, both 2,2,3,4,3,2 and 4,3,1,2,7 are bitonic. Modeling after the `monotonic` function in Section 3.1, write a `bitonic` function.

2. Modify the command-line option processing program in Section 3.2 so that, after all the options have been processed, the nonoption arguments supplied are collected in `argv[1]`, `argv[2]`, and so on consecutively and that `argc - 1` indicates the number of remaining arguments.

3. Add to the `gcd` program so that it can handle any given integers (`int`).

4. Write a function `lcm` that takes two integer arguments and returns the *least common multiple* of all the arguments (e.g., `lcm(15,12)` is 60). (*Hint*: Use `gcd` from Section 3.4.)

5. Examine closely the function `partition` used in our `quicksort` (Section 3.4). Can you show that after the `while` loop the element `a[i]` is not less than `pe`?

6. Given an array of integers, write an efficient program to find the maximum and minimum elements in the array by going over the array only once.

7. Given an array of distinct integers, write an efficient program to find the *median*, the element of the array whose value is in the middle. Namely, roughly half of the elements are over and under the median. (*Hint*: Modify `partition`.)

8. The Fibonacci sequence, $F_0, F_1, \ldots, F_i, \ldots$, is defined by

$$F_0 = 0$$
$$F_1 = 1$$
$$F_i = F_{i-1} + F_{i-2} \quad \text{for } i \geq 2$$

Write a recursive and a nonrecursive function to compute F_i.

9. In a function header, does it make sense to declare `const` any formal parameter other than a pointer? Why?

10. Using `switch`, write a program that counts the number of SPACE, TAB, NEWLINE, and FORMFEED characters in a file.

11. A *stack* is a first-in-last-out buffer. If the numbers 1.0, 2.0, 3.0 are entered into the buffer in that order, then they are taken out of the stack in the sequence 3.0, 2.0, 1.0. The operation `push` enters an item on the top of a stack, and the operation `pop` removes an item from the top of the stack. Only these two operations are allowed to modify a stack. Following the

circular buffer example in Section 3.6, implement the data representation and manipulative routines for a stack of floats.

12. Use the stack in Exercise 11 to implement the UNIX system command **rp** to evaluate a *reverse Polish expression*. For example,

    rp `3.1 5.3 6.7 + *`

    displays the value `(6.7 + 5.3) * 3.1`. (*Hint*: Use **atof**.)

13. In ANSI C, why is it necessary to use the indicator `void` in the prototype of a function that takes no arguments?

14. Is it possible to use the same identifier as both a variable and a function name? What about an `enum` tag? A `typedef` name?

15. List the different purposes that an identifier can serve in a C program, besides being a variable.

16. Consider the declarations

    ```
    const char *str1= "abc";
    typedef char *String;
    const String str2= "def";
    ```

    and the operations `++str1`, `++str2`, `*str1 = 'A'`, and `*str2 = 'B'`. Which ones are legal? Illegal? Why?

17. Compare and contrast an *outside declaration* with an `extern` declaration.

18. Write a recursive implementation of the `string_match` function.

19. Write a program `cedit.c` to simulate command-line editing. It reads one line from standard input, displays the result, and goes back to read the next line. The input line can contain regular characters and the editing characters #, @, and \.

    - The # causes the previous character, if any, to be deleted.
    - The @ causes the line typed so far to be deleted.
    - The \ causes the next character, regular or not, to be taken literally.

20. On System V UNIX, the library function **getopt** accesses command-line arguments (options). Enter

    man `3 getopt`

    at the shell level to find out if your system supports **getopt** and what it can do.

The C Preprocessor

The C preprocessor (CPP) is the first stage of the **cc** command. This
means that your program first goes through the CPP before the
actual compilation takes place. The CPP is a filter, and it makes
certain well-defined transformations on the input (Figure 4.1).

Generally, the CPP provides two types of text transformations,
automatic and *requested*. There are four automatic transformations:
(1) every *trigraph* is replaced (a trigraph is a three-character escape
sequence; see Exercise 1), (2) every comment is replaced by a single
space, (3) every BACKSLASH–NEWLINE pair is deleted, and (4) every
predefined macro is expanded.

Other than the automatic ones, the CPP makes no other
transformations unless specifically requested. You use CPP *directives*
to request transformations. A directive is given with a # as the first
nonblank character on a line followed by a keyword. File inclusion
with #include and symbolic constant with #define are the two
most widely used directives. A directive to the CPP will be deleted
after being processed.

Using the CPP is an integral part of C programming. Because the
preprocessor is part of ANSI C, CPP usage is standardized across
different systems. We will describe important CPP features: header
files, symbolic constants, macros, and conditional text inclusion. The
practical uses of these features are explained. For a first reading of
this chapter, you may browse through the materials rather quickly,
saving many details for later.

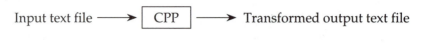

Input text file ⟶ | CPP | ⟶ Transformed output text file

Figure 4.1: The C Preprocessor

4.1   Header Files

The `#include` directive includes another file in a source-code file. We have used

```
#include <stdio.h>
```

to include the standard I/O header in many programs already. In general, the directive

```
#include <filename>
```

is used to include system header files. The given *filename* should be located in one of a list of standard system directories kept by the **cc** command. Almost all standard header files for the C language are located in the directory `/usr/include`.

When the CPP encounters a `#include` line in a file (current file), it does the following:

1. Locates the requested file (the target file) to be included.
2. Reads and processes the target file, which may contain other CPP directives itself. In particular, it may `#include` other files.
3. Inserts the resulting target file into the current file in place of the `#include` line and continues to read the current file.

Therefore, the effect of a `#include` directive is almost as if the target file were physically inserted in place of the `#include` line.

When you use a UNIX system call or a C library function in your C program, you usually need to include certain specific system header files. Required header files will be indicated whenever we describe a new library function or system call. Failing to include the necessary header files will cause errors, and you cannot compile the C program. The header file `stdio.h` is required by C standard I/O library functions such as **putchar, getchar, scanf, fopen,** and **fprintf.** It is common practice to always include `stdio.h` when a program does any input or output.

Besides standard header files, it is also possible to include header files of your own. The preprocessor directive

```
#include "filename"
```

is used to include the file specified. The quotation marks are part of the directive. If *filename* is not given as a full pathname, then it is first sought in

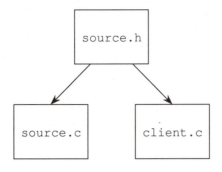

Figure 4.2: Source–Client Relation

the same directory as the input file. If the file is not found there, then the standard system directories are searched.

Now you know how to include header files, but it is still not clear what parts of a program belong in a header file and why. This is our next subject.

4.2 How to Use Header Files

The primary purpose of a header file is to make functions, variables, arrays, and other data objects that are defined in one source-code file accessible from another file. For a file `source.c`, the convention is to use a corresponding `source.h` as its header file. Any file, called a *client*, that wishes to use facilities provided by `source.c` should include the header `source.h`. Furthermore, the file `source.c` itself should also use a `#include` line to incorporate its own header file. This ensures that declarations stay consistent for the source and clients. Figure 4.2 illustrates this source–client relation.

Often in practice, the client file would be using facilities provided by a package consisting of many source-code files. In this case, one header file should declare constructs made available by the package. The `stdio.h` is such a header file. This organization lets you collect information affecting multiple files in one file (the header) so that any modifications can be made easily in one place only. Thus, the impossible question—If I modify this declaration, what other places do I have to make a similar change?—is completely avoided.

So, which declarations should go in a header file and which belong in the source-code file? Use the following rules of thumb:

- Declare in the header any function accessible from another file with a function prototype preceded by the modifier `extern` (see Section 3.5). For example, `extern int gcd(int, int);`.

- Declare in the header any global variables accessible from a client. Also use the `extern` modifier. The same global variable should also be defined with a declaration without the `extern` in one source (`.c`) file.
- Do not put definitions, a declaration that allocates space, in a header file. For example, `int arr[10];` and `float x=3.14f;` are definitions (see Section 3.5).
- Include any `#define` constants to be used by clients in the header file. The constants `NULL` and `EOF` in `stdio.h` are examples.
- Put macros to be used by clients in the header file. The macros **getchar** and **putchar** in `stdio.h` are examples. Macro definitions are discussed in the next section.
- Include data-structure (Chapter 7) and `typedef` (Section 3.9) declarations used by clients in the header file.

In summary, a header file is often the *external interface* of a program package. All necessary declarations should be there so that a client just has to `#include` the header file to access all the facilities provided by the package. On the other hand, nothing that is private to the package should be in the header.

The `cirbuf.h` file (Section 3.6) is one example. Many more example header files can be found in later chapters.

4.3   Symbolic Constants and Macros

The CPP directive `#define` is used to define *symbolic constants* and *macros*. For example, after the definition

```
#define TABLE_SIZE 1024
```

the symbolic constant `TABLE_SIZE` can be used in all subsequent source code instead of the integer `1024`. This makes the program much more readable and easier to modify when the table size must be changed. The general form is

```
#define identifier token ...
```

The preprocessor will then replace the identifier with the given tokens everywhere in subsequent source code, except in string and character constants. Although it is allowable to use any identifier, using all capitals for symbolic constants and reserving all lowercase identifiers for variables, function names, and so on is advisable. This way, distinguishing symbolic constants from other identifiers in a piece of C code is easy. Table 4.1 gives some examples of symbolic constants that also show the various forms of numeric constants. In Table 4.1 note how a character (`FORMFEED`) can be specified with its

`#define PI 3.14159`	`#define NEWLINE '\n'`
`#define DELTA 0.1e-8`	`#define TAB '\t'`
`#define MAXSIZE 200`	`#define NullChar '\0'`
`#define EOF -1`	`#define BACKSLASH '\\'`
`#define TWELVE 014`	`#define TWELVE 0xc`
`#define TRUE 1`	`#define FORMFEED '\014'`
`#define FALSE 0`	`#define NullString ""`
`#define NULL 0`	`#define Low_Bit 01`

Table 4.1: Symbolic Constants

octal ASCII code, a bit pattern (`Low_Bit`) by an octal number, and a special zero pointer (`NULL`) by zero.

Whereas, a symbolic constant provides a fixed substitution, a *macro* is a variable text-substitution mechanism. A macro is defined with parameters in the form

```
#define name(arg1, arg2, ...) definition
```

For example, the macro `SQUARE`

```
#define SQUARE(x)   ((x)*(x))
```

has one parameter and can be used in such forms as

```
area = SQUARE(side);        (becomes area = ((side)*(side));)
r = c/SQUARE(a+b);          (becomes r = c/((a+b)*(a+b));)
```

Macros are *expanded* by the preprocessor using the definition and the supplied parameters.

Another macro `MIN`

```
#define MIN(x, y)    ((x)>(y) ? (y) : (x))
```

takes two arguments x and y and is defined by a conditional expression. The macro call

```
MIN(a + b, c - d)
```

is expanded by the CPP into

```
((a + b)>(c - d) ? (c - d) : (a + b))
```

Although a macro call looks like a function call, it is just an abbreviation to be replaced by its full definition through the preprocessor. Note the use of the extra parentheses around x and y in the definition of `MIN`. This is necessary because x and y can be arbitrary expressions in a macro call. If the definition were given without the extra parentheses, would the above example still be expanded correctly?

Another commonly used macro is absolute value:

```
#define ABS(a)    ((a)>=0 ? (a) : -(a))
```

Technically, a symbolic constant is just a macro with no arguments. Also, the right hand side of a macro may also involve other macros that may or may not be defined yet. When a macro expansion is performed, the result will be scanned again for any macros to be expanded until no more expansion is encountered.

Redefining Macros

Once a macro is defined, it normally should not be defined again. However, the CPP tolerates redefining with the same definition but produces a warning message otherwise. Often, redefining a macro with the same definition is caused by multiple inclusions of the same header file. Avoiding duplicate inclusion is the subject of Section 4.6.

Sometimes it is also useful to undefine a macro, removing its definition entirely with the #undef directive:

```
#undef ABS
```

Once undefined, a macro can then be redefined with no problems.

4.4 Conditional Text Inclusion

The CPP also provides a mechanism to include or exclude certain parts of a program. This facility is useful in many ways. For beginners, the primary use would be in debugging and testing programs.

If #define is given just one token,

```
#define name
```

then *name* becomes *defined* (as opposed to *undefined*). You can request the preprocessor to include or exclude sections of code in your program, depending on whether certain special names are defined or undefined.

Conditional inclusion can be specified in the form

```
any-if-condition
        source-code lines A
#else
        source-code lines B
#endif
```

`if` **Condition**	**Meaning**
`#if` *constant-expression*	True if expression is zero
`#ifdef` *identifier*	True if identifier is `#defined`
`#ifndef` *identifier*	True if identifier is not `#defined`

Table 4.2: CPP Conditionals

where *any-if-condition* can be `#if`, `#ifdef`, or `#ifndef`. The `#else` clause is optional. If the condition is satisfied, then part A will be included; otherwise, part B (if given) will be included. Table 4.2 lists the possible conditions.

Conditional inclusion can be used to include debugging code. For example, the `factorial` function we saw can be revised as follows:

```
int factorial(int i)
{ int ans = 1;
#ifdef DEBUG
      printf("entered factorial with i = %d\n", i);
#endif /* end DEBUG              */
      /* the rest of factorial */
}
```

The point is to perform the diagnostic output only when the program is being debugged. Therefore, such lines don't have to be deleted for regular execution. Note that a comment is supplied after the `#endif` to mark the end, making it easier to see where the conditionally included code starts and ends. This is not a required but a highly recommended practice.

To activate such conditional debug statements, you can either add a line

```
#define DEBUG
```

at the beginning of the source-code file or compile the source-code file with

cc -DDEBUG *file*.c

The -D option tells the preprocessor to define the name DEBUG.

Another frequent use of conditional inclusion is to handle hardware- or system-dependent code. For example,

```
#ifdef AIX
/*  for IBM AIX UNIX */
#define TABLE_SIZE   256
#endif  /* end AIX */
```

```
#ifdef VAX
/* for DEC VAX */
#define TABLE_SIZE   128
#endif  /* end VAX */
```

Here, the symbolic constant TABLE_SIZE is defined differently depending on whether the symbol AIX or VAX is defined.

You can also position extra code for program testing in the source file itself. For example, the lines

```
#ifdef TEST
main()
{   octal_print(0);
    octal_print(-1);
    octal_print(0123456);
    octal_print(-0123456);
    octal_print(999);
    octal_print(-999);
}
#endif  /* end TEST */
```

could be put in the file octal_print.c (Section 2.13), which can then be tested by compiling it with

cc -DTEST octal_print.c

The expression for the #if directive may involve integer and character constants, macros, arithmetic operators, bitwise operations, shifts, relational operators, and the two logical operators && and ||. If the expression involves an undefined token, the token is treated as zero.

Also, #else and #elif directives can be used between a pair of #if and #endif in the obvious way:

```
#if FLAG == 1
   ...
#elif FLAG == 2
   ...
#else   /* default case */
   ...
#endif  /* end else     */
```

You can also use conditional inclusion to exclude code without deleting, as in

```
#if 0
/* This code no longer needed -- John Doe, Date */
```

.
.
.

```
#endif /* end 0 */
```
This technique gives you an easy way to reinstate the code later or to see what has been removed by whom and when.

4.5   More on Macros

The principal benefit of macros and macro calls is run-time efficiency. A macro call can always be replaced by a function call if efficiency is not an important consideration. A macro call looks like a function call and is as easy to read, but it saves the function-call overhead by producing in-line code at compile time.

Let us look at a more complicated macro SYSCALL, which makes a system or library call, and checks for possible failure. In case of an error, it displays a simple error message and calls **exit**(1):

```
#define SYSCALL(val, fn, arglist, errval)               \
    {    val = fn arglist;        /* call fn */          \
         if ( (errval) == val ) /* if error*/            \
         {   fprintf(stderr, "The call %s failed\n", #fn);\
             exit(1);                                    \
         }                                               \
    }
```

The macro SYSCALL takes four arguments

val	The variable to receive the return value
fn	The library or system function to call
arglist	The list, in parentheses, of arguments for fn
errval	The error value for which to check

The macro is on multiple lines through the use of backslashes at the end of each line purely for readability. Remember the CPP deletes the BACKSLASH–NEWLINE pair. So, SYSCALL is, in fact, on one line as all CPP directives should be.

The #fn on the **fprintf** line is worth noting. It turns the argument fn into an equivalent string constant. You can test this macro with a small main program:

```
#include <stdio.h>
/* put SYSCALL macro definition here */
main()
```

```
{ FILE *fp;
    SYSCALL(fp, fopen, ("abc", "r"), NULL)
    printf("After SYSCALL\n");
}
```

If you remove the read permission from the file `abc` and run this program, you should see the correct error message displayed.

To see the expansion of SYSCALL, use the `-P` (CPP-only) or `-E` (expand-only) option of **cc**. You should see that the above SYSCALL becomes something like

```
fp =  fopen("abc", "r");
if ( ( 0 ) == fp )
{   printf("The call %s failed\n", "fopen");
    exit(1);
}
```

only not as neatly formated.

The `#fn`, used earlier, is a case of *stringification*, which means "turning a code fragment into a string." In the definition of a macro with arguments, the notation `#arg` calls for the stringification of the argument `arg`. This advanced feature is new with ANSI C.

In the definition of a macro, you can also use the special notation `##` to concatenate two adjacent tokens into a single one. For instance,

```
#define SOURCE_NAME(file)   #file ## ".c"
```

lets you give `SOURCE_NAME(lowercase)` and obtain the string `"lower-case.c"`. Technically, it produces `"lowercase"".c"`, which is equivalent to the single string because adjacent string constants in C are automatically transformed into one longer string.

4.6   Preventing Multiple Loading of Header Files

In larger C programs, it is common practice to have many source-code and header files. The header files often have `#include` lines to include other headers. This situation often results in the likelihood of certain header files being read more than once during the preprocessing phase. This is not only wasteful but can also introduce CPP errors. To avoid possible multiple inclusion, a header file can be written as a big, conditional inclusion construct:

```
/*  A once-only header file xyz.h */

#ifndef _ _xyz_SEEN_ _
    #define _ _xyz_SEEN_ _
```

```
        /* the entire header file*/
           .
           .
           .

   #endif /* _ _xyz_SEEN_ _ */
```

The symbol _ _xyz_SEEN_ _ becomes defined once the file xyz.h is read by the CPP. This prevents it from being read again due to the #ifndef mechanism. This macro uses the underscore prefix and suffix to minimize the chance of conflict with other macros or constant names.

4.7   Standard Macros

The CPP also maintains a number of built-in macros to make programming easier. The built-in macros available depend on the preprocessor used, but the macros shown in Table 4.3 are standardized in ANSI C. Because these are CPP-defined quantities, the word *current* in Table 4.3 refers to the time when the preprocessor is running. The current input file can be any file being read due to file inclusion.

The standard macros are maintained by the CPP in the sense that their values change as the CPP executes. You can take advantage of these in diagnostic messages such as

```
   fprintf(stderr, "Reached line %d in file %s\n",
               _ _LINE_ _, _ _FILE_ _);
```

Macro	Meaning	Type	Example
_ _FILE_ _	Current input file	String	"stdio.h"
_ _BASE_FILE_ _	Main input file	String	lowercase.c
_ _LINE_ _	Line number in current file	Integer	109
_ _DATE_ _	Current date	String	"Jan 31 1991"
_ _TIME_ _	Current time	String	"21:45:03"
assert(exp)	Assertion testing	Macro call	*See text*
_ _STDC_ _	ANSI C flag, always 1	Integer	#ifdef _ _STDC_ _

Table 4.3: Standard Macros

or in greetings such as

```
printf("Welcome to WonderProgram Created %s, %s\n"
        _ _DATE_ _, _ _TIME_ _);
```

The standard macro `assert`, which requires the header `<assert.h>`, further aids program diagnostics. It is useful for testing various *assertions*, conditions that should hold, at different places in a program. Do this by calling `assert` with any C expression that produces a logical value. If the value produced is zero (false) at runtime, an error message is produced, and execution is aborted.

Here is a small test program to show how to use `assert`:

```
#include <stdio.h>
#include <assert.h>

main()
{ int x=9, y=8;
      assert(x == (y+1));
      printf("first\n");
      assert(x > y);
      printf("second\n");
      assert(x < y);
      printf("third\n");
}
```

Furthermore, the `assert` macro is only active when the symbolic constant `NDEBUG` (no debug) is not defined. This gives you a convenient way of disabling the diagnostics for the production version of your program.

With the materials presented in this chapter, you should be able to write the `assert` macro:

```
#ifndef NDEBUG
#define assert(exp) \
        { if ( !(exp) ) \
          { fprintf(stderr, \
                  "Assertion %s failed: file %s, line %d\n", \
                  #exp, _ _FILE_ _, _ _LINE_ _); \
            abort(); \
          } \
        }
#else                     /* no debug      */
#define assert(ignore)    /* empty         */
#endif                    /* end no debug  */
```

Note that stringification is used. The standard library function **abort**() causes abnormal termination of a program.

4.8 Summary

The C preprocessor (CPP), the first stage of **cc**, performs some important program transformations before the output is sent to the compiling stage. Automatic transformations are trigraphs, comment deletion, BACKSLASH–NEWLINE deletion, and expansion of built-in macros (Table 4.3). Other operations can be requested using CPP directives.

Each directive must take one line and begin with a # followed by the directive keyword. Line continuation is allowed. The #include directive includes both system- and user-supplied header files. Header files themselves may contain #include directives.

The directives #if, #ifdef, #ifndef, #endif, #elif, and #else supply the flexibility to include or exclude portions of a source-code file, depending on conditions that the CPP can check. Multiple inclusion of the same header can be avoided through conditional text inclusion.

The CPP also supplies a macro mechanism to define symbolic constants and to use abbreviations for code sequences. The #define and #undef directives define and undefine macros. The macro assert(exp) is convenient for checking conditions that must hold at key points of your program. This and other features of the CPP, when used effectively, will greatly help the testing and debugging of a program.

Exercises

1. For systems using a reduced character set, the CPP allows the use of the following nine trigraph sequences for the corresponding single character.

   - ??([
   - ??< {
   - ??' ^

   - ??)]
   - ??> }
   - ??! |

   - ??= #
   - ??/ \
   - ??- ~

   The CPP escape sequence ?? takes effect everywhere (including inside single- and double-quotation marks) and is processed before any other CPP transformation. Try a test program with ?? inside a **printf** format string and see what happens. Trigraphs are normally not a concern for anyone using a full-character set such as ASCII.

2. Will the CPP handle circular file inclusion where file1.h includes file2.h, which in turn also includes file1.h? What happens in this situation on your system?

3. Will the CPP handle recursive macro definitions where the definition of a macro xyz directly or indirectly involves xyz itself?

4. Use the -P or -E option of your **cc** command to produce a file containing the output of the CPP. Examine the output and comment on its contents.

5. Consider the code fragment

```
#define buffer_size 1024
#define table_size buffer_size/4
#undef buffer_size
#define buffer_size 512

printf("%d\n", table_size);
```

What will be the `table_size` displayed?

6. Consider multiple files, each containing a test `main` program used for testing the particular file. The test `main` program is conditionally included with `#ifdef`. Devise a convenient scheme that lets you exclude all but a specific `main` program for any particular test run.

7. Rewrite the `assert` macro in Section 4.7 using the ternary ? : conditional operator.

8. Define a macro `ROUND(x)` that produces the usual rounding operation on the floating-point argument x. The returned value is, of course, the nearest integer.

9. The stringification of a sequence of characters results in a C string constant whose value is the sequence. What is the stringification of the code segment `str = "abc\n";`?

10. Does the standard macro _ _TIME_ _ actually change as the CPP executes?

11. What happens when you invoke the `MIN` macro defined in Section 4.3 with `MIN(a++ , b)`? (*Hint*: This side-effect trap has no easy solution in ANSI C.)

12. Is it possible to specify a macro call inside another macro call? Namely, does `MIN(MAX(a,b),c)` do the right thing?

13. Consider the code segment

```
#include <stdio.h>

if ( a > b )
    SYSCALL(x, fopen, ("abc", "r"), NULL);
else
    x = y;
```

where the macro `SYSCALL` is defined in Section 4.5. Does the semicolon at the end of the macro call `SYSCALL` present a problem? If so, how do you propose to cure it?

5

Standard Library
Functions

A *library of functions* is a collection of frequently useful routines that are already written, tested, and debugged. It is a very efficient way of making high-quality code available to programmers so they don't have to "reinvent the wheel" every time a need for one of these functions arises.

Through the years, libraries for C have evolved and matured. With ANSI C, they are also standardized. This means programs written with calls to standard library functions need no modification when ported to another computer system supporting ANSI C. Furthermore, with the wide availability of C, knowledge of these functions will serve you everywhere you go.

When making a call to a library function, you must have the right declarations. Do this by including the necessary header files and then simply call the function and supply it with the required arguments. It is not very different from calling a function of your own, defined in another file. Compiled versions of the standard library functions will be automatically loaded, as needed, into the final executable program.

Frequently used library functions for string manipulation, dynamic memory allocation, variable number of functional arguments, and mathematical calculations are described here. The standard I/O functions will be described in Chapter 8.

5.1   Standard Operations on Strings _____

Although a string is not a basic type, it remains a frequently used construct in C programming. For this reason, a group of standard library functions for string manipulations is available (Tables 5.1 and 5.2). Getting familiar with these library functions will make programming easier in many situations. In Tables 5.1 and 5.2, we employ the notation

s   A character string (terminated by '\0') to be modified by the library function

cs   A const character string not to be modified

n   An integer of type size_t

c   A single char

where size_t (size type) is a typedef (Section 3.9) used for sizes of data items. The type size_t usually means an unsigned integer of a certain size, depending on the computer, and is defined in the standard header file stddef.h. For most purposes, you can regard size_t as unsigned int.

To use any of the string library functions, the standard header file <string.h> must be included. (On some UNIX systems, this header file may be under a different name, most likely <strings.h>.) The functions in Table 5.1 actually alter their first arguments. For copying or concatenating, make sure that there is enough room in s to accommodate the incoming characters.

Function	Description
char *__strcat__(s,cs)	Concatenates a copy of cs to end of s; returns s.
char *__strncat__(s,cs,n)	Concatenates a copy of at most n characters of cs to end of s; returns s.
char *__strcpy__(s,cs)	Copies cs to s including '\0'; returns s.
char *__strncpy__(s,cs,n)	Copies at most n characters of cs to s; returns s; pads with '\0' if cs has less than n characters.
char *__strtok__(s,cs)	Finds tokens in s delimited by characters in cs.

Table 5.1: Destructive String Operations

Function	Description
`size_t` **strlen**`(cs)`	Returns length of `cs` (excluding `'\0'`).
`char *`**strcmp**`(cs1,cs2)`	Compares `cs1` and `cs2`; returns negative, zero, or positive for `cs1` <, ==, or > `cs2`, respectively.
`char *`**strncmp**`(cs1,cs2,n)`	Compares first `n` characters of `cs1` and `cs2`; returns negative, zero, or positive for `cs1` <, ==, or > `cs2`, respectively.
`char *`**strchr**`(cs,c)`	Returns pointer to first occurrence of `c` in `cs`.
`char *`**strrchr**`(cs,c)`	Returns pointer to last occurrence of `c` in `cs`.
`char *`**strpbrk**`(cs1,cs2)`	Returns pointer to first `char` in `cs1` and `cs2`.
`char *`**strstr**`(cs1,cs2)`	Returns pointer to first occurrence of `cs2` in `cs1`. *The four functions all return* NULL *if the search fails.*
`size_t` **strspn**`(cs1,cs2)`	Returns length of prefix of `cs1` consisting of characters from `cs2`.
`size_t` **strcspn**`(cs1,cs2)`	Returns length of prefix of `cs1` consisting of characters *not* in `cs2`.

Table 5.2: Nondestructive String Operations

The **strcmp** functions compare strings lexicographically. For **strncpy**, if `cs` has more than `n` characters, no `'\0'` terminator is copied. The UNIX system library functions **index** and **rindex** are the same as **strchr** and **strrchr**, respectively.

The **strtok** function is a little more involved than the other functions. The purpose of **strtok** is to scan its first argument and break it up into tokens. A *token* is a sequence of characters forming a word such as a variable name or an arithmetic operator. Tokens in a character string are separated from one another by one or more *delimiter characters*. The delimiters are indicated by the second argument `cs`. To extract tokens from a string, a series of calls are made to **strtok**, with each call returning a pointer to the next token as a `'\0'` terminated string. The first invocation of **strtok** supplies a nonempty string `s` and receives the first token. All subsequent calls pass NULL as the first argument and receive successive tokens.

The tokens are returned in place by overwriting the first delimiter character after each token with a `'\0'`. Table 5.3 illustrates how `strtok` breaks `"ls /user/fac/pwang"` into tokens. In Table 5.3, ⊔ stands for a space, ⊗

Call Sequence	Token Found Is Underlined
1 **strtok**(str, del)	<u>ls</u>⊗ ⊔ ⊔/user/fac/pwang⊗
2 **strtok**(NULL, del)	ls⊗ ⊔ ⊔/<u>user</u>⊗fac/pwang⊗
3 **strtok**(NULL, del)	ls⊗⊔ ⊔/user⊗<u>fac</u>⊗pwang⊗
4 **strtok**(NULL, del)	ls⊗ ⊔ ⊔/user⊗fac⊗<u>pwang</u>⊗

str = "ls⊔ ⊔ ⊔/user/fac/pwang" and del = "⊔/"

Table 5.3: Using **strtok**

for a '\0'. Naturally, each token returned contains no delimiter characters. A NULL is returned when **strtok** finds no more tokens. Also, the delimiters contained in cs may be different on each call.

To illustrate matters further, let's examine an implementation of **strtok**:

```
#include          <stddef.h>
#include          <string.h>
typedef char * String;

String strtok(String s, const char *cs)
{ String token;
  int i = 0;
  static String spt;            /* where to search for next token */
      if ( s != NULL ) spt = s; /* new string                     */
      if ( spt[0] == '\0' ) return(NULL);
    /* find beginning of token */
      while ( spt[i] != '\0' && strchr(cs, spt[i]) != NULL ) i++ ;
      token = &spt[i];
    /* find end of token */
      while ( spt[i] != '\0' && strchr(cs, spt[i]) == NULL ) i++;
      spt[i] = '\0';            /* terminator in place            */
      spt = &spt[i+1];          /* record position                */
      return(token);           /* token produced                 */
}
```

A static pointer spt remembers, across calls to **strtok**, the beginning of the string yet to be processed. The library function **strchr** determines whether a character is a delimiter (contained in the string cs) or not. This implementation of **strtok** deserves careful study because of its intricacies in index and pointer handling.

To test **strtok**, use the following `main` program:

```
#define WHITE "\t \n\r"   /* TAB SPACE NEWLINE return */
main()
{ char st1[] = "There it is.";
  char st2[] = "\n \t A string\n \r  of 1 or more    \t tokens";
  String tk;
      tk = strtok(st1, WHITE);
      do
      {      printf("%s\n",tk);
      } while ( (tk = strtok(NULL, WHITE)) != NULL );
      tk = strtok(st2, WHITE);
      do
      {      printf("%s\n",tk);
      } while ( (tk = strtok(NULL, WHITE)) != NULL );
}
```

You should run this program and see what output it produces. Because **strtok** modifies its first argument, it is incorrect to pass a constant string such as `"There it is."` directly in the function call.

In our definition of **strtok**, we could have also used the library functions **strspn** and **strcspn** (Exercise 4). Here we have used subscript notations in manipulating strings. A more concise but less readable alternative is to use *pointer arithmetic*. Pointers will be discussed in detail in Chapter 6.

5.2 String Composition

We already know that string constants can be concatenated by juxtaposition (putting them next to each other) and by the CPP stringification and concatenation features (# and ##). But, sometimes you may need to construct a string out of fixed and variable strings, integers, floating-point numbers, and so on. For this purpose, use the library function **sprintf**. This function works just like **printf**, but instead of producing output, **sprintf** stores the resulting string in its first argument. Naturally, this first argument must be a string with enough space to receive the result:

```
int sprintf(char *result, char *format, arg1, arg2, ...)
```

Let the variable `home_dir` be the home directory, `argv[2]` the base filename, and `version` the version number. Then, we can construct an output filename in the string `outfile` with

```
char outfile[256];
sprintf(outfile, "%s/%s%d.c", home_dir, argv[2], version);
```

and use it to open an output stream

```
if ( (out = fopen(outfile, "w")) != NULL )
{    /* make use of the stream opened */
}
```

This leads us to the topic of the next section, the input and output of character strings.

5.3 String Input and Output

Also contained in the standard library (through `stdio.h`) are functions useful for performing input and output on strings. The function

```
char *gets(char *s);
```

reads a line (including the terminating NEWLINE) from `stdin` into the character array `s`, replaces the NEWLINE by a `'\0'` to make `s` a proper string, and then returns the string `s`. The `gets` function returns NULL upon end of file or error. It is assumed that the result array `s` has been declared with enough space to accommodate the input line.

String output is performed by the library function

```
int puts(char *s)
```

The given string `s` is sent to `stdout`, substituting a NEWLINE for the `'\0'`. The `puts` function normally returns a positive integer but returns EOF upon error. Therefore, `gets` reads an input line and converts it into a proper string, whereas `puts` takes a string and writes it out as a NEWLINE terminated line.

Besides `gets` and `puts` for the standard I/O streams, we have string I/O functions that work with any open stream. The input function

```
char *fgets(char *s, int size, FILE *infile)
```

reads the next input line (up to and including the NEWLINE) from `infile` into the character array `s`. At most, `size-1` characters will be read at a time. The result in `s` is terminated by a `'\0'`; unlike `gets`, we have no NEWLINE substitution here. Normally, a pointer to the string `s` is returned. On end of file or error, NULL is returned.

The output function

```
int fputs(char *s, FILE *outfile)
```

writes `s` to the given `outfile`. It returns zero normally and EOF upon error.

As an example, we can write a function `getline` that reads a line from `stdin` and returns the length of the string:

```
int getline(char *s, int bsize)
{   if ( fgets(s, bsize, stdin) == NULL )
        return(0);
    else
        return(strlen(s));
}
```

The `getline` function returns zero on end of file.

Another application of **fgets** can be found in the interactive calculator example in Section 5.7.

5.4   Operations on Characters

Since a `char` is just a small integer, it can be freely used in arithmetic expressions involving other characters or integers. For example, the expression

```
'8' - '0'
```

yields the integer value 8 because the values of `'0'`, `'1'`, `'2'`, and so on are consecutive and form an increasing sequence. Also the expression

```
'a' - 'A'
```

used in the function `lower` (Section 2.7) works because the corresponding uppercase and lowercase characters are a fixed distance apart. Reliance on such features makes the expression character-set-dependent.

The standard header file `ctype.h` defines a group of useful character macros and functions (Table 5.4) that are character-set-independent. The various testing functions in Table 5.4 return zero for false and nonzero for true.

5.5   Functions with Variable Number of Arguments

Another nice feature supported by the standard library is the ability to specify functions with a variable number of arguments. This ability is vital in situations such as the **printf** function, which takes one or more arguments of different types. Other applications include the functions `sum`, `product`, `max`, and `min`, which naturally take an indefinite number of arguments.

The notation

```
int sum(int argcnt, ...)           (variable args notation)
```

declares `sum` as a function of one or more arguments. The first parameter is `argcnt`, and it is of type `int`. The ellipses (...) are the syntax element called

Function	Test for
`int isupper(int c)`	Uppercase letter
`int islower(int c)`	Lowercase letter
`int isalpha(int c)`	Uppercase or lowercase letter
`int isdigit(int c)`	Decimal digit
`int isalnum(int c)`	`isalpha(c) || isdigit(c)`
`int iscntrl(int c)`	Control character
`int isxdigit(int c)`	Hexadecimal digit
`int isprint(int c)`	Printable character including SPACE
`int isgraph(int c)`	Printable character except SPACE
`int isspace(int c)`	SPACE, FORMFEED, NEWLINE, RETURN, TAB, vertical TAB
`int ispunct(int c)`	Printing character not SPACE, digit, or letter

Function	Meaning
`int toupper(int c)`	Convert to uppercase letter
`int tolower(int c)`	Convert to lowercase letter

Table 5.4: Character Functions

punctuators for indicating that the number and type of the remaining (undeclared) arguments may vary. An indefinite parameter declaration must begin with an explicitly named parameter, such as `argcnt` in this example. A function declared in this way may each time be passed a different number of arguments of arbitrary types.

At run time, when a function with an indefinite number of parameters is actually invoked, the number and type of the arguments being passed in the particular call must somehow be made known to the called function. There are several ways to do this. If the types of the undeclared arguments are fixed, this information can be hard-coded in the called function. Alternatively, the count and types of the unnamed arguments may be supplied in the leading named arguments. For example, the first argument of **printf**, the format string, specifies the number and the type of the remaining arguments. In other cases, the first argument may be an argument count. Instead of the argument count, a terminator marking the end of the unnamed arguments may be appropriate in certain applications.

The principal problem in defining a function to take a variable number of arguments lies in *referencing the unnamed arguments*. For this purpose, macros defined in the standard header <stdarg.h> are used. These macros are

va_start   Variable argument start: Initializes access to unnamed arguments.

va_arg   Next variable argument: Accesses individual unnamed arguments.

va_end   Variable argument end: Cleans up before returning from function.

These concepts can be made clearer with an example. Let's define the function sum:

```
#include   <stdarg.h>        /* header for variable argument list  */

int sum(int argcnt, ...)     /* argcnt supplies count of other args */
{ va_list ap;                /* argument pointer                    */
  int ans = 0;
      va_start(ap, argcnt); /* initialize ap                        */
      while ( argcnt-- > 0 )/* process all args                     */
          ans += va_arg(ap, int);
      va_end(ap);            /* clean up  before function returns   */
      return(ans);
}
```

The type va_list is a macro to declare a variable ap (argument pointer), which is used to refer to each unnamed argument in turn. The macro va_start initializes ap to point to the first unnamed argument. To locate the first unnamed argument, va_start also needs the last named argument, argcnt in this example. Once ap is properly initialized, the macro va_arg returns the next unnamed argument on the argument list. The va_arg macro also advances ap to point to the next argument. To do this, va_arg needs the type, thereby the size, of the unnamed argument. In sum, we provide it with the type int. After all such arguments have been retrieved, the pointer ap is then given to the macro va_end to perform the required cleanup actions.

We should now try to pass a different number of arguments to sum.

```
main()
{ int total;
      total = sum(5, 1,2,3,4,5);
      printf("sum=%d\n", total);
      total = sum(8, 1,2,3,4,5,6,7,8);
      printf("sum=%d\n", total);
}
```

Notice that the second argument of `va_arg` is a type name, not a variable. Therefore, if a function wishes to obtain unnamed arguments of mixed types, different `va_arg` statements, controlled perhaps by a `switch` or `if`, should be used.

Because the number and type of arguments are unknown at compile time, the space to receive incoming arguments must be allocated at run time, a principal job of `va_start`. The main duty of `va_end` is to return dynamic storage used. We'll have more to say about dynamic-storage management in the next section.

5.6   Storage Allocation and Management

When a variable is defined, the compiler allocates storage for it. Thus, variables and arrays you declare in a program have storage allocated at compile time. The management of the compile-time allocation depends on the *storage class* of the variable: *automatic* or *static*.

You already are familiar with how automatic variables are managed. Internal variables with the `static` specifier and all global variables, per file or not, belong to the static-storage class. Objects in the static-storage class are initialized to zero by default. They also retain their storage location and therefore value, regardless of entry or exit of functions and blocks.

Compile-time-allocated data storage is managed implicitly, according to the scoping rules laid down by C. Storage allocation at compile time is efficient and convenient but sometimes too restrictive. To avoid such restrictions, some data storage can also be allocated and explicitly managed at run time, as we will see next.

5.6.1 Dynamic-Storage Allocation

Besides compile-time storage allocation, it is sometimes necessary in a program to allocate storage dynamically or at run time. The latter means, as the program executes, it can request additional memory space for its computational needs. Dynamically allocated data are not subject to the variable scoping rules and will exist until explicitly de-allocated.

One frequent reason for dynamic storage is that certain data sizes are unknown at compile time. Consider a function, `array_add`, that takes two `int` arrays, adds them, and returns the `sum` array. The result, of course, is an array whose size depends on the size of the argument arrays. If the space to hold the answer is to be allocated in the `array_add` function, it must happen at run time. Similarly, if the size of a table is not known beforehand, you can either allocate a huge table at compile time (to guard against all eventual sizes) or use just enough dynamic storage for the job at hand. Run-time storage is allocated from a *free pool* reserved for this very purpose.

The dynamic-storage-allocation technique is often overlooked by beginning C programmers because of the complications involved. But it is extremely important for practical applications. The standard library function **calloc** allocates storage for an array at run time.

```
void *calloc(size_t n, size_t size)
```

The **calloc** function returns a pointer to newly allocated space appropriate to hold an array with *n* elements, each occupying *size* bytes. Also, **calloc** initializes the array elements to zero. NULL is returned if it fails to allocate the requested storage, most likely because of lack of free space. The newly allocated storage has no type yet, the reason why void * (pointer without type) is returned. It can be cast (Section 3.10) into an appropriate type before being used to store and retrieve data. (More information on pointers and the void * type can be found in Chapter 6.)

For the sake of program portability, instead of using a hard-coded constant for *size*, use the compile-time unary operator sizeof to obtain the size of any data type. The compile-time expression

```
sizeof( name )
```

yields a size_t integer equal to the number of bytes required to hold the variable or data type given by *name*. Thus,

```
calloc(n, sizeof(int));
```

creates an integer array of n cells initialized to zero.

Let's put these concepts to use by writing a function vector_add to add two vectors (int arrays) and to return a pointer to the result vector in dynamic-storage space:

```
#include <stdlib.h>
typedef int *Vector;

Vector vector_add(Vector a, Vector b, size_t n)
{ int i;
  Vector ans;
      ans = (Vector) calloc(n, sizeof(int)); /* type cast and calloc */
      for ( i = 0 ; i < n ; i++ )
              ans[i] = a[i] + b[i];
      return(ans);
}
```

The header `stdlib.h` is required by the dynamic-memory-allocation functions. Note how the `void *` returned by **calloc** is cast into type `Vector` before being assigned to the variable `ans`. This is another example of explicit type conversion.

To see how well `Vector_add` works, use the following `main` program:

```
main()
{   int i;
    Vector sum;
    int a[]={10, 20, 30}, b[]={-1, -2, -3};
    int foo[]={1, 2, 3, 4, 5}, bar[]={1, 1, 1, 1, 1};
        sum = vector_add(foo, bar, 5);
        for ( i=0; i < 5; i++ ) printf("%d ", sum[i]);
        printf("\n");
        free(sum);              /* return space to free storage pool */
        sum = vector_add(a, b, 3);
        for ( i=0; i < 3; i++ ) printf("%d ", sum[i]);
        printf("\n");

}
```

Dynamically allocated storage is freed with the standard library function **free** when the space is no longer needed.

> void **free**(void *p)   (p is a pointer of any type)

Freed space goes back to the pool of available space for dynamic allocation. Take care not to free space that has not been dynamically allocated. Otherwise, data and functions in your program can be destroyed in unpredictable ways.

A more basic standard library function

> void ***malloc**(size_t n)

allocates a section of n bytes of *uninitialized* storage. Also, **malloc** takes only one argument rather than two as does **calloc**.

To apply **malloc**, let's write a function `strrev` that takes a character string argument and returns its reverse in dynamic-storage space:

```
#include  <stdio.h>
#include  <string.h>
#include  <stdlib.h>
typedef char *String;

String strrev(String a)
{ register size_t n;
  register int i = 0;
```

```
String ans;
    n = strlen(a) + 1;      /* length of string and terminator */
    ans = (String) malloc(n*sizeof(char)); /* cast + malloc   */
    if ( ans == NULL )      /* test for failure                */
    {   fprintf(stderr,"strrev: malloc failed \n);
        exit(1);
    }
    n -= 2;                 /* so ans[n] gets a[0]             */
    while ( a[i] != '\0' )
        ans[n-i] = a[i++]; /* copy in reverse                 */
    ans[n+1] = '\0';        /* string terminator              */
    return(ans);
}
```

In `strrev`, the standard string function **strlen** (Section 5.1) is used.

The usage of dynamic storage can be summarized as follows:

1. Use `#include <stdlib.h>`.
2. Compute the size of the dynamic storage needed with the `size_of` operator.
3. Cast the pointer returned by **malloc** or **calloc** into a pointer of the desired type and assign it to a pointer variable of the correct type.
4. When the space allocated by **malloc** or **calloc** is no longer needed, use **free** to return it to the pool of available space.

If your system does not have the header `<stdlib.h>`, use `<stddef.h>` instead. It is possible that your system does not require either.

5.7 Numeric Computations

Supported also in the standard library are mathematical functions such as **sin**, **sqrt**, and **log** for floating-point computations. To use these functions, the header file `<math.h>` is needed. Appendix 11 contains a complete description of all the mathematical functions. On UNIX systems, the mathematical library is usually kept in the file `libm.a` in the system directory `/usr/lib`.

The library functions work with type `double` (double-precision floating-point). This means they take `double` arguments and return `double` values. An example is

```
double cos(double x);
```

On some systems, similar libraries are provided for floats of other sizes as well.

If you use functions supplied by a library, you must include such functions in your executable code before it can run correctly. This is done by tell-ing the UNIX linker/loader **ld** to extract the required library functions and combine them with your object code. The **cc** command takes care of supplying the right '-1' option, which is usually `libc.a` for the standard library. On certain systems, the mathematical functions are not contained in the standard library but in a separate `libm.a` file. In this case, the best thing to do is to supply the `-lm` option to the **cc** command (Section 11.2).

Now let's consider an interesting example that deals with floating-point computations.

An Interactive Calculator

We will implement a simple calculator by creating a new UNIX system command **calc**, used at the shell level for interactive calculations. The **calc** command supports the arithmetic operations +, -, *, /, and ^ (exponentiation). It reads infix expressions consisting of numbers and operators separated by white space and computes the result. To avoid complications, expressions are evaluated from left to right without regard to the usual precedence rules. The *clear* operation (the *C* button on a calculator) is also supported.

Here is a typical session with **calc**:

```
calc ready:
0 + 125
125    *    0.25
31.25    - 3.5
27.75 ^D
```

The user input is shown in italic. Numbers and operators must be separated by white space (SPACE, TAB, or NEWLINE). A session ends with ^D.

The **calc** command works with three fundamental quantities:

ans   The answer, the one that normally shows in the liquid crystal display on your hand-held calculator, initialized to `0.0`

op   The operator, initialized to `'+'`, whose left operand is always `ans`

arg   The right operand of `op`, initialized to `0.0`

The outline of the central mechanism used by **calc** is

```
execute   forever
{         arg = get next number
          ans = ans op arg
          display ans
          op  = get next operator

}
```

We break down the program into three parts:

1. Get next number, function `getarg`.
2. Get next operator, function `getop`.
3. Perform the operation, function `main`.

The implementation involves floating-point computations, string manipulations, and use of library functions. Besides the above listed functions, a fourth function `token` is written to extract tokens entered by the user.

The `calc.c` file starts with `#include` files and definitions of global variables `ans`, `arg`, `pname`, `op`, and `line`. User input is received one line at a time and saved in the `line` buffer for processing:

```
/* a simple infix calculator */
#include <stdio.h>
#include <string.h>
#include <math.h>                         /* for pow                    */
#include <stdlib.h>                       /* for atof                   */
#include <stddef.h>
#define SIZE 80                           /* input line buffer size */
static char line[SIZE] = "\0";            /* global line buffer       */
typedef char *String;
static String pname;                      /* program name             */
static double ans = 0.0, arg = 0.0;       /* global variables         */
static char op = '+';
```

The overall computation strategy is reflected in the main function of **calc**:

```
main(int argc, String argv[])
{ static double getarg(void);    /* defined later                   */
  static char getop(void);       /* defined later                   */
      pname=argv[0];
      printf("%s ready:\n%.12g + ", pname, ans);  /* display prompt */
      while( 1 )                 /* repeat forever                  */
      {    arg = getarg();       /* get next number                 */
          switch (op)            /* perform operation               */
          { case '+': ans += arg; break;
            case '-': ans -= arg; break;
            case '*': ans *= arg; break;
            case '/': ans /= arg; break;
            case '^': ans = pow(ans,arg); break;
          }
          printf("%.12g ", ans); /* display answer                  */
          op = getop();          /* get next operator               */
      }
}
```

In the beginning, the screen displays the two-line prompt:

```
calc ready:
0 +
```

All floats in this program are displayed with the .12g format (floating point with 12 digits; see Section 8.3). The while implements the main computation loop in a straightforward manner. The program terminates by exiting when the user input is finished.

The library function **pow**

```
double pow(double base, double expo)
```

computes $base^{expo}$. An error occurs if $base = 0$ and $expo \leq 0$, or if $base < 0$ and $expo$ is not an integer.

It remains only for us to define getop and getarg. The function getop returns the next operator entered by the user, and getarg returns the next number entered by the user. Both getop and getarg follow the general outline:

```
repeat  forever
{       get next token
        check token for correctness
        if  incorrect
                display advisory message
        else
                transform token to correct data type
                return correct result

}
```

Here is the code for getop:

```
static char getop()           /* returns next operator     */
{ char op;                    /* operator                  */
  char *op_ptr;               /* operator pointer          */
  static String token(void);  /* defined later             */
     while ( 1 )              /* forever                   */
     { op_ptr = token();      /* next token from user input */
        if ( strlen(op_ptr) == 1 ) /* insist on one-char operator */
            op = op_ptr[0];
        else
        { printf("%s: %s unknown operation\n", pname, op_ptr);
          printf("%s ready:\n%.12g  ", pname, ans);
          line[0]='\0';             /* require new input         */
          continue;
        }
     }
```

```
        switch( op )                    /* which op is it                    */
        {   case '+': case '-': case '*': case '/': case '^':
                return(op);
            case 'C': case 'c' :   /* clear                                  */
                arg = ans = 0.0;   /* reset global variables                 */
                op = '+';
                printf("%s ready:\n%.12g + ", pname, ans);
                                                            /* prompt */
                line[0] = '\0';
                return(op);
            default:
                printf("%s: %c unknown operation\n", pname, op);
                printf("%s ready:\n%.12g  ", pname, ans);
                                                            /* prompt */
                break;
        } /* end of switch */
    } /* end of while */
}
```

The next token from the user is obtained by calling the function token, and it must be a single-character operator that **calc** understands. Otherwise, getop displays a message and an appropriate prompt. Observe that getop handles the clear operation directly.

The duty of getarg is to obtain the next numeric argument from user input. It calls the function is_number to determine if the next token is a valid number. If so, it calls the standard library function **atof** to convert the number represented by an ASCII string into a double (not float). (Appendix 11 lists such conversion functions.)

```
    static double getarg()
    { String number;
      static int is_number(String);
      static String token(void);
        while(1)
        {   number = token();                      /* get next token */
            if ( is_number(number) )
                return ( atof(number ) );   /* valid number    */
            else                            /* invalid number */
            {   printf("%s: %s nonnumber, please re-enter number\n",
                        pname, number);
                printf("%s ready:\n%.12g  %c ", pname, ans, op);
            }
        }  /* end of while */
    }
```

The string function **strspn** used in `is_number` helps check for a valid number, a sequence of digits with an optional sign, and a possible decimal point:

```
#define DIGITS "0123456789"


static int is_number(String number)
{ int sign = 0, i, j, len;
     /* check for leading sign */
     if ( number[0] == '+' || number[0] == '-') sign = 1;
     len = strlen(number);          /* length of number   */
     i = strspn( &number[sign], DIGITS ) + sign;
     if ( i == len ) return(1);     /* valid number       */
     else if ( number[i] == '.' )   /* with decimal point */
     {     j = strspn( &number[i+1], DIGITS );
          if ( len == i + j + 1 ) return(1);
     }
     else   return(0);              /* invalid number     */
}
```

We have yet to discuss `token`, the function used by both `getop` and `getarg`. The `token` function uses the library function **fgets** (Section 5.3) to read one line at a time from `stdin` into the `line[SIZE]` buffer. The default line `SIZE` is 80 characters. Tokens, separated by white space (`WHITE`), are picked off the array `line` one at a time using the library function **strtok**. Our `token` function refills the line buffer after all tokens are processed:

```
#define WHITE "\t \n\r"


static String token()         /* get next token from user input */
{ String tk;                  /* token                          */
     if (line[0] == '\0')     /* fill empty buffer              */
     {   if ( fgets(line, SIZE, stdin) == NULL ) exit(0);
         tk = strtok(line, WHITE);
     }
     else    tk = strtok(NULL, WHITE);
     if ( tk == NULL )        /* no more tokens on line         */
     {   line[0] = '\0';      /* require new input              */
         return(token());     /* recursive call                 */
     }
     else    return(tk);
}
```

Once all of the source code for **calc** is in the file `calc.c`, the command

```
cc -o calc calc.c -lm
```

compiles `calc.c`, links in the library functions from `libm.a`, and produces an executable file named **calc**. The **calc** program ends when the end of file is encountered. When reading `stdin`, this happens when a **^D** is typed as the lone character on an input line. This is UNIX's convention to signal end of input from the keyboard.

5.8 Environment Variables

The parameters `argc` and `argv` of a main program reference the explicit arguments given on the command line (Section 2.14). Every time a process begins, another array of strings, representing the *user environment*, called the *environment list*, is also passed to the process. This provides a way, besides the command-line arguments, to pass information to a process. When a process is initiated, it receives the environment list of its parent process. If the parent is the shell, then the environment list contains all the environment variables (Section 1.8.3) and their values.

The environment list is always available in the system-defined global variable

```
extern char *environ[];         (environment strings)
```

Each `environ[i]` is an environment string in the form

```
name=value
```

For example,

```
HOME=/users/fac/pwang
PATH=/usr/local/bin:/usr/local:/usr/ucb:/bin:/usr/bin:.
TERM=vt100
```

The last element of the array `environ`, a zero pointer (NULL), serves to mark the end.

Although direct search of the global array `environ` is possible, accessing environment values with the standard library routine **getenv** is simpler:

```
char *getenv(char *variable)
```

This routine searches the environment list for a string whose *name* part matches the *variable* given and returns a pointer to the *value* part. If no match is found, then *variable* is not an environment variable, and NULL is returned.

The function **getenv** makes it easy to retrieve environmental values. A simple version is shown here to illustrate how it works:

```
/*      Searches the global variable environ and
 *      returns a pointer to value associated with str, if any,
 *      else returns NULL.
 */
```

```
#define NULL    0        /* normally defined in stdio.h */
typedef char * String;
extern  String environ[];
String getenv(const char *str)
{ int i = 0;
  /* match is a local function */
  static String match(const char *, const char *);
  String val;    /* value */
      while ( environ[i] != NULL )
              if (( val = match(str, environ[i++]) ) != NULL)
                    return(val);
        return(NULL);
}
```

Our implementation of `getenv` employs another function `match` to check `str` against each environment entry `environ[i]` and returns a pointer to the value part if the match succeeds. Otherwise, `NULL` is returned. Here is an implementation of `match`:

```
/*     Both s1 and s2 are strings:
 *     s1 is a name, s2 is name=value.
 *     If the names match, value is returned, else NULL is returned.
 */
static String match(const char * s1, const char * s2)
{ register int i = 0;
  register int j = 0;
      while ( s1[i] == s2[j++] )
          if ( s1[i++] == '=' ) return( &s2[j] );
      if ( s1[i] == '\0' && s2[j-1] == '=' )
          return( &s2[j] );
      return(NULL);
}
```

Arguments of `match` are declared `const` so that there is no danger of them being modified. This is especially important for the variable `environ`. The automatic variables `i` and `j` are declared `register` for improved performance. The function `match` returns the address of `s2[j]`, a value of the correct type `String`. Observe also how `match` is declared in `getenv`. This declaration is not necessary if the function definition of `getenv` comes after that of `match` in the file. However, omitting function-prototype declarations is a dangerous practice because moving the placement of a function in a file can result in compile-time errors.

To test `getenv`, use the following simple `main` program:

```
main()
{ String val;
      val = getenv("TERM");
      printf("TERM=%s\n, val);
      val = getenv("HOME=");
      printf("HOME=%s\n, val);
}
```

It is also possible to make use of the string library function **strncmp** instead of match for **getenv** (Exercise 16).

5.9   Summary

Standard library functions are tested and debugged routines that come with the C language, ready for you to use. To make library function calls, remember to include the required header files that provide the necessary declarations. Making use of existing library functions rather than writing similar routines on your own is always advisable.

Through the header string.h, a rich set of standard string-manipulation functions are provided: copying (strcpy, strncpy), concatenating (strcat, strncat), comparing (strcmp, strncmp), measuring length (strlen), and separating tokens (strtok). There are functions for obtaining character positions (strchr, strrchr, strpbrk, strstr) and length of prefixes (strspn, strcspn). Also available (with stdio.h) are functions for string composition (sprintf) and string input/output (gets and puts).

A set of character-set-independent functions (or macros) for character operations, such as lowercase to uppercase conversion supported by the header file ctype.h, is available.

The header stdarg.h provides facilities that let you define a function with an indefinite number of arguments. This becomes convenient, sometimes indispensable, in certain applications. The ability to allocate and free storage for data at run time (**malloc, calloc,** and **free**) provides additional flexibility.

Furthermore, C also provides a reasonable assortment of mathematical functions for numeric computation. The header math.h is used. For some systems, the -lm option also has to be supplied to **cc** in order to use these functions. These facilities are augmented by standard library functions to convert ASCII strings to integer and floating-point numbers (stdlib.h).

Environment variables transmit information about the execution environment, such as the terminal type, to programs. The environment values are kept on the system global variable environ, which can be accessed from your program. The standard library function **getenv** provides a convenient way to obtain environment values.

All standard library functions are well documented, as are their error conditions, in Appendix 11. See also Chapter 9 for ways to handle errors resulting from library function calls.

Exercises

1. Examine the following program. Does it work? If not, can you fix it?

```
#include <string.h>

main()
{ char foo[]="abcd";
  char bar[]="EFGHABCD";
      strcat(foo,bar);
      printf("%s\n",foo);
}
```

2. If `str` is a `char *` variable and points to a character string, what is the meaning of the expression `sizeof(str)`? Has it any relation with `strlen(str)`? Why?

3. Write your own implementation of the string functions **strspn** and **strcspn** (Section 5.1).

4. Consider the **strtok** implementation in Section 5.1. Rewrite it using **strspn** and/or **strcspn**.

5. Rewrite the `lowercase` program in Chapter 2 (Section 2.7), using the built-in character functions (Table 5.4).

6. Set several environment variables of your own at the shell level. Then run a program of your own to display the values of these environment variables.

7. Write a function `sum` that produces the total of an indefinite number of arguments uniformly of type either `int`, `float`, or `double`. Make `sum` always return `double` for now.

8. Make Exercise 7 work for mixed types as well. That means dropping the word *uniformly* from the specification of the problem.

9. The **calc** example in Section 5.7 displays floating-point numbers using 12 digits (`%.12g` format). Rewrite **calc**, making this a command-line option so that the user can specify any floating format (e.g., `%.8g`). (*Hint*: Use **sprintf**.)

10. Modify **calc** to use the library function **strtod** (Appendix 11) to process input numbers. What advantages does this bring?

11. Modify **calc** to include more operations such as **sqrt**, **log**, **sin**, and so on. (*Hint*: Modify `getarg`.) In handling these functions, you also need to be careful of domain and range errors (Section 9.5.1).

12. Add to **calc** the ability to save a few intermediate results, in single-letter buffers (*A–Z*), and to reuse them in subsequent computations.

13. The standard library also contains a number of functions dealing with time and dates. The standard header `<time.h>` must be included. Look in this header file and see what time and date functions there are. Find out how to use them to measure the execution time of your program.

14. If you decide to turn the `calc` program into one that uses octal numbers, how can you do that?

15. Can you think of any operations we could add to an octal `calc`? How about << ?

16. Modify the function **getenv** in Section 5.8 to use the library function **strncmp** instead of `match`.

Using Arrays and Pointers

One characteristic of C programming is the extensive use of arrays. Even a string is represented by an array of individual characters. A single array can group many related data items of the same type for easy processing. Arrays we have encountered so far are one-dimensional. Multidimensional arrays are also very useful and are discussed in detail.

A pointer is a value that *points to* the location of another value. Being able to represent and compute with pointers allows us flexibility in organizing and accessing data stored in a program. A very intimate relationship exists between arrays and pointers, which is why we cover them together.

We begin with basic concepts of arrays and pointers. Then, address arithmetic is explained in detail, paving the way to a thorough discussion of two-dimensional arrays. A matrix multiplication routine further illustrates the use of two-dimensional arrays. Next we present some well-selected applications of arrays and pointers to demonstrate how they are used effectively in practice. Included is a complete example for text-line sorting that pulls together many features of C programming presented so far. Then we go into more advanced topics: pointers and function calls, multiple indirection, functional arguments, and pointer arrays. These programming constructs give us the ability to implement a sorting routine to order arbitrary-data entries with a user-supplied comparison function. We also discuss the use of pointers in combination with dynamic-storage allocation.

A beginner may find pointers hard to use, and this is understand-able. A remedy may be to lead into the pointer concept from the simpler array construct and to demonstrate how pointers are used with other constructs in practice. Hopefully, the result is a clear explanation of this key topic.

6.1   Array Concepts and Declarations

The array is the simplest data structure beyond the basic types such as `char`, `int`, and `float`. In earlier chapters, you have seen some use of arrays already. In general, an array is a section of consecutive *memory cells*, each big enough to hold a data element of the same predetermined type. Each cell in an array is also referred to as an *array entry* or *array element*. The declaration

```
char str[10];
```

establishes `str` as a *one-dimensional* array of 10 entries, `str[0]`, `str[1]`,..., `str[9]`, each of type `char`. We know an array can be initialized when declared (Section 2.11). The initializers enclosed in braces (`{ }`) must be con-stant expressions. An array declaration, with or without initialization, can occur anywhere a variable declaration can. The ANSI standard has removed the earlier restriction on initialization of automatic arrays.

The *index* notation `str[n]` refers to the $(n + 1)$th entry of `str`. In gen-eral, if there are k entries, then the index goes from 0 to $k - 1$. The index nota-tion stores and retrieves values in an array:

```
str[0]='A';
putchar(str[0]);
str[1]='B';
putchar(str[1]);
```

In other words, each array entry is used just like a variable of the declared type. The advantage is that array entries are indexed and can therefore be used effectively in loops. Although each array entry is like a variable, the array name is a constant representing the address (memory location) of the first entry of the array. Thus, `str` is a constant whose value is the location of `str[0]`. Because the array name is a constant, its value cannot be changed. Hence, you must not use an array name on the left-hand side of an assign-ment or with an decrement or increment operator such as `str++`.

As an address, an array name can be assigned to a *pointer variable* of the appropriate type. Thus,

```
char *s;
s = str;
s[0] = 'Z';
```

is a roundabout way to assign the character `'Z'` to `str[0]`.

An array name can also be used in a function call as an argument. At the time of the call, the value of the array name (the address of the first entry of the array) is passed to the formal parameter in the called function. Array formal parameters are local variables and are usually used just like pointer variables. To illustrate this, let's write a function that computes the inner product of two vectors. Each vector is represented as an `int` array of specified length. The *inner product* is the sum of the individual products of corresponding components in the two vectors. Thus, for vectors A and B of length *n*, the inner product is

$$A_0 * B_0 + A_1 * B_1 + ... + A_{n-1} * B_{n-1}$$

Here is a definition of the function `inner`:

```
int inner(int a[], int b[], int n)
{ int ans=0;                   /* initialize answer to 0 */
      while ( n-- > 0 ) ans += a[n]*b[n];
      return(ans);
}
```

This is one of those rare occasions when the implementation is simpler than the definition. The formal parameters a and b of `inner` are declared using the array notation. However, they are actually pointer variables, not array names. Thus, a completely equivalent version of `inner` is

```
int inner(int *a, int *b, int n)
{ int ans=0;
      while ( n-- > 0 ) ans += a[n]*b[n];
      return(ans);
}
```

Here is a typical call to `inner`:

```
int y[] = {12,0,-4}, z[] = {2,3,4};
int result ;

result = inner(y,z);
printf("%d\n", result);                /* result should be 8 */
```

Up to now, we have been using indexing with arrays and pointers. The index notation is easy to read and understand, but not the most efficient, as we will see in Section 6.2.

6.2 Pointers and Address Arithmetic

6.2.1 Basic Pointer Concepts

A pointer variable is a variable whose value is the *address* of a memory location where a specific data type is stored. When a pointer variable is declared, the data type it points to is specified. The notations

```
int *a, *b;
char *r, *s;
```

declare a and b as integer-pointer variables and r and s as character-pointer variables. A pointer declaration merely creates the pointer variable; it neither initializes the pointer variable nor allocates memory space for the variable to point to. *Therefore, before it is used, a pointer variable must be assigned the address of an array, of some other variable, or of dynamically allocated space.* For example, the sequence

```
int *a;
int m[]={1,2,3,4};       (m is an integer array)
a = m;                   (pointer variable a assigned address of m)
a[3]= a[0]+5*a[1];       (now entries of m can be referenced through a)
```

results in m[3] being 11. Because a is a pointer variable of type int*, it can be assigned the address of an integer array m. For a char pointer, we would follow the same guidelines:

```
char *s;
s = (char *) malloc(4*sizeof(char));     (s points to allocated space)
s[0]='A';
s[1]='B';
s[2]='C';
s[3]='\0';                               (now s represents "ABC")
```

6.2.2 The Operators & and *

Two unary operators are important in dealing with pointers: &, the address-of operator, and *, the value-of operator. The address-of operator & gives the pointer to (address of) an *object*, a variable, or an array entry in memory. Having already declared int *a;, the statement

```
a = &m[3];
```

assigns to a the address of the int array entry m[3], and we say "a *points to* m[3]." Similarly, if k is an integer variable, then

```
a = &k;
```

assigns the address of k to a. The address-of operator & can be applied only to objects in memory and will not work with constants, register variables, or expressions such as (a + b).

The value-of operator * accesses a data item through a pointer. The * can be used on a pointer variable, a pointer constant, or any expression that produces a valid pointer value. After the above assignment, the notation *a stands for the variable k and behaves exactly the same. Thus, *a has the value of k, and *a = 5; is the same as saying k=5 because it stores 5 at the address where k stores its value. Note that the value of the pointer variable a itself is not changed by this assignment. In general, if p is a pointer of type *, then *p can be used as a variable of that type. The following further illustrates this concept:

```
*a = b - 3        (a is a pointer variable, b integer)
*m += 2           (m is an int array)
b = 5 * *a        (multiplication)
( b >= *a )       (relational operation)
++*a              (or (*a)++, increment *a)
(*m)--            (or --*m, decrement *m)
```

The unary operators * and & have the same precedence as unary arithmetic operators and have higher precedence than binary arithmetic and relational operators. The parentheses are necessary in the last example because unary operators such as *, ++, and -- *associate right to left*. Hence, *a-- would decrement the pointer variable a rather than the integer *a.

Another general observation that can be made of the * operator is that *pointer* is always equivalent to *pointer*[0]. In fact, the C compiler automatically converts the latter notation to the former. Here we have another reason why pointers are closely related to arrays.

6.2.3 Double Indirection

For an integer-pointer variable a, it is clear what *a means. But, what is &a? By definition, it is the address of a. In other words, &a is a pointer to an integer pointer. Thus, the artificial sequence

```
int k, *a, **t;   (t is a pointer to an int pointer)
t = &a;           (t points to a)
a = &k;           (a points to k; same as *t = &k)
**t = 15;         (k gets 15)
```

results in the variable k being assigned the value 15 (Figure 6.1). Here is how it works:

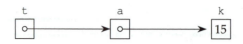

Figure 6.1: Double Indirection

1. Because t points to a, *t is a.
2. Because a points to k, **t is k.
3. Thus, **t = 15 is the same as k = 15.

The same reasoning can be applied to unravel multiple indirections (Section 6.6).

6.2.4 Address Arithmetic

Address arithmetic calculates memory addresses using pointers. Thus, it is also known as *pointer arithmetic*. A pointer is an integer byte count identifying a memory location so many bytes away from a certain reference address, such as the beginning of a program. For instance, 15083 points to byte 15083 from the reference location. A pointer gives the beginning of a *data cell*, which may take 1 or more bytes depending on the data type stored there. The exact number of bytes for each data type is implementation-dependent. On many 32-bit computers, a char takes 1 byte and an int 4 bytes.

In practice, a pointer often accesses a sequence of data cells stored in consecutive memory locations rather than just a single cell. To get from one such data cell to the next, you can use several convenient address arithmetic operations:

- Pointer + integer, resulting in a pointer
- Pointer – integer, giving another pointer
- Pointer – pointer, getting an integer

Each is discussed separately.

Pointer + Integer

Adding an integer quantity to a pointer is not as mysterious as it may seem. In fact, we have been using it implicitly all along. The familiar array notation a[3] retrieves the desired data by calculating its address based on the information that it is the third item down from the cell at a, namely, a[0]. With *explicit address arithmetic*, the same address can be computed by

    a + 3   (&a[3] or address of a[3])

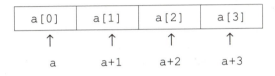

Figure 6.2: Pointer + Integer

The result of this address addition is a pointer to `a[3]` (Figure 6.2). Note, that this is not *adding* 3; rather, it is adding 3 *times* the size of the data cell to the address represented by `a`.

Thus, if `a` is an `int` pointer and is 15083, then the pointer `a+3` has value 15083 + 12 = 15095, assuming that `int` takes 4 bytes. But if `a` is a `char` pointer, then `a+3` becomes 15083 + 3 = 15086. When encountering an address arithmetic expression such as `a+3`, the compiler takes the size of the data cell into account and produces the appropriate code. This arrangement is convenient for programming and makes the program independent of the data type sizes on different computers.

As a result, we have the general rule: If `ptr` is a pointer and `n` an integer, then

```
ptr + n
```

is the pointer for the *n*th data cell from the one pointed to by `ptr`. And the expression

```
*(ptr + n)        (same as ptr[n])
```

is the same as `ptr[n]`, where `ptr` can be a pointer variable or an array name.

The function `inner` given in Section 6.1 can now be rewritten with pointer arithmetic:

```
int inner(const int *a, const int *b, int n)
{ int sum=0;
      while ( n-- > 0 ) sum += *a++ * *b++;    /* pointers advanced */
      return(sum);
}
```

Because of the right-to-left associativity of the operators involved, `*a++` means `* (a++)` rather than `(*a)++`. These terse notations can become hard to read. So, judicious use of parentheses to make the meaning clear is encouraged. It is also good practice to declare, with the `const` specifier, the read-only nature of constructs passed by pointers, as shown in this version of `inner`.

To further illustrate pointer usage, we present a pointer version of the standard library function **strcmp** (Section 5.1), which returns an integer value greater than, equal to, or less than zero if the string r is greater than, equal to, or less than the string s, respectively:

```
int strcmp(const char *r, const char *s)
{    while ( *r == *s )
     {    if ( *r == '\0' ) return (0);   /* strings are equal      */
          r++; s++;                       /* advance pointers       */
     }
     return ( *r - *s );                  /* strings are not equal */
}
```

The definition of strcmp depends on the fact that the string terminator is a zero-valued character.

As another example, let's look at the pointer implementation of the library function **strcpy**, which makes a copy of its second argument into the first argument:

```
char *strcpy(char *s, const char *cs)
{ char *tmp = s;
      while ( *cs != '\0' )
             *tmp++ = *cs++;              /* copy next character */
      *tmp = '\0';
      return(s);
}
```

The pointer variable tmp is first declared and initialized to s. Next, the while loop copies each character on the string cs until '\0' is encountered. Finally, the terminator '\0' is copied, and the pointer s returned. The variable tmp is technically unnecessary because s can serve as a *return parameter* (Section 6.5).

A common source of error in copying by passing pointers is insufficient space to receive the data being copied. In this example, s is assumed to point to the beginning of a reserved space large enough to hold the entire string. The minimum bytes needed is

```
strlen(cs) + 1
```

where the '\0' terminator occupies the final byte. In this case, it is the responsibility of the calling function to ensure that enough space has been provided. If this is undesirable, design the copying function to dynamically allocate space as in the function dstrcpy (dynamic-string copy):

```
char *dstrcpy(const char *cs)
{ char *s, *tmp;
  unsigned size;                                  /* or size_t size      */
```

```
extern char *malloc(unsigned);
    size = strlen(cs)+1;
    tmp = s = malloc(size);            /* allocate space       */
    while ( *cs != '\0' ) *tmp++ = *cs++;  /* copy next character */
    *tmp = '\0';
    return(s);
}
```

Note that the pointer returned by dstrcpy can later be used in a **free** call to return the space to the dynamic-allocation pool.

Pointer – Integer

Subtracting an integer from a pointer is the inverse operation to adding an integer. An example is contained in a pointer implementation of the function match used to consult the environment list in Section 5.8.

```
/*      Both s1 and s2 are strings:
 *      s1 is the target name to find, s2 is in the form name=value
 *      If the names match, value is returned, else NULL is returned.
 */
String match (String s1, String s2)
{    while ( *s1 == *s2++ )
            if ( *s1++ == '=' ) return(s2);       /* field delimiter */
     if ( *s1 == '\0' && *(s2-1) == '=' )
            return(s2);                            /* match found     */
     return(NULL);
}
```

Immediately after the while loop, the last step in determining a match is to pair the terminator of s1 with the field delimiter =, one character before s2. The pointer subtraction *(s2-1) gives exactly the character we need.

  With pointer subtraction, we have the alternative of going backward on a sequence of data cells. For instance, you can think of going from the end of an array to the beginning. This flexibility and power does not come without danger. You must now be careful not to *fall off the left end* of the data cells by going beyond the start.

Pointer – Pointer

It is also valid to subtract one pointer from another. If p and q are two pointers to entries of the same array, then

    n = q - p

is an integer n that is the distance between cells p and q. In other words, p + n is q. Note that n can be positive, negative, or zero. Here is a pointer-based version of **strlen** that uses this feature:

```
int strlen(const String s)
{ char *t = s;
      while( *t++ != '\0' ); /* go to end of string                 */
      return( t - s - 1 );    /* length of string without terminator */
}
```

In this version of **strlen**, the `while` loop, with an empty body, increments t until it reaches the end of the string. Then, the return statement computes the correct length of s via pointer subtraction.

Actually, the pointer variable t is incremented to one character beyond the terminating '\0'. So potentially, t now points to some address that may contain another data type or may even be outside the address space of the program. But this is only a problem if access is attempted, say, with *t.

6.2.5 Valid Pointer Operations

In this section, we summarize valid pointer operations for easy reference. The material here also contains some details not previously mentioned, as well as topics yet to come in this chapter.

Creation   The initial value of a pointer has three possible sources: a constant pointer such as an array name, an address of an object obtained with the & operator, or a value returned by a dynamic-memory-allocation function.

Assignment   Pointers of the same type can be assigned. Pointers of different types, except for `void *`, can be assigned only with an explicit cast (Section 3.10). An array name is a constant pointer and cannot be used on the left-hand side of an assignment. The NULL pointer (zero) can be assigned as a pointer value.

p ± integer   Adding or subtracting an integer from a pointer also includes the operations p++, p--, p += 2, and so on. Such expressions are valid as long as the resulting pointer is within the range of the same array. ANSI C also makes it official that a pointer is allowed to go one beyond the high end of an array. In other words, if p points to the last entry of an array, the pointer p+1 is valid as long as no attempt is made to access the nonexistent entry to which it points. Although most C compilers do not check whether a pointer falls within the range of an array, it is good practice to make sure that you stay within the allowed bounds.

Pointer subtraction Pointers to entries of the same array can be subtracted, yielding an integer that is positive, negative, or zero.

Comparison Pointers to entries of the same array can be compared with ==, <, >, and so on. Any pointer can be checked for equality with the NULL pointer. A function returning a pointer usually would return NULL as an indication of error or failure. The calling function must compare the returned pointer with NULL to detect such an error.

Indirection For a pointer ptr, the notation *ptr stands for the object to which it points and therefore can be used in expressions and on the left-hand side of an assignment.

Indexing A pointer p, whether an array name or a pointer variable, can be used with an index subscript as in p[i], where i is a positive or negative integer. The notation is converted by the C compiler to *(p+i). Again, it is the programmer's responsibility to ensure that the indexing stays within the bounds of the array.

6.3 Two-Dimensional Arrays

Up to now, all the arrays we have seen use a single index or subscript. Such arrays are *one-dimensional*. It is possible to have arrays with more than one subscript. For example,

```
int a[2][4];
```

declares a to be a *two-dimensional array* with the first subscript going from 0 to 1 and the second ranging from 0 to 3. In other words, the array can be thought of as a rectangular grid of two rows and four columns (Figure 6.3). The actual memory organization of a two-dimensional array is still linear: A total of eight entries are allocated in consecutive memory cells (Figure 6.4). The array entries are stored by *rows*, with the first row followed by the second row, and so on. Using pointer arithmetic, the by-row organization also means that the address &a[i][j] is given by

```
&a[0][0] + i*4 + j       (points to cell a[i][j])
```

where the 4 is the number of columns of a. Thus, it is possible to access a[i][j] using the alternative notation

```
int *p = &a[0][0];
*(p + i*4 + j)           (value of a[i][j])
```

a[0][0]	a[0][1]	a[0][2]	a[0][3]
a[1][0]	a[1][1]	a[1][2]	a[1][3]

Figure 6.3: Two-Dimensional Array Logical View

a[0][0]	a[0][1]	a[0][2]	a[0][3]	a[1][0]	a[1][1]	a[1][2]	a[1][3]

Figure 6.4: Two-Dimensional Array Memory Allocation

or equivalently

```
p[i*4 + j]
```

A two-dimensional array can be initialized as follows:

```
int a[][4]= { {0,1,2,3}, {4,5,6,7} };
```

Note that the range of the last subscript must be given explicitly. The initializer is a list of sublists for the rows. No sublist can contain more elements than the range specified in the declaration. Conversely, initializing *less* than the full range for any row is always possible. Some sublists may even be empty ({ }).

One natural question to ask is, Why is the syntax

```
a[i][j]
```

used rather than the common notation for two-dimensional arrays

```
a[i,j]        (not used in C)
```

used in other programming languages? The answer: A two-dimensional array is really just a one-dimensional array of elements that are themselves one-dimensional arrays. Thus, a[i][j] literally means (a[i])[j], and a[i] is a pointer, type int *, pointing to the $i + 1$st row of the two-dimensional array a. The following test program further illustrates many concepts related to pointers and the two-dimensional array:

```
#define RANGE 4
main()
{ int a[][RANGE]= { {0,1,2,3}, {4,5}, {8,9,10,11} };
  int *p = &a[0][0];
  int *q = a[0];                          /* p and q are the same   */
```

```
    int *r = a[1];                     /* pointer to second row  */
    int *s = a[2];                     /* pointer to third row   */
        printf("%d\n", *(p+RANGE+1));     /* a[1][1]              */
        printf("%d\n", *(q+2*RANGE+2));   /* a[2][2]              */
        printf("%d\n", *r);              /* a[1][0]               */
        printf("%d\n", *(r-2));          /* a[0][2]               */
        printf("%d\n", s[3]);            /* a[2][3]               */

}
```

The variable a is created as a 3 × 4, two-dimensional array of consecutive integers. The second row, however, is only partially initialized. The pointers q, r, and s point to the first, second, and third row of a, respectively. A variety of notations have been used to access cells of a to reinforce your understanding of the two-dimensional array representation, as well as pointer arithmetic.

Having a basic understanding of two-dimensional arrays, we are ready to put them to use.

6.3.1 Matrix Multiplication

Using pointer arithmetic, let's write a function matmul to compute the product of two matrices containing integer entries. A matrix is naturally represented by a two-dimensional array. Recall that the product of an $r \times s$ matrix X by an $s \times t$ matrix Y is an $r \times t$ matrix Z. (To appreciate this one, you must *say* the equation.) Each entry $Z_{i,j}$ is given by the inner product (Section 6.1) of row i of X and column j of Y. Here is a simple example:

$$\begin{bmatrix} 1 & 2 \\ 3 & 4 \\ 5 & 6 \end{bmatrix} \cdot \begin{bmatrix} a & b \\ c & d \end{bmatrix} = \begin{bmatrix} a+2c & b+2d \\ 3a+4c & 3b+4d \\ 5a+6c & 5b+6d \end{bmatrix}$$

The matrix-multiplication function matmul is implemented as

```
matmul(int *x, int *y, int* z, int r, int s, int t)
/*  x, y, z are pointers to first entries of
 *  the two-dimensional arrays
 *  r, s, t are array dimensions
 */
{ int i,j;
  int rtc(int *row, int *col, int s, int t); /* prototype          */
      for ( i=0 ; i < r ; i++ )
      {   x += i*s;                           /* x points to next row  */
          for ( j=0 ; j < t ; j++ )
```

```
                *z++ = rtc(x,y+j,s,t);      /* y+j points to col j of y  */
        }
}
```

The function `matmul` takes three pointers x, y, and z to the three two-dimen-sional arrays representing the matrices and the `int` dimensions r, s, and t as input parameters. Nested `for` loops are used to compute elements of the result array z. Each iteration of the outer loop advances x to the next row. Each iteration of the inner loop takes the row x and multiplies it with each column of y to produce an entry of z. The row-column inner product is per-formed by the function `rtc` (row times column) that takes a `row` pointer into the array x and a `col` pointer into the array y and computes the required inner product:

```
/* inner-product row times col */
int rtc(int *row, int *col, int s, int t)
{ int sum=0;
        while ( s-- > 0 )
        {    sum += (*row++) * *col;
             col += t;                      /* next column entry */
        }
        return(sum);
}
```

To get from one entry to the next in the same column of y, the `col` pointer is incremented by t, the column dimension of y. Use the following to test these functions:

```
main()
{ int a[2][3]= { {1,-2,5}, {1,2,3}};
  int b[3][2]= { {9,7},{-2,3},{-1,4}};
  int c[2][2];
        matmul(*a,*b,*c,2,3,2);      /* pass *a rather than a */
        printf("( %d    %d )\n( %d    %d )\n",
                c[0][0],c[0][1],c[1][0],c[1][1]);
}
```

The output of this program is

```
( 8    21 )
( 2    25 )
```

Using a separate function `rtc` to compute the row–column inner product adds to the clarity of the programs but incurs the performance penalty of extra function calls at run time. If execution speed is important, eliminate the function `rtc` by coding the inner-product computation as a third innermost loop in `matmul`.

In our implementation of `matmul`, the arrays are passed into the function as pointers of type `int *`. Receiving two-dimensional arrays as such directly with the function declaration

```
matmul(int a[][3], int b[][2], int c[][2], int r, int s, int t)
```

and using two-dimensional array indexing in the function body are also possible. The disadvantage of using two-dimensional array formal parameters is that the range of the last subscript must be given explicitly in the function header. This means that the function can multiply only matrices with those fixed dimensions, an unreasonable restriction that is avoided by the pointer-based implementation.

At this juncture, we are ready to study some typical applications of arrays and pointers.

6.4   Applications of Arrays and Pointers

In this section, we present some examples that apply the concepts of arrays and pointers. It is important that pointers are not studied in isolation but in conjunction with other constructs to solve problems. By doing so, we make the abstract rules of pointer usage concrete and easy to grasp.

6.4.1 An Implementation of strtok

The standard library function **strtok** was first discussed in Chapter 5. Recall that the function

```
String strtok(String s, const char * cs);
```

returns the next token in the string s. The tokens in s are separated by delimiter characters specified by the string cs. The first call to **strtok** supplies a non-NULL string s and receives the first token. Each subsequent call passes a NULL s to obtain the next token. The parameter cs may be the same or different for each call. An implementation of **strtok** using array indexing was given in Chapter 5. Here we present a pointer-based implementation:

```
#include <stdio.h>
#include <string.h>
typedef char *String;

String strtok(String s, const char * cs)
{ String token;
```

```
    static String spt; /* starting pointer */
        if ( s != NULL ) spt = s;
        if ( *spt == '\0' ) return(NULL);
        /* locate beginning of token */
        while ( *spt != '\0' && strchr(cs, *spt) != NULL ) spt++;
        token = spt;
        /* locate end of token */
        while ( *spt != '\0' && strchr(cs, *spt) == NULL ) spt++;
        *spt = '\0' ;
        spt++;
        return(token);
}
```

The static pointer variable `spt` remembers, across calls to **strtok**, the starting point of the string yet to be processed. The first `while` loop advances `spt` to the first character of the next token. The second `while` loop positions `spt` at the first delimiter character after the token. (See Exercise 5 for a suggested improvement to this definition of **strtok**.)

6.4.2 Polynomial Addition

Let's consider a program for adding polynomials. A one-variable polynomial with integer coefficients has the familiar form

$$a_n x^n + a_{n-1} x^{n-1} + \cdots + a_1 x + a_0$$

where x is the variable and $a_n, a_{n-1}, \ldots, a_0$ are the coefficients. We say that the degree is n and require that the leading coefficient $a_n \neq 0$. For example,

$$3x^5 - 10x^2 + 21x - 8$$

is a fifth-degree polynomial with four terms. Each term is a coefficient multiplied by a power of x. Such a polynomial can be represented by an `int` array recording the power-coefficient pairs of each term. For instance,

```
    int p[] = {5,3,2,-10,1,21,0,-8,-1};
```

gives the fifth-degree polynomial above. The representation p begins with the highest power, its coefficient, followed by the next highest power, its coefficient, and so on. A minus one (–1) is the end marker because no negative power is allowed for a polynomial. Any term with a zero coefficient will not be included in the representation to conserve space. Table 6.1 shows how this representation works.

Representation	Polynomial
`int q[] = {100,1,50,1,0,1,-1};`	$x^{100} + x^{50} + 1$
`int q[] = {20,9,7,-29,-1};`	$9x^{20} - 29x^7$
`int r[] = {0,8,-1};`	8
`int s[] = {-1};`	0

Table 6.1: A Polynomial Representation

Employing this polynomial representation, we can define a function `poly_add` to compute the sum of two polynomials as

```
#define DEG(p) (*(p))          /* macro for the degree of p         */
typedef int *Poly;
Poly poly_add(Poly a, Poly b)
{ Poly c,tmp;
  unsigned len;
      len = 2 * MAX(DEG(a),DEG(b)) + 1;
                              /* compute length of answer          */
      tmp = c = (Poly) calloc(len,sizeof(int));
                              /* allocate space for ans            */
      while ( *a >= 0 )       /* for each term of a                */
      {   while( *b > *a )    /* terms in b of higher power        */
          {   *c++ = *b++;
              *c++ = *b++;
          }
          *c++ = *a;
          if ( *a == *b )     /* add terms of like power    (1)    */
          {   *c = *++a + *++b;
              if ( *c++ == 0 ) c -= 2; /* terms cancel     (2)    */
              b++;
          }
          else *c++ = *++a;               /* no terms to combine   */
          a++;
      }
      while ( *b >= 0 ) *c++ = *b++;  /* add left over terms in b */
      *c = -1;                         /* terminator               */
      return(tmp);
}
```

In `poly_add` the maximum size of the result polynomial is computed and then that much space is allocated with **calloc**. The pointer returned by **calloc** is cast into type `Poly` and assigned to the variable c. To compute the sum, each term of a is added to the unprocessed terms of b with a power greater than or equal to the current term. The resulting terms are stored in c. When two terms from a and b combine (line 1), a check is made to see if the new term is 0 due to cancellation. If so, the c pointer is decremented by 2 to lose the 0 coefficient and its exponent (line 2). The iteration continues until all terms of a and b have been processed. Finally, the −1 terminator is inserted at the end of c, and the pointer `tmp` is returned.

To test this function, various polynomials should be added and the results displayed. For this purpose, we need a function to display a polynomial:

```
void poly_display(Poly p)
{     printf("(");
      while ( *p >= 0 )
            printf("%d, %d", *p, *(p+1));
            p += 2;
            if ( *p != -1 ) printf(", ");
      }
      printf(")\n");
}
```

It is tempting to use

```
printf("%d, %d", *p++, *p++);      (wrong)
```

in `poly_display`. This is incorrect because the order of evaluation of function arguments is unspecified in C.

6.4.3 Sorting Text Lines

The UNIX system **sort** command orders lines in one or more text files. This command provides many options that allow user control over how the lines are ordered. Let's write a simplified version of the **sort** command. Our command, **mysort**, will be used in the form

mysort [*key* **]** < *infile* > *outfile*

It will read all lines from `stdin`, sort the lines by comparing the given *key fields* in the lines, and then write the sorted lines to `stdout`. Each line is assumed to contain one or more fields separated by white spaces. The *key* is an integer indicating which field to use for ordering the lines. If the *key* is unspecified, then whole lines are compared.

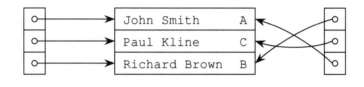

Figure 6.5: Sorting with a Pointer Array

For example, if you have files containing course grades in the form

```
John Smith       A
Paul Kline       C
Richard Brown    B
    .
    .
    .
```

use **mysort** on such files in the following ways:

> **mysort** 2 < grades1 > grades1.byname
> **cat** midterm final | **mysort** 3 > report

The first command sorts the file by last name and the second by letter grades.

To sort the input lines, the strategy is to read each line into a string (character array) and to put the pointer for each string in another one-dimensional array, forming an array of pointers or a *pointer array*. The entries of the pointer-array are sorted and then used in producing the output lines in the right order. The pointer-array approach avoids the actual interchange of text lines by interchanging only the pointers (Figure 6.5). Text-line interchange is expensive because it involves three separate copying operations of character strings.

Therefore, the implementation of the **mysort** command consists of the following major parts:

1. Read input lines and construct an array of strings.
2. Sort the character-pointer array by comparison of keys.
3. Use the pointer array to output the lines in sorted order.

All of this is tied together with a `main` program, which first processes the command-line arguments and then performs the above steps.

This example is more extensive than any we have seen so far. Our description of it is organized following the above outline. It also shows how you can break down a complicated program into manageable parts and then deal with each part separately.

Reading Input Lines for `mysort`

This part of our program is responsible for reading in the text lines from `stdin`, forming a pointer array and filling it with the appropriate pointers. The function `input_lines` will perform these duties.

The function `input_lines` takes a pointer array, `lines`, with entries of type `String`. It reads an input line, copies the line into a dynamically allocated string, then deposits the string pointer into the array `lines`. This is done until there are no more input lines. The return value of `input_lines` is normally the total number of input lines. A –1 is produced if there are too many lines. If an input line is too long, a negative integer equal to –(line number + 1) is returned. This information can be used later in a calling routine for reporting errors. The maximum line length and number of lines are specified by the symbolic constants `MAXLEN` and `MAXLINES`, respectively:

```
int input_lines(String lines[])
{ int k, n=0;
  char buffer[MAXLEN];
  String s;
    while( (k = getline(buffer, MAXLEN)) > 0 )
                                            /* read input           */
    {   if ( ++n > MAXLINES || (s = (String) malloc(k)) == NULL )
            return(-1);                     /* too many lines       */
        else if ( k == MAXLEN-1 && *(buffer+k-1) != '\n' )
            return(-n);                     /* line too long        */
        else
        {   *(buffer+k-1) = '\0';           /* replace \n by \0     */
            strcpy(s, buffer);              /* copy buffer into s   */
            *lines++ = s;                   /* put s on array lines */
        }
    }
    return(n);                              /* total number of lines */
}
```

The value returned by `getline` is the number (at most `MAXLEN-1`) of characters including the final ' \n' read. The functions `strcpy` and `getline` have been discussed in Sections 5.1 and 5.3, respectively.

Ordering Lines for `mysort`

The objective of this part of the program is to take the array `lines` and sort it into order by comparing the appropriate key fields.

Our approach is to adopt the `quicksort` procedure used for integer arrays to sort the array `lines`. The recursive function `quicksort` itself is mostly the same as before. However, the `interchange` function now swaps pointers rather than integers. Furthermore, the `partition` function uses `sortcmp` to compare two lines. The comparison implemented by `sortcmp` will, of course, be based on the user-specified key fields.

```
int partition(String lines[], int l, int r)
{ register int i=l, j=r;              /* for better performance     */
  String piv;
      interchange(lines, (i+j)/2,j);/* choose middle element as pivot */
      piv = lines[j];
      while ( i < j )
      {     while ( sortcmp(lines[i], piv) <= 0 && i < j )
                  i++;
            while ( j > i && sortcmp(lines[j], piv) >= 0 )
                  j--;
            if ( i < j ) interchange (lines,i,j);
      }
      if (i != r) interchange(lines,i,r);
      return(i);                       /* return partition index      */
}


void interchange(String lines[], int i, int j) /* swap lines i and j */
{ String s;
      s = lines[j];
      lines[j] = lines[i];
      lines[i] = s;
}


void quicksort(String lines[], int l, int r) /* sorting text lines   */
{ int k;
      if ( l >= r )   return;
      k = partition(lines, l, r);
      quicksort(lines, l, k-1);                /* recursive calls     */
      quicksort(lines, k+1, r);
}
```

Comparing Keys for `mysort`

Again, we have broken down the line-sorting step into two parts: the quicksort and the key comparison. Applying the divide-and-conquer method repeatedly results in a top-down hierarchy of subproblems that makes program organization logical and implementation easier and more flexible. All we need now is to define `sortcmp` to complete the line-sorting part.

Basically, `sortcmp` performs a `strcmp` on two given key fields. The function `strcmp` cannot be used directly because our fields are delimited by white spaces and possibly by `'\0'` for the last field. Letting the user of **mysort** specify the key field and implementing a separate key-comparison function provides the kind of flexibility that characterizes good programs. On top of this, we can go one step further and allow the field delimiters to be settable, rather than hard-coded. To achieve this, simply keep the delimiters on an external string `delim` that, for the current definition of **mysort**, must contain the characters SPACE and TAB. But we can easily change our minds later and use additional and/or different delimiters such as `'='`, `'.'`, and `':'`. By the way, the colon is an especially frequent field separator on UNIX. It is used in the `password` and `termcap` files, among other things. All the program needs to be able to work with different delimiters is redefining `delim`. What could be more convenient?

```
/* delim and field are external variables */


String key(String s)          /* returns pointer to comparison key    */
{ int i=field;                /* field is user-supplied key indicator */
     while ( --i > 0 )        /* skipping fields                      */
     {   s += strspn(s,delim);
                              /* library string functions        (1) */
         s += strcspn(s,delim);
                              /*                                 (2) */
     }
     s += strspn(s,delim);  /* position on first char of target key */
     return(s);
}
```

Remember the string library functions we used in `key` will need the `<string.h>` header file (Section 5.1). The call on line 1 skips over delimiters and the call on line 2 skips over a field. Finally, the desired key field is found and returned.

The `sortcmp` function will compare, depending on user selection, either whole lines or the appropriate keys:

```
int sortcmp(const char * a, const char * b)
{   if ( field == 0 ) return(strcmp(a,b));
    for( a=key(a), b=key(b) ; *a == *b ; a++, b++ )
        if ( *a == *delim || *a == '\0' )
            return(0);                   /* strings are equal */
```

```
            if ( *a == delim[0] ) return(-1);
            else if ( *b == delim[0] ) return(1);
            else return( *a - *b );
      }
```

Note that `sortcmp` returns positive, zero, or negative for `key(a)` greater than, equal to, or less than `key(b)`, respectively. This is consistent with the way `strcmp` works and is what `partition` expects.

Writing Out Sorted Lines for `mysort`

The hard parts having been done, we can now output the text lines in order. This task simply involves writing out the strings as lines in the order given by the sorted pointer array `lines` and can be performed by a very short function:

```
      void output_lines(String lines[], int n)
      {    while( n-- > 0 )
             printf("%s\n", *lines++);
      }
```

The Main Program for `mysort`

All parts are in place. We must now put them together with a `main` program that processes command-line arguments and calls `input_lines`, `quick_sort`, and `output_lines`:

```
#include <stdio.h>
#include <string.h>

#define MAXLINES 4000
#define MAXLEN 256
#define SPACE ' '

typedef char *String;
static String lines[MAXLINES];  /* define + initialize external vars */
static int field=0;
static char delim[10] = "";

/**** put functions input_lines, output_lines, etc. here ****/

main(int argc, String argv[])
{ int n;
  /* process command-line arguments */
```

```
    if ( argc > 2 )
    {   fprintf(stderr,"%s: takes at most one argument\n",argv[0]);
        exit(1);
    }
    if ( argc == 2 )                        /* user-indicated key    */
    {   field = atoi(argv[1]);
        delim[0] = SPACE;                   /* delim defined here    */
        delim[1] = '\t';
        delim[2] = '\0';
    }
    if ( (n = input_lines(lines)) < 0 ) /* read input lines          */
    {   if ( n == -1 )
            fprintf(stderr,
                "%s: Sorry, input file is too large\n", argv[0]);
        else
            fprintf(stderr,"%s: Sorry, line %d too long\n",
                    argv[0], 1-n);
        exit(1);
    }
    quicksort(lines,0,n-1);                 /* ordering              */
    output_lines(lines,n);                  /* output                */
    return (0);
}
```

When the user gives the **mysort** command with a key, argc becomes 2. In this case, main sets the global variables field and delim appropriately. If the input file is too large or one of the lines is too long, the screen displays an appropriate error message. Section 6.7 and Exercise 9 suggest further improvements on this program.

We have gone from a simple application like strtok to a long and reasonably complicated text-line-sorting program. These examples not only show array and pointer usage but also demonstrate how to break down a problem into chunks that can be handled with ease. The solution processes employed here can serve as models for you in many other situations.

6.5 Pointers and Function Calls

Let's now turn our attention to the usage of pointers and arrays in function calls. All aspects of pointer usage related specifically to function calls are collected in this section for easy reference.

Passing Pointer Arguments

When a function call is made, the value of an actual argument, regardless of its type, is passed to the called function. The value is assigned to the corresponding formal parameter that is a local variable in the called function. When passing a pointer as an argument, the address of the object is passed. In most cases, the address is the memory location of a variable or an array entry. If `x` is a variable, `p` a pointer variable, `a` an array, `b` a two-dimensional array, then the expressions

`&x`	Address of `x`
`p`	Value of pointer variable `p`
`p++`	Value of pointer variable `p`
`a or &a[0]`	Value of constant array name `a`
`a + 2 or &a[2]`	Address of third entry of array `a`
`&b[0][0] or b[0]`	Address of first entry of two-dimensional array `b`
`&b[i][0] or b[i]`	Address of first entry of row $i + 1$ in two-dimensional array `b`

are all valid forms of pointers as arguments.

To specify a simple pointer formal parameter `y` in a function header, the two forms

```
type *y
type y[]
```

equivalent!

are entirely equivalent, and both are commonly used. The first notation is slightly preferable because it better expresses that a formal parameter is a local pointer variable. Extending the above equivalence, the forms

```
type **y
type *y[]
```

equivalent.

are again the same in function headers. Therefore, the command-line argument

    char *argv[]   (or String argv[])

can also be written in a function header as

    char **argv   (or String *argv)

When a pointer passes an object to a function, the called function knows the type and the starting location of the object, but not necessarily where it ends.

For example, the formal parameter int *y receives the address of a single integer or an array of integers. Clearly, some other arrangement must be made. Using a special terminator is a convenient way to define the extent of an object. The conventional terminator '\0' for character strings is a good example. Independent of whether there is a terminator, using another integer parameter to pass the size information into a called function, as in the function output_lines of Section 6.4, is always possible.

There are two possible purposes when passing a pointer into a function:

- To give the called function access to an object without making a copy
- To have the called function initialize or modify the object

The object in question may be global, local to the calling function, or allocated in the scope of some function in the chain of function calls. More details on these two modes of usage are discussed next.

Read-Only and Return Parameters

An object passed by pointer is *read-only* if it is not modified in the called function. The parameter of strlen is a typical example of a read-only pointer; counting the number of characters does not modify a string. The const modifier (Section 3.8) should be used for such a formal parameter, allowing the C compiler to detect any unintended attempt to modify the object. The treatment of such a violation is implementation-dependent, but a warning is usually generated. Furthermore, in making a function call, we often must know whether an object passed by pointer will be modified or not. Used consistently, the presence or absence of const in a function prototype can convey this important information.

One reason for a function to modify an object passed by a pointer is to transmit results computed back to the calling function. Many library functions depend on this feature. For example, to input an int with **scanf** (Sections 2.5 and 8.4), the address of a variable of type int must be supplied in the call, and the value read by **scanf** is deposited into the address provided. Such a parameter transmits computed results back to the calling function and is known as a *return parameter*. The matrix-multiplication routine matmul (Section 6.3.1) uses just such a return parameter for the product matrix. When calling a function with a return parameter, it is the calling function's responsibility to allocate enough space of the correct type to accommodate the returned value.

Functions Returning Pointers

The value returned by a function can be a pointer. The library functions **strcpy, strtok, malloc,** and **calloc,** just to name a few, return pointers.

Take care when you define a function that returns a pointer. The returned pointer must not point to a local variable in the scope of the returning function. An automatic variable in a function is destroyed after the function returns. Certainly, it does not make sense to return a pointer to something that disappears. For example, it is incorrect to use

```
int *bad(int x)
{   int y;
    y = x * x;
    return(&y);      /* wrong */
}
```

This function will produce no syntax error when compiled and would actually execute. Unfortunately, when the returned pointer is used, it may be pointing to a memory cell that has been destroyed (used for other purposes). A pointer that has lost its object in memory is referred to as a *dangling pointer* and should be avoided.

When your function returns a pointer, make sure that it points to either

- Memory cells supplied by the calling function.
- An external object.
- Dynamically allocated space.

The function `poly_add` in Section 6.4.2 is an example where a pointer to memory allocated by **calloc** is returned.

6.6 Multiple Indirection

A variable `x` accesses a memory cell directly (Figure 6.6). The value of `x` is stored in its associated data cell. As stated before, the cell of a pointer variable `ptr`, however, stores the address of another data cell whose content can be accessed *indirectly* through the value of `ptr` using the value-of operator `*`. Treat the quantity `*ptr` just like a variable and use it on the left-hand side of an assignment as well.

We have described one level of indirection. Still another level of indirection is possible if the value of `*ptr` is also a pointer. Referring again to Figure 6.6, the value of `ptra` is the pointer variable `*ptra`, and the value of `*ptra` is an `int` variable `**ptra`, which has the value 15.

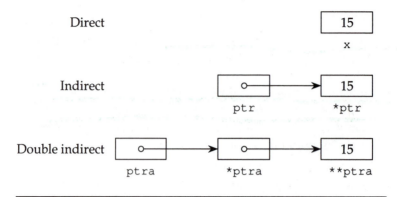

Figure 6.6: Multiple Indirection

The declaration

```
int *ptr;
```

declares the variable `ptr` to be of type `int *`, *not* `*prt` of type `int` as some may mistakenly suppose. Similarly, the declarations

```
char **c;
char ***d;
```

give c type `char **` and d type `char ***`, respectively. A handy example of the type `char **` is the array `char *argv[]` for command-line arguments. Thus, we can use

```
c = argv;
```

In fact, we have seen a few variables of type `char **` already, including the `lines` in the sorting example (Section 6.4.3).

To understand the meaning of d, think of it as the address of an array of different groups of text lines:

```
d[0] is line_group1
d[1] is line_group2
d[2] is line_group3
```

Multiple indirection tends to be confusing and error-prone. The situation can be greatly helped by the appropriate application of `typedef`. Consider

```
typedef char *String;
typedef String *Lines;
typedef Lines *Groups_of_lines;
```

Now the variable d can be declared as

```
Groups_of_lines d;
```

making it much easier to handle: the type of *d is Lines, the type of **d is String, and the type of ***d is char. Section 6.8 contains an example that uses multiple indirection.

By the way, typedef not only helps to decipher multiple indirections but also to simplify other complicated constructs, as we will see in Chapter 7. For the moment, our coverage of pointers continues with the important subject, pointers to functions.

6.7   Functional Arguments

Ordinarily, when we talk about passing an argument to a function, we think of passing data of some type. The called function will perform its preprogrammed procedures depending on what input data it receives. Now we will add a whole new dimension to argument passing—passing functions as arguments in a call. The called function can apply the passed function in conjunction with its own preprogrammed procedures.

An argument that is a function is known as a *functional argument*. The flexibility provided by functional arguments is tremendous. Imagine, now you can write a function that will use different procedures for different invocations. In other words, with functional arguments, your function will not only work with different input data but also use different incoming functions. Just consider how much more a sort program can do if it is supplied with the appropriate comparison function each time it is called.

Because the functional argument is an extraordinary feature, not all languages support it. Fortunately, this feature is available in C, and functional arguments are passed as *pointers to functions*. We will describe in detail how to use functional arguments, how they work, and what they enable you to achieve. Our discussions here ultimately lead to an implementation of quicksort that sorts arbitrary data in any caller-specified ordering. To achieve this goal, we need to present three distinct but related topics: pointers to functions, formal functional parameters, and the type void *.

Pointers to Functions

Once a function is defined, the function name preceded by the & operator is a pointer to the function, namely, the address where the function's definition begins in memory. A function pointer, just like any other pointer, can be assigned as a value to pointer variables of the right type and also passed as an argument in a function call.

For example, if we have a function average defined as

```
int average(int x, int y)
{   return((x+y)/2);}
```

then the following piece of code can be used:

```
int (* fn)(int, int);        (declare function pointer variable fn)
fn = &average;               (function-pointer assignment)
var = (* fn)(14,26);         (function call through pointer)
```

First, the function-pointer variable `fn` is declared to be a pointer to any function that takes two `int` arguments and returns an `int` value. (We will discuss the general syntax for function-pointer declaration presently.) Second, `fn` is assigned the address of the function `average`. Then, `(* fn)` can be used as a function name in making a call to `average`.

To produce a function pointer, the `&` in front of the function name can also be omitted. Thus,

```
fn = average;        (same as fn = &average)
```

is fine, too. This notation is simpler and will be used from now on.

Declaring a function-pointer variable may look complicated, but it is really simple. Just use the function prototype with the function name replaced by the notation `(* var )`. Specifically, the general form

```
value_type (* var )( args );
```

declares the variable `var` to be a pointer to a function that takes the specified arguments and returns a value of the given type.

A function-pointer declaration looks strange because it deviates from the normal syntax of variable declarations. What confuses people is the position of the declared variable relative to the other parts in such a declaration. It may take a little getting used to, but the position is perfectly well defined: The variable is put *where the function name would be* in a function prototype. The examples in Figure 6.7 should help as well.

Because a function-pointer declaration is somewhat long and complicated to look at, we can simplify things greatly by using `typedef`. For instance,

```
typedef int (* INT_FN)(int, int);
```

defines the type name `INT_FN`. Note the type name is placed where the pointer variable would be. `INT_FN` can then be used to declare any function pointer of that type. In particular, we can use it to declare the `fn` pointer used in the `average` example:

```
INT_FN fn;        (alternative declaration for fn above)
```

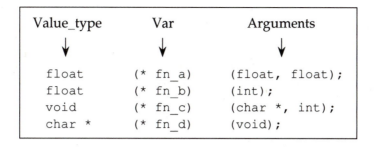

Figure 6.7: Declaring Function Pointers

Formal Functional Parameters

The purpose of a function pointer, almost exclusively, is to pass a function name to another function. To make things easy to understand, we first look at an artificial example:

```
int mystery(int a, int b, int (* fn)(int, int))
{    return( (* fn)(a,b) );
}
```

Here the function `mystery` takes three arguments: two integers and a function pointer `fn`. The declaration of the formal parameter `fn` is the same, as it should be, as declaring a variable of the intended type. Because we already have the type `INT_FN`, a simpler looking version of `mystery` is

```
int mystery(int a, int b, INT_FN fn)
{    return( (* fn)(a,b) );
}
```

The function `mystery` simply calls the function pointed to by `fn` and returns the value of the call. With the ANSI standard, the function call in the above code can be simplified to `fn(a,b)`. Try it on your system. Here are some functions, in addition to `average`, that can be passed to `mystery`.

```
extern int gcd(int a, int b);

int sqsum(int x, int y)
{    return( x * x + y * y );
}
```

The `gcd` function was defined in Section 3.4.

Here is how to make calls to `mystery`. Note that the names `average`, `gcd`, and `sqsum` are pointers to the definitions of the functions:

```
main()
{       printf("%d\n", mystery(16, 30, average));    /* is 23 */
        printf("%d\n", mystery(3, 4, sqsum));         /* is 25 */
        printf("%d\n", mystery(312, 253, gcd));       /* is  1 */

}
```

In fact, any function, local or external, that takes two `int` arguments and returns an `int` can be passed to `mystery`.

We are two-thirds of the way now to the finish line. The one topic that remains on our list is the `void` pointer, a mechanism to pass data of arbitrary type and a necessary complement to the functional argument facility.

Pointer Type `void *`

To write a function that applies the same algorithm in a variety of situations, we need the functional argument mechanism described already. But, in most cases, we also need the ability to receive *arguments of arbitrary*, or *unspecified*, *types*. Let's begin by considering a simple example of determining the length of an arbitrary array. The strategy is to write a function that takes two arguments: an arbitrary array and a test function for the end of the array.

The function `arblen` computes the length of the array `any` without knowing anything about its type. The functional parameter `term` is the supplied function that detects the termination of the given array. What `arblen` does is simply call `term` repeatedly and count the number of calls. The count is then returned when `term` detects the end of the array:

```
typedef int (* TERM_FN) (void *any, int index);

int arblen(void *any, TERM_FN term)
{ int len=0;
        while ( (* term)(any,len) == 0 ) len++;
        return(len);

}
```

A variable or formal parameter of type `void *` (pointer to unknown type) can receive a pointer of any type. This provides a way of passing data of arbitrary type into a function. Because the data type is unknown, there are very few allowable operations on a `void *` variable other than referencing (using the pointer value) and passing it to another function. In particular, indexing, value-of (*), increment, decrement, and other address arithmetic operations are illegal or unsafe on a void * variable. Even so, the void * type is critical to processing arbitrary data, as seen in the function arblen.

To test arblen, let's define two terminator detecting functions, int_term and str_term for nonnegative integer and character arrays, respectively:

```
int int_term(int *a, int i)
{    return( a[i] == -1 );        /* true or false */
}


int str_term(char *a, int i)
{    return( a[i] == '\0' );
}
```

Now, for testing, we can use the following main function:

```
main()
{ char a[]="abcdefg";
  int b[]={1,2,3,4,-1};
  int i;
      i = arblen(a, (TERM_FN) str_term);              /* length 7 */
      printf("length of character string = %d\n", i);
      i = arblen(b, (TERM_FN) int_term);              /* length 5 */
      printf("length of int array = %d\n", i);
}
```

Note that explicit type casting, (TERM_FN), is used on the function pointers to make the argument match the declared formal parameter term of arblen. Generally, the cast has no effect at run time but assures the compiler that all is well.

The preliminaries are now finished. We are ready to consider practical applications culminating in a generalized quicksort.

Applications of Functional Arguments

Our first example is a function that determines if all entries of an array satisfy some given condition. Questions such as

- Is every entry an even or odd number?
- Is every entry positive?
- Is every entry zero?
- Is every character lowercase?

are often asked. We will write one function, and_test, that takes care of them all. The and in the name expresses the concept of logical *and*: All tests must be true before the answer is true:

```
typedef int (* BOOLEAN_FN) (void *any, int index);

int and_test (void *any, BOOLEAN_FN test, TERM_FN term)
{ int len=0;
      while ( (* term) (any, len) == 0 )
      {   if ( (* test) (any, len) == 0 ) return (0);
          len++;
      }
      return (1);
}
```

The type name BOOLEAN_FN also documents that functions of this type must be *boolean* or one that returns a true or false value. The arbitrary boolean test is applied to each array entry successively until the end is found by the supplied terminator detector term. The first failed test causes and_test to return 0 (false). The value 1 (true) is returned after the array is exhausted. Candidate functions to pass to the parameter test are

```
int even (int *ip, int j)
{   return( (ip[j] & 01)   == 0 );}

int odd (int *ip, int j)
{   return( (ip[j] & 01)   == 1 );}

int clower (int *cp, int j)
{   return ( islower(cp[j]) ); }
```

The function or_test is similar but is designed to answer questions like

- Is there an even or odd entry?
- Is there a negative entry?
- Is there a zero entry?
- Is there an uppercase character?

Again, the word or indicates the logical or concept: If at least one test is true, then the answer is true:

```
int or_test (void *any, BOOLEAN_FN test, TERM_FN term)
{ int len=0;
      while ( (* term) (any, len) == 0 )
      {   if ( (* test) (any, len) ) return (1);
          len++;
      }
      return (0);
}
```

Generalized Sort *read this!*

Now, we are ready to write a sorting program that can process a sequence of items of *any type, in any specified order.*

We can achieve this goal by modifying the `quicksort` program to use the following arguments:

1. An arbitrary array
2. A caller-specified comparison function `cmp`
3. A supplied element-interchange function `swap`

The `quicksort` function is revised as

```
typedef int (* COMP_FN) (void *, int, int);
typedef void (* SWAP_FN) (void *, int, int);

void quicksort(void *any, int l, int r, COMP_FN cmp, SWAP_FN swap)
{ int k;
    if ( l >= r ) return;
    k = partition (any, l, r, cmp, swap);
                                    /* call with supplied functions */
    quicksort(any, l, k-1, cmp, swap);
                                    /* recursive calls            */
    quicksort(any, k+1, r, cmp, swap);
}
```

The `partition` function now becomes

```
static int partition(void *any, int l, int r, COMP_FN cmp, SWAP_FN
swap)
{ register int i=l, j=r;
    /* choose middle element as pivot */
    (* swap)(any,(i+j)/2, r); /* pivot element moved to r with swap */
    while ( i < j )
    {    while ( (* cmp)(any, i, r) <= 0 && i < j )
            i++;                                /* use supplied cmp  */
        while( j > i && (* cmp)(any, j, r) >= 0 )
            j--;                                /* use supplied cmp  */
        if ( i < j ) (* swap)(any,i,j);         /* use supplied swap */
    }
    if ( i != r ) (* swap)(any,i,r);            /* use supplied swap */
    return(i);
}
```

Note that indexing of `any` is not possible in `partition` because of its type `void *`. But once passed to the function `(* cmp)` or `(* swap)`, the pointer any is converted back to the right type (via implicit type casting, Section 3.10) and can be used normally again.

After these modifications are made, the new `quicksort` can sort arbitrary arrays with appropriately supplied `cmp` and `swap` functions. To sort integer arrays, the following set of functions can be defined:

```
int cmp_bigger(int x[], int i, int j)
{  return ( x[i] - x[j] ); }

int cmp_smaller(int x[], int i, int j)
{  return ( x[j] - x[i] ); }

void intswitch(int a[], int i, int j)
{      int s;
       s = a[i];
       a[i] = a[j];
       a[j] = s;
}
```

We have defined `cmp_bigger` and `cmp_smaller` as two different comparison functions that conform to the type `COMP_FN`, and we have written `intswitch` to match the type `SWAP_FN`. Now sorting can be done with

```
int a[] = {5,3,-1, 9 , 22, 99};

/* in increasing order */
quicksort(a, 0, 5, (COMP_FN) cmp_bigger, (SWAP_FN) intswitch);

/* in decreasing order */
quicksort(a, 0, 5, (COMP_FN) cmp_smaller, (SWAP_FN) intswitch);
```

It is also a simple matter to convert the text-line-sorting program in Section 6.4.3 to use the new `quicksort` here. For the `keycmp` function, simply replace its first line by the following two lines:

```
int keycmp(String x[], int i, int j)
{ String a = x[i], b = x[j];
```

This change is only needed to make `keycmp` conform to the type `COMP_FN`. With this change, just use

```
quicksort(lines, 0, n-1, (COMP_FN) keycmp, (SWAP_FN) interchange);
```

to do the sorting for **mysort**. Here we are sorting text lines instead of integers with the same generalized `quicksort` function, driving home the point of handling data of arbitrary type.

The `quicksort` defined in this section will be used again in Chapter 7 for other purposes. As you can see, the basic sorting mechanism is in place and will remain unchanged. Its application in a new area is simply a matter of providing the appropriate `cmp` and `swap` functions.

6.8 Pointers and Dynamically Allocated Storage

We have seen some uses of the library functions **malloc** and **calloc** for dynamic storage allocation. However, we have yet to use dynamically allocated space for pointers or pointer arrays, a topic we address now.

Let's consider the representation of days in a month. One way to do this is to use short integers for the individual dates, an array of dates for each week, and an array of pointers to the individual weeks as a structure for the month. The following `typedef`s are helpful:

```
typedef short DATE;
typedef DATE *WEEK;        (WEEK is short *)
typedef WEEK *MONTH;       (MONTH is short **)
```

and the days of the week are   (use Sun = 1)

```
enum DAY {Sun=0, Mon, Tue, Wed, Thu, Fri, Sat};       (see Section 3.7)
```

Employing these types, we can write a function `make_month` that allocates dynamic storage, fills in the dates of the month, and returns a pointer of type MONTH.

The function takes two arguments: ndays, the number of days in the month, and `firstday`, the day of the week on the first of the month:

```
MONTH make_month(DATE ndays, enum DAY firstday)
{ WEEK w[7], wk;
  DATE d;
  enum DAY day;
  MONTH month;
  short j, i=0;
    wk = w[i] = (WEEK) malloc(7*sizeof(DATE));            /* (1) */
    for ( day=Sun ; day < firstday ; day++ ) *wk++ = 0;  /* (2) */
    for ( d = 1 ; d <= ndays ; d++, day++ )              /* (3) */
    {  if ( day > Sat )
       {   i++;
           wk = w[i] = (WEEK) malloc(7*sizeof(DATE));    /* (4) */
           day=Sun;
       }
```

```
        *wk++ = d ;
    }
    while ( day++ <= Sat ) *wk++ = 0;                    /* (5) */
    month = (MONTH) malloc((i+2)*sizeof(WEEK));          /* (6) */
    for ( j=0; j <= i; j++ ) month[j] = w[j];
    month[i+1] = NULL;        /* NULL ptr terminator */
    return(month);
}
```

For each week, seven DATEs are allocated (lines 1 and 4) to record the days of the week. The pointer returned by **malloc** is explicitly cast to type WEEK (short *). Days unused in the first and last week are assigned zero (lines 2 and 5). The dates are filled in by the for loop (line 3).

The automatic array w records the weeks created. A dynamic array month is allocated (line 6), and the entries of w are copied into month before it is returned. Note month is terminated by a NULL pointer (zero). Figure 6.9 illustrates the organization of month.

A typical call to make_month would be

```
MONTH m;
m = make_month(31, Tue);
```

Let's write a main program to display a monthly calendar made by make_month:

```
main()
{ MONTH month;
  WEEK wk;
  enum DAY d;
    month = make_month(31, Tue);
    printf("SUN MON TUE WED THU FRI SAT\n");           /* (1) */
    while ( *month )
    {   wk = *month++;
        for ( d = Sun ; d <= Sat ; d++)
        {   if ( wk[d] ) printf("%3d ", wk[d]);        /* (2) */
            else printf("    ");
        }
        printf("\n");
    }
}
```

After the headings (line 1), the days for each week of the month are displayed. To line up the dates nicely, we have used a field width of four characters for each column of the calendar (line 2). The exact control of output formats is the subject of Section 8.3.

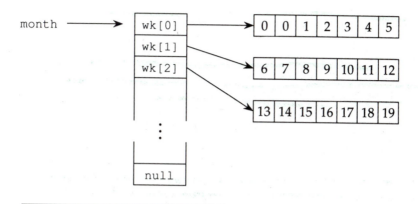

Figure 6.8: The Organization of month, with Pointers

The program produces the following display:

```
SUN MON TUE WED THU FRI SAT
             1   2   3   4   5
  6   7   8   9  10  11  12
 13  14  15  16  17  18  19
 20  21  22  23  24  25  26
 27  28  29  30  31
```

6.9 Summary

An array stores elements of the same type in consecutive memory locations. The array name is a constant pointer to the first array cell. A two-dimensional array is actually a one-dimensional array whose elements are pointers to one-dimensional arrays of the same length. This scheme can be generalized into arrays of higher dimensions.

The unary address-of operator & can be applied to any memory-based variable or array element to obtain a pointer. The unary value-of operator * is applied to a pointer, ptr, to access the value stored at that memory address. Furthermore, the notation *ptr can be used on the left-hand side of an assignment to store a new value at that location. Hence, the combination *ptr can be thought of and used as a variable of the appropriate type.

Pointer arithmetic is convenient to step through the cells of an array. You can perform pointer ± integer and pointer – pointer operations. You are even allowed to go one step beyond the last array cell in pointer arithmetic as long as no attempt is made to use the value of the nonexistent cell. The indexing notation is another way to access values through a pointer. In fact, this is how an array works. Section 6.2.5 summarizes all valid pointer operations.

There are two different reasons to pass a pointer into a function: to avoid copying or to collect values computed. A pointer returned by a function must not point to a local automatic variable in the function.

In dealing with multiple indirection, the notations can become confusing. One way to keep thinking straight is to use the familiar case of `char *argv[]` as a guide. Consistent use of `typedef` can greatly simplify the notations for multiple indirection and in many other situations.

The name of a function is actually a pointer to the function in memory. Thus, a function name can be assigned to an appropriately declared pointer variable or passed to a formal parameter. The function argument together with the unknown pointer type `void *` provides a way to write functions that work on arbitrary-data types. The `quicksort` has been thus modified to sort arbitrary-data items using any supplied comparison function.

Dynamic allocation returns a pointer to the space obtained. This can then be explicitly cast to a specific type before values are stored. Care should be taken to allocate the correct amount of space sufficient for the task at hand.

Exercises

1. Given the declaration

   ```
   int a[]={1,2,3,4,5};
   ```

   what are the values of the expressions (a) `a - &a[3]`, (b) `* (a+4)`, and (c) `* (a+5)`?

2. Explain the meaning of each of the following declarations:

   a. `char a[];`
   b. `char *b;`
   c. `char c[5]="";`
   d. `int d[]={0,1,2};`
   e. `int *e=d+1;`
   f. `int f[20]={0,0,0,0};`
   g. `char *g[];`
   h. `char *g[]={a,b,c};`
   i. `char **a;`
   j. `char **a = &b;`
   k. `typedef int (* C_FN) (String, const String);`

3. Write a program to test the use of negative indices for arrays and pointers.

4. Rewrite the circular buffer example given in Section 3.6 with pointers and pointer arithmetic instead of indexing.

5. The definition of **strtok** can be made much easier to understand and more logical. The idea is to have **strtok** return the first token of the string s and return, in a return parameter, a pointer to the character just beyond the token. To get the next token, **strtok** is called again with the shortened s. So, as far as **strtok** is concerned, there is no difference between a first call and a second call to it. Write a version of **strtok** with this approach.

6. Again, write a function sum that produces the total of an indefinite number of arguments uniformly of type either int, float, or double. The answer produced should be of the same type. (*Hint:* Use a return parameter.)

7. Does the C compiler on your computer allow you to increment a void pointer? If it does, give a good reason why you should not use it.

8. Write a function reverse that takes an integer array and returns an array of the elements in the reverse order.

9. Modify the sorting program for text lines given in Section 6.4.3 to use the more flexible version of quicksort as suggested in Section 6.7.

10. Consider the address-of operator &. List the type of quantities to which it cannot be applied.

11. Consider the value-of operator *. List the type of quantities to which it cannot be applied.

12. Discuss the differences and equivalence of the two notations

```
type x[];
type *x;
```

In what situations are these notations interchangeable?

13. Discuss the differences and similarities of a two-dimensional array and an array of pointers.

14. Write a program that will manipulate a two-dimensional array in the following way:

   a. Creates the array 10 × 10.
   b. Fills in the array with integers 0 through 99.
   c. Deletes any rows or columns indicated by the user at the terminal.
   d. Interchanges any rows or columns indicated by the user at the terminal.
   e. Displays the original 10 × 10 array.
   f. Displays the transformed array.

Use at least three functions, one each for parts c–f. The design of the user input syntax is up to you.

15. Modify the polynomial displaying function `poly_display` in Section 6.4.2 so that it will display an array of polynomials.

16. Write a quadruple-precision integer package with integer arrays and the arithmetic routines: `qint_add`, `qint_sub`, `qint_times`, `qint_quo-tient`, and `qint_display`.

17. Write a function to compute the sum of two three-dimensional integer arrays of compatible sizes.

18. Write a function `arr_apply` that takes an array of arbitrary-data items and applies a supplied operation on each array cell.

19. Write a program to multiply two polynomials.

20. Modify the `matmul` function (Section 6.3.1) so that it returns the result in a two-dimensional array that is dynamically allocated in `matmul`.

7

Structuring Data

Data require organization for easy access and manipulation. Usually, several different pieces of data combine to form an information unit. A bank account consists of an identifying number, customer name, address, transactions, balances, and so on. Even something as simple as a date contains the month, day, and year. When related pieces of data are combined in a logical way, you get information units called *data structures*.

A data structure can make dealing with complicated information easy and efficient. Hence, proper data structures are just as important to good programming as well-written functions and procedures. When dealing with complex information, the data being manipulated must first be represented as data structures. The same information often has many alternative structures, some more suitable for a given application than others. Once the proper data structures have been selected, functions to manipulate the structures can be written to solve the given problem.

C is a compact language that does not provide many built-in, or primitive, data types. For organizing data, a mechanism for defining new data types is used. A new data type, called a *structure*, is composed of existing and/or user-defined data types. The `struct` mechanism for this purpose is the focus of our presentation.

With ANSI C, the treatment of structures has been standardized: Structures can be initialized, copied, assigned to, and passed to and returned by functions. In these respects, user-defined structures are treated the same way as built-in data types. We describe in detail how to establish and use structures. Examples of frequent structures such as tables, lists, and trees are presented with applications.

7.1 Basic Concepts

To explain the basics of data structuring, let's consider the simple problem of computing with fractions. The fraction $\frac{2}{3}$ consists of a numerator (2) and a denominator (3), both integers. How can we represent a fraction as a data structure? Establish a *user-defined data type* that consists of two int quantities, one representing the numerator and the other the denominator.

Declaring Structures

The struct keyword establishes user-defined structures. The declaration

```
struct fraction
{       int num;        (numerator)
        int denom;      (denominator)
};
```

establishes fraction as the name of a *structure* that contains two *members*, num and denom, each of type int. The structure name is also referred to as a structure *tag*. In general, to define a new structure tag, use the form

```
struct tag
{       type1   member1;
        type2   member2;
          . . .
};
```

Once a tag is defined, it can declare variables of that particular type. For example, variables of type fraction can be declared:

```
struct fraction r;
struct fraction s = { 2, 3};
```

The variable r is not initialized, but the variable s is. The keyword struct must be used with a structure tag. However, you can use typedef to establish a single type name:

```
typedef struct fraction Fraction;
```

Then you can simply use

```
Fraction r;
Fraction s = { 2, 3};
```

as shorthand to declare variables of type `struct fraction`.

The members in a structure are accessed with the *dot* (`.`), or member-of, operator.

`s.num`	(a variable of type `int` with value 2)
`s.denom`	(a variable of type `int` with value 3)

Note that each member is accessed directly and independently by its name. A member name is local to a structure and is not confused with other variables outside the particular structure. In other words, you may have another identifier named `num` at the same time, and it won't interfere with the usage of the structure member `s.num`.

It is also true that a structure tag does not conflict with variable or function names. In fact, ANSI C requires that `struct`, `enum`, and `union` (Section 7.10) tags comprise a single *name space*, not confused with other identifiers.

Clearly, the general syntax to access a member is

```
variable.member
```

Basic Structure Operations

Now let's write a function `make_fraction` to construct a `Fraction`. Here the design decision of always keeping the denominator positive is made. Hence, the sign of a fraction is reflected by its numerator:

```
Fraction make_fraction(int n, int d)   /* d is not zero */
{ Fraction x ;
     if ( d < 0 )
     {    x.num = -n;
          x.denom = -d;
     }
     else
     {    x.num = n;
          x.denom = d;
     }
     return(x);
}
```

The variable `x` in `make_fraction` is worth noting. It is the first automatic variable we have used that represents a structure. The function `make_fraction` returns a structure. Therefore, the structure assignment

```
r = make_fraction(4,5);
```

gives `r` a copy of the structure value of `x`, whereas the automatic variable `x` will be destroyed after `make_fraction` returns.

Structure assignment involves copying the value of each corresponding member on the right-hand side to that on the left-hand side. A function returning a structure gives a copy of its value, not a pointer to the structure. In other words, the above structure assignment is no different from an `int` assignment, say,

```
i = factorial(7);
```

Do not confuse a structure with an array. When a function returns an array, a pointer, rather than a copy, is returned. In this case, returning an automatic array would result in a serious mistake, a dangling pointer. There is no such problem with a structure unless a pointer to a structure is returned on purpose, using the `&` operator. In which case, make sure that the returned pointer is not pointing to an automatic variable that will be destroyed after the function returns.

Now we are ready to shape a set of functions for the manipulation of the new data structure `struct fraction`, or `Fraction` for short. As simple examples, we write a display function and a comparison function for fractions. For display, use the function

```
void display_fraction(Fraction x)
{       printf(" %d/%d ", x.num, x.denom);
}
```

It takes one argument `x`, of type `Fraction`, and outputs the integers `x.num` and `x.denom` separated by a division sign. An example call is

```
display_fraction(make_fraction(5,3));
```

It is easy to realize that built-in arithmetic, relational, and other operators do not work with structures. In fact, except accessing members, very few other operations work with structures. Therefore, to compute with fractions, we have to define our own arithmetic operations.

The first such operation is a function to compare two fractions for equality. Because two fractions a/b and c/d are equal if and only if $a * d = c * b$, we can define

```
int equal_fraction(Fraction x, Fraction y)
{       return( x.num * y.denom == y.num * x.denom );
}
```

This is fine if we decide to allow equal but different looking fractions (e.g., $\frac{1}{2}$, $\frac{2}{4}$, $\frac{3}{6}$) to exist. If not, and if we insist that equal fractions must have the same numerator and denominator, then we must modify our `make_fraction` routine. A data representation in which all equal quantities are represented uniquely is known as a *canonical representation*. To have a canonical fraction structure, `make_fraction` is modified to remove the gcd (greatest common divisor; see Section 3.4) between the numerator and denominator as follows:

```
Fraction make_fraction(int n, int d)   /* d is not zero  */
{ Fraction x = {0, 1};                 /* initialization */
   int g;
      if ( n == 0 ) return(x);
      if ( d < 0 )
      {    n = -n;
         d = -d;
      }
      if ( (g = gcd(n,d)) != 1 )       /* remove gcd      */
      {    n /= g;
         d /= g;
      }
      x.num = n;
      x.denom = d;
      return(x);
}
```

To keep the representation canonical, the denominator is forced to 1 if the fraction is actually equal to an integer, 0 included. The function `equal_fraction` now becomes

```
int equal_fraction(Fraction x, Fraction y)
{      return( x.num == y.num && x.denom == y.denom );
}
```

With the canonical representation, we now define addition of fractions:

```
Fraction add_fraction(Fraction x, Fraction y)
{    if ( x.num == 0 )          /* if either arg is 0 return the other */
        return(y);
     else if ( y.num == 0 )
        return(x);
     else                       /* add fractions                       */
        return( make_fraction( x.num * y.denom + y.num * x.denom,
                               x.denom * y.denom ) );
}
```

The function `add_fraction` then relies on the revised `make_fraction` to cancel out any possible gcd between the computed numerator and denominator.

Other operations on fractions (subtraction, multiplication, and division) can be defined similarly.

Structure-Declaration Styles

It is also possible to declare structure variables without first establishing a tag or to define the tag at the same time as the variable declaration. For example, the two forms

```
struct                        struct   complex
{        float real;          {        float real;
         float imag;                   float imag;
}  u, v, w;                   }  u, v, w;
```

are equivalent insofar as the declaration of the variables u, v, and w are concerned. The second form also defines the structure tag complex, which can be used later to declare other complex variables. However, these forms, especially the first one, are not very useful in practice. The recommended style for structure declaration is to

1. Establish the structure tag.
2. Define a type name for the structure tag with typedef.
3. Use the typedef name in all variable declarations.

We have used this scheme in our fraction example and will follow this style throughout the book.

   In summary, a structure tag is declared using the struct keyword and by supplying one or more variable declarations enclosed in {}. Similar to an array, a structure can be initialized when declared with constants enclosed in {}. The members of a structure are accessed with the dot (.) operator. A structure can be assigned to, passed to a function, and returned as value by a function. Consistent use of typedef can help simplify complicated structure declarations.

7.2   Structure Pointers

We have seen how integer and character pointers are used to advantage. Similarly, pointers to structures can be very useful. To study structure-pointer usage, we will revisit the circular, first-in-first-out character buffer discussed in Chapter 3. Recall that a circular buffer has associated quantities such as the size of the buffer and the number of characters still in the buffer. These quantities can be organized, with the character array, into a structure for the circular buffer.

   Following our style conventions, we first establish a cirbuf structure tag

```
struct cirbuf
{        char    *buf;
         unsigned size ;   /* buffer capacity            */
         unsigned head ;   /* first char in buffer       */
         unsigned tail ;   /* first empty space in buffer */
         unsigned length ; /* number of char in buffer   */
};
```

and then the typedef

```
typedef struct cirbuf Cirbuf;
```

For each Cirbuf structure, size indicates the maximum number of characters it can hold. The head is an index for the first character to be consumed and tail the first slot to receive another character. These quantities are unsigned because they are never negative. The character pointer buf will be initialized to a character array with size cells when a cirbuf structure is made.

Now the function make_cirbuf is written to create and return a fresh cirbuf structure of size max:

```
Cirbuf make_cirbuf(unsigned max)    /* create new circular buffer */
{ Cirbuf b = {NULL, 0, 0, 0, 0};
      b.size = max;
      b.buf = (char *) malloc(max*sizeof(char));
      return(b);
}
```

The space for the character buffer is actually allocated dynamically with **malloc**. The character array itself is not part of the structure Cirbuf. The member buf is just a pointer to this character array. The head, tail, and length have been initialized to zero, values consistent with an empty circular buffer.

Characters are put into a circular buffer structure with the produce function and removed from it with the consume function. Macros to test for buffer-full and buffer-empty conditions are also defined:

```
#define EMPTY_CIR(bp) ( bp->length == 0 )
#define FULL_CIR(bp) ( bp->length == bp->size )
```

The function produce puts the character c into a cirbuf structure pointed to by the given pointer bp. The parameter bp cannot be a structure and must be a structure pointer because values in the given buffer structure must be modified. Declaring the second formal parameter of `produce` simply as a `cirbuf` structure is incorrect. Because a `struct` formal parameter gets a copy of the actual argument, any changes made in the called function to the formal parameter do not affect the structure in the calling function.

With a structure pointer such as `bp`, the notations

```
bp->length          (- followed by > as one operator)
(*bp).length        (equivalent notation)
```

are the same. Therefore, the *arrow operator* (`->`) provides the member-of operation for a structure pointer. Because the operators `->` and `.` have the highest precedence (same as `[]`) among all operators, the parentheses in `(*bp).length` are necessary:

```
int produce(char c, Cirbuf *bp)
{    if ( FULL_CIR(bp) )
     {   fprintf(stderr, "produce: buffer full\n");
         return(-1);
     }
     bp->buf[bp->tail++] = c;   /* insert char and increment tail */
     bp->length++;              /* increment length              */
     if ( bp->tail == bp->size ) bp->tail = 0;  /* wraparound     */
     return(0);
}
```

The function `produce` first checks whether the circular buffer is full and returns an error value (–1) if it is. Then, the given character c is put into the character array at the location given by the member `tail`. Both `length` and `tail` are incremented. If `tail` passes the high end of the buffer, it is reset to zero.

Similar techniques are used to implement the `consume` function, which removes the next character from the circular buffer and returns the character as the functional value:

```
int consume(Cirbuf *bp)
{ char c;
      if ( EMPTY_CIR(bp) )
      {   fprintf(stderr, "consume: buffer empty\n");
          return(-1);
      }
      c = bp->buf[bp->head++]; /* remove char and increment head */
      bp->length--;            /* decrement length              */
      if ( bp->head == bp->size ) bp->head = 0; /* wraparound     */
      return(c);
}
```

To round out our implementation, we define three more functions: empty, full, and delete_cirbuf.

```
int empty(Cirbuf *bp)
{       return( EMPTY_CIR(bp) );
}

int full(Cirbuf *bp)
{       return( FULL_CIR(bp) );
}

void delete_cirbuf(Cirbuf b)
{       free(b.buf);         /* free malloc space */
}
```

The purpose of delete_cirbuf is to release the dynamically allocated buffer space to the free pool. This function should be called before any circular buffer variable is destroyed.

7.3   Data Abstraction and Encapsulation

The purpose of defining a structure like cirbuf is to make it available for all kinds of other programs. The recommended practice is to isolate the data-structure definition and all its creation, access, modification, and destruction functions in a single implementation module. The module usually involves two files: a .c file for the manipulation functions and a .h header file. The header supplies all necessary declarations to be included (#include) in any file that may use the structure. Keeping the manipulation routines with the data structure is called *encapsulation*. Although C does not enforce it, encapsulation can still be achieved through good programming practice.

Let's illustrate encapsulation by putting it to practice on the Cirbuf structure. First, we put the routines for circular buffer manipulation in one file and give it an appropriate name such as cirbuf.c. Next, we construct a header file cirbuf.h and put in it all declarations needed for any program, including cirbuf.c itself, to use the cirbuf structure. A #include line is also added to cirbuf.c to include the cirbuf.h header file.

The header file cirbuf.h contains the relevent #define, typedef, struct, and extern declarations as follows.

```
/****** FIFO circular buffer:  file cirbuf.h  *****************/

struct cirbuf
{       char    *buf;    /* pointer to buffer           */
```

```
            unsigned size ;   /* buffer capacity         */
            unsigned head ;   /* first char in buffer     */
            unsigned tail ;   /* first space in buffer    */
            unsigned length ; /* number of char in buffer */
    };

    typedef struct cirbuf Cirbuf;

    extern int empty(Cirbuf *bp);     /* buffer-empty test */

    extern int full(Cirbuf *bp);      /* buffer-full test  */

    /* make_cirbuf returns a new circular buffer of given size */
    extern Cirbuf make_cirbuf(unsigned size);

    /* call delete_cirbuf to free buffer space */
    extern void delete_cirbuf(Cirbuf b);

    /* produce puts c into structure *bp */
    extern int produce(char c, Cirbuf *bp);

    /* consume removes and returns the next char from structure *bp */
    extern int consume(Cirbuf *bp);
    /*************** end of cibuf.h *****************************/
```

In a header file, appropriate comments are absolutely essential to document how to interface to the facilities provided. Therefore, the header file is prepared for any programmer who wishes to use the structure now or in the future.

In the case of cirbuf.h, operations made available through the header file are empty, full, make_cirbuf, delete_cirbuf, produce, and consume (six functions). These routines form the *interface protocol* of the circular buffer. No outside file has a good reason to include code that directly accesses the members of the cirbuf structure.

The other part of the circular buffer module is the cirbuf.c file. It begins with an #include line for the cirbuf.h file, followed by the EMPTY_CIR and FULL_CIR macros and the definitions for the six functions listed before. An object file cirbuf.o, ready to be combined with other files, can also be produced with the **cc** command:

    cc -c cirbuf.c

Let's now write a very simple program, which makes use of the circular buffer, in a separate file testcir.c:

```
#include    <stdio.h>
#include    "cirbuf.h"
main()
{ int i;
  Cirbuf x;
      x = make_cirbuf(5);
      produce('C', &x);
      produce('+', &x);
      produce('U', &x);
      produce('N', &x);
      for ( i=0; i < 3; i++ ) printf("%c", consume(&x));
      produce('I', &x);
      produce('X', &x);
      for ( i=0; i < 3; i++ ) printf("%c", consume(&x));
      delete_buf(x);
}
```

Figure 7.1 shows the buffer status after four `produce` and one `consume` operations. To run this program, first compile and combine it with `cirbuf.o` using the command

    cc `testcir.c cirbuf.o -o testcir`

This command avoids recompilation of `cirbuf.c` and names the executable file `testcir`. Upon successful execution of the above **cc** command, use the shell-level command **testcir** to run the program, which will produce the display C+UNIX.

In summary, a client module of `cirbuf` should ignore the data-structure details as long as it can use the interface protocol provided. The interface protocol hides implementation details such as `size`, `head`, `tail`, `FULL_CIR`, and `EMPTY_CIR`. Direct access of these details by another program is possible

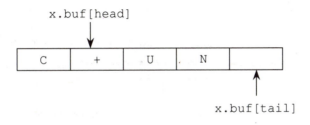

Figure 7.1: Buffer Status

but bad practice. We want to limit knowledge of data-structure details to routines in `cirbuf.c`. The concept of hiding data-implementation details from outside view is called *data abstraction*. Encapsulation and data abstraction reduce program complexity and interdependence, resulting in better software.

7.4 Structure of Structures

The power of structures lies in the grouping of different types into a single data unit. With the `struct` mechanism, uniting not only basic types but also user-defined structures is possible. To illustrate this, let's consider the representation of an address that, for our purposes, contains the following information: name and street address. The name is a structure defined by

```
#define SSIZE 20          /* string size     */
struct name
{     char last[SSIZE];    /* last name       */
      char first[SSIZE];   /* first name      */
      char mi;             /* middle initial  */
      char title[SSIZE];   /* Mr. Ms. Dr. ... */
};
```

and the street address can be represented by

```
struct addr               /* street address  */
{     char street[4*SSIZE];
      char city[SSIZE];
      char state[SSIZE];
      char zip[SSIZE];
};
```

Now the `addr_entry` structure can be defined as

```
struct addr_entry         /* name and address */
{     struct name name;
      struct addr addr;
};
```

We have, on purpose, used the same identifiers for members of `addr_entry` as the existing `struct` tags `name` and `addr`. It shows that structure member names do not conflict with any identifiers outside that particular structure.

With the structures defined, we can now proceed to write some functions for handling addresses. But first, some `typedefs` will be handy:

```
typedef struct addr_entry Addr_entry;
typedef struct addr Addr;
typedef struct name Name;
```

We first want the ability to create new address entries by, say, prompting the user at the terminal. The function `fill` queries the user and obtains input:

```
void fill(char *prompt, char *s)
{        printf("%s :", prompt);
         gets(s);
}
```

To get user input, a function would call `fill` with a character string instructing the user to enter the desired information. The library function **gets** reads one line of user input into the return parameter s. To avoid the run-time overhead of making a function call, defining `fill` as a macro rather than a function is also possible.

The function `mk_name` makes a new `name` structure:

```
Name mk_name()      /* make new Name structure */
{ Name x;
  char line[10];
  void fill(char *prompt, char *s);
      fill("enter last name", x.last);
      fill("enter first name", x.first);
      fill("enter middle initial :", line);
      x.mi = line[0];
      return(x);
}
```

The middle initial is a single character, not a string; therefore, it requires special handling in `mk_name`. Similarly, a new `addr` structure can be made by

```
Addr mk_addr()      /* make new Addr structure       */
{ Addr x;           /* allocates space for structure x */
  void fill(char *prompt, char *s);
      fill("enter zip code", x.zip);
      fill("enter state code", x.state);
      fill("enter city", x.city);
      fill("enter street address", x.street);
      return(x);
}
```

The functions `mk_name` and `mk_addr` are in turn used by the following function to establish a new `addr_entry` structure:

```
Addr_entry mk_addr_entry()
{ Addr_entry x;
  Addr mk_addr(void);
  Name mk_name(void);
      x.addr = mk_addr();      /* structure assignments */
      x.name = mk_name();
      fill("enter title", x.name.title);
      return(x);
}
```

Again, note the use of void to specify the prototype of a function that takes
no arguments.

In dealing with structure of structures, sometimes we need to refer to a
member of a member in a structure. Because the operator . associates left to
right, the notations

```
x.name.title
(x.name).title        (parentheses for readability only)
```

are the same. Use either notation with which you feel comfortable. Similar
comments can be made of the operator ->.

Being able to create address entries, we can now turn our attention to
operations on them. Many different operations can be defined on address
entries, but one essential operation is to display them. Thus we need an
address-label-output mechanism. This is provided by the addr_label function:

```
void addr_label(const Addr_entry *ap)  /* display address label */
{ const Name *name = &ap->name;
  const Addr *addr = &ap->addr;
      printf("%s %s %c. %s\n", name->title,
                             name->first, name->mi, name->last);
      printf("%s\n%s, %s %s\n", addr->street,
                             addr->city, addr->state, addr->zip);
}
```

Notice how the automatic variables name and addr are declared const. This
assures the compiler that members of a const structure stay const.

To test these routines, use the following main function:

```
main()
{ Addr_entry mk_addr_entry(void);
  void addr_label(const Addr_entry *ap);
  Addr_entry a = mk_addr_entry();  /* a is newly made Addr_entry */
      addr_label(&a);              /* display a              */
}
```

In this `main` function, the `mk_add_entry()` call is actually used as part of the declaration to initialize the automatic variable `a`.

7.5   Structure Arrays

An array has two important characteristics: All entries are of the same type, and entries are accessed by indexing at run time. In contrast, in a structure, members can be of different types, and members are accessed by name at *compile time*. The latter may need a little elaboration. For instance, if `frac` is a `Fraction`, the notation

 `frac.denom`

uses a fixed *offset* from `frac`, based on the declaration for `fraction`, to access the member `denom`. Thus, `denom` is a compile-time constant. It is impossible to have `frac.x` where `x` is a run-time variable or expression.

Structures and arrays can be applied in combination to form data structures useful in many applications. In the `addr` structure, we have already an example of a structure involving members that are arrays. In this section, we discuss arrays with entries that are structures.

As a simple example, let's consider keeping a table of foreign-currency exchange rates. Each entry of this table would contain two items of information: foreign-currency name and amount equal to one U.S. dollar:

```
struct rate
{       char *cur;        /* currency name */
        float amt;        /* exchange rate */
};

typedef struct rate Rate;

Rate table[] = { {"Britain (Pound)",         0.5905    },
                 {"Canada (Dollar)",         1.1802    },
                 {"Germany (Mark)",          1.6760    },
                 {"Italy (Lira)",         1233.50      },
                 {"Japan (Yen)",           151.17      },
                 {"Mexico (Peso)",        2827.01      },
                 {"Spain (Peseta)",        104.15      },
                 /*       . . .                        */
                 {"Taiwan (NT $)",          27.40      }
               };

/* total number of rate entries in table */
#define  TABLEN = ( sizeof(table) / sizeof(table[0]) )
```

Note how the array of structures is initialized. To use the rate table, we need a function that takes a currency name and returns a pointer to the appropriate exchange-rate entry. This pointer can then be used to retrieve information or to modify the entry. The function `find_entry` uses a *binary search* to locate the desired entry:

```
Rate *find_entry(char *cur)
{ int low = 0, high = TABLEN-1, mid;
  int test;
      while ( low <= high )
      {    mid = (high + low)/2;
           test = strcmp(cur, table[mid].cur);
           if ( test == 0 )
                return(table+mid);
           else if ( test > 0 )
                low = mid + 1;
           else high = mid - 1;
      }
      return(NULL);    /* no exchange rate found */
}
```

The entries of the rate table are in increasing, lexicographical order. The binary search locates a desired entry by always examining the midpoint in the current search range, between the `high` and `low` indices:

1. If `low` is not less than `high`, then `ent` is not found.
2. Compare `ent` with the entry at the midpoint, `mid` = `(high + low)/2`.
   If `ent` is found, return.
   If `ent` is bigger, `high` = mid + 1.
   If `ent` is smaller, `low` = mid − 1.
3. Repeat steps 1 and 2.

The function `find_entry` returns a `NULL` pointer if the currency is not listed in the table. We now write a function `ex_rate` to retrieve the exchange rate from the table given the currency name `cur`:

```
float ex_rate(char *cur)
{ Rate *tmp = find_entry(cur);
      if ( tmp == NULL )
           return(0.0);              /* rate not available */
      else
           return( tmp->amt );  /* rate from table     */
}
```

A 0.0 exchange rate indicates that the given currency is not on `table`.

Another useful function is `new_rate` that modifies the exchange rate of a certain currency:

```
int new_rate(char *cur, float amt)
{ Rate *tmp = find_entry(cur);
     if ( tmp == NULL )
          return(-1);      /* failed, no such entry */
     else
     {    tmp->amt = amt; /* set new rate          */
          return(0);
     }
}
```

In the currency-exchange example, the entries of `table` are predefined in increasing order of the currency name. To add another entry to the table, we have to modify the source-code file and recompile. In many applications, this would be unacceptable. To provide the flexibility of inserting new table entries at run time, use pointer arrays instead, as we will see in Section 7.6. But before we get there, let's explain the use of `sizeof` in the definition of the symbolic constant `TABLEN`.

The Size of Objects

The C language provides a compile-time unary operator `sizeof` that obtains the size of data objects, built-in or user-defined types. The compiler replaces the expression

```
    sizeof( object or type name )
```

with the number of bytes required to store the given object or an object of the specified type. Table 7.1 shows the typical values of some built-in types and the rules for computing the size of user-defined types. Because some data must be aligned on certain word boundaries in memory, the compiler may supply empty space or *padding* between members in a structure. Therefore, the size of a structure may exceed the sum of its members. The `#define` of `TABLEN` is an example where `sizeof` is used on objects.

7.6   Array of Pointers to Structures _____

Let us extend our address-entry example (Section 7.4) by establishing disk files that store addresses in a well-defined format. We also want to program a shell-level command **addr** to update and retrieve information in any given address file. We can assume that the file is not too large and all address entries can be read into a program for manipulation. Our approach would be

Compile-Time Expr	Typical Value
sizeof(char)	1
sizeof(int)	4
sizeof(long)	4
sizeof(float)	4
sizeof(double)	8
sizeof(*any* *)	4
sizeof(*arrayname*)	*dim**sizeof(*entry*)
sizeof(struct *tag*)	Total size includes padding

Table 7.1: Some sizeof Expressions

to use an array of pointers to struct addr_entry for the in-memory representation of the addresses.

Operations supplied by the shell-level command **addr** should include

- Adding new address entries
- Deleting old address entries
- Modifying existing address entries
- Retrieving specific address entries

These operations can be supported by a few basic routines for inserting, deleting, and ordering entries in an array of pointers to Addr_entry.

In the implementation, MAXLEN is the maximum length of adbook, a global pointer array. The external variable blen, initially zero, records the number of address entries kept in adbook at any given time:

```
#define MAXLEN 1000

static Addr_entry *adbook[MAXLEN];        /* pointer array */
static int blen = 0;   /* total number of existing entries */
```

With appropriate input routines (Section 8.6), the address entries can be read into the adbook array from a disk file. The variable blen will be incremented as entries are put into adbook. We also assume that, initially, all entries in adbook are in sorted order by the name field.

Let's now consider a function find_addr that retrieves an entry from adbook when a Name structure is given.

Following the `find_entry` example in Section 7.5, we again use a binary search to locate the desired address, and we assume that no two entries have the same name. The implementation uses pointer arithmetic rather than indexing as in `find_entry`. Compare the two approaches carefully. The pointer implementation takes great care to avoid generating illegal pointers such as `addbook-1`. Pay special attention to the lines with comments:

```
Addr_entry *find_addr(const Name *name)        /* via binary search   */
{ Addr_entry **high = adbook+blen;             /* beyond end          */
  Addr_entry **low = adbook;
  Addr_entry **mid;
  int test;
      while ( low < high )
      {    mid = low + (high - low) / 2;       /* high + low undefined */
           test = cmp_name(name, &(*mid)->name);
                                                /* -> takes precedence  */
           if ( test < 0 )
                high = mid;        /* high will not fall off left end */
           else if ( test > 0 )
                low = mid + 1;
           else
                return(*mid);
      }
      return(NULL);                 /* not found                       */
}
```

As you may expect, the function `cmp_name` compares two names and returns a positive, zero, or negative integer:

```
int cmp_name(const Name *a, const Name *b)
{ int ans;
      if ( (ans = strcmp(a->last, b->last)) != 0 )
           return(ans);
      else if ( (ans = strcmp(a->first, b->first)) != 0 )
           return(ans);
      else
           return( a->mi - b->mi );  /* compare two characters */
}
```

Now let's turn our attention to building a mechanism for inserting new address entries into `adbook`. For this example, we use a simple approach:

1. Create a new address-entry structure and fill it with the desired data.
2. Put a pointer to the new entry at the end of `adbook`.
3. Sort `adbook`.

The function `new_entry` implements these steps, while ensuring that MAX-LEN is not exceeded and that there is no conflict with an existing entry:

```
int new_entry()
{ Addr_entry *tmp;
  if ( blen + 1 > MAXLEN )        /* no more room, failed       */
          return(-1);
      tmp = (Addr_entry *) malloc(sizeof(Addr_entry));
      /* copy return value into allocated space */
      *tmp = mk_addr_entry();
      if ( find_addr(&tmp->name ) != NULL )
          return(-2);             /* entry already exists, failed  */

      adbook[blen++] = tmp;       /* put entry on array         */
      SORT_ADDR();                /* reorder array              */
      return(0);                  /* normal return              */
  }
```

The **malloc** function allocates memory for the new address entry and puts a pointer to it in the global array `adbook`. The function `mk_addr_entry` has been described in Section 7.4.

The sorting is done with the following routines that make use of the flexible `quicksort` we built in Section 6.7. All we do is to supply the appropriate comparison (`cmp`) and interchange (`swap`) functions:

```
/* compare two address entries */
int cmp_addr(const Addr_entry *x[], int i, int j)
{      return( cmp_name( &(x[i]->name), &(x[j]->name) ) );
}

/* interchange two address entries */
void swap_addr(Addr_entry *x[], int i, int j)
{ Addr_entry *s;
      s = x[i];
      x[i] = x[j];
      x[j] = s;
}

#define SORT_ADDR() quicksort(adbook, 0, blen-1, \
                                (COMP_FN) cmp_addr, \
                                (SWAP_FN) swap_addr)
```

We actually defined a macro `SORT_ADDR()` to sort the global array `adbook` into order. We have continued this long macro definition (with the \s) into multiple lines for readability. Again, the type names `COMP_FN` and `SWAP_FN` have been defined in Section 6.7.[1]

We have shown just a framework and a few key functions for the **addr** command. Other functions for modifying data contained in existing address entries can be added in a similar fashion. For instance, a simple `delete_entry` function would find the desired entry in `adbook` and then shift all entries below up one notch. Finally, the updated `adbook` must be written back to `stdout` or a disk file. We will return to the I/O aspects of the **addr** program in Chapter 8 (Section 8.6).

7.7 Recursive Structures

It has been mentioned that a structure may have members that are also structures. But is it possible or desirable for a structure to have a member that, in turn, has the **same** structure? Very much so. Such structures are called *recursive structures*. In this section, we consider two common recursive structures: the linked list and the binary tree.

Linked List

A grocery list can be thought of as a structure with two members: the name of a grocery item and a grocery list of the remaining items. In fact, this recursive structure is inherent to any list, not just that of groceries.

In C it is impossible for a structure to have an instance of itself as a member *directly* because a structure tag must be defined before it is used in any declaration. But, a *structure pointer* can be used even if the tag is yet to be defined. Therefore, a recursive structure is defined with member *pointers* to the very structure being defined.

As our first example of recursive structures, we consider a *linked list* of integers. Each item of the list contains an integer and a pointer to the rest of the list (Figure 7.2). In other words, each list item also points to the location of the next item, like a "chain of elephants." Each entry on our linked list is a `struct list_item`, defined as follows:

```
struct list_item
{       int                 number;
        struct list_item *next;
};
```

---

[1] A more efficient approach for inserting a new entry into `adbook` uses binary search to locate the point of insertion to avoid a full-scale sort.

Figure 7.2: A Linked List

A list consists of *zero* or *more* entries of type `list_item`. The first entry has a `next` pointer to the second entry, which, in turn, has a `next` pointer to the third entry, and so on. The last entry on a list would have a `NULL` value for its `next` pointer to mark the end of the entire list. A list is always represented by a pointer to its first entry. An *empty list*, one with no entries, is represented by a `NULL` pointer. The following definitions are useful:

```
#define EMPTY_LIST NULL
#define IS_EMPTY(list) ( (list) == EMPTY_LIST )
typedef struct list_item List_item;
typedef List_item *List;
```

We are ready now to write a few functions to manipulate a linked list. First, we need a mechanism to build up a list:

```
List insert_list(List lx, int n)        /* insert in front of a list */
{ List ly = (List) malloc(sizeof(List_item));
                                         /* allocate list cell        */
    ly->number = n;                      /* set number                */
    ly->next = lx;                       /* put in front of list      */
    return(ly);                          /* return new list           */
}
```

The function `insert_list` takes an existing list `lx` and an integer `n` as arguments and returns `ly` with a `list_item` containing the number `n` appended to the front. In this short routine, memory is allocated for a `List_item`, which is assigned the appropriate values and returned. With `insert_list` defined, the sequence

```
List list_x = EMPTY_LIST;
list_x = insert_list(list_x, 3);
list_x = insert_list(list_x, 2);
list_x = insert_list(list_x, 1);
```

builds the linked list `list_x` as shown in Figure 7.2. Such a list can be displayed with `display_list`:

```
void display_list(List a)
{ List b;
```

```
        printf("(");
        for ( b = a ; b != EMPTY_LIST ; b = b->next )  /* idiom */
            b->next ? printf("%d  ", b->number)
                    : printf("%d%d",b->number);
        printf(")\n");
}
```

only supposed to be one "d" → %d

Here, **the `for` loop is a frequent** *idiom* **for following the pointers down a linked list until the end is reached.** The output of `display_list(list_x)` is (1 2 3) and `display_list(EMPTY_LIST)` **gives** ().

Another operation often required on linked lists is **deleting an entry somewhere on the list.** This is implemented by `delete_ent`:

```
List delete_ent(List a, int n)
{ List ans;
        if ( IS_EMPTY(a) )          /* nothing to delete        */
            return(a);
        if ( a->number == n )       /* if entry to delete        */
        {    ans = a->next;         /* delete entry              */
            free(a);                /* return space to malloc pool */
            return(ans);
        }
        a->next = delete_ent(a->next, n); /* recursive call       */
        return(a);
}
```

The function `delete_ent` **finds the entry containing the number** n and **returns a list with the target entry removed**. Recursion is employed to remove the entry n from the given list a:

1. If a is empty, return a. This is the recursion-termination condition when the entry n is not found on the given list.
2. If n is equal to `a->number`, return `a->next`. This action removes the target entry when it is at the head of the list.
3. Otherwise, replace `a->next` by the result returned by `delete_ent(a->next,n)` and return a. This is the recursive call.

Because the list structure is recursive, it works very well with recursive functions. Although **the recursive `delete_ent` is very elegant, its run-time efficiency is not as good as a function that locates and deletes an entry by going down the linked list with, say, a `for`** loop.

We can assume that all entries on the list have been created with the `insert_list` function and that the **individual list cells have been dynamically allocated**. Hence, in `delete_ent` the **removed entry is also freed to return space to the malloc** pool. Now, the sequence

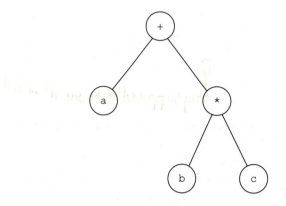

Figure 7.3: A Parse Tree of a + b * c

```
list_x = delete_ent(list_x, 2);
display_list(list_x);
```

results in the output (1 3).

Binary Tree

Another common example of recursive structures is the *binary tree,* a tree with at most two children for each node. Defined recursively, a binary tree is a single node or a node with a left binary subtree and/or a right binary sub-tree.

Let's apply the binary tree in representing and evaluating arithmetic expressions. An arithmetic expression in *infix* notation is usually *parsed* before it is evaluated. The parsing operation produces a binary tree of operator–operand relationships in the arithmetic expression (see Figure 7.3). For simplicity, we will deal with expressions involving integers only.

A binary tree node is a structure with four members:

```
struct tree_node
{    enum Operator      operator;    /* integer-coded operator */
     int                value;       /* associate int value    */
     struct tree_node *left;         /* left subtree           */
     struct tree_node *right;        /* right subtree          */
};

typedef struct tree_node Tree_node;
typedef Tree_node *Btree;
```

Instead of using characters such as '+' for the member operator, we use the more general scheme of integer codes for operators

```
enum Operator {NOOP, PLUS, TIMES, QUOTIENT, DIFFERENCE, MOD, MINUS};
```

allowing easy representation of all types of operators, including user-defined operations such as `gcd`. Of course, in an actual program, the `Operator` declaration must precede the `tree_node`.

The top node in a tree structure is called the *root*. Each node on the tree may have zero, one (left), or two (left and right) child nodes. A node with no children is a *leaf*; otherwise, it is an *internal node*. An internal node represents an operation with an operator and one (`left`) or two operands, each represented by a child node, whereas a leaf node stands for a simple operand consisting of just an integer `value` and no child nodes:

```
#define EMPTY_TREE NULL
enum Child {LEFT, RIGHT};
```

To build a tree, first establish the nodes, link the nodes into subtrees, and link the subtrees into one finished tree structure. The function

```
Btree new_node(enum Operator op, int val)
{ Btree node = (Btree) malloc(sizeof(Tree_node));
      node->operator = op;
      node->value = val;
      node->left = node->right = EMPTY_TREE;
      return(node);
}
```

establishes a new node with dynamic allocation and returns a `Btree` pointer to the node. The left or right subtree relations are established by the function

```
void set_child(Btree b_tree, enum Child id, Btree subtree)
{     if ( id == LEFT )
          b_tree->left = subtree;
      else
          b_tree->right = subtree;
}
```

The `enum` constants `LEFT` and `RIGHT` indicate which subtree to set. A test to see if a node is a leaf is also useful:

```
int is_leaf(Btree b_tree)
{     return(   b_tree != EMPTY_TREE
             && b_tree->left == EMPTY_TREE
             && b_tree->right == EMPTY_TREE );
}
```

We now wish to evaluate a parse tree involving integers and operators. The evaluation employs a recursive procedure:

1. *End condition*: If the tree is a leaf node, then return the value of the node as the answer.
2. *Subproblems*: Recursively, evaluate the left and then the right subtree (if any).
3. *Combine answers*: Apply the operator to the values of the subtrees and return the computed value.

```c
#include <stdio.h>

int eval_btree(Btree b_tree)
{ int l, r;
    if ( b_tree == EMPTY_TREE )
    {   fprintf(stderr, "Cannot evaluate empty tree\n");
        exit(1);
    }
    if ( is_leaf(b_tree) ) return( b_tree->value );
    l = eval_btree(b_tree->left);                    /* recursive call */
    if ( b_tree->operator == MINUS ) return(-l);
    r = eval_btree(b_tree->right);                   /* recursive call */
    switch( b_tree->operator )
    {   case PLUS:          return(l + r);
        case TIMES:         return(l * r);
        case QUOTIENT:      return(l / r);
        case DIFFERENCE:    return(l - r);
        case MOD:           return(l % r);
        default:
            fprintf(stderr, "%s: unknown operator\n");
            exit(1);
    }
}
```

Let's write a simple test program to build a binary tree for the expression 3 + 4 * 5 and then evaluate it with eval_btree:

```c
main()
{ int value;
  Btree node_0 = new_node(PLUS, 0);
  Btree node_1 = new_node(NOOP, 3);
  Btree node_2 = new_node(TIMES, 0);
  Btree node_3 = new_node(NOOP, 4);
  Btree node_4 = new_node(NOOP, 5);

    set_child(node_0, LEFT, node_1);
    set_child(node_0, RIGHT, node_2);
    set_child(node_2, LEFT, node_3);
```

```
        set_child(node_2, RIGHT, node_4);
        value = eval_btree(node_0);
        printf("answer = %d\n", value);
}
```

When a binary tree structure is no longer needed, space can be returned to the dynamic-memory pool with

```
void free_btree(Btree b_tree)          /* deallocate binary tree */
{   if ( b_tree != EMPTY_TREE )
    {   free_btree(b_tree->left);     /* recursion            */
        free_btree(b_tree->right);
        free(b_tree);
    }
}
```

Because each tree node is separately allocated, each has to be individually freed (Section 5.6.1).

Linked List Versus Array of Pointers

We have used a list of integers to illustrate how a linked list works. It is possible, of course, to have linked lists of other data such as character strings, address structures, and so on. A linked list has several advantages over an array of pointers. The space used by a linked list can grow and shrink dynamically with usage. The array, on the other hand, is fixed once it is allocated. Also, inserting and deleting items anywhere on a linked list is relatively easy. The same operations are difficult for arrays.

However, the array has a very crucial advantage of its own. Access to an array entry is direct, and algorithms such as binary search efficiently locate a target entry. With linked lists, information retrieval is a matter of going through the list, entry-by-entry, following the `next` pointers until either the entry is found or the end of the list is reached.

The function `find_list_ent` returns a pointer to the list entry containing the desired integer `i`:

```
List find_list_ent(const List a, int i)
{ List b;
    for ( b = a ; b != EMPTY_LIST ; b = b->next )
                /* idiom again */
    {   if ( b->number == i )
            return(b);
    }
    return( EMPTY_LIST );
}
```

The *linear search* can be very expensive, especially if the list is long. If there are n items, the linear search takes n steps in the worst case, whereas a binary search takes at most $\lceil log_2(n) \rceil$ steps. For $n = 1000$, searching a linked list can take 100 times as long. Such tradeoffs between flexibility and run-time efficiency are frequently encountered in software-design considerations.

The pointer-array and linked-list structures can be combined in a way that maximizes the advantages of both structures, as we see next.

7.8 Hash Table

Discussed in this section is an easy and effective method to store and retrieve data that combine the main advantages of the pointer array and the linked list: the *hash table* data structure.

Our hash table is basically an array of linked lists. To store a piece of data, called a *record*, into a hash table, the record or a part of it, known as a *key*, is used to compute an index into the array where the particular record is stored or retrieved. For instance, the name part in an address record can be the key. A name can be transformed into an integer index by, say, adding the integer representation of its characters together.

The action of turning the key into an integer index is called *hashing*. Hashing is performed by a *hash function*, which takes a key and returns an integer index called the *hash code* whose value must be a valid index in the proper range. The hash function is designed to give different hash codes for different keys, but this cannot be guaranteed. Normally, there is some chance of two keys giving rise to the same hash code. When this happens, we say the two records have *collided*.

The linked list offers a good solution to the problem of collision: The hash table entries are linked lists. Records with the same hash code are stored in the same linked list, located at the hash address in the array. If the hash array has enough entries and if the hash function is well designed, collision should occur infrequently, and the linked lists are kept very small.

Thus, when properly used, the hash table offers a data organization in which most records are accessible directly at their hash code location. Only infrequently will a sequential search down a very short linked list be necessary to locate a record. With the hash table, the need to keep records in sorted order is avoided entirely. Adding new records and removing old ones are simple operations that do not involve reordering or other time-consuming operations. Figure 7.4 illustrates graphically the hash table structure.

If we expect up to 500 records, a hash array slightly larger—say, of dimension 600 to 700— can reduce the chance of collisions.

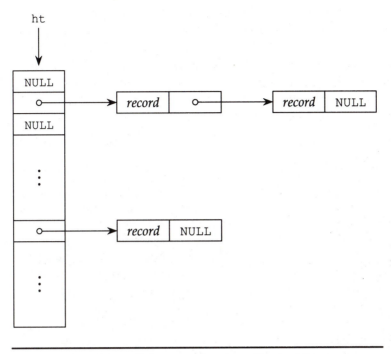

Figure 7.4: A Hash Table of Linked Lists

Hash Table Organization

With a general understanding of the hash table, we are ready to put it to use. Let's consider again the handling of addresses. Here a record is an entire address entry, and the name part is used as the key.

We first establish structures and definitions for a linked list of Addr_entry (Section 7.4), which is defined in the header file addr.h:

```
#include "addr.h"

struct addr_list_item
{       Addr_entry            *addr;
        struct addr_list_item *next;
};

typedef struct addr_list_item Addr_list_item;
typedef Addr_list_item *Addr_list;
#define EMPTY_LIST NULL
```

The definitions closely parallel those for linked lists of integers. The only difference is that now a list item contains a pointer to an address entry rather than just a number.

To establish a hash table, we define the following:

```
#define TABLE_BITS 8                    /* hash table size 2**8 = 256     */
#define TABLE_SIZE 256
#define SHIFT_AMT 8*sizeof(unsigned int) - TABLE_BITS /* shift amt  */
#define HASH_MULT 2640025017u    /* unsigned hash multiplier       */
#define HSTR_LEN 2*(SSIZE+1)     /* max hash string length         */


static Addr_list addr_ht[TABLE_SIZE];                   /* hash table */
```

The hash table is represented by the pointer array `addr_ht`, whose entries are linked lists of address entries (type `Addr_list`). The `TABLE_SIZE` is a power of 2—in this case 256, which can comfortably accommodate about 200 address entries. Because `addr_ht` has been declared `static`, its entries are initially zero (`NULL`). This is just right because we use `NULL` pointers for empty lists and the hash table has all entries empty to begin with.

Let's design a function to produce a hash code based on the `name` part in the address entry. The same name will produce the same hash code. Different names often, but not always, produce different hash codes. In other words, if two names give the same hash code, they may or may not be the same name.

The hashing is done in two stages:

1. Convert the `Name` strings into an `unsigned int`.
2. Hash the `unsigned int` into a hash table index.

The function `str_to_int` takes a string and converts it into an `unsigned int` value. This is done by treating the string as a sequence of `unsigned int` quantities and performing bitwise exclusive or `^` on them.

```
unsigned int str_to_int(const char *str)
{ unsigned value = 0u, tmp = 0u;
  int size = sizeof(int)/sizeof(char);
  int len = strlen(str);
    while ( len >= size )              /* size bytes each time    */
    {     value ^= *(unsigned *)str;   /* xor with explicit cast  */
        str += size;
        len -= size;
    }
    if ( len > 0 )                     /* up to size-1 bytes left */
```

```
    {     strcpy( (char *)&tmp, str );    /* explicit cast        */
          value ^= tmp;
    }
    return(value);
}
```

The `hash` function combines the last name, first name, and middle initial into a single string using the standard library function **sprintf**. Then, `str_to_int` is called to convert the string into an `unsigned int` value `val` (line 1). The actual hash index is then produced by `unsigned` multiplication (Section 2.9) of `val` with the magic hash multiplier `HASH_MULT` and by taking only the leading `TABLE_BITS` bits (line 2) of the product (right shift `SHIFT_AMT` bits):

```
unsigned hash(const Name *name) .
{ char h_str[HSTR_LEN];
  unsigned int val;
      sprintf(h_str, "%s%s%c", name->last, name->first, name->mi);
      val = str_to_int(h_str);                      /* (1) */
      return( (val*HASH_MULT) >> SHIFT_AMT );       /* (2) */
}
```

There is much depth to the selection of the hash multiplier. The one we used here is based on *Fibonacci hashing* and should work well for all 32-bit computers.

Hash Table Operations

The function `hash` is used by other functions that enter, erase, and retrieve information on the hash table `addr_ht`. The `retrieve` function looks up the address entry for a given name:

```
Addr_list retrieve(const Name *name)
{ Addr_list list_a = addr_ht[hash(name)];
      for ( ; list_a != EMPTY_LIST ; list_a = list_a->next )
          if ( cmp_name(name, &list_a->addr->name) == 0 )   /* (1)  */
              return( list_a );                      /* entry found      */
      return( EMPTY_LIST );                          /* entry not found */
}
```

The pointer `list_a` is initialized with the pointer residing at the `hash(name)` location of the array `addr_ht`. Now `list_a` is the linked list of address entries at this particular hash location. A sequential search down the linked list is performed with the `for` loop, comparing the given name with the `name` member in each address entry. The name-comparison function `cmp_name` was defined earlier. If a matching list entry is found, it is returned; otherwise, `EMPTY_LIST` is returned. The `for` loop control has only two parts in this example because `list_a` is already properly initialized. The double pointer access (line 1) to the member `name` is also worth noting.

An existing address entry in the hash table can be removed using the `erase` function:

```
static int found = 0;
int erase(const Name *name)
{ unsigned hashcode = hash(name);
  Addr_list list_a = addr_ht[hashcode];
  Addr_list delete_list(Addr_list, const Name *);
      found = 1;
      if ( list_a != EMPTY_LIST )
      {   addr_ht[hashcode] = delete_list(list_a, name);
          return( found-1 );
      }
      return(-1);        /* no entry to delete */
}
```

The method for erasing an address entry is simple:

1. Set `list_a` to the linked list at the hash location.
2. Delete the target address entry on `list_a` matching the given name.
3. Put the shortened list back in the hash location.

Step 2 is implemented by `delete_list`, which also sets the external variable `found` to 0 if the target entry is not found. This arrangement enables `erase` to return 0 for a successful erasure and –1 for an entry not found. The `delete_list` function is recursive:

```
Addr_list delete_list(Addr_list list_a, const Name *name)
{ Addr_list ans;
      if ( list_a == EMPTY_LIST )                /* if no matching entry */
      {   found = 0;
          return(NULL);
      }
      if ( cmp_name(&list_a->addr->name, name) == 0 )
      {   ans = list_a->next;
          free(list_a);                /* return space to malloc pool */
          return(ans);
      }
```

```
        list_a->next = delete_list(list_a->next, name);
                                                /* recursive call */

        return( list_a );
}
```

The return value of `delete_list` is the shortened list. (This version is a modification of `delete_ent` given in Section 7.7.)

Let's now add a new entry into the hash table. Given a new address node `list_a`, we first look for an entry with the same name. If present, it is replaced by the new entry `list_a`; otherwise, `list_a` is installed on the list at its hash location. The function `enter_add` implements this procedure:

```
    void enter_add(Addr_list a)      /* enter a into hash table */
    { Addr_list b = retrieve(&a->addr->name);
      unsigned hashcode;
          if ( b != EMPTY_LIST )     /* replace existing entry  */
          {   a->next = b->next;
              *b = *a;               /* structure assignment    */
              free(a);
          }
          else                       /* install new entry       */
          {   hashcode = hash(&a->addr->name);
              b = addr_ht[hashcode];
              a->next = b;
              addr_ht[hashcode] = a;
          }
    }
```

The replacing of an old entry is interesting. First, the member `next` of the new entry `a` is assigned the `next` pointer of the old entry `b`. Then the structure `a` is copied into `b` with

```
    *b = *a;        (structure copying)
```

Thus, the list node `b` becomes a copy of `a` as it stays on the same spot on the linked list. The structure `a`, which is presumed to have been created with **malloc**, is freed.

Using the `mk_addr_entry` defined in Section 7.4, we can write `new_entry` to form a new entry and put it into the hash table:

```
    int new_entry()
    { Addr_entry *tmp;
      Addr_list item;
          tmp = (Addr_entry *) malloc(sizeof(Addr_entry));
          *tmp = mk_addr_entry();
```

```
        item = (Addr_list) malloc(sizeof(Addr_list_item));
        item->addr = tmp;
        item->next = EMPTY_LIST;
        enter_add(item);
        return(0);    /* normal return */
    }
```

You should write a main routine to test the above functions. To make it easy to exercise various aspects of the functions, use a very small TABLE_SIZE—say, 2 or 3. Among the things to test are replacing old entries, erasing, and retrieving or erasing nonexistent entries, and so on.

7.9 Structures of Arbitrary Types

Structures such as linked lists or binary trees are useful for organizing many types of data other than just integers. Most of the overall mechanism for dealing with a linked list of integers would be the same for a linked list of floats, doubles, strings, or even structures like addresses. Similar remarks can be made of a binary tree and other *container structures*.

One simple way to get a linked list of floats, for example, is to copy the structure for integers and make a few modifications. But we can do better than that. Establishing a container structure *without specifying what it contains*, resulting in a structure that can be used for different purposes, is possible. Just like the general quicksort in Section 6.7, we can use the void * type and function pointers to fashion structures and their manipulative routines to process arbitrary-data types.

Arbitrary List

To illustrate this technique, we define an arbitrary linked list and see how it can be applied to different types of data. The linked list itself is

```
struct list_item
{   void             *data;      /* arbitrary data item */
    struct list_item *next;
};

typedef struct list_item List_item;
typedef List_item *A_List;

#define EMPTY_LIST NULL
```

If you compare the definitions with the structure for integers, you'll find the only difference is the void *data member declaration. The void * is key in permitting data to point to any type.

To make things work, we also **need a comparison function for the data** we intend to store in the arbitrary container structure. The **comparison function is of type** `CMP_FN`

```
typedef int (* CMP_FN) (void *, void *);
#define L_EQUAL(x,y)    ((* cmp_fn)(x, y) == 0)
```

and **compares the two data items given by the pointer arguments. The result is an integer less than, equal to, or greater than zer**o, depending on whether the first item is less than, equal to, or greater than the second item, respectively. The macro `L_EQUAL` simply makes our program easier to read.

To **find an item on a list, use**

```
A_List find_list(const A_List a, void *item, CMP_FN cmp_fn)
{ A_List b;
    for ( b = a ; b != EMPTY_LIST ; b = b->next )
    {   if ( L_EQUAL(b->data, item) )   /* supplied comparison */
            return(b);
    }
    return( EMPTY_LIST );
}
```

For `find_list`, again, `void *` allows arbitrary data. In addition, the caller-supplied function `cmp_fn` compares data items. Similar techniques are used for deleting from and inserting into a list:

```
A_List delete_list(A_List a, void *item, CMP_FN cmp_fn)
{ A_List ans;
    if ( a == EMPTY_LIST )
        return(a);
    if ( L_EQUAL(a->data, item) )              /* supplied comparison */
    {   ans = a->next;
        free(a);                     /* return space to malloc pool */
        return(ans);
    }
    a->next = delete_list(a->next, item, cmp_fn);/* recursive call */
    return(a);
}


A_List insert_list(A_List a, void *item)/* insert item in front of a */
{ A_List x = (A_List) malloc(sizeof(List_item));
    x->data = item;
    x->next = a;
    return(x);
}
```

We also need to supply a display function that can output a list item of a specific type:

```
typedef void (* DSP_FN)(void *item);   /* item-displaying function */

void display_list(A_List a, DSP_FN dsp_fn)
{ A_List b;
     printf("(");
     for ( b = a ; b != EMPTY_LIST ; b = b->next )
     {       (* dsp_fn)(b->data);
             if ( b->next != EMPTY_LIST ) printf(", ");
     }
     printf(")\n");
}
```

With the caller-supplied `dsp_fn`, the function `display_list` displays a list of arbitrary elements enclosed by parentheses and separated by commas.

List of Fractions

To demonstrate how an arbitrary container structure is applied to a specific data type, let's form and manipulate `A_List` of fractions (Section 7.1). The supplied comparison and display functions are

```
    int cmp_fraction(Fraction *a, Fraction *b)  /* compare fractions */
    {       return( (a->num) * (b->denom) - (b->num) * (a->denom) );
    }


    void display_fraction(Fraction *x)          /* display a fraction */
    {       printf("%d/%d", x->num, x->denom); }
```

and we can use the `main` function to run some tests:

```
    main()
    { A_List s = EMPTY_LIST;
      Fraction a = make_fraction(1,3);          /* make some fractions */
      Fraction b = make_fraction(2,5);
      Fraction c = make_fraction(3,7);
          s = insert_list(s, &a);
          s = insert_list(s, &b);
          s = insert_list(s, &c); /* s now a list of three fractions */
          display_list(s, (DSP_FN) display_fraction);
          s = delete_list(s, &c, (CMP_FN) cmp_fraction);
          display_list(s, (DSP_FN) display_fraction);
    }
```

A list s of three fractions is constructed and displayed. One of the fractions is deleted, and the shortened list is again displayed. In calling `display_list` and `delete_list`, we have applied proper function-type coercion. The output produced is

```
(3/7, 2/5, 1/3)
(2/5, 1/3)
```

To use `A_List` on strings, use the library function **strcmp** as the comparison function and

```
void display_string(char *s)
{      printf(" %s ", s);   }
```

as the display function.

With `A_List` we have the linked-list structure defined once and for all. To use it for any particular data items, just supply the comparison and display functions. The same techniques can be used to establish other, more complicated container structures, resulting in even more flexibility and savings in programming effort.

7.10 Unions

7.10.1 Basic Union Concepts

It is convenient sometimes to have the same variable hold different types of data. A `union` variable has this property and can be declared with the same syntax as `struct`. Once a *union tag* is established, it can define `union` variables. The declaration

```
union int_or_float
{      int    ival;
       float fval;
}
```

creates the union tag `int_or_float`, which can be used in

```
union int_or_float x;
```

to declare a `union` variable x that can hold *both* `int` and `float` values:

```
x.ival = 9;              (x as int variable)
x.fval = 4.321;          (x as float variable, overwrites int value)
```

In effect, a `union` is a `struct` in which all members have offset zero from the base (stored at the same location). A `union` variable is given enough space to hold the largest of the members. Still, a `union` is one variable rather than a structure because it holds only one type of value at a time. The member notations `x.fval` and `x.ival` are used not to get different offsets but to get different interpretations of data stored at the same location. Hence, the compiler treats `x.ival` as an `int` variable and `x.fval` as a `float`, both at the same memory address. Accessing a `union` variable correctly to retrieve the most recently assigned value is the responsibility of the programmer.

Consider a function `divide(int a, int b)`. It would be interesting if we could define this function to return either an `int` or a `float`, depending on whether b divides a evenly:

```
int div_flag = 0;     /* zero for int, nonzero for float */

union int_or_float divide(int a, int b)
{ union int_or_float ans;
    if ( (div_flag = a % b) == 0 )   /* even division */
        ans.ival = a/b;              /* ans is int     */
    else                             /* otherwise      */
        ans.fval =  a / (float) b;   /* ans is float   */
    return(ans);
}
```

The global variable `div_flag` is set correctly so that a calling function of `divide` can examine the value of `div_flag` and determine whether an `int` or a `float` has been returned. Thus, a `test` function can be written as

```
void test(int a, int b)
{ union int_or_float x;
  extern int div_flag;
      x = divide(a,b);
      if ( div_flag ) printf("%d/%d = %g\n", a, b, x.fval);
      else printf("%d/%d = %d\n", a, b, x.ival);
}
```

Then the calls

```
test(8, 4);
test(2, 3);
```

should produce the output

```
8/4 = 2
2/3 = 0.666667
```

Unions can also occur inside arrays and structures just as a `struct` can. The notations for unions are the same as structures. In fact, a union could be redefined as a structure and used without change. The only difference would be the space needed. A union uses less storage because all members are stored at the same location.

The artificial example given here only serves to illustrate the concepts. Now let's study a few actual applications of unions.

7.10.2 Union Applications

In Section 6.4.2, we presented a polynomial representation using an integer array consisting of exponents and coefficients terminated by a −1 (Table 6.1). With the union, we can improve on this data structure by representing a polynomial of degree zero by the integer constant itself, rather than an integer array.

Our new polynomial structure is defined as

```
struct polynomial
{    int             deg;  /* degree of polynomial       */
     union
     {   int  c0;          /* constant when degree is zero */
         int *pl;          /* used when degree is positive */
     }               poly;
};

typedef struct polynomial Polynomial;
```

The structure `polynomial` has two members, `deg` and `poly`. The latter is a union that will be interpreted as an `int` when the degree is zero and as a pointer otherwise. This organization is clean and elegant, besides saving space.

Let's write a display function for our improved polynomial structure. The strategy is to display the polynomial as an integer if it is of degree zero and to call the existing function `poly_display` (Section 6.4.2) otherwise. The `upoly_display` (univariate poly display) implements this procedure:

```
#define DEG(p) (p.deg)

void upoly_display(Polynomial p)
{ void poly_display(int *);          /* existing display function  */
    if ( DEG(p) == 0 )
        printf("%d\n", p.poly.c0); /* display int            (1) */
    else
        poly_display(p.poly.pl);   /* call existing function (2) */
}
```

The union `p.poly` appears in lines 1 and 2.

A union can save space even when it does not take on different data types. Take the binary tree example we discussed in Section 7.7. A `tree_node` can be redefined as

```
enum Node_t {LEAF, UNARY, BINARY};

struct tree_node
{    enum Node_t              type;     /* LEAF, UNARY, or BINARY  */
     union
     {   enum Operator op;             /* integer-coded operator  */
         int            val;           /* associate int value     */
     }                      node;
     struct tree_node       *left;   /* left subtree              */
     struct tree_node       *right;  /* right subtree             */
};
```

where the member `type` indicates whether the tree node is a leaf or a unary or binary operator. This makes tree operations much faster. Since a leaf node has a value and no operator, whereas internal nodes are just the opposite, we can combine the value and operator entries into a union `node`.

Besides `union`, another space-saving device is to use individual bits to represent information. This can be done conveniently with *bit fields*, as we see next.

7.11   Bit Structures

The `struct` notation also lends itself to organizing individual bits in a word. By packing several pieces of data into a single machine word, storage decreases and efficiency increases in certain situations. For example, the UNIX system file uses a 16-bit quantity known as the *file mode* (Section 1.5) to encode file-access permissions (first 9 bits), execution style (next 3 bits), and file type (last 4 bits). Figure 7.5 shows the bit positions.

The declaration

```
struct access
{    unsigned int o_x : 1;     /* execute permission for others */
     unsigned int o_w : 1;     /* write permission for others   */
     unsigned int o_r : 1;
     unsigned int g_x : 1;     /* execute permission for group  */
     unsigned int g_w : 1;
     unsigned int g_r : 1;
     unsigned int u_x : 1;
     unsigned int u_w : 1;
     unsigned int u_r : 1;     /* read permission for owner     */
};
```

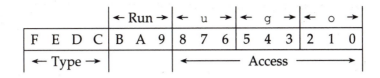

Figure 7.5: The UNIX File-Mode Bits

establishes the *bit-field*, or simply *field*, type access. Each member of a bit field has its width (number of bits) specified after a colon (:). The access structure has nine single-bit members: o_x, o_w, ..., u_r.

The order in which the fields are specified is significant. Usually, the field members occupy bits sequentially in a word, starting from the lowest bit (bit 0). A field with no name (colon and width only) can introduce *padding*. A field width of zero forces alignment at the next-word boundary. If a bit-field structure does not fill a whole machine word, a hole is placed on the high end to make the bit-field structure big enough to pack tightly into arrays and maintain proper alignment. The ANSI standard does not outlaw bit fields that contain implementation-introduced holes after the beginning or that cross word boundaries.

Field members in a structure are accessed in the same way as are members of structures. In general, bit fields behave like *small integers of the specified number of bits* and can be used in expressions just like other integers. Thus, you may specify a bit field signed or unsigned.

Consider the access structure; for example, the fields can be set to 0 or 1 directly to grant or deny access:

```
struct access perm;              (a bit-field variable)
perm.u_r = perm.g_r = 1;         (turn on the 2 bits)
perm.g_w = perm.o_w = 0;         (turn off the 2 bits)
```

The bits may initially be set according to the UNIX system file mode (Section 10.3) st_mode, normally a short int. Bit masks such as the symbolic constants S_IREAD, S_IWRITE, and S_IEXEC (r, w, x for owner; Figure 10.3) are available to extract the desired bits. Thus, we can use

```
perm.u_r = st_mode & S_IREAD;
perm.u_w = st_mode & S_IWRITE;
perm.u_x = st_mode & S_IEXEC;
```

to set the bit-field members. They can also be directly checked:

```
if ( perm.u_r == 1 )
   ...
```

Fields involving different width members can also be used:

```
struct abc
{      unsigned int uu : 3;
          signed int vv : 4;
};
```

Assignments involving field members refer to the low-order bits. For example,

```
main()
{ struct abc x;
       x.uu = 073;
       x.vv = 003;
       if ( x.uu == x.vv ) printf("ok\n");
}
```

will produce the output ok.

Beware that almost everything about bit fields is implementation-dependent. The total number of bits in a word is machine-dependent. The word-alignment requirements and the padding schemes are also implementation-dependent. These factors will affect how external data are picked apart with bit fields.

Also, bit-field members are not stored as variables; therefore, something like &x.uu cannot be used.

The union and field facilities contribute to the *low-level* feel of C. They let you deal conveniently with data representations closer to the machine level than most other languages. Although not important to a beginner, these features are invaluable for systems programmers who implement device drivers, file systems, compilers, and operating systems like UNIX itself.

7.12 Summary

The built-in data types of C can be augmented by user-defined data structures established with the struct declaration, which defines a structure tag and the types of its members. Once a structure tag is defined, it can declare variables (struct fraction x;). A style involving using typedef to simplify structure declarations has been recommended.

A structure can be initialized with constant values for the members (Fraction x={1,3};). Members are accessed with the dot (x.numerator) or arrow ((&x)->denominator) operators. These member-of operators share with array-indexing operator ([]) the highest precedence among all operators. Structures can be assigned, passed as arguments in function calls, and returned as values by functions. In all these cases, full automatic copying is done. To avoid copying, structure pointers can be used.

A data structure should be encapsulated with its manipulation routines. The interface protocol of a particular data structure is put in its header file. Knowledge of structure details should be limited to the data-implementation module. Other programs should respect the abstractness of the data structure.

More complicated data structures include arrays with structure elements, structure with array members, and arrays of pointers to structures. Examples of these have been given.

A recursive structure is a structure with a member that is, directly or indirectly, a pointer to the same structure. Linked lists and binary trees are important examples of recursive structures, and their manipulation has been amply demonstrated. The hash table combines the advantages of an array and a linked list. A full hash table implementation has been described.

A container structure such as a list, a tree, or a hash table can be established without specifying what it contains, resulting in a structure that can be used for different purposes. This is done with the help of `void *` and function pointers.

Regular variables have a fixed type and size. A union is a variable that can hold data of different types or sizes at different times. A union is really a `struct` whose members all begin with offset zero. Only sophisticated applications require unions. With `struct` you can also define bit fields with members involving only a few bits or just 1 bit. The bit-field structure provides a convenient way to pack information into machine words.

Exercises

1. Build a complete set of arithmetic functions for the `fraction` structure. Use a canonical representation.

2. Add to the `fraction` structure a set of relational functions for comparing any two fractions. See Section 2.10.2 for a complete list.

3. A vector in three dimensions (as in geometry) has **x**, **y**, and **z** components. Define a vector structure and implement vector routines `vec_add`, `vec_sub`, and `vec_inner` (inner product).

4. To the vector structure, write a function to test whether two vectors are parallel.

5. A complex number has a real and an imaginary part, each a `double`. Define a structure for complex numbers and define the arithmetic routines including `complex_add`, `complex_sub`, `complex_times`, and `complex_divide`.

6. Follow the circular buffer example and write a first-in-last-out buffer (a stack). Define the data structure with the functions `make_stack`, `push`, `pop`, and `is_empty`.

7. Use a stack to unwind the recursive `quicksort` defined in Section 3.4. Avoid recursion by pushing the subproblems yet to be done onto a stack so that they can be performed later in the correct order by popping them off the stack.

8. Design a data structure to represent a mileage chart like that found in a road atlas. (*Hint*: Use a hash table.) Also implement the routines to retrieve and modify information stored in the hash table.

9. Define a structure `employee` to keep the record related to an employee in a company. It should contain name, address, Social Security number, age, gender, department, salary, and other members.

10. Write a display function for the `employee` record.

11. To the `employee` record, add other functions such as change address, revise salary, modify department, and so on.

12. Build a list of employees and implement functions to add, delete, and look for an employee.

13. Use the foreign-currency exchange structure (Section 7.5) and write functions to compute (a) the U.S. dollar amount for each unit of foreign currency and (b) the currency-one amount for each unit in currency two. For example, yen per mark or dollars per pound.

14. A real exchange table should have different *buy* and *sell rates*. A commission may also be charged on each transaction. With this in mind, redesign the exchange-rate table and the various routines associated with it. Of course, these rates change rapidly with time so we should be able to modify the rates and the commissions at will.

15. An $n \times n$ matrix is upper-triangular if all entries below the main diagonal are zero. For large matrices that are triangular, it is important not to store the zeros. Design a structure to store only the upper-triangular part (in a linear array) and write associate routines to access the elements correctly.

16. Use dynamic allocation in a program that allows the user to perform the following operations on linked lists of integers:

    a. Create a linked list of integers
    b. Find out if a linked list is empty
    c. Insert an element in the list
    d. Delete an element in the list
    e. Reverse a list

    In parts a and c, the program must preserve the sorted order of the list.

17. Can a linked-list node point to itself or to a node earlier in the same list? What would happen if you try to display such a list?

18. A doubly linked list has elements that point to both the next element and the previous element. Redo Exercise 16 with a doubly linked list.

19. Write a program to count the occurrences of words in a file. The output is a list of words in decreasing frequency.

20. Follow the arbitrary-list example and establish an arbitrary-queue structure that can be used for a queue of any data items. Supply the operations `make_queue`, `delete_queue`, `enqueue`, `dequeue`, and `is_empty`.

21. Consider the **addr** command discussed in Section 7.6. Write the functions `delete_entry` and `modify_entry` for it.

22. Consider reimplementing the **addr** facility using (a) an array of pointers and (b) a linked list.

23. What happens if you assign the value 2 to a 1-bit bit field? How about the values 3, 4, or –1? What happens when a bit field overflows?

24. Experiment with `signed` bit fields. How are negative values represented? Can you think of a good application for such bit fields?

25. Test the collision rate (crashes per 100 or 1000 random accesses) with a hash table designed as suggested in this chapter.

Performing
Input and Output

Input and output are the most important aspects of a program. Certainly, a program that produces no output is of little use. With few exceptions, a program whose actions are independent of any input is almost as bad.

I/O facilities have been standardized in ANSI C by including I/O library functions as part of the standard library for the language. These functions support I/O streams, which provide buffered I/O channels to files and other I/O devices. The services provided meet most common I/O requirements. To a large degree, programs can stay with the library I/O functions and be made portable to any system that supports ANSI C. We have already seen some library I/O functions. The emphasis here is on formatted input and output, the specification of formats, input/output of arrays and structures, stream creation and manipulation, direct input/output of blocks of bytes, and other functions not covered so far.

8.1   I/O Streams

We know from the first few chapters that to use library I/O functions, a program must include the header file `stdio.h`:

```
#include  <stdio.h>
```

The standard I/O functions support buffered I/O channels known as *streams*. Although the details are implementation-dependent, a typical stream is a structure defined as

```
#define FILE     struct _iobuf

struct   _iobuf
{    int    _cnt;       /*  number of characters in buffer */
     char *_ptr;        /*  current position pointer        */
     char *_base;       /*  start of buffer pointer         */
     int   _bufsiz;     /*  capacity of buffer              */
     short _flag;       /*  error and eof bits              */
     char  _file;       /*  file descriptor                 */
};
```

Identifiers in library facilities usually have a leading underscore character to distinguish them from user-defined variables. It is good practice not to use such variables in your own programs.

When input/output is buffered on a stream, bytes coming in or going out are collected in the intermediate buffer `_base` to be dealt with collec-

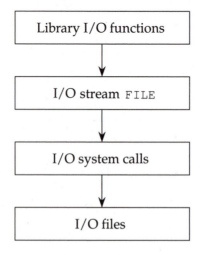

Figure 8.1: StreamI/O Layers

tively rather than individually. For example, an initial **getc** can cause the entire file, or a big chunk of it, to be read into the buffer so that subsequent read operations can simply extract data from the in-memory buffer. Similarly, a **putc** just deposits a character in the buffer. Actual output won't take place until a sufficient number of characters have been accumulated or the buffer is flushed (**fflush**). This buffering substantially reduces I/O overhead and increases efficiency.

The `_file` is a *file descriptor* supported by low-level I/O mechanisms (Section 10.2) supplied by the operating system. Details of the stream structure (`FILE`) are shown here to illustrate how it works, not to encourage accessing its members. In fact, a stream should be manipulated only through calls to routines defined in the standard library (Figure 8.1).

Recall that three preopened streams are standard for each process: `stdin`, `stdout`, and `stderr`. Of these, only `stderr` is not buffered so error messages will be displayed without delay. Other streams to files can be explicitly opened in your program. Some library I/O routines—such as **getchar**, **printf**, and **scanf**—deal with `stdin` and `stdout`. Others, such as **getc**, **fprintf**, and **fscanf**, are called with an argument indicating which I/O stream to use.

8.2 Character and String Input and Output

Tables 8.1 and 8.2 list character and string I/O functions, many of which we have seen already. In these tables, brackets ([ ]) indicate error values returned.

Function	Description
int **getchar**()	Same as **getc**(stdin).
int **putchar**(int c)	Same as **putc**(c, stdout).
int **fgetc**(FILE *stream)	Returns next character of stream as an unsigned char converted to int [EOF].
int **fputc** (int c, FILE *stream)	Writes c out to stream as char and returns c [EOF].

Table 8.1: Character I/O Functions

Function	Description
char ***gets**(char *s)	Reads next line of stdin into s, *replacing terminating* '\n' *with* '\0'; returns s [NULL].
int **puts**(const char *s)	Writes string s to stdout, *replacing terminating* '\0' *with* '\n'; returns nonnegative number [EOF].
char ***fgets**(char *s, int n, FILE *stream)	Reads at most the next n − 1 characters into array s, stopping if a '\n' is encountered; the '\n' is included in the array that is terminated by a '\0'; returns s [NULL].
int **fputs**(const char *s, FILE *stream)	Writes string s to stream; returns a nonnegative number [EOF].

Table 8.2: String I/O Functions

The macro **getc (putc)** is the same as the function **fgetc (fputc)**, except that the macro accesses the stream structure without the extra cost of a function call.

8.3 Formatted Output with printf

The output functions

```
void printf(char *format, arg1, arg2, ...)
void fprintf(FILE *stream, char *format, arg1, arg2, ...)
```

produce output in a user-defined format. These two functions work the same way, except that **printf** assumes stdout. We have used both functions informally; they are described in detail below.

To format output, three pieces of information are needed: the data type of the arguments (arg1, arg2, ...), the exact display representation for each, and the overall form of the output. Based on this information, **printf** will *convert* each argument from its internal representation into a character string and then arrange the output according to the desired format.

The format is a character string consisting of ordinary characters and *conversion modes*. The ordinary characters are copied to the output stream without change, whereas the conversion modes are replaced by the appropriate string forms of arg1, arg2, and so on. There is one conversion mode for each of the zero or more arguments (arg1, arg2, ...).

The simplest form a conversion mode can take is a percent sign (%) followed immediately by a *conversion character*. The familiar modes %s, and %d

Conversion Character	Argument Type	Formatted as
d, i	int	Base 10 number
u	unsigned	Base 10 number
f	double	[–]$m.dddddd$, number of ds given by the precision
s	char *	Characters in a string until ' \0'
c	char	Single character
o	int	Unsigned octal number (no leading zero)
e, E	double	[–]$m.ddd$e±xx or [–]$m.ddd$E±xx
g, G	double	Use %f unless exponent is < -4 or $\geq$ precision
x, X	int	Unsigned hexadecimal (no leading 0x) with a-f or A-F

Table 8.3: Basic **printf** Conversions

are examples. Table 8.3 shows the usual conversion characters. In general, the conversion mode contains several optional entries sandwiched between % and a conversion character c specified in the cryptic form

```
%flagswidth.precisionhlLc
```

without any intervening white space. These options help define the field width, the number of significant digits, the left or right adjustment, padding with spaces or zeros, and so on used for a conversion. A % symbol is always a prefix to a conversion mode unless followed immediately by another %. Thus, a % in the format string as text (not for conversion) is given as %%.

Let's describe each of the available options:

flags   By default the converted argument is displayed right-justified, flush with the right margin in its field width. If the flag – is given, then left justification is used. Table 8.4 shows the available flags. Flags can be given in any order.

width   This is an integer giving the number of character positions allocated. The argument will be displayed in a field at least this wide. If necessary, padding characters (usually white space) are supplied to make up the width.

Flag	Description
–	Left-adjusted in field
+	Display number always with a sign
space	Use a space if first character is not a sign
0:	Padding numbers with leading zeros
#	Alternative format: produce leading 0, 0x, 0X for o, x, X; preserve the decimal point for e, E, f, g, G; trailing zeros not removed for g, G

Table 8.4: **printf** Conversion Flags

.precision   A number preceded by a period specifies the maximum number of characters to be displayed in a string, the number of digits after the decimal point of a floating-point value (default 6), or the minimum number of digits for an integer.

hlL   A single character h, l, or L combines with the conversion character to indicate the argument type to be converted: h for short or unsigned short, l for long or unsigned long, and L for long double.

To provide additional flexibility in formatting, the width and the precision options can also be specified as *. This means the number is supplied by the corresponding argument that must be an integer. For instance,

```
double rate;
int width, precision;
printf("%*.*f", width, precision, rate);
```

will display the double variable rate using width and precision computed in your program at run time.

The **sprintf** function (Section 5.2) uses the same formatting conventions as **printf**.

8.4 Formatted Input with scanf

Similar to **printf**, the input functions

```
int scanf(char *format, ptr1, ptr2, ...)
int fscanf(FILE *stream, char *format, ptr1, ptr2, ...)
```

read characters from the input stream and interpret them according to the given `format`. The input items read will be stored in memory locations specified by the pointer arguments *ptr1*, *ptr2*, and so on. These two functions work the same way, except that **scanf** assumes `stdin`.

The **scanf** format defines the form of the input and how different parts of it are converted into internal data representations such as `int`, `float`, and so on. The `format` is given as a character string consisting of spaces, tabs, ordinary characters, and *conversion modes*. Spaces and tabs in the `format` are ignored. Other characters in the format string must match the next nonwhite characters in the input exactly. (White space in the input includes SPACE, TAB, NEWLINE, RETURN, vertical TAB, and FORMFEED.) A conversion mode specifies the treatment of the next sequence of characters in the input. The result of each conversion is deposited in the memory location given by the corresponding pointer. The total effect is that input, separated by white spaces, is read in correctly and stored in variables.

The simplest form a **scanf** conversion mode can take is a `%` followed immediately by a *conversion character*. The familiar input modes `%d` and `%f` are examples. Table 8.5 shows the usual conversion characters. The general conversion mode may contain several optional entries, sandwiched between `%` and a conversion character *c*,

    %*widthhhlLc

given in order without any intervening white space. To match a percent sign in the input, `%%` is given in the format string. The options are

width This is the number of characters in the input field. The input field for each conversion mode begins with the next nonwhite character in the input stream. The field extends to the next white-space character or until the number of characters reaches the width (if specified). A NEWLINE in the input is simply considered white space.

hlL A single character h, l, or L combines with the conversion character to indicate result data type: h and l may precede d, i, n, o, u, or x to mean `short` and `long`, respectively; whereas, l and L may precede e, f, g to indicate `double` or `long double`, respectively.

* The *skip* indicator, when given, causes the matched conversion field in the input to be skipped over (read but discarded). Thus, use * to ignore certain fields in the input.

The **scanf** function returns when the `format` string is exhausted or when the input fails to match the control information. An integer representing the number of successful conversions is returned. EOF (–1) is returned when the end of the file is reached. Calls to input functions can be mixed, each function picking up the input stream where the previous one left off.

Conversion Character	Pointer Type	Input Data
d	int *	Base 10 number
i	int *	Integer, may be octal (leading zero) or hexadecimal (leading 0x or 0X)
u	unsigned int *	Unsigned base 10 number
o, x e, f, g	int * float *	Octal or hexadecimal with or without prefix float with optional sign, decimal point, and exponent
s	char *	Characters with an added terminator '\0'
c	char *	Characters including white space (default width 1)

Table 8.5: Basic **scanf** Conversions

For example, if the input lines are in the form

```
x    0.0    y    0.0    z    0.0
x    0.5    y    2.5    z    1.0
x    0.8    y    6.4    z    1.6
```

the piece of code

```
float a, b, c;
scanf("x %f y %f z %f", &a, &b, &c);
```

should be used to read each input line.

The **sscanf** function

```
int sscanf(char *s, char *format, ptr1, ptr2, ...)
```

works the same way as **scanf**, except that it takes input from the string s instead.

For some applications, instead of using a complicated **scanf** format, it is more convenient to read a line of input with **gets** (Section 5.3) or readline (Section 2.13) into a string and then use **sscanf** or **strtok** to pick it apart.

We have, in this and Section 8.3, given the basic rules for **printf** and **scanf**. Knowing the rules, however, does not automatically translate into effective use in practice. The additional examples in the following sections should help.

8.5 Array Input and Output _____

Let's first consider the simple task of displaying a two-dimensional array of, say, double-precision floating-point numbers. We want to display the output in a tabular form with aligned rows and columns. For each `double` entry, we elect to use the `%.15e` output format, allowing a total of 16 significant digits, one in front of the decimal point and 15 after. (On 32-bit computers, `double` usually means 16 significant digits.)

The function `display_array` displays a two-dimensional array `x` of dimension $m \times n$:

```
void display_array(double *x,int m,int n)  /* array x of dim m by n */
{ int i, j;
      for ( i = 0 ; i < m ; i++ )           /* (1)                  */
      {   printf("%.15e", x[0]);            /* 1st entry of row      */
          for ( j = 1; j < n; j++ )         /* other entries of row  */
              printf("\t%.15e", x[j]);      /* (2),    \t is tab     */
          printf("\n");                     /* (3)                   */
          x += n;                           /* next row              */

      }

}
```

A `for` loop displays each row of `x` (line 1). To achieve the tabular form, each row is displayed on a different line, and successive entries of the same row are separated by a tab (lines 2 and 3). For example, the array `z`

```
double z[4][3]  =   {{1.0/3.0,  2.0/3.0,  3.0/3.0},
                     {4.0/3.0,  5.0/3.0,  6.0/3.0},
                     {7.0/3.0,  8.0/3.0,  9.0/3.0},
                     {10.0/3.0, 11.0/3.0, 12.0/3.0}} ;
```

can be displayed with the statement

```
display_array(*z, 4, 3);
```

resulting in the following formatted output:

```
3.333333333333333e-01    6.666666666666666e-01    1.000000000000000e+00
1.333333333333333e+00    1.666666666666667e+00    2.000000000000000e+00
2.333333333333333e+00    2.666666666666667e+00    3.000000000000000e+00
3.333333333333333e+00   ·3.666666666666667e+00    4.000000000000000e+00
```

Suppose that the above output is saved in the file `array.data`; we can read the entries into a two-dimensional array again with this function:

```
      void read_array(double *y, int m, int n, FILE *stream)
      { int i;
            for ( i = 0;   i < n*m ; i++ )
                  fscanf(stream, "%le", y + i); /* y+i is a pointer */
      }
```

The library function **fscanf** reads the given `stream`. The `%le` conversion specifies reading of double-precision floats. The successive entries read are stored correctly in the two-dimensional array `y`.

The following routine can test the functions `display_array` and `read_array`:

```
      #include <stdio.h>
      double w[4][3];

      main(int argc, char *argv[])
      { FILE *st = fopen(argv[1],"r");
            read_array(*w, 4, 3, st);
            display_array(*w, 4, 3);
      }
```

After compilation, the command

> **a.out** `array.data`

runs the test program, which should produce the same display as given before.

The above array-input routine is all right if we assume that the program has prior knowledge of the array dimensions. A more flexible arrangement is to record the array dimensions at the beginning of the data file and to have the array-input function allocate a two-dimensional array dynamically (see Section 5.6.1).

The modified input function `input_array` returns a two-dimensional array by reading the input `stream`. The dimensions of the returned array are deposited in the return parameters `m` and `n`:

```
double **input_array(FILE *stream, int *m, int *n)
{ double **arr;
  int i, r, s;
    fscanf(stream, "%d %d", m, n);   /* input array dims         */
    r = *m;                          /* note m and n are pointers */
    s = *n;
 /* dynamic allocation of two-dimensional array */
    arr = (double **) calloc(r, sizeof(double *));          /* (a) */
    arr[0] = (double *) calloc(r*s, sizeof(double));        /* (b) */
```

```
   for (i = 1 ; i < r ; i++)                        /* (c) */
       arr[i] = arr[0] + i * s;
 /* read values into array from stream */
   for (i = 0;  i < r*s ; i++)
       fscanf(stream, "%le", arr[0] + i);
   return(arr);
}
```

The dynamic allocation of an m × n array arr involves allocating space for two sets of array cells: those for arr[i] (line a) and those for arr[i][j] (line b). Also, the array cells arr[0] through arr[m] must be assigned the correct pointer values (line c) (see Section 6.3).

After the creation of arr, its cells can be filled with values read from stream. A similar main function can be used to test input_array:

```
#include <stdio.h>

main(int argc, char *argv[])
{ int m, n;
  FILE *st = fopen(argv[1],"r");
  double **ans = input_array(st, &m, &n);
      display_array(*ans, m, n);
}
```

8.6 Structure Input and Output

Now let's consider input/output of user-defined structures. Consider the structure Name, which we have seen in Chapter 7:

```
#define SSIZE 20
struct name
{       char last[SSIZE];
        char first[SSIZE];
        char mi;
        char title[SSIZE];
};

typedef struct name Name;
```

The display format of a structure depends on the intended purpose. A name can be displayed one way in a list of names and another way as part of an address label. But here we are concerned with an output format that makes it easy to read the structure back into a program again. One approach is to use one line for each individual structure and to separate the structure members with tabs.

For example, the `Name` structure can be written out with the function `display_name`:

```
void display_name(const Name *id)   /* output Name structure */
{    printf("%s\t%s\t", id->last, id->first);
     printf("%c\t%s\n", id->mi, id->title);
}
```

Thus, the statements

```
Name m = {"Smith", "John", 'D', "Mr."};
display_name(&m);
```

will produce this line:

```
Smith    John    D       Mr.
```

This formatted output for `Name`, when stored in a file, can be read back into a program with the function

```
void read_name(Name *id, FILE *stream) /* input Name structure */
{    fscanf(stream, "%s %s %c %s",
             id->last, id->first, &(id->mi), id->title);
         /* note &(id->mi) is a char pointer */
}
```

where `id` points to a `Name` structure supplied by the calling function to be filled in by `read_name`. Alternatively, `read_name` may declare a local structure `Name`, fill it in, and then return it as value.

The method discussed above works well only if the individual data field itself contains no white space. For structures such as an address entry where the street address contains spaces, we must use some other way to separate the structure members in the I/O format. On UNIX systems, common practice is to use the colon (:) as the separator.

Consider input/output involving the structure

```
struct addr
{     char street[4*SSIZE];
      char city[SSIZE];
      char state[SSIZE];
      char zip[SSIZE];
};


typedef struct addr Addr;
```

The function `write_addr` is straightforward. Each `Addr` takes one line, with its members separated by colons:

```
void write_addr(const Addr *add)   /* output Addr structure */
{    printf("%s:%s:", add->street, add->city);
     printf("%s:%s\n", add->state, add->zip);
}
```

Here are a couple of sample output lines:

```
123 Avenue of the Americas:New York City:NY:10036
456 Castro Street:Mountain View:CA:94041
```

A file containing lines formatted this way can be read into `Addr` structures with **fscanf** as shown by the following function:

```
void read_addr(Addr *add, FILE *stream)   /* input Addr structure */
{    fscanf(stream, "%[^:] : %[^:] : %[^:] : %s %*[\n]",   /* (i) */
             add->street, add->city,
             add->state, add->zip);
}
```

The input format specification on (line i) uses two additional **scanf** conversions:

[...]   Reads the longest nonempty input string containing only characters in the set given between the brackets; a terminating '\0' is added.

[^...]   Reads the longest nonempty input string not containing any character in the set given between the brackets; a terminating '\0' is added. (The ^ symbol means *not*.)

Thus, the conversion `%[^:]` gives an input string up to but not including the next : character, and `%*[\n]` consumes and discards the NEWLINE character at the end of an input line.

Here is the way the **scanf** format aligns with an input line:

```
        %[^:]       :         %[^:]     : %[^:] :   %s   %*[\n]
    456 Castro Street : Mountain View :  CA   : 94041   \n
```

Note that this format does not allow any intervening white space between the zip code and the '\n' at the end of a line.

8.7 Standard Operations on Files

In the standard library, some I/O functions such as **getchar** and **printf** assume `stdin` and `stdout`. Other functions such as **fscanf** and **fprintf** use a stream supplied in the argument list. We already know that the functions **fopen** and **fclose** open and close I/O streams to files, respectively. Once

fopen Mode	Meaning
`"r"`	Opens text file for reading.
`"w"`	Opens text file for writing; discards existing contents.
`"a"`	Opens text file for appending at end.
`"r+"`	Opens text file for update (reading and writing).
`"w+"`	Opens text file for update; discards existing contents.
`"a+"`	Opens text file for update; writing at end.

Table 8.6: `fopen` Modes

established, a stream can be passed to other library functions to perform input/output. Moreover, multiple I/O streams can exist at the same time. The maximum number that can be kept at once is system-dependent and is represented by the symbolic constant `FOPEN_MAX` in `stdio.h`.

A file-access mode is specified when a stream is opened (Table 8.6). With the write, append, and update modes, a file is created if it does not already exist. The file is assumed to be a text file unless the mode letter b is given after the initial mode letter (r, w, or a) to indicate a binary file. Input/output with binary files can be very efficient for certain applications, as we will see in Section 8.8. Now let's explain how to use the *update modes*.

File Updating

When the same file is opened for both reading and writing under one of the modes r+, w+, and a+, the file is being updated *in place*. Namely, you are modifying the contents of the file. In performing both reading and writing under the update mode, take care when switching from reading to writing and vice versa. Before switching either way, an **fflush** or a file-positioning function (**fseek**) must be called on the stream. These remarks will become clear as we explain how the update modes work.

The r+ mode is most efficient for making one-for-one character substitutions in a file. Under the r+ mode, file contents stay the same if not explicitly modified. Modification is done by moving a *file-position indicator* (similar to a cursor in a text editor) to the desired location in the file and writing the revised characters over the existing characters already there. A **lowercase** command based on file updating can be implemented using the outline:

1. Open the given file with the r+ mode of **fopen**.
2. Read characters until an uppercase letter is encountered.
3. Overwrite the uppercase letter with the lowercase letter.
4. Repeat steps 2 and 3 until the end of the file is reached.

```
#include <stdio.h>
#include <ctype.h>
#define SEEK_SET 0


int main(int argc, char *argv[])
{ FILE *update;
  int fpos;  /* read or write position in file */
  char c;
      if ( (update = fopen(argv[1], "r+")) == NULL )
      {   fprintf(stderr, "%s: cannot open %s for updating\n",
                          argv[0], argv[1]);
          exit(1);
      }
      while ( (c = fgetc(update)) != EOF )
      {   if ( isupper(c) )
          {   ungetc(c, update);       /* back up one character  (a) */
              fpos = ftell(update);     /* get current position   (b) */
              fseek(update, fpos, SEEK_SET);
                                        /* position for writing   (c) */
              fputc(tolower(c), update);
              fpos = ftell(update);
              fseek(update, fpos, SEEK_SET);
                                        /* position for reading   (d) */
          }
      }
                                /*                              (e) */
      fclose(update);
}
```

After detecting an uppercase character, the file position is on the next character to read. Thus, we need to reposition the write indicator to the previous character in order to overwrite it. Do this by backing up one character with **ungetc** (line a), recording the current position (line b), and setting the write position with **fseek** (line c), before overwriting the uppercase character. Having done that, continue to process the rest of the file. However, set the read position with **fseek** (line d) before switching back to reading again.

The general form of the file-position-setting function **fseek** is

```
int fseek (FILE *stream, long offset, int origin)
```

The **fseek** function normally returns 0, but returns –1 for error. After **fseek** a subsequent read or write will access data beginning at the new position. For a binary file, the position is set to `offset` bytes from the indicated `origin`, which can be one of the symbolic constants

`SEEK_SET` Usually 0: the beginning of the file

`SEEK_CUR` Usually 1: the current position

`SEEK_END` Usually 2: the end of the file

For a text stream, `offset` must be zero or a value returned by **ftell**, which gives the offset of the current position from the beginning of the file.

After the end of the file is reached, any subsequent output will be appended at the end of the file. Thus, if more output statements were given after line e in our example, the output would be appended to the file.

The mode w+ is used for more substantial modifications of a file, especially when parts of the file will be deleted. The file is first wiped clean, allowing you to pick the parts needed to write back out again. The mode a+ gives you the ability to read and write the file, too, but positions the write indicator initially at the end of the file.

Other File Operations

Because the stream provides its own buffering, sometimes there is a need to force any output data that remain in the I/O buffer to be sent out without delay. For this use the function

```
int fflush (FILE *stream)          (flush output stream)
```

This function is not intended to control input buffering.

For I/O redirection, the function

```
#define CSTRING const char *;
FILE *freopen (CSTRING file, CSTRING mode, FILE *stream)
```

connects an existing `stream`, such as `stdin`, `stdout`, or `stderr`, to the given `file`.

There are also operations for erasing and renaming existing files, as well as creating temporary files. The functions

```
int remove (CSTRING filename);                    (erase file)
int rename (CSTRING oldname, CSTRING newname);     (rename file)
```

are handy in many situations. Both **remove** and **rename** return nonzero upon failure.

On UNIX, because there is a **rename** system call, the C library routine of the same name may be implemented identically. Also, the system call **unlink** (Section 10.3) can be used instead of **remove** to erase a file.

In using a temporary file, we must employ a filename that does not conflict with existing files. The library function

    char *tmpnam (char *nambuf)   (make temporary filename)

creates a filename distinct from all existing names and deposits it in the nambuf character array, which should be created with

    char nambuf[L_tmpnam];

where the length L_tmpnam is a library-defined symbolic constant. (The maximum length of a filename allowable is kept in FILENAME_MAX.) To get a temporary file without bothering with a filename, use the library function **tmpfile**

    FILE *tmpfile (void)   (create temporary file stream)

which requires no arguments and returns a temporary stream opened with mode wb+. Note that a binary file can be used as a text file, but not vice versa. The temporary file associated with it is automatically removed when the temporary stream is closed.

8.8 Binary Input and Output

It is usual to think of input/output as dealing with a sequence of characters. However, performing *binary* input/output where you deal with bytes rather than characters is also possible. With binary input/output, you can take a block of consecutive memory locations—for example, an entire array or structure—and write it out, byte for byte, into a file for later retrieval. A binary file contains arbitrary bytes and usually cannot be examined or edited with a text editor. However, it is the most efficient way of reading and writing large amounts of data.

Standard library functions for binary input/output are

    size_t fread (void *ptr, size_t s, size_t n, FILE *stream)
    size_t fwrite (void *ptr, size_t s, size_t n, FILE *stream)

where ptr points to the data area in main memory, s is the size (in bytes) of a binary object, and n is the number of such objects to read in or write out. To illustrate binary input/output, let's look at the function write_obj, which writes an arbitrary object *x of size bytes into a new binary file name:

```
/* output object in binary */
int write_obj(void *x, size_t size, CSTRING name)
{ FILE *stream;
  int flag = 0;
    if ( (stream = fopen(name, "wb")) == NULL )
                                        /* binary write mode      */
    {   fprintf(stderr, "cannot open %s for writing\n", name);
        exit(1);
    }
    fwrite(x, size, 1, stream);
    if ( ferror(stream) ) flag = -1;   /* in case fwrite fails   */
    fclose(stream);
    return(flag);
}
```

This routine simply opens the target binary file for writing, calls **fwrite** to output the object, and then closes the file. The mode `"wb"` opens a binary file for writing. The library function **ferror** (Section 9.5) detects I/O error status.

Similarly, a binary object can be read in from a file:

```
/* input object in binary */
int read_obj(void *x, size_t size, CSTRING name)
{ FILE *stream;
  int flag = 0;
    if ( (stream = fopen(name, "rb")) == NULL )
    {   fprintf(stderr, "cannot open %s\n", name);
        exit(1);
    }
    fread(x, size, 1, stream);
    if ( ferror(stream) ) flag = -1;
    fclose(stream);
    return(flag);
}
```

To experiment with these functions, try to output the array

```
double xx[12] = {1.0/3.0, 2.0/3.0, 3.0/3.0,
                 4.0/3.0, 5.0/3.0, 6.0/3.0,
                 7.0/3.0, 8.0/3.0, 9.0/3.0,
                 10.0/3.0, 11.0/3.0, 12.0/3.0};
```

as a single binary object and then read it back in again with the following `main` program:

```
#include <stdio.h>
#include <stddef.h>

main(int argc, String argv[])
{ double yy[12];
      printf("Array xx\n");
      display_array(xx, 4, 3);
      write_obj(xx, 12*sizeof(double), argv[1]);
      read_obj(yy, 12*sizeof(double), argv[1]);
      printf("Array yy\n");
      display_array(yy, 4, 3);
}
```

Because no number-to-string conversion is done and all bytes are treated at once, the I/O operations are very efficient.

Structures can be handled just as easily. Consider a `Name` structure:

```
Name m = {"Smith", "John", 'D', "Mr."};
```

You can write out its binary image with

```
write_obj(&m, sizeof(m), "filename");
```

or read it back in with

```
Name n;
read_obj(&n, sizeof(n), "filename");
```

More complicated constructs, such as an array of names, can also be written out as a single binary unit.

Although efficient, binary input/output has its limitations. A binary file is system-dependent and usually cannot be moved to a different computer and be useful. Even on the same computer, a binary file can be used only by a program written in the same language that knows its data type. Furthermore, structures such as linked lists that contain pointers cannot use binary input/output because the pointers will be wrong when they are read back in again.

8.9 Summary

The standard C library provides many functions for input/output. These functions support buffered I/O streams and are standard on systems supporting ANSI C. The library provides most commonly required operations including character, string, and binary input/output.

In addition, input/output with (**printf** and **scanf**) allows you to display and read information in a user-designed format. You specify the I/O format with a format string argument containing fixed and variable parts (conversions). File-based and in-memory counter parts of these functions exist (**fprintf**, **fscanf**, **sprintf**, **sscanf**). You can also use formatted input/output to save arrays and structures in files, which can be read back into a program later.

Besides the standard I/O streams supplied automatically for each running program, you can open your own streams to read, write, and update files with the **fopen** function. With the update mode, you can perform both read and write operations on a file and move the position of reading or writing with the **fseek** call. Other file operations include **fclose** (close a stream), **fflush** (empty the buffer of an output stream), **remove** (delete a file), **rename** (change the name of a file), **freopen** (redirect input/output), and **tmpfile** (create a temporary file).

The functions **fread** and **fwrite** support direct binary input/output to read/write a block of consecutive bytes. With binary input/output you have the ability to write out the memory image of arbitrary-data structures into a file and later retrieve them directly. Although efficient, binary I/O operations are usually limited to data, containing no pointers, that are used on the same system.

Exercises _____

1. What happens if you forget to supply enough arguments as required by a **printf** format string? What would `printf("%d\n");` do? Why?

2. Try using **getc** and **scanf** in turn to read from the same input stream. Are there any ill effects?

3. Add to the `make_month` program in Section 6.8 a display function in a monthly calendar form.

4. In displaying a table involving a column containing dollar amounts, usually all decimal points line up for easy reading. Try to format such a column of dollar amounts with **printf**.

5. Write a function to read input from a file of lines containing integers separated by white space. Arrange it to read only the second, fourth, and seventh number on each line.

6. Write a program that, when given an uppercase or lowercase letter, will display on the screen the same letter in BIG poster-style format.

7. Consider the **sprintf** function, the **strcat** function, and the # concatenation mechanism of the CPP. Compare their capabilities and usage.

8. Write a UNIX command **append** that takes two files and appends the second file to the end of the first one using the a+ file mode.

9. Consider updating a file with the r+ mode. Is it possible for the file to become longer? Shorter? Why?

10. Explain why binary input/output is more efficient than formatted input/output.

11. Add to the address-book example (adbook) in Section 7.6 the necessary I/O routines to establish the UNIX command **addr** described in that section.

12. How would you use binary input/output to write out a linked list? You must overcome the problems that the list elements may not be stored consecutively in memory and that, when reading back, the pointer values (the next fields) are incorrect.

13. The standard library functions **setbuf** and **setvbuf** control the buffering of a stream after it is opened and before actual input/output takes place. You may choose full buffering, line buffering, or no buffering. Find out how this works on your system and write a test program to make output to stdout unbuffered.

14. Write a UNIX command **fil**. The usage synopsis is

   fil [*from*] [*to*]

   to transform text from the named file *from* to the named file *to*. If only one file argument is supplied, it is assumed to be the from file. If no file argument is supplied, **fil** uses stdin and stdout. The **fil** command works as follows:

   a. All tabs are replaced by an equivalent number of spaces.
   b. All trailing blanks at the end of each line are removed.
   c. All lines longer than 80 or 132 characters are folded.
   d. A FORMFEED is added for every 66 lines from the previous FORMFEED.
   e. Each control character is converted into two characters: ^ followed immediately by an uppercase character. For example, control-Z becomes the two-character sequence ^Z.
   f. All BACKSPACE and nonprinting characters are removed.

   The choice of the length of each line can be specified as an option (the fold option) on the command line. This filter simulates the transformations that a real line-printer output program performs.

Error Handling and Debugging

After the initial coding, a program is usually still a long way from being fully operational. Program errors, or *bugs*, must be corrected through testing and debugging. The program must also be made robust by including codes that handle many unexpected error situations at run time.

The two broad categories of program errors are compile-time error and run-time error. The former is due to syntax problems that prevent a program from compiling successfully. The C compiler usually provides enough information for you to locate syntax errors. The latter is due to various causes including incorrect logic, overflow, input-data inconsistencies, mistyping == as =, array elements out of range, dangling pointers, and interrupts.

Debugging, finding and fixing bugs, is a significant and integral part of programming. Beginners find debugging difficult, especially for run-time errors. We introduce effective techniques and easy-to-follow rules to make testing and debugging easier. We also introduce **dbx**, an interactive debugging facility popular on UNIX systems. Example debugging sessions illustrate the use of **dbx**.

We also describe the treatment of failed calls to system or library functions at run time and present ways to react and/or recover from such errors.

An *interrupt* is not necessarily an error but an unpredictable event outside of a running program. An interrupt requires the immediate attention of the program or its termination. Such situations include illegal memory references, arithmetic overflow, and user-generated interrupts from the keyboard. We also describe the way UNIX handles interrupts and how you can build into your program reactions to such events.

9.1   Debugging with dbx

Although the C compiler identifies problems at the syntax level, you still need a good tool for debugging at run time. The **dbx** facility is a convenient UNIX utility for source-level debugging and controlled execution of programs. It can be used to debug programs written in any source language such as C, FORTRAN 77, or Pascal, provided that the object files have been compiled to contain the appropriate symbol information for use by **dbx**. On some UNIX workstations, you may find **dbx** available inside a window-menu-oriented debugging package that supplies multiple windows and other useful features for easier debugging. The **dbxtool** on SUN systems is an example.

Other common debuggers include **sdb** and **adb**. These are generally not as easy to use as **dbx**. We describe how to use **dbx** to debug C programs. Once learned, **dbx** should be used as a routine tool for debugging programs. It is much more efficient than inserting **fprintf** lines in the source code. Although not in the scope of this book, the tool can be used in the same way for FORTRAN 77 and Pascal programs.

9.1.1   Interactive Debugging

The **dbx** facility provides an interactive debugging environment and correlates run-time activities to statements in the program source codes. This is why it is called a source-level debugger. Debugging is performed by running the target program under the control of the **dbx** utility. The main features of **dbx** are as follows:

1. Source-level tracing: When a part of a program is *traced*, useful information will be displayed whenever that part is executed. If you trace a function, the name of the calling function, the value of the arguments passed, and the return value will be displayed each time the traced function is called. You can also trace specific lines of code and individual variables. In the latter case, you'll be notified every time the variable value changes.
2. Placing source-level break points: A break point in a program causes execution to suspend when that point is reached. At the break point, you can interact with **dbx** and use its full set of commands to investigate the situation before resuming execution.

3. Single-source-line stepping: When you are examining a section of code closely, you can have execution proceed one source line at a time. (*Note*: One line may consist of several machine instructions.)
4. Displaying source code: You can ask **dbx** to display any part of the program source from any file.
5. Examining values: Values, declarations, and other attributes of identifiers can also be displayed.
6. Editing source files: If you want to correct an error, you can edit source-code files (for later recompilation) from within **dbx**.
7. Object-level debugging: Machine instruction-level execution control and displaying of memory contents or register values are also provided.

To debug a C program using **dbx**, make sure each object file has been compiled with the -g and loaded with the -lg option to **ld**. One simple way to achieve this is to compile all source-code (.c) files at once using the command

    cc -g *source_ files*

This results in an executable a.out file suitable to run under the control of **dbx**. Thus, to use **dbx** on lowercase.c (Section 10.2), first prepare it by using

    cc -g lowercase.c -o lowercase

Then, to invoke **dbx**, simply type

    dbx lowercase

to debug the named executable file. If no file is given, a.out is assumed. When you see the prompt (dbx), the debugger is ready for an interactive session. When you are finished, simply type the **dbx** command **quit** to exit from **dbx**.

A typical debugging session should follow these steps:

1. Invoke **dbx** on an executable file compiled with the -g option.
2. Put in trace and/or break points.
3. Run the program under **dbx**.
4. Examine trace output and display program values at break points.
5. Install new trace and/or break points to discover the bug, deleting old trace and/or break points as appropriate.
6. Resume or restart execution.
7. Repeat steps 4-7 until satisfied.

Having an idea of what **dbx** can do, we are now ready to look at the actual commands provided by **dbx**.

9.1.2 Basic dbx Commands

As a debugging tool, **dbx** provides a rich set of commands. The most often used ones are presented in this section. These should be sufficient for all but the most obscure bugs. The complete set of commands are listed in the **dbx** manual.

To begin execution of the target program within **dbx**, use

(dbx) **run** [*args*] [< *file1*] [> *file2*]   (start execution in **dbx**)

where *args* are any command-line arguments needed by the binary file. It is also permitted to use > and < for I/O redirection. If lowercase is being debugged, then

(dbx) **run** < *input_file* > *output_file*

makes sense.

But before running the program, you may wish to put in traces first. Table 9.1 lists commands for tracing.

In Table 9.1, *exp* can be any valid C expression, allowing you to compute the value of any expression at specific points of the program to help debugging. Lines are specified by line numbers, which can be displayed by the commands in Table 9.2.

Command	Function
trace *line*	Traces execution of the *line*.
trace *function*	Traces calls to *function*.
trace *fun1* **in** *fun2*	Traces calls to *fun1* only inside *fun2*.
trace *var*	Traces changes to *variable*.
trace *exp* **at** *line*	Displays expression when *line* is reached.

Table 9.1: **dbx** Trace Commands

Command	Function
list	Lists the next 10 lines.
list *line1, line2*	Lists the range of lines.
list *function*	Lists a few lines before and after *function*.

Table 9.2: **dbx** Listing Commands

Command	Function
stop at *line*	Suspends execution at *line*.
stop in *function*	Suspends execution just after *function* is called.
stop *var*	Suspends execution if *var* is changed.
print *exp*	Displays the value of *expression*.
cont	Continues execution from where it stopped.

Table 9.3: **dbx** Break-Point Commands

Break points can be associated with line numbers, functions, or variables. Table 9.3 lists commands for break points.

After reaching a break point, you may also single-step source lines with **step** (execute the next source line) and **next** (execute up to the next source line). The difference between **step** and **next** is that if the line contains a call to a function, **step** will stop at the beginning of that function block but **next** will not. You can also use

> **where** [n]

to display the current line number and the sequence of all or the n most recent function calls (on the function-call stack) that led control flow to this break point. If n is not given, the entire stack will be displayed.

As debugging progresses, trace and break points are put in and taken out to localize the bug. Commands to put in trace and break points have been given. For removal, use the command

> **delete** *number*   (remove trace or break point)

to deactivate the trace or break point identified by the *sequence number*. A sequence number is displayed by **dbx** after each **trace** or **stop** command. If you do not remember the numbers, enter

> **status**   (display active trace and break points)

to display all trace and break points currently in effect.

Finally, the command

> **whatis** *name*

displays the declared type of the named identifier.

9.1.3 A Sample Debugging Session with dbx

Let's show a complete debugging session of another version of the lower-case program (Section 10.2), which uses the read and write system calls.

```c
#include <stdio.h>
#include <ctype.h>
#define BUFSIZ 1024

int main(int argc, char *argv[])
{ char buffer[BUFSIZ];
  int nc;                          /* number of characters */
      while (( nc = read(0, buffer, BUFSIZ)) > 0 )
      {    lower(buffer,nc);
           nc = write(1, buffer, nc);
           if ( nc == -1 ) break;
      }
      if ( nc == -1 )      /* read or write failed */
      {    perror(argv[0]);
           exit(1);
      }
      return(0);                   /* normal termination */
}

int lower(char *buf, int length)
{     while ( length-- > 0 )
      {    if ( isupper(*buf) ) *buf = tolower( *buf );
           buf++;
      }
      return(0);
}
```

We now show how **dbx** is used to control the execution of this program. User input is shown after the prompt (dbx). Output from **dbx** is indented. First, compile lowercase.c for debugging and invoke **dbx**:

cc -g lowercase.c -o lowercase
dbx lowercase

Here is the greeting from **dbx** when it starts:

dbx version 5.10
Type 'help' for help.
reading symbolic information ...

Now interact with **dbx**. The **dbx** commands are given on lines with the (dbx) prompt.

```
(dbx) list lower        (display source listing around function lower)
   17              }
   18              return(0);        /* normal termination */
   19    }
   20
   21    int lower(char *buf, int length)
   22    {       while ( length-- > 0 )
   23            {    if ( isupper(*buf) ) *buf = tolower( *buf );
   24                 buf++;
   25            }
   26            return(0);
   27    }
(dbx) trace read        (trace system call read)
   [1] trace read
(dbx) trace write
   [2] trace write
(dbx) trace lower       (trace function lower)
   [3] trace lower
(dbx) stop in lower
   [4] stop in lower            (break point)
(dbx) run < file1 > file2       (run program)
   %2  calling read() from function main
   %2  returning 20 from read
   %2  calling lower (buf = "Now Is The Time For\n", length = 20)
              from function main
   %2  Stopped at breakpoint 4 in lower at line 22
       22   {        while ( length-- > 0 )
(dbx) where         (display function-call stack)
       lower(buf = "Now Is The Time For\n", length = 20),
                  line 22 in "lowercase.c"
       main(argc = 1, argv = 0xfff314, 0xfff31c),
                  line 10 in "lowercase.c"
(dbx) whatis buf
   char *buf;
(dbx) step         (single stepping)
   %2  Stopped after step in lower at line 23
       23            {    if ( isupper(*buf) )
(dbx) print *buf     (display info)
   'N'
(dbx) step
   %2  Stopped after step in lower at line 24
       24                       *buf = tolower( *buf );
```

```
(dbx) step
   %2  Stopped after step in lower at line 25
      25                  buf++;
(dbx) print *buf
   'n'
(dbx) delete 4       (remove break point 4)
(dbx) delete 3       (remove trace 3)
(dbx) status         (what trace and break points are left)
   [1] trace read
   [2] trace write
(dbx) cont           (resume execution)
   %2  returning 0 from lower
   %2  calling write() from function main
   %2  returning 20 from write
   %2  calling read() from function main
   %2  returning 0 from read
   %2  Stopped by Exit in _exit at 0x13a5

(dbx) quit           (exit from dbx)
```

The prefix %2 displayed before trace output lines indicates the *child number* of child processes (lowercase) under the control of **dbx** as we see in Section 9.1.4.

9.1.4 Advanced dbx Usage

After getting to know the basic commands, you are ready to explore the full power of **dbx**. Any of the previously listed trace and stop commands can be followed by

> **if** *condition*

making the tracing and breaking actions effective only if *condition*, given in C syntax, is satisfied. It is also possible to have a *location-independent* break point

> **stop if** *condition*

which suspends execution as soon as the given condition becomes true. For instance, use

> **stop if** queue_length > 100

to get a break in execution when the global variable queue_length becomes larger than 100.

You can also specify **dbx** commands to be executed when a certain condition is true. The commands

when in *function* { *command;* ... }
when *at* *line* { *command;* ... }
when *condition* { *command;* ... }

execute the **dbx** command(s) when `function` is called, `line` is reached, or *condition* is true.

At a break point, you can also invoke any function directly to examine its behavior. To do this, use the command

call *function* (...)   (call function from **dbx**)

to execute the named function. Of course, you must supply the correct arguments so that **dbx** can pass them to the function. In specifying the arguments, use expressions that are constants, variables in the program, or these combined by operators (with C syntax, of course). Depending on the sophistication of your version of **dbx**, other expressions may also be allowed.

Using

dump *function*   (display values related to function)

to display the names and values of local variables and parameters in the current or specified *function* is also possible. Having stopped at the function `lower`, you can enter **dump** and see something like

```
lower(buf = "ABcd EFGH\nIj kL\n", length = 16),
        line 22 in "lowercase.c"
```

Using

set *var* = *expression*

to remember the value of *expression* in a variable for later use is also possible. Again, at the `lower` break point, enter

set n = length
set string = buf
print string

Later the variables `length` and `string` can be used, for example, in a **call** command.

The **dbx** utility also provides a feature similar to job control in the shell. At a break point, you may start another run of the program and therefore create other child processes, which can be controlled in the same way. The command **ps** displays all currently active processes under **dbx** together with their assigned ID numbers. You can also switch between these child processes using the %i command where i is the child ID number.

9.2 Examining Core Dumps

In our preceding example, there were no errors. When your executable program encounters an error, a core-dump file is usually produced. This file, named `core` by default, is a copy of the memory image of your running program taken right after the error. Examining the core dump is like investigating the scene of a crime; the clues are all there if you can figure out what they mean. A core dump is also produced if a process receives certain signals. For example, you can cause a core dump by pressing the quit character (^\) on the keyboard.

The creation of a `core` file may also be controlled by limitations set in your shell. Typing the *csh* command **limit** will display any limits set under that shell. A core dump larger than `coredumpsize` will not be produced. In particular,

> **limit** `coredumpsize 0`

prevents core dumps all together.

If there is a `core` file in the current directory when you invoke **dbx** on the executable file, the information provided by that `core` is also read in for you to examine. The executable file that resulted in the `core` file need not have been compiled with the -g flag as long as the executable file passed to **dbx** was.

Among other things, two pieces of important information are preserved in a core dump: the last line executed and the function-call stack at the time of core dump. Immediately after invoking **dbx**, issue a **list** command to see what the last line was. Also, by giving the **where** command, you can see the sequence of function calls leading up to the error.

Let's look at an example. Consider the following code in file `sample.c`:

```
#include <stdio.h>

int main()
{ int i = 0;
  int a[10];
      while ( i <= 10 )
          a[i++] = -1;
      printf("after while\n");
}
```

If you compile and run this file, you'll find that it takes forever and the program is most likely stuck in some kind of infinite loop. But the only loop is the `while`, and it does not seem to be obviously wrong. So press ^\ to produce a core file and use **dbx** to look into the problem:

cc -g sample.c
dbx a.out

Then perform a debugging session like the following:

```
dbx version 5.10
Type 'help' for help.
reading symbolic information ...
[using memory image in core]

(dbx) list
    7                    a[i++] = -1;
    8              printf("after while\n");
    9   }
(dbx) print i
    9
(dbx) trace 7
    [1]  at 7
(dbx) trace i
    [2] trace i in main
(dbx) run
    %2  initially (at line 4 in "sample.c"):   i = 0
    %2  trace:       7              a[i++] = -1;
    %2  after line 7 in "sample.c":   i = 1
    %2  trace:       7              a[i++] = -1;
    %2  after line 7 in "sample.c":   i = 2
    %2  trace:       7              a[i++] = -1;
    %2  after line 7 in "sample.c":   i = 3
    %2  trace:       7              a[i++] = -1;
    %2  after line 7 in "sample.c":   i = 4
    %2  trace:       7              a[i++] = -1;
    %2  after line 7 in "sample.c":   i = 5
    %2  trace:       7              a[i++] = -1;
    %2  after line 7 in "sample.c":   i = 6
    %2  trace:       7              a[i++] = -1;
    %2  after line 7 in "sample.c":   i = 7
    %2  trace:       7              a[i++] = -1;
    %2  after line 7 in "sample.c":   i = 8
    %2  trace:       7              a[i++] = -1;
    %2  after line 7 in "sample.c":   i = 9
    %2  trace:       7              a[i++] = -1;
    %2  after line 7 in "sample.c":   i = 10
    %2  trace:       7              a[i++] = -1;
```

```
        %2   after line 7 in "sample.c":    i = 0        (aha !!)
        %2   trace:      7            a[i++] = -1;
^C
        %2   Stopped by Interrupt in main at line 7
(dbx) quit
```

Clearly, it was looping infinitely, and the execution had to be stopped inside **dbx** by ^C.

The trace also shows that the variable i became 0 after reaching 10. Looking closer at the while, note that the program goes beyond the last element a[9] and the assignment to a[10] actually changes the value of i! The bug is due to the common mistake of going over the declared bounds of the array subscript. The fix is simple: Change <= to < in the while condition.

When debugging, be on the lookout for any behavior or value that you do not expect based on your program. Find out why it has deviated, and you'll find your bug.

9.3   Instruction-Level Debugging

The **dbx** debugger also provides a set of commands to perform machine-instruction-level debugging. Capabilities provided include tracing and breaking at an instruction address, single machine-instruction stepping, and displaying contents of memory in designated formats. For example,

> **tracei** *address*   (trace instruction at address)

puts a trace on the instruction at the given address, and

> **stopi** *address*   (break point at address)

puts a break point at the machine address.

To display contents of memory locations, use the **dbx** commands

```
/ [count] [format]
address / [count] [format]
address1 , address2/ [format]
```

The contents of memory are displayed starting at the first address and continuing up to the second address or until *count* items are displayed. The *count* and *format* are optional arguments. The default count is 1. The default format is the current format, the one used most recently. The initial format is X (hexadecimal). If no address is specified, the *current address* (following the one displayed most recently) is used.

The single-letter *format* specifies how memory is to be displayed. If it is omitted, the previous format specified is used. Table 9.4 lists the format letters.

Letter	Display Format
i	Machine instruction
s	A null-terminated character string
d, (D)	Short (long) word in decimal
o, (O)	Short (long) word in octal
x, (X)	Short (long) word in hexadecimal
b, (c)	Byte in octal (as character)
f, (g)	Single- (double-) precision real number

Table 9.4: **dbx** Memory-Display Formats

Symbolic addresses are specified by preceding the variable name with an &. An address can also be an expression involving other addresses and +, -, and indirection (unary *). Registers are given as $rN where N is the register number. Refer to the **dbx** manual for more details on instruction-level debugging commands.

9.4 Toward Bug-Free Programs

Unless and until such time when a program can be rigorously proven correct, a certain amount of doubt always exists about whether the program is completely bug-free. The best we can do is to use sound programming techniques and to test the program thoroughly. We present here some rules of thumb to better construct and test programs.

9.4.1 Good Programming Practices

No amount of testing and debugging can turn a badly written program into a good one. So the emphasis should be on how to *write* programs that are less likely to have problems rather than on techniques for debugging. This is not to say that the latter is not important. Furthermore, good programming practice can result not only in fewer bugs but also lower maintenance cost.

In this section, we list helpful conventions and programming techniques found to be valuable for improved program structure and reliability.

1. Avoid writing lengthy functions. Opinions vary, but, in general, any function over one page is too long. Break down large functions into smaller routines that perform well-defined tasks. Use reasonably descriptive names for functions. Use comments before a function to document the meaning of the arguments and the purpose of the function. Use a comment after a larger function to mark its end. If the function implements an algorithm, include a brief description or give a reference.

2. Always declare the result type of functions that return a noninteger result. Use an explicit return statement in each function.

3. Avoid numerical constants in your source program. Use symbolic constants for buffer and table sizes, etc.

4. Functions should check their input parameters for correctness.

5. Always check the returned value of system and library calls for possible errors.

6. Use `typedef` to simplify declarations. Keep structure definitions in header files. Avoid duplicate copies of declarations.

7. Always guard against potential overflow and underflow problems in arithmetic operations.

8. Avoid complicated macros; use functions instead.

9. For system-level programs, always pay attention to how signals and interrupts (Section 9.7) should be handled.

10. Practice data abstraction and procedure encapsulation by grouping data structures and their manipulation routines. Outside functions use the data structure only through functions provided and declared in the associated header file.

11. Use the `static` declaration to keep in-file identifiers from conflicting with outside global names.

12. Keep related routines in one source file; keep logically related source (and object) files in the same subdirectory. Establish a *makefile* for each subdirectory (see Chapter 11).

9.4.2 Testing and Debugging Hints

You already know that functions are the basic building blocks of a C program. A very effective programming technique is to break down the solution of a problem into major steps, each performing a particular task or achieving a specific goal. Each such step is then broken down in the same way until the subgoals are easily implemented. Therefore, well-written programs usually consist of many small functions organized in several files rather than a few big functions in one file.

The individual functions are usually tested separately, and then each file is tested in isolation. After that, the overall program is tested.

1. In testing each function, be sure to supply different kinds of input parameters including extreme cases such as empty strings, zero, negative, very small or large values, and so on.

2. When testing individual functions or small modules that are not self-sufficient, write simple main functions and supply *stubs* for other routines not written or tested yet. Suppose that the functions being tested need to call a random number generator and one has not been written yet. Write a two-line function that will always return, say, 13 to serve as a stub for the random number generator. This technique allows you to better test parts of your program separately.

3. When you do find something wrong, first simplify the test data. This involves trying simpler variations of the test data that produced the error until you get one or a few data sets that all cause the same problem. This usually gives you much more information about the possible nature of the bug as well as which part of your program might be at fault.

4. Armed with a few simple test cases that cause the bug, now isolate it. Through **dbx** (use **where** on a core dump) or some other means, find the sequence of function calls leading to the misbehavior and find (a) the first such function call that is passed with incorrect arguments or (b) a function that produces a wrong answer for the given input. Case (a) means the bug happened before the call and (b) after.

5. In some situations, a program has to run for a long time before reaching the bug. This makes debugging very time-consuming. One way to speed up things is to get into case (b) and record the argument values. Now hunt for the bug by calling a function much closer to the bug with the required arguments. Much time can be saved.

6. In tracing your program, avoid producing voluminous output, which tends to be overwhelming. Rather, select carefully where to put a few traces and move them up or down the chain of function calls to isolate the bug.

7. Some beginners have the tendency to blame the computer for troubles with their program. This is usually wrong. Although it can happen that your bug is due to the compiler or the operating system, don't bet on it.

8. Statistically, most bugs are due to typing errors. Variable and function names can be incorrectly entered. Some typing errors are easier to spot than others. Especially difficult are letters and numbers that look alike (0, O; 1, l) and characters that are not visible (SPACE, TAB, NEWLINE, etc.).

9. Design and implement the code for easy testing. Test individual modules separately. Keep test cases in files and eventually build complete test suites.

10. Finally, some frequent causes of bugs are array index out of bounds, unintended side effects, use of uninitialized variables, case fall-through in a `switch`, problems with indirection or pointers, reversed logic in conditions, and macros that produce incorrect code after substitution.

9.5   Failed System and Library Calls

Standard library functions such as **fopen**, **fclose**, and **remove** return standard error values when they fail. The error indication returned has to be consistent with the return-value type declared for the function. At the same time, the error value must not be anything the function would ever return without failure. For library functions, the standard error values are

EOF   The error value `EOF`, usually –1, is used by functions normally returning a nonnegative integer.

NULL   The error value `NULL`, usually 0, is used by functions normally returning a valid pointer (nonzero).

Nonzero   A nonzero error value is used for a function that normally returns 0.

Again, it is up to your program to check for such a returned value and take appropriate actions. The following idiom is in common use:

```
if ( (value = call(...)) == errvalue )
{   /* handle error here        */
    /* output any error message to stderr */
}
```

Failed UNIX *system calls*, calls to routines contained in the UNIX system, return similar standard errors –1, 0, and so on.

To properly handle system and library-call errors, include the header file `errno.h`:

```
#include <errno.h>
```

This header file defines symbolic error numbers and their associated *standard error messages*. For UNIX systems, Table 9.5 lists some of these quantities. The external variable `errno` is set to one of these error numbers after a system or library-call failure, but it is *not* cleared after a successful call. This variable is available for your program to examine. Use the system/library call

perror(const char *s)

Number	Name	Message
1	EPERM	Not owner
2	ENOENT	No such file or directory
3	ESRCH	No such process
4	EINTR	Interrupted system call
5	EIO	I/O error
6	ENXIO	No such device or address
		. . .
64	ENOTEMPTY	Directory not empty

Table 9.5: UNIX System Errors

to display the standard error message. The call **perror**(s) outputs to standard error

1. The argument string s.
2. The colon (:) character.
3. The standard error message associated with the current value of errno.
4. A '\n'.

The string argument given to **perror** is usually argv[0] or that plus the function name detecting the error. We will see some examples of **perror** in Section 10.2.

Displaying a variant of the standard error message sometimes is desirable. For this purpose, the error messages can be retrieved through the standard library function

> char **strerrpr**(int n)   (obtain error message string)

which returns a pointer to the error string associated with error n. Also, error and end-of-file (eof) indicators are associated with each I/O stream. Standard I/O library functions set these indicators when error or end of file occurs. These status indicators can be tested or set explicitly in your program with the library functions

> int **ferror**(FILE *stream)   Returns true (nonzero) if error indicator is set for stream.

```
int feof(FILE *stream)
```
Returns true if eof indicator is set for stream.

```
void clearerr(FILE *stream)
```
Clears both eof and error indicators of the stream.

We have seen the use of **ferror** to check the stream error status after using **fwrite** in performing binary input/output (Section 8.8).

9.5.1 Error Indications from Mathematical Functions

The standard mathematical functions (Chapter 5 and Appendix 11) also use the variable `errno` to indicate domain and range errors. A *domain error* occurs if a function is passed an argument whose value is outside the valid interval for the particular function. For example, only positive arguments are valid for the **log** function. A *range error* occurs when the computed result is so large or small that it cannot be represented as a `double`.

When a domain error happens, `errno` is set to `EDOM`, a symbolic constant defined in `errno.h`, and the returned value is implementation-dependent. On the other hand, when a range error takes place, `errno` is set to `ERANGE`, and either zero (underflow) or `HUGE_VAL` (overflow) is returned.

9.6 Error Recovery

A run-time error can be treated in one of three ways:

- Exiting: Displays an appropriate error message and terminates the execution of the program.
- Returning: Returns to the calling function with a well-defined error value.
- Recovery: Transfers control to a known point of the program in order to continue execution.

We have seen the first two before. The third way, error recovery, is typified by such programs as **vi**, which returns to its top level when errors occur. Such transfer of control is usually from a point in one function to a point much earlier in the program in a different function. Such *nonlocal*-control transfer cannot be achieved with a goto statement, which only works inside a function. The two standard library routines **setjmp** and **longjmp** are provided for nonlocal jumps. To use these routines, include the header file `setjmp.h`:

```
#include <setjmp.h>
```

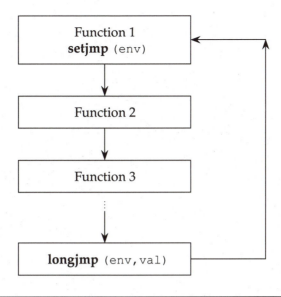

Figure 9.1: A Long Jump

The routine **setjmp**

> int **setjmp**(jmp_buf env)   (set up **longjmp** position)

saves key data defining the current program state in the buffer env for possible later use by **longjmp**. The value returned by the initial call to **setjmp** is zero. The routine **longjmp** uses the saved env to throw control flow back to the **setjmp** statement:

> void **longjmp**(jmp_buf env, int val)   (jump to **setjmp**)

When called with a saved env and an integer val (must be nonzero), **longjmp** will restore the saved state env and cause execution to resume as if the original **setjmp** call has just returned the value val. For this *backtracking* to happen correctly, **longjmp** must be called from a function in a sequence of nested function calls leading from the function that invoked **setjmp** (Figure 9.1). In other words, **setjmp** establishes env as a nonlocal goto label, and **longjmp** is used to transfer control back to the point marked by env.

After the **longjmp** operation, all accessible global and local data have values as of the time when **longjmp** was called. The ANSI standard states that data values are not saved by the **setjmp** call.

Because of the way it works, **setjmp** can be used either alone or inside the test-condition part of if, switch, while, and so on. In a test condition, **setjmp** can be used only in a simple relational expression.

The following template shows how to use **setjmp** and **longjmp**:

```
#include <stdio.h>
#include <errno.h>
#include <setjmp.h>
jmp_buf env;

main()
{   /* initialize and set up things here        */
    /* then call setjmp to mark nonlocal label  */
    if ( setjmp(env) != 0 )
    { /* return spot for longjmp                */
      /* put any adjustments after longjmp here */
    }
    /* proceed with normal processing           */
    func_1(...);
}

func_1()
{   /* normal processing                        */
    ...
    if ( failed ) recover(errno);
    ...
}

void recover(int e)
{   /* adjust values of variables if needed     */
    longjmp(env,e);
}
```

In this example, the function main sets up the eventual **longjmp** called by the function recover. Note that recover **never returns**. It is possible to mark several places env1, env2, ... with **setjmp** and to use **longjmp** to transfer control to one of these marked places.

Besides error recovery, a nonlocal jump can also return a value directly from a deeply nested function call. This can be more efficient than a sequence of returns by all the intermediate functions. However, nonlocal-control transfers tend to complicate program structure and should be used only sparingly.

9.7   Interrupts and Signals

Basic Concepts

We already know that a program executes as an independent process. Yet, events outside a process can affect its execution. The moment when such an event would occur is not predictable. Thus, they are called *asynchronous events.* Examples of such events include illegal memory reference, floating-point exception (overflow or underflow), and interrupts typed in at the keyboard. Asynchronous events are treated in UNIX using the *signal* mechanism. UNIX sends a certain signal to a process to signify the occurrence of a particular event. After receiving a signal, a process will react to it in a well-defined manner. For example, the process may be terminated or suspended for later resumption. A system-defined default action is associated with each signal. A process normally reacts to a signal by following the default action. However, a program also has the ability to redefine its reaction to any signal by specifying its own handling routine for the signal.

There are many different signals. For instance, typing ^\ (control-back-slash) on the keyboard usually generates a signal known as *quit.* Sending the quit signal to a process makes it terminate and produces a *core-image file* for debugging. Each kind of signal has a unique integer number, a symbolic name, and a default action defined by UNIX. Table 9.6 shows some of the many signals UNIX handles. Appendix 12 contains a complete list of all signals.

Symbol	Number	Default Action	Meaning
SIGHUP	1	Exit	Hangup (e.g., lost connection to terminal)
SIGINT	2	Exit	Interrupt (e.g., ^c from keyboard)
SIGQUIT	3	Core dump	Quit (e.g., ^\ from keyboard)
SIGILL	4	Core dump	Illegal instruction
SIGTRAP	5	Core dump	Trace trap
SIGFPE	8	Core dump	Floating-point exception
SIGKILL	9	Exit	Terminate execution (cannot be caught or ignored)
SIGBUS	10	Core dump	Bus error
SIGSEGV	11	Core dump	Memory-segmentation violation
SIGSYS	12	Core dump	Bad argument to system call
SIGVTALRM	26	Exit	Virtual time alarm
SIGPROF	27	Exit	Profiling timer alarm

Table 9.6: Some UNIX Signals

Sending Signals

You can send signals to processes connected to your terminal by typing the
^**, **^z (*csh* and *ksh* only), and the interrupt character (usually **^c**). These signals and their effects are summarized below:

^c   SIGINT   Terminates execution of foreground process.

^   SIGQUIT   Terminates foreground process and dumps core.

^z   SIGSTOP   Suspends foreground process for later resumption.

The tty terminal driver (Section 10.4) detects these special characters and
generates the appropriate signal. Besides these special characters, you can
use the **kill** command at the shell level to send a specific signal to a given
process. The general form of the **kill** command is

>   **kill** [-*sig_no*] *process*

where *process* is a process number (or job ID in *csh*). The optional argument specifies a signal number *sig_no*. If no signal is specified, signal 15
(SIGTERM) is assumed, which causes the target process to terminate. Recall
that we used **kill** in Section 1.7 where we discussed job control.

In a C program, a process uses the standard library function

>   int **raise** (int sig_no)   (send sig_no to a process itself)

to send the signal sig_no to itself. The system call

>   **kill** (int pid, int sig_no)   (send sig_no to process pid)

is used to send a specified signal to a process identified by the given numerical pid.

Signal Delivery and Processing

When a signal is sent to a process, the signal is added to a set of signals pending delivery to that process. Signals are delivered to a process in a manner
similar to hardware interrupts. If the signal is not currently *blocked* (temporarily ignored) by the process, it is delivered to the process following these
steps:

1. Block further occurrences of the same signal during the delivery
   and handling of this occurrence.
2. Temporarily suspend the execution of the process and call the
   handler function associated with this signal.
3. If the handler function returns, then unblock the signal and
   resume normal execution of the process from the point of interrupt.

There is a default-handler function for each signal. The default action is usually exit or core dump (Table 9.6). A process can replace a signal handler with a handler function of its own. This allows the process to *trap* a signal and deal with it in its own way. The SIGKILL and SIGSTOP signals, however, cannot be trapped.

Signal Trapping

After receiving a signal, a process normally (by the default signal-handling function) either exits (terminated) or stops (suspended). In some situations, reacting to specific signals differently is desirable. For instance, a process may ignore the signal, delete temporary files before terminating, or handle the situation with a **longjmp**.

The system call **signal** traps signals. Note that **signal** does not *send* a signal. A better name for this function is, of course, *trap*.

The **signal** call is used in the following way:

```
#include <signal.h>
typedef void (* HANDLER)();
HANDLER old_fn;

old_fn = signal(int sig_no, HANDLER new_fn);
```

where sig_no is the number or name of a signal and new_fn is a function pointer (the name of a function). The handler function of the signal sig_no is replaced by new_fn and a pointer to the old handler function is returned. The old handler function may be one supplied by the system as a default or one placed there by your program through a previous **signal** call. The old handler can be saved for possible restoration later.

The handler can be a routine you write or one that is defined by the system. If new_fn is SIG_DFL, the default action for sig_no is reinstated; Table 9.6 shows default actions of some signals. If new_fn is SIG_IGN, the signal is subsequently ignored, and pending instances of the signal are discarded. The handler function remains until changed by another call to **signal**.

We now give a simple example that uses the **signal** system call to trap SIGINT (interrupt from terminal) and adds one to a counter for each SIGINT signal received:

```
/* this program demonstrates the use of signal to trap interrupts
 * from the terminal. To terminate the program type ^\
 */
#include <signal.h>
```

```
main()
{ void cnt(int sig);
      signal(SIGINT, cnt);
      printf("Begin counting INTERRUPTs\n");
      for(;;);   /* infinite loop */
}

void cnt(int sig)
{ static int count=0;
      printf("Total of %d INTERRUPTS received\n", ++count);
}
```

If the signal-handler function is defined to take an `int` argument (e.g., `sig`), then it will automatically be called with the signal number that caused a trap to this function. Counting the number of signals received is of limited application. A more practical example has to do with cleaning up any temporary files used by a process before terminating due to a user interrupt:

```
#include <stdio.h>
#include <signal.h>
#include <strings.h>
#include <sys/file.h>
FILE *tempfile;

main()
{ void onintr();   /* interrupt handler */
  extern FILE *tempfile;
      /* trap SIGINT only if it is not being ignored */
      if ( signal(SIGINT, SIG_IGN) != SIG_IGN )
          signal(SIGINT, onintr);
      /* open temporary stream for reading and writing */
      tempfile = tmpfile();
      /* other code of the program  */
      ...
      /* remove temporary file before termination */
      fclose(tempfile);
      return(0);
}

void onintr()
{ extern FILE* tempfile;
      fclose(tempfile);
      exit(1);
}
```

In this example, trapping of SIGINT is done only if it is not being ignored. If a process runs with its signal environment already set to ignore certain signals, then those signals should continue to be ignored instead of trapped. For example, the shell arranges a background process to ignore SIGINT generated from the keyboard. If a process proceeds to trap SIGINT without checking to see if it is being ignored, the arrangement made by the shell would be defeated.

A similar usage of **signal** has to do with restoring tty modes (Section 10.4) and/or the terminal display before termination. The interactive menu program (Section 10.6) is an example.

Furthermore, as with interactive utilities such as the **vi** editor and the **lisp** interpreter, using the keyboard interrupt to *abort to the top level* within a program is often desirable. This can be easily done by combining signal trapping with the **longjmp** mechanism:

```
#include <signal.h>
#include <setjmp.h>
jmp_buf top;

main(int arg, char *argv[])
{ void onintr(int);
      if ( signal(SIGINT, SIG_IGN) != SIG_IGN )
          signal(SIGINT, onintr);
      if ( setjmp(top) != 0 )
      {  /* after longjmp */
          ...
      }
      /* top-level loop */
      printf("%s Ready:", argv[0]);
      while(1)
      {  /* process interactive user commands */
      }
}

void onintr(int sig)
{   printf("\n Interrupt--returning to top level\n");
    longjmp(top, sig);
}
```

Generally, when the signal-handler function returns or when a process resumes after being stopped by **^z** (SIGSTOP), a process resumes at the exact point at which it was interrupted. For interrupted system calls, the external errno is set to EINTR, and the system call returns –1. If interrupted while reading input from the terminal (stdin), a process may lose a partially typed line just before the interrupt.

9.8 Summary

The **dbx** package is an interactive debugger that relates program execution to source code lines. A program can be compiled to run under the control of **dbx** allowing tracing, breaking, single-line stepping, and displaying of the function-call stack and memory contents. When a program fails, a core file can be produced. The core file can also be examined with **dbx** to diagnose the problem and to determine the exact nature of the error.

The best way of avoiding bugs is to follow good programming practices. Rules of thumb for writing good programs, efficient testing, and effective debugging have been given.

One source of program-execution error is failed library or system calls. When this happens, standard error values will be returned by the failed call. You should check for such returned values in your program and take appropriate actions. The global variable errno is set after a library or system-call failure, and the library function **perror** can be used to produce a standard error message to stderr.

A run-time error can be treated in three basic ways: exiting, returning an error value, or recovery. A program can recover from an error and return to a known state to continue execution. This can be done by the nonlocal goto facility offered by **setjmp** and **longjmp**.

Unpredictable events outside a program may interrupt the execution of a program. Such events are handled in UNIX by the signal mechanism. There are different types of signals represented by signal numbers (small integers) defined in the system (see Appendix 12). When a particular type of signal is sent to a process, its execution is temporarily suspended, and a handler function associated with the signal is called. Normally, the handler function will treat the signal and then terminate execution. But the handler can also return or **longjmp**, causing the process to resume execution.

Exercises

1. Here is a function parse that uses the library function **strtok** to break apart a string into individual tokens. There is also a simple main program to test it. The only problem is that the program does not work and results in "segmentation fault," meaning the program tried to access an illegal memory location. Use **dbx** to find the bug.

```
/* This program has a bug. Find it with dbx */
#include <stdio.h>
#include <string.h>
#define WHITE "\t \n"
#define MAXARG 20
```

```
typedef char *String;
extern String strtok(String s, const String cs);

String *parse(String cmd, String argv[])
{ int i = 0;
      argv[i++] = strtok(cmd, WHITE); /* to fill in argv */
      while ( i < MAXARG &&
            (argv[i++] = strtok(NULL, WHITE)) != NULL );
      return(argv);
}


main()
{    String cmds[MAXARG];
        parse("name arg1 arg2", cmds);                    /* call parse */
        printf("%s,%s,%s\n",cmds[0], cmds[1],cmds[2]); /* verify ans */
}
```

2. Call **perror** after trying to open a file that is not there or lacks access permissions. What standard error messages do you get?

3. What happens if you execute **longjmp** in a sequence of function calls not containing a **setjmp**?

4. What is the value returned by **setjmp** initially, after a **longjmp**(env,val)? What if val is zero?

5. Write a program that counts the two different keyboard interrupts ^C and ^\ separately.

6. Add to the interactive calculator program in Section 5.7 error recovery from keyboard interrupts.

7. Is it possible to have two different handlers for a particular signal so that they would take turns treating incoming signals?

8. In some situations, a handler function can treat a signal differently depending on whether the user has sent one, two, or more consecutive signals of the same kind. How should such a handler be programmed?

Unix System
I/O Facilities

One of the key services provided by any operating system is the
management of input and output. The C language interfaces to
UNIX particularly well because of their close relationship. In fact, all
UNIX system calls and most libraries are implemented in C. In this
chapter, we cover useful UNIX system I/O facilities for C
programming.

Uniform file, device, and interprocess input/output is a UNIX
hallmark. The same set of system calls supports input and output to
files, to actual I/O devices, and to other running process. The I/O
redirection and pipeline capabilities at the shell level are direct
results of these features.

We explain how I/O descriptors are established and used for
low-level I/O operations. UNIX-supported library and system calls
for the access and manipulation of files and directories are
presented. The I/O system calls provide all the necessary tools to
implement the higher-level I/O facilities offered in C.

UNIX uses a device driver called `tty` to process input/output to and
from a terminal of arbitrary type. It is important to understand the
functionality of `tty` and its modes of operation because all
input/output to the terminal must go through `tty`.

We then move on to cover a library package called `curses`, which
makes controlling input/output to a CRT much easier. Our
presentation leads to the implementation of a complete
window-oriented interactive menu program.

10.1   Directory Access

In the UNIX file system, a directory contains the names and addresses of files stored in it. A number of UNIX library functions are available for accessing directories. To use any of them, include the header file `dir.h`:

```
#include <sys/dir.h>
```

The function

    `DIR `**`*opendir`**`(char *dir_name)`   (**open di**rectory stream)

opens the named directory and associates a *directory stream* with it. A pointer to this directory stream is returned for use in subsequent operations. If the named directory cannot be accessed or if there is not enough memory to hold the contents of the directory, a `NULL` is returned.

Once a directory stream is opened, the function **readdir** sequentially accesses its entries. The routine

    `struct direct `**`*readdir`**`(DIR *dp)`   (**read di**rectory stream)

returns a pointer to the next directory entry. The pointer value becomes `NULL` on error or reaching the end of the directory.

The directory-entry structure is

```
struct direct
{  u_long   d_ino;                /* i-node number of dir entry */
   u_short  d_reclen;            /* length of this record      */
   u_short  d_namlen;            /* length of string in d_name */
   char     d_name[MAXNAMLEN + 1]; /* directory name           */
};
```

The `typedef`s `u_long` and `u_short` are usually defined in the header file `<sys/types.h>`. The symbolic constant `MAXNAMELEN` is the maximum length for directory names on a particular UNIX system. This number is usually 256 but can be 14 on some older UNIX systems. Each file in a UNIX file system also has a unique *i-node number* (Section 10.3).

The function

    closedir`(DIR *dp)`   (**close di**rectory stream)

closes the directory stream `dp` and frees the structure associated with the `DIR` pointer.

To illustrate the use of these library functions, let's look at a function `searchdir`, which searches `dir` for a given `file` and returns 1 or 0 depending on whether the file is found or not. Note that the example uses knowledge of the `direct` structure:

```
#include <sys/types.h>
#include <sys/dir.h>
```

```
int searchdir(char *file, char *dir)
{ int len = strlen(file);          /* length of filename  */
  DIR *dp = opendir(dir);          /* dir pointer         */
  struct direct *entry;            /* dir entry           */
  enum {NOT_FOUND, FOUND} flag = NOT_FOUND;
      /* go through each entry in dir */
      for ( entry=readdir(dp) ; entry != NULL ; entry=readdir(dp) )
      {   if ( entry->d_namlen==len && !strcmp(entry->d_name, file) )
              flag = FOUND;
      }
      closedir(dp);
      return(flag);
}
```

The variable `flag` is an unnamed `enum` (Section 3.7). The `for` loop goes through each entry in `dir` to find `file`. The search is made more efficient by comparing the name strings only after the length of the names match. Note also the logical not (`!`) in front of `strcmp`.

10.2 UNIX System I/O Calls

The standard library I/O routines (Chapter 8) are adequate for most common operations. These high-level library functions are built on top of low-level structures and calls provided by the operating system. On UNIX, the I/O stream of C is built on top of the I/O descriptor mechanism supported by the I/O system calls (Figure 10.1). Getting to know the low-level I/O facilities will not only provide insight on how the library functions work but also let you use input/output in ways not supported by the standard library.

UNIX features a uniform interface for input/output to files and devices, such as a terminal or a line printer, by representing I/O hardware as *special files*. We will discuss input/output to files, understanding they apply also to devices, which are nothing but special files. Besides files, input/output between processes through abstract structures known as *pipes* is also supported. Although files and pipes are different I/O objects, they are supported by many of the same low-level I/O calls explained here.

I/O Descriptors

Before input/output to a file can take place, a program must first indicate its intention to UNIX. This is done by the **open** system call.

```
#include <sys/file.h>
int open(char *filename, int access, int mode);
```

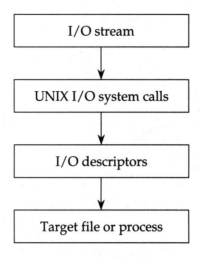

Figure 10.1: I/O Descriptors

This call opens `filename`, for reading and writing, as specified by `access` and returns an integer descriptor for that file. The filename can be given in any of the three valid forms: full pathname, relative pathname, or simple filename. If the file does not exist, **open** creates a new file with the given name. Subsequent I/O operations will refer to this descriptor rather than to the filename. An I/O descriptor is actually an index to a per-process *open-file table*, which contains necessary information for all open files and I/O objects of a process.

For each process, three file descriptors 0, 1, and 2 are preopened, allowing ready access to the standard input, output, and error output channels, respectively.

Arguments to **open** are

`filename`	Character string for the filename
`access`	An integer code for the intended access
`mode`	The protection mode for creating a new file

The `access` code is formed by the logical *or* (|) of the following single-bit values:

`O_RDONLY`	Opens file for reading only.
`O_WRONLY`	Opens file for writing only.
`O_RDWR`	Opens file for reading and writing.
`O_NDELAY`	Prevents possible *blocking*.

O_APPEND	Opens file for appending.
O_CREAT	Creates file if it does not exist.
O_TRUNC	Truncates size to zero.
O_EXCL	Produces an error if the O_CREAT bit is on and file exists.

Opening a file with O_APPEND instructs each write on the file to be appended to the end. If O_TRUNC is specified and the file exists, the file is truncated to length zero. If access is

```
(O_EXCL | O_CREAT)
```

and if the file already exists, **open** returns an error. The purpose is to avoid destroying an existing file.

The file-creation mode is a bit pattern explained in detail in Section 10.3 where the **creat** system call is described.

If the **open** call fails, a –1 is returned; otherwise, a descriptor is returned. A process may have no more than OPEN_MAX (a defined constant, usually 16) descriptors open simultaneously.

Here is a typical usage of the **open** system call. The third argument to **open** is unused because it is not needed for the read-only (O_RDONLY) operation. In this case, any integer can be used as the third argument:

```
#include <stdio.h>
#include <sys/file.h>

main(int argc, char *argv[])
{ int fd;    /* file descriptor */
      /* open argv[1] for reading */
      if ( (fd = open(argv[1], O_RDONLY,0)) == -1 )
      {    fprintf(stderr,"%s: cannot open %s\n",
                        argv[0], argv[1]);
            perror("");
            exit(1);
      }

/* other code */
   }
```

When a system or library call fails, use the call

perror (char* msg)   (display system error)

to display the given message msg, followed by a standard error message associated with the error (Section 9.5).

When a descriptor `fd` is no longer needed in a program, it can be deleted from the per-process open-file table using the call

int **close**(int fd)   (close descriptor)

Otherwise, all open-file descriptors will be closed when the program terminates.

Reading and Writing a File

Reading and writing a file is normally sequential. For each open file, a *current position* points to the next byte to be read or written. After k bytes are read or written, the current position, if movable, is advanced by k bytes. Whether the current position is movable depends on the I/O object. For example, it is movable for an actual file but not for `stdin` when connected to the keyboard.

The system calls **read** and **write** are declared as

int **read** (int fd, char *buffer, int k)   (input from `fd`)
int **write**(int fd, char *buffer, int k)   (output to `fd`)

where `fd` is a descriptor to read from or write to, `buffer` points to an array to receive or supply the bytes, and `k` is the number of bytes to be read in or written out. Obviously, `k` must not exceed the length of `buffer`. The **read** call will attempt to read `k` bytes from the I/O object represented by `fd` and returns the number of bytes actually read and deposited in the buffer. If **read** returns less than `k` bytes, it does not necessarily mean that end of file has been reached. But if zero is returned, then end of file has been reached.

The **write** call outputs `k` bytes from the buffer to `fd` and returns the actual number of bytes written out. Both **read** and **write** return a –1 if they fail.

As an example, we can rewrite the `readline` function (Section 2.13) with low-level **read**:

```
int readline(char s[], int size)
{ char *tmp = s;
  /* read one character at a time */
    while ( 0 < --size && read(0, tmp, 1) != 0
                    && *tmp++ != '\n' );   /* empty loop body */
    *tmp = '\0';        /* string terminator               */
    return(tmp - s);  /* number of characters without terminator  */
}
```

The `while` loop control is intricate and warrants careful study. The `size` argument is the capacity of the array `s`. Again, the function returns the number of characters read, not counting the string terminator.

For a complete program, the **lowercase** command (Section 2.7) has been rewritten with low-level I/O calls:

```
/**** lower command with low-level I/O calls ****/
#include <stdio.h>
#include <ctype.h>
#define BUFSIZ 1024

main(int argc, char *argv[])
{ char buffer[BUFSIZ];
   int nc;                    /* number of characters */
      while ( (nc = read(0, buffer, BUFSIZ)) > 0 )
      {    lower(buffer,nc);
           nc = write(1, buffer, nc);
           if ( nc == -1 ) break;
      }
      if ( nc == -1 )    /* read or write failed */
      {    perror(argv[0]);
           exit(1);
      }
      return(0);            /* normal termination   */
}

int lower(char *buf, int length)
{   while ( length-- > 0 )
    {    if ( isupper(*buf) )
              *buf = tolower( *buf );
         buf++;
    }
    return(0);
}
```

Compared with the version in Section 2.7, which uses **putchar**, the program shows the difference between implicit and explicit I/O buffering.

Moving the Current Position

When reading or writing an I/O object that is an actual file, the object can be viewed as a sequence of bytes. The current position is moved by the **read** and **write** operations in a sequential manner. Furthermore, the system call **lseek** provides a way to move the current position to any location and therefore allows *random access* to bytes of the file. The standard library function **fseek** (Section 8.7) is built on top of **lseek**. The call

```
int lseek(int fd, int offset, int origin)
```

Origin	Position
0	Beginning of a file
1	Current position
2	End of a file

Table 10.1: The **lseek** Origins

Call	Meaning
lseek(fd, 0, 0)	Puts current position at first byte of the file.
lseek(fd, 0, 2)	Moves current position to the end of the file.
lseek(fd, -1, 2)	Puts current position at last byte.
lseek(fd, -10, 1)	Backs up current position by 10 bytes.

Table 10.2: Use of **lseek**

moves the current position associated with the descriptor fd to a byte position defined by (origin + offset). Table 10.1 shows the three possible origins. The offset can be positive or negative. The call **lseek** returns the current position as an integer position measured from the beginning of the file. It returns –1 upon failure. Table 10.2 illustrates several calls. It is possible to **lseek** beyond the end of the file and then **write**. This creates a *hole*, which does not occupy space, in the file. Reading a byte in such a hole returns 0.

In some applications, holes are left in the file, on purpose, to allow easy insertion of additional data into the file later. It is an error to **lseek** a nonmovable descriptor such as the standard input.

10.3   System-Level File Operations

System calls are provided for creating and deleting files, accessing file status information, and obtaining and modifying protection modes or other attributes of a file.

Creating and Deleting a File

To create a new file, use the **open** system call explained in Section 10.2. The older system call

```
int creat(char *filename, int mode)
```
    (**create** a new file)

can also be used. If the named file already exists, it is truncated to zero
length, ready to be rewritten. The returned value of **creat** is a file descriptor
for writing. It is equivalent to

```
open(filename, (O_CREAT | O_TRUNC), mode)
```

The lower 9 bits of mode (for access protection) are modified by the file-creation mask umask of the process. The formula

```
( ~umask ) & mode
```

obtains the file-creation mode . The mode is the *logical or* of any of the basic
modes shown in Table 10.3. The default umask of a process is usually 022,
which clears the write-permission bits for *group* and *other* (Section 1.5). The
umask can be set by the system call

```
int umask(int newmask)
```
    (set file-creation mask)

The returned value is the old umask. For example,

```
umask(077);
```

forces file modes for newly created files to allow file access only for the
owner. This umask setting is inherited by child processes (Chapter 12). After
a file is created, alternative names for it can be given. The call

```
int link(char *file, char *name)
```
    (create file link)

establishes another name for the existing file. The new name, of course, can
be anywhere on the file tree. To remove a link, use the call

```
int unlink(char *name)
```
    (delete file link)

When the link removed is the last one pointing to this file, the file is then
deleted.

Octal Bit Pattern	Meaning
00400	Read by owner
00200	Write by owner
00100	Execute (search on directory) by owner
00070	Read, write, execute (search) by group
00007	Read, write, execute (search) by others

Table 10.3: Basic File Modes

Creating and Removing a Directory

Besides files, establishing and removing directories with UNIX system calls are also possible. The system call **mkdir** is used to create a new directory:

> **mkdir**(char *name, int mode)   (**make a new directory**)

It creates a new directory with the given name. The mode works the same way as in **open**. The new directory's owner ID is set to the process's effective user ID. The directory's group ID is set to that of the parent directory in which it is created. Warning: *If you neglect to pass the mode argument and treat it like the shell-level command of the same name, the permissions will be random garbage.*

To remove a directory, use the system call **rmdir**

> int **rmdir**(char *dir_name)   (**remove a directory**)

to remove the named directory. The directory must be empty (having no entries other than . and ..). For both **mkdir** and **rmdir**, a 0 returned value indicates success, and a –1 indicates an error.

Accessing File Status

For each file, UNIX maintains a set of *status information* such as file type, protection modes, time when last modified, and so on. To access file-status information from a C program, use the system calls

```
#include <sys/types.h>
#include <sys/stat.h>
```
> **stat**(char *file, struct stat *buf)   (get file status of file)
> **fstat**(int fd, struct stat *buf)   (get file status of fd)

The status information for the named file or descriptor is retrieved and placed in buf. The call **stat** does not require read, write, or execute permission of the named file, but all directories listed in the pathname leading to the file must be reachable. The stat structure (Figure 10.2) consists of many members. Additionally, Figure 10.3 shows the symbolic constants for interpreting the value of the stat member st_mode. You can find this information and more in the system header file <sys/stat.h>. The file status is kept with other important information about a file in an *index node* or *i-node structure* kept for each file.

Three *time stamps* are kept for each file:

st_atime   Last access time: the time when the file was last read or modified. It is affected by the system calls **mknod**, **utimes**, **read**, and **write**. For reasons of efficiency, st_atime is not set when a directory is searched.

```
struct stat                              (file-status data structure)
{     dev_t   st_dev;                     (device of i-node)
      ino_t   st_ino;                     (this i-node's number)
   u_short   st_mode;                     (file type and mode)
     short   st_nlink;                    (number of hard links to file)
     short   st_uid;                      (user ID of owner)
     short   st_gid;                      (group ID of owner)
     dev_t   st_rdev;                     (device type, for a is device)
     off_t   st_size;                     (total size of file)
    time_t   st_atime;                    (file last access time)
       int   st_spare1;                   (not used now)
    time_t   st_mtime;                    (file last modify time)
       int   st_spare2;                   (not used now)
    time_t   st_ctime;                    (file last status-change time)
       int   st_spare3;
      long   st_blksize;                  (optimal blocksize for input/output)
      long   st_blocks;                   (actual number of blocks allocated)
      long   st_spare4[2];
};
```

Figure 10.2: File-Status Structure

st_mtime   Last modify time: the time when the file was last modified.
             It is not affected by changes of owner, group, link count, or
             mode. It is changed by **mknod**, **utimes**, and **write**.

st_ctime   Last status-change time: the time when file status was last
             changed. It is set by both writing to the file and changing
             the information contained in the i-node. It is affected by
             chmod, **chown**, **link**, **mknod**, **unlink**, **utimes**, and **write**.

The time stamps are stored as integers, and a larger integer value represents a more recent time. Usually, UNIX uses GMT (Greenwich Mean Time).
The integer time stamp represents the number of seconds since a fixed point
in the past—for example, GMT 00:00:00, January 1, 1970. The library routine
ctime converts such an integer into an ASCII string representing date and
time. The mask S_IFMT is useful for determining the file type. For example,

```
if ( (buf.st_mode & S_IFMT) == S_IFDIR )
```

determines whether the file is a directory.

```
#define   S_IFMT    0170000      (file-type mask)
#define   S_IFDIR   0040000      (directory)
#define   S_IFCHR   0020000      (character special file)
#define   S_IFBLK   0060000      (block special file)
#define   S_IFREG   0100000      (regular file)
#define   S_IREAD   0000400      (read permission, owner)
#define   S_IWRITE  0000200      (write permission, owner)
#define   S_IEXEC   0000100      (execute/search permission, owner)
```

Figure 10.3: File-Status Constants

As an application, let's consider a function `newer` that returns 1 if the last modify time of `file1` is more recent than that of `file2` and returns 0 otherwise. Upon failure, `newer` returns –1:

```
#include <sys/types.h>
#include <sys/stat.h>

/* test if file1 is more recent than file2 */
int newer(char *file1, char *file2)
{ int mtime(char *file);
   int t1 = mtime(file1), t2 = mtime(file2);   /* time stamps */
      if ( t1 < 0 || t2 < 0 ) return(-1);      /* failed      */
      else if ( t1 > t2 ) return(1);
      else return(0);
}

int mtime(char *file)   /* obtain last modify time of file   */
{ struct stat stb;
      if ( stat(file, &stb) < 0 )   /* result returned in stb */
            return(-1);                     /* stat failed    */
      return( stb.st_mtime );        /* return time stamp     */
}
```

The `stb` structure in the function `mtime` is a return argument supplied to the `stat` system call to collect the status information of a file.

Determining Allowable File Access

Determining whether an intended read, write, or execute access to a file is permissible before initiating such an access is possible. The **access** system call is defined as

```
#include <sys/file.h>
int access(char *name, int a_mode)        (file accessibility check)
```

The **access** call checks the permission bits of the named file to see if the intended access given by a_mode is allowable. The intended access mode is a logical or of the bits R_OK, W_OK, and X_OK defined by

```
#define R_OK    4        (test for read permission)
#define W_OK    2        (test for write permission)
#define X_OK    1        (test for execute—search—permission)
#define F_OK    0        (test for presence of file)
```

If the specified access is allowable, the call returns 0; otherwise, it returns –1.

Specifying a_mode as F_OK tests whether the directories leading to the file can be searched and whether the file exists.

Current Working Directory

The UNIX system library routine

```
char *getwd(char *name)        (obtain current directory)
```

copies the full pathname of the current working directory into **name** and returns a pointer to it. For example, the following program displays the current working directory:

```
#include <stdio.h>
/* using getwd */
main()
{ char name[256];     /* buffer for result */
  char *getwd(char *);
      printf("%s\n", getwd(name));
}
```

Use the system call

```
int chdir(char *dir_name)        (change directory)
```

to change the current working directory to the named directory. A value 0 is returned if **chdir** is successful; otherwise, a –1 is returned. Because the current directory is a per-process attribute, you will return to the original directory after the program exits.

10.4 Controlling Input/Output to Terminals

On UNIX systems, each terminal line is represented by a terminal special file under the directory /dev. By convention a terminal special file has a name with a tty prefix (e.g., tty00, tty0a, ttyd4). The *terminal driver* tty is an independently running process that interfaces the terminal and a running program (Figure 10.4). It performs important I/O services for interactions with a user. The terminal driver has three major modes characterized by the amount of processing on the I/O streams: *cooked*, *cbreak*, and *raw*:

cooked   is the normal mode. In this mode, lines of input are collected, and input editing is done. The edited line is made available when it is completed by a NEWLINE or when a ^D is entered. A RETURN is usually made synonymous with NEWLINE in this mode and is replaced by a NEWLINE whenever it is typed. All tty driver functions (editing and interrupt generation for input, delay generation and tab expansion for output, etc.) are enabled in this mode.

cbreak   eliminates the *erase character, kill word*, and *kill line* input editing facilities. The input character is made available to the program as it is typed. Output processing is the same as the *cooked* mode.

raw   eliminates all input processing and makes all input characters available as they are typed. No output processing is done either. Essentially, this mode bypasses the tty driver and gives control of terminal input/output back to a running program.

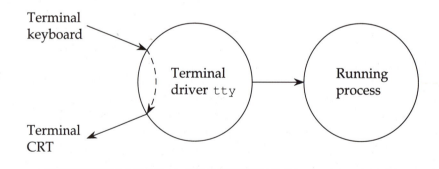

Figure 10.4: The Terminal Driver

Setting Terminal Options

The terminal driver allows flexible treatment of terminal input/output. The user has many settable options to make a program work well with almost any terminal.

At the shell level, use the command

stty [*option*] . . .   (set terminal options)

to set the many terminal options available. For example,

stty crt -tabs kill **^U** intr **^C**

sets these options:

crt   Sets options for a CRT terminal to use backspaces for erasing characters.

-tabs   Replaces a tab by an equivalent number of spaces on output.

kill *c*   Uses character *c* as the *kill-line* character.

intr *c*   Uses character *c* as the *interrupt* character.

Many more options are available; refer to the UNIX documentation on **stty** for details.

Terminal Capability Database

Programs such as **vi** and **more** work on many kinds of terminals that have different characteristics and escape codes. This device independence is achieved through the use of a database containing descriptions of the characteristics and capabilities of most terminals. On Berkeley UNIX systems, the database is usually kept in the file /etc/termcap. On System V UNIX, the terminal information is kept in terminfo. Any program that uses terminal-dependent capabilities can obtain the name of the terminal from the environment variable TERM and retrieve a description of the terminal from the database. A program written this way will work with any terminal that has a terminal-description entry.

The terminal-description entry for a particular type terminal provides all the information for control and input/output to the terminal. For example, it contains the number of lines and columns and the *escape sequences* to move the cursor and to insert and delete characters on the CRT.

Library routines are provided for extracting and using the terminal-description database from C programs. To see what's available on your system, enter

> **man** termcap   (on Berkeley UNIX)
> **man** terminfo   (on System V UNIX)

The termcap/terminfo library routines provide low-level operations that let you write programs independent of the target-terminal type. An even more convenient library package called *curses*, however, provides easier-to-use routines for managing screen input/output, as we see in the next section.

10.5   A Screen Updating Library

The *curses package*, a UNIX-based library of C functions, supplies most common CRT-dependent output operations such as updating the screen, cursor-motion optimization, and so on. The package uses *windows*, which are logical data structures capable of representing the entire terminal screen or a portion of it. If a window is as large as the entire terminal screen, it is referred to as a *screen*. After initialization, curses establishes two built-in *screens*: the current screen curscr and the standard screen stdscr:

> curscr   (for the current state of the terminal screen)
> stdscr   (for the next state of the terminal screen)

After modifications are made to stdscr, a function called to refresh the terminal screen performs all the necessary computations to update the terminal and the curscr. The user is not limited to these screens. In fact, any number of named screens and windows can be established to help manipulate and update the terminal screen. This makes it relatively easy to maintain multiple windows on a CRT screen. One program that uses multiple windows is the UNIX system **talk** command.

To use this library, the line

```
#include <curses.h>
```

must appear at the beginning of the source file. To compile a file with calls to curses functions, use

> **cc** [*flags*] *file* ... **-l**curses

The -l option tells **cc** to include the curses library functions. On some Berkeley UNIX systems, the additional option **-l**termlib must also be supplied to **cc**.

Basic Usage

To use curses in a program, follow four basic steps:

1. *Initializing*. Call **initscr**() to properly initialize curses: obtaining terminal-specific characteristics, establishing the screens curscr and stdscr, and recording the current tty modes for later use.

Among other things, the global variables LINES and COLS are set to the number of lines and columns of the CRT. After calling **initscr**, change the tty modes to suit the application. Often, **noecho**() and **crmode**() are called to stop input echoing and to enter *cbreak* mode.

2. *Establishing windows.* After initialization, establish additional windows, if needed. The call **newwin**(line, col, y, x) establishes a new window, whose upper left corner is at position (y, x), with the given number of lines and columns and returns a window identification (wid) for future operations to reference the window. Note, curses uses (y, x) for the position line y column x in a window.

3. *Performing input/output.* The basic functions that modify stdscr are **move**(y, x) to move the current position to location (y, x) and **addch**(c) to add the character c at the current position. The two operations can be combined to **mvaddch**(y, x, c). A call to **refresh**() will update the terminal screen according to stdscr. The function **getch**() reads a character from the stdscr. For other windows, **waddch**(wid, c) adds a character, and **wgetch**(wid) gets a character.

4. *Finishing.* Before the program terminates, the routine **endwin**() should be called to restore the tty modes recorded by **initscr** and perform other cleanup chores.

To further explain how to use the curses package, a framework program is given here. The usual include files are

```
/* a framework for using curses */
/* usual include files */
#include <curses.h>
#include <ctype.h>
#include <sys/types.h>
```

The main program should initialize curses and set up a *trap routine* in case the program is terminated before running to successful completion. In such a case, the system will call the trap routine first. The **signal** system call (Section 9.7) sets up the trap routine terminate. Once the environment is set up, the processing for the particular application can begin:

```
main()
{ void terminate(int);
     initscr();                     /* initialization   */
     signal(SIGINT, terminate); /* trap signal       */
     /* call principal processing function here       */
     terminate(0);
}
```

```
/* Exit program properly  */
void terminate(int sig)
{    mvcur(0, COLS-1, LINES-1, 0); /* position cursor */
     endwin();                     /* finish curses   */
     putchar('\n');                /* position cursor */
     exit(sig);
}
```

The responsibility of `terminate` is to move the cursor to the lower, right-hand corner of the screen, call **endwin** to exit from curses, output a NEWLINE to position the cursor at the beginning of the next line, and finally terminate the program. Use such a routine, instead of the simple **exit(0)**, to end the program.

The usual purpose of employing curses is to provide a two-dimensional visual user interface for an application such as **vi** or even a game like checkers. In these applications, keyboard input should not be automatically echoed to the CRT. And in most cases, each character must be received by the program as soon as typed. The `drawbox` function shows how to set this up:

```
drawbox()           /* Draws a box on the screen     */
{ WINDOW *b;
     noecho();    /*no echoing of user-typed chars  */
     crmode();    /*enter cbreak mode               */
     b = newwin(17,51,0,0);  /* establish a window  */
     box(b,'|','_');          /* internal box in b   */
     wrefresh(b);             /* display  b on CRT   */
}
```

The curses function **box** draws a rectangular outline around the window with the specified vertical and horizontal characters. To read keyboard input, instead of **getchar**, the input function `readch` works better with curses and is independent of standard input/output. It also returns each character as it is typed:

```
readch()            /* Read a character from the standard input */
{ register int r, cnt=0;
  char ch;
  void terminate(int);
     for (;;)
       { if ( read(0, &ch, sizeof(ch)) <= 0 )
           { if ( ++cnt > 5 )      /* make sure input is closed */
               terminate(0);       /* before terminating        */
           }
```

```
        else if ( ch == CTRL(L) )
        {    refresh();
             mvcur(0, 0, curscr->_cury, curscr->_curx);
        }
        else return (ch);
    }
}
```

10.6   A Simple Menu-User Interface

As an application of the curses package, we will write a program, which can display a menu of items on a CRT, to allow interactive choice on the part of the user. The menu items are labeled sequentially, and the user can choose any item on the menu with different key strokes. The chosen item is highlighted to provide confirmation. The selection can be changed any time before it is finalized. Figure 10.5 shows a menu consisting of a title and a number of items with sequential labels displayed in a box. We will study this program in its entirety.

First, header files and quantities defined globally for this program are listed:

```
#include <curses.h>
#include <signal.h>

#define TOP_MARGIN 4            /* margins around text in menu    */
#define BOT_MARGIN 2
#define SIDE_MARGIN 6
#define INSTR_LINES 2           /* fixed instruction lines        */
#define MAXITEMS  LINES - INSTR_LINES - TOP_MARGIN - BOT_MARGIN
#define LABEL_WIDTH 5           /* number of characters in a label */
#define BELL() printf("\007")
#define MIN(a,b) ((a) > (b) ? b : a)
#define MAX(a,b) ((a) < (b) ? b : a)

typedef char *String;
static int y_0, x_0;            /* y and x position for first label */
```

Note how MAXITEMS, the maximum number of menu items, is defined.

The function menu_select plays a central role in our program. It takes three arguments:

dim   Number of items on the menu

items   An array of strings, each specifying an item

title   Title of the menu

```
 *************************************
 *                                   *
 *            Today's Specials       *
 *                                   *
 *       (1)   Spring Rolls          *
 *       (2)   Fried Rice            *
 *       (3)   Hot and Sour Soup     *
 *                                   *
 *************************************


 TYPE A DIGIT, +, - OR <SPACE BAR> TO REACH AN ITEM,
 <RETURN> TO FINALIZE CHOICE.
```

Figure 10.5: An Interactive Menu

and returns the final choice from the user. This function performs the following major tasks:

1. Constructs and displays the menu (setup_menu).
2. Retrieves user selection (retrieve_choice).
3. Displays confirmation (display_choice).
4. Returns final selection.

```
int menu_select(int dim, String items[], String title)
{ int choice, old_choice = 1;
  char c;
  WINDOW *menu_scr;
  WINDOW *setup_menu(int, String items[], String);
  void display_choice(WINDOW *scr, int choice, int old_choice);
     if ( dim > MAXITEMS )
     {   fprintf(stderr, "too many items on menu\n");
         exit(1);
     }
     menu_scr = setup_menu(dim, items, title); /* set up menu */
     for (;;)                     /* retrieve and display choice */
     {   choice = retrieve_choice(dim, old_choice);
         if ( choice < 0 ) return(old_choice);        /* done */
```

```
                  if ( choice != old_choice )
                  {   display_choice(menu_scr, choice, old_choice);
                      old_choice = choice;
                  }
          }
   }
```

The menu is displayed with `menu_scr`, a curses screen which is established as a subwindow of `stdscr`. The duties of the `setup_menu` function are to

1. Compute menu dimensions, taking into account top and side margins, length of title and items, and horizontal and vertical spaces in the display format.
2. Create the `menu_scr` subwindow.
3. Display menu title, labels, and items, positioning them correctly.
4. Display selection instructions.

```
WINDOW *setup_menu(int dim, String items[], String title)
{ int tlen, maxlen, i, tx, mid_x, menu_lines, menu_cols;
  WINDOW *menu_scr;
/* compute menu dimensions */
      tlen = strlen(title);
      maxlen = max_length(dim,items) + LABEL_WIDTH;
      menu_cols = MAX(tlen, maxlen) + 2*SIDE_MARGIN;
      if ( menu_cols > COLS )
      {   fprintf(stderr, "menu items too long.\n");
          exit(1);
      }
      menu_lines = dim + TOP_MARGIN + BOT_MARGIN;
/* establish menu window */
      menu_scr = subwin(stdscr,menu_lines,menu_cols, 0, 0);
      box(menu_scr,'*','*'); /* draw box to form a window */
/* display title */
      mid_x = menu_cols/2;
      tx = mid_x - (tlen/2);
      wstandout(menu_scr);                /* highlight mode begin    */
      mvwaddstr(menu_scr,2,tx,title);
      wstandend(menu_scr);                /* highlight mode end      */
      y_0 = 3;
/* display all items */
      x_0 = MIN(mid_x - maxlen/2, tx);  /* x-position for each item */
      for( i=1 ; i <= dim ; i++ )
```

```
    {    labeling(menu_scr, i, y_0+i, x_0, i == 1 );
         mvwaddstr(menu_scr, y_0+i, x_0+LABEL_WIDTH, items[i-1]);
    }
/* display fixed instructions */
    mvaddstr(LINES-INSTR_LINES, 0,
            "TYPE A DIGIT, +, - OR <SPACE BAR> TO REACH AN ITEM,");
    mvaddstr(LINES-INSTR_LINES+1, 0, "<RETURN> TO FINALIZE CHOICE.");
    refresh();
    return(menu_scr);
}
```

The curses function **mvwaddstr** positions the menu title and items onto
menu_scr. Modifications of menu_scr are automatically reflected on
stdscr because menu_scr is a subwindow of stdscr. Highlighting is
turned on with **wstandout** and off with **wstandoff**. When the behind-the-
scenes menu construction is done, **refresh** displays everything on the screen,
and menu_scr is returned. Also set in this function are two global variables
y_0 and x_0, the line and column coordinates of the beginning of the first
menu label. Labels are inserted into the window with the function

```
labeling(WINDOW *scr, int no, int y, int x, int standout_flag)
{ char label[LABEL_WIDTH];
    if ( standout_flag ) wstandout(scr);
                                        /* normal or highlight mode */
    sprintf(label, "(%d)\0", no);   /* construct label           */
    mvwaddstr(scr, y, x, label);    /* position label            */
    if ( standout_flag ) wstandend(scr);
                                        /* highlight mode end        */
}
```

which puts a label such as (3) in the given window scr at the (y, x) position specified in either normal or highlight mode. Only one label is highlighted at any time to indicate the current user choice.

After the menu is displayed, the program begins to read user selection
from the keyboard. This is the job of the function

```
    /* read user input */
    int retrieve_choice(int total_items, int old_choice)
    { char c;
      int choice;
        while (c = getchar())
            {   if ( c == '\n' ) return(-1);   /* final choice    */
                if ( c == ' ' || c == '+' )    /* next item       */
```

```
      {   choice = old_choice + 1;
          if ( choice > total_items ) choice = 1;
          return(choice);
      }
      if ( c == '-' )                    /* previous item   */
      {   choice = old_choice - 1;
          if ( choice == 0 ) choice = total_items;
          return(choice);
      }
      choice = c - '0';                  /* 1 thru 9        */
      if ( choice > total_items || choice > 9 )
          BELL();                        /* no such choice  */
      else
          return(choice);
  }
}
```

Recognized key strokes are

Digits 1–9   Selects item specified.

SPACE or plus sign   Selects next item.

Minus sign   Selects previous item.

RETURN   Finalizes selection.

Any other key sounds the bell ($'\007'$), a customary indication of unexpected input.

After receiving the user choice, visual confirmation is made by moving the highlighted label to the one selected by the user. Do this by calling the labeling function once to cancel the highlight on the old choice and a second time to highlight the new one:

```
void display_choice(WINDOW *scr, int choice, int old_choice)
{   labeling(scr, old_choice, y_0 + old_choice, x_0, 0);
    labeling(scr, choice, y_0 + choice, x_0, 1);
    refresh();
}
```

The exact positions of the labels are computed from the global y_0, x_0 values and the label numbers.

Now let's see how this interactive menu program can be tested by fitting it under the framework `main` program discussed earlier:

```
main(int argc, String argv[])
{ void abnormal_end(void);
  int choice;
      initscr();                          /* initialize curses          */
      init();                             /* other initializations      */
      signal(SIGINT, abnormal_end);  /* trap signal (see Chapter 9) */
      choice = menu_select(argc - 2, argv+2, argv[1]);
      normal_end();
      printf("(%d) selected\n", choice);    return(0);
}
```

For experimentation purposes, the title and items of the menu are taken from
the command line. The interactive menu program also uses additional ini-
tializations in the beginning (init()) and cleanup at the end (normal_end):

```
      void init()                /* additional initializations  */
      {    fflush(stdin);
           fflush(stdout);
           noecho();             /* no echo of input characters */
           crmode();             /* set to tty to cbreak mode    */
      }
      void normal_end()
      {    mvcur(0, COLS-1, LINES-1, 0);     /* position cursor */
           clean_up();
           endwin();                         /* finish curses    */
           putchar('\n');                    /* position cursor */
      }


      void clean_up()
      {    clear();                   /* clear stdscr            */
           refresh();                 /* clear terminal screen */
           fflush(stdin);
           fflush(stdout);
      }


      void abnormal_end() /* abnormal exit function              */
      {    normal_end();   /* tidy up as normal before exiting */
           exit(1);
      }
```

Note that the terminal is put in cbreak mode and terminal echo of input characters is disabled for the duration of the interactive menu program. At the end, the terminal screen is cleared, and normal `tty` mode is restored. Assuming this program is in the file `menu.c`, you can then compile it with

cc `menu.c -o menu -lcurses -ltermlib`

Now you are ready to try something like

menu `"Today's Specials" "Spring Rolls" "Fried Rice" "Hot and Sour Soup"`

and make a selection.

10.7 Summary

Input/output covered in this chapter are not part of standard C but are additional facilities standard on UNIX systems. The system and library calls presented allow C programs to interface to UNIX directly.

A set of library functions are available for accessing directories. After including the header `<sys/dir.h>`, call `DIR *`**opendir**`(char *dir_name)` to open a directory stream, `struct direct *`**readdir**`(DIR *dp)` to read the directory stream dp, and **closedir**`(DIR *dp)` to close it.

The system calls shed light on how input/output works and provide a way to bypass the standard I/O library when necessary. UNIX system I/O channels are represented by small nonnegative indices called file descriptors. Three preopened descriptors 0, 1, and 2 give each process access to the standard input, output, and error output channels, respectively. Table 10.4 summarizes file- and directory-related I/O calls.

The UNIX terminal driver program `tty` relays input/output between the terminal and the program. It can deal with any kind of terminal by referring to its description in a system database. The amount of processing `tty` performs on the terminal I/O stream depends on its mode of operation: no processing (raw), some processing (cbreak), and full processing (cooked).

A convenient package called curses displays information on a CRT screen. With curses, programs involving interactions with the user through a window displayed on the screen are much easier to write. A program using curses must include the header `<curses.h>` and be compiled with the `-lcurses` option to **cc** (sometimes also followed by `-ltermlib` option).

Call	Function
`int` **open** `(char *file,` `        int access, int mode)`	Opens `file`; returns descriptor.
`int` **read** `(int fd, char *buffer, int k)`	Inputs from `fd` into `buffer`.
`int` **write** `(int fd, char *buffer, int k)`	Outputs `buffer` to `fd`.
`int` **close** `(int fd)`	Closes `fd`.
`int` **lseek** `(int fd, int offset, int origin)`	Moves the read/write position of `fd`.
`int` **access** `(char *name, int a_mode)`	Tests access permission.
`int` **chdir** `(char *dir_name)`	Changes working directory.
`char` ***getwd** `(char *name)`	Obtains name of working directory.
`int` **link** `(char *file, char *name)`	Creates link.
`int` **unlink** `(char *name)`	Removes link.
`int` **mkdir** `(char *name, int mode)`	Creates new directory.
`int` **rmdir** `(char *dir_name)`	Removes directory.
`int` **stat** `(char *name, struct stat *buf)`	Accesses file status.
`int` **fstat** `(int fd, struct stat *buf)`	Accesses file status.
`int` **umask** `(int newmask)`	Sets file-permission mask.

Table 10.4: A Collection of UNIX System I/O Calls

Exercises

1. Write a simple version of the **ls** command with the directory-access functions explained in Section 10.1.

2. Write your own version of **putc** using a line-buffering data structure and low-level I/O system calls.

3. Add your own version of **fflush** to the mechanism of Exercise 2.

4. Explain the effect of the `umask` values `077` and `022`.

5. Consider how the standard library function **fseek** can be implemented using the basic **lseek** system call.

6. The UNIX command **pwd** displays the current working directory. Write your own version of this command.

7. Write a UNIX command **testaccess** that takes an access flag (-r, -w, etc.) and a filename as command-line arguments and returns an exit status of 0 or 1 depending on whether the specified access is permitted.

8. Write a UNIX command **rmold** that takes a date string and removes all files older than the given date in the current directory. If the command is invoked with the -i flag, then the program will go into interactive mode and asks the user at the terminal for approval before actually deleting a file.

9. Modify the menu.c program so that the menu items are displayed on two columns in the window and the ARROW KEYs on the keyboard can make selections.

10. The game *hangman* is popular on many UNIX systems. If your system has this game, find out how it is played, and write a similar program using the curses package.

11. Using the curses package, write a program to play tic-tac-toe, which has a nice looking board.

12. Expand the menu program by allowing special types of entries that cause the display of a submenu. The program should also have features to let the user elect to go up to a parent menu or back directly to the root menu.

13. Write a program to display the calendar of any given month on the terminal with the curses package.

14. Write an interactive-file browser command **filebr** dir that displays the filenames in the given directory inside a curses window. One entry, the current file, is highlighted, and the highlight can be moved with ARROW KEYs. When the user selection is finalized, the status information of the selected file is displayed. The program terminates only when the user quits.

Program Maintenance

C is an efficient programming tool to implement software packages
for a wide range of applications. A software package consists of
many components including source-code files (.c), object-code files
(.o), header files (.h), test suites, on-line documentation, examples,
installation instructions, and so on.

Program maintenance refers to the compiling, debugging, revising,
updating, testing, documenting, and releasing of a piece of software.
Maintenance is the predominant phase in the overall lifespan of a
large software package, amounting to many times the original cost of
development. The total maintenance cost of a large-scale software
system can be as high as 70 percent of its lifetime cost. Even for
relatively small program packages, maintenance can still be
expensive and time-consuming. Thus, it is important to have
efficient tools for managing and maintaining programs.

Various tasks are involved in maintaining a software package:

- Locating bugs or missing features.
- Defining improvements.
- Modifying source programs.
- Recompiling object codes and rebuilding executable modules.
- Performing tests.
- Modifying documentation.
- Preparing the next *release*, a new version of the software.

These activities constitute the software-maintenance cycle; Figure
11.1 shows a simplified view.

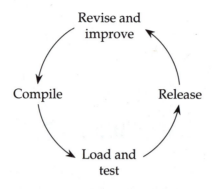

Figure 11.1: Software-Maintenance Cycle

We describe a collection of useful UNIX software facilities for program maintenance: compiling, loading, performance tuning, establishing program libraries, and source-code indexing.

We have written a large number of programs in this book, some with several versions. How will we keep track of them, their interdependencies, and the way each executable program is compiled? The question leads us into the major focus of this chapter: automatic program maintenance with **make**, a convenient, widely used utility that organizes and manages C programs efficiently.

11.1   Stages of Compilation

In Chapter 1, we learned that the **cc** command consists of five stages: preprocessing, compiling, optimizing, assembling, and linking/loading. The compiling phase takes the output of the C preprocessor (CPP) (Chapter 4) and performs *parsing* (syntax checking) and *assembly-code generation*. If the −o option is given, then the code generation will invoke code-optimization routines to improve the efficiency of the generated code. The output of both the compiling and the optimizing phases is assembly code.

The generated assembly code is then processed by the assembler program **as** to produce a *relocatable* object-code file (.o). Relocatable codes can be placed at any starting address in memory rather than being limited to any prespecified location. The relocatable object codes can then be linked together by the loader **ld** to form executable programs.

Linking and Loading

Although linking and loading is the final stage of **cc**, the linker/loader **ld** is an independent command. It is important for C programmers to have a good understanding of how **ld** works.

The linker/loader produces an executable program (the a.out file) by combining user-supplied object files with system-supplied object modules contained in *libraries* (Section 11.4). The **ld** command loads files in the order given on the command line. An object file is relocated and added to the end of the executable binary file under construction. The symbol table of the object file is merged with that of the growing binary file. For a library, **ld** scans the library's symbol table in search of symbols that match undefined function and variable names in the current binary file's symbol table. Object modules in the library that resolve undefined symbols will be added to the binary file. It is therefore important that a library argument be given *after* object files that reference symbols defined in the library.

For example, the **ld** command

> **ld** /lib/crt0.o file1.o file2.o file3.o /lib/libc.a

loads the three object files file1.o, file2.o, and file3.o and produces an executable binary file (a.out by default), which runs under UNIX. The standard object file /lib/crt0.o provides a C program with the necessary UNIX run-time environment, whereas /lib/libc.a is the standard C subroutine library.

Because the **cc** command automatically adds these arguments when it calls **ld**, the following command has the same effect:

> **cc** file1.o file2.o file3.o

After all object and library files have been loaded, **ld** sorts the combined symbol table of the binary file looking for any remaining unresolved references. The final executable module is produced only if no undefined symbols remain.

Options for **ld** can be specified as options of **cc**, which passes any options not processed by the compiling phase on to the later stages as appropriate. The command (Section 10.6)

> **cc** menu.c -o menu -lcurses -ltermlib

asks the loader to use the libraries libcurses.a and libtermlib.a located in system library directories.

The stages of **cc**, the options, the object-code files, and the libraries all contribute to the complexity of program maintenance. Later, in Section 11.6, we show how to automate many such tasks to make management much easier. But first, let's describe some additional **cc** options.

11.2   Options for cc

To better organize, manage, and improve running speed of your C code, knowledge of the various options offered by the C compiler is important. A selected set of frequently used options are described here. On your particular system, the C compiler may provide a few or even many more options.

Because of the close relationship between C and UNIX, the **cc** command has always been a key part of any UNIX system. Through the years, **cc** has provided the *traditional* C compiler, which is still widely available today. But on an increasing number of systems, **cc** now conforms to the ANSI standard. In your installation, you may also find alternatives to **cc**, such as **gcc** (the GNU C compiler from the Free Software Foundation), which provides a good implementation of ANSI C and is used in much the same way as **cc**.

Typically, the **cc** command takes C source files (.c), assembly-source files (.s), and object files (.o) and produces an executable file, typically a.out. The compiling process also produces a corresponding object file (but no assembly file) for each given source file. But, if only one source file is given, the object file is deleted.

You can control the behavior of **cc** by command-line options. A select subset of the available options is described here. A few options we have seen already are included here for completeness:

-c	Produces object (.o) files only. No a.out is produced. This option is used for separate compilation of component modules in a program package.
-g	Generates special symbol table data for and passes the -lg flag to **ld**. The option produces a version of the program for debugging with **dbx**, **sdb**, and other debuggers.
-o *filename*	Names the final, executable output file *filename* instead of a.out.
-O	Activates the optimization stage of the compiling process. The generated code will have improved speed and, most likely, also a smaller size. Optimization algorithms slow the compiler considerably. Apply this option only after your code has been tested and debugged and the code is ready for *production* use.
-l*libname*	Specifies *libname* as a library file to use when linking and loading the executable file. This option is passed by **cc** to **ld**.
-D*name*=*str*	Initializes the **cpp** symbol *name* to the given string *str*. This command-line option is equivalent to inserting #define *name* *str* at the beginning of a source file. If =*str* is omitted, *name* is initialized to 1.

`-Uname`	Undefines the **cpp** symbol *name* to remove its default definition.
`-Idir`	Adds the directory `dir` to the directory list that **cc** searches for `#include` files. The **cc** command searches first in the directory containing the source file, then in any directories specified by the `-I` option, and, finally, in a list of standard system directories. Multiple `-I` options establishes an ordered sequence of additional `#include` file directories.
`-P`	Runs all `.c` files through **cpp** only; the resulting files will carry the `.i` suffix. Inspecting the `.i` files gives you a way to see the source code after substitution and expansion of macros.
`-S`	Generates assembly-language output in files named with the `.s` suffix; no `.o` file or `a.out` is produced.
`-v`	Displays the names and arguments of all subprocesses invoked in the different stages of **cc** (the verbose mode).
`-p`	Prepares to generate an execution profile file to be used by the UNIX **prof** utility to help analyze where a program spends its time.
`-pg`	Prepares to generate an execution profile to be used with the UNIX **gprof** utility.

Consult the on-line manual pages for your C compiler for any deviations or additional options. We describe the profiling of C programs in the next section.

11.3 Performance Tuning

For some programming projects, getting the program implemented, tested, and debugged is followed by efforts to fine-tune the performance of the program for increased execution speed. The objective is simply to make the same basic program run faster. In many cases, time can be saved by reducing calls to I/O functions, eliminating calls to small functions, making recursive functions iterative, and using more efficient data structures.

In the quest for improved performance, one rule of thumb from software engineering is worth noting: *Eighty percent of the time is spent in 20 percent of the code.* Thus, it pays to identify the 20 percent where almost all the time is used. Once these routines are identified, you can target them for improvement and, hopefully, get a marked increase in speed.

11.3.1 Execution Profiling with gprof

How do you really know which routines fall into the 20 percent? UNIX, fortunately, has tools for *execution profiling* to gather information on the amount of time spent in each function, the total number of calls made of any function, and other useful statistics. Two similar commands for profiling are **prof** and **gprof**. Let's describe **gprof** briefly here.

The UNIX command **gprof** helps you digest execution statistics collected, in the file gmon.out, by running an a.out produced with the -gp option to **cc**. To display profiling information on your terminal, simply issue the command

> **gprof** a.out gmon.out

The first part of the displayed information is a *flat profile*: the amount of time and number of calls for each function in the program sorted in decreasing time. From this data, you can already see which individual functions are the most heavily used, and they are, of course, targets for improvement.

The **gprof** command goes one step further and analyzes the *function-call graph*, also represented in gmon.out, of the program. The call graph has nodes representing functions and directed edges representing function calls. In the second part of its display, **gprof** lists the functions with times representing the sum total of times spent in a function and its descendents in the call graph. This information helps identify functions that are used heavily as a group.

Both options -gp (for **gprof**) and -p (for **prof**) depend on the library function **monitor** to collect execution statistics. It is possible to include calls to **monitor** explicitly in your code to gather data on selected functions in a large program instead of on every function as these **cc** options allow you to do. Refer to the manual for **monitor** for more information.

11.3.2 Object Size Reduction with strip

The UNIX **strip** command takes an object file (.o) or an archive file (.a) and removes the symbol table (identifiers and their addresses) and line-number information, resulting in a smaller file. An executable constructed from stripped objects and libraries will be smaller and makes less of a memory demand on a computer.

The command

> **strip** file1.o ...

will replace the named files with the stripped files. This should be done only after the software is completely tested and debugged.

Several options for **strip** control how much information is stripped away. A smaller program may very well also run faster because of time saved on memory management. Producing prestripped object files with the -s option to **ld** (or **cc**) is also possible.

11.4 Libraries and Archives

We have mentioned that **ld** uses libraries in constructing an executable binary file. We also know that the C language itself has a standard library filled with useful functions. Let's take a look at how a subroutine library is created and maintained under the UNIX system. Although our discussion is oriented toward the C language and C functions, libraries for other languages under UNIX are very similar.

A subroutine library usually contains the object-code versions of subroutines that are either of general interest or of importance for a specific project. The idea is to avoid reinventing the wheel and to gather routines that are already written, tested, and debugged in a program library, just like books in an actual library, for all to use. Normally, the library routines are simply loaded with other object files to form the final executable program.

On UNIX a library of object files is actually one form of an *archive file*, a collection of several independent files arranged into the *archive-file format*. A magic number identifying the archive-file format is followed by the constituent files, each preceded by a header. The header contains such information as filename, owner, group, access modes, last modified time, and so on. An archive of object files (a subroutine library) also has a table of contents to identify what symbols are defined in which object files in the archive.

The command **ar** creates and maintains libraries and archives. The general form of the **ar** command is

    ar key [position] archive-name file1 ...

The **ar** command creates, modifies, displays, or extracts information from the given *archive* depending on the *key* specified. The name of an archive file normally uses the .a suffix. Some more important keys are listed here:

r   Puts the given files into the new or existing archive file, *archive-name*. If a file is already in the archive, it is replaced. New files are appended at the end.

q   Quickly appends the given files to the end of a new or existing archive file, *archive-name*, without checking whether a file is already in the archive. This is useful for creating a new archive and adding to a very large archive.

ru
: Same as r except existing files in the archive are replaced only if they are older than the corresponding files specified on the command line.

ri or ra
: After `ri` or `ra`, a *position* argument must be supplied, which is the name of a file in the archive. These are the same as `r`, except new files are inserted before (`ri`) or after (`ra`) the position file in the archive.

t
: Displays the table of contents of the archive file.

x
: Extracts the named files in the archive into the current directory. This, of course, will result in one or several independent files. If no list of names is given, all files will be extracted.

For example, the command

ar `q libme.a file1.o file2.o file3.o file4.o`

creates the archive file `libme.a` by combining the given object files.

For libraries with a large number of routines, searching for the needed modules to load can be time-consuming. On Berkeley UNIX, the command **ranlib** converts an archive file to a form that can be searched more rapidly (required by **ld**). The **ranlib** command does this by adding a table of contents called `_ _.SYMDEF` to the beginning of the archive file. The command

ranlib `lib1.a ...`

converts each library given. You can find many archive files under the system directory `/usr/lib`. On System V, however, there is no need for **ranlib** because the **ar** command does it automatically.

Let's build a library of our own to illustrate the usage of **ar** and **ranlib**. In this example, we take the programs

cir.c
: The circular buffer

strtok.c
: Our implementation of string tokens

arbqsort.c
: Quicksort for arbitrary data items

described in earlier chapters and build them into a library. We first must compile these source-code files by

cc `-c -s -O cir.c strtok.c arbqsort.c`

resulting in `cir.o`, `strtok.o`, and `arbqsort.o`. Now use the command

ar `q libme.a cir.o strtok.o arbqsort.o`

to create the new archive file `libme.a`. Then we must enter

ranlib `libme.a`   (Berkeley UNIX only)

to add the symbol table to `libme.a` so it can be used by **ld**. Finally, move the library file `libme.a` into the system library directory `/usr/lib`. From this point on, the `-lme` option can be given to **cc** or **ld** to use this newly created library.

For instance, you can now compile the line-sorting program `linesort.c` that uses functions supplied by `arbqsort.o` with

    cc `linesort.c -lme`

The command

    ar `tv libme.a`

produces a table of contents of `libme.a`:

```
rw-rw----102/74     178 Nov  7 16:01 1990 _ _.SYMDEF
rw-rw----102/74     448 Nov  7 15:36 1990 arbqsort.o
rw-rw----102/74    1203 Nov  7 15:36 1990 cir.o
rw-rw----102/74     556 Nov  7 15:36 1990 strtok.o
```

If you do not wish or have no permission to locate the `libme.a` file in a system library directory, put the library in your own directory and give the library name explicitly to **cc** (or **ld**) for loading. For the above example, the command sequence becomes

    cc `-c linesort.c`
    cc `linesort.o libme.a`

11.5 Source-File Indexing: Tags File

In managing a software package consisting of multiple source-code files, collecting these files in a single directory is standard practice. On UNIX you can also create a *tags file* in this directory to further facilitate access to source code.

The tags file, once established, lets you use standard editors such as **vi** and **ex** to directly access functions, macros, and `typedefs` without remembering which file contains the desired construct. For instance, the command

    vi `-t qsort`

will use the file `tags` in the current working directory to read into **vi** the correct source file and position the cursor on the function `qsort`. This feature is very convenient for a program with many functions contained in a large number of source-code files.

A tags file can be easily established with the UNIX commands

    cd `dir`
    ctags `*.c *.h`

where `dir` is the directory containing the source-code files. The **ctags** command will create an index file named `tags` containing information about where each function and macro is located. Basically `tags` contains lines in the form

```
name filename pattern
```

where `name` is the function or macro name, `filename` the file containing the construct, and `pattern` a search pattern used by **vi** or **ex** to position the cursor. The `-t` option of **ctags** adds information on `typedefs` to the `tags` file.

The **ctags** command can also produce an index of functions for reference purposes.

11.6 The UNIX make Facility

The UNIX **make** command is a facility to automate the management and maintenance of computer programs. A very useful *software-engineering tool*, **make**, also maintains the UNIX system itself. The **make** program follows a user-prepared description file known as a *makefile* to perform its functions. The contents of makefile describe the dependence relations among the various modules in a package and specify the exact UNIX commands to *update* a module when necessary. A module needs updating when other modules on which it depends have been modified. The makefile descriptions not only direct the actions of **make** but also document the relationships between modules.

The **make** facility (or something like it) is indispensable for any software that will be maintained by a team of programmers. This is especially true when team members come and go frequently or when the software is designed to be reconfigurable (customizable) after distribution. After revisions are made in a software package, the command

make `target`

uses the descriptions provided by the file `Makefile` in the current directory to perform only those actions needed to bring the specified target file up to date. The **make** command carries out the following operations:

1. Finds the description entry for the given target in the makefile.
2. Recursively updates all targets on which the given target depends.
3. Updates `target` if necessary.

A target is usually, but not always, the name of a file in the software package. Whether a target needs updating is determined by comparing the creation/modification time stamps of the target file with those of the files on

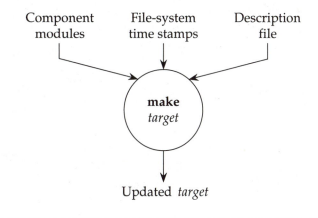

Figure 11.2: Function of **make**

which it depends (as specified by the dependencies contained in the make-file). A file on which a target file depends is called a *component* of that target file. If the target file does not have the most recent time stamp, it needs updating. Figure 11.2 gives an overall picture of the **make** command. The **make** facility automates the rather tedious process of regenerating an execut-able file after modifications have been made to different C source-code mod-ules scattered randomly through a large system. It can also handle other pro-cedures related to the maintenance of the software package, such as running *test suites* (a set of known test cases), generating cross-reference lists, and so on. The **make** command is such a powerful and flexible tool partly because it relies on the UNIX file system for time information and can execute virtually any shell-level commands specified in the makefile.

11.6.1 Makefile Basics

The **make** utility follows the descriptions contained in a makefile to perform its tasks. The makefile specifies two kinds of information about files con-tained in a software package: dependencies among files and exactly how each file is brought up to date. A typical entry in the makefile is of the form

```
target : zero or more components
TABcommand1
TABcommand2
    .
    .
    .
```

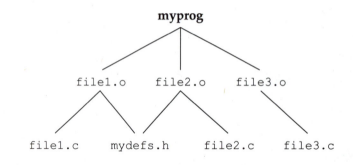

Figure 11.3: A File-Dependence Graph

where *target* and *components* are generally names of files being controlled. On the first line (the dependence line), a target file on the left side of the colon (:) is declared to be dependent on zero or more other files following the colon. The sequence of commands below the dependence line prescribes the actions that must be taken to bring the *target* up to date in case one or more of its components have been modified. The presence of a TAB character is indicated by the word TAB. The first character of each command line must be a TAB.

Consider a small example where the executable **myprog** relies on three object files `file1.o`, `file2.o`, and `file3.o`, each of which in turn depends on the corresponding C source-code file. The files `file1.o` and `file2.o` also depend on a header file `mydefs.h`, as illustrated by the dependence graph in Figure 11.3. The makefile in Figure 11.4 specifies the dependence relationships shown in the dependence graph. The meaning of *dependency* as used by **make** refers only to the chain of updating activities necessary to accommodate modifications made to files in a software package. Because the file `mydefs.h` is included in the files `file1.c` and `file2.c` via `#include`, `file1.c` and `file2.c` will not need updating if `mydefs.h` is modified. Hence, the makefile does not specify `file1.c` or `file2.c` as *dependent* on the header file `mydefs.h`. Instead, `mydefs.h` is a component of the object files `file1.o` and `file2.o` because they need to be recompiled if either the source code or the header file changes.

Entries in Figure 11.4 are more repetitive than they need to be. The **make** utility uses certain default-dependency rules to simplify frequently used entries. For example, without explicit descriptions to the contrary, any object file *name*`.o` is automatically dependent on the corresponding source

```
myprog : file1.o file2.o file3.o
TAB        cc file1.o file2.o file3.o -o myprog

file1.o : file1.c mydefs.h
TAB         cc -c file1.c

file2.o : file2.c mydefs.h
TAB         cc -c file2.c

file3.o : file3.c
TAB         cc -c file3.c
```

Figure 11.4: Dependence Rules

file *name*.c. Default dependencies will be more fully described in a later section. Using such default rules, the description file becomes

```
myprog : file1.o file2.o file3.o
TAB        cc file1.o file2.o file3.o -o myprog

file1.o file2.o : mydefs.h
```

11.6.2 The make Description File

The description file is usually named `makefile` or `Makefile` but is not restricted to these names. The description file can be considered a program that **make** understands. We have seen a simple example where targets represent files. The description file can also contain *fake targets* that do not correspond to files. Instead of file updating, a fake target triggers other actions related to the maintenance of the software package. Examples of such actions are running test cases, installing executables in system directories, generating cross references, and removing unwanted files. Recording the command sequences for these actions in the description file not only automates the actions but also provides documentation. In fact, reading the description file is a good way to understand a software package.

Four kinds of statements are in a description file: macro definitions, dependence rules, commands, and comments.

In a description file, comments begin with the character #. Text from the # until the end of the line is ignored. A statement in the **make** description file must be on one line. A long statement can be continued to the next line by placing a backslash (\\) at the end of a line. In which case, the \\, NEWLINE, and any following TABs or blanks are read by **make** as a single blank.

Let's describe the other three kinds of statements in turn.

Macros

A macro is simply a shorthand used in the description file. (Do not confuse these macros with CPP macros.) You define a macro by

   NAME **=** *value*

where *NAME* is a string of letters and/or digits and *value* is any number of words terminated by a NEWLINE. White space, but no TAB, can precede a macro definition. Some sample macro definitions are

```
OBJS = file1.o file2.o file3.o
SRCDIR = user/john/proj
FLAGS = -c -O
3 = /usr/xyz
NULL =
```

A macro can be used anywhere in the description file after it is defined. To substitute the value of a macro into a statement, use `$(`*NAME*`)` or equivalently `${`*NAME*`}`. For example,

```
prog : ${OBJS}
        echo $3
        cc $(FLAGS) $(SRCDIR)/file1.c
```

If a macro name contains only one character or digit, then it can be used without the surrounding parentheses or braces.

Dependence Rules

The most important part of a **make** description file is the dependence rules. A dependence rule consists of three parts:

- One or more targets
- Zero or more components
- Zero or more commands for updating the targets

The general form of a dependence rule is

```
target1 [target2 ...] :[:] [component1 ...] [; commands]
[ TAB commands ]
        .
        .
        .
```

where, as usual, optional parts are enclosed in brackets. The first line of each dependence rule is a *dependence line*, and it may use either a single or a double colon. Double-colon rules specify different command sequences for different components of a target:

1. When a target is on one or more *single-colon dependence rules*, only one of these dependence rules can have a sequence of commands. If a target needs updating due to any of the dependence rules, the sequence of commands will be executed. For example,

    ```
    prog : file3.o
    TAB     cc file1.o file2.o file3.o -o prog

    prog : file1.o file2.o
    ```

    will recompile prog if any of the three object files have changed.

2. When a target is on one or more *double-colon dependence rules*, each dependence rule can have its own sequence of commands. If the target is out of date on a particular dependence line, the associated commands are executed. For example,

    ```
    prog :: file1.o
    TAB     commands1
    prog :: file2.o
    TAB     commands2
    ```

In a description file, a target can appear on more than one dependence rule of either the single-colon or double-colon type, but not both.

Specifying Commands

Each command can be given on a different line whose first character must be a TAB character (except on the dependence line). Commands can be placed on the same line if they are separated by semicolons (;). Each command is normally displayed before execution. But the display can be suppressed by preceding the command with a @ character (after the leading TAB). Each command line is macro-substituted by **make** before execution by an *sh* shell. A different *sh* shell is used for each line. Commands on the same line are interpreted by the same **sh** shell. Specifying *csh* commands in a makefile is possible. Do this by explicitly calling for *csh* in the command line:

```
TAB    csh command arg1 . . .
```

Because the **make** facility uses the character $ for macro expansion, a shell-level variable $x must be expressed as $$x in the makefile.

11.6.3 Special Macros

When **make** decides that a target needs updating, it also sets the special macros $@, $<, $*, and $?. The settings of these special macros are as follows:

- $@ is set to the name of the target (file to be made).
- $< is set to the component filename generated by **make** when the action is caused by a built-in rule. See the next section for more details.
- $* is set to the common basename of the target and the component. For example, if the target is xyz.o and the component xyz.c, then $* is set to xyz.
- $? is set to the string of components newer than the target.

Here is a section of a description file that involves the special macro $@:

```
CFLAGS= -O
CMD= grep hostid hostname kill ld ln login \  # line continuation
     ls mail mkdir nice

${CMD} mv cp:
TAB      cc ${CFLAGS} -o $@ $@.c
```

Using this description, the command

make grep

for example, results in the updating action

```
cc -O -o grep grep.c
```

because the special macro $@ is set to grep.

11.6.4 Implicit Rules and Suffix Dependency

Earlier we briefly mentioned that **make** has built-in rules to make things easier. This is especially true for maintaining software written in C. Basically, **make** already knows that a .o file is dependent on the corresponding .c file and the command used for updating is to compile the .c file. Furthermore, you can specify the compiler and the options to use because the updating command is implicitly defined as

```
$(CC) $(CFLAGS) -c $<
```

where `$<` is a special macro, which now stands for a `.c` file used to produce a particular target `.o` file. The built-in macros have the default values

```
CC=cc
CFLAGS=
```

By redefining these macros, you can name the compiler and specify options needed. For example,

```
CC=/usr/local/bin/gcc    # GNU C compiler
CFLAGS= -O               # optimize
```

can be included in the makefile.

The **make** command recognizes some other filename suffixes and has additional implicit rules; however, the information presented here should suffice for most C applications.

11.7 Building Makefiles

Based on the materials presented so far, we can list the following rules to help you write your first makefile:

1. Establish a directory and put in it all the source, object, header, executable, test, and documentation files. Depending on the number of files, they can all be in one directory or be grouped and placed into appropriate subdirectories.
2. Write a `Makefile` to control the maintenance of the software package.
3. In the `Makefile`, establish typical macros such as `SRCS` and `OBJS` to collect the names of all source and object files, respectively.
4. Establish a rule to derive the final executable system from all the objects (`$(OBJS)`).
5. Establish a rule to build each object-code file from the source and header files on which it depends. Because of the built-in rules, normally you just need to explicitly declare which object file depends on which header file.
6. If the compiler to be used is not **cc**, then you need to define the macro `CC`.
7. If you need compiler flags such as `-g`, `-O`, then you can define the macro `CFLAGS` appropriately.

These rules usually suffice for simple makefiles, and you can learn the finer details as you get more experience.

11.8 Example Makefiles

Let's now apply what we have learned about **make** and makefiles in a simple but concrete example. Assume that you have a directory `sortdir` containing a program to sort text lines based on `quicksort` (Section 6.7). The files in `sortdir` include

```
Makefile     arbqsort.c    arbqsort.h    arbqsort.o
linesort     linesort.c    linesort.o
```

where `linesort` is the executable file and `Makefile` is the **make** description file shown in Figure 11.5.

Macro definitions are usually put in the beginning of a makefile. The built-in macros `CFLAGS` and `CC` are redefined first. The `CC` definition causes **gcc**, the GNU C compiler, to be used instead of the default value of `CC`. Next come the user-defined macros `OBJS` and `SRCS`, representing a list of all object files and a list of all source files, respectively.

The first dependence rule is for the target `linesort`, the executable file of this program. The components of `linesort` are the object files. When necessary, the command

```
$(CC) $(CFLAGS) -o linesort $(OBJS)
```

(the second to the last line) will update `linesort`. The dependence rule on the very last line in the makefile simply says each of the object files is dependent on the header file `arbqsort.h`. If an updated `arbqsort.h` triggers the updating of an object file, what command is used? The answer is the default

```
# Definitions for built-in macros
CFLAGS= -O
CC= gcc   # gnu ANSI c compiler

# Definitions for other macros
OBJS=arbqsort.o linesort.o
SRCS=arbqsort.c linesort.c arbqsort.h

# Dependence rules
linesort: $(OBJS)
$(CC) $(CFLAGS) -o linesort $(OBJS)

$(OBJS) : arbqsort.h
```

Figure 11.5: Makefile for `quicksort`

command, namely, the action defined implicitly by **make** to update a `.o` file (see Section 11.6).

With the above `Makefile` in place, building a new executable file simply involves the steps

```
cd sortdir
make linesort
```

The **make** command will then automatically carry out all the necessary actions to build `linesort`, displaying each action taken:

```
gcc -O -c arbqsort.c
gcc -O -c linesort.c
gcc -O -o linesort arbqsort.o linesort.o
```

Again, **make** performs only those actions necessary to update the target. If you repeat the same **make** command, you'll get the message

```
'linesort' is up to date
```

If you modify `linesort.c`, but not `arbqsort.c`, and if `arbqsort.o` is up to date, then **make** will only rebuild `linesort.o`.

The same `Makefile` can be used to build an executable file for debugging. Simply enter

```
make "CFLAGS=-g" linesort
```

The command-line definition of `CFLAGS` overrides the corresponding definition inside `Makefile`, resulting in the actions

```
gcc -g -c arbqsort.c
gcc -g -c linesort.c
gcc -g -o linesort arbqsort.o linesort.o
```

11.8.1 Fake Targets

The previous `Makefile` can be expanded to perform additional maintenance tasks. The rules

```
test: linesort
        rm -f test.out
        linesort test.in > test.out

clean:
        rm -f $(OBJS)
        rm -f test.out
```

can be added so that you can use

make test

to test the executable code and produce a new test-output file test.out. Then use

make clean

to remove the test output and all object-code files afterward to free up the disk storage space. The targets clean and test are *fake* because they do not correspond to any real files in the directory. Furthermore, we can add the makefile entry

```
tags: $(SRCS)
        rm -f tags
        ctags -t $(SRCS)
```

to remove the old tags file and produce a new one.

To further automate the maintenance process, add the rule

```
all: linesort test tags
```

to Makefile, allowing you to use

make all

to build linesort, test.out, and tags. You can then simply examine test.out to see if everything is all right. If so, do a

make clean

and you are done.

11.9 Multiple Subdirectories

Our next example has to do with invoking **make** within a makefile. For larger program packages, a number of subdirectories are usually under the main directory where the package is contained. There could be one subdirectory for each major part of the package or one for each member of the programming team. The makefile in the main directory can invoke **make** on its subdirectories. Under this arrangement, the description files can reside in the subdirectories while a **make** call invoked at the main directory can initiate all **make** actions. Here is an example:

```
SUBDIRS = dir1 dir2

CFLAGS = -O
OBJ = dir1/f1.o dir2/f2.o f3.o f4.o f5.o
```

```
chess: ${SUBDIRS} ${OBJ}
        cc -o chess ${OBJ}
        @echo chess done

${SUBDIRS}: /tmp
        cd $@; make ${MFLAGS}
```

The primary target is a chess program. All source files are in C. The two sub-directories `dir1` and `dir2` are under the control of separate makefiles invoked by the makefile here. The `/tmp` simply triggers the actions for the subdirectories because the operating system heavily uses the system directory `/tmp`, which should always have a more recent time stamp than any subdirectory. `MFLAGS` is a **make** built-in macro that is set to any flags specified on the command line. Note that the last line in the above makefile contains two shell-level commands. In general, commands to be executed in the changed-to directory should be given *on the same line* as the **cd** command. This is necessary because each new command line is executed by a different shell.

The entire UNIX system is made exactly this way with a *super makefile*. The results are redirected to a file and examined for errors before releasing for general use.

11.10 The make Command

The simplest way to use the **make** command is first to move to the main directory containing the makefile and the files (and subdirectories) of the software package. Once you are in the main directory, simply type

> **make** [*target* ...]

If no target is specified, the first target in the description that does not begin with a period is used. When multiple targets are given, they are processed sequentially in the order listed.

The general form of the **make** command is

> **make** [*macro* ...] [-f *filename*] [*options*] [*targets*]

The option `-f` specifies a name for the makefile to be used. As mentioned before, the default filename for the makefile is `makefile` or `Makefile` (in that order) in the current working directory. The option `-r` instructs **make** not to use the built-in rules. Another useful option is `-n`, which instructs **make** to display commands, but not to execute them. Even lines beginning with an @ sign are displayed. This is good for testing your own makefile or examining what someone else's makefile does.

11.11 Summary

Coding is only a small part of the overall effort to build and maintain a software system. UNIX provides many useful tools for maintaining C programs, and familiarity with these tools can make you a much more effective programmer.

Many options to the **cc** command have been presented including -c (separate compilation), -o (optimization), -l (library specification), -I (additional #include directory), -g (debugging), and -pg (profiling). The command **gprof** analyzes and displays profiling data collected and lets you identify and improve key parts of your program. The **strip** command removes nonessential information in object and library files to make executables smaller.

The **ar** and **ranlib** commands establish and maintain subroutine libraries. The **ctags** command creates a tags file that is used with the **vi** editor to access C functions, macros, and typedefs directly in many different source files.

Various maintenance tasks can also be automated with the **make** facility. The **make** command works with a user-supplied description file called a makefile. Following the dependence relations and updating commands provided in the makefile, **make** can bring the target files specified by the user up to date or perform other useful tasks.

Commands in the makefile are ordinary sh commands with the added feature of makefile macro expansion. The **make** command also has a set of built-in macros and rules, such as file.o depending on file.c, to capture frequently used dependences. You can override built-in rules with explicit rules. The **make** command is important especially for larger program packages and for programs maintained by more than one person.

Exercises

1. Can the command

    cc file1.o file2.o file2.o

    be replaced by

    ld file1.o file2.o file2.o

    and why?

2. Are the commands

    cc file1.o file2.o -llib1.a -llib2.a
    cc file1.o file2.o -llib2.a -llib1.a

    equivalent? Why?

3. Profile the `linesort` program (Section 6.4.3) with **gprof**.

4. Apply the **strip** command to a program of yours and compare the size of the reduced executable to one not stripped.

5. Establish a tags file in one of your source directories and see how convenient **vi** -t can be.

6. Explain the meaning of the **make** built-in macros `$<`, `$@`, `MFLAGS`, and `CFLAGS`.

7. `LOADLIBS` is also a built-in macro for **make**. Find out how it works (**man** `make`) and write a `Makefile` for the interactive menu program (Section 10.6).

8. Explain the effects of preceding a **make** updating command with an @ or a – character.

9. Explain the meaning of the dependence rule

```
dir1: /tmp
        cd dir1; make
```

and why the artificial component `/tmp` cannot simply be dropped. Also explain why **cd** and **make** must be put on one line.

10. Follow the example in Section 11.4 and establish your own library. Then compile and run a program that requires linking in functions from this library.

12

Multiprogramming _____

The term *multiprogramming* refers to the *concurrent execution* of _____ multiple programs on a computer. The execution of a single program gives rise to a *process* of which there are many in a multi-programming system. The processes are concurrent in the sense that their executions overlap in time. Although not part of the ANSI C, multiprogramming is important for contemporary computer systems. On a time-sharing system with multiple users, multiprogramming is a must. Even for a single-user workstation, concurrent processes usually exist to help operate and manage the system. For example, a window-manager process may be present to handle the window-menu-oriented user interface, a mail program may be constantly monitoring incoming electronic mail, and a networking process may be executing in the background to handle network traffic to and from the workstation. In addition, UNIX itself uses multiprogramming to perform its duties. The `tty` terminal drivers, which constantly update the CRT screens as users type their input, are examples.

In this chapter, we describe the concept of a process in detail and explain how you can control multiple processes. We also explain the creation of a new, independently running *child process* by an existing *parent process*. Multiple child processes can be created to perform different tasks. The parent and child processes can also communicate with each other through a UNIX-provided mechanism called a *pipe*.

The special status C enjoys on UNIX systems is brought home. Many examples of C programs are given, including several complete programs to demonstrate interprocess communication (ipc) using pipes and to help illustrate the inner workings of the UNIX shell-level pipeline mechanism.

The material contained here is at a more advanced level and can be safely omitted for more basic courses.

12.1 UNIX Process Control

We already know that UNIX manages multiple concurrent processes. When created, each individual process has, among other things, memory space allocated for its exclusive use. This memory space is often referred to as the *address space* of a process. The address space is composed of a *text area*, a *data area*, and a *stack area*:

- Text: The machine instructions that represent the procedures or functions in the program. This part of a process will generally stay unchanged over the lifetime of the process.
- Data: The values of variables, arrays and structures. Objects allocated at compile time will occupy fixed memory locations in the data area. Room for dynamically allocated (through **malloc**) space is also part of the data area.
- Stack: A last-in-first-out data structure used to manage function calls, returns, parameter passing, and returned values. The memory used for the stack will grow and shrink with the depth of nesting of function calls.

Besides the address space, each process is also assigned *system resources* necessary for the UNIX kernel, the central part of the operating system, to manage the process.

Each process is represented by an entry in the *process table*, which is manipulated by the kernel to manage all processes. The kernel schedules the CPU and switches from running one process to the next in rapid succession. Thus, the processes appear to make progress concurrently. On a computer with multiple CPUs, a number of processes can actually run simultaneously or in parallel.

A process usually goes through a number of *states* before running to completion. Some of the states are the following:

Running   The process is executing.

Asleep   The process is waiting for an *event* to occur. Such an event could be an I/O completion by a peripheral device, the termination of another process, the availability of data or space in a buffer, the freeing of a system resource, and so on. When a running process has to wait for such an event, it goes to *sleep*. This creates an opportunity for a *context switch*, shifting the CPU to another process. Later, it awakens and becomes *ready* to run.

Ready   The process is scheduled for CPU service.

Zombie   The process no longer exists. After termination of execution, a process goes into the *zombie* state. The data structure left behind contains its exit status and any timing statistics collected. This is always the last state of a process.

A process can go through the intermediate states many times before it is finished.

From a programming point of view, a UNIX process is the entity created by the **fork** system call. When UNIX is booted, there is only one process (process 0) which uses the **fork** system call to create process 1, known as the *init* process. The *init* process is the ancestor of all other processes, including your login shell.

12.1.1 Executable-File Format

An executable file—for example, a.out— is created by compiling and loading source programs and is composed of, in order, five sections:

1. *Header*
2. *Text* and *data* of the program
3. *Relocation information*
4. *Symbol table*
5. *String table*

The header contains information about the executable file. It contains a *magic number* (a long integer), the entry point to the program, and the sizes of the other sections in bytes. The magic number is a code that indicates the type of the executable program. The text and data sections have been described already. The relocation information, symbol table, and string table sections are useful for debugging purposes but are not absolutely necessary for program execution. Therefore, they may be omitted if the program is loaded with the -s option of **ld** or if the executable file has been processed by the **strip** command of UNIX.

The header provides information for **ld** but is not itself loaded into the address space of a process. The text segment begins at location 0 in the process-address space. The exact layout of the text and data segments and whether the text segment is sharable (write-protected) depends on the value of the magic number.

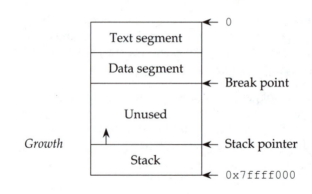

Figure 12.1: Process-Memory Layout

The stack will occupy the highest possible locations in the process-address space and is dynamically extended as required: growing downward from `0x7ffff000` toward the end of the data area (Figure 12.1). A stack pointer to the current top of the stack is kept. The current upper limit of the data segment is known as the *break point*. This break point remains fixed during program execution unless the **brk** system call changes it. The virtual memory addresses between the break point and the stack pointer are not part of the process-address space (see Figure 12.1).

Besides the user areas, each process also has a kernel data and stack area called the `u_area`, which contains additional information for a particular process:

- All open file descriptors
- Open-file table
- Current working and root directories
- System-call parameters, returned values, and error codes
- A pointer to its process-table entry

Data kept in the `u_area` can only be accessed and manipulated by the process while performing operating system functions such as input/output, interrupt handling, and context switching.

12.1.2 The Process Table

A systemwide *process table*, maintained in the UNIX kernel, controls all processes. Each existing process has one table entry. Each process entry contains such information as

- PID: A unique integer process ID.
- UID: Real and effective owner and group IDs of user executing this process.

- State: The current process state.
- Event: Any event for which the process may be waiting (sleeping).
- Size: The size (memory requirement) for the process.
- Locations: Pointers to the `u_area` and to the per-process region table, which contains the pointers to the text, data, and stack regions of the process.
- Priority: Parameters for the scheduling of the process.
- Signals: Signals received but not yet acted on by the process.
- Accounting: Timing information, such as execution time, idle time, kernel-resource utilization, and so on, used for scheduling and billing.

12.2 The ps Command

You can obtain various kinds of information on processes from the shell level. The UNIX command

ps   (display **p**rocess **s**tatus)

displays information about existing processes on your terminal. Because UNIX is a multiuser system and because many system processes perform various chores to keep UNIX functioning, numerous processes are ongoing at any given time. The **ps** command displays a set of reasonable processes that are likely to be of interest to you, and options control what subset of processes are displayed. The **ps** command displays information only for processes belonging to you unless given the option -a (for all). Also, **ps** displays in short form unless given the option -l (for long). For example,

ps -al

displays, in long form, all "interesting" processes. The option -g forces the display to include certain uninteresting processes (e.g., `getty` processes for terminal lines):

ps -ag

Information provided for each process includes the following:

PID	The process ID in integer form
PPID	The parent process ID in integer form
STAT	The state of the process
TIME	CPU time (in seconds) used by the process
TT	Control terminal of the process
COMMAND	The user command that started this process

The state STAT is given by a sequence of four letters, for instance, RWNA. The first letter indicates the runnability of the process (Table 12.1); the second letter indicates whether a process is swapped out (Table 12.2); the third letter indicates whether a process is running with lowered or raised scheduling priority (Table 12.3); the fourth letter indicates any special treatment of the process for virtual memory replacement. This information is usually unimportant for the user. The manual page on **ps** has more details.

First Letter	Process State
R	Runnable
T	Stopped
P	In page wait
D	In disk (or other short-term) waits
S	Sleeping for less than about 20 seconds
I	Idle (sleeping longer than about 20 seconds)

Table 12.1: Process Status

Second Letter	Memory Status
W	Swapped out
Blank	In memory
>	Exceeding soft limit on memory (not swapped)

Table 12.2: Memory Status

Third Letter	Priority Status
N	Reduced priority (NICE)
<	Artificially raised priority
Blank	Normal priority

Table 12.3: Priority Status

If you have a long running program, use **ps** to check its status. System administrators also use **ps** to check for stray background processes and to remove them (with **kill**) from the system.

12.3 Long Running Programs

For a program that takes a long time to complete, you may want to log off and leave the process behind to run in the background. With *csh* do this with

```
command  >& file.out &
```

where *command*, of course, would invoke the long running program. Its standard output and standard error output are redirected to the file `file.out`. The final `&` tells *csh* to put the process in the background and to make it ignore `SIGHUP`, a hangup signal sent to all your processes when you log off.

For the *sh* shell, you can achieve similar effects with

nohup *command* 1> `file.out` 2> `error.out` &

where the **nohup** command explicitly makes the process ignore the hangup signal.

When you log in next time, check on this process you left behind with the **ps** command.

12.4 Process Creation: fork

The **fork** system call, used inside a C program, creates another process. The process that calls **fork** is referred to as the *parent process*, and the newly created process is known as the *child process*. After the **fork** call, the child and the parent run concurrently. The **fork** call is invoked in the form

```
int pid;
pid = fork();
```

The child process created is a copy of the parent process, except that the child process has a:

- Unique PID.
- Different PPID (PID of its parent).

The **fork** is called by the parent but returns in both the parent and the child (Figure 12.2). In the parent, it returns the PID of the child process; whereas in the child it returns 0. If **fork** fails, no child process is created, and it returns −1. Here is a template for using **fork**:

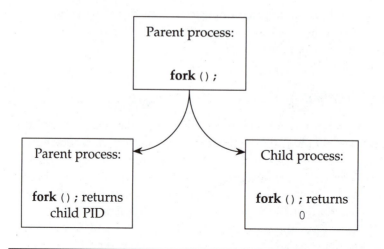

Figure 12.2: Process Creation

```
int pid;
if ((pid = fork()) == 0)
{
     /* put code for child here              */
}
if ( pid < 0 )
{
     /* fork failed; put error handling here */
}
/* fork successful; put remaining code for parent here*/
```

The following simple program illustrates process creation, concurrent execution, and the relationships between the child and the parent across the **fork** call:

```
#include <stdio.h>

main()
{ int pid;
     pid = fork();          /* process creation    */
     if ( pid == 0 )        /* child code begin    */
     {   printf("Child says my pid=%d and my parent pid=%d\n",
               getpid(), getppid());
         _exit(0);          /* child terminates (i) */
     }                      /* child code end      */
     /* remaining parent code */
```

terminates child process

```
        if ( pid < 0 )
        {    fprintf(stderr, "fork failed\n");
             exit(1);
        }
        printf("Parent says child pid = %d\n", pid);
    }
```

After calling **fork**, you suddenly have two processes, the parent and the child, executing the same program starting at the point where **fork** returns.

The child and parent execute different code sections in our example because of the way the program is written. The child only executes the part of the program under if(pid == 0). At the end of the child code (line i), it must terminate execution. Otherwise, the child would continue into the code meant only for the parent. The **_exit** call is slightly different from **exit** and is explained in Section 12.7. Note also that a process can use the system calls **getpid**(void) and **getppid**(void) to obtain the PID of itself and its parent, respectively. The above program produces the following output:

```
Parent says child pid = 2352
Child says my pid=2352 and my parent pid=2351
```

To further illustrate the use of **fork**, we can write a program that uses the child to compute the partial sums and the parent to calculate the partial products of an array of integers:

```
#include <stdio.h>
#define DIM 8

main()
{ int pid, i, ans;
  int arr[DIM]={1,2,3,4,5,6,7,8};
      pid = fork();
      if ( pid == 0 )   /* child code begin */
      {    ans = 0;
           for ( i = 0 ; i < DIM ; i++ )
           {    ans = ans + arr[i];
                printf("Child: sum = %d\n", ans);
           }
           _exit(0);
      }                  /* child code end   */
      if ( pid < 0 )
      {    fprintf(stderr, "fork failed\n");
           exit(1);
      }
```

```
                ans = 1;
                for ( i = 0 ; i < DIM ; i++ )
                {   ans = ans * arr[i];
                    printf("Parent: product = %d\n", ans);
                }
        }
```

Both parent and child have access to their own copies of the array `arr`, the variable `ans`, and so on. The fact that both processes are assigning values to `ans` concurrently does not matter because the programs are running in different address spaces. Here is one possible form of output by this program:

```
Parent: product = 1
Child: sum = 1
Parent: product = 2
Child: sum = 3
Child: sum = 6
Parent: product = 6
Child: sum = 10
Parent: product = 24
Parent: product = 120
Child: sum = 15
Parent: product = 720
Child: sum = 21
Child: sum = 28
Parent: product = 5040
Child: sum = 36
Parent: product = 40320
```

Depending on the relative speed of execution and other system-load factors, the output lines from the parent and the child can be interweaved in a different way.

12.5 Program Execution: exec Routines

The child process is not restricted to executing a subset of the statements in the parent process. It can also execute another program by *overlaying* itself with an executable file. The target executable file is read in on top of the address space of the very process that is executing and overwriting it. Execution continues at the entry point of the target file. The result is that the child process begins to execute a new program, under the same execution environment as the old program, which is now replaced.

The above described program overlay can be initiated by any one of the **exec** routines, including the library functions **execl, execv, exect**, and several others, each a variation of the basic **execv** system call. To avoid confusion, however, we will use the common prefix **exec** when discussing general features of these routines.

To the calling program, the **exec** is a call that never returns. An **exec** call is often combined with **fork** to produce a new process that runs another program:

1. Process A (the parent process) calls **fork** to produce a child process B.
2. Process B immediately calls **exec** to run a new program.

The following attributes stay the same after an **exec** call:

- Process ID
- Parent process ID
- Process group ID
- Access groups
- Working directory
- Root directory
- Control terminal
- Resource usages
- Interval timers
- Resource limits
- File-mode mask (`umask`)
- Signal mask

Furthermore, descriptors that are open in the calling process usually remain open. Ignored signals remain ignored across an **exec**, but signals that are caught are reset to their default values. Signal handling has been discussed in Section 9.7.

The different **exec** routines differ in the type and number of arguments they take. The **execv** system call takes an `argv` array of strings

```
int execv(char *filename, char *argv[])
```

where `filename` is the full pathname of an executable file and `argv` is the command-line arguments, with `argv[0]` being the command name.

This system call overlays the calling process with a new executable program. If **execv** returns, an error has occurred. In this case, the value returned is –1. By convention at least one argument must be present in the `argv` array, and the first element of this array should be the name of the executed program.

A Simple Shell

As an example, let's write a program that is a very simple shell performing the following tasks:

1. Displays a prompt.
2. Reads a command line from the terminal.
3. Starts a background process to execute the command.
4. Goes back to step 1.

The `main` program implements this cycle:

```
#include <stdio.h>
#define MAXLINE 80
typedef char *String;


main()
{ char cmd[MAXLINE];
  void background(String cmd);
      for (;;)
        {   printf("mysh ready%%");   /* prompt                 */
            gets(cmd);                /* read command           */
            background(cmd);          /* start background job */

        }

}
```

The function `background` prepares the `argv` array and starts a child process, which then calls **execv** to perform the given `cmd` while `background` returns in the parent process:

```
#include <string.h>
#define WHITE "\t \n"
#define MAXARG 20


void background(String cmd)
{ String argv[MAXARG];
  int id, i = 0;
      /* to fill in argv */
      argv[i++] = strtok(cmd, WHITE);
      while ( i < MAXARG &&
              (argv[i++] = strtok(NULL, WHITE)) != NULL );
      if ( (id = fork()) == 0 )    /* child executes background job */
      {   execv(argv[0], argv);
          _exit(1);  /* execv failed */

      }
```

```
        else if ( id < 0 )
        {   fprintf(stderr, "fork failed\n");
            perror("background:");
        }
}
```

After the program is compiled, run it and enter a command string after the prompt:

a.out
```
mysh ready% /bin/ls -l
```

The directory listing produced this way should match the one obtained in your usual shell. In fact, virtually any UNIX command executed with a full pathname will behave the same. Type the keyboard interrupt character to quit from the `mysh` program.

The **execl** routine is a convenient alternative to **execv** when the filename and the arguments are known and can be given specifically. The general form is

```
int execl(char *name, char *arg0, char *arg1, ..., char *argn, 0);
```

An example is

```
execl("/bin/ls","ls", "-l",0);
```

Because **fork** copies the entire parent process, it is wasteful when used in conjunction with an **exec** call to create a new execution context. In a virtual memory system, the system call

```
int vfork(void)
```

should be used in conjunction with an **exec** call. Unlike **fork**, **vfork** avoids much of the copying of the address space of the parent process and is therefore much more efficient. Note that **vfork** may not be available on all UNIX systems. Also, don't use it unless immediately followed by **exec**.

12.6 Synchronization of Parent and Child Processes

After creating a child process by **fork**, the parent process may proceed independently or elect to wait for the child process to terminate before proceeding further. The system call

```
#include <sys/wait.h>
int pid = wait(union wait *status);
```

searches for a terminated child (in the *zombie* state) of the calling process. It performs the following steps:

1. If there are no child processes, **wait** returns immediately with the value –1 (an error).
2. If one or more child processes are already in the zombie state (terminated), **wait** selects an arbitrary zombie child, frees its process-table slot for reuse, stores its exit status in the argument variable to **wait**, and returns its PID.
3. Otherwise, **wait** sleeps until one of the child processes terminates and then goes to step 2.

The `union wait` is defined as follows (see Section 7.10 for `union`):

```
union wait
{   int    w_status;
    struct
    {   unsigned short  w_Termsig:7;   /* termination signal       */
        unsigned short  w_Coredump:1;  /* core-dump indicator      */
        unsigned short  w_Retcode:8;   /* exit code if w_termsig==0 */
    }    w_T;                          /* interrupted process status */
    struct
    {   unsigned short  w_Stopval:8;   /* == W_STOPPED if stopped   */
        unsigned short  w_Stopsig:8;   /* signal causing suspension */
    }    w_S;                          /* suspended process status   */
};
```

When **wait** returns after the termination of a child, the argument variable `status` to **wait** is set. Basically, `status` is an unsigned short integer (16 bits). The high byte of `status` contains the low byte of the exit status of the child process. The low byte of `status` contains zero if the child has finished execution normally. If the child's termination is due to a **signal**, then the numerical ID of the signal is contained in the low-order 7 bits. Bit 8 is set only if a core dump of the child has been produced.

A parent process can control the execution of a child process much more closely by using the **ptrace** (process trace) system call. This system call is primarily used for interactive breakpoint debugging such as that supported by the **dbx** command (Chapter 9). When the child process is *traced* by its parent, the **wait** call also returns when the child process is stopped (suspended temporarily). In this case, the low-order byte of the variable `status` is set to the constant `WSTOPPED` (`0177`). The high-order byte contains the signal that caused the suspension.

Let's look at a simple example of the **fork** and **wait** system calls. Here the parent process calls **fork** twice and produces two child processes. Each child simply displays its own PID and terminates. The parent process calls

wait twice to wait for the termination of the two child processes. After each **wait**, the PID and the wait status are displayed:

```
#include <stdio.h>
#include <sys/wait.h>

main()
{ int pid1, pid2, pid;
  union wait status;
      if ( (pid1 = fork()) == 0 )   /* child one */
      {   printf("child pid=%d\n", getpid());
          _exit(0);
      }
      printf("forking again\n");
      if ( (pid2 = fork()) == 0 )   /* child two */
      {   printf("child pid=%d\n", getpid());
          _exit(1);
      }
      printf("first wait\n");
      pid = wait(&status);
      printf("pid=%d, status=%d\n", pid, status);
      printf("2nd wait\n");
      pid = wait(&status);
      printf("pid=%d, status=%d\n", pid, status);
}
```

Note that the second child in this example returns an exit status 1. This causes the parent to display a corresponding wait status 256, which is consistent with how the bytes of the `wait status` are set.

12.7 Process Termination

Every running program eventually comes to an end. A process can terminate execution in three ways:

1. The process runs to completion, and its main program returns.
2. The program calls the library routine **exit** or the system call **_exit**.
3. The process encounters an execution error or receives an interrupt signal, causing its premature termination.

The argument to **_exit/exit** is part of the termination status of the process. Conventionally, a zero argument indicates normal termination, and a nonzero argument abnormal termination. The low-order byte of this argument is put into the second byte (bits 8–15) of the `status` variable returned by a **wait** call.

The system call

```
void _exit(int status)
```

terminates the calling process with the following consequences:

1. All the open I/O descriptors in the process are now closed.
2. If the parent process of the terminating process is executing a **wait** or is interested in the `SIGCHLD` signal, then it is notified of the termination, and the low-order byte of `status` is made available to it.
3. If the terminating process has child processes yet unfinished, the PPIDs of all existing children are set to 1 (the *init* process).

Most C programs call the library routine **exit**, which performs cleanup actions on I/O buffers before calling **_exit**. The **_exit** system call is used by a child process when it is necessary to not interfere with I/O buffers shared by parent and child processes.

12.8 Shell-Level Commands from C Programs

Allowing execution of shell-level commands from within C programs is convenient. With this ability, simply issue a **cp** command to copy a file from a C program rather than writing your own routines. The UNIX library function **system** is used for this purpose:

int **system**(char *cmd_string)   (issue shell-level command)

The **system** call starts a new *sh* process to execute the given command string `cmd_string`. The shell terminates after executing the given command, and **system** returns. The returned value represents the exit status of the given command. Thus, to copy `file1` to `file2`, do

```
char cmd_string[80];
sprintf(cmd_string, "cp %s %s\n", "file1", "file2");
system(cmd_string);
```

The string is, of course, interpreted by the shell before the command is invoked. Any substitution and filename expansion will be done. Also, the shell locates the executable file (e.g., `/bin/cp`) on the command search path. The **system** call waits until the command is finished before returning.

One shortcoming of the **system** function is that it does not allow you to receive the results produced by the command or to provide input to it. This is remedied by the library function **popen**, which invokes an *sh* shell to execute the given `cmd_string` and establishes a read or write stream (FILE *) to it:

FILE **popen**(char *cmd_string, char *mode)

The stream established is either for reading the standard output or writing the standard input of the given command, depending on whether `mode` is `"r"` or `"w"`.

Once opened, the stream can be used with any standard I/O library functions. Finally, the stream created by **popen** can be shut down by

pclose(FILE *stream)

As an application of **popen**, let's write a simple program that counts the total number of words in a list of files given on the command line:

```
#include <stdio.h>
extern FILE *popen(char *, char*);
extern pclose(FILE *);


main(int argc, char *argv[])
{ int i, count, total = 0;
  char cmd[80];
  FILE *in;
      for ( i = 1 ; i < argc ; i++ )      /* for each file given       */
      {    sprintf(cmd, "wc -w %s\n",
                      argv[i]);            /* construct command string */
          in = popen(cmd, "r");           /* execute and read output   */
          fscanf(in, "%d", &count);       /* normal fscanf             */
          total += count;                 /* accumulate total          */
          pclose(in);                     /* close stream              */
      }
      printf("total count is %d words\n", total); return(0);
}
```

The program uses the UNIX command **wc** with the option `-w` to count the number of words in a file. The output is read using **fscanf**, and the total is summed up. This method is definitely easier than having to write your own routines to count words and much simpler than using **exec** and **wait**.

12.9   Communicating Between Processes: pipe

One primary purpose of the system calls **fork, exec, wait,** and **exit** is to employ additional processes to run other existing programs and help perform the tasks at hand. In many such situations, the parent process must also send data to and/or receive data from a child. This can be arranged by establishing a *pipe* between the two processes.

A pipe is a direct (in memory) I/O channel between processes. At the shell level, you can connect commands into a pipeline (Section 1.6). The pipe can be thought of as a first-in-first-out character buffer (Figure 12.3) with a *read descriptor* pointing to one end and a *write descriptor* pointing to the other end.

To establish a pipe, use the system call

```
int pipe(int fildes[2])
```

to obtain a buffer and two descriptors:

```
fildes[0]        (for reading the pipe)
fildes[1]        (for writing the pipe)
```

The **pipe** system call is used in conjunction with subsequent **fork** calls to establish multiple processes having access to the same pipe, thereby allowing them to communicate directly. The **pipe** call returns 0 for success and –1 for failure. Consider this piece of code:

```
int fildes[2];
    pipe(fildes);           /* setting up the pipe     */
    if ( fork() == 0 )
    {   close(fildes[1]); /* child reads fildes[0]   */
        .
        .
        .
        _exit(0);
    }
    close(fildes[0]);       /* parent writes fildes[1] */
```

After the **fork,** both parent and child have their copies of `fildes[0]` and `fildes[1]` referring to the same pipe buffer. The child closes its write descriptor, and the parent closes its read descriptor. Now the child process can read what the parent writes into the pipe.

To perform input/output through a pipe, use the **read** and **write** calls. The **read** call removes characters from the buffer, and **write** deposits them. The capacity of the pipe buffer is usually 4096 characters, but the buffer size is system-dependent. Writing into a full pipe buffer causes the process to be

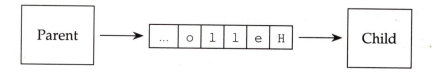

Figure 12.3: Pipe Between Processes

blocked until more space is available in the buffer. Reading more characters than there are in the buffer results in one of the following:

1. Returns end of file (`zero`) if the buffer is empty and the write end of the pipe has been completely closed.
2. Returns what's left in the pipe if the buffer is not empty and the write end of the pipe has been completely closed.
3. Blocks the reading process to await the arrival of additional characters if at least one file descriptor to the write end of the pipe remains open.

The example below shows a parent process writing the message `Hello there, from me.` to a child process through a pipe (Figure 12.3):

```c
#include <stdio.h>
#include <string.h>
#include <sys/wait.h>

main(int argc, char *argv[])
{ int p[2];
  int i, pid, status;
  char buffer[20];
      pipe(p);                              /* setting up the pipe      */
      if ( (pid = fork()) == 0 )            /* child code               */
      {    close(p[1]);                     /* child closes p[1]        */
          while ( (i = read(p[0], buffer, 6)) != 0 )
          {   buffer[i] = '\0';             /* string terminator        */
              printf("%d chars :%s: received by child\n", i, buffer);
          }
          _exit(0);                         /* child terminates         */
      }
  /* in parent */
      close(p[0]);                          /* parent writes p[1]       */
      write(p[1], "Hello there,", sizeof("Hello there,"));
      write(p[1], " from me.", sizeof(" from me."));
      close(p[1]);                          /* finished writing p[1]    */
      while ( wait(&status)!=pid );   /* while loop waiting for pid */
```

```
    if ( status == 0 )  printf("child finished\n");
    else printf("child failed\n");
    return(0);
}
```

After the **fork**, both parent and child have the file descriptors p[0] and p[1]. To establish the parent as the sender and the child as the receiver of characters through the pipe, the child closes its own p[1], and the parent closes its own p[0]. After sending the characters Hello there and from me. in two separate **write** calls, the parent then closes its p[1]. Meanwhile, the child reads the pipe and displays what it gets, six characters at a time (just to show multiple read operations). This program produces the following output:

```
6 chars :Hello : received by child
6 chars :there,: received by child
6 chars : from : received by child
3 chars :me.: received by child
child finished
```

The parent closing its p[1] causes the pipe's write end to be completely closed— processes can no longer write to the pipe. This condition causes the final successful read in the child process to return with the last three characters. The next read by the child returns zero, indicating the end of the file.

Now we are ready to look at a more useful application, to establish a pipe between two processes running arbitrary programs. To do this, we need to combine **pipe**, **fork**, and **exec**. It is best to look at an example.

Pipe Between Two UNIX Commands

A command **mypipe** takes as arguments two command strings separated by a %. It sends the standard output of the first command to the standard input of the second command. Thus,

mypipe /bin/ls -l % /bin/grep pwang

should work as expected (same as ls -l | grep pwang). Of course, we will use a pipe between the two processes, one executing the first command and the other the second. The key in this example is connecting stdin in the second process to the read end of the pipe and connecting stdout in the first process to the write end of the pipe. Do this with the **dup2** system call:

int **dup2**(int fd, int copyfd)

The **dup2** call duplicates the existing I/O descriptor fd, which is a small nonnegative integer index in the per-process descriptor table. The duplicate entry is made in the descriptor table at an entry specified by the index `copyfd`. If the descriptor `copyfd` is already in use, it is first deallocated as if a **close**(`copyfd`) had been done first. The value returned is `copyfd` if the call succeeds; otherwise, the error value returned is –1.

After **dup2**, both `fd` and `copyfd` reference the same I/O channel. In the
f   0 (in child one) with the read
e   ith the write end of the same
p

```
                                                      /* lose argv[0] */
                          i++ )
                          %") == 0 )
                                       /* break into two commands */


                                              /* setting up the pipe */
                          0 )                        /* child one */

                         /* 0 becomes a duplicate of p[0] */

                         gv[i+1]); /* this reads the pipe */
                                      /* bad error execl failed */


                          0 )                        /* child two */

                         /* 1 becomes a duplicate of p[1] */

                                              /* this writes the pipe */
                                              /* bad error execv failed */
                    _exit(1);
              }
      /* parent does not use pipe */
          close(p[0]);
          close(p[1]);
          while ( wait(&status)!=pid2 );          /* waiting for pid2 */
          if ( status == 0 ) printf("child two terminated\n");
              else printf("child two failed\n");
          exit(0);
      }
```

Because open I/O descriptors are unchanged after an **exec** call, the respective programs in the two stages of the pipeline execute as usual, reading standard input and writing standard output, not knowing that these descriptors have been diverted to a pipe. The same principles are used by the UNIX system shell to establish a pipeline.

12.10   Two-Way Pipe Connections

Let's see how a parent process can pass some input to a child process and then receive the results produced. To the parent, the child process is activated like a function call. This can be achieved by establishing a *two-way pipe*, an outgoing and an incoming pipe, between the parent and child processes (Figure 12.4).

The parent uses the outgoing pipe to send input to the child and the incoming pipe to receive results sent back by the child. The function pipe_2way is defined for this purpose. Given the command strings cmd, pipe_2way will establish a process to run the command and return the quantities piped[0] and piped[1], the read end of the incoming pipe and the write end of the outgoing pipe, respectively:

```
pipe_2way(char *cmd[], int piped[])
{ int pid, wt[2], rd[2];
     pipe(rd);                       /* incoming pipe: read from child */
     pipe(wt);                       /* outgoing pipe: write to child  */
     if ( (pid=vfork()) == 0 )   /* child code                     */
     {    close(wt[1]);
          dup2(wt[0],0);             /* 0 identified with wt[0]        */
          close(wt[0]);
          close(rd[0]);
          dup2(rd[1], 1);            /* 1 identified with rd[1]        */
          close(rd[1]);
          execv(cmd[0],cmd);         /* execute given command          */
          perror("execv failed"); /* normally not reached          */
          _exit(1);
     }
     /* in parent */
     close(wt[0]);
     piped[1] = wt[1];
     close(rd[1]);
     piped[0] = rd[0];
     return(0);
}
```

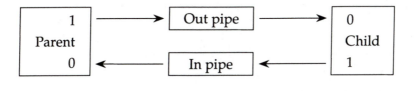

Figure 12.4: A Two-Way Pipe

The return parameter `piped` is filled with the two proper descriptors before the function returns. To test `pipe_2way`, let's write a program that sends characters to the command **lowercase** and receives the transformed string. The latter is performed by the `readl` function

```
#include <stdio.h>
#include <string.h>

int readl(int fd, char s[], int size)
{ char *tmp = s;
      while ( 0 < --size && read(fd, tmp, 1) != 0
                      && *tmp++ != '\n' );
      *tmp = '\0';  /* string terminator */
      return(tmp - s);
}
```

which is only a slight modification of the low-level `readline` implementation we discussed in Section 10.2. Here is the `main` program to test `pipe_2way`:

```
#include <stdio.h>
#define SIZE 256
main()
{ int pd[2];
  char *str[2];
  char test_string[] = "They lived TOGETHER HAPPILY EVER AFTER.\n";
  char buf[SIZE];
  char *tmp = buf;
      str[0] = "./lowercase";
      str[1] = NULL;
      pipe_2way(str, pd);
      /* write to lowercase process  */
      write(pd[1], test_string, strlen(test_string));
      readl(pd[0], buf, SIZE);   /* read from lowercase process */
      printf("Received from lowercase process:\n%s", buf);
}
```

If you compile and run this program, you'll see the display

```
Received from lowercase process:
they lived together happily ever after.
```

12.11   Summary

A process is the abstract agent that carries out the execution of a program. A multiprogramming system allows multiple processes to exist simultaneously, and the available CPUs are switched among the processes.

Each process has its own address space consisting of text, data, and stack areas. Each process is also assigned system resources such as a process-table entry, the u_area, I/O channels, and so on. A process goes through different states as it runs to completion: ready, asleep, running, and zombie.

A running process can be blocked due to input/output or other reasons and will switch from the running state to the asleep state. The CPU is then freed up to run another process. The switching from one process to another is called a context switch.

On UNIX the **fork** and **vfork** system calls create a new process. A process can use any one of the **exec** calls to overlay itself with a new executable file. The **vfork** and **exec** calls are usually used in combination to create new processes to run new programs.

Synchronization between parent and child processes is achieved through the **wait** system call, which sets a 16-bit termination status containing useful information about how a child process terminated.

Direct communication between concurrent processes is possible through the **pipe** system call. When used together with **fork**, **exec**, and **dup2**, **pipe** lets you establish input/output between a parent process and a child process that runs a separate program.

Exercises

1. Modify the simple shell (background) given in Section 12.5 so that it waits until the child process (command) is finished before it gives the next prompt.

2. Write your own version of the **system** function. Instead of *sh*, use *csh* to carry out the command string. Remember to wait for the process to end.

3. Find out what happens if a simple filename instead of the full pathname of an executable file is given to one of the **exec** functions.

4. Write a one-way pipe function that would be similar to **popen**, except that it returns a file descriptor rather than a stream.

5. Construct an example where, if the child uses **exit** instead of **_exit** to terminate, the I/O buffer of the parent is scrambled.

6. Write a program that (a) puts a few new environment variables and values into the global variable `environ` and (b) creates a child process. The child process will display the values on its environment list.

7. Write a program A that produces two child processes B and C. Establish a pipeline A to B, to C, and back to A so that a character written by A into the pipe will be read back by A in a circular fashion.

8. Find out what happens to a child process if its parent process terminates.

9. Experiment with reading from an empty pipe and writing to a full pipe. What happens in these situations?

10. Extend the `pipe_2way` function to tie the standard input/output of the calling process to the two-way pipe established. The result is that the standard input/output of the parent and child process are connected for two-way communication. Add another function `pipe_2way_close` to allow the parent process to recover its standard input/output after it is finished with the two-way pipe.

11. Give at least two ways for a process to send a signal to itself. What possible uses could there be for such signal sending? (*Hint*: See Chapter 9.)

12. Write a program where the parent process suspends and resumes a child process by sending it `SIGSTOP` and `SIGCONT`, respectively, via the **kill** system call.

13. What happens when you try to send a signal to a process not belonging to you?

14. Take the interactive file browser program (Exercise 14, Chapter 10) and add to it the ability of executing any UNIX command on the currently selected file.

1

The emacs Editor

The **emacs** editor originally was developed at the MIT Laboratory for Computer Science. As **emacs** gained popularity, it was ported to UNIX so that today many UNIX systems offer some version(s) of **emacs** in addition to the standard **vi** editor. Some people prefer **emacs** over **vi** for general-purpose text editing as well as writing C programs.

The **emacs** editor is highly customizable. It also means that any general description of **emacs** is likely to be inadequate because commands you enter for the same operations can vary from version to version. Here is a brief introduction to **emacs**.

The four major features of **emacs** are

1. Rather than operating in distinct input and command modes like **vi**, **emacs** operates in only one mode: Printable characters typed are inserted at the cursor position. Commands are given as control characters or are prefixed by **ESC** or **^X**.
2. The **emacs** editor can manage multiple display windows by dividing a CRT screen into two or more horizontal sections. You can cut and paste between windows.
3. The **emacs** editor allows for user definition of editing functions and command keystrokes. Any built-in or user-defined editing function can be *bound* to any keystroke. For example, you can bind the function `delete-character` to the keystroke **^D** to invoke that function. A command can also be invoked by its full name.
4. Some versions of **emacs** have built-in features that help in editing programs written in C, LISP, Pascal, and other languages.

Commands for emacs

Each command of **emacs** has a full name and a one- or two-character *key sequence* used to invoke the command. A key sequence is either a single control character or a two-character combination whose first character is **^X** or **ESC**. The key sequence for any **emacs** command can be changed to a different key sequence to suit the preference of an individual user. Following conventional **emacs** notations, a two-character key sequence will be denoted in this section as two characters separated by a hyphen. Thus,

ESC-*char*   (stands for **ESC**ape followed by any character)
^X-*char*   (stands for **^X** followed by any character)

In **emacs** command listings, a key sequence is usually followed by the full **emacs** function name normally associated with it. A full function name in **emacs** often consists of several words connected by hyphens (e.g., next-line). The full name usually gives a good idea of what a command does.

Two ways invoke the same **emacs** command:

1. Typing the key sequence of the command
2. Typing **ESC-X** followed by the full command name

Entering and Exiting emacs

To invoke **emacs**, simply type

emacs *filename*

where *filename* is either an existing file or a new file. Exit **emacs** by pressing

^C   (exit-emacs, no write)

Because this command does not write out the edited file(s), press

^S   (save-buffer)

to save the current buffer. On some versions of **emacs**, the following also will work:

^F   (write-file-exit)

The emacs Editor Windows

The CRT screen may be divided into one or more *windows*. A buffer is associated with each window, and a part of the buffer is visible through the window. At the bottom of a window is a *mode line*; below the mode line is a *message line*. The message line is used for two purposes: to display messages to the user and to prompt for necessary input from the user.

The mode line, which varies from version to version, contains information about the editing activity in the window. Here is a sample mode line:

```
Buffer: file.c   File: /user/fac/pwang/file.c    27%
```

On most terminals, the mode line is displayed in reverse video (black characters on white) or some other highlight mode. The word Buffer: is followed by a buffer name that is normally the last part of a UNIX file pathname. The `27%` shows the position of the window relative to the whole buffer. In this example, the cursor is 27 percent of the way down from the beginning of the buffer. Sometimes, **emacs** will set up a *help window* that has no file associated with it.

Panic Stop in emacs

Sometimes you may want to stop the currently executing command because it is taking too long, you typed something wrong, or for some other reason. In this circumstance, use

    ^G   (abort)

which immediately stops all activity and returns you to the **emacs** top (command) level.

Frequently Used emacs Commands

The key sequence is followed by the full command name in the following tables.

Cursor Motion			
ESC-<	Beginning-of-file	**ESC->**	End-of-file
^N	Next-line	**^P**	Previous-line
^A	Beginning-of-line	**^E**	End-of-line
^F	Forward-character	**^B**	Backward-character
^T	Scroll-one-line-up	**ESC-z**	Scroll-one-line-down
^V	Next-page	**ESC-v**	Previous-page
^X-1	Goto-line	**ESC-]**	Forward-paragraph
^S	Search-forward	**^R**	Search-reverse

Deletion			
^I	Insert TAB	**^Q**	Quote-character
^J	NEWLINE-and-indent	**^O**	NEWLINE-and-back up
^D	Delete-next-character	**^?**	Delete-previous-character
ESC-d	Delete-next-word	**ESC- DELETE**	Delete-previous-word

Cut and Paste			
`^Y`	Yank-from-killbuffer	`^W`	Delete-to-killbuffer
`^@`	Set-mark		(from mark to point)
`^K`	Kill-to-end-of-line	`ESC-w`	Copy-region-as-kill

Window Operations			
`^X-n`	Next-window	`^X-p`	Previous-window
`^X-1`	Delete-other-windows	`^X-2`	Split-current-window
`^X-z`	Enlarge-window	`^X-^Z`	Shrink-window

File Input/Output			
`^X-^R`	Read-file	`^X-^I`	Insert-file
`^X-^F`	Write-file-exit	`^X-^M`	Write-modified-files
`^X-^S`	Write-current-file	`^X-^V`	Visit-file
`^X-^W`	Write-named-file		

Miscellaneous			
`^L`	Redraw-display	`^G`	Abort-command
`ESC-x`	Full-command-name	`^X-^U`	Undo
`ESC-?`	Apropos	`^Z`	Pause-**emacs**
`^U`	Argument-prefix	`ESC-`*number*	Repeat-command

Cursor Movement in emacs

In **emacs** the editing position is always relative to the current position, which is known as the *point*. The point is not shown on the screen, but it is between the cursor and the character before the cursor. Moving the cursor, and therefore the point, lets you view the file and move to the location where modifications are needed.

For the search commands `^S` and `^R`, **emacs** prompts you with

```
Search for:
```

in the message line and waits for you to type in a character string. (In some versions, **emacs** will carry out the search as you type the search string.) To terminate the search string, press ESC. When responding to a prompt, you may correct typing mistakes with UNIX command-line editing. To repeat a previous search, enter ^S or ^R with an empty search string.

Inserting and Deleting in emacs

There is no need for an *insert* command in **emacs**. Characters insert themselves at the point as you type them.

To insert a control character or the character ESC, precede the character with ^Q (the quote-character command). Two control characters are exceptions to this rule, and they insert themselves: ^I inserts a TAB, and ^J inserts a NEWLINE and tabs it appropriately. The delete commands are self-explanatory. For the delete-word commands, the word deleted is from the point (cursor) to the end of the word. Thus, if the point is in the middle of a word and one of the delete-word commands is typed, only part of the word will be deleted.

2

Quick Reference for vi

Entering and Exiting vi			
vi *file*	Edits *file*.	**vi** -t *tag*	Edits file through *tag* in tags file.
vi +*n file*	Edits *file*, cursor at line *n*.	**vi** +/ *pattern file*	Edits file, cursor at *pattern*.
vi + *file*	Edits *file*, cursor at end.	**view** *file*	**vi** *file*, no modification.
vi -r	Lists system-saved files.	zz	Exits from **vi**, saving changes.
vi -r *file*	Edits system-saved *file*.	^z	Stops vi for later resumption.
vi *file* ...	Edits first *file*; rest via :n.		

Displaying			
Last line	Error messages, echoing input to commands: /, ?, :, !, feedback about I/O and large changes	^*x*	Control characters
@ lines	On screen only, not in file	TABs	Expands to spaces, cursor on last space
~ lines	Lines past end of file		

States	
Command	Executes commands; the normal and initial state; other modes return to command mode; ESC cancels a partial command.
Insert	Entered by a, i, A, I, o, O,, c, C, s, S, R, followed by arbitrary text terminated by ESC; an interrupt aborts an insertion.
Last line	Reads user input for commands /, ?, :, !, which terminates in ESC or RETURN; an interrupt aborts.

Counts Before vi Commands			
Line/column number	z, G, |	Replicate insert	a, i, A, I
Scroll amount	^D, ^U	Repeat effect	Most rest

Basic Commands			
dw	Deletes a word.	i*text*ESC	Inserts *text*.
de	Deletes a word leaving punctuation.	cw*text*ESC	Changes word to *text*.
dd	Deletes a line.	ea*s*ESC	Pluralizes word.
3dd	Deletes three lines.	xp	Transposes characters.
d%	Deletes to matching parenthesis/bracket.		

Interrupting, Canceling, and Shell Interaction			
ESC	Ends insert, input, or incomplete command.	:sh	Runs default shell, then returns.
^?	DELETE; interrupts **vi**.	:!*cmd*	Runs shell-level *cmd*, then returns.
^Z	Suspends **vi** (*csh* and *ksh*).		

File Manipulation			
`:w`	Writes back changes.	`:w` *file*	Writes to *file*.
`:wq`	Writes and quits from **vi**.	`:w!` *file*	Overwrites *file*.
`:q`	Quits from **vi**.	`:n`	Edits next file in argument list.
`:q!`	Quits, discards changes.	`:n` *args*	Specifies new argument list.
`:e` *file*	Edits *file*.	`:f`	Displays current file and line.
`:e!`	Re-edits, discards changes.	`^G`	Synonym for `:f`.
`:e +` *file*	Edits *file*, starting at the end.	`:ta` *tag*	Goes to tags-file entry *tag*.
`:e +n` *file*	Edits *file* starting at line *n*.	`^]`	Same as `:ta`, but current word is *tag*.

Positioning Within File			
`^F`	Moves forward a screen.	`n`	Repeats last / or ?.
`^B`	Moves backward a screen.	`N`	Repeats last / or ? in other direction.
`^D`	Scrolls down half a screen.	*/pattern/+n*	Goes to nth line after *pattern*.
`^U`	Scrolls up half a screen.	*?pattern?-n*	Goes to nth line before *pattern*.
k`G`	Goes to line *k* or last line (default).	`]]`	Goes to next section or function.
*/pattern*ESC	Searches forward for *pattern*.	`[[`	Goes to previous section or function.
*?pattern*ESC	Searches backward for *pattern*.	`%`	Finds matching (,), {, or }.

Adjusting the Screen			
^L	Clears and redisplays.	/*pattern*/z-	Displays line with *pattern* at bottom.
^R	Redisplays, eliminates @ lines.	z*n*	Uses *n* line window.
zRETURN	Displays current line at window top.	^E	Scrolls window down one line.
z-	Displays current line at window bottom.	^Y	Scrolls window up one line.
z.	Displays current line at window center.		

Marking and Returning			
` `	Returns to previous context.	`*x*	Returns to marked position *x*.
' '	Returns to previous context at first nonblank character of the line.	'*x*	Returns to *x* at first nonblank character in line.
m*x*	Marks position with letter *x*.		

Cursor Line Positioning			
:.=	Displays current line number.	-	Moves to previous line.
H	Moves to the first window line.	RETURN	Same as +.
L	Moves to the last window line.	DOWN ARROW or j	Moves to next line, same column.
M	Moves to the middle window line.	UP ARROW or k	Moves to previous line, same column.
+	Moves to next line.		

Cursor Character Positioning			
^	Positions to first nonblank character.	Fx	Finds x backward in current line.
0	Positions to beginning of line (column one).	tx	Moves forward up to x in current line.
$	Positions to end of line (last character).	Tx	Moves backward up to x in current line.
h or LEFT ARROW	Positions to previous character.	;	Repeats last f, F, t, or T
l or RIGHT ARROW	Positions to next character.	,	Same as ;, but in the reverse direction.
^H	Same as LEFT ARROW.	|	Moves to specified column.
SPACE	Same as RIGHT ARROW.	%	Moves to matching (, {,), or }.
fx	Finds x forward in current line.		

Words, Sentences, and Paragraphs			
w	Moves to next word.	(	Moves backward to the beginning of a sentence.
b	Moves backward to the beginning of a word.	{	Moves backward to the beginning of a paragraph.
e	Moves to end of word.	W	Moves to next blank delimited word.
)	Moves to next sentence.	B	Moves backward to the beginning of a blank delimited word.
}	Moves to next paragraph.	E	Moves to end of blank delimited word.

	Corrections During Insert		
^H	Deletes last input character.	*interrupt*	Aborts insert (usually ^c).
^W	Deletes last input word.	^D	Backtabs over blanks supplied by autoindent.
erase	Same as ^H (character erase).	^^D	Kills autoindent; autoindent remains effective for next line.
kill	Deletes entire input line (line kill).	0^D	Kills autoindent, until next indent.
\	Escapes character erase and line kill.	^V	Quotes any special character.
ESC	Ends insertion; goes back to command mode.		

	Insert and Replace		
a	Inserts after cursor.	O	Opens a line for insertion above current line.
i	Inserts before cursor.	r*x*	Replaces current character with x.
A	Inserts at end of current line.	R	Overwrites characters.
I	Inserts before first nonblank character of current line.	~	Changes case of current character.
o	Opens a line for insertion below current line.		

	Operators (Double to Affect Lines)		
d	Deletes text object.	>	Right shifts text object.
c	Changes text object.	y	Yanks text object to buffer.
<	Left shifts text object.		

Miscellaneous Operations			
C	Changes rest of line.	J	Joins lines.
D	Deletes rest of line.	x	Deletes characters.
s	Substitutes characters.	X	Deletes characters before cursor.
S	Substitutes lines.		

Cut and Paste			
p or "xp	Pastes deleted or buffer x text after current position/line.	"xd	Deletes text object into buffer x.
P or "x	Pastes deleted or buffer x text before current position/line.	yy	Yanks current line.
"xy	Copies (yanks) text object to buffer x.	$n$yy	Yanks several lines.

Undo, Redo, and Retrieve			
u	Undoes last change.	.	Repeats last change.
U	Restores current line.	"np	Retrieves nth last delete.

The vi Macros for ANSI C

The definition of the environment variable EXINIT supplied here can be included in your .login file (for *csh*) to give you convenient shorthand for many ANSI C constructs. The **vi** macro definitions let you type three-letter combinations to obtain *templates* for pre-formatted C constructs. For example, if you type ′ma in insert mode, you'll automatically get

```
main(int argc, char *argv[])
{
}
```

with the cursor positioned so that you are ready to type in variable declarations. The indentation and spacing built into these macros follow the formatting style recommended in this book.

For readability we show the definition of EXINIT on multiple lines. When you include it in your file, make sure everything is *on one line* by connecting the lines here without adding any extra characters.

```
setenv EXINIT "set ai to noremap shell=/bin/csh
terse nowarn sm redraw sw=4|
map! #/          /*^M *   ^M*/^[kA|
map! #in         #include <.h>^[2hi|
map! #de         #define |
map! #if         #if ( )i|
map! #en         #endif    /*   */^[hhi|
map! 'ca         case: ^Mbreak;^[kA|
map! 'df         default:^M^T^Mbreak;^[kA|
map! 'fl         float ;^[i|
map! 'do         do^M{   ^M}  while ( );^[kA|
map! 'ei         else if ( )^M{^M}^[kk0f(la|
map! 'el         else^M{   ^M}^[kA|
map! 'en         enum  { };^[4hi|
map! 'fo         for ( ;  ; )^M{^M}^[kk0f(a|
map! 'if         if ( )^M{^M}^[kk0f(la|
```

```
map! 'ma        main(int argc, char *argv[])^M{ ^M}^[kA|
map! 're        return();^[hi|
map! 'st        struct ^M{^M};^[kkA|
map! 'sw        switch ( )^M{  case:^M^T^Tbreak;^M^D^D}^[3k0f(la|
map! 'un        union ^M{^M};^[kkA|
map! 'wh        while ( )^M{^M}^[kk0f(la"
```

If you decide to copy the above into a file, use **vi**. In insert mode, the key sequences for the special symbols are

- **^M**: Control-V RETURN
- **^[**: Control-V ESC
- **^T**: Control-V, control-T

For *sh* and *ksh*, the `setenv EXINIT` should be replaced by `EXINIT=`, the `/bin/csh` by `/bin/sh`, and an extra line `export EXINIT` should be added at the end. The definitions, in this case, should be put in the file `.profile`.

ASCII Character Codes

There are 128 characters in the ASCII (American Standard Code for Information Interchange) character set. For each character, we show a quadruple: (1) *decimal code*, (2) *octal code*, (3) *hexadecimal code*, and (4) *character name*.

The characters are coded with 7 bits as indicated by the octal notations. Not all characters can be entered as a simple key stroke from a regular keyboard. Many are entered as control characters. For example, *bel* is *^G*, *np* (FORMFEED) is *^L*. The control key drops the leading (seventh) bit of the character being typed to zero.

1	2	3	4	1	2	3	4	1	2	3	4	1	2	3	4
0	00	0x0	nul	1	01	0x1	soh	2	02	0x2	stx	3	03	0x3	etx
4	04	0x4	eot	5	05	0x5	enq	6	06	0x6	ack	7	07	0x7	bel
8	010	0x8	bs	9	011	0x9	ht	10	012	0xa	nl	11	013	0xb	vt
12	014	0xc	np	13	015	0xd	cr	14	016	0xe	so	15	017	0xf	si
16	020	0x10	dle	17	021	0x11	dc1	18	022	0x12	dc2	19	023	0x13	dc3
20	024	0x14	dc4	21	025	0x15	nak	22	026	0x16	syn	23	027	0x17	etb
24	030	0x18	can	25	031	0x19	em	26	032	0x1a	sub	27	033	0x1b	esc
28	034	0x1c	fs	29	035	0x1d	gs	30	036	0x1e	rs	31	037	0x1f	us
32	040	0x20	sp	33	041	0x21	!	34	042	0x22	"	35	043	0x23	#
36	044	0x24	$	37	045	0x25	%	38	046	0x26	&	39	047	0x27	'
40	050	0x28	(	41	051	0x29	)	42	052	0x2a	*	43	053	0x2b	+
44	054	0x2c	,	45	055	0x2d	-	46	056	0x2e	.	47	057	0x2f	/
48	060	0x30	0	49	061	0x31	1	50	062	0x32	2	51	063	0x33	3

1	2	3	4	1	2	3	4	1	2	3	4	1	2	3	4
52	064	0x34	4	53	065	0x35	5	54	066	0x36	6	55	067	0x37	7
56	070	0x38	8	57	071	0x39	9	58	072	0x3a	:	59	073	0x3b	;
60	074	0x3c	<	61	075	0x3d	=	62	076	0x3e	>	63	077	0x3f	?
64	0100	0x40	@	65	0101	0x41	A	66	0102	0x42	B	67	0103	0x43	C
68	0104	0x44	D	69	0105	0x45	E	70	0106	0x46	F	71	0107	0x47	G
72	0110	0x48	H	73	0111	0x49	I	74	0112	0x4a	J	75	0113	0x4b	K
76	0114	0x4c	L	77	0115	0x4d	M	78	0116	0x4e	N	79	0117	0x4f	O
80	0120	0x50	P	81	0121	0x51	Q	82	0122	0x52	R	83	0123	0x53	S
84	0124	0x54	T	85	0125	0x55	U	86	0126	0x56	V	87	0127	0x57	W
88	0130	0x58	X	89	0131	0x59	Y	90	0132	0x5a	Z	91	0133	0x5b	[
92	0134	0x5c	\	93	0135	0x5d	]	94	0136	0x5e	^	95	0137	0x5f	_
96	0140	0x60	`	97	0141	0x61	a	98	0142	0x62	b	99	0143	0x63	c
100	0144	0x64	d	101	0145	0x65	e	102	0146	0x66	f	103	0147	0x67	g
104	0150	0x68	h	105	0151	0x69	i	106	0152	0x6a	j	107	0153	0x6b	k
108	0154	0x6c	l	109	0155	0x6d	m	110	0156	0x6e	n	111	0157	0x6f	o
112	0160	0x70	p	113	0161	0x71	q	114	0162	0x72	r	115	0163	0x73	s
116	0164	0x74	t	117	0165	0x75	u	118	0166	0x76	v	119	0167	0x77	w
120	0170	0x78	x	121	0171	0x79	y	122	0172	0x7a	z	123	0173	0x7b	{
124	0174	0x7c	|	125	0175	0x7d	}	126	0176	0x7e	~	127	0177	0x7f	del

5

Collection of UNIX Commands

UNIX Command	Purpose
a.out	Executes `a.out`.
ar	Establishes program archive.
as	Invokes assembler.
cat [*file ...*]	Concatenates files.
cc `myprog.c`	Compiles C program.
chmod *mode file*	Changes file mode.
cpp	Invokes C preprocessor.
cp *file1 file2*	Copies *file1* into *file2*.
csh, ksh, sh	Invokes *csh, ksh, sh*.
ctags	Establishes tags file.
dbx	Invokes source-level symbolic debugger.
gprof	Displays performance profiling data.
grep *pattern file ...*	Looks for *pattern* in files.
kill [`-9`] *job-id*	Terminates job.
ld	Invokes linker/loader.
lpr *file*	Produces printout of file.
ls [*directory*]	Displays working (or given) directory.
make	Initiates makefile-based program maintenance.
man *command-name*	Consults documentation for command.
more *file*	Displays *file* on CRT nicely (**less** is similar).
mv *file1 file2*	Renames *file1 file2*.
ps	Displays information on processes.

UNIX Command	Purpose
pwd	Displays name of working directory.
ranlib	Transforms archive file into program library.
rmdir *dir ...*	Removes empty directory.
rm *file1 file2 ...*	Removes files.
script [*file*]	Records terminal session.
strip	Removes extra symbolic information from executable file.
stty	Sets `tty` terminal driver options.
vi	Invokes visual editor.
who	Displays current users.

Shell Command	Purpose
cd [*directory*]	Changes directory.
fg *job-id*	Brings job to foreground.
jobs	Displays all jobs.
logout	Ends terminal session.
set *var = string*	Sets *csh* variable.
var=string	Sets *sh* or *ksh* variable.
printenv	Displays environment values (*csh*).
setenv *VAR string*	Sets environment variable (*csh*).

APPENDIX

6

Operator Precedence

All C operators are listed here according to their relative precedence. An operator on an earlier line takes precedence over any that comes after. Operators on the same line have the same precedence. An expression involving operators of the same precedence is evaluated according to the *associativity rule* of the operators. Most operators associate left to right. The ones that associate right to left are indicated by ← in the table.

Note also that the unary operators +, -, and * (value-of) take precedence over the binary forms.

Operator	Associativity
() [] -> .	
!~ ++ -- + - * & (type) sizeof	←
* / %	
+ -	
<< >>	
< <= > >=	
== !=	
&	
^	
|	
&&	
||	
?:	←
= += -= *= /= %= ^= |= <<= >>=	←
,	

7

Summary of Constructs

Function Definition

```
valuetype fn_name ( type arg1, type arg2, ... )
{ variable declarations
        statements
}

/* valuetype can be void; argument list can be empty */
/* zero or more declarations, statements            */
```

The if Statement

```
if ( exp1 )
    statement-1
else if ( exp2 )  /* optional */
    statement-2
...
        . . .
else    /* optional */
    statement-i
```

Iteration Statements

```
while ( continuation condition ) body

for ( init-exp ; cont-cond ; incr-exp ) body
    /* all parts optional */

do body while ( continuation condition );
```

The `switch` Statement

```
switch ( expression )
{      case constant-exp1 :
            statements  /* zero or more */
       case constant-exp2 :
            statements

       . . .

       default:           /* optional */
            statements
}
```

The `goto` Statement

```
label:  statement
...
goto label;
```

Array Declarations

```
type array_name[10];           /* linear array            */
type array_name[10][20];       /* two-dimensional array    */
type array_name[10][20][30];   /* three-dimensional array  */
```

The `enum` Declaration

```
enum name { symbol₁[ = val₁],
            symbol₂[ = val₂],
            ...
          };
```

The Function Prototype

```
value_type fn_name(type1, type2, ...);
void fn_name(type1, type2, ...);  /* returns no value   */
value_type fn_name(void);         /* takes no arguments */
```

The Function Pointer

```
value_type (* fn_ptr) (type1, type2, ...);
```

The `struct` Declaration

```
struct tag
{       type1   member1;
        type2   member2;
           . . .
};
```

The `union` Declaration

```
union tag
{       type1   member1;
        type2   member2;
           . . .
};
```

The Bit-Field Declaration

```
struct tag   /* bit fields */
{       type1   member1 : n1 ;
        type2   member2 : n2 ;
           . . .
};
```

Keywords in C

32

auto	break	case	char
const	continue	default	do
double	else	enum	extern
float	for	goto	if
int	long	register	return
short	signed	sizeof	static
struct	switch	typedef	union
unsigned	void	volatile	while

Some implementations also reserve the words `asm` and/or `fortran`.

8

Implicit Type-Conversion Rules

When the two arguments of an operator have different types, automatic type conversion is performed before the operation is carried out. The conversion rules summarized here are applied in the order given:

1. If one operand is `long double`, convert other operand to `long double`.
2. If one operand is `double`, convert other operand to `double`.
3. If one operand is `float`, convert other operand to `float`.
4. If one operand is `long int`, convert other operand to `long int`.

After carrying out the above rules, *integral promotions* are applied on both operands. Integral promotions upgrade a `char`, a `short int`, an `int` bit field (or their signed or unsigned varieties), or an enumeration object to type `int`. Then, the following rules are used:

5. If one operand has type `unsigned long int`, then convert the other operand to the same.
6. If one operand has type `long int` and the other `unsigned int`, convert the latter to `long int` if this type can accommodate all values of type `unsigned int`; if this is not the case, convert both operands to `unsigned long int`.
7. If one operand has type `long int`, convert the other to `long int`.
8. If one operand has type `unsigned int`, convert the other to `unsigned int`.
9. Both operands must now have type `int`.

9

Command Summary for dbx

Command	Meaning
run	Begins execution of the program.
cont	Continues execution.
step	Single steps one line.
next	Steps to next line (skips over calls).
trace *line*	Traces execution of the line.
trace *function*	Traces calls to the function.
trace *var*	Traces changes to the variable.
trace *exp* at *line*	Displays *exp* when *line* is reached.
stop at *line*	Suspends execution at the line.
stop in *function*	Suspends execution when *function* is called.
status	Displays trace/stops in effect.
delete *number*	Removes trace or stop of given number.
call *function*	Calls the function.
dump *function*	Displays values related to the function.
where	Displays currently active functions.
set *var* = *exp*	Sets variable to value of the expression.
print *exp*	Displays the value of the expression.
whatis *name*	Displays the declaration of the name.
list *line, line*	Lists source lines.
edit *function*	Edits file containing *function*.
quit	Exits **dbx**.

10

Standard Library Functions for Input/Output

Library functions summarized here use the header file <stdio.h> and support buffered I/O streams (FILE *) defined in the header. The symbolic constants stdin, stdout, stderr, EOF, NULL, and others are defined in the header. The error value returned by each library function is indicated in brackets [].

The #define CSTR const char * is used.

Operations on Files

```
FILE *fopen(CSTR filename, CSTR mode)   [NULL]
```

opens filename for read, write, or update as indicated by the given mode:

Mode	Meaning
"r", "rb"	Open text/binary file for reading.
"w", "wb"	Open text/binary file for writing, discard existing contents.
"a", "ab"	Open text/binary file for appending at end.
"r+", "rb+"	Open text/binary file for *update* (reading and writing).
"w+", "wb+"	Open text/binary file for update, discard existing contents.
"a+", "ab+"	Open text/binary file for update, writing at end.

```
FILE *freopen(CSTR filename, CSTR mode, FILE *stream) [NULL]
```

opens filename for read, write, or update as fopen but reuses an existing stream, which is returned. This function is often used to redirect stdin, stdout, and stderr.

```
int fclose(FILE *stream) [EOF]
```

closes the given `stream` after flushing any unfinished output, discarding unread input, and freeing allocated buffer space.

```
int fflush(FILE *stream)
```

forces all unfinished output of the given stream to be sent out.

```
int remove(CSTR filename) [nonzero]
```

deletes the given file.

```
int rename(CSTR oldname, CSTR newname) [nonzero]
```

changes the name of `oldname` to `newname`.

```
int setvbuf(FILE *stream, char *buf, int flag, size_t size) [nonzero]
```

sets the buffering mode for `stream` using the supplied buffer `buf`. If `buf` is `NULL`, the buffer will be allocated when necessary. The `flag` specifies the buffering mode: `_IOLBF` (line buffering), `_IONBF` (no buffering), or `_IOFBF` (full buffering).

```
void setbuf(FILE *stream, char *buf)
```

turns off buffering on `stream` if `buf` is `NULL`. Otherwise, full buffering on `stream` is done with the supplied buffer (size at least `BUFSIZ`).

```
FILE *tmpfile(void) [NULL]
```

creates a temporary file with mode `"wb+"`, which will be automatically deleted when closed.

```
char *tmpname(char name[L_tmpnam]) [NULL]
```

`tmpname(NULL)` returns a unique heretofore unused name string as a pointer to an internal static array. The name is also copied into `name` if supplied.

Formatted Input

```
int scanf(FILE *stream, CSTR format, ...) [EOF]
```

reads input according to the given `format`. Conversion modes for `scanf` are as follows:

Conversion Character	Pointer Type	Input Data
d	int *	Base 10 number
i	int *	Integer, may be octal (leading 0) or hexadecimal (leading 0x or 0X)
u	unsigned int *	Unsigned base 10 number
o, x	int *	Octal or hexadecimal with or without prefix
e, f, g	float *	Float with optional sign, decimal point, and exponent
s	char *	Characters with an added terminator '\0'
c	char *	Characters including white space (default width 1)
p	void *	Pointer value as displayed by printf("%p")
n	int *	Number of characters read so far
u	unsigned *	Unsigned decimal integer
[...]	char *	Longest nonempty input string consisting only of characters given in []
[^...]	char *	Longest nonempty input string consisting only of characters *not* given in []
%		No input assignment, matches a literal %

Formatted Output

```
int fprintf(FILE *stream, CSTR format, ...) [negative]
```

outputs to stream according to the given format and returns the number of characters sent out. Conversion modes in the format are as follows:

Conversion Character	Argument Type	Formatted as
d, i	int	Base 10 number
u	unsigned	Base 10 number
f	double	[–]$m.dddddd$, number of d's given by the precision
s	char *	Characters in a string until ' \0'
c	char	Single character
o	int	Unsigned octal number (no leading 0)
e, E	double	[–]$m.ddd$e±xx or [–]$m.ddd$E±xx
g, G	double	Use %f unless exponent is < –4 or ≥ precision
x, X	int	Unsigned hexadecimal (no leading 0x) with a–f or A–F
p	void *	A pointer value (implementation-dependent)
n	int *	No output, the number of characters output so far is *stored* into the argument
%		Displays a %, no argument needed

For printf the possible conversion flags are

Flag	Description
–	Left-adjusted in field
+	Display number always with a sign
space	Use a space if first character is not a sign
0 :	Pad numbers with leading zeros
#	Alternative format: produce leading 0, 0x, 0X for o, x, X; preserve the decimal point for e, E, f, g, G; trailing zeros not removed for g, G

Character Input/Output

`int getchar()`	Same as `getc(stdin)`.
`int putchar(int c)`	Same as `putc(c, stdout)`.
`int getc(FILE *stream)`	Same as `fgetc`; if implemented as a macro it may evaluate stream more than once.
`int putc(FILE *stream)`	Same as `fputc`; if implemented as a macro it may evaluate stream more than once.
`int fgetc(FILE *stream)`	Returns next character of `stream` as an `unsigned char` converted to `int` [EOF].
`int fputc(int c, FILE *stream)`	Writes `c` out to stream as `char` and returns `c` [EOF].
`int ungetc(int c, FILE *stream)`	Pushes `c` back onto `stream` for next read; only one character can be pushed back per `stream`; returns `c` [EOF].

String Input/Output

`char *gets(char *s)`	Reads next line of `stdin` into s, *replacing terminating '\n' with '\0'*; returns s [NULL].
`int puts(const char *s)`	Writes string s to `stdout`, *replacing terminating '\0' with '\n'*; returns nonnegative [EOF].
`char *fgets(char *s, int n, FILE *stream)`	Reads at most the next $n-1$ characters into array s, stopping if a '\n' is encountered; the '\n' is included in the array, which is terminated by a '\0'; returns s [NULL].
`int fputs(const char *s, FILE *stream)`	Writes string s to `stream`; returns a nonnegative [EOF].

Binary Input/Output and Error Status

```
size_t fread(void *ptr, size_t s size_t n, FILE *stream)
```

reads at most n objects of size s into space pointed to by ptr. The number of objects read is returned, which may be less than s. Use feof and ferror to determine status.

```
size_t fwrite(const void *ptr, size_t s size_t n, FILE *stream)
```

outputs n objects of size s from array pointed to by ptr. The number of objects written is returned, which is less than s only if there is an error.

```
int feof(FILE *stream)
```

returns nonzero if the end of file indicator of stream is set.

```
int ferror(FILE *stream)
```

returns nonzero if the error indicator of stream is set.

```
int clearerr(FILE *stream)
```

clears the end-of-file and error indicator of stream is set.

Moving File Read/Write Position

```
int fseek(FILE *stream, long offset, int org) [nonzero]
```

sets the file position for stream as given by offset from the origin org. For a binary file, the position is moved to offset bytes from org, which can be SEEK_SET (beginning of file), SEEK_CUR (current position), or SEEK_END (end of file). For a text file, offset must be zero or a value obtained by ftell (relative to SEEK_SET).

```
void rewind(FILE *stream)
```

is the same as fseek(stream, 0L, SEEK_SET); clearerr(stream).

```
long ftell(FILE *stream) [EOF]
```

returns the current file position as an offset from SEEK_SET.

```
int fgetpos(FILE *stream, fpos_t *ptr) [nonzero]
```

marks the current file position in ptr for later use by fsetpos.

```
int fsetpos(FILE *stream, fpos_t *ptr) [nonzero]
```

moves the file position to that marked by ptr.

11

Standard Library Functions

Character and String Functions

Character-set-independent functions (or macros) are supplied to deal with characters. Use the header `<ctype.h>`.

Function	Test for
`int isupper(int c)`	Uppercase letter
`int islower(int c)`	Lowercase letter
`int isalpha(int c)`	Uppercase or lowercase letter
`int isdigit(int c)`	Decimal digit
`int isalnum(int c)`	`isalpha(c) || isdigit(c)`
`int iscntrl(int c)`	Control character
`int isxdigit(int c)`	Hexadecimal digit
`int isprint(int c)`	Printing character including SPACE
`int isgraph(int c)`	Printing character except SPACE
`int isspace(int c)`	SPACE, `\f, \n, \r, \t, \v`
`int ispunct(int c)`	Printing character not SPACE, digit, or letter
Function	**Meaning**
`int toupper(int c)`	Converts to uppercase letter.
`int tolower(int c)`	Converts to lowercase letter.

A large set of string manipulation functions are available. The header `<string.h>` (or `<strings.h>` on some nonstandard systems) should be used.

Function	Description
`char *strcat(s,cs)`	Concatenates a copy of cs to end of s; returns s.
`char *strncat(s,cs,n)`	Concatenates a copy of at most n characters of cs to end of s; returns s.
`char *strcpy(s,cs)`	Copies cs to s including '\0'; returns s.
`char *strncpy(s,cs,n)`	Copies at most n characters of cs to s; returns s; pads with '\0' if cs has less than n characters.
`char *strtok(s,cs)`	Finds tokens in s delimited by characters in cs.

Function	Description
`size_t strlen(cs)`	Returns length of cs (excluding '\0').
`char *strcmp(cs1,cs2)`	Compares cs1 and cs2; returns negative, zero, or positive for cs1 <, ==, or > cs2, respectively.
`char *strncmp(cs1,cs2,n)`	Compares first n characters of cs1 and cs2; returns negative, zero, or positive for cs1 <, ==, or > cs2, respectively.
`char *strchr(cs,c)`	Returns pointer to first occurrence of c in cs.
`char *strrchr(cs,c)`	Returns pointer to last occurrence of c in cs.
`char *strpbrk(cs1,cs2)`	Returns pointer to first char in cs1 and in cs2.
`char *strstr(cs1,cs2)`	Returns pointer to first occurrence of cs2 in cs1. *These four functions all return* NULL *if the search fails.*
`size_t strspn(cs1,cs2)`	Returns length of prefix of cs1 consisting of characters from cs2.
`size_t strcspn(cs1,cs2)`	Returns length of prefix of cs1 consisting of characters *not* in cs2.

Arbitrary Objects as Character Arrays

Processing data of other types as a sequence of characters in consecutive memory locations is sometimes convenient. A set of library functions exists for this purpose.

```
void *memcpy(void *target, const void *source, size_t n)
```

copies n characters from source to target, which is returned.

```
void *memmove(void *target, const void *source, size_t n)
```

is the same as `memcpy` but works even if s and ct overlap.

```
int memcmp(const void *cs, const void *ct, size_t n)
```

compares the first n characters of cs with ct and returns a positive, negative, or zero value (as `strcmp`).

```
void *memchr(const void *cs, const char c, size_t n)
```

returns a pointer to the first character c in cs or NULL if c is not among the first n characters.

```
void *memset(void *s, const char c, size_t n)
```

sets each of the first n characters of s to c and returns s.

Floating-Point Calculations

To use the functions listed here, include the header file <math.h>. To check possible domain and range errors, you also need the header <errno.h> which defines EDOM, ERANGE, and HUGE_VAL (Section 9.5.1). In the following, the variables xx, yy are of type double, and i is an int. All functions return double.

`sin(xx)`	Sine of xx
`cos(xx)`	Cosine of xx
`tan(xx)`	Tangent of xx
`sinh(xx)`	Hyperbolic sine of xx
`cosh(xx)`	Hyperbolic cosine of xx
`tanh(xx)`	Hyperbolic tangent of xx
`exp(xx)`	e^{xx}
`log(xx)`	Natural logarithm $ln(xx), xx > 0$
`log10(xx)`	Base 10 logarithm $log_{10}(xx), xx > 0$
`asin(xx)`	$sin^{-1}(xx)$ in range $[-\pi/2, \pi/2], xx \in [-1,1]$
`acos(xx)`	$cos^{-1}(xx)$ in range $[0, \pi], xx \in [-1,1]$
`atan(xx)`	$tan^{-1}(xx)$ in range $[-\pi/2, \pi]$
`atan2(xx, yy)`	$tan^{-1}(xx/yy)$ in range $[-\pi, \pi]$
`sqrt(xx)`	Square root of xx, $xx \geq 0$
`ceil(xx)`	Ceiling of xx as double
`floor(xx)`	Floor of xx as double

`fabs(xx)`	Absolute value of xx
`ldexp(xx,n)`	$xx \cdot 2^n$
`pow(xx,yy)`	xx^{yy}; if $xx=0$ and $yy \leq 0$ or if $xx < 0$ and yy is not equal to an integer, a domain error results

Besides the above, the functions for fractional parts and floating remainder are the following:

- `frexp(xx, int *exp)` computes the fractional and exponent parts of xx. The fractional part (fr) is normalized ($0.5 \leq fr < 1$) and returned. The power-of-2 exponent is stored in `exp` so that $xx = fr \cdot 2^{(*exp)}$. If xx is zero, both parts of the result are zero.
- `modf(xx, double *ip)` computes the fractional and exponent parts of xx. The fractional part fr has the same sign as xx and is not normalized. The integer part is stored in `ip` so that $xx = {}^*ip + fr$.
- `fmod(xx,yy)` computes a remainder of xx by subtracting yy from xx an integral number of times. The result is less than xx in magnitude and has the same sign. $\wedge D$

Variable-Length Argument Lists

The header `<stdarg.h>` provides the capability to define functions with an indefinite number of arguments of unknown type. This is done through the use of an argument pointer (type `va_list`) and the three macros `va_start`, `va_arg`, and `va_end` (Section 5.5).

Here is a template-function definition with unnamed arguments:

```
int fn_name(/* named args */, lastarg, ...)
/* lastarg  is the last fixed argument */
{ va_list ap;                    /* argument pointer        */
     va_start(ap,lastarg);       /* initialize ap           */
     /* ... */
     va_arg(ap, type);           /* return next arg of given type  */
                                 /* and advance ap to next argument */

     /* ... */
     va_end(ap);                 /* clean up  before function returns  */
     return(answer);
}
```

Error- and Signal-Handling Functions

```
#include <stdio.h>
perror(CSTR s)
```

displays the string s and an implementation-defined error message corresponding to the value of the global variable errno to stderr.

```
#include <stdlib.h>
void exit(int status)
```

causes normal termination of program. The value status is passed to the environment.

```
void abort(void)
```

causes abnormal termination of program as if by raise(SIGABRT).

```
int atexit(void (* fn)(void)) [nonzero]
```

registers the function fn to be invoked when the program terminates normally. Multiple calls to atexit set up a sequence of such functions executed at exit time, in the reverse order as registered.

```
#include <setjmp.h>
int setjmp(jmp_buf env)
```

sets up env for a later longjmp nonlocal-control transfer (Section 9.6).

```
#include <setjmp.h>
int longjmp(jmp_buf env, int val)
```

restores the program state saved in env and transfers control to the corresponding setjmp call, which returns val.

```
typedef void (* H_FN)(int)
H_FN signal(int sig, H_FN new_handler)
```

replaces the handler function of the given signal sig with the function new_handler. The old handler function is returned (Section 9.7). Valid signals are sigabrt, sigfpe, sigill, sigint, sigsegv, and sigterm. All except SIGABRT, which causes the executing program to terminate abnormally, are also recognized by UNIX as valid signals.

```
int raise(int sig)
```

sends sig to the program itself.

String to Number Conversions

```
double atof(CSTR str)
```

converts string str into a double, which is returned.

```
int atoi(CSTR str)
```

converts string str to an int, which is returned.

```
long atol(CSTR str)
```

converts string `str` to a `long`, which is returned.

```
double strtod(CSTR str, char **rest)
```

converts the prefix of the string `str` to a `double`, ignoring any leading white space. It also stores in `*rest` a pointer to the rest of the string after the consumed prefix, unless `rest` is NULL. Overflow and underflow are detected, and ERANGE is set.

```
long strtol(CSTR str, char **rest, int base)
```

treats the prefix of `str` as a number of the given `base` and converts it to `long`. It is otherwise similar to `strtod`. If `base` is zero, the C integer constant notations are recognized.

```
unsigned long strtoul(CSTR str, char **rest, int base)
```

is the same as `strtol`, except the result is `unsigned long`.

Dynamic-Storage Allocation

```
#include <stdlib.h>
void *malloc(size_t n)  [NULL]
```

allocates space for an object of size `n` and returns a pointer to the memory space, which is not initialized.

```
#include <stdlib.h>
void *calloc(size_t m, size_t n)  [NULL]
```

allocates space for `m` objects each of size `n` and returns a pointer to the memory space whose bytes are initialized to zero.

```
#include <stdlib.h>
void *realloc(void *ptr, size_t n)  [NULL]
```

changes the size of the previously allocated space pointed to by `ptr` to `n`. A pointer to the new space is returned. The content of the space (up to the minimum of the new and old spaces) is unchanged. This is useful for adding more room to the end of previously allocated space without disturbing the contents.

```
#include <stdlib.h>
void free(void *ptr)
```

deallocates previously allocated space pointed to by `ptr` and returns the space to the pool of free space for future allocation.

Date and Time

The header <time.h> defines structures, macros, and functions for manipulating date and time. The date is kept according to the Gregorian calendar (in common use). Date and time can be represented in calendar time, local time, or Daylight Saving Time (DST).

The *broken-down* time structure struct tm includes the following members:

int tm_sec;	Seconds after the minute (0–59)
int tm_min;	Minutes after the hour (0–59)
int tm_hour;	Hours since midnight (0–23)
int tm_mday;	Day of the month (1–31)
int tm_mon;	Months since January (0–11)
int tm_year;	Years since 1900
int tm_wday;	Days since Sunday (0–6)
int tm_yday;	Days since January 1 (0–365)
int tm_isdst;	DST flag

The value of tm_isdst is positive if DST is in effect, zero if not, and negative if unknown. There are also clock_t and time_t, which are arithmetic types capable of representing time.

```
clock_t clock(void)
```

returns the processor time used by the program since the beginning of its execution or -1 if unavailable. Use clock()/CLOCKS_PER_SEC to convert to seconds. To measure the time spent in a program, the clock function should be called at the start of the program, and its return value subtracted from subsequent calls.

```
time_t time(time_t *tptr)
```

returns the current calendar time in an implementation-defined encoding of type time_t or -1 if not available. The value is also assigned to *tptr if tptr is not NULL.

```
struct tm *localtime(const time_t *tptr)
```

converts the given calendar time *tptr and creates a broken-down time structure representing the corresponding local time. A pointer to the structure is returned.

```
double difftime(time_t t1, time_t t2)
```

returns `t1 - t2` in seconds.

```
time_t mktime(struct tm *tptr)
```

takes the (partial) local-time information contained in the given structure `*tptr` and determines the values of all members in calendar-time form (`*tptr` is modified). It also returns the calendar time as encoded by `time` (or -1). This is useful to obtain the broken-down calendar time for a future or past date.

```
char *asctime(const struct tm *tptr)
```

converts the broken-down time in `*tptr` into a string in the form

```
Sun  Dec   23  15:35:22  1990\n\0
```

```
char *ctime(const time_t *tptr)
```

is the same as `asctime(localtime(tptr))`.

```
struct tm*gmtime(const time_t *tptr) [NULL]
```

converts the calendar time `*tptr` into Coordinated Universal Time (UTC) and returns the broken-down structure.

```
size_t strftime(char *s, size_t slen, CSTR fmt, const struct tm
                *tptr)
```

formats data and time given by `*tptr` into the string s (maximum length is `slen`) according to the format specified by `fmt`. The format is analogous to that for `printf`.

`%a`, `%A`	Abbreviated or full weekday name
`%b`, `%B`	Abbreviated or full month name
`%c`	Local date and time representation
`%d`	Day of month (01–31)
`%H`, `%I`	Hour (00–23) or (01–12)
`%j`	Day of the year (001–366)
`%m`	Month (01–12)
`%M`, `%S`	Minute, second (00–59)
`%p`	Local equivalent of A.M. or P.M.
`%U`, `%W`	Number of weeks/year (Sunday/Monday as first day of week)
`%w`	Day of week (0–6; Sunday is 0)

%x, %X Local date, time representation

%Y, %y Year with, without century

%Z   Time-zone name, if any

%%   %

Utility Functions

Functions listed here all use the header `<stdlib.h>`.

```
int abs(int n)
long labs(long n)
```

returns the absolute value of n.

```
div_t div(int num, int denom)
```

computes the quotient and remainder of `num` divided by `denom` and stores the results in `quot` and `rem`, `int` members of the structure `div_t`.

```
ldiv_t ldiv(long num, long denom)
```

computes the quotient and remainder of `num` divided by `denom` and stores the results in `quot` and `rem`, `long` members of the structure `ldiv_t`.

```
void rand(void)
```

returns the next random integer in a pseudorandom sequence based on a seed given by a prior call to `srand`. The default seed value is 1. The random integers are in the range 0– `RAND_MAX`.

```
void srand(unsigned int seed)
```

sets the seed value for a new random sequence to be used by subsequent calls to `rand`. The same seed value gives rise to the same random sequence.

```
void *bsearch(const void *key, const void *base,
              size_t n, size_t size
              int (*cmp) (const void *key, const void *datum))
```

searches an array located at `base` with n elements, each of size `size`, for an element matching the given `key`. The supplied comparison function `cmp` takes a key and an array element and produces a negative, zero, or positive `int` value as `strcmp`. The array must be already in increasing order as defined by the same comparison function.

```
void qsort(void *base, size_t n, size_t size,
           int (*cmp) (const void*, const void *))
```

sorts an array located at `base` with n elements each of size `size` with the supplied comparison function `cmp`, which takes two array entries and returns a negative, zero, or positive `int` as `strcmp`.

```
int system(CSTR cmd)
```

passes the string `cmd` to the operating system for execution. If `cmd` is `NULL`, then `system` returns zero if there is no command processor. Otherwise, the return value is implementation-dependent.

```
char *getenv(CSTR name)
```

returns the environment string associated with the given `name` or `NULL` if no such string exists.

Implementation-Defined Data Limits

The header `<limits.h>` contains symbolic constants for implementation-defined size limits for integer quantities. The limits must not be more restrictive than the following values:

CHAR_BIT	Bits per character	8
MB_LEN_MAX	Byte per character	1
SCHAR_MIN	signed char **minimum**	−127
SCHAR_MAX	signed char **maximum**	127
UCHAR_MAX	unsigned char **maximum**	255U
CHAR_MIN	0 or SCHAR_MIN	
CHAR_MAX	SCHAR_MAX or SCHAR_MAX	
SHRT_MIN	short int **minimum**	−32767
SHRT_MAX	short int **maximum**	32767
USHRT_MAX	unsigned short int **maximum**	65535U
INT_MIN	int **minimum**	−32767
INT_MAX	int **maximum**	32767
UINT_MAX	unsigned int **maximum**	65535
LONG_MIN	long int **minimum**	−2147483647
LONG_MAX	long int **maximum**	2147483647
ULONG_MAX	unsigned long int **maximum**	4294967295U

Constants and limits related to floating-point computations are contained in `<float.h>`. The minimum values are listed here. Actual values are defined by each implementation.

`FLT_RADIX`	Radix of exponent representation	2
`FLT_ROUND`	Rounding mode for addition	
`FLT_DIG`	Number of decimal digits for `float`	6
`FLT_MANT_DIG`	Number of base `FLT_RADIX` digits in mantissa for `float`	
`FLT_EPSILON`	Smallest `float` ε that $1.0 + \varepsilon \neq 1.0$	1E-5
`FLT_MAX`	Maximum `float`	1E+37
`FLT_MIN`	Minimum normalized `float`	1E-37
`FLT_MAX_EXP`	Maximum n such that $FLT\_RADIX^{n}-1$ is representable	
`FLT_MIN_EXP`	Minimum n such that $FLT\_RADIX^{n}-1$ is a normalized `float`	
`DBL_DIG`	Number of decimal digits for `float`	10
`DBL_MAX`	Maximum `double`	1E+37
`DBL_MIN`	Minimum normalized `double`	1E-37
`DBL_MANT_DIG`	Number of base `FLT_RADIX` digits in mantissa for `double`	
`DBL_EPSILON`	Smallest `double` ε that $1.0 + \varepsilon \neq 1.0$	1E-9

There are other similar constants. The values for `FLT_ROUNDS` controls how rounding is done for floating-point addition:

0	Round toward zero
1	Round to nearest
2	Round toward $+\infty$
3	Round toward $-\infty$
-1	Indeterminable

12

UNIX Signals

Symbol	Number	Default Action	Meaning
SIGHUP	1	Exit	Hang up
SIGINT	2	Exit	Interrupt
SIGQUIT	3	Core dump	Quit
SIGILL	4	Core dump	Illegal instruction
SIGTRAP	5	Core dump	Trace trap
SIGIOT	6	Core dump	IOT instruction
SIGEMT	7	Core dump	EMT instruction
SIGFPE	8	Core dump	Floating-point exception
SIGKILL	9	Exit	Kill (cannot be caught or ignored)
SIGBUS	10	Core dump	Bus error
SIGSEGV	11	Core dump	Segmentation violation
SIGSYS	12	Core dump	Bad argument to system call
SIGPIPE	13	Exit	Write on a pipe with no one to read it
SIGALRM	14	Exit	Alarm clock
SIGTERM	15	Exit	Software-termination signal
SIGURG	16	Discard	Urgent condition present on socket
SIGSTOP	17	Suspend	Stop (cannot be caught or ignored)
SIGTSTP	18	Suspend	Stop signal generated from keyboard
SIGCONT	19	Discard	Continue after stop

Symbol	Number	Default Action	Meaning
SIGCHLD	20	Discard	Child status has changed
SIGTTIN	21	Suspend	Background read attempted from terminal
SIGTTOU	22	Suspend	Background write attempted to terminal
SIGIO	23	Discard	Input/output is possible on a descriptor
SIGXCPU	24	Exit	CPU time limit exceeded
SIGXFSZ	25	Exit	File-size limit exceeded
SIGVTALRM	26	Exit	Virtual time alarm
SIGPROF	27	Exit	Profiling timer alarm

Index

FIGURES AND TABLES

FIGURES

TABLES

SERIES FOREWORD

Immanuel Wallerstein

The Political Economy of the World-System Section of the American Sociological Association was created in the 1970s to bring together a small but growing number of social scientists concerned with analyzing the processes of world-systems in general, and our modern one in particular.

Although organizationally located within the American Sociological Association, the PEWS Section bases its work on the relative insignificance of the traditional disciplinary boundaries. For that reason it has held an annual spring conference, open to and drawing participation from persons who work under multiple disciplinary labels.

For PEWS members, not only is our work unidisciplinary, but the study of the world-system is not simply another "specialty" to be placed beside so many others. It is instead a different "perspective" with which to analyze all the traditional issues of the social sciences. Hence, the themes of successive PEWS conferences are quite varied and cover a wide gamut of topics. What they share is the sense that the isolation of political, economic, and sociocultural "variables" is a dubious enterprise, that all analysis must be simultaneously historical and systemic, and that the conceptual bases of work in the historical social sciences must be rethought.

PREFACE

Latin America is in the midst of great transformations. Institutional reforms in the 1980s and 1990s have sought to promote a more competitive position for the region in the world-economy. These reforms have sought to achieve greater economic efficiency by curtailing the ability of states to regulate the production and distribution of wealth. Often, these reforms have been perceived as entailing painful social adjustments (as manifested, for example, in the persistence of poverty and the exacerbation of income inequalities). At the same time, Latin America has experienced the consolidation of democratic transitions and the emergence of new political dynamics characterized by distinct organizational arrangements and novel forms of collective action. To probe the contours, scope, and implications of these dramatic transformations, the North-South Center at the University of Miami hosted the nineteenth annual Conference on the Political Economy of the World-System. The essays included in this volume were originally presented at the conference, which was held in Coral Gables on April 20–22, 1995.

We would like to thank all the conference participants for their contributions during three exhausting, but highly stimulating, days of discussion and debate. In addition to the authors of the chapters included in this volume, conference participants included Caren Addis, Frank Bonilla, Marcelo Cavarozzi, Norma Stoltz Chinchilla, Paul Ciccantell, Susan Eckstein, Nancy Forsythe, Walter L. Goldfrank, Ramón Grosfoguel, Nora Hamilton, Jeffery Paige, Edward Mc-Caughan, John M. Talbot, Richard Tardanico, Beatrice Wallerstein, and Immanuel Wallerstein.

On behalf of all the conference participants, we wish to express our great appreciation to those who made this project possible. For the necessary financial support for the conference and the simultaneous publication of hardback and paperback editions, we owe special thanks to the North-South Center, particularly to Ambler H. Moss, Jr.; Robin Rosenberg; and Jeff Stark.

This volume would not have been possible without the collaboration of our respective institutions, colleagues, students, and staff. We would like to acknowledge the help provided by the Department of Sociology (especially Kevin Barth, Darrin Helsel, Cyndi Mewborn, Timothy Moran, and Mildred Yen) and the Latin American Studies Center at the University of Maryland in College Park. At the University of Miami, the assistance of students at the Graduate School of International Studies (particularly Holly Pierce, Julie Diehl, Vanessa Gray, María Eugenia Mujica, and Mariela Córdoba) was essential in the organization and smooth operation of the conference. We also appreciate the support and encouragement of Immanuel Wallerstein, editor of the Political Economy of the World-System (PEWS) series, and the the patient work of James Ice, the book's editor at Greenwood Press. Above all, this book was made possible by the critical assistance of Nancy Forsythe.

LATIN AMERICA IN THE WORLD-ECONOMY

1

A GREAT TRANSFORMATION?

Roberto Patricio Korzeniewicz and William C. Smith

Latin America is in the midst of dramatic transformations. Stabilization and structural adjustment programs are dismantling state regulation of the economy in an effort to extend the reach of markets and construct a new framework for growth and development. Advocates of these programs expect neoliberal restructuring to enhance economic efficiency by shifting responsibility for the allocation of resources from states to markets, enterprises, and households.[1] Simultaneously, the consolidation of the democratic transitions of the 1980s has been followed by the emergence of a new and distinct (albeit still inchoate) matrix of political dynamics and modes of organization, as some of the most influential forces of the past (such as trade unions or the military) have experienced a significant erosion of their bargaining power, while other actors (such as nongovernmental organizations [NGOs]) have found a new voice. Together, these political and economic changes signal the emergence of new institutional arrangements.[2]

Not all observers share the optimism of advocates of current reforms as they evaluate the depth and resiliency of these new arrangements. Some critics fear that economic restructuring will expose vulnerable sectors of the population to rising levels of poverty and that market mechanisms ultimately will fail to ensure the sustainable development of human and natural resources under democratic conditions (Bresser Pereira, Maravall, and Przeworski, 1993, 1994). Others cast doubt on the extent to which the consolidation of democratic regimes has enhanced full citizenship (particularly in contexts of increased economic hardship among the poor), or the degree to which democratic institutions have overcome enduring legacies of authoritarianism and privilege in many spheres of public and private life (O'Donnell, 1994b; Smith, 1993).

The chapters included in this book provide a critical evaluation of several crucial dimensions of the institutional transformations experienced in Latin America during the 1980s and 1990s. Some contribute to such an evaluation by providing detailed insights into the organizational changes undergone within the region by households, enterprises, and states. Other chapters focus more closely on changes in world-economic flows (e.g., the movement of people or capital across national borders). This introductory chapter reviews the contributions made by the essays in this volume, focusing on the conceptual areas in which a world-systems perspective might be particularly useful in advancing our understanding of emerging patterns of social and political change in Latin America.

ECONOMIC GROWTH, SOCIAL EQUITY, AND DEMOCRACY

The 1990s have witnessed a strong endorsement of stabilization and structural adjustment programs throughout Latin America. The implementation of these programs has had a profound impact on prevailing institutional arrangements. At a superficial level, market mechanisms have continued to displace state regulation in coordinating the production and distribution of resources. More profoundly, new institutional arrangements privilege a greater separation in the spheres of action of enterprises, states, and households. These patterns of institutional change in Latin America during the 1990s are intricately linked to the unraveling and collapse of import-substitution industrialization and state-centric models, as manifested in three legacies of the 1980s: stagnant economic growth, an exacerbation of social inequalities, and the consolidation of democratic transitions. Among these, economic crisis and stagnant growth were perhaps the most important legacy, as they led to a thorough reevaluation of existing institutional arrangements.

Characterized by unprecedented levels of economic crisis and instability, the 1980s in Latin America came to be termed a "Lost Decade" (see Table 1.1). The cumulative change in gross domestic product (GDP) per capita between 1981 and 1990 was −7.9 percent in the region as a whole, including, for example, −21.2 percent in Argentina, −18.6 percent in Bolivia, −3.6 percent in Brazil, −4.3 percent in Mexico, −33.5 percent in Nicaragua, −28.9 percent in Peru, −19.4 percent in Venezuela, and −1.4 percent in Uruguay (ECLAC, 1994, 1995; see also World Bank, 1993b: table 1). Only two countries in mainland Latin America experienced an increase in their cumulative GDP per capita during this period: Chile (11.7 percent) and Colombia (17.9 percent) (ECLAC, 1994; for similar data on GNP per capita, see World Bank, 1993c: table 1).

Economic crisis in many of the Latin American countries in question was often accompanied by traumatizing bouts of hyperinflation. In Argentina, for example, the average annual rate of inflation between 1980 and 1993 was 374.3 percent, and it reached the astonishing rates of 3,079.2 percent in 1989 and 2,314.0 percent in 1990. Likewise, annual inflation rates in Brazil reached an average of 423.4 percent between 1980 and 1993, and moved into four-digit

Table 1.1
Some Leading Economic Indicators, Selected Latin American Countries,
1980–1995

| | Cumulative Growth, GDP per Capita | | Urban Unemployment 1995 (percent) | Average Inflation 1995 (percent) |
	1981–1990 (percent)	1991–1995 (percent)		
Argentina	-21.1	23.6	18.6	1.8
Bolivia	-17.4	6.1	5.8	10.7
Brazil	-4.6	4.8	4.7	22.0
Chile	12.4	29.7	5.6	8.3
Colombia	17.9	13.2	8.6	20.0
Costa Rica	-5.8	10.1	4.3	24.9
Cuba	27.8	-33.4	NA	NA
Ecuador	-6.6	6.0	8.4	22.2
El Salvador	-18.8	16.0	7.5	11.4
Guatemala	-18.2	5.8	4.3	8.6
Honduras	-8.2	1.6	4.5	28.6
Mexico	-4.3	-5.8	6.4	48.5
Nicaragua	-33.5	-11.1	20.2	10.8
Panama	-2.4	14.6	14.3	0.8
Paraguay	-0.8	0.9	4.8	10.4
Peru	-28.9	19.3	8.2	10.4
Uruguay	-1.4	14.8	10.7	36.8
Venezuela	-19.4	2.5	10.3	52.9
Latin America & Caribbean	-7.5	5.1		

Source: ECLAC (1995).

territory in 1989, 1990, and 1992–1994. In Bolivia, the average annual rate of inflation between 1980 and 1993 was 187.1 percent, and it reached an average rate of 1,300.0 percent in 1984 and 11,804.8 percent in 1985. Similarly explosive bouts of inflation were experienced prior to 1992 in Nicaragua and Peru (for these figures, see Inter-American Development Bank, 1994: 284; World Bank, 1995: 163).

There is considerable evidence that macroeconomic instability and inflationary spirals produced an environment that led to a deterioration of virtually all indicators of social equity. During the "Lost Decade," poverty became accentuated throughout the region (CEPAL, 1992). Bonilla (1990: 215), for example, has indicated that the incidence of poverty among households in Latin America increased from 33 percent to 39 percent between 1980 and 1985 alone. Furthermore, the data suggest a rapid increase in the incidence of poverty during recessionary periods, but a slow reduction of poverty during periods of economic growth (CEPAL, 1992: 5). For these reasons, compared to the 1970s, there came to be a significantly higher number of households lacking sufficient income to meet basic needs (CEPAL, 1992: 7).[3]

Similar patterns characterize recent changes in the distribution of income. Available data indicate that inequalities became significantly more pronounced in Argentina, Bolivia, Brazil, Guatemala, Mexico, Peru, and Panama. On the other hand, the distribution of income became slightly more equitable in Colombia and Uruguay. Reviewing the evidence on changes in income distribution in Latin America since the early 1980s, Morley (1994: 10) argued, "Inequality in almost every case is strongly countercyclical, rising in recession and falling in recovery."[4] Providing some support to such an interpretation, recent patterns of income distribution in Chile, Costa Rica, and Venezuela appear to have shifted according to the economic cycle (CEPAL, 1994; see also Lustig, 1995; Fiszbein and Psacharopoulos, 1995; Morley, 1995b; Psacharopoulos, 1993; Raczynski and Romaguera, 1995).

The profound impact of economic stagnation and hyperinflation gave a number of governments throughout the region considerable political leeway in their efforts to implement adjustment and restructuring programs. Using this leeway, administrations such as those of Carlos Menem in Argentina, Fernando Collor in Brazil, and Alberto Fujimori in Peru were able to implement reforms that had been considered impossible only a few years before (Acuña, 1994; Sola, 1994; Roberts, 1995).[5] The implementation of these reforms has generated considerable opposition from forces claiming to represent those sectors most affected by the adjustment and restructuring programs, including, most notably, the Chiapas insurrection in Mexico, but no coherent alternative agenda had emerged on a regional basis by the middle of the 1990s (Zermeño, 1996).

What are the long-term political concomitants of these trends in poverty and inequality? More specifically, how can we explain why stabilization plans and market-driven restructuring associated with recent patterns of poverty and inequality have been implemented so aggressively by democratic leaders chosen in competitive elections? Are not widespread poverty and growing social inequality antithetical to the consolidation of democratic regimes?

Although common sense would lead us to expect economic "hard times" to threaten new democracies (and economic prosperity to facilitate democratic transition and consolidation), the relationship between democracy and economic conditions is not so simple or linear. In fact, Latin America's conjunction of democratic transitions and a context of economic crises and regressive income distributions is consistent with a broader pattern experienced elsewhere in the semiperiphery of the world-economy since the 1970s. For example, the transitions of the southern European semiperiphery (Spain, Greece, and Portugal) took place precisely in a context of economic stagnation. Moreover, current political transitions elsewhere in the semiperiphery (e.g., Eastern Europe and Russia) are occurring in even more desperate circumstances of crisis, austerity, and the collapse of living standards. If anything, economic growth and employment (as well as salary levels) appear typically to have fallen during transitions from authoritarian rule to more open, competitive polities. In these cases, macroeconomic conditions adverse to the social welfare of the majority of the population posed a challenge to democratic stabilization, and it is tempting simply to conclude that democratic "consolidations" have taken place in spite of economic hardships. This conclusion is true as far as it goes, but an alternative formulation might highlight a less obvious, but more interesting, relationship; namely, that profound economic restructuring has been advanced despite its high social costs and precisely *because* new democracies have both legitimated harsh economic policies and demobilized much of the anti-systemic opposition.[6]

This somewhat counterintuitive relationship between democracy and economic trends is complemented, in contemporary Latin America, by the equally paradoxical elective affinity between neoliberal restructuring and neopopulism, as well as the more obvious linkages of poverty, inequality, and personalistic governing styles, with the symbols and formal rituals of representative democracy. In contrast with the emphasis on *substantive* reforms designed to assure social equality, economic justice, and the broadened political participation characteristic of previous waves of democratization, the democratic discourse of the 1980s and 1990s has generally stressed the "Schumpeterian" or *procedural* components of the competitive struggle between rival elites for the people's vote. Concomitantly, demands for fundamental structural reform and expanded participation take a back seat and are frequently portrayed as leading to excessive and inefficient state intervention, predatory rent seeking, and ungovernability. In these circumstances, dominant economic and political actors, as well as many less privileged sectors, come to share the conviction that dictatorial regimes are unpredictable and that democracies are more reliable in securing adequate conditions for capitalist growth. Citizenship and political participation are thus largely limited to elections and the act of voting, while the market is enshrined as the most efficient means through which consumers can express economic preferences.[7]

In these circumstances it is perhaps hardly surprising that "the most natural political correlate to the neoliberal era may actually be populism, the option most widely seen as its antithesis" (Roberts, 1995: 112).[8] As O'Donnell recently observed, under such conditions, powerful plebiscitarian and majoritarian tendencies are likely to prevail over weak liberal and representative impulses. As a result,

the more properly political, *democratic* freedoms are effective: uncoerced voting, freedom of opinion, movement, and association. . . . But for large sections of the population, basic *liberal* freedoms are denied or recurrently trampled [and] . . . individuals are citizens in relation to the only institution that functions close to what its formal rules prescribe, elections. In the rest, only the members of a privileged minority are full citizens. (O'Donnell, 1996: 45)

Personalist mobilization of the populace is the counterpoint to the weakness of representative institutions such as legislatures, political parties, and labor unions. Moreover, the rapidity of economic restructuring erodes traditional social and political identities and accelerates the disarticulation of forms of social organization that, during the previous state-centric model of development, had formed the basis for the collective action of the subaltern sectors of society. Along with the emergence of "national saviors," particularistic interests flourish and the weakening of the "state-as-law" allows archaic authoritarian practices to reassert themselves, thereby reinforcing, in the strongly hierarchical societies, already egregious asymmetries in power and privilege.

While these transformations may facilitate the emergence of more efficient and dynamic circuits of production and distribution, they are probably incompatible with the broad-based type of class compromise (e.g., New Deal or social democracy) that characterized the historical consolidation of democracies in the core of the world-economy. Nevertheless, neoliberal reforms are not only compatible with democracy but may even facilitate the eventual consolidation of a democratic political order in much of Latin America. The key question is no longer authoritarianism versus democracy, but precisely what *type* of democratic systems are likely to develop in the near future in such semiperipheral areas of the world-economy.[9]

The specific institutional arrangements and the social bases of posttransition democratic regimes in Latin America will vary considerably. A variety of alternative politico-economic scenarios is possible (Smith and Acuña, 1994).[10] As institutional arrangements in each nation are transformed by the implementation of market-oriented reforms, collective outcomes may not produce a modal pattern for the region as a whole. In this sense, profound alterations in social and economic structures probably foreshadow growing social, economic, and political diversity within the region.

Diversity can also be found in recent patterns of economic growth (see Table 1.1). At one end of the spectrum, Chile has continued to be characterized by extremely high rates of economic growth and a similar, if less dynamic, pattern has characterized the case of Colombia. At the other end of the spectrum, a considerably slower pace of economic growth has characterized cases such as Bolivia, Brazil, and Mexico. The most striking pattern of change has characterized countries such as Argentina and Peru, where the profound recession and instability of the 1980s was followed by considerable growth (although, as in other countries in the region, with considerable susceptibility to shifts in financial flows, as demonstrated by the recessionary tendencies manifested in the so-called "Tequila effect" following the Mexican crisis in 1994). In most of these cases, structural reforms have achieved considerable success in reducing inflation to historical lows, thus providing considerable legitimacy to the regimes in question. Nevertheless, in some countries, such as Argentina, structural reforms continue to be accompanied by painful social costs (i.e., excessive unemployment rates and measures of income inequality, which recently reached historically high levels), while in other countries, such as Chile, most of these social indicators have improved.

Notwithstanding these divergencies, the region as a whole has undergone major changes in existing institutional arrangements, including a new hegemonic ascendancy of liberal ideology in the design and implementation of economic policies, far-reaching changes in the regulatory capacity of the state, and an apparent erosion in the bargaining power of established political parties, social movements, and collective actors. Are these new institutional arrangements indicative of a "Great Transformation"? A little over 50 years ago, Karl Polanyi (see Polanyi, 1957) introduced the term to describe the rise and demise of a self-regulating market economy.[11] According to Polanyi, the rise of a self-regulating market economy in the middle of the nineteenth century generated social and political responses that led to its eventual demise between World War I and World War II, to be succeeded by new forms of state regulation and class compromise, as embodied in the "Keynesian" formulas of core countries and the statist and populist strategies pursued in the semiperiphery. Are the current changes in Latin America of such a magnitude that they indicate a new Great Transformation reintroducing a self-regulating market economy? The chapters in this volume serve to outline three key areas of inquiry that a world-systems perspective can explore to answer this question.

EVALUATING STRATEGIES FOR GROWTH: COMMODITY CHAINS IN THE WORLD-ECONOMY

From different perspectives and disciplines, scholars have observed that the trends that characterized Latin America during the 1980s are particularly striking when compared to regional patterns of development in East Asia. In comparison to the crisis, instability, and precipitous deterioration in economic performance that most of Latin America experienced during the "Lost Decade," the East Asian nations indeed appeared as success stories. Between 1980 and 1993, in the midst of the Latin American crisis, the average annual growth rate of gross national product (GNP) per capita was 8.2 percent for South Korea, 5.4 percent in Hong Kong, and 6.1 percent in Singapore (World Bank, 1993c: table 1). This striking divergence stimulated a large of body of empirical and comparative studies seeking to distill the strategies and policies that explain East Asian success (e.g., Amsden, 1989; Appelbaum and Henderson, 1992; Balassa et al., 1986; Evans, 1995; Gereffi, 1989, 1995; Wade, 1990; Whitehead, 1989; World Bank, 1987, 1993a).

We should be cautious about our ability to abstract recipes for such success. After all, in the 1960s and 1970s, there came to be considerable consensus that industrialization and self-reliance were important ingredients for growth, and the "economic miracles" that served as models in those decades were countries such as Yugoslavia or Brazil. Industrialization prescribed very clear strategies (e.g., in terms of investments, tariff and trade arrangements, and infrastructure) to be pursued by enterprises, households, and state agencies in order to promote economic growth and development. True, there were already conflicting interpretations over the specific mechanisms that should be implemented to promote effective industrial growth (e.g., in regard to the precise extent of state regulation of trade or the degree to which price supports or taxes were to be extended to agriculture or manufacturing). In overall terms, however, and particularly as compared to later developments in the 1980s and 1990s, there was relative consensus over the importance of industrialization as an engine of growth to drive the whole model of development.[12]

The postwar model of development that prevailed until the 1980s, which was based on industrialization and statist/populist modes of regulation, had clear difficulties in delivering its promise of promoting economic growth and rapid convergence with high-income nations. Already apparent, these difficulties prompted many debates in the 1960s and 1970s (e.g., Suttcliff, 1972, 1984). Until the 1980s, however, these debates did not fundamentally challenge the premise of industrialization as an engine of development. After the debt crisis and Latin America's "Lost Decade," on the other hand, the Asian experience became widely perceived, in policy-making circles and elsewhere, as providing a contrasting pattern of development and growth. In this new model, the pursuit of industrialization as a general strategy was displaced by a more specific emphasis on particular modes of organization (e.g., flexible specialization) and market integration (e.g., export-oriented growth rather than continued reliance on protected internal markets).

Efforts to derive a new model of development from the East Asian experience are tempered by considerable debates over how to interpret the role of enterprises and the state in promoting growth. For advocates of neoclassical prescriptions for economic restructuring, the East Asian experiences serve as an indictment of state regulation and inward-oriented industrialization (e.g., Balassa et al., 1986; World Bank, 1987, 1993a). For example, the World Bank suggested that in the East Asian experience, government regulation "was subjected to international competition and market-related checks and balances," trade regimes "remained highly outward-oriented," and government regulation of markets was "more moderate than in most other developing countries" (1991: 39). Some critics have countered that successful development did entail active intervention in markets on the part of effective state bureaucracies (Amsden, 1989; Evans, 1992, 1995; Wade, 1990).[13] For yet others, countries in East Asia and Latin America underwent distinct paths of industrialization, some of which (e.g., import-substitution industrialization oriented toward domestic markets) generated institutional constraints that made it difficult for states and enterprises to promote greater economic integration or move into more complex areas of production (Appelbaum and Henderson, 1992; Gereffi, 1989, 1995; Whitehead, 1989). Such a range of interpretations reflects considerable disagreement as to the crucial variables that might explain the success of the East Asian experience.

Often inherent in the effort to scrutinize the East Asian experiences in search of an effective model of growth is the assumption that success in the economic arena is derived from the *replicable* construction of certain capabilities (e.g., at the level of the firm or state agencies) that are best suited to exploit available opportunities. Alternatively, a world-systems perspective emphasizes the *relational* character of the economic transformations that have alternatively led to economic growth and/or stagnation. "Success" and "failure," from such a perspective, are related outcomes of a *singular* process of world-economic accumulation.

Historically, social and economic rigidities and institutional constraints operating in some areas of the world-economy have generated competitive opportunities that could be exploited by enterprises and state agencies in countries where innovations could be adopted relatively free from these rigidities and constraints.[14] These innovations sometimes have involved new organizational linkages to production and/or market niches within Global Commodity Chains (GCCs).[15] Innovative practices, however, have not been limited to enterprises, as they often have involved the organization of state regulation around new strategic objectives.

This type of focus on innovation allows us to emphasize the relational character of world-economic processes, thus focusing on the spatial dimensions of the processes of competition and exploitation shaping GCCs.[16] Such a perspective primarily emphasizes the fact that the relative command over wealth secured by specific patterns of organization and exchange (or by particular configurations of production processes, commodities, and services) is likely to change significantly over time. In this sense, successful growth policies in the 1980s and 1990s, as generated by both enterprises and states, have been characterized, not by specific forms of organizing production and/or trade, but by the organizational capacity to mold and shift strategic goals according to rapidly changing opportunities and constraints. The nature and characteristics of these patterns must be assessed empirically, which is the concern of several of the articles in this volume.

Amy E. Bellone, for example, carries out a detailed study of the organization of the cocaine commodity chain in Chapter 2. As in previous world-system studies of this chain (e.g., Wilson and Zambrano, 1994), Bellone points out that although the final product within this commodity chain commands a high value, wealth is very unevenly distributed within the chain. Overall, growers and agents involved in the earlier, labor-intensive stages of production and distribution are able to capture only a relatively small share of profit. However, some agents have been more successful than others in extending their role and share of profits. To illustrate this point, and also to identify the characteristics that made some agents more successful than others, Bellone compares coca producers in Bolivia and Peru. She indicates that these efforts by farmers and intermediaries to expand their role were often well received by the actors involved in the higher stages of refining and distribution, for risks were more diffused by the active role of small firms. However, Bolivian producers were better able than their Peruvian counterparts to control the refining of coca paste into cocaine. Bellone argues that this was because in Bolivia, there was an already-existing group of local elites in possession of the trade networks and capital required to engage in refining.

Changing patterns of competitive pressures are also highlighted in Chapter 3 by Miguel E. Korzeniewicz. The author begins by focusing on the success of Brazilian shoe manufacturers in capturing substantial niches in the global shoe market. He draws a comparison to shoe producers in Argentina in order to highlight several variables that help account for the comparative success of Brazilian producers. First, their concentration in geographically specific industrial districts has facilitated the emergence of organizations and informal ties that facilitated collective action on behalf of their interests. Second, a growing specialization in women's shoes allowed these shoe producers to target production to a specific world market niche. Third, the state played an important role in promoting these exports. Finally, Brazilian business firms were particularly successful in developing effective linkages, both backward (e.g., securing access to raw materials and labor) and forward (e.g., developing formal channels for marketing and distribution). However, although organizational choices along each of these dimensions served to enhance the competitiveness of Brazilian shoe producers prior to the 1990s, Korzeniewicz observes that this competitive edge began to erode in the 1990s, as producers in other countries (such as mainland China) made significant inroads in the market niches in question.

In Chapter 4, David Spener enhances our understanding of the competitive pressures that characterize GCCs by highlighting the importance of social capital in providing competitive advantages to small firms. As indicated by the author, ''ethnic Mexican entrepreneurs' reliance on transborder social capital to extend commodity chains from the United States into Mexico was as much a strategy to compensate for their lack of other kinds of capital—human, physical, and financial—as it was a strategy that built on their natural strengths.'' Spener's study helps us to develop a better understanding of the conditions that are likely to strengthen and weaken this type of social capital: with the North American Free Trade Agreement (NAFTA), for example, as ''state rules are lifted or made less stringent, the demand for the kinds of social network conditions that permitted the circumvention of the old trade barriers is reduced.'' Social capital is very important, but it is more unstable and vulnerable than usually assumed in the literature.

In Chapter 13, Alvaro Díaz tackles the case of Chile, which (along with Colombia, as indicated in Table 1.1) was among the few countries in Latin America to experience economic growth during the 1980s; moreover, high rates of growth have prevailed in the 1990s. The Chilean case has often become appealing as a model of development because its trajectory since the early 1980s can be used to justify the often-painful costs of adjustment and restructuring as temporary, and yet necessary, steps on the road to economic recovery. After all, in the early 1980s, Chile was characterized both by stagnant economic growth and by rapidly growing unemployment and poverty. In the 1980s, however, rates of economic growth achieved record heights, unemployment and poverty rates underwent a steady decline, and real wages grew rather substantially from the troughs they had reached in the early 1980s. Nevertheless, overall levels of income inequality remain essentially unchanged (Raczynski and Romaguera, 1995).

The Chilean case has been hailed as a model of development in order to emphasize the need to use exports as a platform for economic growth, to replace the state regulation of economic activities with entrepreneurial efforts regulated primarily by the market, and to reshape the political sphere so that state policies cease to respond to centralized decision making, unproductive rent seekers, and particularistic claims on resources. Advocates of the model claim that it alone provides the substantial reforms necessary to sustain economic development into the twenty-first century. Opponents of the model, however, argue that its social costs were such that they could only be incurred in Chile by a military dictatorship, and that efforts to implement a similar model under democratic regimes are only likely to undermine democratic rule by generating profound discontent or undermining the historical rights endowed by citizenship (Vergara, 1986, 1994).

Díaz suggests that the very success of strategies of economic growth in Chile is generating new constraints. First, while the adoption of technological and organizational innovations has provided enterprises in Chile with a considerable competitive edge in world markets, the very growth of exports and the accompanying influx in foreign investments have exposed the country to "Dutch Disease," in which the overvaluation of the currency can have a severe negative impact on other economic activities (particularly manufacturing). Second, income distribution remains highly skewed, an asymmetry that may undermine the future pace of economic growth. Finally, the persistence of many of the same authoritarian enclaves that allowed for the initial implementation of the prevailing model of economic growth may undermine the ability to continue the political and institutional reforms required for continued growth. These constraints represent a growing asymmetry between internationalization and democratic transition, on the one hand, and on the other, "the rigidity and obsolescence of the political and economic institutions inherited from the previous authoritarian regime and its neoliberal economic policies." Resolving such an asymmetry, according to Díaz, will be required to consolidate economic growth and deepen democracy.

The insights gained from these chapters on patterns of competition speak for caution in endorsing export strategies as the centerpiece of a model for economic growth. Furthermore, the magnitude of the changes required to *initiate* an export-centered strategy of growth in countries such as Argentina, Brazil, or Mexico (where exports account for a relatively small proportion of overall economic activity) is likely to be significantly greater than the *maintenance* of such a strategy is in countries such as Chile or Costa Rica, where exports have come to play a central role in the overall economy.[17] Furthermore, the overall size of the economy in countries such as Argentina, Mexico, or Brazil implies that increasing the relative importance of exports to the degree achieved in countries such as Chile would require a much larger transformation.

The promise that wealth would be forthcoming through the adoption of specific combinations of production processes, trade patterns, and institutional arrangements has often encouraged enterprises and states to pursue an impossible race. In fact, this was the most important lesson drawn from the failure of postwar industrialization to deliver greater approximation to the standards of wealth enjoyed in high-income or core nations (Arrighi, 1991). If greater control over wealth has been an outcome of innovation rather than specific commodities or production processes, there is no single model or specific strategy to be derived from the successful experiences (e.g., East Asia, Spain, or Chile).[18] In fact, the very implementation of innovative practices initiates their diffusion, their inevitable (albeit eventual) elimination as innovations, and the emergence of new technological, organizational, and institutional rigidities. However, this skepticism regarding the ability of the world-economy to deliver a more even distribution of wealth between nations in the near future should not distract us from the profound changes accompanying economic restructuring.

One of the most significant changes has involved the emergence of new world-economic organizational networks coordinating the production and distribution of goods and services. Observers in recent decades have frequently proclaimed these global economic networks to constitute a "new international division of labor" and have generally attributed the creation of these linkages to the action of multinational enterprises based in core countries. Regardless of the extent to which this "international division of labor" is actually "new" (such an argument is certainly challenged by the world-systems literature), the chapters in this volume suggest that enterprises in peripheral and semiperipheral nations should also be considered as crucial actors in the creation of these new arrangements.[19]

To some extent, the new role of peripheral and semiperipheral enterprises within GCCs is linked to changes in the organization of markets (hence following Adam Smith's dictum that the division of labor is determined by the extent of the market). Future world-systems research, however, might explore the degree to which the extent of markets is itself a consequence of the space allowed by an existing division of labor. In this sense, comparatively slow organizational changes among local enterprises outside the core prior to the 1980s might have prepared the terrain for the accelerated transformations of the 1980s and 1990s.[20]

Both Bellone and Korzeniewicz suggest in their respective chapters that the adoption of organizational innovations allowed local enterprises to capture important production niches within GCCs. Corroborating the findings of the broader literature on export strategies in East Asia, these contributions also suggest that local enterprises play an active role in gaining greater access to core markets (either directly or by developing new links to multinational corporations). However, beyond the crucial role of these local enterprises in allowing for the formation of the new production and distribution networks that are often characterized as a "new" internationalization, networks of peripheral and semiperipheral enterprises might themselves be moving in the direction of becoming large multinational corporations. For example, large business conglomerates in Chile have used direct foreign investments to expand elsewhere in the continent (particularly in Argentina, Bolivia, and Peru). As suggested in this volume and elsewhere by Alvaro Díaz (1996), the new control gained by these enterprises over processes of accumulation (following restructuring and privatization), represents, not so much a growing prevalence of market arrangements, but a shift from one type of command (as previously exercised by state agencies) to another (as currently deployed by large corporations).

THE LOGIC OF RULE AND THE RECASTING OF STATE POWER

Although states play an important role in shaping processes of accumulation, they are often driven by the dynamics of a separate logic of rule. As indicated by Arrighi (1994) in his recent contribution to world-systems theory, the relationship between accumulation and rule can be more effectively probed by acknowledging these distinctions. The essays included in this collection make an important contribution in probing the logic and processes of rule and the recasting of state power at different levels of action and organization.

In Chapter 9, Bruce M. Podobnik uses a comparison between Peru and Cambodia to probe the processes giving rise to revolutionary violence. He argues that the emergence and expansion of the Khmer Rouge in Cambodia and the Shining Path in Peru were tied to the linkage between sectarian dissident groups and a generation of youth that found few employment opportunities. A political vacuum (resulting, to some extent, from the failure of reformist efforts in previous decades) and the existence of institutional and geographical spaces (such as universities or isolated rural areas) allowed for the relatively free operation of the new groups. Regardless of the relative appeal or rejection inspired by the organizations involved, Podobnik suggests that revolutionary violence will remain one of the forms adopted by those in resistance to world-economic processes of accumulation and rule.

Dealing with a different arena of political demands, J. Timmons Roberts, in Chapter 10, focuses on the current deterioration of the environment in Latin America. Roberts indicates that this deterioration can be traced back at least to import-substitution industrialization and argues that future changes in environmental conditions will be shaped by several variables. For example, the initiatives associated with export-led strategies of growth certainly have a potential for further environmental degradation, but economic growth might generate resources that can be channeled (given sufficient pressure from interested parties) to improve the environment. A similar ambivalence is likely to result from the adoption of global environmental standards (for example, as dictated in international trade agreements). Most important, according to Roberts, will be the pressures brought to bear on governments, enterprises, and state agencies by an environmental social movement that has become increasingly international in character.

Such a perspective, which calls attention to the unhinging of the logic of rule from the logic of accumulation, can play an important role in clarifying contemporary political changes and the impact of market-oriented restructuring. In Chapter 11, A. Douglas Kincaid and Eduardo A. Gamarra examine the political challenges stemming from the illegality, huge profits, and violence manifested, for example, in Brazilian *favela* gangs or Bolivian coca growers. They argue that efforts to come to terms with the interaction between drug-trafficking networks and the erosion of state capacity, both of which are manifestations of particularly perverse forms of integration into the world-economy, are key to understanding emergent patterns of reorganization of the means of violence. A chief characteristic of a "new Latin American mode of public security," according to the authors, is growing recourse to military intervention in support, or in place, of the conventional roles of the police. Their case studies of Bolivia, Brazil, and Honduras probe three fundamental features of this redefinition of state and the market with regard to the provision of public security: a process of *militarization*, in which threats of major civic disorder are repressed but crime flourishes and citizen security erodes; a simultaneous *informalization* of some security functions, including the formation of paramilitary neighborhood groups and the rise of a "parallel state" of shantytown criminal organizations; and a *privatization* of security as a commodity to be purchased on the market by the privileged and powerful. Kincaid and Gamarra warn that despite initiatives to promote the demilitarization of public security, the toll exacted by neoliberal reforms and the transnational drug economy threatens to bring about a generalization of public disorder that will prove deeply inimical to democratic politics.[21]

A more nuanced understanding of the relations between the logics of accumulation and rule can also contribute to a more adequate interpretation of the recasting of state power as national political institutions are whipsawed between the growing hegemony of marketplace logic, which is reinforced by the exigencies of the world-economy, and by pressures to expand citizenship rights and popular participation. It is generally recognized that the collision between globalization and national and local actors has resulted in a sharp erosion of the national state's capacity to manage major macroeconomic variables. The difficulty is that such affirmations to the effect that state power is "weakening" actually say very little.[22]

Underlying the question of state and societal power, there is, in fact, a striking contradiction (Kahler, 1990, 1992; Bierstekker, 1995). On the one hand, neo-utilitarian and neoclassical prescriptions call for rolling back the state and weakening governmental mechanisms of macroeconomic regulation; on the other hand, the state apparatus must argument its power capabilities to impose a market-driven model of accumulation under conditions of growing globalization and intranational competition. Greater economic orthodoxy, under these circumstances, may well require, not less, but *more* autonomy, particularly from specific entrepreneurial and trade union interests. Similarly, greater orthodoxy may imply, not less, but *more* effective coordination and regulation of the private sector (e.g., overseeing the stock and financial markets, broadening the tax base, upgrading skills of workers, promoting technological innovations and competitiveness, and so on). Similarly, "market-friendly" growth strategies frequently seem to go hand-in-hand with the concentration of augmented administrative power in the hands of state managers and technocratic elites.[23]

To go beyond a simple recognition of this neoliberal paradox, we need carefully crafted comparative studies of state reform focusing on particular agencies and institutional arrangements. Sergio Berensztein's discussion of taxation policies in Chapter 12 is a valuable example of this needed research. Berensztein eschews the Manichean rhetoric surrounding the debate on neoliberalism and the state in which some tout the efficiency of international financial markets while others warn that the implacable discipline imposed by the globalization of financial flows has deprived states—even those at the core of the world-economy—of the instruments and resources to regulate the economy. Without ignoring these constraints, the author focuses on the institutional design of the semiperipheral Latin American states. On the basis of a detailed analysis of fiscal reforms in Argentina and Mexico, the author argues that theoretical perspectives emphasizing shifts in the international division of labor, the peripheralization of industrial activities, and the logic of competition in the world-economy should give greater weight to the continuing importance of domestic actors, state agencies, and processes of rule. By the same token, however, Berensztein is fully cognizant of the fragility of institutional reforms intended to enhance state capacity. Of course, as the Mexican collapse of 1994 reminds us, speculative movements of capital can wreak havoc in the form of recessions and political instability, and rising interest rates can spark a surge of tax evasion capable of threatening to reverse all efforts to bolster state capacity.[24]

These chapters illustrate that, while obeying their own separate dynamics, the logic of accumulation and the logic of rule clearly remain intertwined. Seen from this perspective, the recasting of the state in Latin America should be understood, not merely in terms of the shrinkage and more "efficient" operation of state administrative agencies, but as a manifestation of a more fundamental redrawing of the existing boundaries between "politics" and "economics" and between the "public" and the "private." This will be a wrenching experience during which many organized societal interests are, in effect, "expelled" from the regulated spheres to fend for themselves as individuals in the market.[25] A state more impermeable to societal demands will require a more "authoritative" administrative apparatus capable of neutralizing the reaction of adversely affected groups. The concentration of power in the executive agencies of the state (characterized by *decretazos*, or presidential decrees, of dubious legality and with clear authoritarian overtones), which is characteristic of current market-oriented reforms in Latin America, highlights a central aspect of the political and economic dynamics present in the transition from the Keynesian and Fordist modes of reproduction of consent to more "liberal" models of accumulation and of political domination and rule.

However, once the transition has been completed, will the state be stronger or weaker than before the market-driven restructuring? In all likelihood, state institutions and public authority in the future will be *both* stronger and weaker.[26] Depending on the specific issue area or public policy arena, for example, neo-liberal restructuring may lead to a severe retrenchment of the public sphere's traditional "entrepreneurial" functions that are related to direct ownership and the management of productive enterprises, thus resulting in a smaller and much "weaker" state apparatus. Simultaneously, however, in other arenas, such as the capacity of civilian elites to exercise civilian control over the armed forces (e.g., formulation of national security policies, severe cuts in military budgets, and so on) or to impose labor market flexibilization and other restrictions on the prerogatives of workers and trade unions, public authority may be strengthened significantly, surpassing even the power and autonomy achieved by state elites during earlier populist and authoritarian periods. Even with respect to the market, it is not clear that neoliberal strategies necessarily imply a weaker state. For example, in order for markets to function properly and with the efficiency and transparency required by private investors, strong legal norms protecting private property must be guaranteed and effective mechanisms of state regulation that were previously absent must be put into place.

These observations make it clear that rather than trying to formulate overarching generalizations regarding the relative strength of the state in Latin America following restructuring, it will be fruitful for future empirical research to examine particular state agencies and specific public arenas.[27] The key role of local actors and institutional arrangements across the region should be stressed, but without losing sight of the fact that the dynamics and logic informing the choices of local actors and the recasting of state power necessarily incorporate transformations in the world-economy.

EVALUATING HOUSEHOLDS, COMMUNITIES, AND RESISTANCE

Some observers attribute growing poverty and income inequality to changes in the structure of production. Clearly, and particularly among the wealthiest Latin American countries, manufacturing and industrial activities lost relative importance to services.[28] In Argentina, for example, the share of industry in the gross domestic product declined from 44 percent in 1970 to 31 percent by 1993 (and manufacturing, from 32 percent to 20 percent during the same period), while services enhanced their share from 47 percent to 63 percent over the same years. Similar patterns, albeit with different degrees of intensity, can be observed in Uruguay, Chile, and Brazil (World Bank 1995: 166–167). In effect, such trends constitute a form of deindustrialization that is strikingly familiar to any observer acquainted with the dramatic decline of industrial job opportunities in the Rust Belt of the United States or similar regions elsewhere in the core of the world-economy.[29]

Other analysts have sought to emphasize the relationship between social welfare and alternative long-term and short-term variables. As a long-run determinant of social welfare, some have sought to emphasize the crucial importance of education (Morley, 1994, 1995a, 1995b). The World Bank, for example, noted that "education is the most important single variable influencing income inequality," and asserted that "when markets work well, greater equity often comes naturally" (1991: 138). As a short-term determinant of social welfare, this interpretation emphasizes the importance of economic growth. Hence, Morley, for example, has argued that in the short term, "changes in the level of per capita income are the key determinants of changes in the level of poverty" (1994: 1).[30]

One of the most striking features of recent patterns of economic and political change in Latin America is the fact that the growth of poverty and unemployment, as well as rising income inequality, have often been accompanied by a demobilization of civil society. In Chapter 13, for example, Díaz refers to "the (apparent) silence of civil society" in Chile (see also Tironi, 1986). The author calls our attention to the fact that economic restructuring involves both an initial decomposition of existing social and political arrangements and the eventual ascendance of new social and political actors. He suggests that in the case of Chile, the highest levels of collective organization and mobilization have characterized the areas most affected by recession or decline. By the same token, areas characterized by rapid growth and profound social recomposition have so far been characterized by lower levels of mobilization—an outcome, for Díaz, of the "inchoate" character of "collective social actors still in the process of formation."[31]

Distinguishing the social impact of economic restructuring in terms of demobilization and recomposition makes sense within a world-systems analytical framework that has often emphasized differences in the types of resistance elicited by exclusion as opposed to exploitation (e.g., Arrighi, 1978: 20). Such a line of analysis opens interesting areas of research on current patterns of mobilization and protest. Are protest movements in Chiapas or the provinces of the interior of Argentina indicative of the type of resistance associated with areas in economic decline? Does the new importance of transnational NGOs (e.g., organized around gender or environmental issues) reflect new modes of organization among the social actors most affected by processes of growth and reconstitution?

Several chapters in this volume focus on alternative efforts by households to gain greater leverage. In Chapter 5, José Itzigsohn focuses on economic strategies within the informal sector, differentiating four types of activities: petty marketers, suppliers, subcontractors, and the informal proletariat. To what extent do linkages to multinationals prevail in the new informal economy of the 1980 and 1990s, and to what extent are different patterns associated to the extent of state regulation? Itzigsohn calls for a nuanced study of these issues, as market conditions (for labor and products) and patterns of state regulation vary a great deal across different types of economic activities. Thus, product market opportunities are restricted for Costa Rican garment producers (who move into supplying and subcontracting arrangements), but not for their Dominican counterparts (who have greater bargaining power due to the existence of alternative outlets). For craft producers oriented to the tourist trade, on the other hand, state regulations lead to a restricted market for Dominican producers, while greater opportunities enhance the bargaining power of their Costa Rican counterparts. Thus, the ability of producers to maintain autonomy and capture a greater share of income is related to their relative bargaining power vis-à-vis purchasers.

In fact, the strategies adopted within the informal sector bear considerable similarity to the entrepreneurial strategies reviewed in the first section of this chapter. In both cases, "success" entails the adoption of organizational strategies that can exploit the opportunities and constraints of prevailing institutional arrangements. The successful deployment of such a strategy suggests that what is generally read as a "silence" of civil society might actually reflect the viability (under current conditions and for some sectors of the population) of what Albert Hirshman (1970, 1994) would characterize as an exercise of "exit" rather than "voice."

An alternative form of practicing the "exit" option involves migration, and several of the chapters included in this volume analyze patterns of change in this particular arena. For example, Susanne Jonas, in Chapter 6, argues that the migration patterns of some Latino communities (such as those of Salvadorans or Guatemalans) are transforming certain regions into "trinational spaces" that include the home countries of these migrants, Mexico, and areas of the United States. Furthermore, Jonas argues that these transnational spaces are constructed through informal networks that are particularly impervious to state regulation, and for this reason, she expresses skepticism regarding the likelihood that current efforts in the United States to restrict migration from Latin America will succeed in their larger objective. Jonas also warns that such policies might lead to exclusionary politics that restrict the practice of citizenship among important sectors of the population and undermine more generally the consolidation of democratic practices in the region as a whole, including the United States.

In Chapter 8, reproducing his noteworthy keynote address to the PEWS conference, Alejandro Portes argues that the current emphasis on processes leading to the globalization of capital should be complemented with a better understanding of the constitution of transnational communities. While analyses of transnationalization generally emphasize how geographic mobility enhances the bargaining power of capital, Portes seeks to call equal attention to the manner in which communities may use migration to exploit the opportunities that result from "the differentials of advantage created by political boundaries." These opportunities are generally exploited through "grassroots transnational enterprises" that rely on informal social ties centered around kin and friendship networks. For Portes, this is a relatively new phenomenon in both scale and relative importance. The potential significance of these communities is that they might serve to challenge "a strategy of capitalist accumulation based on wage differential and information asymmetries between different regions of the world."

Focusing on Garifuna migration to the Los Angeles metropolitan area, Linda Miller Matthei and David A. Smith, in Chapter 7, argue that gender relations constitute a crucial dimension of the way in which households participate in the world-economy. Their chapter highlights shifting migration patterns, characterized by declining opportunities for male workers (as a consequence of falling demand for manufacturing labor) but rising opportunities for female workers (particularly in service occupations and new types of manufacturing jobs). According to the authors, networks developed among women allowed their households (and the individuals contain therein) to expand their social capital and served as transnational linkages to the United States. These networks often included child care in Belize when parents migrate to the United States (in exchange for a share of remittances). In short, households appear as active as enterprises in constructing the transnational linkages that have emerged as a striking feature of recent decades.

A focus on shifts in the construction of gender is particularly important to understanding social movements and communities of resistance. Much of the theorizing on social movements in Latin America was built on the specific features that these movements appeared to exhibit through the course of the twentieth century: they seemed to be built primarily around class interests, they were geared primarily to alter the rule of states, and their principal sphere of action appeared to involve a public (rather than private) arena. The incorporation of gender as an important (if not central) concern in the contemporary social sciences has led to a reevaluation of these premises, highlighting the importance of cleavages other than class in guiding the construction of social identities, probing into the crucial impact on politics of everyday and informal organizational networks, and challenging the boundaries between public and private arenas (Bose and Acosta-Belén, 1995; Folbre, 1994; Jaquette, 1989; Jelin, 1990; Moser, 1993; Ward, 1993). This shifting analytical focus does not merely make visible what was always there, but also responds to a shift to women as the epicenter of a different "kind" of transnational community (Forsythe, 1995).

CONCLUSION

The institutional arrangements that prevailed in Latin America for most of the postwar period are being disassembled at a precipitous pace, to be replaced by a deepening differentiation in the arenas of operation of enterprises, states, and households (Korzeniewicz, 1996). Enterprises appear to exercise greater control over processes of accumulation, in a shift that has entailed the organization of new networks linking production and market niches within global commodity chains.[32] However, the adoption of neoliberal strategies does not necessarily imply a weaker state, as state agencies generally become involved in implementing effective mechanisms of state regulation and strong legal norms guaranteeing private property. Markets, in this sense, continue to require state regulation for their very survival. Social actors affected by such changes seek to maintain or enhance their relative bargaining power by alternatively moving among strategies designed to enhance "exit" and/or "voice" options.

These institutional transformations are reshaping the fundamental questions that currently guide intellectual discourse in the social sciences. What is the path to sustainable growth, and through what mechanisms can it ensure improvements in social welfare? What is the likely future of democracy, and to what extent does its strength depend on the practice of citizenship and the assertion of social rights? What are the new categories of identity emerging in the region, and to what extent are they likely to promote either existing or new social movements? In short, what are the crucial elements of the new constellation of institutional arrangements and social practices currently emerging in Latin America?

Returning to a question posed earlier in this chapter, the magnitude and simultaneity of the changes at hand do reveal a critical juncture that closely resembles a "Great Transformation" of Latin America. However, it is far too early to assess the extent to which new institutional arrangements and social practices will come to revolve around a self-regulated market "directed by market prices and nothing but market prices" (Polanyi, 1957: 43), or what will be the precise role of the state and political institutions in regulating the production and distribution of wealth. A world-systems perspective, with its emphasis on space and time as delineating the boundaries of change, does not offer definitive predictions but suggests instead useful and interesting ways of raising the pertinent questions, expecting the answers to be contingent on the courses of action and strategic choices adopted by the relevant actors.

NOTES

This chapter has benefited from comments by Nancy Forsythe and Aldo Vacs.

1. See Cavarozzi (1992, 1994) for illuminating analyses of the collapse of state-centric models of development. For authoritative statements of the so-called "Washington Consensus," see Williamson (1990a, 1993). See Fannelli, Frenkel, and Rozenwurcel (1994) and Bresser Pereira, Maravall, and Przeworski (1994) for criticisms.

2. Douglass North, who is grounded in neoclassical economics and focuses on the analysis of transaction costs, argues: "Institutions are the rules of the game in a society or, more formally, are the humanly devised constraints that shape human interaction. In consequence they structure incentives in human exchange, whether political, social, or economic" (1990: 3). A more "sociological" definition is advanced both by the French

Regulation school (e.g., Aglietta, 1979; Brenner and Glick, 1991) and the "social structures of accumulation" (SSA) school, which is advanced by some U.S. economists (cf. Kotz, McDonough, and Reich, 1994).

3. The data suggest differences between urban and rural areas during the 1980s, as in several countries (e.g., Argentina, Brazil, Costa Rica, Guatemala, Mexico, and Peru) poverty indicators rose in urban areas while declining in rural areas (CEPAL, 1992: 6). Moreover, while the *relative* incidence of poverty is still generally higher in rural areas, most of the poor in Latin America today reside in urban areas.

4. Similar conclusions had been provided earlier in a preliminary report of the World Bank that included Samuel Morley as an author (see Psacharopoulos et al., 1993).

5. For a review of the variety of political and economic features (e.g., hyperinflation, the political "honeymoon," etc.) that facilitate the adoption of free-market reforms, see Williamson and Haggard (1994).

6. For a discussion of recent transitions in southern and Eastern Europe and Latin America that call attention to these points, see Linz and Stepan (1991) and Przeworski (1991). See Acuña and Smith (1994) for an analysis focusing on the microfoundations of individual and collective responses under conditions of market-oriented structuring implemented by democratic regimes.

7. See Vacs (1994a) for a detailed exploration of these questions, which contrasts the contemporary period with earlier waves of democratization.

8. Roberts (1995) provides an extensive discussion of the similarities and differences between the classic populism of Juan Perón, Getúlio Vargas, and Lázaro Cárdenas, and the recent "new caudillos," such as Carlos Menem, Fernando Collor de Mello, Carlos Salinas, and Alberto Fujimori. In addition, useful analyses of the affinity between neoliberal reform and this new-style neopopulism can be found in Zermeño (1989, 1996), Dresser (1991), Cavarozzi (1994), Vacs (1994b), and Weyland (1994). For a broader analysis of the collapse of the "national-popular" model in Latin America and its consequences for modes of rule, see Touraine (1989).

9. Guillermo O'Donnell's recent work (1994a, 1994b, 1996) offers a provocative theorization of what he refers to as "informally institutionalized" polyarchies.

10. For detailed analyses of neoliberal reform and democratization in Argentina, Bolivia, Brazil, Chile, and Mexico, see the country studies in Smith, Acuña, and Gamarra (1994). On Venezuela, see Karl (1995) and McCoy and Smith (1995); and on Peru, see Roberts (1995), Mauceri (1995), and Pastor and Wise (1992). For a provocative treatment of the Andean region, which stresses broader comparative implications, see Conaghan and Malloy (1995).

11. Polanyi argued that in all modes of social organization prior to the nineteenth century, human interactions (e.g., economic transactions) had been regulated through customary moral arrangements, maintaining economies "submerged in . . . social relationships" (1957: 46). The Great Transformation of the nineteenth century involved the construction of a self-regulated market, with transactions becoming "directed by market prices and nothing but market prices" (1957: 43), and where "social relations are embedded in the economic system" (1957: 57). This self-regulating market revolved around three principal commodities (labor, land, and money), which were entirely fictitious, in that "[n]one of them is produced for sale" (Polanyi, 1957: 72). The use of these resources as commodities "subordinate[d] the substance of society itself to the laws of the market" (Polanyi, 1957: 71).

12. This model of development, which emphasizes industrialization as a key engine

of growth, also suggests rather clear paths of political transformation. Both the modernization and dependency literatures, for example, have tended to agree that industrialization should produce the various agents that would generate democracy over the long run. Of course, there were crucial differences in the interpretation of who were the key new agents of democratization (e.g., the middle class or the labor movement) and in their view of what would be the final appearance of democratic rule (e.g., capitalism with electoral democracy or socialism with "popular participation"). Most interpreters agreed, however, that industrialization and economic growth would generate or strengthen precisely those social classes, interest groups, and organizations that would, over the long run, promote greater electoral participation or generate more democratic styles of policy making and state organization (O'Donnell, 1973; Borón, 1977, 1995; Moore, 1966; de Schweinitz, 1964; Dos Santos, 1971).

13. There is a long tradition of studies that have emphasized the active role played by states in promoting industrialization among the later-developed nations (Hirschman, 1965; Gershenkron, 1962; de Schweinitz, 1964). Later, similar notions were incorporated into the literature on dependent development (Evans, 1979; Cardoso and Faletto, 1979) and the Bureaucratic-Authoritarian state (O'Donnell, 1973; Collier, 1979), as well as into literature on developmental states (Amsden, 1989; Evans, 1995; Wade, 1990).

14. To draw on Hirschman, "[T]he very process of decline activates certain counterforces" (1970: 4).

15. These GCCs are networks of households, enterprises, and states that serve to articulate production, distribution, and consumption as world-economic processes. Within these networks, the ability of individuals and organizations to appropriate wealth is unevenly distributed (Wallerstein, 1983; Hopkins and Wallerstein, 1986; Gereffi, Korzeniewicz, and Korzeniewicz, 1994; as well as the essays in Gereffi and Korzeniewicz, 1994). On innovations as new patterns of state regulation, see Cumings (1984) and Wade (1990).

16. Within these networks, production processes and commodities "have had 'production cycles,' starting off as core products and eventually becoming peripheral products" (Wallerstein, 1983: 36; see also Cumings, 1984; Arrighi and Drangel, 1986; Arrighi, 1991). This interpretation shares similarities with Schumpeter (1934, 1942), for whom innovative processes were at the root of the "creative destruction" that characterizes capitalism as a system. More recently, this focus on innovation (rather than industrialization) as the basis for comparative advantages in the world-economy has been at the fore of influential studies on economic organization (Vernon, 1979; Porter, 1985, 1990).

17. In Argentina, the value of exports rose 61.6 percent between 1984 and 1993 (from $8.1 to $13.1 billion), but accounted for a mere 5.1 percent of GDP by 1993. Likewise, exports in 1993 accounted for merely 8.7 percent of GDP in Brazil, 8.8 percent in Mexico, and 8.3 percent in Peru. On the other hand, in Chile, for example, the value of exports rose 152.1 percent between 1884 and 1993 (from $3.6 to $9.2 billion), to account for 21.4 percent of GDP by 1993 (likewise, exports account for 22.1 percent of GDP in Venezuela, and 38.4 percent of GDP in Costa Rica) (World Bank, 1995).

18. Even within countries, efforts to imitate successful strategies will often fail to produce the expected results. For example, farmers in Chile in the early 1990s sought to replicate the successful experience of grape exporters by engaging in kiwi production, but the outcome was a world glut and falling prices of kiwis in subsequent years.

19. This is not to diminish the role that the reduction of exchange risks has played in increasing the willingness of global investors to expand their exposure in Latin American markets.

20. For example, this is the argument implicit in Evans (1995), who discusses the role of local firms, in the 1990s, in allowing for new linkages to transnational corporations.

21. Likewise, Bellone, in Chapter 2, suggests that core-like activities may be pursued by organizations that challenge the monopoly of the state over the means of violence.

22. In fact, such generalizations obscure differences between those countries in which the state is unable to carry out the neoliberal policies favored by state elites and others in which, notwithstanding its "weakening," the state still possesses sufficient power to impose economic reform and disarticulate unruly social actors. See Acuña and Smith (1994) for an effort to rethink the relation between politics and economics in the context of economic restructuring.

23. For a discussion of the neoliberal prescriptions for shrinking the state advanced by the International Monetary Fund and the World Bank, see Bierstekker (1990).

24. In view of Latin America's recent authoritarian past (and the persistence of authoritarian enclaves under the current democracies), many critics of economic orthodoxy are perhaps rightly suspicious of the recent discovery (by institutions such as the World Bank) of the need for augmented state capacity. Nevertheless, as O'Donnell (1994b) has pointed out, the sharp erosion of the "state-as-law" in Latin America and the former socialist bloc vitiates any notion of genuine democratic politics and is particularly detrimental to the poor and powerless, who are left to the predations of powerful and unaccountable political elites and economically dominant classes.

25. The social and economic intervention of the Keynesian welfare state blurred the "liberal" limits between politics and economics and between the public and private spheres. As Offe (1974, 1975, 1984) and Przeworski (1990) have pointed out, this intervention (in fiscal and monetary policy, public investment, labor market regulation, educational and social welfare policies, the public production of goods and services, and so on) removed the market as the main mechanism for the resolution of conflicts of interest, and placed them under state tutelage in response to priorities determined by political and electoral objectives. The post-1930s politicization of the market prompted the mobilization and organization of societal interests to influence state policies. Conversely, the marketization of politics in the contemporary period frequently results in the erosion of traditional collective identities and the disarticulation of political and social organization, along with a decline in capacities for collective action. See Acuña and Smith (1994), Díaz (1996), and Zermeño (1996) for discussions of the implications of these trends for democratic politics in Latin America.

26. A (physically) "smaller" state can be "weaker" (control fewer resources, lose entrepreneurial functions, etc.) but simultaneously more autonomous, more coherent, and more effective in regulating macroeconomic and microeconomic behaviors. For an evaluation of some of these issues, see Huber (1995).

27. In carrying forth this effort, much is to be gained by developing closer linkages between the world-systems literature and other critical theoretical perspectives, such as those developed in international political economy or the field of economics proper.

28. Among the poorer Latin American countries, despite the explosion of the tertiary sector, the share of industrial and manufacturing activities has continued to increase, particularly in relation to a declining agricultural sector.

29. Such trends have generated a considerable amount of literature focusing on the impact of economic adjustment programs on household reproductive strategies (e.g., Benería and Roldán, 1987; De Vos, 1987; Folbre, 1994; García and Oliveira, 1994; Jelin, 1991; Moser, 1993; Pérez-Sáinz and Menjívar Larín, 1994; Roberts, 1994).

30. Regardless of the analytical framework used to explain trends in poverty and income distribution, the literature at hand suggests a noticeable shift in the underlying agenda. Partly as an outcome of the resource constraints imposed by structural reforms, but also reflecting some of the concerns raised by NGOs at both the local and international levels, the social sciences in Latin America have begun to evaluate more systematically the extent to which social programs funded by states can effectively reach their intended beneficiaries (e.g., the "truly disadvantaged").

31. On the possibilities of collective action under neoliberal restructuring, see Díaz (1996), Roxborough (1996), and Acuña and Smith (1994).

32. As suggested by scholars such as Arrighi (1995), the emergence of these new networks are also indicative of a broader shift in hegemony from the United States to Asia.

REFERENCES

Acuña, Carlos H. 1994. "Politics and Economics in the Argentina of the Nineties (Or Why the Future No Longer Is What It Used to Be)." In *Democracy, Markets, and Structural Reform in Latin America: Argentina, Bolivia, Brazil, Chile, and Mexico*, ed. William C. Smith, Carlos H. Acuña, and Eduardo A. Gamarra, pp. 31–74. New Brunswick, NJ: North-South Center/Transaction.

Acuña, Carlos H., and William C. Smith. 1994. "The Political Economy of Structural Adjustment: The Logic of Support and Opposition to Neoliberal Reform." In *Latin American Political Economy in the Age of Neoliberal Reform: Theoretical and Comparative Perspectives for the 1990s*, ed. William C. Smith, Carlos H. Acuña, and Eduardo A. Gamarra, pp. 17–66. New Brunswick, NJ: North-South Center/Transaction.

Aglietta, Michel. 1979. *A Theory of Capitalist Regulation: The U.S. Experience*. London: Verso.

Amsden, Alice H. 1989. *Asia's Next Giant: South Korea and Late Industrialization*. New York: Oxford University Press.

Appelbaum, Richard P., and Jeffrey Henderson, eds. 1992. *States and Development in the Asian Pacific Rim*. Newbury Park, CA: Sage.

Arrighi, Giovanni. 1978. "Towards a Theory of Capitalist Crisis." *New Left Review* 111: 3–24.

———. 1991. "World Income Inequalities and the Future of Socialism."*New Left Review* 189: 39–65.

———. 1994. *The Long Twentieth Century: Money, Power, and the Origins of Our Times*. London: Verso.

Arrighi, Giovanni, and Jessica Drangel. 1986. "The Stratification of the World-Economy: An Exploration of the Semiperipheral Zone." *Review* 10: 9–74.

Balassa, Bela, Gerardo Bueno, Pedro-Pablo Kuczynski, and Mário Henrique Simonsen. 1986. *Toward Renewed Economic Growth in Latin America*. Washington, DC: Institute of International Economics.

Benería, Lourdes, and Martha Roldán. 1987. *The Crossroads of Class and Gender: In-*

dustrial Homework, Subcontracting, and Household Dynamics in Mexico City. Chicago: University of Chicago Press.

Bierstekker, Thomas J. 1990. "Reducing the Role of the State in the Economy: A Conceptual Exploration of IMF and World Bank Prescriptions." *International Studies Quarterly* 34: 477–492.

———. 1995. "The 'Triumph' of Liberal Economic Ideas in the Developing World." In *Global Change, Regional Response: The New International Context of Development,* ed. Barbara Stallings, pp. 174–198. New York: Cambridge University Press.

Bonilla, Elssy. 1990. "Working Women in Latin America." In *Economic and Social Progress in Latin America: 1990 Report,* pp. 207–256. Washington, DC: Inter-American Development Bank.

Borón, Atilio. 1977. "El fascismo como categoría histórica. En torno del problema de las dictaduras en América Latina." *Revista Mexicana de Sociología* 39.

———. 1995. *State, Capitalism, and Democracy in Latin America.* Boulder, CO: Lynne Rienner.

Bose, Christine E., and Edna Acosta Belén, eds. 1995. *Women in the Latin American Development Process.* Philadelphia: Temple University Press.

Brenner, Robert, and Mark Glick. 1991. "The Regulation Approach: Theory and History." *New Left Review* 11: 45–119.

Bresser Pereira, Luiz Carlos, José María Maravall, and Adam Przeworski. 1993. *Economic Reforms in New Democracies: A Social-Democratic Approach.* New York: Cambridge University Press.

———. 1994. "Economic Reforms in New Democracies: A Social-Democratic Approach." In *Latin American Political Economy in the Age of Neoliberal Reform: Theoretical and Comparative Perspectives for the 1990s,* ed. William C. Smith, Carlos H. Acuña, and Eduardo A. Gamarra, pp. 181–212. New Brunswick, NJ: North-South Center/Transaction.

Cardoso, Fernando Henrique, and Enzo Faletto. 1979. *Dependency and Development in Latin America.* Berkeley: University of California Press.

Cavarozzi, Marcelo. 1992. "Beyond Democratic Transitions in Latin America." *Journal of Latin American Studies* 24: 665–684.

———. 1994. "Politics: A Key for the Long Term in Latin America." In *Latin American Political Economy in the Age of Neoliberal Reform: Theoretical and Comparative Perspectives for the 1990s,* ed. William C. Smith, Carlos H. Acuña, and Eduardo A. Gamarra, pp. 127–156. New Brunswick, NJ: North-South Center/Transaction.

Comisión Económica para América Latina y el Caribe (CEPAL). 1992. *El perfil de la pobreza en América Latina a comienzos de los años 90.* Santiago: CEPAL.

Collier, David, ed. 1979. *The New Authoritarianism in Latin America.* Princeton, NJ: Princeton University Press.

Conaghan, Catherine M., and James M. Malloy. 1995. *Unsettling Statecraft: Democracy and Neoliberalism in the Central Andes.* Pittsburgh: University of Pittsburgh Press.

Cumings, Bruce. 1984. "The Origins and Development of the Northeast Asian Political Economy." *International Organization* 38: 1–40.

de Schweinitz, Karl. 1964. *Industrialization and Democracy: Economic Necessities and Political Possibilities.* New York: Free Press.

De Vos, Susan. 1987. "Latin American Households in Comparative Perspective." *Population Studies* 41: 501–517.

Díaz, Alvaro. 1996. "New Developments in Social and Economic Restructuring in Latin America." In *The Politics of Social Change and Economic Restructuring in Latin America*, ed. William C. Smith and Roberto Patricio Korzeniewicz. Boulder, CO: North-South Center/Lynne Rienner.

Dos Santos, Theotonio. 1971. *Socialismo o fascismo: El nuevo carácter de la dependencia y el dilema latinoamericano.* Santiago: Centro de Estudios Sociales.

Dresser, Denise. 1991. *Neopopulist Solutions to Neoliberal Problems.* San Diego, CA: Center for U.S.-Mexican Studies.

Economic Commission for Latin America and the Caribbean (ECLAC). 1994. *Preliminary Overview of the Economy of Latin America and the Caribbean 1994.* New York: United Nations.

————. 1995. *Preliminary Overview of the Economy of Latin America and the Caribbean 1995.* New York: United Nations.

Evans, Peter. 1979. *Dependent Development: The Alliance of Multinational, State and Local Capital in Brazil.* Princeton, NJ: Princeton University Press.

————. 1992. "The State as Problem and Solution: Predation, Embedded Autonomy and Structural Change." In *The Politics of Adjustment: International Constraints, Distributive Justice and the State*, ed. Stephan Haggard and Robert Kaufman, pp. 139–181. Princeton, NJ: Princeton University Press.

————. 1995. *Embedded Autonomy: States and Industrial Transformation.* Princeton, NJ: Princeton University Press.

Fanelli, José María, Roberto Frenkel, and Guillermo Rozenwurcel. 1994. "Growth and Structural Reform in Latin America: Where We Stand." In *Latin American Political Economy in the Age of Neoliberal Reform: Theoretical and Comparative Perspectives for the 1990s*, ed. William C. Smith, Carlos H. Acuña, and Eduardo A. Gamarra, pp. 101–126. New Brunswick, NJ: North-South Center/Transaction.

Fiszbein, Ariel, and George Psacharopoulos. 1995. "Income Inequality Trends in Latin America in the 1980s." In *Coping with Austerity: Poverty and Inequality in Latin America*, ed. Nora Lustig, pp. 71–100. Washington, DC: Brookings Institution.

Folbre, Nancy. 1994. *Who Pays for the Kids?* London: Routledge.

Forsythe, Ann Elizabeth. 1995. "Old and New Anti-Systemic Movements: Accumulation, Rule and Resistance in Latin America." Paper presented at the nineteenth Annual Conference of the Political Economy of the World-System, University of Miami, Coral Gables, FL.

García, Brígida, and Orlandina de Oliveira. 1994. *Trabajo femenino y vida familiar en México.* México, DF: El Colegio de México.

Gereffi, Gary. 1989. "Rethinking Development Theory: Insights from East Asia and Latin America." *Sociological Forum* 4, 4: 505–533.

————. 1995. "State Policies and Industrial Upgrading in East Asia." *Revue d'economie industrielle* 71: 79–90.

Gereffi, Gary, and Miguel Korzeniewicz, eds. 1994. *Commodity Chains and Global Capitalism.* Westport, CT: Greenwood Press.

Gereffi, Gary, Miguel Korzeniewicz, and Roberto Patricio Korzeniewicz. 1994. "Introduction: Global Commodity Chains." *In Commodity Chains and Global Capitalism*, ed. G. Gereffi and M. Korzeniewicz, pp. 1–14. Westport, CT: Greenwood Press.

Gerschenkron, Alexander. 1962. *Economic Backwardness in Historical Perspective.* Cambridge: Harvard University Press.

Hirschman, Albert O. [1958] 1965. *The Strategy of Economic Development.* New Haven, CT: Yale University Press.

―――. 1970. *Exit, Voice, and Loyalty: Responses to Decline in Firms, Organizations, and States.* Cambridge: Harvard University Press.

―――. 1995. *A Propensity to Self-Subversion.* Cambridge: Harvard University Press.

Hopkins, Terence K., and Immanuel Wallerstein. 1986. "Commodity Chains in the World-Economy prior to 1800." *Review* 10: 157–170.

Huber, Evelyne. 1995. "Assessing State Strength." In *Latin America in Comparative Perspective: New Approaches to Methods and Analysis,* ed. Peter H. Smith, pp. 163–194. Boulder, CO: Westview Press.

Inter-American Development Bank. 1994. *Economic and Social Progress in Latin America: 1994 Report.* Washington, DC: Johns Hopkins University Press.

Jaquette, Jane, ed. 1989. *The Women's Movement in Latin America: Feminism and the Transition to Democracy.* Winchester, MA: Unwin Hyman.

Jelin, Elizabeth, ed. 1990. *Women and Social Change in Latin America.* London: Zed.

―――. 1991. *Family, Households, and Gender Relations in Latin America.* London: Kegan Paul International.

―――. 1996. "Emergent Citizenship or Exclusion? Social Movements and Non-Governmental Organizations in the 1990s." In *The Politics of Social Change and Economic Restructuring in Latin America,* ed. William C. Smith and Roberto Patricio Korzeniewicz. Boulder, CO: North-South Center/Lynne Rienner.

Kahler, Miles. 1990. "Orthodoxy and Its Alternatives: Explaining Approaches to Stabilization and Adjustment." *In Economic Crisis and Policy Choice,* ed. Joan Nelson, pp. 33–62. Princeton, NJ: Princeton University Press.

―――. 1992. "External Influence, Conditionality, and the Politics of Adjustment." In *The Politics of Economic Adjustment: International Constraints, Distributive Conflicts, and the State,* ed. Stephan Haggard and Robert R. Kaufman, pp. 89–138. Princeton, NJ: Princeton University Press.

Karl, Terry Lynn. 1995. "The Venezuelan Petro-State and the Crisis of 'Its' Democracy." In *Venezuelan Democracy under Stress,* ed. Jennifer McCoy, William C. Smith, Andrés Serbin, and Andrés Stambouil, pp. 59–76. New Brunswick, NJ: North-South Center/Transaction.

Korzeniewicz, Roberto Patricio. 1996. "The Deepening Differentiation of Enterprises, States and Households." In *The Politics of Social Change and Economic Restructuring in Latin America,* ed. William C. Smith and Roberto Patricio Korzeniewicz. Boulder, CO: North-South Center/Lynne Rienner.

Kotz, David, Terrence McDonough, and Michael Reich. 1994. *Social Structures of Accumulation: The Political Economy of Growth and Crisis.* Cambridge: Cambridge University Press.

Linz, Juan J., and Alfred Stepan. 1996. *Problems of Democratic Transition and Consolidation: Southern Europe, South America, and Post-Communist Europe.* Baltimore: The Johns Hopkins University Press.

Lustig, Nora, ed. 1995. *Coping with Austerity: Poverty and Inequality in Latin America.* Washington, DC: Brookings Institution.

Mauceri, Philip. 1995. "State Reform, Coalitions, and the Neoliberal Autogolpe in Peru." *Latin American Research Review* 30, 1: 7–38.

McCoy, Jennifer L., and William C. Smith. 1995. "Democratic Disequilibrium in Venezuela." *Journal of Inter-American Studies and World Affairs* 37, 2: 113–180.

Moore, Barrington, Jr. 1966. *Social Origins of Dictatorship and Democracy: Lord and Peasant in the Making of the Modern World*. Boston: Beacon Press.

Morley, Samuel. 1994. *Poverty and Inequality in Latin America: Past Evidence, Future Prospects*. Washington, DC: Overseas Development Council.

———. 1995a. *Poverty and Inequality in Latin America: The Impact of Adjustment and Recovery in the 1980s*. Baltimore: The Johns Hopkins University Press.

———. 1995b. "Structural Adjustment and the Determinants of Poverty in Latin America." In *Coping with Austerity: Poverty and Inequality in Latin America*, ed. Nora Lustig, pp. 42–70. Washington, DC: Brookings Institution.

Moser, Caroline O. N. 1993. *Gender Planning and Development*. New York: Routledge.

North, Douglass C. 1990. *Institutions, Institutional Change and Economic Performance*. New York: Cambridge University Press.

O'Donnell, Guillermo. 1973. *Modernization and Bureaucratic-Authoritarianism: Studies in South American Politics*. Berkeley, CA: Institute of International Studies.

———. 1994a. "Delegative Democracy." *Journal of Democracy* 5 (January): 55–69.

———. 1994b. "On the State, Democratization and Some Conceptual Problems (A Latin American View with Glances at Some Post-Communist Societies)." In *Latin American Political Economy in the Age of Neoliberal Reform: Theoretical and Comparative Perspectives for the 1990s*, ed. William C. Smith, Carlos H. Acuña, and Eduardo A. Gamarra, pp. 157–181. New Brunswick, NJ: North-South Center/Transaction.

———. 1996. "Illusions About Consolidation." *Journal of Democracy* 7 (April): 34–51.

Offe, Claus. 1974. "Structural Problems of the Capitalist State." *German Political Studies* 1: 31–56.

———. 1975. "The Theory of the State and the Problem of Policy Formation." In *Stress and Contradiction in Modern Capitalism*, ed. Leon Lindberg, pp. 124–144. Lexington, KY: D. C. Heath.

———. 1984. *Contradictions of the Welfare State*. Cambridge: MIT Press.

Pastor, Manuel, and Carol Wise. 1992. "Peruvian Economic Policy in the 1990s: From Orthodoxy to Heterodoxy and Back." *Latin American Research Review* 27, 2: 83–117.

Pérez-Sáinz, J. P., and R. Menjívar Larín. 1994. "Central American Men and Women in the Urban Informal Sector." *Journal of Latin American Studies* 26: 431–447.

Polanyi, Karl. 1957. *The Great Transformation: The Political and Economic Origins of Our Time*. Boston: Beacon Press.

Porter, Michael. 1985. *Competitive Advantage: Creating and Sustaining Superior Performance*. New York: Free Press.

———. 1990. *The Competitive Advantage of Nations*. New York: Free Press.

Przeworski, Adam. 1985. *Capitalism and Social Democracy*. Cambridge: Cambridge University Press.

———. 1990. *The State and the Economy under Capitalism*. New York: Academic Publishers.

———. 1991. *Democracy and the Market: Political and Economic Reforms in Eastern Europe and Latin America*. Cambridge: Cambridge University Press.

Przeworski, Adam, et al. 1996. "What Makes Democracies Endure?" *Journal of Democracy* 7: 39–55.

Psacharopoulos, George, et al. 1993. *Poverty and Income Distribution in Latin America:*

The Story of the 1980s. Latin America and the Caribbean Technical Department Report No. 27. Washington, DC: World Bank.

Raczynski, Dagmar, and Pilar Romaguera. 1995. "Chile: Poverty, Adjustment, and Social Policies in the 1980s." In *Coping with Austerity: Poverty and Inequality in Latin America*, ed. Nora Lustig, pp. 275–333. Washington, DC: Brookings Institution.

Roberts, Bryan. 1994. "Informal Economy and Family Strategies." *International Journal of Urban and Regional Research* 18: 6–23.

Roberts, Kenneth M. 1995. "Neoliberalism and the Transformation of Populism in Latin America: The Peruvian Case." *World Politics* 48: 82–116.

Roxborough, Ian. 1996. "Citizenship and Social Movements under Neoliberalism." In *The Politics of Social Change and Economic Restructuring in Latin America*, ed. William C. Smith and Roberto Patricio Korzeniewicz. Boulder, CO: North-South Center/Lynne Rienner.

Schumpeter, Joseph A. 1934. *The Theory of Economic Development*. Cambridge: Harvard University Press.

———. 1942. *Capitalism, Socialism and Democracy*. New York: Harper and Row.

Smith, William C. 1992a. "Hyperinflation, Macroeconomic Instability, and Neoliberal Restructuring in Democratic Argentina." In *The New Democracy in Argentina*, ed. Edward C. Epstein, pp. 3–21. New York: Praeger.

———. 1992b. "State, Market and Neoliberalism in Post-Transition Argentina: The Menem Experiment." *Journal of Interamerican Studies and World Affairs* 33, 4: 45–82.

———. 1993. "Neoliberal Restructuring and Scenarios of Democratic Consolidation in Latin America." *Studies in Comparative International Development* 28, 2: 3–21.

Smith, William C., and Carlos H. Acuña. 1994. "Future Politico-Economic Scenarios for Latin America." In *Democracy, Markets, and Structural Reform in Latin America: Argentina, Bolivia, Brazil, Chile, and Mexico*, ed. William C. Smith, Carlos H. Acuña, and Eduardo A. Gamarra, pp. 1–28. New Brunswick, NJ: Transaction.

Smith, William C., Carlos H. Acuña, and Eduardo A. Gamarra, eds. 1994. *Democracy, Markets, and Structural Reform in Latin America: Argentina, Bolivia, Brazil, Chile, and Mexico*. New Brunswick, NJ: Transaction.

Sola, Lourdes. 1994. "The State, Structural Reform, and Democratization in Brazil." In *Democracy, Markets, and Structural Reform in Latin America: Argentina, Bolivia, Brazil, Chile, and Mexico*, ed. William C. Smith, Carlos H. Acuña, and Eduardo A. Gamarra, pp. 1–28. New Brunswick, NJ: Transaction.

Suttcliff, R. B. 1972. *Industry and Underdevelopment*. London: Addison Wesley.

———. 1984. "Industry and Underdevelopment Reexamined." *Journal of Development Studies* 21: 121–133.

Tironi, Eugenio. 1986. "Para una sociología de la decadencia: El concepto de disolución social." *Proposiciones* 6 (October–December).

Touraine, Alain. 1989. *Palavra e Sangue: Política e Sociedade na América Latina*. São Paulo: Editora da UNICAMP.

Vacs, Aldo C. 1994a. "Convergence and Dissension: Democracy, Markets, and Structural Reform in World Perspective." In *Latin American Political Economy in the Age of Neoliberal Reform: Theoretical and Comparative Perspectives for the 1990s*, ed. William C. Smith, Carlos H. Acuña, and Eduardo Gamarra, pp. 67–100. New Brunswick, NJ: North-South Center/Transaction.

————. 1994b. "The Unanticipated Merger of Liberal Democracy, Neo-Liberalism, and Neo-Populism in Argentina." Paper presented at the annual meeting of the American Political Science Association, New York, September 1–4.

Vergara, Pilar. 1986. *Auge y caída del neoliberalismo en Chile*. Santiago: Facultad Latinoamericana de Ciencias Sociales.

————. 1994. "Market Economy, Social Welfare, and Democratic Consolidation in Chile." In *Democracy, Markets, and Structural Reform in Latin America: Argentina, Bolivia, Brazil, Chile, and Mexico*, ed. William C. Smith, Carlos H. Acuña, and Eduardo A. Gamarra, pp. 237–262. New Brunswick, NJ: North-South Center/Transaction.

Vernon, Raymond. 1979. "The Product Cycle Hypothesis in a New International Environment." *Oxford Bulletin of Economics and Statistics* 41: 255–267.

Wade, Robert. 1990. *Governing the Market: Economic Theory and the Role of Government in East Asian Industrialization*. Princeton, NJ: Princeton University Press.

Ward, Kathryn. 1993. "Reconceptualizing World System Theory to Include Women." In *Theory on Gender/Feminism on Theory*, ed. Paula England, pp. 43–68. Hawthorne, NY: Aldine.

Wallerstein, Immanuel. 1983. *Historical Capitalism*. London: Verso.

Weyland, Kurt. 1994. "Neo-Populism and Neo-Liberalism in Latin America: Unexpected Affinities." Paper presented at the annual meeting of the American Political Science Association, New York, September 1–4.

Whitehead, Laurence. 1989. "Tigers in Latin America?" *The Annals* 505: 142–151.

Williamson, John, ed. 1990a. *Latin American Adjustment: How Much Has Happened?* Washington, DC: Institute for International Economics.

————. 1990b. *The Progress of Policy Reform in Latin America*. Washington, DC: Institute of International Economics.

————. 1993. "Democracy and the 'Washington Consensus.' " *World Development* 21, 8: 1329–1336.

Williamson, John, and Stephan Haggard. 1994. "The Political Conditions for Economic Reform." In *The Political Economy of Policy Reform*, ed. John Williamson, pp. 525–596. Washington, DC: Institute for International Economics.

Wise, Carol. 1994. "The Politics of Peruvian Economic Reform: Overcoming the Legacies of State-Led Development." *Journal of Interamerican Studies and World Affairs* 36, 11: 75–126.

Wilson, Suzanne, and Marta Zambrano. 1994. "Cocaine, Commodity Chains, and Drug Politics: A Transnational Approach." In *Commodity Chains and Global Capitalism*, ed. G. Gereffi and Miguel Korzeniewicz, pp. 297–315. Westport, CT: Greenwood Press.

World Bank. 1987. *World Development Report 1987*. New York: Oxford University Press.

————. 1991. *World Development Report 1991*. Washington, DC: Oxford University Press.

————. 1993a. *The East Asian Miracle: Economic Growth and Public Policy*. New York: Oxford University Press.

————. 1993b. *Social Indicators of Development 1993*. Baltimore: Johns Hopkins University Press.

————. 1993c. *World Development Report 1993*. New York: Oxford University Press.

————. 1995. *World Development Report 1995*. New York: Oxford University Press.

Zermeño, Sergio. 1989. "El regreso del líder: Crisis, neoliberalismo y desorden." *Revista Mexicana de Sociología* 51 (October–December).

———. 1996. "State and Society in Dependent Neoliberalism: The Mexican Case." In *The Politics of Social Change and Economic Restructuring in Latin America*, ed. William C. Smith and Roberto Patricio Korzeniewicz. Boulder, CO: North-South Center/Lynne Rienner.

2

THE COCAINE COMMODITY CHAIN AND DEVELOPMENT PATHS IN PERU AND BOLIVIA

Amy E. Bellone

Between 1980 and 1985, the amount of cocaine hydrochloride consumed by North Americans tripled from 34 to 100 metric tons per year (Healy, 1986: 110). In 1986, by the time the chemical reached the circulatory system of users, each metric ton generated an estimated $250 million in profits (conservatively) for an intricate network of producers, processors, traders, and transporters throughout the hemisphere (Healy, 1986: 110; Hargreaves, 1992: 159; Henkel, 1986: 59).[1] A crop traditionally cultivated for use in rituals enforcing social cohesion has been transformed into an international commodity funnelling an estimated $.8 to $1.5 billion a year into the Bolivian economy and $1.2 billion into the Peruvian economy (Henkel, 1986: 75; Morales, 1989: 48). The cocaine commodity chain generates more revenue than any other Bolivian product or enterprise (Healy, 1986; Henkel, 1986; Hargreaves, 1992; Blanes, 1989). The value of cocaine exports from Bolivia was twice that of all legal Bolivian exports in 1984 and 1987 and almost equal to that of all legal exports in 1989 (De Franco and Godoy, 1992: 376). Already in 1986, 5 percent of the Bolivian labor force was involved in harvesting coca leaves, and it is now estimated that one in five Bolivians receives income somehow associated with the production and trade of coca or cocaine (Healy, 1986: 110; Hargreaves, 1992: xi; De Franco and Godoy, 1992: 376). In 1987 an estimated 200,000 Peruvians (or 2.9 percent of the labor force) were directly employed in cocaine production (De Franco and Godoy, 1992: 376).

The expansion of cultivation, processing, and trade occurred in a context of severe economic crisis in the national economies of Peru and Bolivia. Bolivia's debt of almost $5.8 billion in 1987 represented between 45 and 50 percent of its GDP (Queiser Morales, 1992: 156). This debt burden was accompanied by a cycle of insufficient foreign exchange earnings, hyperinflation, and severe unemployment (Queiser Morales, 1992: 155–160; Healy, 1986). Peru's economy was also debilitated by high rates of inflation, a decline in export earnings, and decreased access to foreign credit and exchange.

Coca producers in both Bolivia and Peru have differed in their ability to engage the higher value-added niches of the cocaine commodity chain. These differences are explored through the use of the "commodity chain" approach (see Gereffi, 1989; Gereffi and Korzeniewicz, 1990, 1994; Truelove, 1992) to conduct a systematic analysis of the links between the local processes and the regional economic and social structures. Like that of Wilson and Zambrano (1994), this analysis places the cocaine trade in a framework of global exchange by employing a commodity chain framework to uncover the local and international links involved in production and distribution. Unlike the 1994 analysis, which focuses on implications for eradication and law enforcement efforts, this chapter seeks to explain how the "white gold rush" can be characterized and conceptualized in terms of uneven organizational development. In doing so, this analysis focuses on the early stages of the cocaine commodity chain rather than international trafficking and sales, topics on which most discussions of the drug trade focus. The cocaine commodity chain presents an interesting case because it encompasses agricultural production, transport, chemical processing, export, and trade in a chain operating outside government regulation in a manner which, unlike most agricultural commodities, has proven to be quite flexible in terms of production processes.

Placing the coca trade in the context of the global capitalist system is more than an academic exercise. If the international goals of control of the cocaine trade and development in Latin America are to be seriously considered, the precedents to, and operation of, the trade need to be identified. Furthermore, how we conceptualize the trade in terms of the type of enterprise it represents conditions the solutions advocated to curb efforts to cultivate the leaves, process them into cocaine, and market the final product. The world-system's commodity chain approach provides a framework clearly illustrating the aspects of the trade that are characteristic of dependent development and the junctures and characteristics that divert from traditional conceptualizations. Analyzing the structure of the cocaine commodity chain illustrates the proliferation of a global demand for cocaine, the accumulation of economic surpluses, how new actors and political environments contribute to the dynamism of particular production processes, and the futility of supply-side solutions. Such analysis also shows how relationships emanating from political culture and the organization of labor contribute to the form of cultivation, processing, sale, and trafficking of the coca leaf and cocaine in Peru and Bolivia and the ways that they are inserted into the global production process.

COLONIZATION AND THE BURGEONING COCAINE COMMODITY CHAIN

The often-harsh economic and social forces influencing life in the Andean Mountains have been mediated through time by the use of coca leaves as a traditional vehicle for regulating these forces at the individual, community, and spiritual levels. To those from the highlands of Peru and Bolivia, coca mastication is a ritual affirming individual identity and fostering social cohesion. Allen (1988, 1986) and other authors (Mitchell, 1991; Morales, 1989) have documented the importance of the coca leaf as a symbolic vehicle acting as an intermediary between the people and deities associated with the earth. It is seen as having a power that, when directed through prayer to specific places or deities, invokes these powers to aid the group. The physiological effects of coca mastication allow an individual to endure the hardships of poverty; of long, intense working days at high altitudes; and of limited resources. As a central element of Andean society, coca is also widely used for medicinal purposes and as a veritable prerequisite for celebrations (Morales, 1989: 19–24). In addition, coca leaves are often part of the wages received for day labor and of reciprocal labor arrangements whereby employers supply music, rations of coca, alcoholic beverages, and food (Morales, 1989: 147).

Prior to the beginning of the coca ''boom'' of recent decades, coca cultivation was confined primarily to the satisfaction of domestic demand in Peru and Bolivia. In Peru, cultivation was concentrated in the eastern slope of the Andes (known as the ''Ceja de Selva'' or ''eyebrow of the jungle''), in the valley of the Huallaga River. In Bolivia, Las Yungas, a small region in the department of La Paz, supplied most of the coca for that country until the 1960s (Healy, 1986: 102). The Chapare region, in the department of Cochabamba, has become the primary area of cultivation and now supplies 90 percent of the leaves grown in Bolivia (Hargreaves, 1992: 32). The coca plant is native to these regions, as they provide the lower altitudes necessary for growth (500 to 2,000 meters above sea level depending on the variety) (Plowman, 1986). Thus, the primary locational constraint involved in the cocaine commodity chain has traditionally been, and continues to be, the climate necessary for the growth of the plant.

The first steps toward the international commodification of the coca leaf occurred with the parallel commencement of colonization efforts in Peru and Bolivia and the increasing U.S. demand for cocaine. Both Peru and Bolivia embarked on government-led efforts to colonize the jungle regions east of the Andean plateau, which was accompanied by spontaneous colonization (primarily because of land pressures in the highlands) and the growth of the coca trade. In Bolivia, the 1953 agrarian reforms, coupled with later assistance from the U.S. Agency for International Development, initiated colonization projects directed at Las Yungas, the Chapare region, and the department of Santa Cruz in order to promote national integration and self-sufficiency in staple crops (Sanabria, 1986: 82, 86; Healy, 1986: 102). Many highland farmers were granted titles to land in these target areas, while others either bought land or accompanied and worked for other landowners (Sanabria, 1986). Because the agricultural cycles of traditional highland crops and the coca plant are complementary, coca quickly became the primary crop in the colonized valleys.

Expanding cultivation of the plant required an increased labor supply: one hectare of coca requires about 260 days of labor annually, while rice and coffee, the next two most labor-intensive crops appropriate to the valleys of the Andean plateau, require, respectively, only 84 and 88 days (Sanabria, 1986: 92, 95). As more highlanders permanently moved to the Chapare, the system of bizonal cultivation declined and was coupled with an "influx of peasant laborers from different parts of Bolivia without secure access to land in the lowlands" (Sanabria, 1986: 99). By 1981, the net stock of migrants to the Chapare region was 68,000, and "as many as 420,000 people—7 percent of Bolivia's total population—travelled to the Chapare to work in coca cultivation or cocaine production" (De Franco and Godoy, 1992: 383). Thus, locational constraints and an inability to manipulate the rate of production dictated the organization of the labor needed to cultivate coca leaves, resulting in intensive travel in and out of the Chapare region.

During the agrarian reforms of the 1950s, large cattle ranchers in the department of Beni and owners of sugar and cotton estates in the department of Santa Cruz not only avoided the expropriation of their land, but enjoyed "favorable pricing, export, credit, marketing and investment policies of the Bolivian state" (Healy, 1986: 105, 107). These enterprises served as a platform for the boom of agricultural exports in the 1960s and 1970s. While these estates are north and east of the area that is appropriate for growing coca, the power and international export experience developed by these entrepreneurs created a powerful elite whose resources were available when the illicit market for coca emerged in the 1970s (Hargreaves, 1992: 52–56; Healy, 1986: 104–107; MacDonald, 1989: 67–70).

Similar changes in patterns of migration and human settlement characterize the case of Peru. In the late 1950s, increasing land pressures led the Peruvian government to seek a solution to excessive migration to Lima and the coast through the colonization of the less-populated land available in Eastern Peru. Upon being promised credits for citrus, coffee, and cattle production (as well as a highway to Lima), many residents of the highland areas voluntarily moved to the Ceja de Selva. Many migrants were unfamiliar with the agricultural techniques necessary for the climate and soil of the jungle, and the promised credit, marketing channels, and technical assistance never materialized. Nevertheless, the population density in the upper Huallaga Valley (now Peru's center for coca cultivation) grew from one person per square kilometer in 1961 to ten in 1981 (Morales 1990: 631).

The increases in population density in both the Huallaga Valley in Peru and the Chapare region in Bolivia are directly related to an increase in the cultivation and processing of coca leaves. Between 1962 and 1972, land devoted to coca

Figure 2.1
Commodity Chain for Cocaine

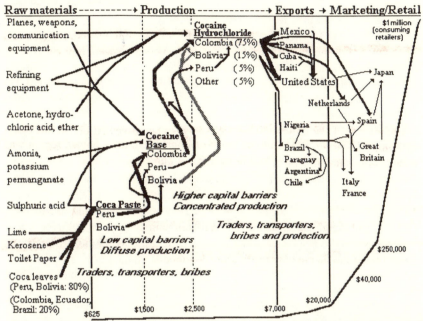

Line represents the rough value of inputs used at each stage to make 1 kilogram of cocaine (U.S. market prices, 1986)

in the Huallaga Valley doubled to 3,000 hectares, and by 1989, at least 75,000 hectares were used to grow coca (the amount of land needed to harvest leaves to make at least 85 tons of cocaine, or 40 percent of the world's supply) (Kaswell, 1989a: 24, 1989b: 13; Campodonico, 1989: 235; Craig, 1987: 13). Arable land devoted to coca cultivation in Bolivia's Chapare region *exploded* to 48 percent in the period between 1977 to 1985, compared to only 24 percent of land between 1970 and 1977 (De Franco and Godoy, 1992: 395).

TRACKING THE TRAFFICKING

Tracing the cocaine commodity chain from the cultivation of the initial raw material (the coca leaf) to the marketing and distribution of cocaine demonstrates how this international commodity links small farmers and landless entrepreneurs to the world capitalist system, offering opportunities, at various junctures, to exploit forward linkages and value-added profits. The productive structures involved in the various stages of the commodity chain illustrate the ways that this particular commodity chain encompasses aspects of both agricultural and industrial production, the nonmarket forces involved in its operation, and the reasons for its growth and resiliency.

The commodity chain for cocaine is illustrated in Figure 2.1, in which estimates of the degree of profits enjoyed at the various stages are included.[2] Key aspects of this chain include the informal nature of each node and connection, narrow roles for actors involved in the chain, continuous exchanges between inputs, and expenditures for bribes, transport, and trade, which are encountered at every link and connection. In addition to bribes, individuals receive coca-related profits through a vast array of activities in coca-growing regions. Among these activities are the transport and resale of inputs by a host of landless entrepreneurs in the regions, as well as the resale of confiscated goods by government personnel trying to augment extremely low salaries. Therefore, all inputs in the chain are essentially illegal goods.

The effects of the commodity chain may also be witnessed outside its direct operation in terms of forfeited taxes, degraded working environments, the growth of contraband markets, and capital flight. In Bolivia, "[a]ccording to some economists, the size of illegal economic transactions is comparable to that of the official balance of trade" (Blanes, 1989: 139; see also Wilson and Zambrano, 1994). Even though the aggregate effect of informal trade of this magnitude is a destabilization of the national economies, the informal diffusion of profits to virtually all elements in the society makes unlikely the existence of a collective will to dismember the cocaine commodity chain. Furthermore, without such a will, pursuit of a path of development more strongly based on welfare seems quite elusive.

Raw-material supply networks for the cocaine commodity chain may be characterized as "procurement networks," based "upon personal ties, common ethnic backgrounds, and a history of previous common transactions," as opposed to vertically integrated networks (Gereffi and Korzeniewicz, 1990: 57). The narrowly defined productive roles of each link and, at the raw material and initial production stages, the use of exchange (both of which are characteristic of the trade) are not only the result of an exploitation of comparative advantages as suggested by Gereffi (1989), but also brought about by the relatively small amounts of capital necessary at most nodes of production and by the entire enterprise's illegality. As a commodity chain operating outside regulation and constantly pursued by legal authorities, actors in each link of the chain minimize risks by sticking to one or few roles, and production is carried out in small quantities, thus impeding market domination by one actor.

Although yields of coca crops cannot be increased significantly through technology or other inputs, and although large amounts of labor are needed for harvesting, its ability to grow interspersed with other crops and the fact that these plants, which last 20 to 35 years, may be harvested up to six times per year after only twelve months, make the crop particularly attractive and easy to manage (Plowman, 1986). Unlike most other agricultural commodities for export, coca is generally grown on plots of only a few hectares. Additionally, because of the bulkiness of the dried leaves, they are generally processed into coca paste and sometimes further refined before being transported for final processing into cocaine and export. In this sense, the locational constraint of a limited area appropriate for cultivation enables agricultural production to be linked to the first steps of refining. This initial processing, along with the need for secret transport in small quantities, provide value-added profits for the Peruvians and Bolivians involved. In comparison to the profits enjoyed by *narcotraficantes* (drug traffickers), however, the commodity resembles other traditional exports more closely (with only 0.5 percent of the final value accruing to farmers) (McClintock, 1988: 128; Hargreaves, 1992: 38).

The low capital barriers involved in cultivating coca leaves and procuring and selling other raw material inputs result in the existence of widespread small-scale enterprises. Even once the coca leaves enter the production stages of the commodity chain, networks of buyers, sellers, and transporters are employed with relatively low amounts of capital and high profits. With the exception of planes and refining and communications equipment, the bulk of raw materials needed to make and market coca paste (the first stage of refining after harvesting the leaves) are supplied from within Bolivia and Peru. This demonstrates the generation of backward linkages throughout the national economies within the cocaine commodity chain. Another very unique feature of the cocaine commodity chain is the fact that inputs are often exchanged in place of cash, as for example, in the common exchange of coca paste for weapons (Hargreaves, 1992).

The cultivation and harvest of coca plants, along with their preparation for transport, generate employment and income for a whole set of laborers. Clearing land before planting, preparing seedlings, planting, and harvesting are all activities that could be done by individual farmers yet, because of the influx of workers to the jungle, tend to be done by specialized workers (see Morales, 1989; Healy, 1986). Transforming coca leaves into coca paste not only requires labor, but materials such as toilet paper (used as a filter), kerosene, sulfuric acid, and lime. The prices of these products are high, due in part to demand, but also because the final price includes bribes, transport costs, and markups incurred in the journey to the coca pits, where leaves are transformed into coca paste.[3] Therefore, forward and backward linkages involved in the chain include numerous exchanges rather than one transfer at each node. Furthermore, the linkages involved in providing raw materials illustrate how individuals who are considered otherwise employed become integrated into the illicit commodity chain.

Once the leaves are harvested, the first stage of processing consists of turning the coca leaves into coca paste. Because the leaves are bulky, 80 percent of all coca paste is made in Peru and Bolivia (Henkel, 1986: 54). Coca paste is made in a pit, which can be constructed simply of plastic sheets and tree branches, thus requiring little capital. Paste making, however, is a labor-intensive and risky activity, which involves serious health hazards.[4] Thus, it is relegated to the vast labor supply of native individuals willing to take such risks with little profit compared to the final value of cocaine. Bolivian *pisacocas*, or leaf stompers (many of whom are ex-miners), receive seven to fifteen dollars for a night's work, amounting to wages four times those of other agricultural labor associated with coca and eight to twelve times greater than those of labor for other agricultural crops (Hargreaves, 1992: 39; Healy, 1986: 123; K. Healy, personal communication, March 28, 1995).

In conceptualizing the production networks of commodity chains, the size of firms and the labor patterns and organization of production are key (Gereffi and Korzeniewicz, 1990). According to Morales (1989) and Kaswell (1989a, 1989b), coca farmers in Peru's upper Huallaga Valley are economically and socially stratified according to the extent to which the leaves are processed. Some farmers only cultivate and dry coca leaves and are therefore excluded from value-added profits gained from linking with the production node of the commodity chain. Others remain involved in the process until the leaves have been converted to coca paste and are ready to be sold to refiners and traffickers. To date, the proportion of farmers engaging in different levels of processing in Peru and Bolivia is unknown.

Prior to the 1980s, the decision to make coca paste was not an issue for Bolivian and Peruvian farmers, who instead tended to sell their leaves to intermediaries for resale to traffickers and refiners (Morales, 1989). In Bolivia, operating "paste pits went against the way of thinking of many campesinos who were used to subsistence on the land, not being entrepreneurs" (Hargreaves, 1992: 36). While difficult to investigate empirically, this kind of social consideration is key in understanding how nonmarket factors condition a commodity chain. In Bolivia, increasing cultivation in the 1980s led to a drop in the price of leaves and an influx of labor to the jungle regions (Hargreaves, 1992). Because transforming the leaves into paste offered considerable profits and labor was abundant, many farmers were willing to take the risk of venturing into the blatantly illegal stage of production (Hargreaves, 1992).

The shift by Peruvians and Bolivians to a forward link and increased value-added profits was not perceived as competition by actors in the nodes further along in the commodity chain but rather as a boon, as the further refined the product is before they buy it, the less risk there is (Hargreaves, 1992: 36). The value-added profits for links farther away from the retail stage are insignificant compared to the profits received from transporting and selling refined cocaine hydrochloride. Diffusing risks associated with early stages of production among small entrepreneurs in the jungles decreases those of future links which, in turn, allows the latter to operate on a larger scale. In this way, participants from peripheral economies receive less profit because they are far removed from the final sale of the commodity, while their engagement allows participants closest to the consumption stage to earn greater profits.

The networks and labor relations involved in harvesting leaves and transforming them into coca paste are based on mutual reliance, ensuring that the farmers and paste-making "chemists" act as links in the productive process rather than dominant powers in a vertically structured commodity chain (Gereffi and Korzeniewicz, 1990). Even if a farmer is a chemist, the inability to farm large tracts of land with coca, the need for a diverse pool of material inputs, and the illegal sale and transport of the paste mean that the individual is intimately linked to a complex production process, which includes "infrastructure sharing," pooling for the purchase of the necessary inputs, and the sharing of "coca pits."

When choosing a level of processing, the decisions of farmers are influenced in part by their access to production networks and their level of risk-acceptance or -aversion. Even though the additional inputs and labor needed to make paste are expensive, the profits for the value they add are comparatively high, and coca farmers may usually pay for them in leaves, thus lessening the need for large capital outlays. Price fluctuations, as well as the possibility that the paste could be confiscated after investing in its production, create a "risk factor" that individual farmers must weigh. Unlike coca leaves, coca paste cannot be stored because it loses weight and thus drops in value (Morales, 1989). Furthermore, although selling leaves is easy because they may readily be exchanged or sold to a large group of landless individuals and entrepreneurs for processing, selling paste (to which value has been added with low capital barriers) limits the market for the farmer's product.

Entrepreneurs who buy leaves from farmers and then process them also receive a relatively large profit because, since the leaves are dried and thus can last longer, they are able to engage in year-round processing. "Besides constant production, this type of operation is often connected to the next chemical step, refining centers" (Morales, 1989: 74). Year-round processing offers this type of entrepreneur more opportunities to establish forward and backward linkages in processing and to exploit economies of scale, making up for the costs of not cultivating coca. Since processing does not only occur in the coca growing regions, these entrepreneurs are also liberated from the locational constraint associated with agricultural production. Coca pits can be set up virtually anywhere, including the back of trucks, to allow for mobility in escaping law enforcement personnel (Hargreaves, 1992).

The refining of coca paste into "cocaine base" is the next stage in the production process. Making cocaine base (and then cocaine hydrochloride) tends to be done on a larger scale than paste-making because it requires more tools (lamps, tables, bowls), an indoor location, additional chemicals, and planes for transport of the base and refined cocaine (Hargreaves, 1992: 65). In August 1991, the price of the amount of coca paste needed to make a kilogram of cocaine was $250, while refining this paste into base earned the seller six to seven times that amount (Hargreaves, 1992: 66; Henkel, 1986). In August of 1991, a kilogram of cocaine hydrochloride could be sold to traffickers in Bolivia for anywhere from $1,600 to $2,500 (Hargreaves, 1992: 66). This same kilo might cost $7,000 in Colombia; $20,000 in Miami; $40,000 in Detroit; and $250,000 by the time it is sold to dealers (Hargreaves, 1992: 159). Once it has been broken into batches as small as an eighth of a gram and cut with baking soda or other substances, consumers in the United States may end up paying about a million dollars.

The transition to refining stages represents a larger scale of production, a less labor-intensive organization, an increased need for capital investments, and significantly higher risks and value added. This chapter argues that the extent to which this transition included an internationalization of the commodity chain was a consequence of the availability of local organizational capacities. In this sense, the transition represents the point in the chain where cross-national differences emerge between Peru and Bolivia due to factors such as the strength of local elites and existing political climates.

FORWARD LINKAGES AND POSITIONS IN THE INTERNATIONAL NETWORK

In 1989 and 1990, a law enforcement clampdown in Colombia resulted in difficulties for Peruvians and Bolivians in selling their paste at high prices (Hargreaves, 1992: 66). Up until this point, Bolivia and Peru had been restricted to the raw material and primary processing stages. Paste was then flown to Colombia, where it was further refined and then smuggled to its international destinations. Even though the Colombian drug traffickers had the networks needed to operate the chain, the fact that coca appropriate for cocaine grows only in Peru and Bolivia required that international networks be created to gain access to those leaves—but why Colombia? Why did Peruvians and Bolivians fail to seek such greater value-added profits? To answer this, we must once again consider nonmarket factors influencing production. Henkel has suggested that Colombia's domination of the later links of the commodity chain was the result of an already-existing and highly organized supply network of marijuana for the United States (Henkel, 1986: 54; Hargreaves, 1992: 65–66). Not only were the chemicals needed for later refining stages available in Colombia, this network also ensured direct connections by air and sea to the United States (Henkel, 1986: 55).

By the late 1980s, however, the law enforcement efforts in Colombia and the increasing availability of chemicals and technical expertise in Peru and Bolivia led to a shift in the productive structure of the cocaine commodity chain. More and more labs for refining coca paste into cocaine were erected in Bolivia and, to a lesser extent, in Peru (Henkel, 1986; Hargreaves, 1992; Morales, 1989). The involvement of Peruvians in the commodity chain is primarily through the generation of raw materials and the first productive process (Morales, 1989: 86). Since only 5 percent of the world supply of cocaine hydrochloride is estimated to be produced in Peru, while Bolivia (which cultivates about half the amount of leaves) generates 15 percent of all cocaine, it can be reasonably inferred that refining is much more prevalent in Bolivia than in Peru (Hargreaves, 1992: 54; Henkel, 1986: 56; Strug, 1986). While this may have changed in recent years, one distinct feature of the production network in Peru is that subsequent production stages beyond the stage of paste making are dominated by either Colombians or Peruvians working under close Colombian supervision (MacDonald,

1989: 59–60; Morales, 1989: 89; Kaswell, 1989b). Hence, Peru has been less successful in exploiting opportunities for value-added profits enjoyed in the later links of the commodity chain.

The nature of the *narcotraficantes* is somewhat different in Bolivia. The booming market for cocaine was accompanied by U.S. pressure to control coca production in the Chapare (Sanabria, 1986: 57). The effect of this increased enforcement was to drive coca paste production into the Beni and Santa Cruz departments. In these departments, colonization projects and the promotion of agro-industry and ranching had solidified the political and economic hegemony of a rural elite during the 1960s and 1970s, whose cotton, soy, and cattle enterprises had received credit and marketing assistance, largely through foreign loans (Healy, 1986: 105; Sanabria, 1986: 108–109).[5] By the late 1970s, these elites had developed both a strong experience in international trade and local political clout. Many of the cattle ranches in the remote Beni region, which were established through colonization projects, faced a troubled export market for cotton and therefore became involved in refining operations (K. Healy, personal communication, March 28, 1995).

The linkages between raw materials and production were facilitated by the remoteness of the regions and the capital available from local elites. The capital enabled the Bolivian actors to extend forward linkages into refining facilities, thereby decreasing their reliance on Colombian export connections, capital, and transportation networks (Sanabria, 1986; Hargreaves, 1992; Healy, 1986; Henkel, 1986). These Bolivian labs were able to exploit a number of locational advantages, including proximity to raw materials, avoidance of law enforcement personnel, and availability of infrastructure (such as airstrips that had been originally constructed to develop agro-industrial production in the regions). Air transport to Colombia was much easier from these areas than via land from the Chapare, enabling the Bolivian refining "industry" to engineer productive arrangements to exploit their locational advantages (Henkel, 1986; Hargreaves, 1992). Furthermore, unlike the cartels controlling the Colombian end of the trade, the Bolivian "narcobourgeoisie" have avoided violence with the community outside the commodity chain and have often financed public works projects, thus solidifying their support in their communities of operation (Hargreaves, 1992: 58).

The results of this control of forward linkages in Bolivia are manifested in several ways. Though much of the capital earned by the higher value contributed to the Bolivian product probably flees the country or is reinvested in the illicit economy, it still has a greater chance of remaining in Bolivia than in Peru (where Colombian cartels capture these profits). Nevertheless, the effects of the cocaine trade were extremely deleterious for Bolivia's economy. The weakness of the state, coupled with escalating trade and economic crises, has caused significant portions of the economy to go "further underground" (Blanes, 1989). The acute financial crisis experienced by Bolivia between 1982 and 1985 severely restricted credit for legitimate businesses, some of which sought "narcodollars" to continue their operations which, due to their secure access to foreign exchange, increased the political and economic influence of the narcobourgeoisie (Henkel, 1986: 66). The power this narcobourgeoisie gained throughout the 1980s crippled efforts to control and capture traffickers and strengthened the efforts of the traffickers themselves. Not only were they protected by high-level contacts and economic power, but the thousands of Bolivians working for them were somewhat protected as well.[6] In contrast, the absence of an indigenous elite in Peru meant that the government was less intimately tied to the interests of traffickers.

This is not to suggest that the forces with which the Peruvian government must contend are manageable. Sendero Luminoso, a Maoist Peruvian guerrilla group, has presented a completely separate and forceful variable in Peruvian efforts to control the cultivation and processing of coca leaves. Speculations about its uncertain role in the commodity chain range from categorical declarations by state agencies that towns engaged in the production and transport of coca leaves and paste are under the ''de facto political authority'' of Sendero Luminoso (Kaswell, 1989a) to speculations that absolutely no influence is enjoyed by the group (Morales 1989, 1990).[7] Whether Sendero Luminoso enjoys an ideological influence in the coca-growing areas of Peru almost becomes a moot point when one considers that the mere perception of a powerful guerrilla threat facilitates the networks of the illicit commodity chain, because the Peruvian military (in charge of controlling Sendero) has adopted a laissez-faire stance toward the drug trade as a means to contain guerrilla movements (Reid, 1989: 158). For the drug traffickers, framing terrorist actions as if they were committed by guerrilla groups shifts attention away from the violence they commit and reinforces a fear of the spread of Sendero Luminoso (Morales, 1989). Thus, efforts to contain guerrilla movements can result in a relaxation of efforts to control the coca trade and facilitate its functioning.

The resistance to eradication efforts in Bolivia takes a very political form, including hunger strikes, protest marches, and roadblocks.[8] The Confederation of Peasant Worker Unions of Bolivia (CSUTCB) operates at the community, regional, and national levels to express peasant interests (Healy, 1986).[9] Since the 1970s, membership in CSUTCB organizations in the Chapare region has included an increasing number of coca farmers. These groups have proven very strong relative to other branches of the confederation, as members have not only more income to support leaders and activities, but also strong interests to defend (i.e., the right to grow coca). With the development of coca cultivation on a large scale, peasant organizations have become extremely vocal and effective in expressing opposition to Bolivian and U.S. governmental efforts to quell the trade.

Each initiative by either the Bolivian or U.S. government to reduce the amount of coca being cultivated has been met with opposition from CSUTCB and other concerned unions and organizations (Healy, 1986; Henkel, 1986; Hargreaves, 1992). In recent years, union activity has gone beyond defensive measures and now includes coca leaf "chew-ins," rallies, and large-scale marches to bring the issue of the right to grow coca to the forefront of the national agenda (Healy, 1991). These mobilizations undoubtedly hinder government efforts to take strong and effective eradication measures. Not only does the coca growers' militancy improve their ability to grow the leaf, but CSUTCB's efforts have been framed in terms of cultural preservation and revitalization, national themes with an appeal beyond the population receiving profits from the coca trade (K. Healy, personal communication, March 28, 1995). Furthermore, the traffickers working with the growers are well aware of the benefits that accrue to them because of CSUTCB's activism. Thus, they often make concessions to the growers. Hargreaves reported that each time a plane lands in a village to pick up paste or base, the traffickers donate about $120 to the local union for "public works" (1992: 63).

The experiences of Peru and Bolivia illustrate how political culture, historical circumstances, and class structure may condition a commodity chain. These factors determine the extent to which otherwise similar actors are able to exploit differing degrees of locational advantages, forward linkages, and value-added profits. The experiences described here also illustrate the flexible nature of productive organization that is inherent to the production and exporting stages of the commodity chain. As the chain thrives despite efforts to curb the trade, modifications may constantly be made to adapt to the new environments to which its structure is subjected. Adjustments are made through human agency, modifying productive structures, sharing of infrastructure and power, and exploiting locational advantages, all of which are central elements of the structure of industrial, and not necessarily agricultural, production.

CONCLUSION: FIVE PENNIES FOR A DIME OR A NEW DEVELOPMENT PATH?

In examining the effect of the cocaine commodity chain in Peru and Bolivia, the focus has been on the first two of the chain's four stages. These stages (raw material supply and production) are characterized by low capital barriers, small-scale enterprises, continuous exchanges between actors, extensive forward and backward linkages, and diffuse production. Informal links are pervasive throughout the chain, as both the final commodity (cocaine) and its principal components (cocaine paste and base) are illegal. Compared to the profits enjoyed in the postproduction stage, profits for the growth of coca and for the production of cocaine and its components are very low. Like other commodity chains, the value of the product in peripheral areas is lower than in core nations (Gereffi and Korzeniewicz, 1994).

Unlike other commodity chains, however, the differential profits are only partially attributable to increased value added and higher capital barriers. The cocaine commodity chain is conditioned, not only by the labor and materials necessary for its operation, but also by social networks, political conditions, and social attitudes about the actual product. This demonstrates the importance of considering factors not directly related to production when using the commodity chain approach to examine the distribution of profits among core and peripheral economies. As Wilson and Zambrano (1994) have pointed out, the bulk of profits are in the nodes of the chain that occur in core countries, despite the fact that production is complete before export.

The cocaine commodity chain challenges traditional conceptions about development that suggest the nation-state is the primary motor and unit of the development of growth strategies and a capital base. While the nation-state is certainly an important actor in the operation of the cocaine commodity chain, its role is primarily in reaction to the chain's operation. Regulation and taxation are not the responses to its growth but, rather, international political and legal issues. The tangible products of the commodity chain and the accumulated profits remain largely informal, illegal, and transnational in nature. For countries such as Peru and Bolivia, the effect has been that national efforts to plan development must be made in response to the illegal classification of the commodity rather than efforts to incorporate its enormous profits into national revenues.

Examining cocaine as a transnational commodity also demonstrates the way its production process diverts from traditional agricultural-export crops. While supplying the primary input of the final commodity resembles agricultural production, it is also unique in the hardiness of the plant, the large amounts of labor necessary for harvesting, the small plots on which it is grown, and the highly inelastic demand for cocaine as an international commodity. Moreover, cultivators of the leaf have found it relatively easy to insert themselves into later links of the commodity chain, thus affording them more control over the type of production in which they engage.

Locational constraints conditioning the cocaine commodity chain demand extensive transportation costs and the development of routes and vehicles. Because this must be done outside the law, it tends to occur on a small scale and involves narrow roles for participants. This results in the creation of significant forward and backward linkages for local producing economies that are involved in the international commodity chain. In the sense that the coca trade is a response to externally generated demand, it resembles traditional commodity exports fairly closely. Production for the exclusive purpose of export results in the trade's removal from the consumption needs of the producing society. However, as Healy observed: "[F]armers control the raw material within an economic structure of small-plot agriculture. This point appears to contradict the theory that treats peasant farmers as passive and manipulated 'masses,' victimized by a dependent development process dominated by the State and the national and international bourgeoisie" (1986: 126). It can also be argued that because of the highly inelastic demand for cocaine, the market is (at least so far) much less affected by external constraints of market dependence. While coca producers are price takers, the high demand usually ensures a high price and secure market.

Furthermore, as the Bolivian case suggests, the commodity chain is so flexible that it can sometimes be manipulated so as to be internally controlled.

The procurement of other raw materials necessary to make cocaine; the production of coca paste, cocaine base, and cocaine hydrochloride; and the mechanisms governing the export and sale of cocaine resemble an industry more closely than an agricultural enterprise. The locational constraints conditioning cultivation are not as strong in these later stages, nor is the need for intensive labor. The production of coca paste and cocaine can occur wherever the law does not disable it and the capital is available. For the later stages in production (refining paste into base and cocaine), the necessary social connections and capital result in its operation in a more concentrated manner, also making it more closely resemble an industry.

Although the organization of labor in the chain is constrained by the location of the main raw input, the contrast of these networks in Peru and Bolivia suggests that there is some latitude in the chain's establishment. Elite structures are, therefore, key to understanding the geography of the cocaine commodity chain. While the business in Peru has been dominated by a Colombian power structure and production that is relatively contained in the Huallaga Valley, in Bolivia, the organization of labor has become controlled by a national elite spread all over the remote areas of the Beni and Santa Cruz regions. In turn, through their participation in the cocaine commodity chain, these elites have reconfigured themselves into a new group, termed the "narcobourgeoisie."

If coca cultivation did more closely resemble that of traditional crops, controlling the coca trade would consist of isolating the area of cultivation. Instead, the small plots, low capital barriers, large profits, and flexibility of organizational and production networks render this strategy futile. "Like any business, it responds to changing market conditions by altering management and location. . . . Finding employees to run the gauntlet of smuggling cocaine supplies across international borders, however risky, will never be difficult given the enormous sums the druglords can afford to pay" (Hargreaves, 1992: 188). As can be seen in Figure 2.1, given the remarkably higher profits in the export and marketing stages, the structure of the commodity chain is such that any decrease in the final consumer prices can be absorbed by the links closer to the retail stages without rendering the chain unprofitable. As long as the demand for coca remains relatively inelastic, and the price many times higher than that of alternative crops, the cultivation of this export crop will be the choice for many. Furthermore, eradication and control efforts aimed at curbing the drug supply seem to ignore the flexibility of the productive structure following the stage of raw material supply.

Even though the U.S. market for cocaine seems to be shrinking, recent evidence suggests that other, more profitable ones are opening up. "Between 1989 and 1990 the amount of cocaine confiscated in Europe more than doubled, from 6 to 14 tons. Given that police estimate they seize a maximum of 10 percent of the total, that means that in 1990 Europe was awash with at least 140 tons of

[the drug]'' (Hargreaves, 1992: 8). Moreover, cocaine entering the rapidly expanding markets in Japan and Europe fetches up to three times more than that
exported to the United States (Hargreaves, 1992: 188). Human agency is certainly involved in finding networks and processes to satisfy the incredible demand. Furthermore, given recent increases in illegal synthetic drugs, the
eradication of the coca used for cocaine will probably neither end these international networks nor erase demand for illicit drugs. Given the impracticality
of supply-side solutions demonstrated in this chapter, a government wishing to
address a national drug problem would be wiser to focus on demand and, as
recommended by Wilson and Zambrano (1994), on efforts at making it more
difficult for cocaine to penetrate national borders.

Clearly, the cocaine commodity chain is of tremendous economic importance
in both Peru and Bolivia. De Franco and Godoy reported that ''work as an
unskilled labourer in cocaine production pays 20 times more than work as a
public employee'' and that ''landless rural labourers in the Chapare earn three
to five times more by working in the drug industry than working in their home-
lands'' (1992: 386). Thus, even though only about 0.5 percent of $1 million
that cocaine users may pay for a kilogram of cocaine goes to the growers of
the main raw material, for many, the cocaine commodity chain appears as the
most viable development path in the face of a lack of alternate export crops and
economic destitution. As explained by a U.S. Drug Enforcement Agency official,
''These people are not addicted to coca, they are addicted to eating'' (quoted
in Hargreaves, 1992: 190).

NOTES

The author wishes to thank J. Timmons Roberts for several sets of comments and
numerous ideas; John Hite, Bill Smith, and Roberto P. Korzeniewicz for comments and
editorial assistance; and Tulane University for supporting travel to the Political Economy
of the World-System (PEWS) conference.

1. Due to the illicit nature of the cultivation, processing, and trade of the coca leaf,
these and virtually all the other figures used in this chapter are largely speculative: they
are derived through local surveys, information collected by law enforcement agencies in
the United States and Latin America, satellite photos, estimates derived from seizures,
and development agencies. Here, every effort has been made to compare statistics with
as many sources as possible. The data and descriptions of the social relations of production presented here are drawn heavily from ''micro'' analyses. Therefore, regional
generalizations made on the basis of specific anecdotes and particular cases, while extremely illustrative, are also primarily speculative.

2. While the line representing the price of the components necessary to produce a
kilogram of cocaine is a very rough estimate, the proportion of profits enjoyed at each
stage is represented fairly accurately.

3. For example, in 1986 a roll of toilet paper cost nine times more in Chapare than
in the nearby city of Cochabamba, and about 2,000 individuals made a living buying,
selling and transporting toilet paper in Bolivia alone (Healy, 1986: 118).

4. Those who stomp on the leaves mixed with sulfuric acid may experience burns on the soles of their feet, often resulting in amputation (Hargreaves, 1992: 39).

5. In 1975, when prices of cotton dropped, the "Cotton Growers' Association" (controlled by the Santa Cruz elites) was granted millions of dollars in credit as compensation (Sanabria, 1986; Hargreaves, 1992: 57). It is suspected that much of this money was funneled to finance the development of the cocaine-trafficking infrastructure (Hargreaves, 1992: 57).

6. While alignment with the Bolivian narcobourgeoisie allows for some degree of protection, in both Bolivia and Peru, arrests are primarily symbolic acts against agents in the early stages of the chain rather than against those who control refining and transport.

7. Morales argued that the ideologies of those involved in the drug trade are inherently opposed to those of a revolutionary movement and that Peruvians enjoying profits from the trade have little interest in Sendero Luminoso's radical ideological agenda (1990: 103, 136).

8. For a detailed account of the development of a political consciousness among coca growers in the Bolivian Chapare region, see Healy (1991). He reported that Bolivian growers are developing more sophisticated political tactics designed to preserve the legality of coca growing, gain legitimacy among national union groups, and advance issues such as international legalization and the preservation of Bolivia's sovereignty in the face of U.S. pressure for eradication.

9. "The peasant sindicato organizations [local CSUTCB groups] have employed sophisticated means of using the news media, print, radio and television to represent the interests of Bolivia's peasant majority and to embarrass and pressure the relevant government ministries" (Healy, 1986: 135).

REFERENCES

Allen, Catherine J. 1986. "Coca and Cultural Identity in Andean Communities." In *Coca and Cocaine: Effects on People and Policy in Latin America*, ed. Christine Franquemont and Deborah Pacini, pp. 35–48. Boston: Cultural Survival.

————. 1988. *The Hold Life Has: Coca and Cultural Identity in an Andean Community*. Washington, DC: Smithsonian Institution Press.

Blanes, José Jiménez. 1989. "Cocaine, Informality and the Urban Economy in La Paz, Bolivia." In *The Informal Economy: Studies in Advanced and Less Developed Countries*, ed. Alejandro Portes, Manuel Castells, and Lauren Benton, pp. 135–149. Baltimore: Johns Hopkins University Press.

Campodónico, Humberto. 1989. "La política del avestruz." In *Coca, cocaína y narcotráfico: Laberinto en los Andes*, ed. Diego García-Sayán, pp. 225–258. Lima: Comisión Andina de Juristas.

Craig, Richard B. 1987. "Illicit Drug Traffic: Implications for South American Source Countries." *Journal of Interamerican Studies and World Affairs* 29, 2: 1–34.

De Franco, Mario, and Ricardo Godoy. 1992. "The Economic Consequences of Cocaine Production in Bolivia: Historical, Local, and Macroeconomic Perspectives." *Journal of Latin American Studies* 24: 375–406.

Gereffi, Gary. 1989. "Rethinking Development Theory: Insights from East Asia and Latin America." *Sociological Forum* 4, 4: 505–533.

Gereffi, Gary, and Miguel Korzeniewicz. 1990. "Commodity Chains and Footwear Exports in the Semiperiphery." In *Semiperipheral States in the World Economy*, ed. William G. Martin, pp. 45–68. Westport, CT: Greenwood.

———, eds. 1994. *Commodity Chains and Global Capitalism*. Westport, CT: Greenwood.

Hargreaves, Clare. 1992. *Snowfields: The War on Cocaine in the Andes*. New York: Holmes and Meier.

Healy, Kevin. 1986. "The Boom within the Crisis: Some Recent Effects of Foreign Cocaine Markets on Bolivian Rural Society and the Economy." In *Coca and Cocaine: Effects on People and Policy in Latin America*, ed. Christine Franquemont and Deborah Pacini, pp. 101–144. Boston: Cultural Survival.

———. 1991. "Political Ascent of Bolivia's Peasant Coca Leaf Producers." *Journal of Interamerican Studies and World Affairs* 33 (Spring): 87–121.

Henkel, Ray. 1986. "The Bolivian Cocaine Industry." In *Drugs in Latin America*, ed. Edmundo Morales, pp. 53–80. Williamsburg, VA: College of William and Mary.

Kaswell, Jo Ann. 1989a. "The Addict Economies." *NACLA Report on the Americas* 22, 6: 33–38.

———. 1989b. "The Real Green Revolution." *NACLA Report on the Americas* 22, 6: 12–19.

Macdonald, Scott B. 1989. *Mountain High, White Avalanche: Cocaine and Power in the Andean States and Panama*. New York: Praeger.

McClintock, Cynthia. 1988. "The War on Drugs: The Peruvian Case." *Journal of Interamerican Studies and World Affairs* 30, 2/3: 127–142.

Mitchell, William P. 1991. *Peasants on the Edge: Crop, Cult, and Crisis in the Andes*. Austin: University of Texas Press.

Morales, Edumundo. 1989. *Cocaine: White Gold Rush in Peru*. Tucson: University of Arizona Press.

———. 1990. "The Political Economy of Cocaine Production: An Analysis of the Peruvian Case." *Latin American Perspectives* 17, 4 (Fall): 91–109.

Plowman, Timothy. 1986. "Coca Chewing and the Botanical Origins of Coca (Erythroxylum SPP) in South America." In *Coca and Cocaine: Effects on People and Policy in Latin America*, ed. Christine Franquemont and Deborah Pacini, pp. 5–29. Boston: Cultural Survival.

Queiser Morales, Waltraud. 1992. *Bolivia: Land of Struggle*. Boulder, CO: Westview Press.

Reid, Michael. 1989. "Una región amenazada por el narcotráfico." In *Coca, cocaína y narcotráfico: Laberinto en los Andes*, ed. Diego García-Sayán, pp. 133–169. Lima, Peru: Comisión Andina de Juristas.

Sanabria, Harry. 1986. "Coca, Migration and Social Differentiation in the Bolivian Lowlands." In *Drugs in the Americas*, ed. Edumundo Morales, pp. 81–124. Williamsburg, VA: College of William and Mary.

Strug, David L. 1986. "The Foreign Politics of Cocaine: Comments on a Plan to Eradicate the Coca Leaf in Peru." In *Coca and Cocaine: Effects on People and Policy in Latin America*, ed. Christine Franquemont and Deborah Pacini, pp. 73–88. Boston: Cultural Survival.

Truelove, Cynthia. 1992. "The Fetishism of Commodity Chains: Social Embeddedness, Social Regulation and Economic Restructuring Reconsidered." Unpublished paper presented at the American Sociological Association's 87th Annual Meeting, Pittsburgh, PA, August 20–24, 1992.

Wilson, Suzanne, and Marta Zambrano. 1994. "Cocaine, Commodity Chains, and Drug Politics: A Transnational Approach." In *Commodity Chains and Global Capitalism*, ed. Gary Gereffi and Miguel Korzeniewicz, pp. 297–315. Westport, CT: Greenwood Press.

Uncertainty, Innovation, and Global Competitiveness: The Brazilian Footwear Industry

Miguel E. Korzeniewicz

In the 1990s, Latin America has undergone profound economic, social, and political transformations. Many governments in the region have implemented policies involving the privatization of state assets, an emphasis on the role of free markets, and trade liberalization, thus seeking a greater integration into the international economy. The global landscape itself has changed dramatically in the past few years. New capitalist markets have surfaced in Eastern Europe and the former Soviet Union, North America and Western Europe have established trading blocs, and greater East Asia (including the People's Republic of China) has emerged as the most dynamic and fastest-growing economy in the world.

The nature and evolution of these global trends, and their consequences for individuals and communities, can only be grasped by an analytical framework that integrates local, national, and international dimensions. This chapter examines the Brazilian footwear industry to illustrate the linkages between industrial districts, state export policies, and world-market competitiveness.

In the 1970s and 1980s, Brazilian footwear manufacturers became highly successful exporters. In those two decades, the U.S. domestic production of shoes declined drastically as factories closed or became distributors of imports. During the 1980s, U.S. consumption of footwear grew rapidly, and this demand was met largely by production sites in Brazil, South Korea, and Taiwan. Within a cluster of small towns in southern Brazil, a tightly knit industrial district with the support of governmental export-promotion policies captured the profitable niche of mid-priced women's leather shoes. In the 1990s, however, competition from the People's Republic of China and the decline of state support has atomized firms within the district and eroded the communitarian character that had led to its success.

The objective of this chapter is to explore the nature and consequences of insertion in the global economy by specifying the conditions that underlie the emergence, transformation, and eventual decline of export-oriented manufacturing industries in semiperipheral countries such as Brazil. I suggest that the study of local organization and state support shows that they play an important role in competitive success. A Global Commodity Chains (GCC) approach helps cast light on the critical importance of the integration of backward and forward linkages. However, new theoretical and conceptual insights are needed to understand the conditions that lead to industrial decline.

The first section of this chapter reviews theoretical issues associated with the study of transnational linkages and manufactured exports. Next, I summarize data on three components of Brazilian export success: consumption patterns in the core, the consolidation of industrial districts, and the role of state incentives. The third section reviews the concept of GCC and its application to the case study. In the fourth and final section, I discuss both the empirical and the conceptual challenges of trends of global competitiveness in the 1990s.

TRANSNATIONAL ECONOMIC LINKAGES AND EXPORTS

In 1965 and 1966, Fernando Henrique Cardoso conducted a survey of firms and firm managers in Argentina and Brazil. The results were published in 1972 under the title of *Ideologias de la burguesia industrial en sociedades dependientes (Argentina y Brasil)*. The study was a very nuanced exploration of the relationship between the degree of "internationalization" of firms and their ideology and political orientation. Among other conclusions, Cardoso wrote that "from the moment in which the international capitalist system of industrial production becomes 'internationalized,' there is no longer a necessary relation between 'development, national independence and industrial bourgeoisie' " (1972: 221). A few years later, in *Dependency and Development in Latin America*, Cardoso (1979) defined both the extrinsic and intrinsic dimensions of dependency: "[I]mperialist penetration is a result of external social forces. . . . [T]he system of domination reappears as an 'internal' force, through the social practices of local groups and classes which try to enforce foreign interests" (1979; cited in Brown, 1994: 7).

Even in their subtle and sophisticated formulation, Cardoso's interpretations of the international economy and the international system reflect the perceptions prevalent in the intellectual and political agendas of the Latin American left in the 1960s and 1970s. From the standpoint of both history and contemporary trends, societal linkages to the outside world were cast in a detrimental light. In the twentieth century, the most visible manifestations of external linkages were the penetration of multinational corporations in domestic economies and foreign aid (in currency and arms) tied to U.S. political objectives of promoting and supporting "friendly" regimes. Even linkages originating at home (exports, primarily of raw materials) were seen as part and parcel of the overall structure of domination by core countries.

Thirty years after his earlier publications, Fernando Henrique Cardoso reformulated his assessment of external linkages:

The international system is a field of opportunities, of resources that must be sought. . . . The process of liberalization of the economy and opening toward the outside world will continue, not an objective in and of itself, but as a strategic element in the modernization of our economy. (cited in Brown, 1994:7)

Currently, the majority of sociologists and the political leaders, especially those from developing countries, identify the integration to, and the participation in, the international system with the solution to their problems rather than with the cause of their difficulties. (cited in Grosfoguel, 1995: 2)

Such a reassessment of the possibilities of development is characteristic of broader trends within the development literature. In the 1970s and 1980s, the impressive growth and relative equity of the development patterns of some East Asian nations led to a reevaluation of the role of external linkages in national development (Evans, 1987; Gereffi and Wyman, 1990). National ties to the world economy were defined as transnational economic linkages (TNELs) and categorized as consisting of four types: foreign aid, exports, direct foreign investment, and loans. The main argument underlying these types of analyses is that the specific conditions of dependency and inequality are contingent on both the mix and the management of these international linkages. In Latin America, foreign direct investment (primarily by U.S. multinationals) and commercial loans have been predominant, whereas in the East Asian nations, foreign aid and exports have driven their insertion in the world economy.

The ''lost decade'' of the 1980s in Latin America stood in sharp contrast with the growth of GNP per capita and trade in South Korea and Taiwan. There have been two different readings of the East Asian success. A ''market'' approach argues that the reason for their success lies in free and open merchandise and financial markets, a minimal role of the state, and the reliance on comparative advantages for their insertion in the world economy. An alternative reading of the success of East Asian economies focuses on the historical and institutional conditions that shaped its incorporation into the world economy (Johnson, 1982; Haggard, 1989; Cummings, 1987).

These theoretical interests coincide with an effort to study the institutional causes and effects of successful export strategies in Latin America (CEPAL, 1990, 1991; Goldfrank, 1989, 1990; Schwartz, 1991) and an interest in lessons that can be learned from other nations that have engaged in export-led development strategies (Fishlow, 1989; Gereffi and Wyman, 1990; Whitehead, 1989). To approach such themes, scholars from a variety of fields have called for a cross-disciplinary approach to the study of comparative development and organizational behavior (Evans and Stephens, 1988; Scott, 1983; Pfeffer, 1987; Starr, 1988).

Manufactured exports have come to be increasingly regarded as critical influences on national economies, and for several interrelated reasons. An export orientation may increase employment, provide currency, and force manufacturers to become competitive. Rubinson and Holtzman examined several studies of trade and found that a concentration on export commodities and reliance on raw-materials exports have a negative effect on development (Rubinson and Holtzman, 1982). Trade and international competitiveness have been related to issues of distribution and equity (Krueger, 1985; Baer and Gillis, 1983). Some scholars have argued that "patterns of trade in manufactured goods provide better insights into the efficiency of the institutions and policies of a country than do patterns of trade in primary products or services" (Olson, 1987: 252–253). Others indicate that the expansion of manufactured exports involves an expansion of overall employment and industrial activity, by contributing to the achievement of economies of scale (Tavares de Oliveira, 1987; Baldinelli, 1990; de Paula Pinto, 1983) and by exposing exporting firms to theoretically quasi-infinite markets (Lim, 1981). A detailed study of exports in Brazil found a substantive contribution of exports to savings and investment (Baumman Neves, 1985). The need to generate foreign currency to meet debt payments and interests has stimulated interest in manufactured exports because they are considered to be more stable in the long run, compared to the price and demand fluctuations that affect primary-product exports (CEPAL, 1989).

In previous studies, colleagues and I have identified cases of successful export industries in Latin America and analyzed the various social and economic factors that underlie their performance (Korzeniewicz et al., 1995; Goldfrank, 1994; Korzeniewicz, 1990; Lee and Cason, 1994; Wilson and Zambrano, 1994). Brazilian footwear is an archetype of a successful export commodity. Exports grew from U.S. $6 million in 1970 to $390 million in 1980 and $1.4 billion in 1992 (see Figure 3.1). Placed in the context of footwear exporters to the U.S. market, Brazil has maintained a share of between 10 and 15 percent of the total, which in 1994 amounted to almost $10 billion (see Table 3.1). What are the sociological insights that help account for this growth? The following two sections explore the role of industrial communities, state policies, and global commodity chains.

BRAZILIAN FOOTWEAR EXPORTS IN THE 1970s AND THE 1980s

During the 1980s, U.S. consumption of imported shoes grew at an astounding rate. Shoe imports tripled between 1975 and 1995 (U.S. Department of Commerce, various years–c). Twenty-five years ago, one out of every five pairs of shoes purchased in the United States was imported; fifteen years ago, one out of every two pairs was imported; and by 1989, four out of every five pairs of shoes purchased in the United States were made abroad (FIA, 1990; Mutti, 1980; U.S. Department of Commerce, various years–a).[1]

Table 3.1 shows the total current dollar value amount of footwear imports and the distribution of market share by country where exports originate. Between

Figure 3.1
Exports of Brazilian Footwear, 1970–1992

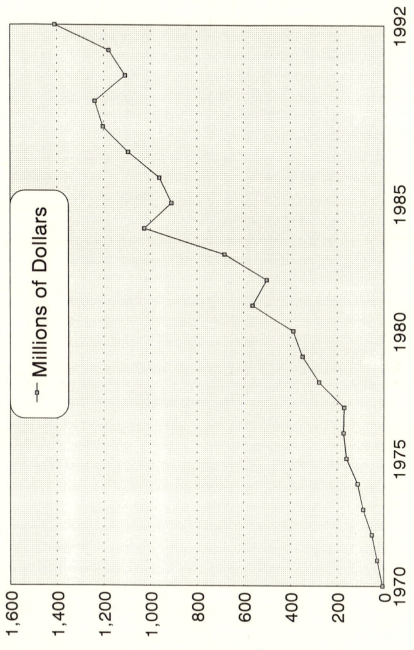

Source: United Nations, *International Trade Statistics Yearbook* (various years).

Table 3.1
Market Share of U.S. Footwear Imports, Selected Countries, 1967–1994 (Thousands of Dollars)

Year	TOTAL	Japan	Spain	Italy	Korea	Taiwan	Brazil	Indonesia	P.R.C.
1967	263,220	23	9	39	3	3	0	-	-
1968	388,135	21	12	41	3	4	1	-	-
1969	488,172	17	15	41	2	4	0	-	-
1970	629,402	15	13	42	2	6	1	-	-
1971	758,095	13	17	38	4	9	3	-	-
1972	915,014	6	19	37	5	11	5	-	-
1973	1,079,166	2	18	34	6	13	8	-	0
1974	1,153,391	1	17	28	9	15	8	-	-
1975	1,301,404	2	18	26	10	16	9	-	0
1976	1,724,547	1	14	20	16	21	8	-	0
1977	1,805,824	1	12	20	16	24	7	-	0
1978	2,584,979	2	11	22	15	23	7	-	0
1979	2,859,446	1	10	28	13	21	8	-	1
1980	2,807,937	1	7	19	17	30	9	-	1

Year									
1981	3,019,374	1	7	17	18	27	12	–	1
1982	3,437,455	1	7	18	22	27	10	–	0
1983	4,009,541	1	6	17	21	30	13	–	0
1984	5,034,436	1	7	16	19	29	17	–	–
1985	5,955,634	–	7	15	19	30	15	–	1
1986	6,472,891	0	6	14	23	32	13	0	1
1987	7,546,765	0	5	11	23	32	13	0	2
1988	8,406,340	–	4	10	28	29	12	0	4
1989	8,380,755	–	4	10	26	24	12	1	9
1990	8,408,472	–	4	11	26	16	12	3	15
1991	8,311,911	–	4	9	20	12	11	5	27
1992	8,587,509	–	3	9	12	8	13	7	35
1993	9,256,221	–	3	8	7	5	15	8	42
1994	9,889,570*	–	2	7	4	3	14	7	46

*Projected.

Sources: U.S. Department of Commerce, *U.S. General Imports* (various years); *Foreign Trade Highlights* (1987, 1989); *National Trade Data Bank* (April 1991); U.S. International Trade Commission, *Nonrubber Footwear Quarterly Statistical Report* (various years).

1967 and 1994, the distribution of exports shows a distinct pattern. In the late 1960s, Japan, Italy, and Spain were the dominant exporters to the U.S. market, accounting for 74 percent of total imports in 1967. As these countries' economies matured and labor costs increased, the production of footwear relocated to Korea, Taiwan, and Brazil. By the mid-1980s, these three countries accounted for two-thirds of all imported footwear into the U.S. market.

The world footwear industry is segmented in terms of price and type-of-shoe niches. Data on shoe imports between 1970 and 1987 show that Korea has been highly specialized in the production of mid-priced athletic footwear; Taiwan concentrated on the lower-price plastic/rubber category; and Italy and Brazil were dominant in the women's leather shoes segment, at the high- and mid-price ranges, respectively. The consolidation of export niches in terms of type, gender, and cost of shoes is a key component of the success of Brazil and other semiperipheral countries in world markets. "Export niches help explain how South Korea, Taiwan and Brazil captured large shares of the American footwear market by specializing in products that were well suited to their raw material supply networks and domestic industrial capabilities" (Gereffi and Korzeniewicz, 1989: 24–25).

Women's footwear is the driving segment of the footwear industry. A majority of the dollars spent on shoes in the United States are spent on women's shoes, and a majority of the pairs of shoes bought in this country are women's shoes ("Footwear," 1989: 40–46). The growth in consumption of women's shoes helps explain the export success of Brazilian manufacturers. In 1970, Italian manufacturers were responsible for 70 percent of all the imported women's leather shoes sold in this country. By 1987, Brazil was the dominant exporter of women's leather shoes, accounting for 39 percent of the value and 50 percent of all the pairs sold. Within Brazil, footwear manufacturers have increasingly specialized in the women's shoe niche. In 1970, women's shoes comprised 41 percent of all the shoes Brazil exported to the United States; in 1980, the share was 67 percent; and in 1987, it was 83 percent (U.S. Department of Commerce, various years–b).

Two factors help account for the success of Brazilian exporters: industrial communities and state policies.

The Constitution of Geographically Bound Industrial Districts

Brazilian footwear producers are concentrated in distinct regional clusters. Data is drawn from a directory of Brazilian footwear firms (CTCCA, 1983), which, in its 1983 edition, lists 4,059 Brazilian firms. To identify geographical distribution, I first selected only those firms located in a city with ten or more producers, which yielded a sample of 3,140 firms, or 77.61 percent of the total directory.

Over 90 percent of producers are located in just five states (Minas Gerais,

Rio de Janeiro, Rio Grande do Sul, Santa Catarina, and São Paulo), and about 84 percent are located in only three states.

The Brazilian footwear industry thrives in nonurban areas. In the state of São Paulo, only 265 firms, or 27 percent of the total, are located in the city of São Paulo, while 431 firms, or close to half the state total, are located in the smaller city of Franca. Finally, within the state of Rio Grande do Sul, only nine firms (1.19 percent) are located in its capital of Porto Alegre, while 309 (41 percent) are located in the smaller city of Novo Hamburgo. This regional concentration of the footwear industry also encompasses a range of suppliers of tanned leather, component parts, chemicals, and machinery (Schmitz, 1995).

The region of Vale dos Sinos is by far the most important footwear-exporting locality in Brazil. Total footwear exports in Brazil increased by 700 percent between 1973 and 1988. Throughout this period, the share of Rio Grande do Sul (RGS) over the Brazilian total has remained relatively constant, oscillating between 75 and 80 percent of the Brazilian total, although with a slight declining tendency. The region of Vale dos Sinos accounts for the overwhelming majority of RGS exports. In 1973, it accounted for 99.12 percent of all RGS exports. Since that year, however, it has declined slightly but consistently, and for the last four years of the series (1985–1988), it has accounted for about 90 percent of the state total. In sum, the region of Vale dos Sinos remains the preeminent exporting area in Brazil, accounting for well over two-thirds of all exports throughout the period of highest growth for the footwear-export business.

Brazilian firms are also very concentrated in terms of the type of products manufactured. Firms in the Vale dos Sinos area are highly specialized in the production of women's shoes for export, and this product concentration has increased over time. In 1974, about 85 percent of all shoes produced in the Vale do Rio dos Sinos area were women's shoes. In 1985, the share was closer to 98 percent (ACI, various years). On the one hand, specialization in ladies' shoes may be associated with highly dynamic organizational structures, since the quantity and quality of demand for ladies' shoes changes more and faster than for any other segment of footwear. On the other hand, a reliance on one segment hinders the capacity to diversify markets and renders producers dependent on specific marketing and distribution channels.

A critical component of industrial districts is what may be called *competitive collectivism*, which refers to the remarkable combination of collective-oriented actions—namely, the sharing of new technology and information—and competitive-oriented actions—namely, individual-firm production and marketing. One indicator is the consolidation of collective trade associations that provide benefits to their members, and a second is the existence of ethnically based informal ties that enhance economic competitiveness.

Brazil's collective organizations are old, effective, and consistent, particularly in terms of training and of research and development. There are two types of collective organizations: training/R&D organizations, and lobbying organizations. The Vale dos Sinos area, in southern Brazil, contains five well-established collective organizations. The Feira Internacional do Calçado (FENAC), or International Shoe Fair, organized its first fair in the Novo Hamburgo area in 1963 and became institutionalized in 1973. Its purpose has been to provide a showcase for Brazilian products and to serve as meeting point for Brazilian sellers and international buyers. The Serviço Nacional de Aprendizagem Industrial (National Industrial Apprenticeship Service) (SENAI) is a national organization in charge of instruction and training in technical areas, which maintains a footwear school (Escola do Calçado) in Novo Hamburgo. The Centro Tecnólogico do Couro, Calçado, e Afins (CTCCA), or Technological Center for Leather, Footwear, and Related Items, which is located in the city of Novo Hamburgo, is a private institution created by initiative of the producers of the Rio Grande do Sul area. Their main activity consists of ensuring quality controls of components and chemical products and lending technological assistance to their associates or to other firms requesting their services (Klein, 1986).

One example of interfirm networking is illustrated by the response to competitive challenges. At a time when Taiwanese shoe exports were beginning to be perceived as a potential threat because they were entering segments of the market in which Brazil had been dominant, the CTCCA chaired a roundtable with the participation of producers and importers to discuss the problem (Tecnicouro, 1987: 3–8). The Associação Comercial e Industrial do Novo Hamburgo (ACI/NH), or Industrial and Commercial Association of Novo Hamburgo, is the oldest trade association in Novo Hamburgo (founded in 1920). Most of its members (87 in 1989) are small- and medium-sized producers, and the main functions of the organization are lobbying, representing area industrialists, technical consulting, and maintaining a data bank. The Associaciao das Indústrias do Calçado do Rio Grande do Sul (ADICAL), or Association of Footwear Industries of Rio Grande do Sul, which was founded in 1983, consisted of 121 members as of 1989. ADICAL is primarily a lobbying group, and many of its members were among the largest firms in the Vale dos Sinos area at the time when ADICAL retained the services of Anthony Motley, former U.S. ambassador to Brazil and a former ranking State Department official, as a paid consultant to advance the interests of footwear producers in Washington.

Interviews with footwear industry people in Brazil and the United States indicate that a common German heritage of residents of the Vale dos Sinos area of Brazil has been a key component of the region's economic success in footwear manufacturing. The city of Novo Hamburgo—the largest in the Vale dos Sinos area—received its name after large numbers of Germans settled the area in the eighteenth and nineteenth centuries. Between the early 1800s and early 1900s, about 400,000 Germans migrated to Brazil, and by far the largest number settled in the state of Rio Grande do Sul, home of the Vale dos Sinos (Luebke, 1987: 14). In the late nineteenth and early twentieth centuries, many Germans or their second-generation descendants began to specialize in leather products. In the mid-1920s, Germans constituted about one-eighth of the overall population of nearby Porto Alegre, but they accounted for nearly one-third of the commerce and industry there. Even as far back as 1915, Germans and their descendants dominated the shoe and leather-goods businesses (Luebke, 1987: 29, 214). Today, a high percentage of Brazilians involved in the footwear industry are of German descent.

There is in the region a competitive spirit that is very healthy, but at the same time, we continue to have a gregarious spirit, of unity and collaboration, perhaps because of the German descent/colonization. Community action is impressive. You can easily manage to get the participation and the support of people for common activities. Large firms are conscious about the need of small and medium firms because of their agility in attending certain orders. (Klein, 1986)

The Role of the State

Governmental policies have played a key role in the development of footwear exports in Brazil. There are two fundamental types of policies through which the state carries out policies of export promotion: the administration of the exchange rate and the use of financial and fiscal incentives for exporters. Elsewhere (Korzeniewicz, 1990), I have shown that exchange rates and export incentives were relatively stable in Brazil throughout the 1970s and most of the 1980s. Virtually all producers interviewed in Brazil agreed that these were two stable features of their broader environment. The stability of these two variables is explained by the relative strength and cohesiveness of the Brazilian state.

The rate of foreign-currency exchange, or exchange rate, is of fundamental importance to the promotion of exports because it is one of the most important of the factors that determine the competitiveness of the locally produced good in the world market. Considerations about the exchange rate are a key aspect of a firm's decision to invest and produce. This is especially true of developing countries, such as Brazil. Throughout the 1970s and 1980s, the Brazilian state maintained its currency at a slightly undervalued rate, which favored exports of manufactures. Such a strategy was part of a broader Brazilian industrial policy designed to stimulate foreign trade.

Throughout the 1970s and 1980s, the promotion and management of exports in Brazil was concentrated in a relatively small but highly efficient agency: the Carteira do Comércio Exterior (CACEX), a division of Banco do Brasil. CACEX was characterized by an unusual degree of coordination with other agencies related to international economic policy making. Its effectiveness was due in part to its particular institutional configuration, as a "kind of strategic vertice of different governmental agencies and private interests . . . [with] evident dexterity to occupy 'empty spaces' in the administration . . . and assimilate entrepreneurial practices without losing its governmental mission" (Martins, 1985: 156). One of the institutional advantages of CACEX was its location, by virtue of its association with Banco do Brasil, vis-à-vis financial loci of power. The availability of resources allowed export programs to be financed consistently, and the bargaining power of CACEX in relation to both public and private interests was enhanced.

In summary, the Brazilian state's policies of export promotion in the 1970s and part of the 1980s met Meyer-Stamer's (1995: 5) definition of one condition of sustained competitiveness: "[T]he existence of stable framework conditions is crucial to industrial activity that goes beyond profit-maximization in the shortest possible term."[2] While the role of industrial districts and state policies are important components of the explanation of Brazilian success, a Global Commodity Chains approach helps shed light on the critical areas of backward and forward linkages.

COMMODITY CHAINS

Global Commodity Chains (GCC) are conceptual devices that examine related networks of organizations, activities, and social relations. They help illustrate and describe some of the master institutions underlying the structures of contemporary global capitalism.

A GCC consists of sets of interorganizational linkages, formed in the production and distribution of a commodity or product, that integrate trends in the global economy with their consequences on regions, nations, local industrial districts, communities, and the workplace. A "commodity chain," as defined by Hopkins and Wallerstein, refers to "a network of labor and production processes whose end result is a finished commodity" (1986: 159). In building a commodity chain, one begins with the final production operation for a consumable good and moves sequentially backward until reaching the raw-materials inputs (Hopkins and Wallerstein, 1986: 160–163).

The complexity of commodity chains for the kinds of export-oriented manufacturing industries in countries like Argentina, Brazil, and Chile requires extending the model proposed by Hopkins and Wallerstein (1986). It is extremely important to include forward as well as backward linkages from the production stage in the commodity chain. In the example of the global leather-footwear industry, a full commodity chain spans the entire spectrum of activities in the world economy: from Argentine raw materials to Brazilian manufacturing and then to the critical area of marketing and distribution in the U.S. market.

The concept of GCCs helps clarify the interplay of local, national, and international dimensions of organizations, classes, and politics. It can also help explore and explain the social, political, and economic dynamics that shape this global division of labor. By using a Global Commodity Chains perspective, we ask how and why firms, industries, localities, and/or countries incorporate themselves into the world economy and what the social consequences of these patterns of integration will be. GCCs help capture new trends in worldwide economic organization, as well as their consequences on society. The models focus on the organization of production in global industries enables us to make assessments about how and where wealth is generated and accumulated in the world-economy.

A GCC analysis also allows us to estimate the relative strength and importance of each of the chain's segments and to assess the possible consequences for the organizations and individuals involved. In the case of the leather footwear chain, while links are interdependent, U.S. importers and distributors have held the initiative in determining the volume and timing of purchases. The critical link provided by Brazilian marketing intermediaries illustrates the utility of Global Commodity Chains in highlighting simultaneously domestic and global dimensions of social and economic organization.

The commodity chains approach provides a helpful taxonomic device to understand how export networks are organized. However, these models tend to focus on the descriptive analyses of static components of particular chains, providing a snapshot of one point in time but neglecting processes and change over time (Humphrey, 1995: 151).

Backward Linkages

Tanned leather is one of the key inputs in leather footwear production. How, when, and what kind of tanned leather becomes available are fundamental factors underlying competitive export patterns. The processed leather must be of a quality appropriate to the intended quality and price of the finished product. The quantity of the leather must be sufficient to make the number of shoes required in a particular purchase order. Finally, the leather must be delivered in time to meet the appropriate deadlines.

Leather is by far the most important raw material utilized in the manufacturing of Brazilian shoes, and it is also an important component in the manufacturing of soles. The share of all-leather upper shoes in Vale dos Sinos exports (where the vast majority of Brazilian exports originate) has increased substantially between 1980 and 1987, from about half of all shoes produced to about 65 percent. In 1980, about 70 percent of all shoes exported from Vale dos Sinos had all-leather or nearly all-leather uppers, and by 1987, the share had risen to about 80 percent. Leather is the most important raw material supply for Argentine and Brazilian producers, and its importance has been increasing (ACI, 1980, 1985).

Interviews with Brazilian footwear producers show that informal as well as formal linkages allow them to purchase Argentine leather, which is considered more prestigious and of higher quality than Brazilian leather (Klein, 1986). Brazilian footwear producers have been successful in developing input networks to secure the best quality of processed leather in appropriate delivery schedules.

Labor is also an additional key input in the shoe industry of Brazil. The industry remains characterized by labor-intensive production, particularly as compared to related activities such as leather production. Among the firms interviewed in a recent study of shoe exporters (henceforth, the UIIC [Uncertainty, Innovation, and International Competitiveness] study),[3] where the labor force

ranged from 262 to 2,200 workers, productivity levels showed no clear corre-
lation with either the overall size or magnitude of sales of each particular enterprise. The largest firm, for example, had levels of productivity that placed it
among the overall average of the sample, while one of the smallest firms (with
320 workers) had the second highest level of productivity. Without exception,
all the firms reported no problems in securing a steady supply of labor and
characterized their overall labor relations as stable.

Forward Linkages

Shoe manufacturers in Brazil have organized production primarily in terms
of their export market. Among the seven enterprises interviewed in the UIIC
study, for example, all except one derived over 90 percent of sales from the
export market (and the remaining enterprise derived 73 percent of sales from
exports). Such a pattern differs significantly from the industry's Argentine coun-
terpart, where the export market constitutes, at best, a supplemental source of
demand for firms that are primarily oriented toward their domestic market. Shoe
producers in Brazil are also overwhelmingly directed toward the North American
market. In the UIIC sample, for example, six of the seven producers cited the
United States as their principal market (in most cases, capturing over 70 percent
of overall exports), and the remaining producer cited Canada as the principal
market (capturing 40 percent of overall exports). By contrast, only one of the
shoe producers interviewed in Argentina had made any inroads into the North
American market.

The differences between Brazil and Argentina are partially explained by the
relative importance of their domestic markets. In the case of Argentina, domestic
demand continues to constitute the principal market for shoe producers. In the
case of Brazil, on the other hand, local market opportunities are characterized
by greater constraints and export markets often provide the only available avenue to greater volumes of sales. These differences are reflected in the UIIC
interviews: five of the seven Brazilian firms in the study cited the instability of
the domestic market or the "low purchasing power of Brazilians" as the principal reason for moving into export markets, while none of their counterparts
in Argentina mentioned the characteristics of the domestic market as an incentive
for promoting exports.

The success of Brazilian footwear manufacturers is also explained by their
ability to rely on an intermediary "corps" of individuals who act as linkages
between the local producers and consumer markets in the United States and
other destination markets. The seven Brazilian shoe producers interviewed in
the UIIC study all identified these *intermediarios* ("intermediaries") or "export
agents" as the primary channel used to gain access to markets in the United
States and Europe.

These agents fulfill several key roles in the exporting sequence of the footwear
industry in Brazil. Formally, they act as trading intermediaries between local

domestic producers and foreign buyers, but in practice, they also cover a wide range of additional activities. For example, the agents act as product consultants; they study and follow fashion trends in Paris, Milan, New York, and other leading centers and then design shoes that meet changing consumer trends (Schuster, 1985). In a personal interview, an exporting agent in Brazil described his functions as including shoe design, cost estimation, production-sequence programming, leather quality control, raw-materials procurement, and economic and financial advice (Pochintesta, 1988).

The crucial role of intermediary agents is reflected in their symbiotic relationship with the tight-knit community of producers, particularly in the Brazilian Vale dos Sinos area. Comments made during the interviews in the UIIC study suggest that personal *trust* is a crucial component of the transactions conducted between local producers and export agents.

It is interesting to note differences between the cases of Brazil and Argentina. In Argentina, where shoe producers have been much less successful in capturing niches in the world market, the export agents that characterize the case of Brazil are altogether absent. In the UIIC study, the strategies used by four producers of shoes and related products in Argentina to seek markets abroad involved arrangements developed by either personal visits by firm owners to foreign stores or the use of appointed representatives abroad. A similar pattern characterized the strategies used by the Argentine leather exporters interviewed in the UIIC study. In these cases, the absence of formal channels of commercialization appears to be an important variable in explaining the limited access of Argentine producers to foreign markets.

The importance of analyzing the role of export agents lies in the fact that it allows us to link the success of exporters in Brazil to the changes experienced by the industry in the United States through a single organizational variable. That is, the two sets of observations—the success of exporters in Brazil and the decline of the industry in the United States—are equally central to the transformations experienced by this industry on a world-economic scale. Furthermore, both processes often arise out of a single shift in organizational strategy, as when corporations in the United States closed local production and replaced it with new contractual relations developed through agents abroad.

THE 1990s: GLOBAL COMPETITION, DEMISE OF THE DEVELOPMENTAL STATE AND THE LIMITS OF COMMUNITARIANISM

In the late 1980s and early 1990s, there have been three key developments in the global production of footwear. First, the People's Republic of China (PRC) has redrawn the map of the international division of labor in the production of light manufactures. The PRC now accounts for about half the value of all shoe exports to the United States (see Table 3.1).

The second major development of the 1990s is intrinsically related. Footwear firms have relocated from Taiwan and Korea to peripheral locations. Firms from Taiwan have relocated primarily to sites in the People's Republic of China, and Korean firms have relocated primarily to Indonesian sites. Part of the reason for this relocation is the increase in labor mobilization that accompanied the reinstitution of democratic regimes in Taiwan and South Korea. In addition, the pool of available labor for light manufacturing factories shrunk as these countries' economies became more diversified and the proportion of service activities increased. In contrast, the authoritarian regimes of Indonesia and the PRC have provided the appropriate combination of a low-paid workforce, incentives in the form of infrastructure and fiscal concessions, and the means for social control.[4]

A third characteristic that emerges from Table 3.1 is that in each of the first two waves of footwear exports, one country has maintained an important share of the market. Italian footwear firms continued to export a significant value of shoes through the 1980s. In the second wave of major exporters, the share of Korean and Taiwanese-made shoes dropped precipitously, but Brazil has not followed the trajectory of its semiperipheral counterparts. Instead, the data shows that Brazil has maintained its share of exports to the U.S. market.

The Demise of the Developmental State

The central question facing the Brazilian footwear industry is whether resources and actions can be mobilized to achieve "systemic competitiveness" (Meyer-Stamer, 1995: 7–8). Beyond labor cost advantages, supporting environments need to be consolidated and new patterns of state-firm relationships must be created. In 1994, the Brazilian state set in motion a set of programs designed to fundamentally transform the economic system and the trade regime. The basic cornerstone of these programs has been control over the inflation rate. Tight monetary policies, privatization of state-owned enterprises, and the influx of foreign capital have combined to substantially appreciate the domestic currency.

Domestic currency appreciation has two immediate consequences: first, it automatically renders locally produced goods more expensive in world markets (and, hence, less competitive) and second, it renders imported goods cheaper. The reduction in cost of the imported goods has two important consequences for industrial production and industrial exports: on the one hand, it can help industrial firms renovate or expand their capital goods and equipment, while on the other, it encourages imports of consumer goods. In other words, firms have the strategic option of either strengthening or weakening their competitiveness in global markets.

In terms of state incentives for exports, de Castro (1994) gave an excellent overview of what he calls the "Demise of State-Led Development" in Brazil (for a broader and compelling assessment of the dynamics involved in the social, economic and political outcomes of neoliberal reforms, see Smith, Acuña, and Gamarra, 1994). Over the past few years, there has been a gradual retrenchment of state expenditures on items like the promotion of manufactured exports (including the dissolution of CACEX). Many of the most important fiscal and financial incentives that gave that industry a boost in the late 1970s and early 1980s had been either phased out gradually or been subject to policy-originated fluctuations through the 1980s. Brazil's balance of trade has deteriorated in the mid-1990s. Between 1989 and 1993, Brazil's exports grew by $4.4 billion, but its imports grew by $7.4 billion (Brazil Country Report, 1994: 1–5).

The Limits of Communitarianism

The effect of competition from Asia and the loss of governmental incentives on the Brazilian footwear industry have been twofold. Some firms have found locations with relatively inexpensive labor and fewer labor organizations in the hinterland within the Brazilian borders. In the industry as a whole, there has been a process of atomization between firms able to compete successfully under these new conditions and those that have been unable to adjust.

Data from the 1980s already showed a pattern of firm relocation. In particular, the two most important municipalities in the area show a declining share of total Vale dos Sinos exports. Between 1976 and 1987, the share of exports originating in the municipality of Novo Hamburgo declined by 40 percent, while in the same period, the share of Campo Bom declined by about 25 percent. On the other hand, there was a cluster of four municipalities—mostly small—that noticeably increased their share of Vale dos Sinos exports. Sapiranga increased its share, between 1976 and 1987, by about 50 percent. The other three municipalities—Igrejinha, Dois Irmaos, and Ivoti—increased their share from a combined total of 5.3 percent to 15.5 percent—an increase of 300 percent. The relative increases and decreases in the two clusters are fairly consistent over time but became more accentuated throughout the 1980s.

This data suggests that these two clusters of municipalities reproduce, *within a single industrial district*, patterns of sequential change from manufacturing to service activities. Newer, less urbanized municipalities with lower labor costs become more industrialized, while older, more developed municipalities come to specialize in services. In the words of one Brazilian businessman, "Novo Hamburgo has become the New York of Vale dos Sinos" (Korzeniewicz, 1990: 125).

The Brazilian footwear industry is facing some of the constraints and challenges that the Italian footwear industry confronted in the 1970s. Faced with competition from lower wage sites in Brazil and Asia, producers strengthened their advantages in the areas of image, fashion content, and design, upgrading the average unit-value of their shoes (Rabellotti, 1995: 31). In Brazil, some of the larger firms are trying to modify their marketing in order to diversify both export destinations and distribution and retail patterns (Schmitz, 1995: 15). The central question facing the Brazilian footwear industry is whether resources and actions can be mobilized to achieve "systemic competitiveness" (Meyer-Stamer, 1995: 7–8).

While a number of small and medium producers are expected to downsize or close down in the near future, "a small handful of factories, well-financed and well-administered, have reinvested profits for decades and have thrived and grown. These factories will continue their path of perfecting their product, technology, skills and efficiency, with their average price climbing, to replace those surviving Italian factories in a specific quality level" (Geller, 1995: 2). Additionally, faced with changing trends in demand and foreign competition, firms may either attempt to move into different niches or to redefine their position within their commodity chain (Humphrey, 1995: 158).

During the 1970s and most of the 1980s, the cohesiveness of trade associations in the Brazilian footwear industry played a major role in the success of exports. However, in the course of interviews conducted in 1992, Brazilian shoe manufacturers reported almost unanimously that their entrepreneurial environment was characterized by a combination of confrontational and cooperative elements. One firm owner remarked that "our system is confrontational. We have a system of agents that buy from the cheaper supplier. Each time, Americans are getting lower and lower prices." According to another, "[S]mall firms are left aside when the most important decisions get made." Another explained: "Abicalcados [the Brazilian Association of the Footwear Industry] does not help us. It's only for an elite. They don't help with cancelled orders. . . . [T]he weak point in the system is the factory, but they don't help with the relationship between factories and buyers. I pay my dues, but what they talk about has nothing to do with me" (UIIC study).

CONCLUSION

Scholars in the areas of social and economic development have increasingly turned their attention to the role of external linkages (such as manufactured exports) in shaping local, regional, and national patterns of growth. This chapter described the success of Brazilian footwear in global markets during the 1970s and 1980s and the competitive challenges that have surfaced in the 1990s. It focused on three main explanations. First, the constitution of industrial districts based on cooperative and communitarian action facilitated effective and expedient economic transactions. However, these sets of relationships have become strained as firms atomize in the face of increased competition. Second, the Brazilian state's policies of export promotion through fiscal incentives and management of the exchange rate provided a stable macroeconomic environment conducive to trade transactions. However, by the mid-1990s, developmental policies and resources have become drastically curtailed in the context of major economic reforms, which also resulted in the appreciation of the domestic currency. Finally, the consolidation of commodity chains that linked production with backward and forward linkages played a major role in the success of the Brazilian footwear industry.

This chapter raised theoretical and conceptual issues that suggest venues for future research. Taxonomically, I highlighted the importance of integrating macro- and micro-levels of analysis by linking communities, state policies, and the global environment. The use of a commodity chains approach is particularly helpful in mapping out the geography and organization of transnational activities. For example, the focus on export agents as a component of forward linkages helps shed light on both the access of Brazilian manufacturers to global markets and the transformation of American footwear producers into importers and distributors.

Perhaps the most germane and promising questions, however, arise out of the dynamic changes that these global linkages and structures undergo over time. The rise of the People's Republic of China as a major exporter of footwear directs our attention to geographical cycles of competitiveness. The decline of the Brazilian state's policies of export promotion suggests that the relationship between state and industrialization in Latin America has changed drastically and needs to be analytically redefined. Last, but not least, recent data for the Vale Dos Sinos area show patterns of industry consolidation, firm relocation, product upgrading, and transition to service activities. These patterns indicate that semiperipheral, "newly industrializing" regions and countries can replicate, to some extent, the cycles of industrial growth, maturation, and decline typically associated with developed countries. Assessing and measuring these changes, their consequences, and the social and organizational responses that follow should prove to be a very valuable contribution to our understanding of development.

NOTES

1. Between 1988 and 1992, however, the consumption of imported footwear in the United States remained stagnant. It again grew in 1993 and 1994, but at a much slower pace compared with the 1980s.

2. By contrast, state policies in Argentina were characterized by considerable shifts over the past two decades.

3. This study is composed of 27 interviews with managers of firms associated with the shoe-exporting business in Brazil and Argentina.

4. While Taiwan and South Korea contend with a relatively confined geographical setting, Brazilian companies continue to expand within the national territory. In recent months, firms have relocated as far as northeast Brazil to take advantage of lower labor costs and concessions by local state and city governments (Geller, 1995: 3).

REFERENCES

Associação Comercial e Industrial do Novo Hamburgo (ACI/NH). 1980, 1985, 1989. [census data.] Novo Hamburgo, Brazil: Associação Comercial e Industrial do Novo Hamburgo.

Baer, Werner, and Malcolm Gillis, eds. 1983. *Export Diversification and the New Protectionism*. Champaign: University of Illinois Press.

Baldinelli, Elvio. 1990. *Exportar, el Camino de los Paises que Crecen*. Buenos Aires: Fundacion de Investigaciones Economicas Latinoamericanas.

Baumann Neves, Renato. 1985. *Exportacoes e Crescimento Industrial do Brasil*. Rio de Janeiro: Instituto de Planejamento Economica e Social.

Brown, Ken. 1994. "Having Left Campus for the Arena, Winner in Brazil Shifts to Right." *New York Times*, November 20, 1994, sec. 4.

Capecchi, Vittorio. 1989. "The Informal Economy and the Development of Flexible Specialization in Emilia-Romagna." In *The Informal Economy*, ed. Alejandro Portes, Manuel Castells, and Lauren Benton, pp. 189–215. Baltimore: Johns Hopkins University Press.

Cardoso, Fernando Henrique. 1972. *Ideologias de la Burguesia Industrial en Sociedades Dependientes (Argentina y Brazil)*. Mexico: Siglo XXI editores.

Cardoso, Fernando Henrique, and Enzo Faletto. 1979. *Dependency & Development in Latin America*. Berkeley: University of California Press.

Centro Tecnologico do Couro, Calçados e Afins (CTCCA). 1983. *Anuario da Industria Nacional do Couro, Calçados, e Afins*. Novo Hamburgo, Brazil: CTCCA.

Comision Economica para America Latina y el Caribe (CEPAL). 1989. *Proceso de Industrializacion y Dinamica Exportadora: Las Experiencias de las Industrias Aceitera y Siderurgica en la Argentina*. Buenos Aires: CEPAL.

———. 1990. *Changing Production Patterns with Social Equity*. Santiago: CEPAL.

———. 1991. *Los Canales de Comercializacion y la Competitividad de las Exportaciones Latinoamericanas*. Santiago: CEPAL.

Cummings, Bruce. 1987. "The Origins and Development of the Northeast Asian Political Economy: Industrial Sectors, Product Cycles, and Political Consequences." In *The Political Economy of the New Asian Industrialism*, ed. Frederic Deyo, pp. 44–83. Ithaca, NY: Cornell University Press.

de Castro, Antonio Barros. 1994. "Renegade Development: Rise and Demise of State-Led Development in Brazil." In *Democracy, Markets, and Structural Reform in Latin America*, ed. William Smith, Carlos Acuña, and Eduardo A. Gamarra, pp. 183–209. Miami, FL: Transaction Publishers.

de Paula Pinto, Mauricio Barata. 1983. *Exportaçoes Brasileiras de Manufacturados: Crescimento e Mudanca de Estrutura*. São Paulo: Instituto de Pesquisas Economicas.

Economist Intelligence Unit. 1994. *Brazil: Country Report 1994*. London: The Economist.

Evans Peter. 1987. "Class, State, and Dependence in East Asia: Lessons for Latin Americanists." In *The Political Economy of the New Asian Industrialism*, pp. 203–226. Ithaca, NY: Cornell University Press.

Evans, Peter, and John Stephens. 1988. "Development and the World Economy." In *Handbook of Sociology*, ed. Neil Smelser, pp. 739–773. Beverly Hills, CA: Sage.

Fishlow, Albert. 1989. "Latin American Failure against the Background of Asian Success." *Annals* 505 (September): 117–128.

"Footwear." 1989. Fairchild Factfile. New York: Fairchild Publications, Market Division.

Footwear Industries of America (FIA). 1990. *Current Highlights*. Washington, DC: FIA.

Geller, Lawrence, President of Celerity-Comercio International Ltda., Novo Hamburgo, Brazil. 1995. Personal interview via fax.

Gereffi, Gary, and Miguel Korzeniewicz. 1990. "Commodity Chains and Footwear Exports in the Semiperiphery." In *Semiperipheral States in the World Economy*, ed. William Martin, pp. 45–68. Westport, CT: Greenwood Press.

Gereffi, Gary, and Donald Wyman, eds. 1990. *Manufacturing Miracles: Paths of Industrialization in Latin America and East Asia.* Princeton, NJ: Princeton University Press.

Goldfrank, Walter. 1989. "Harvesting Counterrevolution: Agricultural Exports in Pinochet's Chile." In *Revolution in the World-System*, ed. Terry Boswell, pp. 189–198. Westport, CT: Greenwood Press.

———. 1990. "State, Market and Agriculture in Pinochet's Chile." *Semiperipheral States in the World-Economy*, ed. William Martin, pp. 69–77. Westport, CT: Greenwood Press.

———. 1994. "Fresh Demand: The Consumption of Chilean Produce in the United States." In *Commodity Chains and Global Capitalism*, ed. Gary Gereffi and Miguel Korzeniewicz, pp. 267–279. Westport, CT: Greenwood Press.

Grosfoguel, Ramón. 1995. "From Cepalismo to Neoliberalism: A World-System Approach to Conceptual Shifts in Latin America." Manuscript presented at the Political Economy of the World-System XIX Annual Conference: Latin America in the World-Economy, University of Miami, April 20–22.

Haggard, Stephan. 1989. "The East Asian NICs in Comparative Perspective." *Annals* 505 (September): 129–141.

Hearn, Frank. 1988. "Part Three: Beyond the Management Model of Industrial Organization." In *The Transformation of Industrial Organization*, ed. Frank Hern. Belmont, CA: Wadsworth Publishing Company, pp. 193–204.

Hopkins, Terence K, and Immanuel Wallerstein. 1986. "Commodity Chains in the World-Economy prior to 1800." *Review* 10, 1: 157–170.

Humphrey, J. 1995. "Industrial Reorganization in Developing Countries: From Models to Trajectories." *World Development* 23, 1: 149–162.

Johnson, Chalmers. 1982. *MITI and the Japanese Miracle.* Stanford, CA: Stanford University Press.

Klein, Enio, Director of the Technologicial Center for Leather and Footwear (CTCCA). Novo, Hamburgo, Brazil. 1986. Personal interview.

Korzeniewicz, Miguel. 1990. "The Social Foundations of International Competitiveness: Footwear Exports in Argentina and Brazil." Ph.D. diss., Department of Sociology, Duke University, Durham, NC.

Korzeniewicz, Roberto P., Walter Goldfrank, and Miguel E. Korzeniewicz. 1995. "Vines and Wines in the World-Economy." In *Food and Agrarian Orders in the World-Economy*, ed. Philip McMichael, pp. 113–138. Westport, CT: Greenwood Press.

Krueger, Anne. 1985. "The Experience and Lessons of Asia's Super Exporters." In *Export Oriented Development Strategies*, ed. Vittorio Corbo, Anne Krueger, and F. Ossa, pp. 187–212. Boulder, CO: Westview Press.

Lazerson, Mark. 1988. "Organizational Growth of Small Firms: An Outcome of Markets and Hierarchies." *American Sociological Review* 53, 3 (June): 330–342.

Lee, Naeyoung, and Jeffrey Cason. 1994. "Automobile Commodity Chains in the NICs: A Comparison of South Korea, Mexico, and Brazil." In *Commodity Chains and*

Global Capitalism, ed. Gary Gereffi and Miguel Korzeniewicz, pp. 223–244. Westport, CT: Greenwood Press.

Lim, Youngil. 1981. *Government Policy and Private Enterprise: Korean Experience in Industrialization*. Berkeley: University of California Press.

Luebke, Frederick C. 1987. *Germans in Brazil*. Baton Rouge: Louisiana State University Press.

Martins, Luciano. 1985. *Estado Capitalista e Burocracia do Brasil Pos-64*. Rio de Janeiro: Paz e Terra.

Meyer-Stamer, Joerg. 1995. "Governance in the Post-Import Substitution Era: Perspectives for New Approaches to Support Industrial Competitiveness in Brazil." Unpublished manuscript.

Mutti, John H. 1980. *Output and Employment in a "Trade Sensitive" Sector: Adjustment in the U.S. Footwear Industry*. Washington, DC: World Bank.

Olson, Mancur. 1987. "Economic Nationalism and Economic Progress." *World Economy* 10, 3: 240–261.

Pfeffer, Jeffrey. 1987. "Bringing the Environment Back In: The Social Context of Business Strategy." In *The Competitive Challenge: Strategies for Industrial Innovation and Renewal*, ed. David J. Teece, pp. 119–135. Cambridge, MA: Ballinger.

Piore, Michael J., and Charles F. Sabel. 1984. "The Second Industrial Divide." New York: Basic Books.

Pochintesta, Alberto, President of STEPS, Inc. 1988. Personal interview, Ivoti, Rio Grande do Sul, Brazil, March 13.

Rabellotti, Roberta. 1995. "Is There an 'Industrial District Model'? Footwear Districts in Italy and Mexico Compared." *World Development* 23, 1: 29–41.

Rubinson, Richard, and Deborah Holzman. 1982. "Comparative Dependence and Economic Development." In *Comparative Sociological Research in the 1960s and 1970s*, ed. J. Michael Armer and Robert Marsh, pp. 86–101. Leiden, The Netherlands: E. J. Brill.

Schmitz, Hubert. 1995. "Small Shoemakers and Fordist Giants: Tale of a Supercluster." *World Development* 23, 1: 9–28.

Schuster, Lynda. 1985. "Brazil Captures a Big Share of the U.S. Shoe Market." *Wall Street Journal*, August 27.

Schwartz, Hugh H. 1991. *Supply and Marketing Constraints on Latin American Manufacturing Exports*. Washington, D.C.: Interamerican Development Bank.

Scott, W. Richard. 1983. "The Organization of Environments: Network, Cultural and Historical Elements." In *Organizational Environments: Ritual and Rationality*, ed. John W. Meyer and W. Richard Scott, pp. 155–175. Beverly Hills, CA: Sage.

Smith, William L., Carlos H. Acuña, and Eduardo A. Gamarra, eds. 1994. *Latin American Political Economy in the Age of Neoliberal Reform*. New Brunswick, NJ: Transaction Publishers.

Starr, Martin K. 1988. *Global Competitiveness: Getting the U.S. Back on Track*. New York: W. W Norton.

Tavares de Oliveira, Carlos. 1987. *Exportaçao: O Modelo Ideal*. Rio de Janeiro, RJ, Brazil: Editors de Fundacao Getulio Vargas.

Tecnicouro. 1987. "Brasilestá Começando a Perder Mercado nos Sapatos Baratos." *Tecnicouro* (Brazil) 9 (March-April).

U.S. Department of Commerce. Various years–a. *U.S. Foreign Trade Highlights*. Washington, DC: Bureau of the Census.

————. Various years–b. *U.S. General Imports.* Washington, DC: Bureau of the Census.

————. Various years–c. *U.S. Industrial Outlook.* Washington, DC: Bureau of the Census.

————. Various years–d. *Nonrubber Footwear Quarterly Statistical Report.* Washington, DC: Bureau of the Census.

Whitehead, Laurence. 1989. "Tigers in Latin America." *The Annals of the American Academy of Political and Social Science.* 505 (September): 142–151

Wilson, Suzanne, and Maria Zambrano. 1994. "Cocaine, Commodity Chains, and Drug Politics: A Transnational Approach." In *Commodity Chains and Global Capitalism,* ed. Gary Gereffi and Miguel Korzeniewicz, pp. 281–296. Westport, CT: Greenwood Press.

4

Small Firms, Social Capital, and Global Commodity Chains: Some Lessons from the Tex-Mex Border in the Era of Free Trade

David Spener

The United States–Mexico border is a unique geographical zone of articulation between a dominant state in the capitalist core and a subaltern state in the traditional periphery of the world-system.[1] Social, cultural, economic, and political relations—indeed practically the entirety of social life in the region—are starkly colored by the international division of labor that is enforced by the militarized political boundary between Mexico and the United States. The last few years have been an especially interesting conjuncture for studying the border region as Mexico, under the administrations of Miguel de la Madrid and Carlos Salinas, attempted to move from the periphery and into the semiperiphery of the world-economy, becoming what the current U.S. administration deemed one of the world's major "emerging markets." During this period, the border region has received a great deal of attention in the research literature on globalization in capitalist development. Most of the effort has gone into studying the Border Industrialization (*maquiladora*) Program, and important insights have been gained for the export-oriented industrialization of Latin America as a whole. Much less attention has been paid, however, to the role played by small- and medium-scale enterprises in the region, which employ half or more of the private sector working population on both sides of the international border.

In this chapter, I relate the effects that Mexico's unilateral trade liberalization of the late 1980s and early 1990s had on entrepreneurs operating small businesses in the Texas portion of the U.S.-Mexico border region and explain how these entrepreneurs—most of whom were of Mexican ancestry—responded by using the social and cultural resources at their disposal.[2] The analysis will: (1) describe how Texas border entrepreneurs helped, not only U.S., but also Asian and European manufacturers to extend commodity chains into Mexico in the period prior to that country's trade opening in a limited, informal way; (2) how, subsequent to the trade opening, they played a crucial role in the rapid elaboration of more complete distribution networks for these goods in Mexico; and (3) how the same social and cultural resources that served Texas border entrepreneurs well in the initial period of Mexican liberalization soon proved inadequate to defend their traditional role as brokers of binational trading relationships.

There are several senses in which the border entrepreneurs discussed in this chapter occupied what Wright (1985) has referred to as a "contradictory class location." First, they were owners or managers of businesses, and hence, generally bourgeois in their outlook, yet in most cases they had only limited capital and labor at their disposal. They thus found themselves in an extremely vulnerable position relative to larger-scale enterprises, which had a much greater capacity to dominate the markets served by both. Second, most of the border entrepreneurs, as either Mexican-Americans or Mexican immigrants, were members of a U.S. minority group and binational diaspora that had suffered a long history of discrimination and subordination at the hands of the dominant Anglo majority in the United States. At the same time, they had been treated with great ambivalence by the Mexican ruling elites as well. Thus, their perspectives on the structure of U.S. society and their opportunities within it, as well as toward the Mexican state and society, were different than those of Anglo businesspeople in the United States and Mexican businesspeople across the border. Third, unlike many large U.S. manufacturers, most entrepreneurs in the Texas border region viewed Mexico mostly as a geographically accessible, coethnic market to be sold to, and not as a low-wage production site to either exploit or from which to fear competition. Amid these contradictions, the business organizations in which border entrepreneurs participated became strong advocates of the North American Free Trade Agreement (NAFTA). The agreement was viewed as beneficial for the Mexican consumers and firms who were their own customers, and they hoped it would strengthen the binational brokering role they had already been playing within the limits imposed by the restrictive trade regime that was in place prior to NAFTA.

By looking at the particular conjunctural situation of Texas border entrepreneurs in the period leading up to NAFTA, I also attempt to shed some theoretical light on the participation in general of small-scale retail/wholesale firms in global commodity chains. Gereffi, Korzeniewicz, and Korzeniewicz (1994) have described how in many industries it is not multinational manufacturers who direct the market in goods, but rather global merchandisers who organize, not only the promotion and distribution of goods sold under their auspices, but also their production through a system of flexible subcontracting. What remains undertheorized in this formulation are many of the forward commercial linkages of not only producer-driven, but also buyer-driven commodity chains. It is frequently forgotten that it is not always the manufacturer or global merchandiser who organizes the local distribution of globally traded products, but rather a plethora of small firms whose detailed knowledge of local markets is drawn

from the many webs of socioentrepreneurial relationships in which their personnel are enmeshed. As Sayer and Walker (1992) and others (Crook, Pakulski,
and Waters, 1992; Reich, 1991) have pointed out, small firms have traditionally
carried out vital commercial, distribution, and maintenance/repair services that
larger concerns cannot perform as profitably.

Moreover, these many small firms add considerable value to the final product
by delivering it to the buyer and servicing it thereafter in what analysts of the
post modern condition remind us is an increasingly fragmented global consumer
market (Harvey, 1989). The existence of these firms and the persons operating
them should not be assumed, nor should it be viewed as incidental to the overall
process of elaborating commodity chains. Large corporations playing directive
roles in global commodity chains do not simply conjure up these smaller firms;
instead, small firms actively seek to insert themselves in these global commodity
chains, and they do so for particular sets of reasons and with specific kinds of
resources at their disposal. Finally, how successfully small firms are able to
insert themselves or defend their existing positions in global commodity chains
has serious repercussions for the local communities in which they are located,
not only in terms of employment levels (since small firms are generally more
labor intensive than their larger-scale counterparts) but also in terms of the social
reproduction of the local (mostly petty) bourgeoisie. The experiences of Texas
border entrepreneurs provide an interesting case study of this process.

THE TEXAS BORDER REGION BEFORE MEXICAN TRADE
LIBERALIZATION

The urban areas of the border region of Texas have long been among the
poorest in the United States (Cárdenas, Chapa, and Burek, 1993; Maril, 1989;
Montejano, 1987; Valdez, 1993).[3] Geographically isolated from and economically marginal to the rest of the United States, the border region could be referred to as "Mexican" Texas as well, for the large majority of its nearly 3
million inhabitants are of Mexican ancestry (63 percent were Latinos, and 57
percent spoke Spanish at home in 1990).[4] Historically, the economies of the
cities in this region were dependent on farm production, ranching, mining, and
government employment (particularly the military), and in the case of El Paso,
garments and other light manufacturing (Institute for Mining and Materials Management, 1991). As the population in northern Mexico grew between 1960 and
1980, brought about in part by the Border Industrialization Program (the *maquiladora* program), Texas cities on the international line itself also increasingly
specialized in commerce and distribution services for production and consumption needs across the border (Corona Vásquez, 1990; Curtis, 1993; Savage and
Blankmeyer, 1990; Tamayo and Fernández, 1983). While the San Antonio metropolitan area is not normally thought of as a "border town" (it is located more
than 100 miles from the international line) the city serves as the economic and
cultural capital of the region, and it has especially strong historical and contem-

porary ties to Mexico (Arreola, 1987; Dunigan, 1992; Landolt, 1976; "Casa San Antonia," 1994). San Antonio also increasingly attracted Mexican shoppers, tourists, and immigrants during this period and, as the region's largest city, was a net exporter of services to the border towns in its "hinterland" (Geyer, 1990; Gilmer, 1990).

Even though the Texas border region's trading relationship with Mexico was of a limited nature during this period, its urban economies were still quite dependent on sales to Mexican nationals, many of whom resided in Mexican border cities immediately across the international line and regularly shopped on the U.S. side. When the Mexican peso crashed in 1982, the effect on business revenues and employment in the Texas border cities was devastating (Harrell and Fischer, 1985), leading two commentators to note that the "monetary and fiscal policies of the Mexican government have a greater impact on the border merchant than do the fiscal and monetary policies of the United States" (Savage and Blankmeyer, 1990: 76). By that time, the avenues for new, autonomous economic growth in the Texas border region were quite limited. Mechanization had eliminated much of the need for farm labor in South Texas (Maril, 1989; Montejano, 1987); moreover, the region's existing manufacturing base was small (14.3 percent of workers in 1980) and government employment was large (24.6 percent) relative to other major Texan urban centers. Opportunities for industrial expansion in the region were limited by competition with the Mexican *maquiladoras* for assembly operations (low wages) and by already established manufacturing in Dallas and Houston (which benefited from existing plant and equipment and better access to U.S. and world markets, as well as sources of finance). The region was not blessed with abundant natural resources, nor did it have a vast potential as a tourist attraction for residents of either the United States or Mexico. The low education levels and poverty of the border region's workers compared to those in Dallas and Houston also limited the region's internal market for services (see Table 4.1), since the growth of retail trade and other personal services depends on high disposable incomes on the part of a substantial part of the population. The history of anti-Mexican racism in Texas (Foley, 1988; Maril, 1989; Montejano, 1987), as well as nearly continuous cross-border migration by Mexican nationals, resulted in poverty and lack of education being especially concentrated among Mexican-Americans and Mexican immigrants in the region.

Given these conditions, trade in goods with Mexico was one of the few viable entrepreneurial niches for nonelite members of the border region's majority Mexican ancestry population. This was especially so to the extent that such trade could be built on social network and cultural connections with Mexico—Mexican *social capital*—that could be substituted for other kinds of capital (financial, physical, and human), which were in short supply in the community.[5] Indeed, physical proximity to the border with Mexico and Texas's social and cultural connections to Mexico were not only what defined the Texas border region as a *region*, but also constituted its principal economic *resource* in the

Table 4.1
Selected Characteristics of the Employed Population, Texas Border Region,
Dallas, and Houston, 1980

Border Region Urban Areas			
Group	Percent with college degree	Percent living in poverty	Mean annual income*
All persons	17.2	10.7	$13,138
White Anglo natives	29.5	3.9	$17,103
Latino natives**	9.8	12.4	$10,974
Latino immigrants	4.9	24.9	$9,336

Dallas			
Group	Percent with college degree	Percent living in poverty	Mean annual income*
All persons	23.1	4.4	$16,594
White Anglo natives	25.6	2.9	$17,853
Latino natives**	8.7	7.7	$12,571
Latino immigrants	7.0	12.0	$11,064

Houston			
Group	Percent with college degree	Percent living in poverty	Mean annual income*
All persons	24.5	4.6	$18,119
White Anglo natives	28.9	2.6	$21,886
Latino natives**	7.9	6.5	$13,923
Latino immigrants	8.6	11.4	$10,697

*For persons who worked at least 1,600 hours in 1979 (40 weeks times 40 hours per week).
**Nearly all Latinos in the border region of Texas are of Mexican origin; however, many Mexican-ancestry persons identify themselves simply as "Hispanic" on the census questionnaire.
Source: U.S. Bureau of the Census (1980), 5 Percent Public Use Microdata Sample.

capitalist world-system. The hundreds of *maquiladora* plants in Ciudad Juárez, for example, were located in the middle of the Chihuahuan desert, isolated from major population centers, ports, and transportation hubs, *only* because the border existed and functioned as a peculiar zone of articulation between the capitalist core and periphery and featured both physical proximity to the U.S. market and cheap Mexican labor. In addition, many of the El Paso economy's producer and distributive services—which were mostly controlled by the same multinational corporations that run *maquiladoras* themselves—were ancillary to the *maquiladora* industry immediately across the border. Similarly, the central business districts in Laredo and McAllen owed their existence to the border and the way in which it served to divide two quite distinct economic spaces, one featuring a wide variety of high-quality consumer products at low prices, and the other with fewer and less appealing products at higher prices. Unlike the case of *maquiladora*-based development, however, commerce in the form of brokering U.S. commodities into Mexico offered the Texas border's regional population at least some chance to establish its own, autonomous enterprises.

Research literature on the Mexican diaspora in the southwestern United States in general, and in Texas in particular, has shown that throughout this century, active transborder social networks have abounded, connecting both Mexican Americans and Mexican immigrants to persons and places immediately across the border in northern Mexico (Alegría, 1992; Arreola, 1993; Martínez, 1994; Portes and Bach, 1985). It has also documented a significant entrepreneurial tradition among Mexicans, in spite of the fact that the global *rates* of entrepreneurship for the Mexican-ancestry population have tended to be dramatically lower than for Anglos and other ethnic groups and immigrants in the region (Alvarez, 1990; Cárdenas, De la Garza, and Hansen, 1986; Chapa and Cárdenas, 1991; Torres, 1990). Given (1) their geographic location on the border; (2) the binational nature of the social, cultural, and linguistic resources at their disposal; and (3) the lack of other lucrative alternatives in the region, playing a brokering role for U.S. goods flowing into Mexico seemed almost a "natural" role for border entrepreneurs to assume. In fact, Latino entrepreneurs in the region in 1980 were especially concentrated in retail/wholesale trade (50 percent operated businesses in this sector), which was heavily dependent on sales to Mexican firms and consumers.

Before undertaking trade liberalization in the mid-1980s, Mexico's policy of protecting domestic industries substantially limited its imports of consumer goods and many intermediate goods from other countries.[6] Imports were limited through tariffs of up to 100 percent, extensive import-licensing requirements, the government subsidy of some industries, and a system of official reference prices (Lustig, 1992; Pastor and Wise, 1994; Ros, 1992; Ten Kate, 1992; United States International Trade Commission, 1990; Wright, 1971). Exporters from the United States, which provided up to 70 percent of Mexican imports (Lustig, 1992; Weintraub, 1990), bore the brunt of these restrictions, which were quite onerous. They were so onerous, in fact, that most smaller enterprises seeking to access the Mexican market *legally* found it nearly impossible to do so, given the costs involved (both in terms of paying the tariffs and the resources that had to be invested in obtaining the required permissions).

Nonetheless, many small businesses in Texas border cities, such as Laredo, McAllen, and El Paso, did "export" substantial quantities of goods to Mexico in the period before trade liberalization was undertaken. These exports occurred in a peculiar and informal way, however. Texas entrepreneurs would open formal retail and wholesale establishments and receive customers and clients from the Mexican side, who would return to Mexico with their purchases. Much of the merchandise entered Mexico without being taxed (or counted as imported value) because it was carried by private consumers, whose purchases fell under the duty-free limit ($50 per person for border residents, $300 per person for residents of the interior). Goods purchased by Mexican businesses were frequently smuggled back across the border in small quantities or allowed to enter without proper authorizations or tariffs by Mexican customs officials who had been bribed. A leading wholesaler whom I interviewed in El Paso described the business environment there before trade liberalization as "a field of dreams: build it and they will come."[7] An electrical parts salesman in Laredo put it this way:

People, when they can't get something in Mexico, normally they come to the border. And that's how we've been in the business for forty years! So they know that we can get whatever they need. . . . We've never taken care of how things get back into Mexico. The customers themselves would take care of it. The Mexican government had a lot of barriers. And more restrictions on imports. . . . Before you had to get government permits and pay so much for the permit that by the time you got it across it'd cost you 100 percent in duties! But also, in those days, people had ways to go, without having to go through the big thing, you know, go around. . . . They would get the things across. (personal interview, August 12, 1993)

Of course, some entrepreneurs on the Texas side also actively smuggled goods into Mexico themselves and made a handsome profit doing so; their more colorful exploits have been documented in the popular press (see Miller, 1981, for example).

MEXICAN TRADE LIBERALIZATION AND THE TEXAS BORDER BOOM, 1988–1994

Although Mexico's restrictive trade regime created some specific and fairly lucrative opportunities for a few Texas border entrepreneurs, there is little doubt that more Texas border entrepreneurs would have been exporting far greater quantities of goods into Mexico had trade restrictions not been in place. Following the onset of its debt crisis and the collapse of the peso in 1982, Mexico abandoned its import-substitution development model and became a party to the General Agreement on Tariffs and Trade (GATT) in 1986. By 1988, Mexico had implemented measures that brought it largely into compliance with GATT norms, and in so doing it effectively ushered in the era of (so-called) free trade with the United States several years before negotiations of a formal free-trade pact were undertaken (Lustig, 1992; Pastor and Wise, 1994; Ros, 1992; Ten Kate, 1992). The elimination of formal trade barriers and the peso's subsequent recovery provoked a sharp increase in imports. As demonstrated in Table 4.2,

Table 4.2
Mexican Imports, 1980–1994, in Millions of U.S. Dollars

	Dollar Amount	Percent Change
1980	18,895	
1981	23,950	26.8
1982	14,436	-23.6
1983	8,549	-54.8
1984	11,255	-40.4
1985	13,219	-30.0
1986	11,135	-41.1
1987	12,223	-35.3
1988	18,895	0.0
1989	23,411	23.9
1990	29,799	57.7
1991	38,100	101.6
1992	62,100	228.8
1993	65,400	246.0
1st Qtr. 1993	15,400	---
1st Qtr. 1994	18,100	---

*Excludes *maquiladora* inputs.
Sources: Ten Kate (1992); Banco de México (1994): 281, 564.

by 1990 Mexico's non-*maquiladora* imports were nearly 60 percent higher than they were in 1980, and by 1993 they were nearly three and a half times higher than before the trade opening. U.S. exports to Mexico rose from just under $20 billion in 1988 to over $40 billion by 1993, and Texas's share of U.S. exports to Mexico grew from 40 percent to over 50 percent, as shown in Table 4.3. Not only did over half of U.S. exports originate in Texas by 1993, but nearly 80 percent of the dollar value of all U.S. surface exports to Mexico were funneled through the Texas border region (Stolp, 1994). From 1990 to 1992, annual growth in payrolls (8.4 percent), the number of business establishments (3.2 percent), and private sector employees (3.6 percent) in the border region far exceeded that experienced by Dallas and Houston, as the border became the first region in Texas to emerge from the 1980s recession.[8] The business press did not miss this development, and frequent articles began to appear describing the trade "boom" on the Texas border (Dunigan, 1992; "Mexican-American Border," 1991; "Texan-Mexican Trade," 1992; Holt, 1991; Palmieri, 1994; Schusler, 1991a, 1991b).

BORDER ENTREPRENEURS' SUPPORT FOR NAFTA

As the Bush and Salinas administrations began to discuss the accession of Mexico to a North American Free Trade Area (NAFTA), the Texas border

Table 4.3
U.S. and Texan Exports to Mexico, in Millions of U.S. Dollars

Year	U.S. Exports to Mexico	Texas Exports to Mexico	Texas Percent of Total
1983	$8,755	NA	---
1984	11,461	NA	---
1985	13,084	NA	---
1986	11,925	NA	---
1987	14,045	$5,659	40.3
1988	19,853	8,241	41.5
1989	24,117	11,011	45.7
1990	27,468	13,288	48.4
1991	32,279	15,485	48.0
1992	39,605	18,839	47.6
1993	40,265	20,380	50.6

Note: NA = not applicable.
Sources: U.S. Department of Commerce (1994); Texas Department of Commerce (1988–1994); U.S. International Trade Commission (1990).

region appeared to be at the cutting edge of free trade, and border entrepreneurs became some of its most ardent exponents. An official of the El Paso Hispanic Chamber of Commerce described his organization's support of a free trade agreement in the following terms:

One of the reasons we're grateful for NAFTA is the fact that because of NAFTA, all of a sudden we're getting noticed here on the border! And a lot of people are turning their attention to the border! . . . Our local Hispanic businesses, if they're not already doing business in Mexico, if they don't have joint ventures, then they've got sales people going into Mexico. We speak the language, we understand the culture. The majority of the time we've got relatives that are still in Mexico that can help us out as far as the networking aspect. So we've got a leg up on the rest of the business, on the rest of US business, we've got a leg up on them because of all these contacts. And NAFTA will give us an advantage! (personal interview with Hispanic business leader in El Paso, April 1, 1993)

Border entrepreneurs and their business organizations were active participants in the political action committee, Texans for NAFTA, which was instrumental in garnering nearly unanimous support for the agreement among members of the Texan congressional delegation. The Texas Association of Mexican American Chambers of Commerce and the U.S. Hispanic Chamber of Commerce lobbied other Latino/Hispanic organizations to endorse passage of NAFTA by the U.S. Congress. In the end, the leadership of organizations such as the National Council of La Raza and the Mexican American Legal Defense Fund were convinced of the benefits of NAFTA to Latino businesses and offered their qualified support for the agreement. The Latino Summit on NAFTA, a political event that was carefully orchestrated to hush voices from within these same organizations who opposed NAFTA (and who were generally from other areas of the country where unionized industries were likely to be hurt by the agreement), articulated the following justification for its conveners' endorsement of NAFTA:

Under the proper conditions, NAFTA can foster greater economic growth, job creation, and ownership opportunities in the Latino community. . . . NAFTA may very well stimulate Latino entrepreneurship. Small business, including Latino-owned enterprises, which are incubators for product and technological innovation, created most of the new jobs in recent years, and offer wealth and ownership opportunities. . . . NAFTA offers an obvious potential for Latino business formation and growth and greater involvement and participation, including joint ventures, with the mainstream economy. (Latino Summit on NAFTA, 1993: 23)

San Antonio, as the border region's economic and cultural capital, played a particularly important role in the push for NAFTA. Its Hispanic Chamber of Commerce was the largest Hispanic chamber in the state of Texas and, together with the Greater San Antonio Chamber of Commerce, the San Antonio World Trade Association, and the city planning department, it aggressively promoted San Antonio as a major North American trade hub via frequent missions to and from Mexico. The San Antonio Hispanic Chamber also organized commercial expositions, invited Mexican businesses and government trade delegations to locate in the city, lobbied the federal government for passage of NAFTA, and pressed for the location of key NAFTA institutions—mainly, the North American Development Bank—in San Antonio. The city's position was also enhanced by the fact that the Mexican government hired former mayor and future U.S. cabinet secretary Henry Cisneros to be one of its principal NAFTA lobbyists in Washington, D.C., a move that reflected Mexico's growing recognition that enlisting the support of ethnic Mexicans in the United States could advance its own interests before the U.S. government (De la Garza and Vargas, 1992). It was no accident, therefore, that San Antonio was the place where Presidents Bush and Salinas and Prime Minister Mulroney of Canada signed the draft NAFTA agreement in 1991 and was subsequently chosen as the site for the new North American Development Bank following NAFTA's approval by Congress.

The congressional passage of NAFTA was in doubt right up to the time of the final vote in November 1993. The lobbying efforts of Texas border businesspeople who believed their interests would be advanced by the agreement were ultimately a key force in assuring its passage, a point that was strongly emphasized by U.S. Representative Esteban Torres (a California Democrat who was one of the principal players in the last round of congressional wrangling

on NAFTA) when he visited San Antonio shortly after the agreement was rat-
ified (Torres, 1994). It is worth noting, in this regard, that the majority of Mexicans in Texas live in the border region, as do the majority of the state's
Mexican-ancestry entrepreneurs. Moreover, while Mexican immigrants and
Mexican Americans are not dramatically more likely to be entrepreneurs in the
border region than elsewhere in Texas, their close proximity to Mexico has given
many of them a better understanding of the potential of its market (Spener,
1995).

With the establishment of the North American Free Trade Area and the rise
in the hemispheric status of Mexico to that of junior partner to the United
States, Mexican-ancestry entrepreneurs in the Texas border region seemed
poised to finally "cash in" on the advantages of their dual Mexican/American
identity. Their position seemed to be ideal in many ways. They were geographically closer to the major Mexican industrial centers and consumer markets than
anywhere else in the United States. They shared a common language and culture with the *madre patria* (mother country), and many maintained family and
social ties on the other side of the border. Many already had considerable experience selling to Mexican private consumers and businesses at a time when
relatively few other entrepreneurs in the United States did and they were a
known site of provisioning for many Mexican businesses in the interior. With
regard to free trade with Mexico, the Texas Mexican entrepreneurs seemed to
be at the cutting edge: they were the right people in the right place at the right
time.

TEXAS BORDER ENTREPRENEURS AND U.S. MEXICAN
ECONOMIC INTEGRATION

Survey results and in-depth interviews conducted in 1993 tend to confirm that
Texas border entrepreneurs built on their social networks and cultural knowledge
to extend their businesses' sales into Mexico. Logit regression results (Spener,
1995; Spener and Roberts, 1994) from a survey of small business operators in
El Paso, Laredo, and San Antonio showed that, net of other factors such as
branch of industry, businesses were much more likely to make sales calls in
Mexican territory if their operators had lived in Mexico as adults, had immediate
family currently living in Mexico, were first- or second-generation Mexican
immigrants, or spoke Spanish while growing up. In all three cities, Mexican-
American and Mexican-immigrant entrepreneurs cited the importance of their
social network connections in Mexico for conducting business in the major
cities, particularly in light of a Mexican way of doing business that they viewed
as both much more personalistic *and* more bureaucratic than in the United States.
In this regard, they concur with the anthropologists (Alvarez, 1990; Lomnitz,
1977; Vélez-Ibáñez, 1983, 1988) on the importance of *confianza* (trust) and
compadrazgo ("godfathering," a common male fictive-kinship relation) in economic relations among Mexicans, and with Lomnitz (1990) in particular on the

persistence of informal modes of exchange within bureaucratic systems in Mexico. One Laredo wholesaler, for example, described his attempts to set up a joint venture with a company in Mexico City by investing not only his financial capital, but his social capital as well:

That's where culture comes [in]to play. And as you might know, in Mexico, *el compadrazgo*—and that's everybody getting a little bit of everything. . . . Because the *compadre le va a pasar la mano* [your *compadre* will give you a hand]. . . . The other thing that they have to do is they have to trust us. And I think that being *mexicano* is an advantage. Because you know my family, I have an uncle and extended family that live in Mexico City. Well, what I want to do, is I'll call my uncle and his family to make sure that I get, you know, straight information. That I have access to some officials, you know, when it's needed. Because he's a *judicial*, so he belongs to the *judicial*, which is the federal police. He's a functionary there, and he should make it easier for us to to to get along. . . . He'll be able to tell us how to handle the bureaucracy and . . . it's *big*. And they'll all want something. And my uncle will tell me, you know, how to get to the right people. . . . He'll know which bureaucrats to talk to [to] get reports, to get reports, to get information, to get statistics, because those are very hard to come by in Mexico. You always need some contact to show you the way. . . . [Still] you're going to have to rely on a lot of friendships and other relationships to show you the ropes. (Personal interview)

With regard to the position of Mexican-ancestry entrepreneurs in the Texas border region in the period of "silent integration" (Ros, 1992) immediately preceding NAFTA, it is important to remember that the Mexican government's removal of formal restrictions on trade in the latter half of the 1980s did not by itself guarantee that new trade would proceed automatically (Alarcón González, 1994). Distribution networks for U.S. goods needed to be established in Mexico, and in many cases these networks had to be built using existing networks for Mexican goods of the same type. These existing networks, in turn, were often controlled by Mexican businesspeople who traditionally had obtained a variety of parts and supplies from merchants on the Texas border. By beginning to sell to the Mexican market via a "middleman" in the Texas border region, or by increasing the volume of Mexican sales passing through that border broker, U.S. manufacturers could meet rapidly expanding demand in Mexico without extending credit to Mexican firms of still unknown reliability and without either having to invest in establishing their own operations in Mexico or in recruiting an appropriate Mexican joint venture partner. Many U.S. companies had long known that their sales through distributorships or manufacturers' agents in the border region were much greater than the official sales territory being covered on the U.S. side could support. It was natural, therefore, for them to explore the Mexican market further by working through small companies that had already been serving Mexico for them. Similarly, the owners of many small Mexican firms knew that their most direct point of access to U.S. products was through Texas merchants. As a result, in the first years of the export boom to Mexico, thousands of traders flocked to Laredo, McAllen, and San Antonio, not only from Monterrey, but from as far away as Mexico City and Guadalajara, to supply the demand in Mexico for newly affordable consumer goods—a demand that was readily served by Texas entrepreneurs because of their unique geographical, cultural, and linguistic position. At the same time, the more forward-looking border entrepreneurs began to extend their own sales networks forward into the major Mexican cities, building on their existing networks of customers and other social or familial contacts across the border.

Although local entrepreneurs on the Tex-Mex border had pioneered the elaboration of many trans-frontier trade networks, by the eve of NAFTA's passage, their very success in doing so began to bring them significant new competition. First, major retail warehouses such as Wal-Mart, Sam's Warehouse, K-Mart, Best Buy, and Home Depot began to open mega-stores in border cities, mainly to serve the Mexican market. The low prices, large inventories, and high profile of such stores cut into the sales of smaller businesses, both wholesale and retail, as they had done elsewhere in the United States. In the huge parking lots of these stores in Laredo in the fall of 1992, one could see hundreds of cars with Nuevo León license plates, reflecting the extent to which Monterrey consumers and businesses stocked up on goods in Texas. Second, by 1993, many of these same companies had begun opening branches in Mexico, starting first in Monterrey and Mexico City but then fanning out rapidly to Guadalajara and many second-tier Mexican cities, such as San Luís Potosí, León, and Aguascalientes (for example, by the summer of 1994, Wal-Mart already had about 40 Mexican stores either in operation, under construction, or in the planning stages). While some Texas "middlemen" who served specialized market niches felt that this competition would not harm them, many others had already lost customers to the local branches of these mega-stores and worried about losing additional customers to the new stores opening in Mexico.

In addition to competition from discount chain stores, the take-off of the Mexican export market brought with it other threats to the position of Texas border traders. While the middleman role that these entrepreneurs played in the initial phases of the elaboration of distribution networks from the United States into Mexico may have been crucial, such a position was inherently precarious. The go-between who introduces two trading partners and mediates their relationship at the outset of commercial relations can soon become a costly "third wheel" in the transaction. Once U.S. manufacturers became convinced of the profitability and stability of the Mexican market, had workable distribution networks in place, and had established professional and personal contacts of their own in Mexico, their need for intermediaries on the border diminished. Indeed, one of the principal complaints of border middlemen was that they were being cut off by suppliers who decided either to contract with distributors in major Mexican cities or to open their own distributorships or factory outlets in Mexico. One angry Laredo businessman, who was a Mexican-American, put it this way:

Because if I buy from a company . . . and I was taking care of my customers and that company, I've built my sales for their product to this customer, and then all of a sudden they—a lot of companies are doing this, they jump me and go sell to the customer that I've built for them, without even asking me, "What are you going to do with Mexico? Can you do something better? Let's work together." They just jump me and go directly to my customers! And that's killing me after *I've* built the business! . . . A lot of companies are doing that, and we don't think it's fair. (Personal interview)

Efforts to cut out the middleman at the border were also initiated by Mexican businesses. Field interviews conducted with manufacturers and wholesalers in Mexico City, Guadalajara, and Monterrey in July and August 1994 revealed that even before trade liberalization was undertaken, the heads of small Mexican businesses frequently traveled to the United States to attend trade shows, visit suppliers, and vacation. They regularly received trade publications and company catalogues from the United States and, in spite of their often-weak English language skills and lack of familiarity with U.S. business practices, did not hesitate to make "cold calls" on U.S. suppliers in search of needed parts and equipment. When Mexican entrepreneurs were obliged to avail themselves of the services of a border wholesaler or manufacturer's representative, they often did so in the hopes that the relationship would be a temporary first step on the way to a direct relationship with a manufacturer.

In addition, a number of Mexican business operators whom I interviewed "confessed" to their own *malinchismo*; they maintained that they would rather deal with real *americanos* (i.e., Anglo businesspeople from the "real" United States, and not the border) than with Mexican businesspeople in Texas.[9] Their feelings stemmed in part from a desire to interact with the leadership of U.S. companies, whose headquarters were far from the border region, and in part from a general feeling that although they were more cold and ruthless, Anglos were also more reliable and trustworthy than Mexican businesspeople. Some of the Mexican businesspeople also reserved particular contempt and suspicion for Mexican-*American* entrepreneurs on the border, whom they regarded as unscrupulous in their business dealings with Mexico and who were, in their eyes, of doubtful cultural affinity. As one Mexico City manufacturer told me, *"Ni sabemos qué son, si son mexicanos o americanos u otra cosa, como les decimos: pochos."*[10]

These entrepreneurs also discounted the importance of Mexican cultural sensitivity on the part of U.S. businesspeople, noting that "business is business" and that they understood that the *americanos* had different customs than their own. Moreover, they said, they were looking to the United States principally to do business, not to make friends.[11] A few Texas businesspeople whom I interviewed in 1993 themselves acknowledged that their Mexican "cultural capital" (i.e., general knowledge of language, customs, and business practices) was of limited value in a free-trade environment on the border, although they did not mention enmity between Mexican citizens and Mexican-Americans as a reason for this:

When you get down to brass tacks, and you talk business and you talk free trade, and you talk free enterprise, I don't think that [culture] is going to matter a lot, basically. I mean, businessmen do business where it's more convenient to do business. . . . And the bottom line always is—yes, we've got the language, and we've capitalized on that—but I think they [Mexicans] are always looking for good business. This is a place where a Mexican can come in and it's the fastest crossing point, he'll save money on the transaction and then, of course, it helps that we speak Spanish. But if we didn't speak Spanish, he'd still save money and he'd still do it. . . . Because once you become global, once you're dealing in a global community, those guys from Mexico now are trained in Harvard. I mean they know our system better than we do! [Laughs.] So now those guys are looking for the best deals. They can speak English, or find people who speak English for them, and that kind of thing. I think it's part of progress. (Mexican-American official of a border business organization, personal interview)

Of course, I also interviewed other Mexican businesspeople who professed affection for Texas and their *paisanos* living there; my point here is simply that the Mexican cultural capital of Mexican-ancestry entrepreneurs based in Texas is not uniformly valued in Mexico itself. Furthermore, it is important to recognize that free trade does not only involve U.S. businesspeople learning about how Mexicans do business, but also involves Mexican businesspeople learning how gringos do business. In fact, the asymmetrical power relationship between the two countries suggests that Mexicans must learn gringo ways to a greater extent than Texans must learn Mexican ways.

Following the opening of the Mexican market, in addition to contending with larger, better-financed competitors with a greater "global reach," entrepreneurs in the Texas border region experienced a depreciation of the fungibility of their Mexican social capital. There were several reasons for this. First, the lifting of certain kinds of trade restrictions by the Mexican government reduced the need for special favors from Mexican officials in order to get goods into Mexico. Principal among these changes was the elimination of most import-licensing requirements, which formerly had required intensive politicking of the government trade ministry with little certainty of obtaining the license unless one had the needed inside contacts (Wright, 1971). The reduction of tariffs on goods going into Mexico, like the lifting of import-licensing requirements, lowered incentives for smuggling goods into Mexico and, in so doing, also had the effect of diminishing the importance of *confianza* between Texas border traders and their Mexican customers who conspired to move goods into Mexico without paying duties on them. Second, some real advances were made by the Salinas administration in its efforts to eliminate corruption and increase the transparency of trade-related regulations. Business operators on both sides of the border gave Salinas particular credit for cleaning up the Mexican customs service by firing corrupt agents en masse and replacing them with new, better-paid, and more professional personnel (see also Holt, 1991; MacDonald, 1993). The reorganization of the Mexican customs service did not necessarily make it easier to get goods into Mexico (the new agents quickly developed a reputation for being overly stringent in enforcing the remaining import regulations), but it did make it much more difficult either to bribe or trade favors with agents in order to clear customs. Third, the formal trade-promoting activities of state and federal governments and business associations on both sides of the border made it considerably easier for smaller firms without Mexican social capital to enter the Mexican market. These activities included not only workshops and seminars, but also frequent trade missions and exhibitions, the opening of trade offices by various Mexican states in San Antonio and by the state of Texas in Mexico City, and the development of match making on-line databases for prospective traders. While state programs are perhaps ultimately not a substitute for *confianza*, they could facilitate the establishment of cross-border business relationships in the first instance, and thus substitute for a border "middleman" in some cases.

None of the depreciation of the Mexican social capital of border businesses contradicts Granovetter's (1985) assertion that all economic relations are embedded in social contexts. It suggests, rather, that the forms of state regulation of economic activity constitute an important element of those contexts and that changes in state policy also alter the *social* contexts in which economic activities take place. Portes (1994a, 1994b), Roberts (1978), and Lomnitz (1990) have all noted that state regulation and informal economic activity define one another in a dialectical relationship. As Portes put it:

By definition, informal economic activities bypass existing laws and the regulatory agencies of the state. It follows therefore that the more pervasive the enforcement of state rules and the greater the penalties for violation, the more socially embedded must informal transactions be. This is so because their success in highly repressive situations depends not only on preventing malfeasance by partners but in avoiding detection by the authorities. Secrecy in these situations demands a high level of mutual trust and the only way this can be created is through the existence of social networks. (1994b: 431)

In the context of trade liberalization on the border, the converse also seems to hold true: to the extent that state rules are lifted or made less stringent, the demand for the kinds of social network connections that permitted the circumvention of the old trade barriers is reduced. Other things being equal, the kind of social capital that is more fungible under conditions of relatively unrestricted trade has rather less to do with having useful personal contacts in the right places and rather more with one's professional reputation for honesty and reliability, a company's track record in the market, and the quality of the product being sold. This latter kind of social capital may be possessed (and put to good use in a free-trade environment) by the personnel of large, multinational corporations as well as by local entrepreneurs whose operations are of a much smaller scale.

We must also remember that the Texas border entrepreneurs' reliance on trans-border social capital to extend commodity chains from the United States into Mexico was as much a strategy to compensate for their lack of other kinds of capital—human, physical, and financial—as it was a strategy that built on their natural strengths. Moreover, while they are not perfect substitutes, different forms of capital may be substituted for one another in production such that an economic actor with greater endowments of human, physical, and financial capital may be able to get by with a smaller endowment of social capital. The implication of this formulation is that border entrepreneurs who are richly endowed with Mexican social capital can be outcompeted by rivals who are better trained, equipped, and financed. Once these competitors for the Mexican market appeared on the scene—essentially, as soon as the Texas border-region entrepreneurs had demonstrated the profitability of that market—the comparative advantages of the border entrepreneurs diminished considerably.

Although competitors for the Mexican market came from all over the United States, it seemed that the border entrepreneurs' chief competition came from Texas's two largest metropolitan centers, Dallas–Fort Worth and Houston. While trade liberalization and improved transportation and communications do, in principle, make borders and physical location less important to economic success, Texas's capture of the lion's share of U.S. exports to Mexico demonstrates nonetheless the continued advantages of physical proximity to markets. With large and diversified manufacturing bases, world-class transportation and warehousing facilities, and substantial concentrations of financial and other producer-services firms, Dallas and Houston are in a better position to benefit from NAFTA-related export activity than any other part of the state (Gilmer, 1990; Stolp and Weintraub, 1993; Weintraub and Boske, 1991). Indeed, as has been suggested by a number of books and articles in the popular press, Texas has been witnessing an economic expansion of the border region to include these two large "interior" Texas cities (Myerson, 1994; Orme, 1993; Palmieri, 1994). While Mexican-ancestry entrepreneurs in Dallas and Houston may able to take advantage of this reorientation of export activity away from the border, the majority of the state's Mexican-ancestry population and entrepreneurs live in the border region. Moreover, the wholesale, transportation, and manufacturing markets of Dallas and Houston are dominated by large-scale national and international companies, and the leading professional service firms are Anglo-owned and -operated.

CONCLUSIONS

It is an irony of the first order that the entrepreneurs in the Texas border region, who played such a crucial role in the initial opening of the Mexican market and the political push for passage of NAFTA, were already beginning to find themselves bypassed by the process of binational economic integration even before the formal consummation of the free trade pact. We must also bear in mind, however, that many kinds of border businesses have not been bypassed as a result of trade liberalization between the United States and Mexico.

- The many retailers in the Texas border cities on the international line itself who served the daily consumption needs of cross-border shoppers from the "twin" cities on the Mexican side of the border have been little affected by integration, though the competition from large-scale discount chains remains as serious a threat to them as to small merchants anywhere in the United States.

- Those border wholesalers who sold relatively small quantities of specialized parts and equipment for industry may have found niches in which to remain protected from competition from larger concerns, especially to the extent that they serve markets in smaller Mexican cities close to the northern border. Numerically speaking, however, such wholesalers employed less than 5 percent of the border region's workforce in 1990 (U.S. Bureau of the Census, 1990); their survival is probably not crucial to the region's overall economic well-being.

- Professional-service providers located in the border region—including engineers, architects, and management consultants, who accounted for a growing share of total employment (15.3 percent in 1990)—probably stood to benefit most from economic integration, as NAFTA allowed them to serve a binational market running in a 360-degree (instead of a 180-degree) radius around them, especially given that quality services of these kinds had been in short supply outside the major cities in Mexico. Entry into these professions, however, requires educational credentials that are in particularly short supply among the majority Mexican-ancestry population in the region— by 1990, only 12.3 percent of Mexican Americans and 6.0 percent of Mexican immigrants who were employed in the border region had graduated from college, compared to 35.9 percent among Anglo natives. (U.S. Bureau of the Census, 1990)

Perhaps the increased volume of goods passing through the border region would have made up for its decreased centrality to the overall process of integration had the Mexican import boom been sustained beyond the first year of the free-trade area's existence. Of course, the liquidity crisis that left the Mexican economy prostrate in 1995 rendered the question moot. In commercial terms, the Texas border region has seen a repeat of 1982, with retail sales in Laredo and El Paso down 60 to 80 percent in January 1995 compared with January 1994 (Texas Comptroller, 1995); moreover, it remains to be seen what significant role, if any, Mexican-ancestry and other border entrepreneurs will play in a future resurgence of exports to Mexico. Whether such a resurgence in exports occurs will most certainly depend on decisions made by members of elite social networks to which border residents barely have access.

At the theoretical level, the experiences of entrepreneurs in the Texas border region demonstrate several points about the role of small-scale firms in global commodity chains. First, the operators of such firms do, in fact, actively seek to insert themselves into global chains and do so in a way that is reflective, not of the will of the large firms directing the chains, but rather of their own social and economic trajectories. These trajectories, in turn, are bound up in contexts that are simultaneously local and transnational insofar as they are determined by both the personal networks of local community members and the impersonal forces of global political economy. Second, small-scale firms insert themselves into global chains in accordance with the resources they have at their disposal. Relative to larger firms, small businesses often depend more heavily on social capital deriving from the personal networks and lived experiences of their owners/operators and less heavily on financial, physical, and human capital investments or other types of social capital deriving from institutional rather than personal networks.

Finally, in the context of global free trade, social capital may be a more valuable substitute for other forms of capital as part of a *subsistence* strategy involving intrafirm relations (e.g., use of unpaid family labor) or exchange relations at a local, community level (e.g., rotating credit associations, in-kind barters, etc.) than as part of a *competitive* strategy for meeting challenges from rivals who are better endowed with those other forms. Thus we can see that the economic activities of small firms in global commodity chains are embedded in social contexts that involve, not only the "horizontal" exchange relations among members of local communities or migrant diasporas, but also the "vertical" power relations that are intrinsic to the capitalist world system. The latter relations exert an inexorable pressure on the former, while the former relations adapt and persist in ways that often place our assumptions about the functioning of the system in doubt.

NOTES

1. Research for this chapter was conducted with generous support from the Ford Foundation and the Institute for Latin American Studies of the University of Texas at Austin. Computing services were funded in part by the National Institute for Child Health and Development's core grant to the Population Research Center of the University of Texas. I also wish to acknowledge helpful comments on an earlier version of this chapter that I received from Robert G. Cushing, Rodolfo de la Garza, Roberto Patricio Korzeniewicz, Humberto González, Bryan Roberts, and Chandler Stolp.

2. In relating this story, I rely on results of my own field research in the Texas border region from 1992 to the present, as well as official statistics published or made available electronically by the governments of the United States, Mexico, and the state of Texas. For simplicity of presentation in the narrative I often use the terms "border business" and "border entrepreneur" as short-hand expressions for businesses that sell to Mexican firms or private consumers and the people who operate those businesses. Not all businesses located in the border region can be regarded as "border businesses," since many serve immediate local markets. Similarly, not all entrepreneurs in the region qualify as "border entrepreneurs," whatever their national heritage. In this regard it should also be noted that not all "border entrepreneurs" who use the cultural and social resources at their disposal to do business with Mexico are themselves of Mexican ancestry. Just as Mexican-ancestry entrepreneurs learn and become expert in the language and culture of business in Anglo-majority communities, Anglos and other non-Latinos can, and do, become expert in the language (Spanish) and culture (Mexican or Tex-Mex) of the border region. Indeed, in spite of the fact that the region's working population is mainly of Mexican ancestry, the entrepreneurial community is disproportionately composed of white Anglo natives, European Jews, and Asian immigrants.

3. By the "Texas border region," I refer to the urban areas of El Paso, Del Rio, Eagle Pass, Laredo, McAllen, Brownsville-Harlingen, and San Antonio.

4. Demographic data on the working populations of the border region, Dallas, and Houston are taken from the 5 Percent Public Use Micro Samples of the 1980 and 1990 United States Censuses of Population and Housing. Figures for the border region do not include Del Rio and Eagle Pass.

5. My use of the term "social capital" in this chapter derives from Coleman (1988).

6. *Maquiladora* inputs were of course exempted from this general policy. However, as noted earlier, inputs, and ancillary services to the *maquiladoras* on the northern border were not generally supplied by local entrepreneurs in the Texas border region. For my purposes here, the real story has to do with Mexico's *overall* policy on imports.

7. This characterization of the border business environment before Mexican trade liberalization is drawn from a popular Hollywood movie of the 1980s. *Field of Dreams* stars Kevin Costner as an Iowa farmer who is obsessed with baseball and who is visited by the ghost of a great player of the past. The ghost instructs him to clear one of his cornfields and create a baseball field so that the ghosts of other legendary players can appear and play there. When Costner states his skepticism about the plan, the ghost replies, "If you build it, they will come." This phrase is repeated at key moments throughout the remainder of the movie, as Costner does the ghost's bidding—and, being a Hollywood movie, the ghosts do indeed come.

8. These figures are derived from U.S. Bureau of the Census, *County Business Patters* (1990, 1992), electromagnetic tape data.

9. La Malinche was the Aztec mistress of Hernán Cortes, the Spanish conqueror of Mexico. To accuse a Mexican of *malinchismo* is to accuse him or her of treason to his or her own country and people.

10. Translation: "We don't know what they are, whether they're Mexicans or Americans, or something else, like we call them: *pochos*." The term *pocho* is a derogatory term used by Mexicans in Mexico to describe Mexican immigrants or Mexican Americans in the United States who have abandoned Mexican ways.

11. This comment is especially interesting given that many border entrepreneurs on the Texas side insisted on the importance of knowing the proper Mexican customs and way of socializing in a business context. This theme is overstated a great deal in the business press. See, for example, Barnstone (1993).

REFERENCES

Alarcón González, Diana. 1994. *Changes in the Distribution of Income in Mexico and Trade Liberalization*. Tijuana, Mexico: El Colegio de la Frontera Norte.

Alegría Olazábal, Tito. 1992. *Desarrollo urbano en la frontera México–Estados Unidos*. Mexico City: Consejo Nacional para la Cultura y las Artes.

Alvarez, Robert. 1990. "Mexican Entrepreneurs and Markets in the City of Los Angeles: A Case of an Immigrant Enclave." *Urban Anthropology* 19, 1–2: 99–124.

Arreola, Daniel D. 1987. "The Mexican American Cultural Capital." *Geographical Review* 77, 1: 17–34.

———. 1993. "Mexico Origins of South Texas Mexican Americans, 1930." *Journal of Historical Geography* 19, 1: 48–63.

Banco de Mexico. 1994. *Sumario Estadístico*. Mexico, DF: Author.

Barnstone, Robert. 1993. "Viva la diferencia!" *Texas Monthly*, October, pp. 66–74.

Cárdenas, Gilberto, Jorge Chapa, and Susan Burek. 1993. "The Changing Economic Position of Mexican Americans in San Antonio." In *Latinos in a Changing U.S. Economy: Comparative Perspectives on Growing Inequality*, ed. Rebecca Morales and Frank Bonilla, pp. 160–183. Newbury Park, CA: Sage Publications.

Cárdenas, Gilberto, Rodolfo O. De la Garza, and Niles Hansen. 1986. "Mexican Immigrants and Chicano Ethnic Enterprise: Reconceptualizing an Old Problem." In *Mexican Immigrants and Mexican Americans: An Evolving Relation*, ed. Harley Browning and Rodolfo O. De la Garza, pp. 157–174. Austin: Center for Mexican American Studies, University of Texas at Austin.

"Casa San Antonio: Blazing the Trail to Free Trade." 1994. *Public Management* 76, 8 (June): 23–24.

Chapa, Jorge, and Gilberto Cárdenas. 1991. *The Economy of the Urban Ethnic Enclave*. Austin: Lyndon B. Johnson School of Public Affairs and Tomás Rivera Center, University of Texas at Austin.

Coleman, James. 1988. "Social Capital in the Creation of Human Capital." *American Journal of Sociology* 94 (supplement): s95–s120.

Corona Vásquez, Rodolfo. 1991. "Principales características demográficas de la zona fronteriza del norte de México." *Frontera Norte* 3, 5: 141–155.

Crook, Stephen, Jan Pakulski, and Malcolm Waters. 1992. *Postmodernization: Change in Advanced Society*. London: Sage Publications.

Curtis, James R. 1993. "Central Business Districts of the Two Laredos." *Geographical Review* 83, 1: 54–65.

De la Garza, Rodolfo O., and Claudio Vargas. 1992. "The Mexican-Origin Population of the United States as a Political Force in the Borderlands: From Paisanos to Pochos to Potential Political Allies." In *Changing Boundaries in the Americas: New Perspectives on the U.S.-Mexican, Central American, and South American Borders*, ed. Lawrence Herzog, pp. 89–111. San Diego: University of California at San Diego, Center for U.S.-Mexican Studies.

Dunigan, Andrew. 1992. "Texas Looks South: The Lone Star State Meets Mexico, Once Again." *Business Mexico*, December, pp. 32–33.

Foley, Douglas E. 1988. *From Peones to Políticos: Class and Ethnicity in a South Texas Town, 1900–1987*. Austin: University of Texas Press.

Gereffi, Gary, Miguel Korzeniewicz, and Roberto P. Korzeniewicz. 1994. "Introduction: Global Commodity Chains." In *Commodity Chains and Global Capitalism*, ed. Gary Gereffi and Miguel Korzeniewicz, pp. 1–14. Westport, CT: Praeger.

Geyer, Anne. 1990. "Strengthening Trade Connections." *Business Mexico*, September, pp. 22–23.

———. 1991. "Credit Card Surge: Mexicans Are Finding Plastic to Be a Handy Way to Spend Money." *Business Mexico*, June, pp. 4–7.

Gilmer, Robert W. 1990. "Identifying Service-Sector Exports from Major Texas Cities." *Economic Review*, July, pp. 1–16.

Granovetter, Mark. 1985. "Economic Action and Social Structure: The Problem of Embeddedness." *American Journal of Sociology* 91, 3: 481–510.

Harrell, Louis, and Dale Fischer. 1985. "The 1982 Mexican Peso Devaluation and Border Area Employment." *Monthly Labor Review* 108, 10: 25–32.

Harvey, David. 1989. *The Condition of Post-Modernity*. Oxford: Basil Blackwell.

Holt, Stanley. 1991. "Clearing Customs: U.S. and Mexican Customs Services Struggle to Meet the Challenges of Increasing Trade." *Business Mexico*, May, pp. 46–48.

Institute for Mining and Materials Management. 1991. *Paso del Norte Regional Economy: Socioeconomic Profile.* El Paso: University of Texas at El Paso.

Landolt, Robert Garland. 1976. *The Mexican American Workers of San Antonio, Texas.* New York: Arno Press.

Latino Summit on the North American Free Trade Agreement (NAFTA). 1993. *Latino Consensus Position on NAFTA.* Washington, DC: Latino Summit on NAFTA.

Lomnitz, Larissa. 1977. *Networks and Marginality: Life in a Mexican Shantytown.* San Francisco, CA: Academic Press.

———. 1990. "Redes informales de intercambio en sistemas formales: Un modelo teórico." *Comercio Exterior* 40, 3: 212–220.

Lustig, Nora. 1992. *Mexico: The Remaking of an Economy.* Washington, DC: Brookings Institution.

MacDonald, Christine. 1993. "Customs' Unsung Hero? Francisco Gil Díaz Cleans Up Customs." *Business Mexico*, April, pp. 27–29.

Maril, Robert Lee. 1989. *The Poorest of Americans: The Mexican Americans of the Lower Rio Grande Valley of Texas.* Notre Dame, IN: University of Notre Dame Press.

Martínez, Oscar. 1994. *Border People: Life and Society in the U.S.-Mexico Borderlands.* Tucson: University of Arizona Press.

"The Mexican-American Border: Hi, Amigo." 1992. *Economist*, December 12, pp. 21–25.

Miller, Tom. 1981. *On the Border: Portraits of America's Southwestern Frontier.* New York: Harper and Row.

Montejano, David. 1987. *Anglos and Mexicans in the Making of Texas, 1836–1986.* Austin: University of Texas Press.

Myerson, Allen R. 1994. "The Booming, Bulging Tex-Mex Border." *New York Times*, August 7, p. C1.

Orme, William A., Jr. 1993. *Continental Shift: Free Trade and the New North America.* Washington, DC: Washington Post Company.

Palmieri, Christopher. 1994. "Laredo's Giant Sucking Sound." *Forbes*, April 25, p. 78.

Pastor, Manuel, and Carol Wise. 1994. "The Origins and Sustainability of Mexico's Free Trade Policy." *International Organization* 48, 3: 459–489.

Portes, Alejandro. 1994a. "By-passing the Rules: The Dialectics of Labour Standards and Informalization in Less Developed Countries." In *International Labour Standards and Economic Interdependence*, ed. W. Sensenberger and D. Campbell, pp. 159–176. Geneva, Switzerland: Institute for Labour Studies.

———. 1994b. "Paradoxes of the Informal Economy: The Social Basis of Unregulated Entrepreneurship." In *Handbook of Economic Sociology*, ed. Neil Smelser and Richard Swedberg, pp. 426–449. New York: Russell Sage Foundation.

Portes, Alejandro, and Robert Bach. 1985. *Latin Journey.* Berkeley: University of California Press.

Reich, Robert B. 1991. *The Work of Nations: Preparing Ourselves for 21st Century Capitalism.* New York: Random House.

Roberts, Bryan. 1978. *Cities of Peasants: The Political Economy of Urbanization in the Third World.* London: Edward Arnold.

Ros, Jaime. 1992. "Free Trade Area or Common Capital Market? Notes on Mexico-U.S. Economic Integration and Current NAFTA Negotiations." *Journal of Interamerican Studies and World Affairs* 34, 2: 53–92.

Savage, V. Howard, and Eric Blankmeyer. 1990. "A Test of Purchasing Power Parity: Texas Border Retail Trade and the Value of the Peso, 1976–1987." *Journal of Borderlands Studies* 5, 1: 67–78.

Sayer, Andrew, and Richard Walker. 1992. *The New Social Economy: Reworking the Division of Labor.* Cambridge, MA: Blackwell Publishers.

Schusler, Ralph. 1991a. "Border Boom Town: Laredo Ready for Action as Free Trade Paves the Way for Growth." *Business Mexico*, November, 28–31.

———. 1991b. "Getting Ready: U.S. Businessmen on the Border Gear for Free Trade." *Business Mexico*, March, pp. 16–19.

Spener, David. 1995. "Entrepreneurship and Small-Scale Enterprise in the Texas Border Region: A Sociocultural Perspective." Ph.D. dissertation, University of Texas at Austin.

Spener, David, and Bryan Roberts. 1994. "Social Networks and Trade on the Texas-Mexico Border: The Role of Small-Scale Enterprise in the Integration of Transnational Space." Paper presented at the annual meeting of the Latin American Studies Association, Atlanta, GA, March 9–13.

Stolp, Chandler. 1994. "The LBJ School of Public Affairs Model of NAFTA Impacts." Unpublished mimeo, Austin, Texas.

Stolp, Chandler, and Sidney Weintraub. 1993. "NAFTA: Challenges and Opportunities for a 21st Century Texas." *Texas Lyceum* 10, 1: 16–23.

Tamayo, Jesus, and Jorge Luis Fernández. 1983. *Zonas fronterizas.* Mexico City: Centro de Investigación y Docencia Económicas.

Ten Kate, Adriaan. 1992. "El ajuste estructural de México: Dos historias diferentes." *Comercio Exterior* 42, 6: 519–528.

"Texan-Mexican Trade: Optimists All." 1991. *Economist*, August 17, pp. 25–26.

Texas Comptroller. 1995. "Peso Fiasco: Texas Exports Feel the Brunt of Mexico's Fiscal Woes." *Fiscal Notes*, March, pp. 3–6.

Texas Department of Commerce. 1988–1994. *Texas Exports.* Austin: Author.

Torres, David. 1990. "Dynamics behind the Formation of a Business Class: Tucson's Hispanic Business Elite." *Hispanic Journal of Behavioral Sciences* 12, 1: 25–49.

Torres, Esteban. 1994. "NAFTA Owes Texas." *Fiscal Notes*, June 1994, p. 6.

U.S. Bureau of the Census. 1980. *1980 Census of Population and Housing: 5 Percent Public Use Microdata Sample.* Washington, DC: Author. Electromagnetic tape data.

———. 1990. *1990 Census of Population and Housing: 5 Percent Public Use Microdata Sample.* Washington, DC: Author. Electromagnetic tape data.

———. 1990, 1992. *County Business Patterns.* Washington, DC: Author. Electromagnetic tape data.

U.S. Department of Commerce. 1994. *National Trade Database.* Washington, DC: Author. CD-ROM database.

U.S. International Trade Commission. 1990. *Review of Trade and Investment Liberalization Measures by Mexico and Prospects for Future United States-Mexico Relations. Investigation No. 332–282: Phase I: Recent Trade and Investment Reforms Undertaken by Mexico and Implications for the United States.* Washington, DC: United States International Trade Commission.

Valdez, Avelardo. 1993. "Persistent Poverty, Crime, and Drugs: U.S.-Mexican Border Region." In *The Barrios: Latinos and the Underclass Debate*, ed. Joan Moore and Raquel Pinderhughes, pp. 173–194. New York: Russell Sage Foundation.

Vélez-Ibáñez, Carlos G. 1983. *Bonds of Mutual Trust: The Cultural Systems of Rotating Credit Associations among Urban Mexicans and Chicanos*. New Brunswick, NJ: Rutgers University Press.

———. 1988. "Networks of Exchange Among Mexicans in the U.S. and Mexico: Local-level Mediating Responses to National and International Transformations." *Urban Anthropology* 17, 1: 27–51.

Weintraub, Sidney. 1990. *A Marriage of Convenience: Relations between Mexico and the United States*. New York: Oxford University Press.

Weintraub, Sidney, and Leigh Boske. 1991. *US.-Mexico Free Trade Agreement: Economic Impact on Texas*. Austin: University of Texas, Lyndon B. Johnson School of Public Affairs.

Wright, Erik Olin. 1985. *Classes*. London: Verso.

Wright, Harry K. 1971. *Foreign Enterprise in Mexico: Laws and Policies*. Durham: University of North Carolina Press.

5

GLOBALIZATION, THE STATE, AND THE INFORMAL ECONOMY: THE LIMITS TO PROLETARIANIZATION IN THE LATIN AMERICAN PERIPHERY

José Itzigsohn

Proletarianization is one of the central characteristics of the capitalist world-system. As the world-economy expands, it leads to the commodification of the labor force in the newly incorporated regions. As Wallerstein (1983) pointed out, however, the proletarianization of the peripheral labor force is always partial. Not all the labor force of the periphery of the world system is incorporated into modern wage relations, as this would put on capital's shoulders the full cost of its reproduction. The result of the process of partial proletarianization is the rise of a variety of non–fully proletarian income-producing activities that are commonly referred to as the informal economy.

Individual workers are rarely isolated economic actors. Instead, for most people, the basic economic unit is the household. Households in the periphery very rarely, in fact, depend totally on proletarian wages. The modal type of peripheral household usually depends on a combination of wages and petty market operations (Smith and Wallerstein, 1992). Peripheral households usually have different members working on a diverse array of formal and informal activities. The question arises, then, how these different types of activities are related to each other in the functioning of peripheral urban economies.

The focus of this chapter is on the roles of informal economic activities within the urban economies of Latin America and the Caribbean, and on how those informal activities are related to the process of proletarianization in the region. During the last two decades, Latin America and the Caribbean have gone through a process of social and economic change. This process, which has been alternatively labeled structural adjustment, economic restructuring, or export-oriented development (EOD), amounts to a restructuring of the mode of insertion of the region in the world-economy. In previous periods, the region was a provider of raw materials for core production and, in a few cases, a provider of some industrial products or markets for transnational companies. Presently, however, a central role of the region in the world-economy is that of a provider of cheap labor and services for an increasingly globalized production system.

This chapter compares the articulations of formal and informal firms in the Dominican Republic and Costa Rica in order to address these questions. However, it should be asked whether linkages to multinationals prevail as a general pattern in the new informal economy of the 1990s, or whether there are alternative patterns of informal arrangements that reflect variables such as the particular extent and type of state regulation that prevail in different local environments. The two countries discussed here have applied export-oriented policies during the last fifteen years and have opened their economies to international trade. They have also emphasized a focus on the informal economy as a cornerstone of their social policies. This chapter examines different ways in which informal and formal economic activities are related to each other and explores the effects of the mode of insertion of these two countries in the world-economy and the action of their respective states on the boundaries between the formal and informal economies. The goal is to achieve an understanding of the functioning of peripheral urban economies and of the relationship between the processes of formation of a proletarian and an informal labor force in Latin America in the present period of globalization of the world-economy.

THE INFORMAL ECONOMY IN THE LATIN AMERICAN PERIPHERY

During the period of import-substitution industrialization, Latin America witnessed a growth in both formal proletarianization and the informal economy. Employment in manufacturing, the public sector, and modern services grew very fast. In spite of this, the informal economy did not disappear; on the contrary, it encompassed a large part of the economically active population. Moreover, the proletariat created by the process of industrialization did not always correspond to the image of factory wageworkers. Part of the proletariat was, in fact, an informal proletariat, which was employed in small workshops and lacked legal protection (Portes, 1985). Nevertheless, its members were still part of commodity chains that linked them to the formal economy. Several researchers have documented how informal, and apparently marginal, economic activities are linked to modern formal production or distribution (Birckbek, 1978; Bromley, 1978; Moser, 1994; Portes and Schauffler, 1994). These scholars have shown that the informal economy was part and parcel of peripheral capitalism.

The social and economic crisis that hit Latin America and the Caribbean in the beginning of the 1980s reversed the trends of the previous decades. Stable and protected employment in manufacturing and the public sector decreased, and the continent witnessed a rise in precarious forms of employment encompassing temporary, part-time, and unprotected jobs in sectors such as export manufacturing and in the public sector. This crisis also gave way to the rise of a large array of informal activities. The last decade, therefore, saw a partial reverse in the process of proletarianization in the Latin American periphery.

In this context, the informal economy has acquired a renewed interest. After years of being considered a result of an incomplete process of industrialization, the informal economy has come to be hailed as a reservoir of true market forces and a potential solution for the problems of unemployment and poverty in the region (De Soto, 1989; Rakowski, 1994). These views, however, do not take into account the roles that the informal economy plays in the process of capital accumulation. In order to understand the roles of the informal economy, it is necessary to examine the forms of articulation of informal and formal economic activities. This is, in fact, an old, but always present, question in political economy: how capitalism, as it expands, organizes production and distribution. In other words, it focuses on the types of labor relations, firms, and markets that emerge as the world capitalist economy searches for new forms of capital accumulation.

The informal economy is defined in this chapter as comprising those economic activities that are carried out in spite of existing regulations that restrict those types of activities. In order to reduce the scope of the definition, I will consider informal only those activities that violate existing labor regulations. This definition, however, is still very broad. The informal economy is, in fact, a label that encompasses a multitude of different economic actors and social relations. Its use is widespread because it is an easy way to refer to activities that depart from the legal and "expected" norms regarding working conditions and the structure of firms in industrialized economies. Nevertheless, the types of economic activities and linkages encompassed under this label vary in different contexts. In order to make sense of such diverse economic activities, we need to analyze their roles within the urban economy. The rest of this section relates the different functions of the informal economy to the particular types of linkages found between formal and informal activities. This, in turn, allows the development of a typology of informal economic actors in relation to those linkages and functions.

The informal economy performs two main functions within the urban economic system. The first function is to supply low-cost goods and services for working-class and middle-class consumers. In this way, the informal economy subsidizes the formal firms: by lowering the costs of consumption of basic needs, formal firms are able to pay lower salaries than they would have to pay if consumption were carried on only through formal means. The second function of the informal economy is to allow formal firms a direct reduction of labor costs through the practices of subcontracting parts of their production or marketing tasks and through off-the-books hiring (Portes and Walton, 1981). In this way, formal firms can avoid the burdens imposed by labor and social security laws concerning minimum wages, working conditions, and other fringe benefits that they are forced to pay their permanent formal workers.

The production and marketing of any good or service is the outcome of different sets of linkages that include, among others, securing sources of capital, raw materials, and supplies, as well as finding outlets for the final product. These linkages can be horizontal, such as arm's-length market relationships between different firms; they can also be vertical, as when a branch of a firm supplies or sells the goods of another branch of the same firm. They can be linkages of subordination (e.g., subcontracting relationships) or linkages of cooperation, such as those described for industrial districts (Portes and Schauffler, 1994). The sum of the linkages of a business constitutes its articulation with the urban economy.

The two different functions of the informal economy are associated with different types of linkages among formal and informal economic units. The subsidizing of consumption is related to two main types of linkages. The first is between informal sellers of goods or services and final consumer markets (e.g., the independent informal street vendors, informal workers who perform home services such as gardening or painting, or informal workshops that repair everything from tape recorders to cars). I call these informal actors *self-employed petty marketers.* The second type of linkage is between informal firms and formal markets (e.g., an informal shoemaker who supplies one or more formal shoe stores). I call these informal actors *suppliers.* In these ways, informal firms supply consumers with cheap goods and reduce the amount of money needed to meet the needs of the household.

The direct reduction of the labor-cost function is also related to two main types of linkages. The first involves subcontracting chains between a formal firm and one or more informal firms or self-employed people. The latter work for the formal firm, producing certain products, performing particular parts of the production process, or selling the final product. I call this group of informal actors *subcontractors*. The second type of linkage involves the hiring of informal workers by informal or formal firms. The latter often resort to the hiring of temporary or off-the-books workers who do not enjoy the wages and benefits of most of the firm's labor force. These informal workers constitute the *informal proletariat* proper.

Table 5.1 schematically presents the different types of articulation between the formal and informal economies. The basic difference between the linkages under the two functions is that those under function (1) are basically horizontal linkages; in other words, linkages between independent economic actors in different markets.[1] The linkages under function (2) are vertical linkages; that is, linkages where the informal economic actors are vertically articulated into formal commodity chains. In the two functions, however, the second type of linkage expresses a more subordinate relation than the first type. It is easy to see why this is so. The fact that two economic units are related by horizontal linkages does not necessarily mean that they have equal power. The markets of those informal firms that supply formal firms—the second type of linkage—are often oligopolic or oligopsonic. Hence, the informal entrepreneurs have a clear disadvantage vis-à-vis their formal partners. Furthermore, casual, "off-the-

Table 5.1
Articulations among the Formal and Informal Economies

	Function 1: Horizontal articulation. Subsidize consumption by formal workers and middle classes.	Function 2: Vertical articulation. Reduce labor costs of formal firms.
Less-Subordinated Articulation	"petty marketers"— Informal sellers, or producers selling informal products in consumer markets.	"subcontractors"— Informal producers performing part of the production process for formal firms, or informal sellers selling the products of formal firms.
More-Subordinated Articulation	"suppliers"— Informal producers supplying formal retailers with the goods they produce.	"informal workers"— Informal workers working temporarily off-the-books for formal firms, or employees of informal firms.

book'' workers are in a relation of more direct subordination than those informal producers who perform subcontracted work for other firms, as the latter can engage in such relations with several different firms or sell part of their product independently.

Table 5.1 underscores the heterogeneous character of the informal economy, which encompasses a continuum of economic actors from off-the-books workers to self-employed people and small entrepreneurs; the social relations include informal proletarians, independent workers, and informal employers. Therefore, in order to understand the functioning of peripheral urban economies, it is necessary to look at the types of activities and social relations that predominate at any particular moment of the expansion or contraction of the world-economy. In other words, it is important to examine what causes the rise of particular forms of informal activities and what role they fulfill. In this way, we can find out the forms, extent, and limits to the process of proletarianization in the periphery.

GLOBALIZATION, THE STATE, AND THE INFORMAL ECONOMY

As we analyze the interaction between global and local processes in the formation of particular forms of articulation between formal and informal activities, two issues are of particular interest: the presence and extent of international subcontracting linkages, and the role of the state in shaping the boundaries between formal and informal activities.

The existing literature often suggests that the globalization of the economy is accompanied by the proliferation of international subcontracting chains linking corporate headquarters in the core to informal producers or homeworkers in the periphery. Commodity chains of this sort were documented by several researchers (Beneria and Roldán, 1990; Portes and Schauffler, 1994). There is some evidence that during the last decade, informal firms with a certain capacity of accumulation due to their connections with producers or consumers in the United States have emerged in Latin America. My interest is in finding out to what extent commodity chains spanning from international firms to informal workshops are common within the new informal economy.

The role of the state in shaping the boundaries between formal and informal activities has been emphasized by Portes (e.g., Portes and Schauffler, 1994), who proposed that a state that regulates labor relations strictly will lead formal firms to try to evade those regulations through subcontracting or off-the-books hiring, thus creating a tight articulation in production or marketing between formal and informal activities. In a less regulated context, however, there will be fewer incentives to integrate informal activities in production or marketing, and therefore, their role will tend to be that of a supplier of cheap consumer goods. To evaluate these propositions, I assess whether a more regulated context accentuates the labor-cost reduction function of the informal economy, while a less regulated context accentuates the consumption subsidy function.

To permit analysis of these issues, this chapter compares the linkages between formal and informal firms in San José, Costa Rica, and Santo Domingo (the Dominican Republic). These two countries share a series of common characteristics due to similarities in their insertion in the world-economy (in terms of the structure of their trade) and social structures. Both countries were latecomers to industrialization, as serious industrialization efforts were not attempted until the 1960s. At that point, both countries had small economies that depended on the export of a few commodities for growth: sugar, in the Dominican case, and coffee and bananas in Costa Rica. Both countries applied an import-substitution industrialization (ISI) model during the 1950–1980 period, and both switched to an export-oriented development (EOD) model during the 1980s (Lozano and Duarte, 1992; Rovira Más, 1985). The two countries differ, however, in the type and degree of state regulation of economic activities and labor relations and in the size of their informal economies. Costa Rica has a more extensive regulation of economic activities and labor relations than the Dominican Republic. Moreover, in Costa Rica, the existing regulations are more consistently applied than in the Dominican Republic.[2]

The economic crisis of the early 1980s and the new, export-oriented model of development strongly affected formal sources of employment. The protected industries were hit by the opening of the economies to international trade, and employment and income in the import-substitution–manufacturing sector were reduced. During the economic crisis, the public sector performed a counter-cyclical function, absorbing some of the workers who were expelled from the private formal sector. This increase in employment caused a large reduction in the salaries of the sector. As the decade went on and structural adjustment programs were applied, employment in the public sector also decreased (Infante and Klein, 1991). On the other hand, the fastest-growing employment sectors have been export assembly manufacturing, tourism, and the informal economy. This general trend toward socioeconomic internationalization and informalization constitutes the context within which to analyze the articulations of the informal economy (Portes, Itzigsohn, and Dore, 1994.).

Based on a series of interviews with informal microentrepreneurs, this section contrasts what emerged as the most typical situations of articulation of formal and informal firms in the two cities.[3] The results have an exploratory character, and therefore, the conclusions should be taken as hypotheses for further research. In spite of these limitations, the access to direct sources provides important insights about the roles of informal economic actors in the urban economy. The interviews provide in-depth information on issues such as forward and backward linkages and the histories of the informal microenterprises and the microentrepreneurs. I focus on the results of interviews with informal microentrepreneurs producing garments and crafts (the latter refers to those crafts that are produced for selling to tourists). The choice of these two trades is due to their inclusion in two increasingly internationalized economic sectors: garment production and tourism. It is important to look at the formal-informal linkages in more than one sector. The articulations of formal and informal firms may vary, not only between the two cities, but also within the two cities themselves (e.g., the contrast between the two cities in the articulations of informal garment production is different than the contrast among craftspersons). This occurs because the effects of different types of state regulations interact with the characteristics of the markets for the products of the different industries within each city (such as the openness of the local market to the import of goods that compete with informal production, or the presence or absence in the local markets of oligopolistic national producers). The remainder of this section presents the basic patterns of linkages found in each city.[4]

Garments

The garments sector is one of the most interesting in which to look at the economic articulations of informal businesses. The international garment and textile industry has been ''globalized'' during the last two decades. Large assembly factories have moved from the core to the periphery, where they are concentrated in export zones. In the core countries, garment production has moved underground to informal sweatshops (Portes and Sassen-Koob, 1987). Linkages have been found between formal factories in core countries and small, informal workshops in peripheral countries, such as those described by Pérez Sainz (1994) between formal garment firms in California and informal workshops in the Mayan village of San Pedro Sacatepequez (near Guatemala City). Thus, in this trade we can expect to find a large array of different economic actors, from people who make clothes for their neighbors to informal producers engaged in international commodity chains.

In Santo Domingo, I found a certain progression in the forms of articulation of the informal garment producers. Small producers begin selling to the public, to informal peddlers, or to middlemen. They secure their position by obtaining some secure contracts with formal shops. The latter stage of growth comes when they are able to diversify their clientele and manage to have a number of vendors going around the city or the country and sell their production. Thus, they begin as sellers in final consumer markets (or selling to people who sell in final consumer markets), continue as suppliers or subcontractors, and then return as independent sellers in consumer markets.

Of course, not all of the informal garment producers go through these stages. In fact, most of them do not, remaining instead at the first or second stage. However, although the number of microenterprises that ''make it'' is small, the results of the interviews indicate that there are several market options for garment producers in Santo Domingo. These options are related to the presence of a large number of people trying to make a living by selling whatever they can. There is, in fact, an informal producer–informal retailer articulation that provides an outlet for informal products. Nevertheless, what seems to be a bonus for informal producers may be a curse for informal retailers.

The interviews in San José show both a common element and a clear difference in comparison to Santo Domingo. The common element is that in both cities, the subcontracting of garment production to informal workshops is extensive. The big difference is that in San José, the market for informal garment production is much narrower than in Santo Domingo and the informal businesses are in a much more subordinated position. The reasons for this are, on the one hand, the much larger presence in Santo Domingo of informal retailers, who offer an outlet for informal goods, and on the other hand, the lower purchasing power of large segments of the population in the Dominican Republic, which leads them to buy cheap goods that are produced locally. In Santo Domingo, the informal producers provide the low-income consumer markets with cheap goods that are marketed, to a large extent, through informal retailers. In San José, due to the higher level of earnings and the presence of cheap imports, people buy mainly in formal outlets. Informal retailers also provide cheap goods for popular consumption, but the demand for them is lower than in Santo Domingo. Most informal products are marketed through formal outlets. In the terms of Table 5.1, we can say that in Santo Domingo, there is a larger presence of ''petty marketers'' within the informal economy, while in San José there is a larger presence of ''suppliers.''

This explanation is based on variations in the consumer-goods markets that are caused by the different structures of the labor markets rather than differences in the burden of labor costs. In both cities, formal businesses subcontract their production to informal businesses. In Santo Domingo, though, informal businesses have more alternatives that allow them to escape the more subordinated type of relationships. It is important to note that most of the subcontracting work does not come from factories, but from retail chains. To be sure, in both cities there are factories that subcontract to small workshops. However, most of the subcontracting arrangements that I found were between retail chains or independent stores that cater to low-income sectors and the informal firms.

According to this interpretation, state regulation affects the linkages of informal microentrepreneurs in the garment sector more through its effects on the labor and consumer markets than through its effect on labor costs. Nevertheless, that is not the whole story. The informal labor force in San José is not entirely unprotected, as informal workers can use the threat of complaining to the ministry of labor in order to obtain better working conditions (a threat that is completely irrelevant in Santo Domingo). As a result, informal entrepreneurs in Costa Rica also need to escape high labor costs as well as the threat of an increase in their payroll that they cannot withstand. For this reason, the informal commodity chains in San José have more stages than in Santo Domingo. In San José I found two types of relationships that I did not find in Santo Domingo: (1) the subcontracting of production by the informal firms to homeworkers and (2) informal middlemen specializing in the design of products and the subcontracting of their production to informal firms.

All the examples presented so far concern cases of subcontracting by local firms. In both cities, I asked all my informants whether they had ever taken subcontracting jobs for international firms or knew about such cases. In all the cases but one, the answer was that small firms did not get those kinds of jobs because international firms have schedules and quality demands that small workshops cannot fulfill. For that reason, international subcontracting work is carried out in export zones in Santo Domingo and in big *maquila* factories in San José.[5] International subcontracting exists, but it stays at the level of the medium-sized firms and does not reach the level of the microenterprises and small informal workshops.

These results can be explained by the existence of a secondary labor market within the formal economy, which is composed mainly of cohorts of young women who were previously not employed. This sector offers international subcontractors access to a pool of cheap labor coupled with the advantages of large-scale production and tight control over the production process. The Dominican and Costa Rican states have encouraged this "informalization" of formal work through their policies of promoting export assembly-manufacturing, using cheap labor costs as an incentive for investment.

Craftspeople

Craftspeople linked to the tourism industry in the two cities provide an interesting counterpoint. In garments, we have seen a more favorable market situation for informal enterprises in Santo Domingo. In this sector, the situation is reversed. Most of the informal crafts producers in Santo Domingo find themselves pressed between an oligopsonic market for their products and monopolistic prices for their raw materials (Lozano, 1994). These craftspeople can sell only to a small number of gift shops, often through intermediaries who have connections with those shops. The latter, therefore, have the power to arbitrarily determine the prices of the products of the informal producers. Those informal entrepreneurs who have a direct connection with the gift shops have more power in the market because they are able to skip one link in the commodity chain: they are able to sell more when demand is up. Even those craftspeople, however, are in a position of subordination in relation to the gift shops.

The situation is different in San José, where the market for "souvenirs" is larger than in Santo Domingo. In San José, there are more outlets for crafts, and they are sold in more areas of the city than in Santo Domingo. Moreover, there is also the street selling of crafts products in San José—this is the one type of product that is not sold in the streets of Santo Domingo. In Santo Domingo, the link with the tourist sector is monopolized by a small number of shops, while in Costa Rica, crafts products for tourists have a larger and less controlled outlet. This is, in part, the result of the fact that the Dominican state has kept street sellers out of the main areas where tourists concentrate, and in that way it has precluded access to the market by craftspeople.[6]

In this sector, we find that the predominant type of actor in San José is the "petty marketer," while in Santo Domingo, "suppliers" predominate. These suppliers, however, confront a market that is so limited that they are almost totally subordinated to the buyers. In this case, the linkages between the global and informal economies are mediated through the domination of the market by local formal traders. The state intervenes in consolidating this subordination through its regulations and control of street trading. This subordination transforms these self-employed people into disguised workers of the traders. Nevertheless, even though their market situation and income are very unstable, the craftspeople whom I interviewed in Santo Domingo would not take up a formal job, since the income they could obtain in their trade was higher than any wage employment they could access. This suggests that in the present situation of general informalization of labor relations, partial or "disguised" proletarianization is, for many, a preferable alternative to full proletarianization (Itzigsohn, 1994; Murphy, 1990).

CONCLUSION

This chapter describes common trends between the two countries, as both respond to global pressures in quite similar ways. The qualitative interviews did not show major differences between the articulation of formal and informal enterprises in the two cities. In both cities, informal firms act mainly as suppliers or petty marketers. Most of the subcontracting chains that encompass informal microenterprises involve retailers who cater to the low-income sectors, rather than large multinational firms.

The sourcing by formal stores that cater to low-income sectors from informal enterprises may be explained by the need of the former to guarantee low prices, given the constraints of the markets in which they operate. As a result, they organize production in a sort of "putting-out" system in which formal stores provide informal enterprises with raw materials that are assembled by the latter at lower costs. Given the instability of the markets for informal goods, informal enterprises have no alternative but to accept the deals proposed by this type of formal business, which, in most cases, are unfavorable to informal producers. International subcontracting does not reach the small, informal workshops but rather remains at the level of the medium firms. In the two cities, international subcontractors have access to cheap labor in large factories—in the export zones in Santo Domingo and in the *maquilas* in San José. For that reason there is no incentive to extend the commodity chains to include informal microenterprises. Moreover, the latter lack the capacity to meet the quality and schedule demands of the international subcontractors.

The explanation of these similarities lies in a leveling between the formal and informal conditions of work in both cities. In Santo Domingo, the formal/informal divide is quite blurred due to the deterioration of formal working conditions during the last ten years. As a result, formal labor is not much more expensive than informal labor, and hence, there is no stimulus for formal firms to subcontract parts of their production (a finding that was expected). In San José, labor regulations make a difference even for informal workers, who are not completely unprotected. On the other hand, within the formal sector there is a secondary subsector whose working conditions differ little from those in the informal economy. Thus, for certain productive sectors (mainly light industries), the costs of secondary formal and informal labor are nearly the same.

What do these findings show concerning the relationship between informality and proletarianization? This chapter suggests a reorganization in the relationship between capital, the state, and labor in Latin America under the new mode of the insertion in the world-economy. By reducing labor regulations or their enforcement, states "informalize" the labor markets. In this context, capital has access to cheap sources of formal labor and is free of any pressure to "go informal." The role of the informal economy in this context is that of a subsistence sector that subsidizes the low cost of labor for capital. This role is not a new role for the informal economy, which fulfilled a similar role under import-substitution industrialization. The difference is that during the import-substitution period, although the informal economy partially subsidized the costs of proletarianization, access to formal wage work meant access to relatively decent wages and stable jobs. Thus, proletarianization implied an increase in the costs of the labor force for capital.

Under the new, export-oriented model, there is a process of general informalization of labor relations. The export-oriented development model that emerged during the last two decades is indeed associated with the formation of a global proletariat, but it is a heterogeneous rather than a "traditional" one, as the scattered productive units embedded in global commodity chains encompass different types of labor relations (Barkin, 1985; Broad, 1991; Sanderson, 1985). Access to formal employment in either the new, growing sectors or the public sector does not mean additional access to stable employment or a decent level of income. Income from informal activities, as well as remittances, has acquired a central role in the household economic strategies, while an increasingly precarious formal employment is being relegated to a secondary role (Itzigsohn, 1994).

As Smith and Wallerstein (1992) showed, in periods of economic contraction of the world-economy (such as the present), there is a reduction in wage employment opportunities and a rise in informal activities. This, however, is not the whole story. There is, in fact, a reversal in the importance of the different types of income for household subsistence. The incomes derived from formal and informal activities change in favor of the latter as shifting the costs of the reproduction of the labor force toward informal activities significantly cheapens the costs of wage labor. The growing process of informalization renders the use of full proletarian labor a cheap alternative for capital.

Peripheral proletarianization, thus, is not only a partial, but also an ever-shifting, process.[7] As capital searches for cheaper labor costs, it commodifies the labor of populations that were previously excluded from wage work. This process takes place by expanding industrial work into nonindustrialized peripheral areas or incorporating into industrial production populations that were not previously part of the active industrial labor force in industrialized areas. At the same time, new populations are proletarianized and segments of the population that were previously included in the labor force are deproletarianized and forced into informal activities to make their living. In the present context, these informal activities are mainly of the petty marketer and supplier type. The persons engaged in these activities participate in the reproduction of the newly proletarianized labor force. In this way, the creation of a cheaper proletariat, which combines the advantages of low cost as well as high control of the labor process, is related to the expansion of certain types of informal activities.

This process is occurring in both cities, as it is the result of global structural pressures. The process of informalization, however, is much more advanced in Santo Domingo than in San José. In the latter city, labor protections still make a difference in favor of formal employment. The action of the state is, after all, an important intermediary variable that affects the form that global processes take in each locale. This suggests that the growing calls for flexibilization of the labor market will not solve the problems of unemployment and underemployment. Therefore, the presence of effective state regulation, while not a solution, is needed to slow the pace of the deteriorating of living conditions of the popular sectors.

Since state action is a relevant variable, a final word is necessary with regard to the policies aimed toward the informal economy, which have been extremely popular in the last decade. The informal economy fulfills an increasingly important role in guaranteeing the reproduction of the labor force, suggesting that a policy focus on the informal economy is indeed necessary. Nevertheless, the results of this study show that the informal economy is not a panacea for growth, as suggested by De Soto (1989) and several international institutions. It does not seem that, under the present economic model, the informal economy can be absorbed by the formal sector. As shown by De Oliveira and Roberts (1994) rather than being more integrated into international chains of production and distribution, the informal economy is becoming increasingly marginalized. Therefore, a policy directed toward the informal economy cannot, and should not, pretend to transform informal activities into an engine of accumulation. The main tool available to informal economic actors to improve their situation, within the limits imposed by the local and global socioeconomic context, is their social networks. A successful policy directed toward the informal economy has to take into account, and promote, the organization of informal economic actors on the basis of their social networks and common interests.

NOTES

1. In fact, informal firms can often be classified as subcontractors or suppliers at the same time, or at different periods in the history of the business. Likewise, petty marketers often change their status between true self-employed and "disguised" workers. It is important to note that so-called suppliers do not always reduce the price of goods; sometimes, they retain an extra profit by acting as intermediaries.

2. In spite of these extensive regulations, or perhaps because of them, the informal sector in Costa Rica is considerably smaller than in the Dominican Republic (Itzigsohn, 1994).

3. The empirical base for the analysis is a series of semistructured interviews with informal microentrepreneurs conducted in the two cities during the summers of 1992 and 1993. The people interviewed were reached through the use of the snowball technique with multiple points of entry. I conducted 44 interviews in Santo Domingo, of which 9 were with microentrepreneurs and workers in the garments sector and 9 in the crafts sector. In San José, I conducted 46 interviews, including 22 with microentrepreneurs and workers in the garment sector and 4 in the crafts sector. These interviews cannot be taken as representative of the entire population of informal entrepreneurs in the two cities due to the limitations of the sample.

4. For a detailed description of the cases, see Itzigsohn (1994).

5. The only exception I found confirms this statement. It was a case of a cooperative of women in a popular area west of San José. The cooperative had 23 workers, most of them members, and the production process was organized with strict discipline as to working hours and production standards. Hence, more than an informal workshop, it was a small informal factory with the capacity to meet the tight standards of international firms.

6. The reference to the state here is not misguided, as, in the last ten years, Dominican president Joaquín Balaguer has taken on himself the management of the city of Santo Domingo.

7. This is a characteristic of proletarianization in general, as shown by the rise of temporary employment, sweatshops, and structural unemployment in the core regions. The differences are in the different forms that this process takes in the core and the periphery.

REFERENCES

Barkin, David. 1985. "Global Proletarianization." In *The Americas in the New International Division of Labor*, ed. Steven E. Sanderson, pp. 26–45. New York: Holmes and Meier.

Beneria, Lourdes, and Martha Roldán. 1987. *The Crossroads of Class and Gender: Homework, Subcontracting, and Household Dynamics in Mexico City*. Chicago: University of Chicago Press.

Birkbeck, Chris. 1978. "Self-Employed Proletarians in an Informal Factory: The Case of Cali's Garbage Dump." *World Development* 6: 1173–1185.

Broad, Dave. 1991. "Global Economic Restructuring and the (Re)Casualization of Work in the Center." *Review* 14, 4: 555–592.

Bromley, Ray. 1978. "Organization, Regulation and Exploitation in the So-Called 'Urban Informal Sector': The Street Traders of Cali, Colombia." *World Development* 6: 1161–1171.

Castells, Manuel, and Alejandro Portes. 1989. "World Underneath: The Origins, Dynamics, and Effects of the Informal Economy." In *The Informal Economy: Studies in Advanced and Less Developed Countries*, ed. Alejandro Portes, Manuel Castells, and Lauren A. Benton, pp. 11–37. Baltimore: Johns Hopkins University Press.

De Oliveira, Orlandina, and Bryan Roberts. 1994. "The Many Roles of the Informal Sector in Development: Evidence from Urban Labor Market Research, 1940–1989." In *Contrapunto: The Informal Sector Debate in Latin America*, ed. Cathy A. Rakowski, pp. 51–71. Albany: State University of New York Press.

De Soto, Hernando, 1989. *The Other Path*. New York: Harper and Row.

Infante, Ricardo, and Emilio Klein. 1991. "The Latin American Labour Market, 1950–1980." *CEPAL Review* 45 (December): 121–135.

Itzigsohn, José. 1994. "The State, the Informal Economy, and the Reproduction of the Labor Force." Ph.D. dissertation, Johns Hopkins University, Department of Sociology.

Lozano, Wilfredo. 1994. "La Vida Mala: Economía informal y pobladores urbanos en Santo Domingo." Unpublished manuscript, Johns Hopkins University, Department of Sociology.

Lozano, Wilfredo, and Isis Duarte. 1992. "Proceso de urbanización, modelos de desarrollo y clases sociales en República Dominicana 1960–1990." In *Urbanización en el Caribe*, ed. Alejandro Portes and Mario Lungo, pp. 213–349. San José, Costa Rica: Facultad Latinoamericana de Ciencias Sociales.

Moser, Caroline. 1994. "The Informal Sector Debate, Part 1: 1970–1983." In *Contrapunto: The Informal Sector Debate in Latin America*, ed. Cathy A. Rakowski, pp. 11–29. Albany: State University of New York Press.

Murphy, Martin. 1990. "The Need for a Re-evaluation of the Concept of 'Informal Sector': The Dominican Case." In *Perspectives in Economic Anthropology*, ed. M. E. Smith, pp. 161–181. Lanham, MD: University Press of America.

Pérez Sainz, Juan Pablo. 1994. "Apatía y esperanza: Las dos caras del área metropolitana de Guatemala." Unpublished manuscript, Johns Hopkins University, Department of Sociology.

Portes, Alejandro. 1985. "Latin American Class Structures: Their Composition and Change During the Last Decades." *Latin American Research Review* 20, 3: 7–39.

Portes, Alejandro, José Itzigsohn, and Carlos Dore. 1994. "Urbanization in the Caribbean Basin: Social Change during the Years of the Crisis." *Latin American Research Review* 29, 2: 3–37.

Portes, Alejandro, and Saskia Sassen-Koob. 1987. "Making it Underground: Comparative Material on the Informal Sector in Western Market Economies." *American Journal of Sociology* 93 (July): 30–61.

Portes, Alejandro, and Richard Schauffler. 1994. "Competing Perspectives on the Latin American Informal Sector." *Population and Development Review* 19 (March): 33–60.

Portes, Alejandro, and John Walton. 1981. *Labor, Class, and the International System.* New York: Academic Press.

Rakowski, Cathy A., ed. 1994. *Contrapunto: The Informal Sector Debate in Latin America.* Albany: State University of New York Press.

Rovira Más, Jorge. 1985. *Costa Rica en los años 80.* San José, Costa Rica: Editorial Porvenir.

Sanderson, Steven. 1985. "A Critical Approach to the Americas in the New International Division of Labor." In *The Americas in the New International Division of Labor*, ed. Steven E. Sanderson, pp. 2–25. New York: Holmes and Meier.

Smith, Joan, and Immanuel Wallerstein, eds. 1992. *Creating and Transforming Households: The Constraints of the World-Economy.* Cambridge: Cambridge University Press and Maison des Sciences de l'Homme.

Wallerstein, Immanuel. 1983. *Historical Capitalism.* London: Verso.

Transnational Realities and Anti-Immigrant State Policies: Issues Raised by the Experiences of Central American Immigrants and Refugees in a Trinational Region

Susanne Jonas

This chapter suggests an interdisciplinary, cross-border conceptual framework for research about the second and third largest groups of Latinos in California (after Mexicans): Salvadoran and Guatemalan immigrants and refugees of the 1980s and 1990s. The upsurge in the movement of Salvadorans and Guatemalans across borders in recent years is analyzed here in relation to the configuration of a "trinational region" or "space" that includes their home countries in Central America, the "intermediate space" of Mexico, and the United States (focusing here on California). In conforming transnational communities, Salvadorans and Guatemalans have established cross-border circuits and linkages that are difficult to break, even in the face of anti-immigrant state policies. Furthermore, their experiences in a "trinational region" are transforming the identities and behavior of Salvadoran and Guatemalan immigrants, making many of them actors in more than one nation (particularly as some return, by choice or coercion, to their countries of origin).

In addition to sketching the outlines of this specific research, the chapter explores the effects of anti-immigrant state policies in an age of transnational realities. Because the research draws on a particular case study and the policies in question are themselves changing rapidly, this chapter does not propose definitive or generalized conclusions. However, the research reported in the study, together with other recent contributions, does raise questions about both the effectiveness of restrictive state policies in actually stopping or controlling immigration and the collateral political effects of such policies (for the immigrants themselves as well as in their different sites of residence and action).

The approach presented here is regional in scope in that it draws on the experiences of Salvadoran and Guatemalan refugees and immigrants who have crossed two borders within a trinational region that is becoming ever more integrated. These two borders (Guatemala/Mexico and Mexico/United States) are becoming nodal points in the contradictory pressures between economic transnationalization, on the one hand, and restrictive immigration policies imposed by nation-states, on the other hand. Cross-border flows of capital and goods (many of them state-promoted or -assisted), as well as U.S. foreign policies affecting the case of Central Americans, are among the realities that have made these borders more porous and stimulated increased immigrant flows. At the same time, however, the U.S. government is attempting to stem the flow of migrants (both labor and political) through increasingly restrictive immigration and refugee policies and is pressuring the Mexican government to prevent Central Americans in particular from ever reaching U.S. soil. Hence, this chapter suggests broader questions about the contradictory roles of the state in relation to cross-border movements of capital and people—a central concern of immigration research within a world-systems framework.

Like the migrations being studied, this research adopts a regional, cross-border perspective. The backdrop for this study involves the rapidly changing economic and political conditions in all three parts of this region. During the 1980s, the prolonged civil wars in El Salvador and Guatemala, which were characterized by widespread violence and repression, both combined with and intensified economic crises that left over 85 percent of the population living below the poverty line in both countries. These conditions generated a new, much larger wave of immigrants to Mexico and the United States. In the 1990s, the prospects for and obstacles to stable peace and development in the home countries continue to appear as crucial variables in shaping the decisions of Salvadorans and Guatemalans about cross-border migrations in both directions. Within the region, Mexico has played a very particular (and increasing) role as a space and a player mediating between the United States and Central America—all the more so in the age of the North American Free Trade Agreement (NAFTA) and its projected extension to Central America. Today, the endless complexities and contradictions of Mexico itself are affecting the conditions for Central American transmigrants to the United States. Finally, rapidly changing events in the United States (in this case, in California) also continue to have repercussions for Salvadorans and Guatemalans throughout the region.

This chapter is organized in four principal sections. The first section establishes a structural context, referred to as the emergence of a trinational region. The second section describes briefly some of the insights about recent migration patterns derived from in-progress, empirical research projects. The third and fourth sections suggest that the study of the Salvadoran and Guatemalan experiences can contribute toward addressing two broader questions. First, how effective are anti-immigrant state policies in the face of transnational realities within an increasingly integrated region? Second, if their effectiveness is only relative, what are the other political consequences of these policies for the region? The chapter ends by suggesting briefly some theoretical implications for cross-border reconceptualizations of democracy in the Americas and for immigration research grounded in world-systems perspectives.

TRINATIONAL REGION AS THE STRUCTURAL CONTEXT

The structural context for changing migration patterns involves the emergence of a trinational region that is undergoing a process of integration, spanning the United States (particularly California), Mexico, and Central America, and becoming interlinked economically, politically, and socioculturally. With regard to economic integration, there is already an extensive literature written by world-systems scholars (e.g., Immanuel Wallerstein, Alejandro Portes, María Patricia Fernández-Kelly, Robert Bach, Saskia Sassen, Paul Ong, Edna Bonacich, and Lucie Cheng) that focuses on the complementarity of capital and labor flows, particularly within economic arrangements characterized by relations of unequal exchange. This topic has attracted wide discussion, most recently in relation to NAFTA (e.g., the linkages created by this agreement, as well as the disruptive and/or displacing effects of economic integration for some sectors of the population on each side of the border).

Throughout the 1980s, economic crises in the region increased migratory flows, and such trends are likely to continue in the 1990s. Of equal or greater importance, the demand continues for the low-waged labor of Central Americans as well as Mexicans (both in agricultural and urban/service activities), even at the height of economic recession and anti-immigrant sentiment in the United States. In this sense, economic integration is itself important in explaining the rise of migration from Central America over recent decades.

In this region, however, the process of integration includes political, social, and cultural dimensions, and not merely economic linkages. Politically, the civil wars in Guatemala and El Salvador during the 1980s contributed to the integration of the region through the deep involvement of both the United States and Mexico (each in its own way, and directly or indirectly) in those civil wars and their peace processes. These linkages are hence based primarily on security and diplomacy considerations. Ironically, the Reagan administration's policies of supporting counterinsurgency wars during the 1980s served indirectly to stimulate the exodus of Central Americans to Mexico and the United States. The role of Mexico as a site for Central American refugees, as well as Mexican diplomacy in the region, also increased significantly during the same period. Other political linkages were forged by opponents of U.S. policy (sanctuary cities, church activists, asylum lawyers, and human rights groups in the United States and Mexico). Today, the construction of peace (the volatile peace of El Salvador and the endlessly difficult efforts to reach peace in Guatemala) has become a factor whose progress will affect people's living conditions in their home countries and, in turn, their migration decisions.

Socially, the movement of people has itself become a structural factor. Prior Central American migrations have created "bridges" (based on kinship, household, and community networks) that new migrants are crossing today.[1] These prior relationships and interactive networks have increasingly contributed to the integration of the United States, Mexico, and Central America as a trinational social region through which people move north and return. As with other transnational communities, older generations of Salvadorans and Guatemalans frequently paved the way for the 1980s refugees, who in turn have laid the groundwork for the 1990s immigrants.[2] An important concrete indicator of the significance of these transnational family and community networks is the fact that remittance flows from the United States to the home countries have become a pillar of the economies of both El Salvador and Guatemala (estimated, respectively, at $1 billion and over $.5 billion a year); in the Salvadoran case, remittances have become far greater than revenues from coffee exports.

A final point about this region is that today it is a zone of multiple conflicts and growing instabilities—from the wars and uncertain peace in Central America to the compounded crises of 1994–1995 in Mexico and economic recession in California and elsewhere in the United States. Anti-immigrant initiatives, such as California's Proposition 187 (denying education, health, and social services to undocumented immigrants), can also be expected to increase social conflict and have destabilizing consequences. This entire complex, then, forms the material basis or framework for understanding the cross-border movements of Central American immigrants and refugees as social actors.

SALVADORANS AND GUATEMALANS IN CALIFORNIA AND MEXICO

Within this trinational region, most Salvadoran and Guatemalan migrants to the United States have had two borders to cross, generating two different sets of passage (and, in some cases, adaptation) experiences. Moreover, while some Central American migrants seek a rapid passage to the United States, others end up in California only after an extended stay in Mexico. Furthermore, taking households as the unit of analysis, some migrants (especially Guatemalans) have family members in all three countries. Our in-progress research seeks to establish how migrants are transformed by their trinational experiences and, to complete the circle, how those who return to El Salvador or Guatemala may play new roles there as a result of their experiences in Mexico and California. Our research suggests the constitution of new social actors (binational or even trinational), whose behavior and identities are being redefined in a variety of ways.[3]

The Salvadoran and Guatemalan immigrants/refugees of the 1980s and 1990s, as opposed to previous generations, are characterized not only by greatly increased numbers, but by a distinct class background (generally lower-middle class, working class, or peasant rather than professional or entrepreneurial). The vast majority of these Central American migrants entered the United States via Mexico and without documentation. In some cases of indigenous Guatemalans, entire communities came collectively and continue to live collectively in "daughter communities." Given the close association between the political and economic disasters leading to their emigration, as documented in the vast literature on Central America during the 1980s, the line between political and economic motivations is often blurred. (Hamilton and Chinchilla, 1991, and Stanley, 1987, address this question directly.) In general, however, we can say that political violence was a more important factor in the 1980s than in the 1990s, particularly for Salvadorans.[4]

Precise numbers regarding Central Americans in the United States are virtually impossible to establish because a high proportion of these residents are undocumented. All counts, however, show a dramatic increase in the number of Central American immigrants during the 1980s. Although estimates vary considerably, some mid-1990s approximations suggest that up to 1.2–1.5 million Salvadorans and 800,000–1 million Guatemalans (including permanent legal residents, those in legal limbo with temporary work permits, and undocumented migrants) have entered the United States.[5] The main increase in legal immigrants for both groups occurred in 1989 and 1990 (resulting from a combination of new admissions and legalizations). For both groups, at least half are estimated to be undocumented. The data provided by the U.S. Immigration and Naturalization Service (INS) greatly underestimate the numbers involved (because they are based on a count of "deportables apprehended"), but INS data do clearly show an increase in immigration, in the mid-1980s for Salvadorans, and in the late 1980s and early 1990s for Guatemalans. For both groups, by far the largest numbers of both documented and undocumented immigrants are in California. According to the 1990 U.S. Census, almost 60 percent of Salvadorans and Guatemalans resided in this state; 1992 INS statistics suggest that the shares are even higher for undocumented immigrants.[6]

Since the civil wars were a major factor in the exodus of the 1980s, many migrants originally came as refugees but entered the United States via Mexico without refugee status and without documentation of any kind. Such a pattern contrasts with the experience of refugees from other countries such as Cuba, who generally entered the United States directly and with refugee status. Among those who applied for asylum once they were in the United States, 97 percent of Salvadorans and 99 percent of Guatemalans were turned down during the 1980s—a situation that only began to be rectified with the ABC class action lawsuit (*American Baptist Church v. Thornburgh*), which was won in December 1990, and the granting of Temporary Protected Status (TPS) to Salvadorans in 1991.[7] Even at the end of fiscal year 1994, there were some 126,500 asylum cases pending for Guatemalans (30 percent of all pending asylum cases) and 72,000 for Salvadorans, plus 187,000 TPS cases (as explained in note 7). These numbers do not include the many thousands of immigrants who never applied for asylum out of fear. The accumulation of pending asylum cases suggests that restrictive U.S. immigration policies since the mid-1980s, and U.S. hostility toward these asylum seekers specifically, did very little to deter Salvadorans and

Guatemalans from deciding to leave their home country and undertake a violent and dangerous trip through Mexico and into the United States. In fact, the largest numbers of arrivals came during the years when the INS was systematically denying asylum to virtually all applicants from these two countries who sought such a status.[8]

The passage of immigrants through Mexico represents a crucial moment in the migration circuit, especially for Guatemalans. (This section builds on the extensive research about the largest group, Guatemalan migrants and transmigrants, which was conducted by Manuel Angel Castillo at the Colegio de Mexico and Rodolfo Casillas at FLACSO/Mexico during the last decade, and which focused primarily on Mexico's southern border, in Chiapas and the surrounding states.) Our research includes as many as 150,000 Guatemalan migrants and refugees of the 1980s who were never incorporated into the camps of the United Nations or recognized in Mexico as refugees.[9] Some have become integrated into Mexican society and its labor force, and do not plan to return to Guatemala. Many have gone from the southern border states of Mexico to the cities or other points north, and some end up in the United States. Given the instability of southern Mexico and their inability to attain refugee status in Mexico, some Guatemalans who initially remained in southern border areas may now be more likely to move on to the United States.

We also focus on Guatemalan transmigrants who consciously pass through Mexico in order in order to enter the United States—often through networks that are extremely exploitative and abusive, especially for women and children. Reliable statistics are even more difficult to obtain in Mexico than in the United States, but the studies by Casillas and Castillo leave no doubt that the number of transmigrants is also growing and that experiences in Mexico are significant for some migrants who end up in California.

We now turn from the migrants' initial decisions, to leave their home countries and traverse Mexico to the United States, to their decisions to remain in the United States, return to their home countries, or move back and forth. This is the focus of our collaborative study in northern and southern California.[10] The project involves interviews with 600 Salvadorans and Guatemalans in the metropolitan areas of Los Angeles and San Francisco, two of California's "global cities." This survey attempts to determine how a number of variables, including the winding down of the 1980s civil wars in their home countries, is affecting the decisions of these Central American migrants to stay in the United States or return home. Other variables include the legal status of the Salvadorans and Guatemalans in question, their arrival date and length of stay, the strength of their family and community networks, and the changing political-economic climate in California.[11]

The survey is beginning to suggest one possible trend: even after the war is over, many Salvadorans are not deciding to return to their home country in the near future.[12] The formal end of the war is no longer the primary consideration in making the decision to stay or return—for some, they have become incorporated here; for others, because of doubts about their economic future in El Salvador. If they came largely as refugees, the determinants of their decision to remain or return are far more complex, and may vary along gender and generational lines. The findings also suggest that Salvadorans have not been induced to return permanently by anti-immigrant policies or denial of asylum—even in California's current hostile political climate (although this climate might lead many residents to advise their friends and relatives not to come to California in the immediate future). Certainly, these migrants retain very close ties to El Salvador and closely follow events in their home country. Consequently, those residents who have the option may choose to move back and forth between El Salvador and the United States. However, the situation and mind-set of the Guatemalans are quite different since the low-intensity civil war there is not fully over and political violence remains widespread.

ANTI-IMMIGRANT STATE POLICIES AND TRANSNATIONAL REALITIES

What does this case suggest about the effectiveness of anti-immigrant state policies within an increasingly integrated region—particularly in the era of an expanded NAFTA that will incorporate Central America, and of state-promoted cross-border flows of capital and goods? Specifically, in the medium or longer range, how effective are U.S. anti-immigrant policies (now complemented by Mexican policies) in relation to Central American migration through Mexico to the United States? It will take many years to have definitive answers, but I can suggest some preliminary working hypotheses.

Since the mid-1980s, U.S. immigration policies have become increasingly restrictive.[13] During the 1980s, the denial of virtually all asylum requests from Salvadorans and Guatemalans in particular was largely a function of a U.S. foreign policy that supported the counterinsurgency armies of those two governments and regarded refugees as "subversives." In the post–Cold War era of the 1990s, it is primarily for domestic political reasons that these asylum seekers and immigrants are being treated as if they constituted a threat to U.S. "national security." The post–Cold War redefinition of U.S. national security doctrine actually includes immigration as a top priority concern. Salvadorans and Guatemalans are particularly affected by all the border-focused anti-immigrant measures and by increasingly restrictive "reforms" of asylum laws, as well as by the end of TPS for Salvadorans.

An additional component that has surfaced since the mid-1980s is growing U.S. pressure on Mexico to collaborate in keeping Central Americans out of the United States. The INS has been working with Mexican migration agents (particularly on Mexico's southern border) to turn back Central Americans before they can ever come through Mexico to cross into the United States, where some could exercise the right to seek asylum and others would find work. The Mexican government denies this collaboration, but it is documented in the United

States, with Congress openly allocating funds to reimburse Mexico for the expenses of interdiction and deportation (see Frelick, 1991, and more recent congressional documents). In any case, Mexican deportations (mainly of Central Americans) have increased one hundredfold, from 1,308 in 1987 to around 130,000 a year since 1990 (Casillas, 1995:12).

A word about Mexico itself: because of its historic role as a mediator between the United States and Central America, as well as its geographic position as an "intermediate space," Mexico is caught in a complex dilemma between its diplomatic and national security concerns vis-à-vis Central Americans. Within this trinational region, Mexico's relative weight in Central America has been on the increase throughout the 1980s and 1990s. Mexico has been not only a space through which Central Americans pass, but also a major player in the Central American peace negotiations, with its own interests and definitions of "national security" (and in this regard, often an opponent rather than a supporter of U.S. policy). In addition, Mexican business interests now project increasing investment, and therefore seek greater stability, in Central America. Today, however, the situation is vastly complicated by Mexico's own crises, especially in the context of the Chiapas uprising and greater militarization on the border with Guatemala. In short, just at the moment when Mexico is becoming the centerpiece of this trinational region, its policies toward Central Americans are more contradictory and less predictable than ever.

Despite the escalation of anti-immigrant measures by both the United States and Mexico, it is far from clear how effective state policies that treat immigration as a "national security" issue will prove in the medium or long range in actually keeping out Salvadorans and Guatemalans. Clearly, a hostile U.S. reception did not stop them from coming during the 1980s. Since then, the pace of regional economic integration has greatly quickened, while the demand for cheap labor in the United States remains as high as ever; and by now, preexisting immigrant social networks are already in place. As Espenshade (1994), Kossoudji (1992), and others have suggested, the threat of apprehension at the United States–Mexico border has only a limited deterrent effect unless it is applied massively and absolutely (which would make border areas literally a police state)—although we can expect that the deterrent effect will be greater for Central Americans, who risk deportation to their home country, than for Mexicans. Increased interdictions and deportations by Mexican authorities have not stopped the influx of Salvadorans and Guatemalans, although they have doubtless reduced the numbers. Moreover, in terms of those already in the United States, it seems likely that, short of massive deportations or the passage of extremist legislation, many individuals and families who have the option will do what they can to remain (including naturalization), while maintaining ties to their home countries.

In short, anti-immigrant state policies do not necessarily control the actual behavior of people whose lives have been transnationalized. These measures may temporarily affect the direction of the flow, but they will not decrease cross-border movements of people, disrupt the migration circuits, or stop the process of regional integration. In the case of Salvadorans and Guatemalans specifically, the numbers of new migrants will be significantly affected by the extent to which the end of the civil wars brings stable peace and economic opportunity—equitable, rather than neoliberal, development. Apart from that, migration will doubtless continue through established and, to some extent, self-perpetuating networks and patterns.[14] Furthermore, even if the end of the wars, combined with the crackdown in the United States, were to encourage a larger number of Central Americans to return home (by free choice or increased deportations), the binational or trinational practices and collective cross-border links and circuits that have developed during the last fifteen years are likely to persist, with Salvadorans and Guatemalans continuing to move back and forth across the borders in this trinational region.

The final contradiction of anti-immigrant state policies, which undermines or relativizes their effectiveness perhaps more than all other factors discussed here, is that labor migrants are not truly "unwanted" in the United States. Consequently, proposals for a new Bracero-type program are now emerging precisely at the height of anti-immigrant measures, which is an oft-repeated pattern in the immigration history of the United States. Today, as Portes remarks in Chapter 8 of this volume, "Core-bound immigration is not an optional process, but one driven by the structural requirements of advanced capitalist accumulation." Public perceptions in the United States that immigrants are "taking American jobs" or "over using public services" must be understood largely as a function of the fact that the costs of immigration are socialized (worse yet, at a time of economic recession), while the benefits are privatized. Clearly, there are many different agendas in regard to immigration policy, but those who advocate stopping the flow are less likely to prevail, in the long run, than those who seek to control it (in ways adverse to the immigrants themselves).

POLITICAL EFFECTS AND THEORETICAL IMPLICATIONS

All the issues discussed here raise serious questions about the medium- or long-range effectiveness of anti-immigrant state policies, but there are other consequences as well. The creation of an integrated region is already in process; but what kind of region will it be, politically? Treating immigration as a national security issue, I suggest, will likely have serious antidemocratic and destabilizing consequences. Specifically, it subjects the migrants involved to conditions of greater vulnerability, with diminished human and civil rights. Just as banning abortion only leads to coat-hanger abortions, so, too, the criminalization of border crossings does not stop them; bans might reduce border crossings, but above all, they make them far more dangerous and abusive to those involved. To put it another way, anti-immigrant state policies can certainly punish undocumented entrants, regardless of the effectiveness in restricting their entry.

More broadly, these anti-immigrant policies also lead to exclusionary politics in the United States. Castañeda (1993), writing about Mexican immigration, postulated a "de-democratization" of California, referring to the creation of a two-tiered system of citizens/non citizens as a form of electoral apartheid. Furthermore, de-democratization has had a spread effect in California and elsewhere in the United States. The measures began by treating undocumented immigrants as a national security problem, but they have rapidly spread to attacks on legal resident immigrant communities, and they could ultimately affect Latino citizens. (We should not forget the massive deportations of Mexican-American citizens during the 1930s). Even beyond that, however, given the multiple initiatives to change the Fourteenth Amendment of the U.S. Constitution so as to deny citizenship to children born in the United States of undocumented parents, a basic principle of "American democracy" is in danger of being profoundly undermined.

Anti-immigration policies also have broader implications for Latin America. Even in terms of the stated goals of U.S. policy for the hemisphere, both Mexico and Central America will be politically and economically destabilized rather than stabilized as a consequence of these measures. To cite only the most obvious example, cutting off remittances from immigrants (one of the survival mechanisms of economies in crisis) will surely undermine economic stabilization programs in both Mexico and Central America. By contrast, permitting free movement of peoples would build a more stable, as well as a more humane, integrated region. That is the European approach, at least among the European Community (EC) countries.[15] Nor can the economies of these countries absorb a major influx of deportee labor. Furthermore, treating immigration as a national security issue actually serves to undermine rather than promote democracy in Latin America, since it institutionalizes new forms of exclusionary politics in inter-American relations and in the countries involved (e.g., the militarization of Mexico's borders).

In the case presented here, Salvadorans and Guatemalans have begun to play a role in struggles for democratization in all three areas of this region and are engaging in "transnational grassroots political practices," as some (e.g., Smith, 1994) have called them.[16] In addition, having begun as targets of exclusionary politics in their countries of origin, some of these Salvadorans and Guatemalans are carriers of resistance strategies, which they are learning to adapt and use against exclusionary politics in the United States (e.g., working in coalitions around immigration issues).

These immigrant groups will need solid support from progressive movements in the United States and Mexico. In the United States, this suggests the need to build a new civil rights movement with an internationalist orientation to fight for the rights of Latino and other immigrants and to build cross-border coalitions and alliances. Such a movement would go beyond defensive focuses (e.g., against restrictive legislation) to initiate campaigns for the strict application of international refugee conventions, an international charter or bill of rights (even an ombudsman), and international unions representing workers who move across borders (including their treatment at those borders). This movement would also push for hemispheric codes establishing and enforcing minimum wage rates, basic working conditions, and so forth—in short, setting limits on the degree of exploitation of Latin American workers within the United States as well as in their home countries. These should be among the priority concerns of twenty-first-century, U.S.-based citizens of an increasingly integrated transnational region.

Finally, let us consider briefly some of the theoretical implications. First, the great upsurge in cross-border immigration suggests the limitations of the nation-bound concept of democracy as nothing more than elections—and even more so, the neoliberal idea that the internationalization of capital will automatically "democratize" these regions (which is the working assumption of NAFTA and of U.S. policy in Latin America generally). On the contrary, free-trade agreements can only be compatible with a more integral notion of democracy that includes its social dimension if they are based on an upward harmonization of wage, environmental, and political standards rather than downward harmonization, as is currently the case. Furthermore, in a transnational era, democracy must include mechanisms to ensure the accountability of states to civil society across borders, and thus to counter the undemocratic tendencies of, and pressures from, transnationalized capital. More generally, as I argue in more detail elsewhere (Jonas, forthcoming), democracy and citizenship must be substantially reconceptualized for the twenty-first century in order to address the rights of people who move across borders and of transnational populations as de facto citizens of an increasingly integrated region.

Second, just as immigration research grounded in a structural world-systems framework has been greatly enriched by enthnographic and network research and perspectives, so too it can gain a new dimension from examination of the political implications of anti-immigrant state policies and the new opportunities for political action on this issue by individual and collective actors in civil society. This more explicit political focus can be useful, not only to activists, but also to researchers and theorists developing a multidimensional paradigm or approach to immigration. It can shed light on the contradictory roles of the state as it seeks to enhance cross-border flows of capital and goods while restricting cross-border movements of people, and on the intersection of transnational realities and state policies—both ongoing concerns of world-systems analysis.

Third, at a more general level, we need a thoroughly interdisciplinary approach. The project described here combines structural and policy analyses with survey research, ethnographic interviews, and statistical analysis. This particular study, and immigration research more generally, exemplifies the broader need and the opportunity (already identified by leading world-systems scholars) for a new paradigm for the social sciences—including its interaction with what has traditionally been considered the "humanities."[17]

A final note on levels of analysis goes back to our starting point: this chapter has attempted to present an approach that is multilevel—that is regional as well as global and local. By themselves, global structural analyses risk explaining too little by explaining too much. Strictly community or local focuses, on the other hand, can become problematic when their conclusions are generalized too readily. However, a combination of both that additionally incorporates a "middle," or regional, cross-border level permits a focus on the specific dynamics of a particular area, such as the trinational region examined here. This multidimensional spotlight seems particularly appropriate to illuminate the complex dynamics of immigration in the Americas of the twenty-first century.

NOTES

I wish to thank the North-South Center of the University of Miami and the Chicano-Latino Research Center of the University of California (UC) at Santa Cruz for the funding that made this research possible. Thanks also go to John Marshall for valiant research assistance on statistical materials, and many thanks go to the organizers and participants in the PEWS conference (especially Bill Smith), as well as colleagues at UC Santa Cruz (John Isbister, Pat Zavella) and elsewhere (particularly Nestor Rodríguez, Manuel Angel Castillo, and Frank Bonilla) for invaluable comments on earlier versions of this chapter. As always, they bear no responsibility for the final product.

1. As Fernández-Kelly and Portes (1992: 253) put it, "Migrants walk across the invisible bridges created by particular capital flows and political linkages." From a different vantage point, Basch, Schiller, and Blanc referred to "the creation of social fields that cross national boundaries," in which people link nations (1994: 22).

2. The pioneering work by Frank Bonilla and the Centro de Estudios Puertorriqueños (1986) about "circuits and cycles of migration" has proven useful for understanding transnational Latino communities. In the case of Salvadorans and Guatemalans, see note 10 below.

3. In a recent review of the immigration literature, Massey et al. referred to the emergence over time of a "culture of migration that is distinct from the culture of both sending and receiving countries" (1994: 738).

4. The importance of civil wars and political violence in the case of Salvadorans and Guatemalans (and Nicaraguans, although they are not included in our study) can be seen by contrasting their large wave of immigration during the 1980s with the far smaller migration from Honduras, where poverty levels were similar but were not accompanied by civil war or an equivalent level of political violence.

5. The 1990 U.S. Census reported 565,081 Salvadorans and 268,779 Guatemalans; in addition to generally recognized undercounting (in large part, because of the high proportion of undocumented migrants), this does not include post-1990 entrants—which is particularly problematic in the case of Guatemalans, because their migration increased more during the late 1980s and early 1990s.

6. Los Angeles has become the second capital city to both groups, with 300,000–500,000 Salvadorans and 250,000–400,000 Guatemalans by 1994 (estimates vary significantly)—in both cases, and especially for Guatemalans, far more than the number counted in the 1990 census.

7. The ABC class-action lawsuit (*American Baptist Church v. Thornburgh*), which was won in December 1990, established that the INS had "wrongfully discriminated" against Salvadoran and Guatemalan asylum applicants (by arbitrarily dismissing their

cases on foreign policy grounds), and called for their cases to be reheard. Several hundred thousand Central Americans were saved from deportation pending a new hearing; today, over four years later, they remain in a legal limbo but do have work permits. Given the huge backlog of cases pending, it is likely that some will find a way to regularize their status. Those who came after 1990, however, are not protected by the ABC decision. Between 1991 and 1994, Salvadorans had another avenue: Temporary Protected Status/ Deferred Enforced Departure (TPS/DED)—temporary safe-haven programs. However, as of 1995, the TPS program was ended, giving 187,000 Salvadorans thirteen months to find another way to legalize their status. Meanwhile, Guatemalans never enjoyed any TPS or DED program, and efforts to gain such a program failed—despite the lack of a peace accord to end the 35-year civil war, and despite the continuing high level of political violence and repression there. From 1992 through 1994, the number of Guatemalan asylum applications was by far the highest for any country in the world (42 percent of the total in 1992 and 23 percent in 1994). In a year when 44,000 applications were received (1992), only 63 were granted.

8. The influx of Salvadoran asylum seekers slowed in 1992, when the civil war was ended. With the termination of the TPS program in 1995, the number of asylum cases will likely increase, but the end of the war will make their cases far more difficult to win. Moreover, both Salvadoran and Guatemalan asylum seekers will face an even more difficult situation in the future: among the current asylum "reforms" is the denial of work permits to applicants awaiting a decision, and far more drastic proposals are making their way through the U.S. Congress.

9. In regard to Guatemalans in Mexico, this section does not focus on the seasonal contract laborers who come across the Guatemala/Mexico border "legally" (50,000–60,000 a year are involved in something like a bracero program) or border residents who move back and forth across that border (some on a daily basis). Nor does it focus on the 45,000 Guatemalan political refugees of the 1980s who have been living in the UN camps in southern Mexico and whose goal is collective and organized return to Guatemala (which is now in progress).

10. This study on Salvadorans and Guatemalans in California is being conducted by Nora Hamilton, Norma Chinchilla, Carlos Córdova, and myself. It will complement research being conducted by Nestor Rodríguez and Jacqueline Hagan in Texas, Allen Burns in Florida, Terry Repak in Washington, D.C., and Sarah Mahler on Long Island, New York—and previous and ongoing work being conducted in California by various researchers (see References).

11. Our questionnaire is quite broad and will yield much additional information about these transnational individuals, families, and communities. We are currently conducting the interviews (300 in each area)—primarily with those who came during the 1980s and 1990s, but also including some from earlier migrations, in order to see the contrast. Snowball sampling is used, with an orientation toward a stratified sample that will replicate data from the 1990 census with regard to national group and similar parameters. Our interviews include both documented and undocumented migrants and are drawn from a wide range of networks, including soccer clubs, business associations, refugee assistance organizations, and churches; moreover, they are distributed over gender and generational groupings, as well as between Salvadorans and Guatemalans. In addition to the interviews, we will be integrating available statistical information from the census, the INS, and other sources—despite the limitations of such information when taken by itself. A second phase of this project will attempt to assess the multiple impacts of the decisions

to either remain or return on families and communities, both in the United States and "back home," as well as the creation of transnational identities.

12. This confirms informal surveys reported in 1993 on Univisión (Spanish-language television news in the United States) in the *San Francisco Chronicle*, and in *La Opinión* (Los Angeles) to the effect that a very high percentage no longer considered themselves refugees. For earlier studies, see Chávez, Flores and López-Garza (1990) and Córdova (1987).

13. For the purposes of policy analysis, these observations shift from the California to the U.S. level because national laws have far greater impact than state laws; additionally, anti-immigrant initiatives that premiered in California are spreading to other states and being taken up in Congress.

14. Sarah Mahler (1995) went even farther, arguing that Salvadoran society has become so "vested in migration"—so permeated by the culture and industries of migration—that the flow will be only minimally deterred by restrictionist U.S. policies or the end of the war. Studies by Nestor Rodríguez and others have emphasized, in addition, the role of rapid travel and communications. On these points more generally, see Chapter 8 in this volume, by Portes, which focuses on the role of transnational entrepreneurs. The latter contribution and Massey et al. (1994: 699–751) have both referred to the "cumulative" and "self-perpetuating" nature of migration.

15. As Luis Guarnizo concluded in his study of Dominican return migration, "While the formal Dominican economy is restructuring itself to redefine its mode of insertion into the world economy, migrants are laying the groundwork to further this process of globalization: a growing Dominican population overseas with a thriving ethnic economy, plus a continuous flow of tangible and intangible resources between both countries, are apt pillars to support this process" (1993: 44).

16. To cite just one incipient example, a group of Guatemalan "Displaced Persons living in the United States" gained representation in the multisectoral Assembly of Civil Society in Guatemala, which is deeply involved in the peace process and the democratization of Guatemala; in the United States, this same group has been part of a coalition seeking to gain TPS status for Guatemalans. Like other transnational Latino communities described by Basch, Schiller, and Blanc, "by living their lives straddling several nation-states, they are affected by, pose special challenges to, and contribute to hegemonic processes in several separate states" (1994: 15).

17. See, among others, Gulbenkian Commission (1992), Quijano and Wallerstein (1992), and Bonilla (1994). On the last point, which has received increasing attention in cultural studies, Quijano and Wallerstein have noted that the Americas are undergoing a "growing decolonization of the production of culture, of the arts, and of scientific knowledge," despite the pressures from globalizing capital (1992: 549–557).

REFERENCES

Bach, Robert L. 1992. "Hemispheric Migration in the 1990s." In *The United States and Latin America in the 1990s: Beyond the Cold War*, ed. J. Hartlyn, L. Schoultz, and A. Varas, pp. 262–281. Chapel Hill: University of North Carolina Press.

Basch, Linda, Nina Glick Schiller, and Cristina Szanton Blanc. 1994. *Nations Unbound: Transnational Projects, Postcolonial Predicaments, and Deterritorialized Nation-States*. Langhorne, PA: Gordon and Breach.

Bonilla, Frank. 1986. "Ethnic Orbits: The Circulation of Capitals and Peoples." In *Industry and Idleness*, ed. Frank Bonilla and Ricardo Campos. New York: Centro de Estudios Puertorriqueños.

———. 1992. "Circuits and Cycles: A Century of Puerto Rican Migration." Connecticut Humanities Council.

———. 1994. "The Global Society and the Latino Community: Changing the Americas from within the U.S." Unpublished manuscript.

Burns, Allan. 1993. *Maya in Exile: Guatemalans in Florida*. Philadelphia: Temple University Press.

Casillas, Rodolfo. 1995. "Se mueve la frontera al Suchiate?" *Este País*, April, pp. 9–12.

———, ed. 1992. *Los Procesos Migratorios Centroamericanos y Sus Efectos Regionales*. Mexico, DF: Facultad Latinoamericana de Ciencias Sociales/Mexico.

Casillas, Rodolfo, and Manuel Angel Castillo. 1994. *Los flujos migratorios internacionales en la frontera sur de México*. México, DF: Secretaría del Trabajo y Previsión Social, Consejo Nacional de Población.

Castañeda, Jorge. 1993. "Mexico and California: The Paradox of Tolerance and Dedemocratization." In *The California-Mexico Connection*, ed. A. Lowenthal and K. Burgess, pp. 34–47. Palo Alto, CA.: Stanford University Press.

Castillo, Manuel Angel. 1995. "Politicas de Refugio y Politicas de Immigración: ¿Posibilidades de Conciliación?" Unpublished manuscript.

Chávez, Leo, Estevan Flores and Marta López-Garza. 1990. "Here Today, Gone Tomorrow? Undocumented Settlers and Immigration Reform." *Human Organization* 49, 3: 193–205.

Córdova, Carlos. 1987. "El Salvadorean Immigrants in the San Francisco Bay Area." *Journal of La Raza Studies* 1, 1: 9–37.

Espenshade, Thomas. 1994. "Does the Threat of Border Apprehension Deter Undocumented U.S. Immigration?" *Population and Development Review* 20, 4 (December): 871–892.

Fernández-Kelly, M. Patricia, and Alejandro Portes. 1992. "Continent on the Move: Immigrants and Refugees in the Americas." In *Americas: New Interpretive Essays*, ed. Alfred Stepan, pp. 248–274. New York: Oxford University Press.

Frelick, William. 1991. "Running the Gauntlet: The Central American Journey through Mexico." Washington, DC: U.S. Committee for Refugees.

Guarnizo, Luis. 1993. "Going Home: Class, Gender and Household Transformations among Dominican Returned Migrants." Report prepared for Commission for Hemispheric Migration and Refugee Policy, Georgetown University.

Gulbenkian Foundation Commission. 1992. "Report." *Fernand Braudel Center Newsletter* (State University of New York at Binghamton) 17 (August).

Hagan, Jacqueline. 1994. *Deciding to be Legal: A Maya Community in Houston*. Philadelphia: Temple University Press.

Hamilton, Nora, and Norma Chinchilla. 1991. "Central American Migration: A Framework for Analysis." *Latin American Research Review* 26, 1: pp 75–110.

Jonas, Susanne. Forthcoming. " 'National Security,' Regional Development, and Citizenship in U.S. Immigration Policy: Reflections from the Case of Central American Immigrants and Refugees." In *Transnational Realities and Nation States: Trends in International Migration and Immigration Policy in the Americas*, ed. M. Castro. Miami, FL: North-South Center.

Kossoudji, Sherrie. 1992. "Playing Cat and Mouse and the U.S.-Mexican Border." *Demography* 29, 2 (May): 159–180.

López, David, Eric Popkin, and Eddie Telles. 1995. "To Earn a Living: The Occupational World of Central American Immigrants in Los Angeles." Unpublished manuscript.

Mahler, Sarah. 1995. "Vested in Migration: Salvadorans Challenge Restrictionist Policies." Unpublished manuscript.

Massey, Douglas, Joaquín Arrango, Graeme Hugo, Ali Kouaquci, Adela Pellegrino, and J. Edward Taylor. 1994. "An Evaluation of International Migration Theory: The North American Case." *Population and Development Review* 20, 4 (December): 699–751.

Ong, Paul, Edna Bonacich, and Lucie Cheng. 1994. *The New Asian Immigration in Los Angeles and Global Restructuring*. Philadelphia: Temple University Press.

Portes, Alejandro and Ruben Rumbaut. 1990. *Immigrant America*. Berkeley: University of California Press.

Quijano, Aníbal, and Immanuel Wallerstein. 1992. "Americanity as a Concept, or the Americas in the Modern World-system." *International Social Science Journal* 44, 4 (November): 549–557.

Rodríguez, Nestor. 1987. "Undocumented Central Americans in Houston: Diverse Populations." *International Migration Review* 21, 1 (Spring): 4–26.

Sassen, Saskia. 1988. *The Mobility of Labor and Capital*. Cambridge: Cambridge University Press.

Smith, Michael Peter. 1994. "Can You Imagine? Transnational Migration and the Globalization of Grassroots Politics." *Social Text* 39 (Summer): 15–33.

Stanley, William. 1987. "Economic Migrants or Refugees from Violence?" *Latin American Research Review* 22, 1: 132–153.

Torres Rivas, Edelberto and Dina Jiménez. 1985. "Informe sobre el estado de las migraciones en Centroamerica." *Anuario de Estudios Centroamericanos* (San José, Costa Rica) 11, 2: 25–57.

Wallerstein, Immanuel. 1992. "The Collapse of Liberalism." In *Socialist Register 1992*, ed. Ralph Miliband and Leo Panitch, pp. 96–110. New York: Monthly Review Press.

## 7

Women, Households, and Transnational Migration Networks: The Garifuna and Global Economic Restructuring

Linda Miller Matthei and David A. Smith

The world-system perspective provides a powerful conceptual framework for the analysis of global processes that give rise to and structure migration. Unlike "modernization" theories, which explain migration flows as the cumulative responses of individuals to "push" factors (e.g., high unemployment) in sending areas and unrelated "pull" factors (e.g., high labor demands) in receiving areas, world-system analyses focus explicitly on the structural inequalities that link societies in a single system: the capitalist world-economy (Portes and Walton, 1981; Sassen-Koob, 1981a). Migration, from this perspective, is generated by the penetration and expansion of capitalism and represents a mechanism for the allocation of labor in the global economy (Sassen-Koob, 1981b; Fernández-Kelly 1981).

Though the historical-structural approach developed in world-system analyses significantly advances our understanding of the linkages between migration and global economic forces, it is sometimes criticized for its singular emphasis on the economic *functions* of labor migrants in capitalist development and a lack of attention to migrants as active participants in the migration process (Bach and Schraml, 1982; Massey et al., 1987). As Bach and Schraml have pointed out, in historical-structural analyses, migration is often reduced to a purely economic process in which the migrants themselves are treated "like empty grocery carts, wheeled back and forth between origin and destination under the hungry intentions of world capital. The migrants themselves engage in very little action" (1981: 324).

World-system analyses are also criticized by feminist scholars who argue that macrostructural research often presents an impoverished view of women in international labor migration and in the world-system in general (Grasmuck and Pessar, 1991; Pedraza, 1991; Georges, 1990; Ward, 1993). In numerous studies of international labor migration, women are overlooked completely or treated as secondary migrants who move only at the behest of male decision makers (e.g., Massey et al., 1987; Portes and Bach, 1985; Piore, 1979). This neglect of gender issues in migration research, feminists argue, perpetuates the ideological assumption that "women do little worth writing about" (Pedraza, 1991: 302).

Those macroeconomic studies that *do* examine gender as a dimension of international labor migration generally focus on the global restructuring of production processes and the increasing demand for female labor in low-wage services and the garment and electronic industries (Morokvasic, 1983; Sassen-Koob, 1981a, 1988). The recognition that women are not simply "along for the ride" but are indeed labor migrants in their own right is a significant one. However, these studies, too, tend to limit their analyses to the economic functions of female migrants, and we are left with the impression that the only real difference between men's and women's migration lies in the fact that women represent a more exploitable source of labor. Still absent is any sense of women as active participants in the migration process. "The woman remains silent and invisible, present as a variable, absent as a person" (Morokvasic, 1983: 18).

This chapter is based on an ethnographic study of a "transnational community" (see Portes, Chapter 8 of this volume): the Garifuna of Belize, Central America and Los Angeles. It examines the political-economy of global restructuring and the way in which structural forces shape migration processes, but our primary focus is more "micro"—focusing on what Portes (Chapter 8 of this volume) terms the "everyday networks and patterns of social relationships" that develop in response to more global forces. More specifically, we question the adequacy of approaches that focus on the household as the fundamental unit of analysis in migration research. Such approaches, we argue, obscure women's roles in building and maintaining the transnational networks that pave the way for migration.

In seeking to establish a conceptual link between individuals and the macroeconomic forces that shape migration flows, many migration researchers settle on the household as the "appropriate" unit of analysis (e.g., Wood, 1981; Pessar, 1982). Typically, households are conceptualized as income-pooling and decision-making units that ensure their viability through the strategic allocation of labor (e.g., Wood, 1981; Smith, Wallerstein, and Evers, 1984). In migration research, this "generic" household model has been applied uncritically across societies to explain how migration is planned and how resources are marshaled at ground level. However, these efforts to fit a temporally and culturally specific model of household structure and behavior to all locales and times assume a uniformity and stability that do not hold up to empirical scrutiny (Guyer and Peters, 1987; Moser, 1993). Cross-cultural research indicates, for example, that there is a good deal of variability in levels of income pooling within households. Factors such as marital instability, ethnicity, individual household members' access to employment opportunities, and varying inheritance and marital patterns all contribute to patterns in which household members find it strategically beneficial to maintain "separate purses" (Treas, 1991; Fapohunda, 1988; Beneria and Roldan, 1987).

The conceptualization of households as monolithic units in which members selflessly subsume their individual interests and desires for the good of the collectivity also fails to bring to light inequalities and competing interests that give rise to conflict between household members (e.g., Wolf, 1988, 1992; Blumberg, 1991; Wong, 1984). Feminist scholars are particularly critical of the model's lack of attention to the unequal gender distribution of resources and access to power within the household (e.g., Benería and Roldán, 1987; Blumberg, 1991; Wolf, 1992). Treated as a wholly cooperative unit, the household has been cast as *the* actor in migration decision making, and as a result, the negotiations and conflicts that characterize gender relationships within households are left unexamined. Consequently, any woman "who seeks a paying job, earns a wage, or migrates is interpreted as doing so as part of a household strategy" (Wolf, 1992: 12). In fact, however, numerous studies from a variety of migration-sending societies show that women often use migration as an avenue of escape from marital relationships that are exploitative and oppressive (e.g., Chávez, 1992; Grasmuck and Pessar, 1991: 146–147; Foner, 1986: 139).

Recent efforts to address international migration as a social process have resulted in renewed attention to migration as "a process of network-building" (Portes and Walton, 1981: 60) through which migrants organize their moves, gain access to the economic opportunities that await in receiving societies, and pave the way for a subsequent return to sending communities (Portes and Bach, 1985; Massey et al., 1987). However, as Monica Boyd pointed out:

To date much of the recent research on networks is indifferent to gender. Some studies emphasize the experiences of male migrants or all migrants undifferentiated by sex, while others emphasize group behavior as represented in household decisionmaking [*sic*] strategies. Such emphasis is consistent with a general research orientation which assumes that women migrate as part of family migration. As a consequence, little systematic attention is paid to gender in the development and persistence of networks across time and space. (1989: 655)

This lack of attention to female participation in migration networks, we argue, is perpetuated by studies that fail to examine migration as a process of *intra*-household negotiation and decision making, and to question the long-held assumption that migration and migration decision making are, by and large, the province of males (e.g., Massey et al., 1987: 124; Portes and Bach, 1985: 60). Even feminist scholars often treat women as "passive victims" of patriarchal domination (Wolf, 1992: 20). Kathryn Ward, for example, in summarizing research on the impact of migration on women, emphasized their "disadvantaged" status relative to males and suggested that when women accompany their migrant mates, they "lose access to kin-support networks that were essential for economic subsistence and social support in the rural areas" (1985: 308). Moreover, nonmigrant women, if they are considered at all, are characterized simply as "women who wait" (Peattie, 1977: 126), or "women left behind" (Gordon, 1978).

Limiting the focus of research on migration and gender to the social and economic "consequences" for women fails to recognize their active participation in the process of transnational network building. A large body of cross-cultural literature documents the central role that "women-centered" networks play in facilitating the flow of goods, services, and information between households in both industrialized and less-developed societies (e.g., Yanagisako, 1977; Neuhouser, 1989; Grieco, 1987; Stivens, 1984). Why, then, should we assume that women's social ties are severed by migration or that men necessarily assume the primary responsibility for building transnational networks?

Our findings suggest that in their efforts to ensure some level of economic security, both migrant *and* nonmigrant Garifuna women engage in building and maintaining transnational networks, much as they do at the local level in Belize. Therefore, it is critical to consider, not only intrahousehold relationships and negotiation in studies of migration decision making, but also the networks that link sending and receiving societies. Moreover, our findings indicate that transnational networks need *not* weaken over time and distance. On the contrary, social and economic pressures experienced by migrants in the United States can motivate them to strengthen their relationships with those back home.

GARIFUNA MIGRATION IN HISTORICAL CONTEXT

The Garifuna are a product of European colonial expansion into the Caribbean. Throughout their history, their economic fortunes have been inextricably linked to labor demands in the capitalist world-economy, and as a result, they exhibit a history of wage-labor migration extending back to the early nineteenth century. According to historical accounts, the Garifuna emerged as a distinct ethnic group after African slaves escaped the wreckage of two Spanish ships in 1635 and took up residence with the indigenous Carib Indians on the island of St. Vincent, in the eastern Caribbean. In 1797, after an unsuccessful uprising aimed at dislodging the island's British colonizers, the Garifuna were exiled to the Bay of Honduras and quickly began to migrate to the Central American mainland (Shephard, [1831] 1971). By 1800, they began to establish small settlements along the coast from Nicaragua to Belize, maintaining a peaceful, but uneasy, coexistence with the British colonists.

Their autonomy was short-lived, however. Following slave emancipation in 1834, chronic labor shortages in Belize made the Garifuna an attractive source of labor for British forestry and agricultural enterprises. Through a series of legislative measures that restricted their access to land, the British ensured Garifuna availability to the wage labor market (Bolland, 1977). However, by permitting the Garifuna to continue to occupy lands for traditional subsistence activities, the British reduced their labor costs substantially. During off-seasons in forestry and agriculture, the men returned to their home communities, where women provided support through their traditional horticultural activities.

Until the 1940s, male wage-labor migration was, by and large, temporary as men pursued seasonal employment in Central America's forests and plantations. However, World War II and resulting labor shortages in the United States created new employment markets for Garifuna men, who were recruited by the U.S. Labor Department to replace U.S. workers involved in the war effort. About half the men stayed on at war's end (Vernon, 1990), thus paving the way for a sustained flow of Belizeans to the United States.

As males began to travel farther and stay away longer, Garifuna women adapted their economic strategies to the changing patterns of male migration. Unable to maintain sufficient horticultural production without the assistance of men, they turned increasingly to marketing and domestic service in order to supplement their incomes. During the 1960s, however, structural changes in the U.S. economy resulted in a shift from a goods-producing to a service-based economy, creating a substantial demand for low-wage female labor (Tienda, Jensen, and Bach, 1984; Singlemann and Browning, 1980), and leading Garifuna women to quickly join their male counterparts in international wage-labor migration.

Garifuna men and women recall the 1960s and early 1970s as a boom period for both documented and undocumented workers seeking employment in Los Angeles. Not only were jobs plentiful, employers were relatively unconcerned about the immigration status of prospective employees. However, as restructuring in Los Angeles progressed, traditional blue-collar manufacturing jobs were largely replaced by downgraded manufacturing and low-wage service jobs. In the Los Angeles metropolitan area, some 75,000, mostly unionized, relatively high-wage manufacturing jobs disappeared due to plant closures and indefinite layoffs from 1978 to 1982 (Soja, 1987: 182), while garment-manufacturing and low-wage services that rely heavily on female immigrant labor made huge gains (Sassen, 1988; Soja, 1987).

Having grown accustomed to finding reasonably high-paying, blue-collar jobs with relative ease, Garifuna men found it difficult to adapt to the transformed labor market in Los Angeles, where the kinds of jobs they used to get (semi-skilled factory and warehouse work and commercial maintenance work) were no longer available to them. Today, men arriving in Los Angeles often spend two or three months looking for employment and then are likely to find only low-paying, irregular work as parking lot attendants or security guards. Understandably, Garifuna migrants living in Los Angeles are more inclined to offer their assistance to women seeking to migrate, since these women are likely to be able to find work quickly and will not need to rely on the hospitality and financial resources of kin for extended periods of time after their arrival. James, a man in his mid-30s living in Belize, said, "We keep getting the message from there, 'It's best you stay on your job where you are there than come here to waste time and live on somebody else's back.' " As opportunities diminished,

men began to relinquish their traditionally dominant role in the migration process to women, who continue to enjoy a strong demand for their labor in Los
Angeles' low-wage service industry.

Since most Garifuna women who migrate to Los Angeles are relatively unskilled—and, as often as not, undocumented—their opportunities in Los Angeles are largely limited to low-wage, service-sector jobs. To understand why
women actively seek jobs that most women in the United States would reject
out of hand, a Garifuna woman in Belize explained, "You have to compare
'hard' in the States to 'hard' here [in Belize]." In the following section, we
briefly describe the research setting and then examine the current economic
situation in Belize and the narrow range of employment options available to
women there.

WOMEN AND HOUSEHOLDS IN THE SOURCE COMMUNITY

Although Belize was initially a producer of forestry products, its economy is
now primarily dependent on export agriculture. Sugar (grown in the northern
districts) and citrus and bananas (from the south) constitute more than 70 percent
of the total value of Belize's domestic exports. Employment opportunities and
the earning power of Garifuna men is limited by the low-wage, mostly seasonal,
labor demands of the citrus and banana industries, and also by longstanding
ethnic discrimination in the Belizean labor market. The average wage of unskilled agricultural workers ranges between U.S. $.69 and U.S. $1.12 per hour
(Labor Department, 1987).

Although there is no cultural resistance to women's employment outside the
home and women are eager to take any available jobs, there are very few opportunities for them in the local wage-labor market. The unemployment rate of
38.8 percent for women in the district where the research was carried out is the
highest in Belize. The women's high jobless rate is due, at least in part, to the
preference of agricultural employers for male workers. A 1990 labor force survey indicated that males outnumbered females four-to-one in agricultural employment (Government Information Service, 1992).

The gender wage gap in Belize is also significant. Average wages for unskilled women range from $.58 to $.68 per hour, and even when they do the
same work, women typically earn one-quarter to one-third less than their male
counterparts (Bolland, 1986; Kerns, 1982). According to government estimates,
in 1992, 59 percent of employed males earned less than $3,000 annually, com-
pared to 75 percent of females (Government Information Service, 1992).[1] The
employment difficulties experienced by women in Belize come into even sharper
focus when we consider that one-third in Belizean households are headed by
women (Government Information Service, 1992: 45). In the southern districts
where Garifuna are concentrated, this figure has reached 40 percent (Ministry
of Education, 1984: 15).

To further probe into employment and migration patterns, this section reports the findings of our study of a coastal settlement in Belize. Most contemporary Garifuna communities in Central America are coastal settlements, with small numbers of Creoles (descendants of the slave population), East Indians, and Chinese in residence. We use the fictitious name "Seaview" to refer to a town (population 7,000) where Professor Matthei did her Belizean fieldwork. A commercial and transportation hub, it serves as a major staging area for U.S.-bound migrants from throughout southern Belize.[2]

The dearth of full-time employment opportunities makes it necessary for most Garifuna to employ a strategy of "occupational multiplicity" (Comitas, 1973). That is, they work at several income-generating activities in order to make ends meet. For men, occupational multiplicity often involves migration between temporary formal-sector jobs in various areas of Belize supplemented by fishing and odd jobs during their stays in Seaview. The lack of formal-sector employment for women requires that they engage in a variety of informal-sector activities (e.g., taking in laundry, sewing, vending a variety of low-cost goods, and taking in boarders). Though women often devalue their activities, referring to them as simply "turning over a little cash," both men and women agree that women are particularly resourceful at generating cash in the informal sector. The local social-service officer estimates that women are the primary sources of household income in more than half of her town's households.

The composition of Garifuna households is fluid and flexible, and as a result, it is often difficult to determine to which household an individual does, in fact, "belong" at any given time. For instance, it is not uncommon for a man to carry on simultaneous relationships with two or more women, dividing his time (and economic contributions) among them (González, 1969). Moreover, though most men and women spend some part of their lives in one form of conjugal relationship or another, such unions are not necessarily regarded as permanent, and both men and women often have more than one marital partner during their lifetimes (González, 1969; Kerns, 1983). Households also expand and contract with the periodic comings and goings of adult kin who find themselves *between* marital relationships. Since conjugal relationships are often transitory, Garifuna men and women retain substantial autonomy in their domestic relationships. Even within stable households, marital partners maintain separate purses, and they only rarely hold property in common (Miller, 1992; Kerns, 1983). In Seaview, for example, an examination of applications for residential lots from 1959 through 1990 revealed that only 11 of 1,481 applications were made jointly (780 were made by individual males, and 690 by individual females) (Government Information Service, 1959–1990).

Although couples do typically contribute a portion of their incomes to meet household expenses, neither partner has direct access to the other's earnings, nor does one spouse necessarily know exactly how much the other earns (see Benería and Roldán, 1987, and Treas, 1991, on similar patterns in Latin America and the United States). The wife typically controls the pooled budget to purchase food and take care of daily household expenses, but any additional purchases are made on an individual basis (usually by the wife), without consultation between partners. Interviews with Garifuna women revealed that perceived inequities in household contributions are a common source of domestic conflict. They complain that men withhold substantial portions of their income for their personal use and fail to contribute adequately to the household (see Benería and Roldán, 1987). Thus, they argue that they must protect themselves and their children by maintaining control of their own incomes. For example, in explaining why she kept her own finances separate, one informant clearly called into question the assumptions of unity and solidarity proffered in typical household models: ''Whatever women make stays in the home. Men have five or ten places for their money. It's us against them!''

Although the household model posits discrete, independent units, among the Garifuna relationships with extra domestic kin are frequently stronger and more enduring than marital ties (Kerns, 1983; González, 1969). For women in particular, relationships beyond the level of the household are vital sources of support during periods of crisis (cf. Wong, 1984). Most Garifuna women find themselves responsible for dependent children and without a mate more than once during their lifetimes (Kerns, 1983: 112), and they must often depend on relatives, either for child care when they are working or for temporary support and refuge when marital relationships end. However, because they themselves are often unemployed and in poor economic circumstances, the assistance that kin are able to provide is usually limited. To broaden their potential resource base, women in Seaview also forge cooperative relationships with female friends and neighbors. Food, clothing, small loans, and child care services are exchanged with the assumption that debts will be repaid at some point in the future. During periods of relative plenty, women share any surplus they may acquire within their networks, thus building accounts of social capital on which they can draw when circumstances demand.

Personal networks outside the household are particularly crucial to women, who depend on income-generating activities in the informal sector. With very limited financial resources and few formal skills, they must actively seek out opportunities. In Belize, Garifuna women frequently recruit five or six friends to pool their limited financial resources and labor in a variety of small income-generating enterprises. The networks also function as important conduits for information regarding potential employment opportunities elsewhere, and in addition to their local networks, women assiduously cultivate ties throughout Belize. The relatively recent introduction of telephone service in outlying areas greatly enhances the ability of individuals to maintain frequent contact with friends and relatives in urban centers like Belize City and Belmopan, the nation's capital, where domestic and commercial service jobs are more plentiful. Thus, women who are unable to find work locally often turn to their contacts in other communities for employment information and for temporary living quarters while they look for work.

Garifuna women's personal networks have traditionally served as channels for the exchange of material goods, services, and employment information in Belize, but they have also adapted their support networks to meet the exigencies of international migration. Expanded transnationally, these networks serve as vital conduits that facilitate migration, the exchange of employment information, and remittances. Conceptual models that arbitrarily define the household as the locus of migration decision making overlook the vital role that such extra domestic networks play in the migration process. Moreover, as the following section illustrates, it is often women who are the central actors in building and maintaining these networks.

TRANSNATIONAL NETWORKS OF GARIFUNA WOMEN IN BELIZE

The most obvious and immediate benefits of maintaining strong transnational ties are perhaps clearest for nonmigrant women seeking to ensure a regular flow of remittances from migrant kin. Among the Garifuna, ties between mothers and daughters are particularly strong, as women must often seek maternal aid when their marital relationships fail. Even though daughters may migrate, these bonds tend to remain strong. In Los Angeles, the Garifuna women interviewed named their mothers as recipients of their remittances more frequently than any other kin, including children. Though most daughters remit to their mothers, in many cases a migrant daughter's obligation is reinforced because she has left her children in the care of her mother in order to seek work in the United States. Thus, children often serve as critical links in women's transnational networks and ensure a regular flow of remittances (cf. Soto, 1987).

Although children are most often placed with their maternal grandmothers, other female kin (usually sisters) also actively seek the opportunity to "foster" the children of migrants. In most cases, the caretaker receives some sort of remittance (either cash or material goods) in exchange for her child care services. However, there are other potential benefits as well—a woman who fosters the children of migrants builds a reservoir of social capital on which she can draw in the future. Mutual obligation is implicit in the fostering relationship, and it is understood that the woman for whose children she has cared is obligated to help should she or a member of her family seek to come to the United States at some point. In some cases, women who migrate have jobs waiting for them upon their arrival in the United States. In others, migrant women meet their obligations to nonmigrant kin through what might be described as "job sharing." If the mother of fostered children works as a domestic in the United States (a common pattern of employment among Garifuna women), she will sometimes arrange for their caretaker to travel, at her expense, to the United States to fill in at her job while she returns to Belize to spend time with her children. In addition to the money she earns, the foster mother gains some useful domestic experience that she may well use should she herself migrate in the future.

Nonmigrant women's roles as critical anchors in the transnational networks that link sending and receiving communities secure for them significant control in migration decision making. Because they maintain the ties that link potential migrants to opportunities in the United States, they ultimately hold a good deal of power in determining which members of their household will be selected for migration. Presented with the opportunity to launch the migration of one of her children, for example, a woman will, more often than not, elect to invest her network resources in a daughter, who will "remember" her with remittances, rather than a son who, it is assumed, will eventually transfer his affections and earnings to his wife and her family.

As in other source communities, migration to the United States becomes an important means of escape for women who find themselves in unhappy conjugal relationships. Under these circumstances, a woman's access to transnational ties is crucial. Typically, the woman makes the decision to migrate and organizes the move surreptitiously, with the cooperation and financial assistance of kin in the United States.

Nonmigrant women's transnational ties serve much the same function as the ties that they use on a day-to-day basis in Belize. In addition to helping them to meet immediate economic needs, reciprocal ties to migrant kin also serve as investments in the future. The mutual obligations of close kin are implicit in the relationship, although the ties can be strengthened through child fostering and the transnational exchange of goods and services. Women may tap into their networks to facilitate their own migration, or they may transfer their social capital to their daughters so that they both may benefit: the daughters through employment in the United States, and the mother through the remittances sent home.

Those who stress the role of households in migration decision making may fail to recognize that the decision to migrate is often conditioned by prospective migrants' ability to marshal the support and assistance of kin already settled in the receiving country. As migration opportunities became more accessible to Garifuna women, they actively worked to build systems of support in the United States. As a result, they now play a central role in organizing their own, and their children's, migration.

MIGRANT WOMEN'S TRANSNATIONAL NETWORKS

In general, scholars argue that as migrants accumulate time in sending societies, they put down increasingly deeper social and economic roots, so that over time, there is a gradual weakening of ties to their home communities as they begin to view themselves as "settlers" rather than "sojourners" (Chávez, 1991; Massey et al., 1987). However, among the Garifuna, even women who have lived in Los Angeles for 25 to 30 years generally maintain close ties to their home communities through remittances, periodic visits, and economic investments in homes and businesses. It might be argued that as the traditional "kin keepers,'' women feel stronger emotional bonds to the kin who are left behind, but our findings suggest that social and economic pressures also induce Garifuna women to foster strong relationships with those back home.

Although some women establish careers as teachers, clerical workers, and nurses in Los Angeles, most arrive with few skills and spend their years working in the informal sector as domestics, nurse's aides, and nannies. For the latter group, retirement pensions are nonexistent, and they must eventually either return to Belize to take advantage of the lower cost of living or find a way to supplement their U.S. earnings. With this in mind, most women set aside a portion of their earnings to buy or build houses in their home communities in Belize.[3] Others invest their earnings in businesses back home. In 1990, for example, Matthei found that a hotel, two clothing stores, and a restaurant in Seaview were owned by migrant women living and working in the United States (see Portes, Chapter 8 of this volume, for similar findings).

Social pressures in the United States also motivate women to nurture their links to Belize. The Garifuna are concentrated in South-Central Los Angeles, an area that in recent years has become a national symbol of the economic decay and unrest plaguing America's inner cities. As economic conditions in the South-Central area have worsened over the years, crime rates (especially those associated with gangs and drugs) have soared, and the area has the highest homicide rate in the city (Silverstein and Brooks, 1991). In response to an open-ended question regarding what they disliked most about living in Los Angeles, 34 of 51 (67 percent) Garifuna men and women identified gangs, drugs, and drive-by shootings as the major drawbacks (Miller, 1992). As the levels of drug activity and gang violence have intensified over the years, Garifuna parents have grown increasingly wary of raising children in Los Angeles. Some have extended the period of time that their children remain in Belize, and others sent offspring born in Los Angeles back to be raised by kin. Still others send adolescent sons to Belize "under punishment" because they have gotten involved in gang-related activity in Los Angeles.

Although a few families have acquired the financial means to move their families out of South-Central Los Angeles, most have not. Unskilled, single women with children find it nearly impossible to leave the area. They lack the financial resources to pay the much higher rents in other parts of the city, and few enjoy the job security needed to commit to long-term leases. Under these circumstances, the availability of kin in Belize who are willing to take on child care responsibilities is critical.

Contrary to findings that suggest that migrants' ties to their home societies wither as they accumulate time abroad, our research suggests that geographic separation and the resulting decrease in frequency of contact need not lead to a weakening of ties. The extraordinary stresses associated with life in South-Central Los Angeles motivate Garifuna migrants to foster their links to Belize even after absences of decades. Given the social and economic instability that characterizes their lives in Los Angeles, women are particularly unwilling to burn their bridges to Belize. Indeed, most carefully nurture their transnational ties, which provide potential "safety nets" for them and their children and which may, for some at least, pave the way for their eventual return migration.

CONCLUSION

A growing body of migration research documents the increasing participation of women in international labor migration as a consequence of global economic restructuring and the "feminization" of low-wage labor markets in the United States (e.g., Simon and DeLey, 1986; Sassen, 1988; Pedraza-Bailey, 1991). Even in Latin America, where migration streams have long been dominated by males, there is a clear trend toward greater female participation in labor migration to the United States (Donato, 1994; Fernández-Kelly, 1988). Though migration research is beginning to acknowledge women as an increasing "presence" in international migration, we still know relatively little about them as "actors" in the migration process.

Much of the blame for this blindness to female agency is caused by a misplaced theoretical emphasis on households as the unit of analysis in migration studies. As currently conceived, this model fails to take into account the variability of household forms cross-culturally, and thus lacks empirical validity. It presents us with assumptions regarding how households *should* operate, but fails to consider a large body of empirical evidence suggesting that household behavior is far more complex than suggested by the model. Moreover, by treating the household itself as a social actor, important intrahousehold conflicts and divisions based on gender are hidden from view.[4] However, feminist approaches that cast women as powerless victims of the migration process are problematic, too, as they tend to overlook the ways in which women build significant bases of informal power through personal networks extending beyond the household.

It is time that migration studies move away from facile assumptions regarding gender roles in international labor migration. We claim that women, as anchors of extradomestic and transnational networks, play a significant role in determining which of their household members are selected for migration. Although labor migration may once have been the relatively exclusive domain of males, this is no longer the case. We must begin to consider the broader implications of a trend in which women migrate and men are increasingly the ones "left behind." Moreover, as migration becomes institutionalized over time and a substantial proportion of individuals in sending societies gain access to ties in the United States, the transnational network, rather than the household, becomes the primary locus of migration decision making.

There may be an even more general lesson in this chapter. In recent essays, both Ward (1993) and Böröcz and Smith (1995) have decried the lack of dialogue between researchers working from a feminist "women in development" approach and world-system analysis. At least part of the problem involves a preference for different levels and modes of analysis. Feminists tend to favor ethnographic views of women's everyday lives, while world-system analysts opt for macrostructural, political-economic explanations. A focus on the gendered structure of the everyday networks making up the sinews of particular transnational communities could provide an important theoretical bridge between these scholarly camps. Smith-Lovin and McPherson have presented an interesting argument (though implicitly based on advanced industrial societies) to the effect that the socialization processes and webs of interpersonal relationships in which people find themselves create differences in behavior and outlook that lead to "dramatic levels of gender segregation and inequality" (1993: 223). Our research reveals distinct male and female networks for migration and job seeking among Garifuna men and women, too. We believe that these Garifuna patterns are quite *different* in nature from those Smith-Lovin and McPherson described, and that this is due to the particular macrohistorical context of this community, including the way in which it was incorporated into the modern world-system and how it currently experiences global restructuring. To fully understand the "embedded" nature of transnational communities, we need to arrive at synthetic views that capture *both* the micro/everyday aspects of personal relationships *and* the macro/historical dynamics of global political-economy.

NOTES

Linda Miller Matthei gratefully acknowledges the research support provided by a National Science Foundation dissertation grant (BNS–8918803) and by a Rockefeller Foundation Post-Doctoral Fellowship at the Institute of Latin American Studies, University of Texas, Austin.

1. Women are not only paid less than men, they also work for a shorter portion of their lives. Most full-time employment in Belize carries a mandatory retirement age of 55 for both sexes, but traditional employment practices make it nearly impossible for women to find any sort of waged employment past the age of 50 (Kerns, 1982).

2. A fictitious name is used for this town, which is a major staging area for both documented and undocumented migration to the United States.

3. A social worker estimated that since the 1960s, women had built 65 percent of the new homes in the town where the research was done. The perception that women are more likely to build homes than men is held by both sexes. In fact, men's tendency to burn their bridges with their home communities is a topic of jokes, folktales, and music in the community. In Los Angeles in 1990, a Catholic bishop visiting from Belize chastised migrant men during his sermon for failing to maintain ties and build homes as women have done.

4. Moser made a similar argument, claiming that constructive attempts to formulate policies must "disaggregate households and families on the basis of gender" (1993: 15). While we limit our focus to migration, the scope of her thesis is broader, with generic implications for policies and planning for Third World development.

REFERENCES

Ashcraft, Norman. 1973. *Colonialism and Underdevelopment: Processes of Political Economic Change in British Honduras.* New York: Teachers College Press, Columbia University.

Bach, Robert L., and Lisa A. Schraml. 1982. "Migration Crisis and Theoretical Conflict." *International Migration Review* 16, 2: 320–341.

Benería, Lourdes, and Martha Roldán. 1987. *The Crossroads of Class and Gender: Industrial Housework, Subcontracting and Household Dynamics in Mexico City.* Chicago: University of Chicago Press.

Blumberg, Rae Lesser, ed. 1991. "Introduction: The 'Triple Overlap' of Gender Stratification, Economy and the Family." In *Gender, Family, and Economy: The Triple Overlap*, ed. Rae Lesser Blumberg, pp. 7–32. Newbury Park, CA: Sage Publications.

Bolland, O. Nigel. 1977. *The Formation of a Colonial Society: Belize, from Conquest to Crown Colony.* Baltimore: Johns Hopkins University Press.

————. 1986. *Belize: A New Nation in the Making.* Boulder, CO: Westview Press.

Böröcz, József, and David A. Smith. 1995. "Introduction: Late Twentieth-Century Challenges to World-System Analysis." In *A New World Order? Global Transformations in the Late Twentieth Century*, ed. David A. Smith and József Böröcz, pp. 1–15. Westport, CT: Greenwood.

Boyd, Monica. 1989. "Family and Personal Networks in International Migration: Recent Developments and New Agendas." *International Migration Review* 23, 1: 638–670.

Central Statistical Office. 1990. *Abstract of Statistics, 1990.* Belmopan, Belize: Central Statistical Office.

Chávez, Leo R. 1991. "Outside the Imagined Community: Undocumented Settlers and Experiences of Incorporation." *American Ethnologist* 18, 2: 257–278.

————. 1992. *Shadowed Lives: Undocumented Immigrants in American Society.* Fort Worth, TX: Harcourt Brace Jovanovich College Publishers.

Comitas, Lambros. 1973. "Occupational Multiplicity in Jamaica." In *Work and Family Life: West Indian Perspectives*, ed. Lambros Comitas and David Lowenthal, pp. 157–174. Garden City, NJ: Anchor Press.

Donato, Katharine M. 1994. "U.S. Policy and Mexican Migration to the United States, 1942–92." *Social Science Quarterly* 75, 4: 705–729.

Fapohunda, Eleanor R. 1988. "The Nonpooling Household: A Challenge to Theory." In *A Home Divided: Women and Income in the Third World*, ed. Daisy Dwyer and Judith Bruce, pp. 143–154. Stanford, CA: Stanford University Press.

Fernández-Kelly, Maria Patricia. 1981. "Mexican Border Industrialization, Female Labor Force Participation, and Migration." In *Women, Men, and the International Division of Labor*, ed. June Nash and Maria Patricia Fernández-Kelly, pp. 205–223. Albany: State University of New York Press.

Foner, Nancy. 1986. "Sex Roles and Sensibilities: Jamaican Women in New York and London." In *International Migration: The Female Experience*, ed. Rita James Simon and Caroline B. Brettell, pp. 133–151. Totowa, NJ: Rowman and Allanheld.

Georges, Eugenia. 1990. *The Making of a Transnational Community: Migration, Devel-*

opment and Cultural Change in the Dominican Republic. New York: Columbia University Press.

González, Nancie. 1969. *Black Carib Household Structure*. Seattle: University of Washington Press.

———. 1984. "Rethinking the Consanguineal Household and Matrifocality." *Ethnology* 23, 1: 1–12.

Gordon, Elizabeth. 1978. *The Women Left Behind: A Study of Migrant Workers in Lesotho*. World Employment Program Working Paper. Geneva, Switzerland: International Labor Office.

Government Information Service. 1959–1990. *Government Gazette*. Belize: Government Printery.

———. 1992. "Women in the Workforce." *Belize Today* (Government Information Service, Belmopan, Belize) 6 (October): 44–46.

Grasmuck, Sherri, and Patricia R. Pessar. 1991. *Between Two Islands: Dominican International Migration*. Berkeley: University of California Press.

Grieco, Margaret. 1987. *Keeping It in the Family: Social Networks and Employment Chance*. London: Tavistock.

Guyer, Jane I., and Pauline E. Peters. 1987. "Introduction." *Development and Social Change* 18, 2: 197–214.

Kerns, Virginia. 1982. "Structural Continuity in the Division of Men's and Women's Work Among the Black Carib (Garifuna)." In *Sex Roles and Social Change in Lower Central American Societies*, ed. Christine A. Loveland and Franklin O. Loveland, pp. 23–43. Urbana: University of Illinois Press.

———. 1983. *Women and the Ancestors: Black Carib Kinship and Ritual*. Urbana: University of Illinois Press.

Labour Department. 1987. *Annual Report of the Labour Department*. Belmopan, Belize: Government Printery.

Lee, Everett S. 1966. "A Theory of Migration." *Demography* 3, 1: 47–57.

Massey, Douglas S., Rafael Alarcón, Jorge Durand, and Humberto González. 1987. *Return to Aztlán*. Berkeley: University of California Press.

Meillasoux, Claude. 1972. "From Reproduction to Production." *Economy and Society* 1, 1: 93–105.

Miller [Matthei], Linda R. 1992. "Bridges: Garifuna Migration to Los Angeles." Ph.D. dissertation, University of California, Irvine.

Ministry of Education. 1984. *Belize Today: A Society in Transformation*. Belmopan, Belize: Sunshine Books.

Morokvasic, Mirjana. 1983. "Women in Migration: Beyond the Reductionist Outlook." In *One Way Ticket: Migration and Female Labour*, ed. Annie Phizacklea, pp. 13–31. London: Routledge and Kegan Paul.

Moser, Caroline O. N. 1993. *Gender Planning and Development: Theory, Practice and Training*. New York,: Routledge.

Neuhouser, Kevin. 1989. "Sources of Women's Power and Status among the Urban Poor in Contemporary Brazil." *Signs* 14: 685–702.

Peattie, Lisa. 1977. "Migrants and Women Who Wait: Introduction." In *Women and National Development*, ed. Wellesley Editorial Committee. Chicago: University of Chicago Press.

Pedraza, Silvia. 1991. "Women and Migration: The Social Consequences of Gender." *Annual Review of Sociology* 17: 303–325.

Pessar, Patricia. 1982. "The Role of Households in International Migration and the Case of U.S.-Bound Migration from the Dominican Republic." *International Migration Review* 16: 342–364.

Piore, Michael J. 1979. *Birds of Passage: Migrant Labor and Industrial Societies.* London: Cambridge University Press.

Portes, Alejandro, and Robert L. Bach. 1985. *Latin Journey: Cuban and Mexican Immigrants in the United States.* Berkeley: University of California Press.

Portes, Alejandro, and John Walton. 1981. *Labor, Class, and the International System.* Orlando, FL: Academic Press.

Sanford, Margaret. 1971. "Disruption of the Mother-Child Relationship in Conjunction with Matrifocality: A Study of Child-Keeping among the Carib and Creoles of British Honduras." Ph.D. dissertation, Catholic University of America.

Sassen, Saskia. 1988. *The Mobility of Labor and Capital: A Study in International Investment and Labor Flow.* Cambridge: Cambridge University Press.

Sassen-Koob, Saskia. 1981a. "Labor Migration and the New Industrial Division of Labor." In *Women, Men, and the International Division of Labor*, ed. June Nash and María Patricia Fernández-Kelly, pp. 175–204. Albany: State University of New York Press.

———. 1981b. "Towards a Conceptualization of Immigrant Labor." *Social Problems* 29, 1: 65–85.

Shephard, Charles. [1831] 1971. *An Historical Account of the Island of St. Vincent.* London: Frank Cass and Company.

Silverstein, Stuart, and Nancy Rivera Brooks. 1991. "South L.A. Shoppers Need Stores." *Los Angeles Times*, November 24.

Simon, Rita J., and Margo C. DeLey. 1986. "Undocumented Mexican Women: Their Work and Personal Experiences." In *International Migration: The Female Experience*, ed. Rita J. Simon and Caroline B. Brettel. Totowa, NJ: Rowman & Allanheld.

Singlemann, Joachim, and Harley Browning. 1980. "Industrial Transformation and Occupational Change in the U.S., 1960–1970. *Social Forces* 59: 246–264.

Smith, Joan, Immannuel Wallerstein, and Hans Dieter Evers, eds. 1984. *Households and the World-Economy.* Beverly Hills, CA: Sage Publications.

Smith-Lovin, Lynn, and Miller McPherson. 1993. "You Are Who You Know: A Network Approach to Gender." In *Theory on Gender/Feminism on Theory*, ed. Paula England, pp. 223–251. New York: Aldine De Gruyter.

Soja, Edward W. 1987. "Economic Restructuring and the Internationalization of the Los Angeles Region." In *The Capitalist City: Global Restructuring and Community Politics*, ed. Michael Peter Smith and Joe R. Feagin, pp. 178–198. New York: Basil Blackwell.

Soto, Isa Maria. 1987. "West Indian Child Fostering: Its Role in Migrant Exchanges." In *Caribbean Life in New York City: Sociocultural Dimensions*, ed. Constance R. Sutton and Elsa M. Chaney, pp. 131–149. New York: Center for Migration Studies.

Stivens, Maila. 1984. "Women, Kinship and Capitalist Development." In *Of Marriage and the Market: Women's Subordination Internationally and its Lessons*, ed. Kate Young, Carol Wolkowitz, and Roslynn McCullagh, pp. 178–192. London: Routledge and Kegan Paul.

Tienda, Marta, Leif Jensen, and Robert L. Bach. 1984. "Immigration, Gender and the

Process of Occupational Change in the United States, 1970–1980.'' *International Migration Review* 18: 1021–1044.

Treas, Judith. 1991. ''The Common Pot or Separate Purses? A Transaction Cost Interpretation.'' In *Gender, Family, and Economy: The Triple Overlap*, ed. Rae Lesser Blumberg, pp. 211–224. Newbury Park, CA: Sage Publications.

Vernon, Dylan. 1990. ''Belizean Exodus to the United States: For Better or For Worse.'' In *SPEAR Reports 4: Second Annual Studies on Belize Conference*, pp. 6–28. Belize City: Society for the Promotion of Education and Research (SPEAR).

Ward, Kathryn. 1985. ''Women and Urbanization in the World-System.'' In *Urbanization in the World-Economy*, ed. Michael Timberlake, pp. 305–323. New York: Academic Press.

———. 1993. ''Reconceptualizing World-System Theory to Include Women.'' In *Theory on Gender/Feminism on Theory*, ed. Paula England, pp. 43–68. New York: Aldine De Gruyter.

Wolf, Diane L. 1988. ''Father Knows Best About All in the Household: A Feminist Critique of Household Strategies.'' Paper presented at the Sex & Gender Session of the American Sociological Association Meetings, August.

———. 1992. *Factory Daughters: Gender, Household Dynamics, and Rural Industrialization in Java*. Berkeley: University of California Press.

Wong, Diana. 1984. ''The Limits of Using the Household as a Unit of Analysis.'' In *Households and the World-Economy*, ed. Joan Smith, Immanuel Wallerstein, and Hans Dieter-Evans, pp. 56–63. Beverly Hills, CA: Sage Publications.

Wood, Charles. 1982. ''Equilibrium and Historical-Structural Perspectives on Migration.'' *International Migration Review* 16: 298–319.

Yanagisako, Sylvia Junko. 1977. ''Women-Centered Kin Networks in Urban Bilateral Kinship.'' *American Ethnologist* 3: 207–226.

## 8

Transnational Communities: Their Emergence and Significance in the Contemporary World-System

Alejandro Portes

The aphorism, "capital is global, labor is local," sits at the base of an edifice built relentlessly during the last half century. From different theoretical quarters, this edifice has been celebrated as the final triumph of free trade and economic rationality as well as denounced as the tomb of proletarian rights and national liberation. Whatever the outlook, the narrative that follows portrays an increasingly bound global economy in which capital criss-crosses the earth in search of accumulation. The success of these initiatives correlates inversely, in most cases, with the economic autonomy achieved by national states and the economic prerogatives of local labor. For the most part, however, the momentum acquired by global capitalist expansion tends to sweep away everything in its path, confining past dreams of class equity and autonomous national development to the dustbin of history.

The process of capital going abroad in search of valorization is, of course, nothing new; it is, indeed, the cloth from which numerous accounts of the growth of the modern world-system have been fashioned. What is new at present are the modalities and intensity of the process, which today are driven by technological improvements in communications and transportation. Today, instantaneous investments and disinvestments are made in the bourses of remote Asian and Latin American countries and, as Castells (1980) puts it, a garment design conceived in New York can be transmitted electronically to a factory in Taiwan and the first batches of the product received in San Francisco in a week's time. The advantages of the process seem to be entirely on the side of those able to avail themselves of the new technologies, thus turning globalization into the final apotheosis of capital against its adversaries, be they state managers or organized workers.

However, as sociologists we are professionally trained to look at the dialectics of things and hence, understand that a social process of this magnitude cannot be all one-sided. By its very momentum, the process is likely to trigger various reactions giving rise to countervailing structures. In the end, the technology-driven revolution that we are witnessing at century's end may not usher in the era of unrestrained global capitalism after all, but rather a new form of that age-old struggle of exchange versus use values or, put differently, of the formal rationality of law versus the substantive rationality of private interests.

As a contribution to this analysis, I attempt here to give theoretical form to the concept of *transnational communities*, as a less noticed, but potentially potent, counter to the more visible forms of globalization described in the recent literature. I embark on this task with some hesitation since the concept of transnationality, like that of globalization itself, threatens to become part of one of the passing fads that grip social scientist's attention for a while, only to then fade into oblivion. I believe, however, that there is enough real substance here to make the effort worthwhile. If successful, the concept may actually perform double duty as both part of the theoretical arsenal with which we approach the modern world-system and as an element of a more neglected enterprise, namely, the analysis of the everyday networks and patterns of social relationships that develop in and around that system. The latter goal belongs in the realm of a mid-range theory of social interaction, which I will seek to outline after considering two past initiatives in the same general direction.

FAILED MID-RANGE EFFORTS: LABOR STANDARDS AND FLEXIBLE SPECIALIZATION

From policy and academic quarters, there have already been efforts to come to terms with the new mobility of capital by finding ways to rein in its footloose ways. One of these efforts has seen institutional economists, industrial sociologists, and trade unionists deplore the consequences of deindustrialization in the developed world and call for governmental measures to reverse it. This approach pits the regulatory capacity of national states against the global opportunities for profit created by new technologies drawing on vast differentials in wage levels. The result has been the Labor Standards movement, which seeks to restrict imports produced under conditions that violate the labor rights commonly accepted in the First World. In the words of one of the movements' most prominent academic supporters:

[N]ew communication technologies have virtually eliminated international barriers to trade. They have brought the most extreme income disparities in the world into play, and this change has happened very rapidly.... If you let the market play itself out, it could undermine our capacity to redeploy the economy towards high-wage productive strategies. We can't get to the high-wage business strategy because it ... is continually being undermined by the attraction of essentially a Third World system. (Piore, 1990: 48–49)

This contest of domestic and globalized interests has so far produced some interesting ironies such as North American industrialists, formerly notorious opponents of organized labor, becoming ardent advocates of trade unions and workers' rights abroad. Spearheaded by such powerful organizations as the International Labour Office, the effort to reproduce the achievements of two centuries of labor struggles in Europe and North America in the newly industrialized countries of the periphery has met with some notable *formal* successes.

Since the mid-1980s, for example, the United States Congress has enacted four different laws that make access to the U.S. market contingent on respect of "internationally recognized labor rights." The United States has also sought to introduce the issue of international labor rights into multilateral trade agreements. In the European Union, workers' rights were taken up in 1989 in the community's Charter of Fundamental Rights of Workers. Although provisions vary widely, they are all guided by the same premise: that poor working conditions in one country will adversely affect labor and competitiveness in others (Lawyers Committee for Human Rights, 1991).

These impressive declarations contrast markedly with their failure to alter conditions on the ground. The fundamental reason is that the task of enforcing such lofty goals falls on peripheral governments that are seldom keen to do so. Officials in these nations know that excessive zeal in applying imported labor standards will only lead to the exodus of foreign investments to an adjacent labor-surplus country. Their position is buttressed by arguments about the long-term consequences of labor-intensive export industrialization. Linda Y. C. Lim, a Chinese Singaporean economist, puts this argument succinctly:

While initially low labor standards may be one of the factors attracting investors, export manufacturing itself tends to raise these standards. . . . In Thailand, as in other developing countries, successful export manufacturing has rapidly expanded the industrial proletariat and labor organization, arguably at an earlier stage of development than occurred historically in the developed countries themselves. (Lim, 1990: 93)

The attempt to impose First World standards on less-developed countries leads to another perverse consequence, namely, the transfer of many productive activities to the informal sector. Though well-concealed from public view, informal subcontracting and off-the-books hiring represent important mechanisms in labor-surplus economies by which to escape costly state regulation. Formal industry and commerce in these countries commonly avail themselves of this strategy, creating in the process a working class segmented between a relatively high-paid and protected minority and a mass of unprotected workers employed in numerous informal activities (Benería and Roldán, 1987; Castells and Portes, 1989).

In these contexts, the "underutilization" of labor by the formal sector is, in many cases, more apparent than real. The literature documents a number of instances in which the problem is not the absorptive capacity of the modern economy, but the ways in which it utilizes labor in order to bypass relatively advanced regulatory structures (Fortuna and Prates, 1989; Birbeck, 1979; Davies, 1979). A dense network of formal-informal relations is characteristic of peripheral economies with extensive rules and indicates, in turn, the futility of attempting to equalize labor market conditions on the basis of externally imposed standards. By the same token, this situation points to a theoretical dead end, namely, the effort to apprehend a global process on the basis of normative structures designed to regulate national economies.

A second mid-range approach to productive globalization was pioneered by economists Michael Piore and Charles Sabel, who theorized the experience of the small-firm economy of central Italy into a new model of industrial organization. In their view, the old model of mass production based on Taylorist principles is being superseded by new forms of flexible production based on smaller units, which are better able to adapt to changes in the world-market. This structural change coincides with the globalization process and makes use of the same technologies. It is precisely through these technologies that formerly centralized assembly-line production can be parceled out to smaller units and thereby made more flexible (Piore and Sabel, 1984; Sabel, 1982, 1986).

Simultaneously, flexible specialization opens up new opportunities for artisans and small producers to insert themselves into the networks of global trade. This is what happened in the central Italian region of Emilia Romagna, where networks of skilled workers and artisans managed to create a competitive export economy based on technological prowess and cooperative relations. Italian students of this experience have been skeptical about the possibility of reproducing in other national contexts the industrial know-how and bounded solidarity on which it is based (Capecchi, 1989; Brusco, 1982). Nevertheless, Piore and Sabel forged ahead, defining the process as universal and identifying numerous other ''industrial districts'' where, in their view, it is also taking place. Sabel went as far as suggesting that informal activities in Latin America and other Third World regions may be converted, under certain conditions, into models of flexible specialization, thus reproducing the small firm successes in central Italy. In his words:

The second surprising setting in which flexible specialization might emerge is the immeasurably vast and poorly understood informal sector in Latin American economies. . . . It would not be the first time that such a thing happened: many of the small firms in the Third Italy that today vaunt their numerically controlled machines and foreign customers had their start when large firms decentralized production in the early 1970s to avoid growing union control. (Sabel, 1986: 48)

The problem with this optimistic scenario is that it finds few instances of empirical support. Examples of communities of successfully integrated producers and exporters are exceptional; they are particularly rare in Latin American countries. The global wave of industrial restructuring has not substituted Fordist production in the deindustrializing areas of the advanced countries for flexibly specialized districts in the backward ones. Instead, restructuring has, for the most part, merely transplanted assembly-line production that is organized along typical Taylorist lines to export zones in the Third World. The production regime in these zones can be every bit as harsh and mind-numbing as those documented at the height of assembly-line production in the industrialized countries (Fernández-Kelly, 1983; Deyo, 1989; Pérez-Sainz, 1994).

Back in the First World, there is evidence that the experiences of successful small firms do not so much oppose as complement the long-term plans of large corporations. Although portrayed as organizational dinosaurs by some advocates of flexible specialization, many corporations have proven quite adept at appropriating the ideas of small innovators. As Bennett Harrison (1994) noted in his recent critique of the flexible specialization school, such appropriation can occur either through the direct acquisition of successful small companies or through copying and internalizing their technological breakthroughs. Although the founders of the raided small companies can benefit from these transactions, their activities do not provide a systemic counter to the dominance of large-scale capital.

In fairness to Piore and Sabel, they show themselves quite aware of the depredations of runaway industries in the periphery as well as of the ability of some large firms to implement flexible and innovative production arrangements in the advanced countries (Piore and Sabel, 1984; Sabel, 1986). However, if their analysis were limited to these points, it would be no different from the many reports of global restructuring or competition among factory regimes in North America, Europe, and Japan. The core point that makes their argument attractive is the vision of an emerging opportunity for grassroots economic actors to gain a niche in an expanded global system (Harrison, 1994). Unfortunately, this is also the most doubtful part of their story.

Hence (like the effort to stop the excesses of transnational capitalism with nationally imposed labor standards), the promise of a new economic order where the coordinated activities of artisans and small entrepreneurs can outcompete the corporate giants falls short. Although one perspective comes from the practical realm of trade unions and the other from the academic field of institutional economics, the two coincide in keeping labor local while conceding globality to large-scale capital ventures. Neither national laws nor cooperative efforts of small producers are enough by themselves to counterbalance that age-old tool of the moneyed class: complete mobility, which permits it to identify profitable options worldwide and seize them or buy out those initially profiting from them. To be effective, any social reaction to current trends must have some of the same elements of geographic mobility and, more important, it must be driven by the same forces promoting industrial restructuring rather than running counter to it.

THE ONSET OF TRANSNATIONAL NETWORKS

The popular response to the globalization of capital has been more subtle than the imposition of labor standards and more widespread than the emergence of flexible industrial districts. It consists of the gradual growth of communities that sit astride political borders and that, in a very real sense, are "neither here nor there." The economic activities that sustain these communities are grounded precisely on the differentials of advantage created by political boundaries. In this respect, they are no different from the large global corporations, except that these enterprises emerge at the grassroots level.

A group of well-informed social anthropologists has pioneered the identification of this phenomenon in the attempt to make theoretical sense of it. In their words:

We define "transnationalism" as the processes by which immigrants forge and sustain multi-stranded social relations that link together their societies of origin and settlement. We call these processes transnationalism to emphasize that many immigrants today build social fields that cross geographic, cultural, and political borders. . . . An essential element . . . is the multiplicity of involvements that transmigrants sustain in both home and host societies. We are still groping for a language to describe these social locations. (Basch, Glick Schiller, and Blanc-Szanton, 1994: 6)

Their puzzled attitude toward this emergent phenomenon is understandable when we begin to grasp the array of activities that it comprises and the potential for social and economic transformation that it holds. The existing literature suggests three tentative theoretical points: (1) The emergence of these communities is tied to the logic of capitalism itself. (2) While following well-established sociological principles of the development of social structures, these communities represent a distinct phenomenon at variance with traditional patterns of immigrant adaptation. (3) Because the phenomenon is fueled by the dynamics of globalization itself, it has greater growth potential and offers a broader field for popular initiatives than alternative social structures.

Let us begin by looking at the origins of these communities. As the preceding quote indicates, they are composed of immigrants and their friends and relatives. Public opinion in the advanced countries has been conditioned to think that contemporary immigration stems from the desperate quest of Third World peoples seeking to escape poverty at home. In fact, neither the poorest of the poor migrate, nor is their move determined mainly by individualistic calculations of advantage.[1] Instead, contemporary immigration is driven by twin forces that have their roots in the dynamics of capitalist expansion itself. These are, first, the labor needs of First World economies, and second, the penetration of less-developed countries by the productive investments and consumption standards of the advanced societies.

Contrary to widespread perceptions, immigrants come to the wealthier nations less because they want to than because they are needed. A combination of social and historical forces has led to acute labor scarcities in these economies. In some instances, these are real, absolute scarcities such as the dearth of industrial workers in Japan and the deficit in certain professions, such as nursing and engineering in the United States. In other instances, however, the scarcity stems from the culturally conditioned resistance of native-born workers to accept the low-paid, menial jobs commonly performed by their ancestors (Piore, 1979; Gans, 1992; Portes and Guarnizo, 1991). The list of such stigmatized occupations is large and includes, among others, agricultural labor, domestic and other personal services, and garment sweatshop jobs (Sassen, 1989).

By 1990, the foreign-born population of the United States had reached almost 20 million, the largest absolute total in the century (Fix and Passel, 1991; Rumbaut, 1994). The legislated loopholes of the Immigration Reform and Control Act (IRCA) of 1986, plus new, generous provisions in the 1990 Immigration Act, virtually guarantee that this absolute number and the proportion that immigrants represent in the total U.S. population will increase significantly by the century's end.[2] In Germany and France, despite the official termination of the foreign guestworker program in the 1970s, immigrant communities have continued growing through a variety of legal loopholes and clandestine channels (Zolberg, 1989; Bade, 1995). Today, Germany has a foreign population of 7 million, or roughly 9 percent of the total, which is quite similar to that in the United States (Münz and Ulrich, 1995; Rumbaut, 1994). Even in ethnically homogenous Japan, labor scarcity has prompted a variety of legal subterfuges, including the use of foreign-company "trainees" and visa overstayers to perform line-industrial jobs. By 1990, the foreign-born population of Japan numbered about 1.1 million. This is still an insignificant proportion of the total, but the number was expected to double during the decade (Cornelius, 1992).

The other side of the equation involves the effects of the globalization process in the supply of potential immigrants. The drive of multinational capital to expand markets in the Third World and, simultaneously, to take advantage of its reservoirs of labor has had a series of predictable consequences. Among them are the remolding of popular culture on the basis of external forms and the introduction of consumption standards bearing little relation to local wages (Alba, 1978). The process presocializes prospective immigrants about life abroad and encourages them to move because of the gap between local realities and imported consumption aspirations. Paradoxically, this process does not so much affect the very poor as the working- and middle-class sectors, which are frequently the most exposed to marketing messages and cultural symbols beamed from the advanced world (Grasmuck and Pessar, 1991; Portes and Bach, 1985).[3]

The fundamental point is that contemporary, First World–bound immigration is not a contingent process, but one driven by the very dynamics of global capitalism. For this reason, the immigration flow to the developed world can be confidently expected to continue in the years ahead. This foreign population provides, in turn, the raw material out of which transnational communities develop.

THE RISE OF TRANSNATIONAL ENTERPRISE

Immigrant workers attracted by the growing demand in the advanced countries for fresh sources of low-wage labor soon become aware that the pay and labor conditions in store for them do not go far in promoting their own economic goals. To bypass the menial, dead-end jobs that the host labor market assigns them, they must put into play their networks of social relationships. Immigrant social networks display two characteristics that those among domestic workers generally lack. First, they simultaneously are dense and extend over large geographical distances, and second, they often generate high levels of solidarity by virtue of uncertainty. The sociological principle that exchange under conditions of uncertainty creates stronger bonds among participants applies particularly well to immigrant communities (Kollock, 1994). Their economic transactions in the receiving country tend to occur with little initial information about the trustworthiness of exchange partners and the character and reliability of state regulation. This high uncertainty creates the need to remain loyal to trustworthy partners, regardless of tempting outside opportunities (Guarnizo, 1992).

Geographically extended and solidary networks among immigrants can be put into play for a number of strategic initiatives. A first initiative, discussed by Sassen (1994), leads to long distance, cross-national labor markets where job opportunities in far-away locations are identified and appropriated. A second, described by Zhou (1992), leads to living arrangements designed to lower consumption costs and produce savings for business or real estate acquisition abroad. A third, which has been extensively studied by Light (1984; Light and Bonacich, 1988), leads to the emergence of credit associations where pooled savings are allocated on a rotating basis. A fourth initiative, which is the present topic of inquiry, consists of appropriating the price and information differentials between sending and receiving countries through the creation of transnational enterprises.

Grassroots transnational enterprise benefits from the same set of technological innovations in communications and transportation that underlie large-scale industrial relocations. A class of immigrant entrepreneurs who shuttle regularly across countries and maintain daily contact with events and activities in them could not exist without these new technologies and the options and lower costs that they make possible. Put more broadly, these grassroots initiatives do not rise in opposition to global restructuring or technological innovation, but are driven by them. Through this strategy, labor (initially, immigrant labor) joins the circles of global trade by imitating, often in ingenious ways, the initiatives of large corporate actors.

This parallel between the strategies of corporations and immigrant entrepreneurs is only partial. Though both make extensive use of new technologies and depend on price and information differences across borders, corporations rely primarily on their financial muscle to make such ventures feasible, while immigrants must depend entirely on their social networks (Guarnizo, 1992; Zhou and Bankston, 1994). The long-distance ties that underlie the viability of such initiatives are constructed through a protracted, and frequently difficult, process of adaptation to a foreign society, which gives them their distinct characteristics. In turn, the onset of this economic strategy strengthens such networks. Hence, transnational entrepreneurs expand and thicken, in a cumulative process, the web of social ties that originally made their activities possible.

THE CONSTRUCTION OF TRANSNATIONAL COMMUNITIES

The cumulation of activities across national borders by former immigrants may lead eventually to a qualitatively distinct phenomenon. This qualitative leap, which has been adumbrated by the recent experience of a few immigrant groups, is what the concept of transnational community attempts to capture. Before discussing its formal characteristics, a few examples from the recent literature are presented to flesh out these abstract considerations.

There exist today in the Dominican Republic literally hundreds of small and medium enterprises that are founded and operated by former immigrants to the United States. They include small factories, commercial establishments of different types, and financial agencies. What makes these enterprises transnational is not only that they are created by former immigrants, but that their existence depends on continuing ties to the United States. A study of 113 such firms conducted in the late 1980s found that their mean initial capital investment was only $12,000, but that approximately half continued to receive periodic capital transfers from abroad, averaging $5,400. Monies were remitted by kin and friends who remained in the United States and were partners or co-owners of the firm. In addition to capital, many firms received transfers in kind, producer goods, or commodities for sale (Portes and Guarnizo, 1990: 16).

In the course of fieldwork for this study, we found a second mechanism for capital replenishment, namely, owners' periodic trips abroad to encourage potential new immigrant investors. Such promotions may take place directly, through existing kin and friendship networks, or through the mediation of Dominican-owned financial and real estate agencies in New York City. These trips are also used by factory owners and managers to sell part of their production abroad. Proprietors of small garment firms, for example, regularly travel to Puerto Rico, Miami, and New York to sell their wares. It is common practice to have a prearranged verbal agreement with buyers abroad, including small clothing stores. On their way back to the Dominican Republic, the informal exporters fill their empty suitcases with inputs needed for business, such as garment designs, fabrics, and needles.

To the untrained eye, these loaded-down international travelers appear as common migrants visiting and bearing gifts for their relatives back home, but in reality, they are engaged in a growing form of transnational informal trade. The information requirements for this traffic are invariably transmitted through kin and friendship networks spanning the distance between places of origin and destination. By the same token, it is clear that the men and women who operate these firms are not "return immigrants" in the traditional sense of the term. Instead, they make use of their time abroad to build a base of property, bank accounts, and business contacts from which to organize their return home. The result is not final departure from the United States, but rather a cyclical, back-and-forth movement through which the transnational entrepreneur makes use of differential economic opportunities spread across both countries (Portes and Guarnizo, 1990: 21–22).

A similar story, but with a unique cultural twist, is told by David Kyle (1994) in his study of the Otavalan indigenous community in the highlands of Ecuador. Traditionally, the region of Otavalo has specialized in the production and marketing of clothing, developing and adapting new production skills since the time of the colonial period under Spain. During the last quarter of a century or so, Otavalans have taken to traveling abroad to market their colorful wares in major cities of Europe and North America. By so doing, they appropriate the exchange value pocketed elsewhere by middlemen between Third World indigenous producers and final consumers. After years of traveling abroad, they have also brought home a wealth of novelties from the advanced countries, including European and North American wives. In the streets of Otavalo, it is not uncommon to meet these women attired in traditional indigenous garb.

During the same period, semipermanent Otavalan enclaves began to appear abroad. Their distinct feature is that their members do not make their living from wage labor or even local self-employment, but from the sale of goods brought from Ecuador. They remain in constant communication with their hometown in order to replenish supplies, monitor their *telares* (garment shops), and buy land. The back-and-forth movement required by this trade has turned Otavalans into a common sight, not only at the Quito airport, but also in street fairs in New York, Paris, Amsterdam, and other large cities. According to Kyle (1994), Otavalans have even discovered the commercial value of their folklore and groups of performers have fanned throughout the streets of First World cities.

The sale of colorful ponchos and other woolens accompanied by the plaintive notes of the *quena* flute have been quite profitable. The economic success of these indigenous migrants is evident in their near-universal refusal to accept wage labor abroad and in the evident prosperity of their town. Otavalo is quite different in this respect from other regions in the Andean highlands. Its indigenous entrepreneurs and returned migrants comprise a good portion of the local upper stratum, reversing the traditional pattern of dominance by white and mestizo elites.

A third variant involves immigrants of considerably greater economic power. For example, the growth of Asian communities in several U.S. cities has created opportunities for moneyed entrepreneurs from Taiwan, Hong Kong, and South Korea to invest profitably in the United States and, in the process, themselves become part of the transnational community. Smith and Zhou (1995) explained, for example, how the rapid growth of Chinese home ownership in the New York City suburb of Flushing has been largely financed by new Chinese banks established with Taiwanese and Hong Kong capital. Members of the rapidly growing Chinese population in Flushing and adjacent cities in the borough of Queens are very motivated to acquire their own homes but lack the knowledge of English and the credentials needed to seek credit from mainstream institutions. To meet the burgeoning demand for housing loans processed in the immigrants' own language, local entrepreneurs went to Taiwan and Hong Kong to pool capital for new banks, and new investors came to the United States bearing the necessary resources. As a result, Chinese-owned banks in Flushing proliferated. Although small by conventional standards, they serve simultaneously the economic interests of the immigrant community and those of overseas investors.

Three thousand miles to the west, the city of Monterey Park, California, has been transformed into the "first suburban Chinatown," largely by the activities of well-heeled newcomers (Fong, 1994). Many Taiwanese and Hong Kong entrepreneurs established businesses in the area, less for immediate profit than as a hedge against political instability and the threat of a Chinese communist takeover. Opening a new business in the United States facilitates obtaining permanent residence permits, and as a result, many owners are able to bring their families along to live in Monterey Park, while they themselves continue to commute across the Pacific.

The activities of these "astronauts" (as they are dubbed in Chinese in reference to the frequency of their air travel) adds a new layer of complexity to the transnational community. In this instance, returned immigrants do not invest U.S.-accumulated savings in enterprises at home; instead, immigrants bring new capital to invest in firms in the United States. The birth of a child on American soil guarantees the offspring U.S. citizenship and securely anchors the family in their new setting. As a result of the twin processes of successful investments and citizenship acquisition, Chinese immigrants have moved swiftly from the status of marginal newcomers in Monterey Park to the core of the city's business class (Fong, 1994).

A fourth instance of transnationalization illustrates another facet of the process, namely, the political and social influence that immigrant groups can acquire over the sending communities. The example is based on Smith's (1992) study of a small farming community in the Mixteca region of Mexico, near the city of Puebla. Smith described the excitement of members of the Ticuani Potable Water Committee on learning that new tubing had arrived, and with it, the long-awaited solution to the town's water problem. They immediately made plans to go inspect the new materials and organize their installment. Smith commented:

On first sight, this is no more than an ordinary civic project. . . . Yet when we consider certain other aspects of the scene, the meaning becomes quite different. The Committee and I are not standing in Ticuani, but rather on a busy intersection in Brooklyn. . . . The Committee members are not simply going to the outskirts of the town to check the water tubes, but rather they are headed to JFK airport for a Friday afternoon flight to Mexico City, from which they will travel the five hours overland to their pueblo, consult with the authorities and contractors, and return by Monday afternoon to their jobs in New York City. (1992: 1)

As it turns out, the potable water project was only the latest of a series of public works in Ticuani to be initiated and paid for by its New York immigrants. For this particular project, the expatriate community contributed more than $50,000, which was gathered in donations of $100 or less. The waterworks also marked the twentieth anniversary of the successful completion of the first transnational public project, and for this occasion, the New York Committee unveiled a new seal, to be used in all future correspondence and public events. It reads: *"Por el Progreso de Ticuani: Los Ausentes Siempre Presentes. Ticuani y New York"* ("For the Progress of Ticuani: The Absent Ones, Always Present. Ticuani and New York") (Smith, 1992: 1–2).

I have dwelled on these examples at some length to give credibility to a phenomenon that, when initially described, strains the imagination. A multitude of similar examples could have been used, as illustrated in the pioneering collection by Basch and her collaborators (Basch, Glick Schiller, and Blanc-Szanton, 1994). The central point that these examples illustrate is that once started, the phenomenon of transnationalization can acquire a cumulative character, expanding not only in numbers, but also in the qualitative character of its activities. Hence, while the original wave of these activities is economic and their initiators can be properly labeled transnational entrepreneurs, subsequent activities encompass political, social, and cultural pursuits as well.

Alerted by the initiatives of immigrant entrepreneurs, political parties and even governments have established offices abroad to canvass immigrant communities for financial and electoral support. Not to be outdone, many immigrant groups organize political committees to lobby the home government or, as in the case of the Mexican community studied by Smith, influence the local municipality on various issues. To provide yet another example, Colombian and Dominican immigrants in New York City organized during the 1970s and 1980s to demand the right to vote in elections in their respective countries and to obtain the support from their home governments to combat negative stereotypes in the U.S. media (Sassen, 1979).

Churches and private charities have joined the traffic between home country and immigrant community with a growing number of initiatives involving both.

Finally, the phenomenon can acquire a cultural veneer as home performers and artists use the expatriate communities as platforms to break into the First World scene and returnee artists popularize cultural forms learned abroad.[4] The end result of this cumulative process is the transformation of the original pioneering economic ventures into transnational communities, which are characterized by dense networks across space and by an increasing number of people who lead dual lives. Members are at least bilingual, move easily between different cultures, frequently maintain homes in two countries, and pursue economic, political, and cultural interests that require a simultaneous presence in both. It bears repeating that the onset of this process and its development are nurtured by social forces unleashed by contemporary global capitalism. Paralleling Marx's description of the proletariat as created and placed into the historical scene by its future class adversaries, today's roaming capitalist ventures have given rise to the conditions and incentives for the transnationalization of labor.

THE STRUCTURE AND LONG-TERM CONSEQUENCES OF TRANSNATIONALIZATION

If conditions confronting today's U.S.-bound immigrants bore some similarity to those faced by their European predecessors at the turn of the century, one could wager that today's immigrants would not have moved so decisively in the direction of transnationalization. That earlier era featured two conditions significantly different from today: a plethora of relatively well-paid wage jobs in industry and the limitations imposed by the costly and time-consuming nature of long-distance transportation. The first condition militated against widespread entrepreneurial ventures and gave rise over time to stable working-class ethnic communities. For example, most Poles and Italians in the United States became workers and not entrepreneurs because labor market opportunities in the industrial cities where they arrived made this an attractive option. By contrast, today's uncertain and minimally paid service-sector jobs strongly encourage immigrants to seek alternative automonous paths.

Second, communications and transportation technologies were such as to make it prohibitive for turn-of-the-century immigrants to make a living out of bridging the cultural gap between countries of origin and destination or to lead simultaneous lives in both. No trans-oceanic commuting was possible, and thus, no means were available for Polish peasants to check how things were going at home over the weekend and be back in their New York jobs on Monday.

Contemporary transnational communities are distinguished from comparable activities of earlier immigrant waves by three features: First, the instantaneous character of communication across vast geographic distances; second, the large numbers involved in these activities; and third, the tendency for these activities to become normative in the immigrant community, driven by the numbers who take part and the dearth of alternative opportunities in the host society. Just as in the past migration abroad became the norm in certain regions of the Third

World (Massey and Garcia España, 1987), today, participation in transnational enterprises is turning into ''the thing to do'' among certain groups of immigrants.

It must be emphasized that transnational communities do not emerge in opposition to global capitalism, nor is there anything in their operation that is set explicitly against the designs of large corporations. In this sense, the analogy with Marx's account of the emergence of the industrial proletariat breaks down. Grassroots transnational enterprises and the manifold social and political activities that follow them are not necessary for the structures of global capital accumulation; they represent instead the means through which some members of the working class escape the hold of these structures.

Over time, however the process can acquire novel characteristics and lead to unexpected consequences. As more and more common people become involved in transnational activities, they come to subvert one of the basic premises of contemporary capitalist globalization, namely, that labor stays put and that its reference point for wages and work conditions remains local. Immigrant workers who become transnational entrepreneurs not only deny their own labor to businesses abroad and at home, they become conduits for information about different labor conditions and novel economic opportunities. The growth of socio-political and -economic ties across national borders can also provide a measure of protection for immigrant workers against the vulnerability of cultural isolation and an inferior legal status in the developed world. Flows of capital from newly industrialized countries of Asia to North American cities work in the same direction by facilitating home ownership and a swift move into self-employment in the immigrant community.

The significance of transnationalization is already apparent in the smaller labor-exporting countries. In the peripheral nations of the Caribbean Basin, as well as those Asian countries with long ties to the United States (such as Taiwan, South Korea, and the Philippines), the entire economy has been remolded by the twin processes of corporate globalization and immigrant transnationalization. Scarcely a family exists that does not have a relative abroad, and the back-and-forth movement of people, information, and investment has become integral to family economic strategies. Consumption patterns and lifestyles are shaped as much by the global media as by the activities of former immigrants who have been transformed into transnational entrepreneurs. Even governments get into the act by seeking, as in the case of President Jean Bertrand Aristide of Haiti, to transform the immigrant community into a symbolic ''10th Department'' (in addition to the existing nine) in search of its contributions and political support (Glick Schiller, Basch, and Blanc-Szanton, 1992).

It is still too soon to predict the long-term implications of the process of transnationalization. While in smaller peripheral countries it already has great importance, in larger labor-exporting nations, such as Mexico, its visibility and significance remain limited. Nonetheless, as the process continues, it may become a significant factor in modifying a strategy of capitalist accumulation based on wage differentials and information asymmetries between different regions of the world. The main reason for this expectation is that, unlike labor standards or flexible specialization, the emergence of transnational communities places everyday people in the same plane as the corporate actors who are engaged in global restructuring. The level of information and expertise thus acquired may partially neutralize the power of First World employers to simultaneously exploit Third World populations at home and their immigrants abroad. Whether the process comes to acquire this systemic consequence or not, the spectacle of common people criss-crossing the world in search of opportunities that are otherwise denied to them possesses enough intrinsic appeal to deserve attention.

EDITOR'S NOTE

This chapter was the keynote address delivered at the nineteenth annual conference on the Political Economy of the World-System, "Latin America in the World-Economy," North-South Center at the University of Miami, April 21, 1995.

NOTES

1. This statement cannot be fully justified here without derailing the reader's attention from the central focus of the analysis. The argument has been documented fully in several earlier writings. See Portes (1978) and Portes and Böröcz (1989).

2. Some 2.5 million formerly unauthorized aliens were legalized under IRCA. Subsequent legislation contained generous provisions for newly legalized immigrants to bring their relatives. More importantly, IRCA retained a large loophole allowing for the continuation of the unauthorized flow by requiring employers to check prospective workers' documents but not to establish their validity (Portes and Zhou, 1995).

3. Sassen (1988) has developed a variant of this argument whereby runaway industries located in peripheral export zones stimulate outmigration by presocializing their work forces in First World cultural practices. Most of the labor force in these industries is formed by young people, who are commonly dismissed after a few years. The combination of the skills and aspirations learned during their employment with their economic redundancy converts them into a ready pool for future migration. Sassen provided little empirical evidence, but subsequent research in a number of Latin American countries indicates that Sassen's thesis has some validity (see Pérez-Sainz, 1994; Itzigsohn, 1994).

4. Latin American artists have taken to using the city of Miami, Florida, in this way because of its large and diversified Spanish-speaking community, which is anchored by the Cuban ethnic enclave. Latin-owned recording studios, galleries, and theaters, plus a large resident artist community, offer newcomers access to opportunities that are unavailable elsewhere in the United States (Sassen and Portes, 1993).

REFERENCES

Alba, Francisco. 1978. "Mexico's International Migration as a Manifestation of Its Development Pattern." *International Migration Review* 12 (Winter): 502–551.

Bade, Klaus J. 1995. "From Emigration to Immigration: The German Experience in the 19th and 20th Centuries." Paper presented at the German-American Migration and Refugee Policy Group, American Academy of Arts and Sciences, Cambridge, MA, March 23–26.

Basch, Linda G., Nina Glick Schiller, and Cristina Blanc-Szanton. 1994. *Nations Unbound: Transnational Projects, Post-colonial Predicaments, and De-territorialized Nation-States.* Langhorne, PA: Gordon and Breach.

Benería, Lourdes, and Marta I. Roldán. 1987. *The Crossroads of Class and Gender: Homework, Subcontracting, and Household Dynamics in Mexico City.* Chicago: University of Chicago Press.

Birkbeck, Chris. 1979. "Garbage, Industry, and the 'Vultures' of Cali, Colombia." In *Casual Work and Poverty in Third World Cities*, ed. R. Bromley and C. Gerry, pp. 161–183. New York: John Wiley.

Brusco, Sebastiano. 1982. "The Emilian Model: Productive Decentralization and Social Integration." *Cambridge Journal of Economics* 6, 2 (June): 167–184.

Capecchi, Vittorio. 1989. "The Informal Economy and the Development of Flexible Specialization." In *The Informal Economy: Studies in Advanced and Less Developed Countries*, ed. A. Portes, M. Castells, and L. A. Benton, pp. 189–215. Baltimore: Johns Hopkins University Press.

Castells, Manuel. 1980. "Multinational Capital, National States, and Local Communities." Institute of Urban and Regional Development working paper. University of California, Berkeley.

Castells, Manuel, and Alejandro Portes. 1989. "World Underneath: The Origins, Dynamics, and Effects of the Informal Economy." In *The Informal Economy: Studies in Advanced and Less Developed Countries*, ed. A. Portes, M. Castells, and L. A. Benton, pp. 11–37. Baltimore: Johns Hopkins University Press.

Cornelius, Wayne A. 1992. "Controlling Illegal Immigration: Lessons from Japan and Spain." Working paper. University of California, San Diego, Center for U.S.-Mexico Studies.

Davies, Rob. 1979. "Informal Sector or Subordinated Mode of Production? A Model." In *Casual Work and Poverty in Third World Cities*, ed. R. Bromley and C. Gerry, pp. 87–104. New York: John Wiley.

Deyo, Frederic C. 1989. *Beneath the Miracle, Labor Subordination in the New Asian Industrialism.* Berkeley: University of California Press.

Fernández-Kelly, M. Patricia. 1983. *For We Are Sold, I and My People: Women and Industry in Mexico's Frontier.* Albany, NY: State University of New York Press.

Fix, Michael, and Jeffrey S. Passel. 1991. "The Door Remains Open: Recent Immigration to the United States and a Preliminary Analysis of the Immigration Act of 1990." Working paper. The Urban Institute and the Rand Corporation.

Fong, Timothy P. 1994. *The First Suburban Chinatown: The Remaking of Monterey Park, California.* Philadelphia: Temple University Press.

Fortuna, Juan Carlos, and Suzanna Prates. 1989. "Informal Sector versus Informalized Labor Relations in Uruguay." In *The Informal Economy: Studies in Advanced and Less Developed Countries*, ed. A. Portes, M. Castells, and L. A. Benton, pp. 78–94. Baltimore: Johns Hopkins University Press.

Gans, Herbert. 1992. "Second-generation Decline: Scenarios for the Economic and Ethnic Futures of the Post-1965 American Immigrants." *Ethnic and Racial Studies* 15 (April): 173–192.

Glick Schiller, Nina, Linda Basch, and Cristina Blanc-Szanton. 1992. "Transnationalism:

A New Analytic Framework for Understanding Migration." *Annals of the New York Academy of Sciences* 645: 1–24.

Grasmuck, Sherri, and Patricia Pessar. 1991. *Between Two Islands: Dominican International Migration.* Berkeley: University of California Press.

Guarnizo, Luis E. 1992. "One Country in Two: Dominican-Owned Firms in the United States and the Dominican Republic." Ph.D. dissertation, Department of Sociology, The Johns Hopkins University.

Harrison, Bennett. 1994. *Lean and Mean: The Changing Landscape of Corporate Power in the Age of Flexibility.* New York: Basic Books.

Itzigsohn, Jose A. 1994. "The Informal Economy in Santo Domingo and San Jose: A Comparative Study." Ph.D. dissertation, Department of Sociology, The Johns Hopkins University.

Kollock, Peter. 1994. "The Emergence of Exchange Structures: An Experimental Study of Uncertainty, Commitment, and Trust." *American Journal of Sociology* 100 (September): 313–345.

Kyle, David. 1994. "The Transnational Peasant: The Social Structures of Economic Migration from the Ecuadoran Andes." Ph.D. dissertation, Department of Sociology, The Johns Hopkins University.

Lawyers Committee for Human Rights (LCHR). 1991. "Protection of Workers' Rights." Draft. LCHR, New York.

Light, Ivan. 1984. "Immigrant and Ethnic Enterprise in North America." *Ethnic and Racial Studies* 7 (April): 195–216.

Light, Ivan, and Edna Bonacich. 1988. *Immigrant Entrepreneurs: Koreans in Los Angeles 1965–1982.* Berkeley: University of California Press.

Lim, Linda Y. C. 1990. "Singapore." In *Labor Standards and Development in the Global Economy*, ed. S. Herzenberg and J. Perez-Lopez, pp. 73–95. Washington, DC: U.S. Department of Labor.

Massey, Douglas, and Felipe García España. 1987. "The Social Process of International Migration." *Science* 237: 733–738.

Münz, Rainer, and Rolf Ulrich. 1995. "Changing Patterns of Migration, the Case of Germany, 1945–1994." Paper presented at the German-American Migration and Refugee Policy Group, American Academy of Arts and Sciences, Cambridge, MA., March 23–26.

Pérez-Sainz, Juan Pablo. 1994. *El dilema del Nahual.* San José, Costa Rica: FLACSO Editores.

Piore, Michael. 1979. *Birds of Passage.* Cambridge: Cambridge University Press.

———. 1990. "Labor Standards and Business Strategies." In *Labor Standards and Development in the Global Economy*, ed. S. Herzenberg and J. Perez-Lopez, pp. 35–49. Washington, DC: U.S. Department of Labor.

Piore, Michael J., and Charles F. Sabel. 1984. *The Second Industrial Divide.* New York: Basic Books.

Portes, Alejandro. 1978. "Migration and Underdevelopment." *Politics and Society* 8: 1–48.

Portes, Alejandro, and Robert L. Bach. 1985. *Latin Journey: Cuban and Mexican Immigrants in the United States.* Berkeley: University of California Press.

Portes, Alejandro and József Böröcz. 1989. "Contemporary Immigration: Theoretical Perspectives on Its Determinants and Modes of Incorporation." *International Migration Review* 23 (Fall): 606–630.

Portes, Alejandro, and Luis E. Guarnizo. 1990. "Tropical Capitalists: U.S. Bound Immigration and Small Enterprise Development in the Dominican Republic." Working paper no. 57. Commission for the Study of International Migration and Cooperative Economic Development, Washington, DC.

————. 1991. "Tropical Capitalists: U.S.-Bound Immigration and Small Enterprise Development in the Dominican Republic." In *Migration, Remittances, and Small Business Development: Mexico and Caribbean Basin Countries*, ed. S. Díaz-Briquets and S. Weintraub, pp. 101–131. Boulder, CO: Westview Press.

Portes, Alejandro, and Min Zhou. 1995. "Divergent Destinies: Immigration, Poverty, and Entrepreneurship in the United States." In *Poverty, Inequality, and the Future of Social Policy*, ed. K. McFate, B. Lawson, and W. J. Wilson, pp. 489–520. New York: Russell Sage Foundation.

Rumbaut, Rubén G. 1994. "Origins and Destinies: Immigration to the United States Since World War II." *Sociological Forum* 9, 4: 583–621.

Sabel, Charles. 1982. *The Division of Labor in Industry*. Cambridge: Cambridge University Press.

————. 1986. "Changing Modes of Economic Efficiency and Their Implications for Industrialization in the Third World." In *Development, Democracy, and Trespassing: Essays in Honor of Albert O. Hirschman*, ed. M. S. McPherson, A. Foxley, and G. O'Donnell, pp. 27–55. Notre Dame, IN: Notre Dame University Press.

Sassen, Saskia. 1979. "Formal and Informal Associations: Dominicans and Colombians in New York." *International Migration Review* 13 (Summer): 314–332.

————. 1988. *The Mobility of Labor and Capital: A Study in International Investment and Labor Flow*. New York: Cambridge University Press.

————. 1989. "New York City's Informal Economy." In *The Informal Economy: Studies in Advanced and Less Developed Countries*, ed. A. Portes, M. Castells, and L. A. Benton, pp. 60–77. Baltimore, MD: Johns Hopkins University Press.

————. 1995. "Immigration and Local Labor Markets." In *The Economic Sociology of Immigration: Essays in Networks, Ethnicity, and Entrepreneurship*, ed. A. Portes, pp. 87–127. New York: Russell Sage Foundation.

Sassen, Saskia, and Alejandro Portes. 1993. "Miami: A New Global City?" *Contemporary Sociology* 22 (July): 471–477.

Smith, Christopher, and Min Zhou. 1995. "Flushing: Capital and Community in a Transnational Neighborhood." Manuscript. Russell Sage Foundation, New York.

Smith, Robert C. 1992, October. "Los ausentes siempre presentes: The Imagining, Making, and Politics of a Transnational Community between New York City and Ticuaní, Puebla." Manuscript. Columbia University, Institute for Latin American and Iberian Studies.

Zhou, Min. 1992. *New York's Chinatown: The Socioeconomic Potential of an Urban Enclave*. Philadelphia: Temple University Press.

Zhou, Min, and Carl L. Bankston. 1995. "Entrepreneurship." In *The Asian American Almanac: A Reference Work on Asians in the United States*, ed. S. Gall and I. Natividad, pp. 511–528. Detroit: Gale Research, Inc.

Zolberg, Aristide R. 1989. "The Next Waves: Migration Theory for a Changing World." *International Migration Review* 23 (Fall): 403–430.

Revolutionary Terrorism in the Periphery: A Comparative Analysis of the Shining Path and the Khmer Rouge

Bruce M. Podobnik

The particularly brutal form of revolutionary violence that continues to haunt Peru and Cambodia is a forceful reminder of the dangers inherent in a global system characterized by growing inequality and the increasing marginalization of vast segments of the population of peripheral societies. Caught in an international context marked by wrenching economic restructuring, chronic austerity, and the apparent collapse of alternative development strategies, entire generations of youth in less-developed countries such as Peru and Cambodia face futures of grinding poverty and social dislocation. While the majority of the youth of these countries continue in their attempts to survive within the framework of the contemporary capitalist world-system, small but determined groups of Shining Path and Khmer Rouge guerrillas have chosen to reject any accommodation with such a system, and instead have embarked on radical projects of autonomous socialist development.

An examination of the recent history of the Shining Path and the Khmer Rouge, however, highlights the dangers involved when revolutionary forces within peripheral nations attempt to undertake policies of autarkic development. In both Peru and Cambodia, transitory periods of popular support for guerrilla campaigns against oppressive elites or occupying military forces gave way to widespread resistance in the face of the destructive policies of autarky and social reconstruction imposed by Shining Path and Khmer Rouge guerrillas. Imbued with an apparently limitless faith in the accuracy of their revolutionary analyses, Shining Path and Khmer Rouge cadre refused to accommodate their policies to existing realities and instead systematically assassinated representatives of virtually all state institutions, peasant leaders, labor organizers, and most other activists who would not submit to the radical demands of their movement. In a pattern that resembles those of other recent revolutionary conflicts, the struggles of the Shining Path and the Khmer Rouge degenerated into increasingly incomprehensible, and ultimately self-defeating, orgies of violence and terror.[1]

The comparative analysis that follows is intended to shed light on the conditions that produced movements willing to employ violence against virtually all social groups in their efforts to achieve revolutionary transformations. As this chapter will argue, structural problems common to most peripheral societies led to the emergence of a generation of youth in Peru and Cambodia with few viable employment opportunities in either rural or urban areas. Although mentioned in passing in previous writings on peripheral revolutions, my analysis emphasizes the key role of such youth in the contemporary revolutionary struggles of Peru and Cambodia.[2] In addition to examining the emergence of these strata of detached youth, I investigate specific social, political, and cultural conditions that led dissident elite groups within each country to adopt extremist, uncompromising stances toward existing political and social structures. The institutional settings in which such leadership factions could engage in the intensive ideological training of alienated rural and urban youth are then described, followed by an analysis of the regional political and social vacuums into which embryonic radical parties could expand and generate wider bases of social support.

THE EMERGENCE OF A GENERATION OF DETACHED YOUTH

The penetration of capitalist enterprise into rural areas in Cambodia and Peru has led to the disruption of local subsistence economies, the concentration of landownership, and the growth of a sector of the peasantry that is compelled to migrate in search of employment. Combined with the destructive impact of regional wars and internal civil conflict, these pressures have led to the dislocation of large segments of the rural populations of both countries. Demographic growth, spurred by the introduction of modern health services, has served to heighten the social tensions inherent in contexts of increasing class inequality and foreign exploitation, while the urban industrial sectors have proven incapable of providing avenues out of poverty for the majority of the citizens of either country. These, I will argue, are the structural roots of the emergence of revolutionary terrorist movements in Cambodia and Peru.[3]

The imposition of French colonial rule over Cambodia in 1863 marked the definitive end of that country's political autonomy and the beginning of its incorporation into an expanding capitalist world-system as an exporter of agricultural commodities. Plantations established by the French in the Mekong Delta had, by the 1930s, transformed Cambodia into an important exporter of rubber and cotton, while an influx of foreign capital from France, the United States, the Soviet Union, and China in the years following World War II financed the expansion of port facilities and transportation systems and allowed for steady increases in Cambodian agricultural production during the period of 1950–1966 (Chandler, 1991: 89).

When measured in terms of its export sectors' performance, the Cambodian economy appeared to be relatively dynamic into the mid-1960s. Modest successes in Cambodia's export performance, however, masked growing internal structural imbalances. The expansion of large landholdings and plantations in the country's most fertile regions brought about the dislocation of rural populations, so that during the period 1950–1970, the percentage of Cambodians forced to work as sharecroppers or landless migrant laborers grew from 4 to 20 percent (Kiernan, 1982: 4). Rapid demographic expansion produced high rates of rural out-migration in Cambodia as well. It is interesting to note that while approximately 590,000 people resided in urban areas in 1962, by 1967 that number had risen to 880,000 (Banister and Johnson, 1993: 107). By the late 1960s, a sizable class of impoverished rural inhabitants with few ties to the land had emerged. As in other peripheral societies, it was precisely this confluence of structural changes that provoked serious social conflict in rural Cambodia.

The first revolutionary tremors broke out in April 1967, with the beginning of the Samlaut Rebellion in the central rice plains of Cambodia. Located in Battambang province, the Samlaut region was the site of increasing land pressure during the 1950s and 1960s as fruit and cotton plantations encroached on peasant holdings. What appears to have begun as a largely spontaneous peasant revolt sparked off by these multiple threats to local subsistence activities had, by 1969, expanded to become the most extensive outbreak of violence seen since anti-French uprisings had swept through Cambodia following World War II.

While tensions were growing in those parts of central Cambodia that were most integrated into the national and international market systems, conditions in the country's peripheral mountain and jungle regions were deteriorating as well. Inhabited primarily by non-Khmer tribal minorities, the remote areas of northeastern, southwestern, and eastern Cambodia remained largely untouched by commercial influence into the 1960s. In the mid-1960s, however, the central government began moving lowland Khmer peasants into the northeastern zone in an apparent attempt to "Khmerize" the independent hill tribes, and thus establish some control over the region. The threats to local ethnic customs and subsistence activities posed by these new colonists provoked a series of tribal revolts throughout the northeast in 1968 and 1969, eventually leading many of the non-Khmer minorities to join the Khmer Rouge's war against lowland, urban Cambodia (Burgler, 1990: 23).

By the late 1960s, in short, both the central and the more remote regions of the country were already exhibiting most of the social tensions characteristic of societies undergoing processes of peripheral development. The expansion of the Indochina War into Cambodia brought profound disruptions to the society and accelerated revolutionary processes within the country. In an effort to shut down the North Vietnamese supply lines that stretched along Cambodia's eastern frontiers, the United States initiated covert bombing raids into the country in early

1969. The bombing campaign expanded relentlessly, so that by the time the U.S. Congress halted military operations in Cambodia in August 1973, approximately 500,000 tons of explosives, or more than three times that dropped on Japan during all of World War II, had been unleashed on the nation (Markusen, 1992: 159). In addition to killing an estimated 275,000 Cambodians, the U.S. bombing campaign destroyed most of the country's rural infrastructure, disrupted agricultural production, and generated an immense refugee population. As a result, by 1975, the population of the country's capital city, Phnom Penh, had surged to approximately 3 million, or over 40 percent of Cambodia's entire population (Banister and Johnson, 1993: 107). It was precisely in this context of rural collapse and widespread destruction that the Khmer Rouge was able to recruit a young cadre to perpetuate its revolutionary war.

Although Peru has avoided provoking the direct wrath of a core state in the contemporary period, its initial mode of incorporation into the modern world-system was itself an extremely violent process. The impact of European military campaigns, enslavement, and contagious diseases provoked an Andean demographic collapse of dramatic proportions, while the exploitation of Peru's mineral and agricultural resources during the ensuing centuries further threatened Andean societies. It is estimated that only about 6 percent of Peru's land mass is suitable for agriculture, and although indigenous communities developed networks of exchange in order to integrate distinct ecological niches into sustainable systems, such subsistence economies have proven vulnerable to the expansion of capitalist markets, predatory landowners, and demographic pressures.

The penetration of railroads and other transportation networks into the central Andes during the 1940s and 1950s precipitated structural changes that, over the long term, undermined these Andean subsistence economies (Slater, 1989). The availability of improved transportation systems encouraged large landowners to bring fertile land into intensive production for urban markets, which meant driving segments of the peasantry off their land. Even those indigenous communities that managed to retain control over communal lands began to experience growing internal pressures as the spread of public health services generated a demographic expansion throughout the central Andes in the postwar period. That a growing number of peasants were desperate for land is evidenced by the wave of land invasions that began in the mid-1950s and which, by 1968, had involved the participation of over 300,000 peasants (García-Sayán, 1982: 13).

A further indication of the poverty and subsistence crises sweeping through the countryside can be found in an analysis of rates of out-migration. During the 1940–1981 period, out-migration rates from the central Andean provinces of Ayacucho, Apurimac, Ancash, and Huancavelica were consistently the highest in the nation (Degregori, 1990: 32). In this period, in fact, Peru underwent a fundamental transition: whereas in 1940, only 17 percent of the nation's population resided in urban areas, by 1980, this percentage had grown to 65 percent.

In 1980, fully one-quarter of the country's 17 million people resided in the capital city of Lima.

By invading marginal urban land, constructing homes, and then organizing to demand the provision of such services as water and electricity, Lima's new residents managed to begin a process of achieving limited upward mobility during the 1950s, which lasted into the 1970s. A portion of the city's working class was absorbed by expanding formal industrial enterprises, while the rest sought employment in an informal sector that flourished in Lima's streets and neighborhoods. Moreover, for the children of these new migrants, state-funded education offered a new avenue toward upward mobility: while in 1960 there were only 30,000 university students nationwide, by 1970 there were 109,000, and by 1982 the number had expanded to 305,000 (Cotler, 1986: 110).

Migrating to Lima and other urban areas resulted in better living conditions and employment prospects for most individuals into the 1970s. However, the onset of a protracted economic crisis in 1976 began to undermine the capacity of Peru's lower classes to generate alternative forms of limited upward mobility. The increasing saturation of urban spaces and the urban informal economy led to intensified competition among impoverished residents for shrinking resources (Stein and Monge, 1988). Meanwhile, a collapse of formal industrial employment severely limited the ability of high school and university graduates to find adequate employment. As a result of this collapse, by 1982, fully 63.4 percent of Lima residents aged 15 to 24 were either underemployed or unemployed (Cotler, 1986: 114).

By 1980, in sum, structural inequalities and demographic pressures in rural and urban areas were undermining the future prospects of an entire generation of Peruvians. Much as in Cambodia, processes of uneven development in Peru were resulting in the emergence of a class of youth with few attachments to the land and also with limited opportunities for upward mobility in urban areas. These conditions resulted in heightened levels of political and social turmoil over the following decades.

THE CONSOLIDATION OF SECTARIAN LEADERSHIP GROUPS

In addition to producing a generation of rural and urban youth with few employment opportunities, the particular forms of uneven development that have taken place in Cambodia and Peru produced exclusionary social systems that failed to incorporate newly emergent classes of professionals and educated individuals into meaningful political participation.[4] It was precisely out of these marginalized strata that the core leadership factions of the Khmer Rouge and the Shining Path emerged.

From 1941 until 1970, the Cambodian political system was dominated by the idiosyncratic rule of one individual, Prince Norodom Sihanouk. Although nominally democratic parliamentary procedures were instituted in the mid-1950s,

Sihanouk ensured that most of his chosen candidates ran unopposed in elections during the subsequent decade. A new class of entrepreneurs in Phnom Penh found itself shut out of the Cambodian political arena, while a growing number of young university graduates encountered few opportunities for suitable employment as the Cambodian economy stagnated (Chandler, 1991).

This closed political and social order came under increasingly severe criticism from a select group of Cambodians who studied together in France in the early 1950s and then returned to their native country, only to find most avenues of upward social mobility blocked.[5] Saloth Sar (who later adopted the guerrilla name Pol Pot), Ieng Sari, Son Sen, and Khieu Samphan were sent to Paris for technical training but became immersed in the radical political environment created by a large Asian expatriate community in the French capital. Upon their return to Phnom Penh, a series of elements converged to further intensify the political extremism of this faction. First, throughout the 1950s and 1960s, Prince Sihanouk appropriated much of the moderate left's political rhetoric by adopting an anti-imperialist, anti-American stance, and by supporting the Non-Aligned Movement. Pol Pot and his allies initially echoed Sihanouk's critiques of exploitative international powers, but they eventually went further and demanded a complete cut in ties with virtually all foreign powers.

In 1963, following widespread protests mounted by students and disaffected urban residents, Sihanouk unleashed his military on the Cambodian Communist Party, thereby driving the entire Khmer Rouge leadership into the remote northeastern mountains. From 1963 until 1975, Pol Pot and his faction lived among the isolated hill tribes of this northeast region, depending on the assistance of these tribal people for their very survival (Burgler, 1990: 17). This experience more than any other nurtured the anti-urban, Maoist orientation of the original Khmer Rouge leadership, thus producing a revolutionary group that was fundamentally different from any other oppositional faction in Cambodia. In sum, by the 1960s, a closely knit, ideologically distinct Khmer Rouge leadership group had coalesced within a context marked by closed political and social institutions, a violent and repressive central government, and a sustained immersion in rural Cambodian society.

A very similar set of conditions produced an equally sectarian, extremist leadership group in the Andean highlands of Peru. Although the modern political history of Peru is more complex than that of Cambodia in part because elected civilian governments alternated with de facto military regimes throughout the century, a few constants can nevertheless be identified. First, until very recently the central government itself has been dominated by a *criollo* elite, with cultural roots in Lima as well as economic ties to key export sectors linking Peru to the world-economy. This political and economic orientation toward the coast produced a second constant in Peruvian politics and society: the neglect of the marginally productive, culturally isolated central Andean regions. Well into the twentieth century, sections of the Andean highlands remained largely outside the sphere of influence of the Peruvian central government; instead, large landowners exercised ideological, economic, and political domination over the regional populations. In a uniquely Andean phenomenon termed *gamonalismo*, the indigenous populations of such provinces as Ayacucho, Apurimac, and Huancavelica were subjected to intense forms of coercion by powerful hacendados who, in addition to imposing feudalistic obligations on the peasants they employed, frequently controlled local municipalities, legal officials, and even church clergy (Manrique, 1990: 82).

Within this oppressive political and social context, an emergent mestizo class of provincial university professors and students began to elaborate critiques of the inequalities embedded in Andean society.[6] Key among this elite group of dissidents was Abimael Guzmán Reynoso, a professor of philosophy who arrived in Ayacucho in 1962 and soon distinguished himself as a particularly dogmatic activist within the local political scene. A visit to China during the height of the Cultural Revolution intensified Guzmán's ideological extremism, and by late 1969, he and a small group of allies, including key future leaders such as Oscar Morote, Julio Mezzich, and Antonio Díaz Martínez, had split from another local Maoist party to form the Peruvian Communist Party–Shining Path (Gorriti, 1990).

The sectarian nature of the Shining Path began to reveal itself immediately. Labeling all other splinter groups in Ayacucho "revisionists," the group proceeded to argue that there was no possible accommodation with the "bureaucratic capitalist, fascist state" that they claimed ruled Peru. Drawing on Mao Tse-tung's theory of guerrilla warfare, Guzmán called the mobilization of the peasantry in a massive assault on urban society the only correct strategy for true revolutionaries in Peru (Peruvian Communist Party, 1982). Militants of the Shining Path physically attacked members of other radical parties in Ayacucho who rejected such a strategy, accusing these more moderate activists of confusing the masses with revisionist doctrines (Gorriti, 1990: 32–33).

Aside from the possible psychological idiosyncrasies of the core leadership of the Shining Path, there are specific social and political conditions that pushed the party to adopt such uncompromising positions. Much like Prince Sihanouk in Cambodia, the reformist military regime of Juan Velasco Alvarado, which seized power in Peru in 1968, appropriated the moderate left's political agenda by attacking U.S. business interests, denouncing foreign imperialism, and instituting an agrarian reform. The failure of most of these reforms, which was evident by 1976, lent added weight to the Shining Path's attacks on all versions of political revisionism. Additionally, the abortive guerrilla struggles waged in Ayacucho in 1965 by a handful of Cuban-inspired urbanites convinced Shining Path militants that long-term efforts would be required to establish the rural connections necessary for carrying out a peasant-based guerrilla war in the Andes.

Much like the Khmer Rouge, therefore, the original leaders of the Shining Path consolidated their position within a context of closed political and social systems, a heritage of pervasive local oppression, and long-term interaction with rural populations. Moreover, like the Khmer Rouge, the Shining Path leadership came to reject reformist policies in favor of a strategy of peasant-based guerrilla warfare.

INSTITUTIONAL CONTEXTS

Having examined the emergence of populations of detached youth in Cambodia and Peru, along with the consolidation of extremist leadership factions in each country, I now turn to an analysis of the institutional contexts in which these two social groups came into sustained contact with each other. Particular attention will be directed toward identifying precisely which kinds of individuals responded to the political messages being advanced by the leaders of the Khmer Rouge and the Shining Path.

The core leaders of what was to become the Khmer Rouge were able to begin the long-term task of recruiting militants on their return from Paris in the 1950s, when they assumed positions within key universities in Phnom Penh. In 1956, Pol Pot took a teaching position in the private Chamraon Vichea (Progressive Study) school, while Khieu Samphan and Ieng Sari joined the faculty at Kambubot College, an institution that had already earned a reputation as a site of radical political activity. The success of the original leadership of the Khmer Rouge in mobilizing support within these university contexts is revealed by Chandler:

The roles played by teachers at Kambubot and Chamraon Vichea are crucial to the development of Cambodian radicalism. . . . By the late 1960s, when a Communist-led rebellion had broken out in much of Cambodia, many guerrilla bands were made up in part of former teachers and their students who had followed them into the forest. (1991: 110–111)

Frustrated by the closed nature of Cambodia's political system and class structure, teachers and students in Phnom Penh became actively engaged in oppositional activities by the late 1950s. Prince Sihanouk responded by clamping down on the Communist Party, forcing Pol Pot and his key allies to flee into the remote northeast provinces of the country in 1963. In 1967, a renewed crackdown on urban Maoists in Phnom Penh drove hundreds of young students and intellectuals into the jungle, facilitating the expansion of Khmer Rouge influence in rural areas. By 1968, the Khmer Rouge had established a network of contacts throughout the country that allowed them to begin their armed struggle against the Cambodian state.

Although the Khmer Rouge received little support from the middle peasantry located in the central rice plains and along the Mekong River, they did gain adherents among the impoverished hill tribes where for years, party members had worked the land, dug irrigation canals, and provided basic medical care. Young peasants with no access to land in these peripheral regions became the movement's main converts (Frieson, 1993: 37). Indeed, the party found the young to be the most committed revolutionaries. Party documents indicate that by 1970, efforts were being made to organize special military- and political-training camps for the poorest peasant youth in Khmer Rouge base areas (Etcheson, 1984: 161). Once sent to the front lines to battle government troops, these youth were isolated from their families, and their dependence on the party thus became complete. The harshness of the war, including saturation bombing of the countryside by U.S. B-52 bombers, had a profound psychological impact on these youth, inuring them to brutality and generating hatred for the members of the urban elite who were orchestrating the destruction of rural Cambodia.[7] It was precisely these young cadres who marched into Phnom Penh in April 1975, ready to carry out the radical policies of the Khmer Rouge leadership.

The history of the Shining Path shares striking similarities to that of the Khmer Rouge, though there are important differences as well. As with the Khmer Rouge, the leadership of the Shining Path was able to initiate its recruitment efforts in a university context. Unlike the Khmer Rouge, however, the Shining Path did not find bases of support solely among the poorest segments of the peasantry. Instead, the movement's most consistent militants were provincial and urban youth with relatively high levels of education but few viable opportunities for upward social mobility.

One of the sad ironies of Peruvian history is that changes that were fundamentally progressive often resulted in heightened social conflict over the long term. Thus, although the Agrarian Reform of 1969 succeeded in eradicating an exploitative class of rural landowners, these same measures undermined investments in Andean agriculture and led to an intensification of the subsistence crisis assailing the central sierra. Similarly, while the reopening of the University of San Cristóbal de Huamanga in the provincial capital of Ayacucho in 1959 brought new educational and professional opportunities to an impoverished region, this same university also became the epicenter of the most violent guerrilla movement in Peru's history.

From 1969 until 1973, the Shining Path dominated key institutions within the University of San Cristóbal. With Guzmán installed as director of university personnel and Díaz Martínez as director of student affairs, the party was able to exercise control over hiring and admissions decisions regarding professors and students. With the partial support of university resources, Shining Path activists began their own outreach programs into the surrounding Andean countryside in the early 1970s, spending long periods of time providing rudimentary medical, teaching, and technical services to impoverished rural inhabitants. In contrast to other leftist factions, which remained encased within urban areas, by the late 1970s, Shining Path militants had dispersed themselves throughout Ayacucho and neighboring provinces, thus extending the influence of the party into rural communities (Degregori, 1990: 184).

In 1976, Guzmán resigned from the University of San Cristóbal and returned to Lima. The Shining Path slowly increased its influence in the capital, especially within the University of San Marcos. As an institution, San Marcos provided a safe haven for radical political activism in the capital, since under the legal autonomy enjoyed by all Peruvian universities, police and military personnel are prohibited from entering the grounds without a warrant. As early as 1965, Maoists had won student elections at San Marcos, and the student body proved receptive to the radical critique of Peruvian society advanced by Shining Path militants in the 1970s (Montoya, 1992).

From their positions within universities in Ayacucho and Lima, Shining Path leaders undertook long-term efforts at recruiting larger numbers of militants. A study by Chávez de Paz (1989), which examined the background of 183 individuals imprisoned in Lima for terrorist acts during the period 1983–1986, provides one snapshot of the social characteristics of these early Shining Path members. According to his findings, 60 percent of those arrested on terrorist charges had been born in the rural provinces. Furthermore, whereas only 7.7 percent of Peru's total population had achieved some university education, a full 35.5 percent of the accused terrorists had attained that educational level or higher. An unusually large number of the prisoners were women, and the educational levels attained by these female accused terrorists were generally much higher (including graduate and postgraduate studies) than those of male accused terrorists or the general Peruvian population (Chávez de Paz, 1989: 34–43).

These findings generally support the conclusion that the Shining Path recruited the majority of its core militants from the ranks of male and female provincial university students. Culturally alienated from their rural communities through their educational experiences, these youth found few avenues for upward social mobility in a society characterized by an enduring economic crisis and persistent racism. By the late 1970s, networks of extremely dedicated militants recruited from this social strata had been established in the regions surrounding Ayacucho, and in the capital of Lima as well. It was this organizational strength that encouraged the Shining Path to begin its armed struggle in 1980, just as Peru was returning to democratic rule.

EXPANSION INTO REGIONAL POLITICAL AND SOCIAL VACUUMS

The final task in this comparative analysis is to describe the expansion of the armed struggles of the Khmer Rouge and the Shining Path. Both guerrilla movements were able to take advantage of political and social vacuums in order to impose military control over wide segments of Cambodia and Peru. While ideologically committed cadres of the Khmer Rouge and the Shining Path proved effective in carrying forward such military struggles, the totalitarian characteristics of each party's revolutionary policies alienated rural and urban populations. Organized civilian resistance in the face of such policies provoked an increasingly violent response from Khmer Rouge and Shining Path cadres, leading to the escalation of terrorism and the eventual weakening of each party's revolutionary projects.

The large-scale bombing of Cambodia carried out by the United States had been designed both to disrupt North Vietnamese supply lines and to prop up a Cambodian state that was faltering in the face of the guerrilla campaign being waged within the country. Rather than reinforce the Cambodian state, however, this massive deployment of military firepower had the unintended consequence of forging what had been a fractured nationalist/communist insurgency into an extremely radical, Khmer Rouge-dominated revolutionary army (Etcheson, 1984: 118). Although backed by massive U.S. financial and military assistance, the Cambodian military was decimated in 1970 and had to withdraw from most of northeastern Cambodia. By 1973, the Cambodian state had essentially disintegrated and its leaders were confined to Phnom Penh, which was itself subjected to repeated attacks by Khmer Rouge forces.

On April 17, 1975, Khmer Rouge forces took control of Phnom Penh. Reports indicate that most party cadres appeared to be under fifteen years of age and were illiterate, and although many technicians and educated urban citizens offered their assistance to the party, such conciliatory advances were rejected by the Khmer Rouge. Armed cadres instead began evacuating Phnom Penh and other cities, so that within two months, between 2 and 3 million people had been forced into the Cambodian countryside.

Once in the countryside, people found themselves in a radically transformed environment dominated by the Khmer Rouge's network of party members and sympathizers. Money was abolished, markets were closed, most personal property was confiscated, and virtually everyone was forced to don the black clothing traditionally worn by peasants. Religious orders, including Buddhism, Islam, and Catholicism, were suppressed, and concerted efforts were made by the Khmer Rouge to dismantle the traditional Cambodian family structure by separating children from their parents and sending relatives to work in different regions. A 1976 party document graphically summarized the central aim of the Khmer Rouge in the following terms:

All the exploiting classes who had previously been beaten down were beaten and cut down again. . . . As for individualism, whether of feudalists, capitalists, or of other classes not particularly poor, such as independent farmers, independent workers, and independent manual laborers, we have dug down and uprooted even more of this in 1976. We won't allow individualism to rise again. (Communist Party of Kampuchea, 1976: 182)

In 1976, the Khmer Rouge leadership inaugurated a four-year plan of economic development that involved the collectivization of all agriculture and the undertaking of massive irrigation projects. Malnutrition increased throughout 1976, however, and by 1977–1978, famine conditions became widespread as poorly planned irrigation systems silted up, agricultural machinery broke down, and Khmer Rouge confiscations of rice supplies intensified. The policies of complete autarky imposed on Democratic Kampuchea by Pol Pot and his key allies led to the rejection of all foreign humanitarian and technical assistance, bringing about the collapse of the country's mechanical infrastructure and an expansion of malaria during this period.

The totalitarian regulations imposed by the Khmer Rouge led hundreds of thousands of Cambodians to seek refuge in neighboring countries, while many who were trapped inside the country attempted to resist Khmer Rouge policies. Dissent and criticism were not tolerated in Democratic Kampuchea, however, and teenage cadres began executing peasants, workers, and intellectuals. Conditions became so extreme that by late 1976, a number of provincial Khmer Rouge leaders came to the conclusion that Pol Pot and his advisors were bringing about the destruction of Democratic Kampuchea, and attempts were apparently made on Pol Pot's life. In response, the hard-line group led by Pol Pot began to carry out internal purges within the Khmer Rouge. As a result, between 1976 and 1978, as many as 20,000 party members were interrogated, tortured, and then killed in Tuol Sleng, a former school in Phnom Penh (Etcheson, 1984: 178). In addition, purges directed against party members in Cambodia's eastern provinces claimed approximately 100,000 lives.

In an apparent attempt by the Khmer Rouge leadership to deflect internal criticism by inciting xenophobic hatred of an old adversary, military raids were initiated against Vietnamese villages in 1977. The attacks eventually provoked a full-scale invasion by the Vietnamese army, however, and an estimated 30,000 Khmer Rouge troops proved no match for the well-equipped Vietnamese forces. By January 1979, the Vietnamese army had surrounded Phnom Penh, forcing Pol Pot to flee by helicopter and bringing about the downfall of the Khmer Rouge regime.

Although a core group of Khmer Rouge leaders and cadres succeeded in imposing their revolutionary agenda on the Cambodian people during the period 1975–1978, the totalitarian nature of such transformations, which in the end led to the death of over a million Cambodians, alienated most of the population and many within the party's own ranks, thus fatally weakening the Khmer Rouge. Interestingly, a similar pattern emerged in many of the rural and urban areas that fell under the influence of the Shining Path of Peru.

The central Andean departments of Ayacucho, Andahuaylas, and Huancavelica were the site of the Shining Path's first extensive military campaigns. Shining Path guerrillas began threatening and killing police, judges, and other government officials in 1980, so that by 1982, many rural regions in the central Andes had been "liberated." Peasant accounts of what transpired in "liberated" villages during this period have been recorded by anthropologists, and such testimonies consistently describe the same general pattern of events.[8] Shining Path militants typically entered villages and, based on their familiarity with specific communities, executed cattle thieves, hacendados, or government officials who were particularly hated by local peasants. Party members also imposed strict codes of behavior on these villages, punishing individuals who drank to excess, committed adultery, or abused family members. This imposition of social order in communities that had suffered long histories of abuse at the hands of local landlords and corrupt officials was initially welcomed, and rural support for the Shining Path grew during the early stages of the party's military campaign.

However, in accordance with its Maoist-inspired guerrilla strategy of surrounding urban areas and strangling them, the Shining Path began closing down peasant markets and prohibiting all commerce between villagers and nearby towns. Such policies generated widespread opposition, but when peasant leaders voiced disagreement, they were accused of being in collaboration with the government and threatened or killed by Shining Path cadres. From 1981 through 1983, increasingly bloody confrontations took place between organized peasants and the Shining Path in the central sierra (Gorriti, 1990: 254).

These early attempts by Andean communities to expel the guerrilla movement were completely subverted by the arrival of the Peruvian military in late 1982. Instead of targeting actual guerrilla cadres, state security forces from the coast proceeded to carry out indiscriminate assaults on the Andean peasantry itself. As a result of this state-sponsored terrorism, the death toll in the Peruvian civil war rose abruptly; whereas in 1982 there were 170 confirmed deaths as a result of political violence, by 1983 this number had risen to 2,807, and it jumped to 4,319 in 1984 (Americas Watch, 1992: 14).

Although the military occupation of Ayacucho and surrounding departments led to the massacre of entire peasant communities and the generation of a large population of displaced persons, it did not halt the expansion of the Shining Path. Guerrillas moved into the strategically important Mantaro Valley in Junin (a key source of hydroelectric power and agricultural products for Lima), and also penetrated deep into the upper Huallaga Valley, a center of Peruvian coca production. By the mid-1980s, electrical power in Lima was regularly disrupted by Shining Path dynamite attacks, and in 1987 the guerrillas dramatized their presence in the Huallaga Valley by launching widespread attacks on police stations and halting traffic on most roads in the jungle region (Gonzáles, 1992: 109).

While the Shining Path's ability to project its military influence into these new regions was certainly impressive, the party's political success at the village level was more qualified. Peasant communities in the Mantaro Valley, which have experienced some economic progress by selling agricultural products in Lima's central markets, have consistently resisted the Shining Path's attempts to sever all commerce with the capital (Kent, 1993). Similarly, attempts by the Shining Path to expand into the southern department of Puno were met with resistance from moderate, progressive political and church organizations, which favored more peaceful forms of protest (Berg, 1992). By the late 1980s, both the Mantaro Valley and the regions surrounding Puno had become the site of intense confrontations between peasants and insurgents, indicating again the deep-seated resistance among wide sectors of the Peruvian lower and middle peasantry to the revolutionary policies that the Shining Path was attempting to impose.

The final front in the Peruvian civil war has been fought in the capital, Lima. Beginning in 1989, the Shining Path dramatically escalated its military actions in the capital, and by 1991 more than half the nation's incidents of political violence were occurring in the city (Kent, 1993: 452). From May to September 1992, the Shining Path conducted a terrorist offensive in Lima that included the regular detonation of large explosive devices, spreading fear throughout the city's civilian population. This deployment of violence, however, concealed underlying weaknesses in the Shining Path's bases of support in the capital. Although the party had generated some sympathy in isolated shantytowns by spearheading a number of land invasions, most of the city's community organizations rejected the violent and dogmatic behavior of Shining Path militants. The fact that the Shining Path had assassinated many of Lima's most respected progressive leaders and killed hundreds of citizens at random in car bomb attacks further undermined urban support for the movement.

Due to its increasingly indiscriminate use of violence in both rural and urban areas, the Shining Path came under attack from peasant and urban groups that might otherwise have formed the social basis for a future expansion in the party's guerrilla war. Instead, as Degregori (1994: 89) noted, by 1993 approximately 300,000 peasants had joined civic defense committees and, armed with an estimated 10,000 rifles provided by the Peruvian military, were engaged in driving Shining Path columns away from their communities. Meanwhile, throughout Lima's shantytowns, neighborhood watch groups have attempted to protect their own activists by expelling Shining Path militants. The September 1992 capture of Abimael Guzmán and most of the Shining Path's Central Committee severely shook an already-fragile guerrilla movement, terminating whatever slim chance the party had of overthrowing the Peruvian state and imposing its unpopular revolutionary agenda.

CONCLUSION

This comparative analysis of the Khmer Rouge and the Shining Path reveals a fundamentally problematic feature of the contemporary world-system. On the one hand, growing numbers of rural and urban youth throughout the periphery face futures of poverty and social dislocation. The disruption of rural subsistence economies, whether as a result of wartime destruction in Cambodia, demographic pressures in Peru, or environmental degradation in many other regions is accelerating, while urban industries continue to prove incapable of providing young men and women with stable employment. The global expansion of educational systems in the postwar era has done little to improve the employment opportunities for youth in peripheral societies, and may instead increase relative levels of frustration and political radicalism.[9]

Although many requisite elements are in place to foster new social upheavals in specific countries in Latin America and throughout the periphery, the experiences of the Shining Path and the Khmer Rouge highlight the destructive paths that can be taken by isolated, sectarian groups in the name of revolution. As world-system theorists have long argued, the constraints imposed by the capitalist world-economy and the rules enforced by advanced industrial states make it exceedingly difficult for individual parties in dependent nations to seize state power and carry out lasting, progressive transformations.[10] When reformist, quasi-socialist regimes such as those of Sihanouk in Cambodia and Velasco in Peru fail to bring about real change, political and ideological spaces are opened for extremist parties that espouse total revolution of one kind or another.

The Shining Path and the Khmer Rouge may represent, therefore, instances of a kind of revolutionary violence that may become increasingly common in peripheral societies. Faced with the collapse of reformist regimes on a global level, segments of the youth of Latin America and the periphery appear to be turning to messianic political or religious movements that claim to offer new alternatives to harsh social realities. The best hope for reducing the danger of the emergence of new revolutionary terrorist movements in such a global context lies in the efforts spearheaded by progressive groups to increase popular participation in decisions made regarding political, economic, and social matters. It may only be through such grassroots campaigns for participatory democracy that the populations most susceptible to extreme political radicalization—the youth of the world who are subjected to unrelenting economic shocks—may be integrated into constructive revolutionary struggles rather than the self-destructive, totalitarian forms of revolutionary terrorism represented by the Shining Path and the Khmer Rouge.

NOTES

I would like to thank Bill Smith, Beverly Silver, Mahua Sarkar, and Dag MacLeod for comments on earlier versions of this chapter. I am especially indebted to Mirella Podobnik for her assistance during my research in Peru and in the following years.

1. A partial list of movements with roughly similar histories would include Renamo of Mozambique, the Naxalite movement of India, and the Tamil Tigers of Sri Lanka.

2. While Wolf (1969: 281) noted the increasing difficulty of contemporary peasant societies in absorbing new generations of youth, and Wickham-Crowley (1992: 29) empirically documented the prevalence of youth in Latin American guerrilla movements during the postwar era, the role of peasant or urban youth in revolutionary struggles remains largely unexamined.

3. My understanding of the structural roots of revolution draws on the work of such theorists as Goldfrank (1979), Paige (1975), Walton (1984), and Wolf (1969).

4. Goodwin and Skocpol's (1994) analysis of the regime types that appear most susceptible to revolutionary overthrow sheds light on the experiences of Cambodia and Peru. Cambodia typifies the neopatrimonial state, which they identify as being most vulnerable, while Peru highlights the greater resiliency of quasidemocratic regimes, even in the face of strong guerrilla uprisings.

5. The most sophisticated of these Khmer Rouge critiques is that of Samphan (1959).

6. See Díaz Martínez (1985) for the Shining Path's interpretation of Peru's developmental problems.

7. While crucially important in explaining the viciousness of Khmer Rouge cadre, the experience of being subjected to sustained aerial bombardment must be seen as only one of the necessary conditions that produced the revolutionary terrorist movement in Cambodia. The inhabitants of Laos, after all, were subjected to a higher per-capita level of bombing than were their Cambodian neighbors, but the Pathet Lao, who took power in 1975, manifested few of the totalitarian characteristics of the Khmer Rouge. A more detailed comparison of the Khmer Rouge and the Pathet Lao remains to be carried out.

8. See Isbell (1992), Manrique (1990), and Smith (1992) for particularly good descriptions of Shining Path behavior in peasant communities.

9. John Meyer and Michael Hannan (1979) have documented the expansion of global education systems.

10. See the volume edited by Boswell (1989) for an introduction to a world-systems approach to understanding revolutions.

REFERENCES

Americas Watch. 1992. *Peru under Fire: Human Rights since the Return to Democracy.* New Haven, CT: Yale University Press.

Banister, Judith, and Paige Johnson. 1993. "After the Nightmare: The Population of Cambodia." In *Genocide and Democracy in Cambodia*, ed. Ben Kiernan, pp. 65–139. New Haven, CT: Yale University, Southeast Asia Studies Program.

Berg, Ronald. 1992. "Peasant Responses to Shining Path in Andahuaylas." In *The Shining Path of Peru*, ed. David Scott Palmer, pp. 83–104. New York: St. Martin's Press.

Boswell, Terry, ed. 1989. *Revolution in the World-System.* Westport, CT: Greenwood Press.

Burgler, Roeland. 1990. *The Eyes of the Pineapple: Revolutionary Intellectuals and Terror in Democratic Kampuchea.* Saarbrucken, Germany: Verlag Breitenbach Publishers.

Chandler, David. 1991. *The Tragedy of Cambodian History: Politics, War, and Revolution Since 1945.* New Haven, CT: Yale University Press.

Chávez de Paz, Dennis. 1989. *Juventud y terrorismo: Características sociales de los condenados por terrorismo y otros delitos.* Lima, Peru: Instituto de Estudios Peruanos.

Communist Party of Kampuchea. 1976. "Report of Activities of the Party Center According to the General Political Tasks of 1976." Translated and reprinted in *Pol Pot Plans the Future: Confidential Leadership Documents from Democratic Kampuchea, 1976–1977*, ed. David Chandler, Ben Kiernan, and Chanthou Boua, pp. 177–212. New Haven, CT: Yale University Southeast Asia Studies.

Cotler, Julio. 1986. "The Political Radicalization of Working-Class Youth in Peru." *CEPAL Review* 29: 107–118.

Degregori, Carlos. 1990. *Ayacucho 1969–1979: El surgimiento de Sendero Luminoso.* Lima: Instituto de Estudios Peruanos.

———. 1994. "Shining Path and Counterinsurgency Strategy since the Arrest of Abimael Guzmán." In *Peru in Crisis: Dictatorship or Democracy?* ed. Joseph Tulchin and Gary Bland, pp. 81–100. Boulder, CO: Lynne Rienner Publishers.

Díaz Martínez, Antonio. [1965] 1985. *Ayacucho: Hambre y esperanza.* Reprint. Lima: Mosca Azúl Editores.

Etcheson, Craig. 1984. *The Rise and Demise of Democratic Kampuchea.* Boulder, CO: Westview Press.

Frieson, Kate. 1993. "Revolution and Rural Response in Cambodia, 1970–1975." In *Genocide and Democracy in Cambodia,* ed. Ben Kiernan, pp. 33–50. New Haven, CT: Yale University, Southeast Asia Studies Program.

García-Sayán, Diego. 1982. *Tomas de tierras en el Peru.* Lima: Centro de Estudias y Promoción del Desarrollo.

Goldfrank, Walter. 1979. "Theories of Revolution and Revolution without Theory: The Case of Mexico." *Theory and Society* 7, 1 (January–May): 135–165.

Gonzáles, José. 1992. "Guerrillas and Coca in the Upper Huallaga Valley." In *The Shining Path of Peru,* ed. David Scott Palmer, pp. 105–125. New York: St. Martin's Press.

Goodwin, Jeff, and Theda Skocpol. 1994. "Explaining Revolutions in the Contemporary Third World." In *Social Revolutions in the Modern World,* ed. Theda Skocpol, pp. 259–278. Cambridge: Cambridge University Press.

Gorriti, Gustavo. 1990. *Sendero: Historia de la guerra milenaria en el Peru.* Lima: Editorial Apoyo.

Isbell, Billie. 1992. "Shining Path and Peasant Responses in Rural Ayacucho." In *The Shining Path of Peru,* ed. David Scott Palmer, pp. 59–81. New York: St. Martin's Press.

Kent, Robert. 1993. "Geographical Dimensions of the Shining Path Insurgency in Peru." *Geographical Review* 83, 4 (October): 441–454.

Kiernan, Ben. 1982. "Introduction." In *Peasants and Politics in Kampuchea, 1942–1981,* ed. Ben Kiernan and Chanthou Boua, pp. 1–28. New York: M. E. Sharpe.

Manrique, Nelson. 1990. "Formas de acción de sendero y su relación con el campesinado." In *Las condiciones de la violencia en Peru y Bolivia,* ed. Heidulf Schmidt and Carlos Toranzo, pp. 75–87. La Paz: ILDIS.

Markusen, Eric. 1992. "Comprehending the Cambodian Genocide: An Application of Robert Jay Lifton's Model of Genocidal Killing." *Psychohistory Review* 20, 2 (Winter): 145–169.

Meyer, John, and Michael Hannan, eds. 1979. *National Development and the World System: Educational, Economic, and Political Change, 1950–1970.* Chicago: University of Chicago Press.

Montoya, Luis. 1992. *El lado oscuro de la luna: Las percepciones de los jóvenes en los 70 y 90.* Lima: Centro de Estudios y Promoción del Desarrollo.

Paige, Jeffery. 1975. *Agrarian Revolution: Social Movements and Export Agriculture in the Underdeveloped World.* New York: Free Press.

Peruvian Communist Party (Shining Path). 1982. "Desarrollemos la guerra de guerrillos!" Clandestine mimeograph.

Samphan, Khieu. [1959]. *Cambodia's Economy and Industrial Development.* Reprint and translation. Ithaca, NY: Cornell University, Southeast Asia Program, Department of Asian Studies.

Slater, David. 1989. *Territory and State Power in Latin America: The Peruvian Case.* London: Macmillan.

Smith, Michael. 1992. "Taking the High Ground: Shining Path and the Andes." In *The Shining Path of Peru*, ed. David Scott Palmer, pp. 15–32. New York: St. Martin's Press.

Stein, Steve, and Carlos Monge. 1988. *La crisis del estado patrimonial en el Perú*. Lima, Peru: Instituto de Estudios Peruanos.

Walton, John. 1984. *Reluctant Rebels: Comparative Studies of Revolution and Underdevelopment*. New York: Columbia University Press.

Wickham-Crowley, Timothy. 1992. *Guerrillas and Revolution in Latin America: A Comparative Study of Insurgents and Regimes since 1956*. Princeton, NJ: Princeton University Press.

Wolf, Eric. 1969. *Peasant Wars of the Twentieth Century*. New York: Harper and Row.

10

Global Restructuring and the Environment in Latin America

J. Timmons Roberts

> Controversy over development of heavy oil reserves in Ecuador's Oriente rain forests has escalated to the point where environmentalist and native groups have routinely picketed company offices in Quito, Ecuador's capital, and used mass fund raiser mailings in North America. Other major industry/ environment conflicts are taking shape in Brazil and Peru, and in Venezuela the state oil company has initiated the kind of broad environmental initiatives usually seen among U.S. and European multinational petroleum firms.
> *Oil and Gas Journal* (July 6, 1992: 46)

> I don't think we can afford to have the [nature] reserve anymore—we need jobs. We're a third-world country with first-world environmental laws.
> Carlos Estrada, Mexican Land Developer, 1995

As Latin America turns from strongly protected and state-regulated economies to economies more open to market forces, are environmental conditions likely to improve or decline? Can the impacts of increasing export production be mitigated by the growing number of international treaties and business initiatives concerning the environment? What forces generate pressure to protect the environment in Latin America, and how durable and significant are they?

The goal of this chapter is to introduce Latin American environmental questions to world-systems scholars and to incorporate the insights of the world-system perspective in our understanding of environmental problems in the region. While globally, a virtual consensus is emerging that assessments of national development cannot ignore issues of ecological sustainability, writings in the world-system tradition have remained nearly silent on issues of the natural environment (see Smith, 1993; Grimes, Roberts, and Manale, 1993; Chew,

1995). Quite simply, we cannot understand Latin America's place in the world-economy without examining what has too long been treated as an externality by neoclassical and Marxian economic analysis alike: the environment (Bunker, 1985).

In spite of this silence, the world-system perspective has significant potential to provide insights into the interaction between national actors and the international forces implicated in environmental issues. For example, world-systems research has focused on how ties to the world-economy—through historical patterns of colonial conquest, productive investments, and external debt, to name a few—influence national class structures, social movements and types and levels of government repression. Grimes, Roberts, and Manale (1993) have argued that, therefore, a nation's links to the world-economy have critical implications for its environment and for the likely success of environmental social movements.

Some environmental impacts are characteristic of countries at one position in the global stratification (core, semiperiphery and periphery) and others of countries moving up or down in the hierarchy.[1] In simple terms, the pollution of poverty is different than the pollution of affluence, as was pointedly remarked at the United Nations Conference on the Environment, held in Stockholm, Sweden, nearly a quarter century ago. Of course, many factors are operating to subtly influence the relationship between position in the international system and environmental degradation, such as efficiency of production, level of infrastructure, internal political struggles, and norms of consumption, all of which vary with global region and culture. My intent here is to examine how changes in national links to the world-economy and world-system influence the direction of environmental conditions in the Latin American periphery and semiperiphery.

Latin America is taken here in its broadest sense, including Caribbean nations as well as those countries south of the United States without Iberian origins. This region is tremendously diverse in cultural and ecological terms; in world-system terms, it ranges from lower periphery (Haiti) to upper semiperiphery (Argentina, Venezuela, Brazil, Mexico). As the next section describes, environmental issues vary tremendously by country, but overall, conditions are serious and deteriorating throughout the region. How can we account for those differences and predict the direction of environmental conditions with respect to current changes in the world-system?

To assess the influence of international forces on environmental conditions in Latin America, we need to analyze trends in three separate areas as well as the effects of their convergence: the shift to export-oriented strategies of growth, the internationalization of the environmental movement, and the internationalization of environmental regulation.

First, quite apart from the widespread devastation to the environment associated with import-substitution industrialization (ISI), Latin American countries have turned from inward-focused development strategies to policies of free trade and export promotion as a consequence of oil shocks, massive external debt, and persistent economic crises. In order to minimize imports, countries often continued to employ inefficient, domestically produced technologies long after "cleaner-tech" versions were available elsewhere. Pollution controls and impact statements were often neglected in pursuing projects of national development. Subsidized energy prices were kept so low that they eventually favored terrible inefficiencies (World Bank, 1992). ISI policies were also heavily urban biased, and they left a legacy of poverty, deforestation, and soil erosion in the rural environment.[2] However, much the same can be said for the effects of export projects in the region during the postwar period, as well as many current export initiatives.

Throughout Latin America, plantation agriculture designed for export often forced peasants out of fertile lowlands onto more marginal soils or into cities. The region became attractive as a site for core-based firms wishing to avoid labor and environmental regulations and penetrate new markets. Environmentalists have increasingly tied foreign direct investment (FDI) to air pollution, toxic contamination, and worker exposure throughout the region. They have also criticized chemically intense agriculture; sloppy oil extraction, mining, lumbering and ranching projects; and highly polluting factories in the region's cities and across the *maquiladora* belt along the U.S.-Mexican border.[3] Export initiatives often require the exploitation of resources in the national hinterlands, and this, in turn, requires infrastructure such as roads, highways, and railroads. These "rainforest corridors" frequently bring lumberers, miners, ranchers, and squatters along their penetration routes.[4]

With this in mind, it can be said that in the post-ISI era, Latin America's relationship with the world-economy is becoming both more intense and more complex. Some countries have diversified their export profiles to include "nontraditional" products, but small nations have been far less able to substitute manufactured imports, and most countries continue to be dependent on a fairly narrow range of "traditional" exports such as coffee, bananas, cacao, oil, and minerals.[5] The region's economies (with a few exceptions) have grown in absolute terms over the last fifteen years, albeit sporadically. While a point may be reached at which Latin American countries can afford greater pollution controls, it appears that for most nations, economic growth will pose a multitude of urgent environmental problems.[6] Several authors also argue that increasing openness to trade is likely to intensify precisely the *type* of growth that is driven by foreign productive technologies and brings with it unsustainable imported consumption values (e.g., Serbin, De Lisio, and Ortiz, 1993; Barkin, 1995).

To consider only economic forces, however, would be to miss what I will argue is the main engine driving environmental initiatives of all types in Latin America: the internationalization of the environmental movement. Nongovernmental organizations (NGOs) dedicated to environmental causes mushroomed in number and in size during the years leading up to the UN 1992 Conference on Environment and Development in Rio de Janeiro (also known as UNCED, the Earth Summit, or EcoRio). The official and unofficial meetings that took place at the conference brought together representatives of hundreds of countries and thousands of nongovernmental organizations. Across the region, and around the world, the movement has sagged somewhat since Rio, and the significance and permanence of its accomplishments remain an open question. However, most observers believe that the event, as well as the proliferation and growth of electronic networks (such as ECONET, BIODIV-L, and ELAN), have helped "globalize" the environmental movement by allowing NGOs of many types to interact and build communications and support networks. There is little doubt that overall, internationalization has strengthened the position of many Latin American environmental movements by providing them new leverage vis-à-vis the transnational corporations and their own states. Besides examining the potential of the international environmental movement to react effectively to the restructuring of capital, we need to examine how global connections between environmental NGOs affect the direction and durability of the "green" movement in Latin America.

Finally, we cannot ignore the growing number of international environmental agreements that have been advanced, on their own and also in conjunction with the explosion of free-trade agreements, both in the region and around the world. Thirty years of major environmental treaties include the Montreal Protocol on chlorofluorocarbon (CFC) emissions, the CITES treaty on the endangered species trade, and the UN Framework Convention on Climate Change. Each of these treaties has important implications for economic growth in noncore countries and raises specific environmental enforcement problems for Latin American states. Their impact is unclear: while signing an environmental treaty certainly can be no more than an empty promise, efforts for their enforcement are gaining strength. Ironically, more may be at stake in economic integration treaties such as the North American Free Trade Agreement (NAFTA), the General Agreement on Tariffs and Trade (GATT), the Caribbean Basin Initiative, MERCOSUR, and the Pact of the Americas. Environmental issues constantly arise during these negotiations. World-systems research must consider whether these political initiatives, in combination with those begun by the business community itself in response to demand for "green" products, have the potential to create global environmental standards that could establish limits on capital's attempts to flee regulation.

In attempting to gauge the interaction of these three currents, this chapter first reviews the origins and scope of environmental problems in Latin America. It then examines the role of Latin American public opinion concerning environmental questions and the strength and direction of environmental movements in the region. Finally, the chapter analyzes environmental treaties, side agreements to trade treaties, and industrial initiatives. Because its scope is so wide, this chapter constitutes, by necessity, an exploratory effort at synthesizing the environmental impacts of a diverse set of globalizing influences.[7] The task has elements of crystal ball gazing: with Latin American development paths, environmental social movements, and global agreements on the environment changing so rapidly, we can use current and past trends only to project possible future scenarios. The picture that emerges is of a world-economy and state system exerting complex, and often contradictory, pressures on the environment and environmental social movements in Latin America.

THE SCOPE OF ENVIRONMENTAL PROBLEMS IN LATIN AMERICA

The environment in Latin America is beset by a series of dire threats, although there is little agreement on which issues are most important. Popular concern from outside the region has focused almost entirely on the destruction of the rainforest, especially the Amazon.[8] Common local concerns focus on more immediate hazards to human health, such as sewage treatment and urban air and water pollution (Roberts, 1994; Keck, 1995).

The acuteness of these urban environmental problems is reflected in emergencies leading to driving bans and the closure of factories on days with high pollution inversion in Mexico City, São Paulo, Santiago, Bogotá, and Caracas (World Health Organization and UN Environment Program, 1992). Comparative urban air-pollution data is not available outside these cities, but estimates of per capita emissions of carbon dioxide (presented in Table 10.1) demonstrate that Trinidad, Venezuela, Suriname, Mexico, and Argentina are the biggest emitters in Latin America relative to their populations.

The recent cholera epidemic affecting Peru, Ecuador, Colombia, and Brazil drew attention to the fact that sewage treatment and safe drinking water are currently the exception rather than the norm in the region. For example, in São Paulo, the continent's most powerful industrial center (with more than 15 million people and over a quarter of Brazil's entire gross national product), more than 80 percent of the population lacks sewage treatment.[9] The situation is similar or worse in most other Latin American cities; across the region 20 to 80 percent of national populations officially lacked sewage treatment in 1990.[10]

Many chemicals banned long ago in the United States continue to be used in the region, some of which are exported from the United States itself or produced by U.S. firms in Latin America. Poor training and equipment for handling toxic chemicals are responsible for dangerous exposures to humans and the environment in industry and agriculture throughout the region. This is reported to be especially true in export agriculture and in assembly and chemical factories, such as in the *maquiladora* belt along the U.S.-Mexico border.

Land degradation is severe, especially of the marginally arid and hilly farming and grazing lands, and particularly in Mexico and Central America. The Sonoran, Patagonian, and Atacama deserts are at risk of spreading due to continued unsustainable land use, and the northeast of Brazil is in a severe and extended drought (World Wildlife Federation, 1990: 54–55). Most countries have over half their land classified by Conservation International and the World Resources Institute as "disturbed by human action." Recent reports are that 40 percent of

Table 10.1

Indicators of Environmental Policies and Conditions in the Americas

Country	(1) % w/ Sanit-ation Urban 1990	(2) % w/ Sanit-ation Rural 1990	(3) Fossil Fuel CO_2 per capita 1991	(4) Defor-estation Rate 1981-90	(5) % Land w/medium or high disturb. 1993	(6) # Env'l treaties signed (of 9) 1963-89	(7) % CITES treaty require-ments met 1990	(8) % of Land in Pro-tected Areas 1993
Argentina	100	29	3.6	..	64	4	82	3.4
Belize	76	22	1.4	0.2	64	..	55	12.7
Bolivia	38	14	0.8	1.1	22	3	62	8.4
Brazil	84	32	1.4	0.6	33	5	41	3.3
Canada	..	..	15.2	..	7	7	100	5.0
Chile	100	6	2.4	..	44	6	65	18.1
Colombia	84	18	1.8	0.6	33	4	64	8.2
Costa Rica	100	93	1.1	2.6	88	4	76	12.1
Cuba	100	68	3.2	0.9	98	2	50	8.1
Dom. Republic	95	75	0.8	2.5	82	4	80	21.5
Ecuador	56	38	1.6	1.7	53	3	76	39.3
El Salvador	85	38	0.5	2.1	100	1	20	0.9
Guatemala	44	17	0.4	1.6	75	6	83	7.6
Guyana	97	81	1.1	..	2	1	53	0.3
Haiti	44	17	0.1	3.9	95	1	na	0.3
Honduras	89	42	0.4	1.9	68	4	29	4.8
Jamaica	14	..	1.9	5.3	100	1	na	0.1
Mexico	85	12	3.9	1.2	77	6	100	5.1
Nicaragua	32	..	0.6	1.7	68	3	80	7.3
Panama	100	68	1.5	1.7	..	8	86	17.2
Paraguay	31	60	0.4	2.4	16	3	60	3.6
Peru	76	20	0.9	0.4	40	5	59	3.2
Suriname	64	36	4.7	0.1	9	5	100	4.5
Trin. & Tobago	100	92	14.7	1.9	50	4	67	3.4
United States	..	..	19.5	0.1	75	8	88	10.5
Uruguay	60	65	1.4	..	100	6	59	0.2
Venezuela	97	72	6.2	1.2	100	5	79	30.2

Sources: sewage disposal: World Resources Institute (WRI) (1994). Note that definitions may vary (some include pit toilets, others only flush toilets); CO2 per capita: WRI (1994); deforestation and levels of human disturbance: WRI (1994: 307, 319); environmental treaties: Dietz and Kalof (1992: 360); CITES treaty (trade in endangered species) requirements met: WRI (1994: 327); protected areas: WRI (1994: 317).

the land in Central America and Mexico has seen its productivity reduced by erosion; this figure reaches a frightening 77 percent in the case of El Salvador.[11] Coastal pollution and the destruction of mangroves and reefs are less well known problems, which carry critical ramifications for the ecology and for the fishing and tourism industries.

Finally, deforestation and other habitat loss has wiped out about 70 percent of Central America's rain forests and almost 93 percent of Brazil's Atlantic Coast forest. Small remnant forests in Trinidad, Jamaica, Haiti, Costa Rica, the Dominican Republic, and Paraguay are disappearing rapidly (Rudel and Roper, 1994). Meanwhile, some of the rain forest areas were, until recently, considered relatively "safe" with respect to deforestation, due to their size or inaccessibility. However, the most recent estimates for the Amazon region (both in Brazil and in the other eight countries that contain Amazon forests) show continuing deforestation, although about 80 to 90 percent remains uncleared overall (Skole and Tucker, 1993; Kasa, 1993). As South and East Asian countries deplete their supplies of lumber, they have increased their reliance on Latin American suppliers. Reports are now coming out of the Guyanas (Suriname, French Guiana, and Guyana) of huge lumber concessions to Korean, Indonesian, and Malaysian companies (Linden, 1995). Timber deals involving exports have also been reported in Nicaragua, Panama, Honduras, Guatemala, and Peru. Assuming that 5 million species inhabit the tropical moist forests of the world (the majority of which are in Latin America), E. O. Wilson (1988) estimated that 17,500 species are being driven to extinction each year by deforestation.

War, poverty, and the increasing concentration of landholdings have combined to drive refugees and profiteers into the region's remaining wild lands to farm, lumber, grow and smuggle coca, drill for oil, and pan for gold (Faber, 1993; Butler, 1985; Hecht and Cockburn, 1990). Indigenous populations have suffered these incursions in the form of disease, degraded environments, and cultural loss. Because of peoples' desperation and the difficulty of policing, areas that are officially "protected" in national, indigenous, or extractive reserves are often nothing but "paper parks."[12] On average, about 8 percent of the land in Latin American countries is now officially "protected" in parks and other reserved areas. National variation is great, however: while Belize, Costa Rica, Dominican Republic, Panama, Chile, Venezuela, and Ecuador have over 10 percent of their land in protected areas, Jamaica, Uruguay, Haiti, Guyana, and El Salvador have protected less than 1 percent.

Tracing the roots of all these environmental problems in Latin America is beyond the scope of this chapter (see Hajek, 1991; Maguire and Brown, 1986), but some points can be made. Latin America's incorporation into the world-system was essentially in the role of an extractive periphery (Bunker, 1985; Cardoso and Faletto, 1979). As such, the region's mineral and agricultural resources have been devastated for centuries by colonial and, later, neocolonial powers. While a few parts of the region were settled in earnest, others were considered only temporary stopping places from which to make one's fortune and return to the homeland. Often, the export of its natural resources left precious little by way of an integrated social infrastructure capable of absorbing the impact of subsequent waves of capital expansion, extraction, and contraction (Wolf and Hansen, 1972; Bunker, 1985). Concern was seldom paid to the sustainability of production under such conditions.

Twentieth-century efforts by Latin American states to integrate their national territories and substitute imports with locally made products were precisely attempts to break with the negative pattern typical of extractive peripheries. In order to accumulate sufficient capital to fund these efforts, many countries adopted state-led strategies and borrowed heavily from overseas. Large loans from foreign banks and multilateral agencies, such as the International Monetary Fund (IMF) and the World Bank often went to fund development mega-projects. One dramatic example of the relation between mega-projects and debt was the massive Itaipú Dam in Brazil, which cost that nation U.S. $20 billion, one-fifth of its foreign debt at the time (Green, 1991). Mega-projects have also included airports, highways, industries, and mining, colonization, agribusiness, and ranching projects. Many of these projects have combined an export orientation with essentially ISI objectives such as opening bottlenecks in national infrastructure or heavy industry.

Poverty and economic crisis, worsened by the pressure of debt-service payments, have certainly sharpened the logic of searching for quick export commodities that may ultimately damage the environment. Mega-projects are easy to begin, but because weak states have extreme difficulty in enforcing environmental regulations, environmental and social calamities may spin out of control.[13] Many mega-projects have had devastating environmental consequences, and some have been strongly criticized for their questionable benefits for human welfare. Corruption as well as class and urban biases have been widely reported, and many externally financed mega-projects are thought to have benefited mainly political elites and well-connected government subcontractors. The complexity of environmental enforcement for such mega-projects is shown by the Brazilian case: environmental impact analysis was formally adopted by the nation in 1986, but the biggest projects, with the greatest potential environmental impacts, are government directed, and the government exempts itself from preparing environmental impact statements. Strong political pressure from environmentalists has been necessary for any credible impact analyses to be carried out.

ENVIRONMENTAL SOCIAL MOVEMENTS: THEIR SUPPORT AND LINKAGES

The impact of export-led development strategies on Latin America's environment will depend substantially on the extent to which its citizens express opinions and mobilize in favor of environmental causes. The shape, strategy, and direction of environmental movements depend, in turn, on their class makeup and their relations with national elites and international environmentalists.

Environmental social movements in core nations have often been characterized as elitist, and while support for environmental causes crosses class lines, activists in the mainstream groups tend to be highly educated, urban, and of above-average income (Morrison and Dunlap, 1986).[14] While Leff (1986) pointed out the complexity of the environmental movement in Latin America and its potential to bridge social strata, Viola's (1992) research has suggested that Brazilian environmental activists tend to be urban professionals.[15] The groups are well connected with universities, government agencies, policy networks, and international financial institutions. Highly educated technicians and administrators are leading these advocacy and research organizations, increasingly making the movement a professional one.[16] Supporting this view is a recent poll in Brazil showing that the degree of interest in the environment "increases proportionally to education and family income" (MAST/CNPq, 1992: 5).

How widespread is environmental concern in the broader populations of Latin America? Cross-national research on environmental concern and participation in environmental groups has been scarce, but the Gallup Institute's 1992 "Health of the Planet Survey" asked a series of questions to national samples in 24 nations, including Mexico, Brazil, Chile, and Uruguay (cited in Dunlap, Gallup, and Gallup, 1993). Over the 1990–1993 period, the World Values Survey asked a consistent battery of questions to national samples in 43 nations, including the same Latin American countries as the Dunlap/Gallup study (except that Uruguay was replaced by Argentina) (Ingelhart, 1995). Both studies are biased in favor of the countries in the region with the highest world-system positions, but they provide the only existing cross-national data. The surveys show that approval of the environmental movement and concern about the environment both reach levels that are, in some places, even *higher* than in core countries. This is especially true for local environmental issues such as air and water pollution. According to the Dunlap/Gallup poll, the most serious local issue for respondents in all four countries was inadequate sewage treatment. In this poll, concern over global issues was at a level similar to that for the core countries.

There is also some evidence that a majority of citizens in these semiperipheral countries might value environmental protection over economic gain. Given the choice between placing a priority *either* on protecting the environment *or* promoting economic growth, 64 percent of Chileans and Uruguayans and 71 percent of Mexicans and Brazilians chose protecting the environment, at levels *higher* than found in the United States (Dunlap, Gallup, and Gallup, 1993). Over half of respondents in each country said they were "willing to pay higher prices to protect the environment."[17] Rates of reported "green consumerism" (that is, avoiding certain products that harm the environment) were low in the region, however, and the percent of the population saying they were active in environmental groups varied from 4 percent in Brazil to 10 percent in Chile (one of the world's highest rates).[18] While these polls must be taken extremely cautiously, they do show why environmental NGOs in Brazil have grown in number from just 2 groups in 1971 and about 40 in 1980 and over 1,000 in 1992 (Viola, 1992; Movimento Ecológico Mater Natura, 1992; Landim, 1992). Other nations have seen substantial, albeit less spectacular, rates of growth; in particular, Costa Rica and Ecuador have especially strong environmental movements.

Some grassroots groups, such as those made up of rubber tappers, small farmers, and shantytown dwellers, have also taken up environmental causes. These groups differ in their approach and interests from mainstream environmental groups in much the same ways as U.S. grassroots and environmental justice groups differ from the big national groups such as the Sierra Club: they tend to be interested more in health, social justice, and/or economic welfare issues rather than habitat preservation (Bullard and Wright, 1992; Freudenberg and Steinsapir, 1992). These grassroots groups also often prefer direct action, such as protests and education campaigns, rather than lobbying and legal work. These findings are supported by a 1992 survey by the Brazilian Institute for Public Opinion Research (IBOPE), which found that overall levels of *interest* in environmental issues did not vary significantly by class or education (although profiles of public supporters and activists did tend to differ). The IBOPE survey found that less-educated respondents are more practical and interested in the conservation of local resources, while higher education people are "more idealistic" and interested in national and international environmental issues (Pedro Leitão, interview, June 22, 1993).

Environmental NGOs in Latin America share a common problem. In North America and Europe, hundreds of thousands of dues-paying members provide independence, power, and legitimacy to their environmental leaders, but in Latin America there is a smaller potential constituency of dues-paying members. While the World Wildlife Fund in Britain has 1,200,000 members, each donating varying amounts, a nationwide publicity campaign by Brazil's largest group, S.O.S. Mata Atlántica, only recruited 1,000 new members (although this represented a doubling of the membership, to 2,000).[19] The World Wildlife Fund in Brazil itself has virtually no dues-paying members in the sense of U.S. or European groups.

Thus, Latin American NGOs are forced to look for other sources of funding, primarily from international groups, corporate sponsors, or government contracts (Roberts, 1994). Each option opens new doors at the cost of a certain loss in autonomy (Viola, 1992: 62–63). An undeniable result of the UNCED conference was the massive presence of NGOs at official and unofficial parallel events. When these links involve money, they have sometimes obliged Latin American groups to focus on issues distant from their own priorities, for example, species or habitat preservation instead of urban pollution and the environmental effects of poverty. In short, due to their greater dependence on overseas funding, some Latin American environmental groups may be forced to focus on preserving large, "charismatic" species that sell calendars and bring in pledge money in the United States and Europe.

"The whole world is watching" is a common cry of protest movements, and with the expansion of electronic networks (which include both Latin American and northern environmentalists, academics, and journalists), this is increasingly true. Action alerts have been disseminated across Internet services such as ECONET and the Environment in Latin America Network on pressing environmental issues from the Ecuadoran Amazon and the Galapagos to Mexico's southern and northern border regions, as well as in Guatemala, Costa Rica, Venezuela, and Brazil. Usually these alerts call for letter writing, phone calls, and other forms of outside pressure on corporations, funding agencies, and Latin American states to protect the environment. Their success at generating this pressure has not been studied, but even the circulation of information often prevents a state from so easily committing environmentally and socially degrading actions.

The effect of the exchange of information between Latin American environmentalists and their colleagues in the core can be seen in two examples from the Brazilian Amazon, both of which were pivotal in redirecting the lending strategy of the World Bank. First, a photograph of the western Amazon taken one evening from the U.S. space shuttle showed over 5,000 fires. That photo covered an area of the state of Rondônia, where a huge colonization project funded by the World Bank and Inter-American Development Bank, called Polonoroeste, was underway. In 1985, after a public outcry and a campaign by environmentalists to stop the project, the World Bank halted money for the project, the first time it had ever done so for environmental reasons.

A second example is the huge Carajás project. With the help of the World Bank, the Brazilian state planned to turn the massive Carajás iron deposits in the eastern Amazon into an immense regional development project (Bunker, 1989). The most controversial part of the plan involved 22 pig-iron factories that were to run on charcoal from the native rainforest (Anderson, 1990). In fighting the projects, international environmentalists worked with local groups, such as peasant leagues and indigenous peoples, to focus attention on the international press, the United States Congress, and other lenders such as the European Economic Community (EEC) and the Inter-American Development Bank. Hearing of the potential devastation through pressure from environmentalists, who dubbed the Carajás project potentially one of the world's five worst ever, the EEC boycotted Carajás iron and the World Bank issued warnings about future funding for Brazil. Later, after the struggles with Chico Mendes's group of rubber tappers and peasant farmers, funds for the paving of a critical highway in Acre were also suspended several times.

Battles over a number of projects related to the Carajás complex still continue, but since 1985, the environmental evaluation components of these loans have pressured Latin American states to more actively enforce *some* environmental laws and even to expand their areas under preservation (Gross, 1990).[20] The continuing importance of the environment to the international banks remains clear in the 1990s. For example, the U.S. deputy assistant secretary for inter-American affairs reported that the United States has encouraged multilateral lenders to increase their focus on the environment (Gelbard, 1992). As an indicator of change in what is now the world's largest creditor nation, the Japan Development Bank has begun "directing its efforts toward solving worldwide environmental problems" (Amano, 1993: 20). Whether bank pressures inspire genuine efforts or empty gestures merely "for the English to see" (as the Brazilian saying goes) is hotly debated. This tension—between the appearance of protection and actual action—was revealed in a statement about the Amazon by Brazil's president, Fernando Henrique Cardoso, shortly after he assumed office in 1995. Cardoso observed that Brazil would not be able to obtain low-cost loans from such sources as the World Bank "if we don't have a sense that we are responsible before the rest of mankind for preserving nature, for preserving indigenous culture'' (Reuters News Service, March 31, 1995).

Outside pressure over environmental issues provoked a sometimes-strident nationalist backlash in Latin America. For a long time, Brazil's government claimed that outside pressure was part of a plot to keep Brazil from becoming a developed country.[21] These backlashes typically come from the political right, business interests, and militaries of Latin America, but they often gain the support of much wider segments of the population. Such appeals invoke sentiments of national sovereignty and reveal a weakness in externally imposed and top-down environmental regulations and activism, such as their external cash dependency and heavy reliance on (and pressure from) outside funding and regulatory agencies.

In sum, then, public opinion appears to have ''greened'' significantly in those Latin American nations for which survey data is available. The region's many environmental groups have made significant advances, but many remain tied to, and dependent on, northern environmental groups. These ties provide leverage that local groups can use in their battles with their states and with transnational corporations. Their links provide leverage, of course, only to the extent that they represent the genuine threat of poor publicity for governments and firms, which depends directly on the extent to which they can generate mobilization in the wealthier nations. Their ability to mobilize those letters, phone calls, protests, and boycotts in the North will generally be limited to issues that inspire Northerners. This circuitous route of pressuring Latin American states and high-polluting transnational firms, however, does not provide much leverage over national firms (especially those that do not export to the core).

INTERNATIONAL AGREEMENTS AND INITIATIVES

Beyond considering economic restructuring and the expansion of the role of environmental NGOs, when assessing the influence of international forces on environmental conditions in Latin America we must consider the effects of treaties and other types of multinational agreements. What explains the rapid proliferation of these accords? Do these pacts have the potential to create globally standardized environmental regulations, eliminating disparities and thereby modifying the trajectories of capital movements?

Four types of international environmental agreements must be examined: binational agreements, multilateral treaties, side agreements to trade pacts, and industry's own initiatives to create ''green'' standards. Binational agreements tend to be limited in scope, attempting to resolve disputes such as transboundary air or water pollutants between neighboring countries. However, they have often provided frameworks for the initial discussion of issues that later are incorporated into wider, regional pacts. Multilateral environmental treaties such as those on ozone protection, climate change, endangered species, and nuclear testing attempt to create a consensus among the largest possible number of nations on issues considered most critical to humanity's collective survival. Since so many environmental issues are global in scope (Stern, Young, and Druckman, 1992), solving them requires that a majority of nations sign. While these treaties are normally proposed and drafted by core nations, Third World nations have some bargaining power since they can threaten to deny drafters the consensus they see as necessary for their success (Miller, 1995a, 1995b).

Latin American nations vary tremendously in their level of participation in environmental treaties such as those just mentioned.[22] Of the nine major global treaties negotiated over the 1963–1987 period, Haiti, Guyana, El Salvador, and Jamaica had signed only one of the nine treaties by 1992, while Panama, Guatemala, Chile, Mexico, and Uruguay signed six or more, with the other nations falling in between (see Table 10.1).[23] Elsewhere I have reported that worldwide, there is a strong positive relation between a country's position in the world-system (or its GDP per capita) and the likelihood that it signed the nine treaties (Roberts, 1996). This is true also for Latin America, which demonstrates that the wealthier semiperipheral states tend to be more interested in, or able to participate in, global eco-diplomacy.[24] The actual importance of these treaties is unclear for several reasons, including the fact that many countries sign and then proceed to flaunt them, and also because of the weakness of their enforcement and dispute-resolution mechanisms (Biggs, 1993). Moreover, even when they possess the political will, Latin America's governments may, in fact, not be *able* to effectively enforce the protection of their environments, especially in the face of recent efforts to ''shrink the state.'' I return to this issue in the concluding section.

Meanwhile, the opening of Latin American economies and the explosion of free-trade agreements across the region are the harbingers of both greater environmental perils and of new leverage for enforcing protection. For example, the environmental side agreement to the North American Free Trade Agreement (NAFTA) includes explicit directives regarding the ''harmonization'' of environmental protection in Canada, the United States, and Mexico. In the years just prior to January 1, 1994, when NAFTA took effect, Mexico substantially increased environmental regulations and spending, as well as the enforcement of environmental laws. A considerable official oversight structure is being put into place along the border and in Washington, Mexico City, and Ottawa, bringing together government officials, academics, and activists.[25] The success and permanence of these efforts remains to be seen, especially as national and international attentions shift elsewhere. The crisis in Mexico involving devaluation of the peso and the land developer's quote at the outset of this chapter show how a pact can restructure trade and the deeper structures of production, the consequences of which can far outlive popular support for, and watch-dogging of, environmental safeguards.

While many environmentalists have decried the lack of solid protection for the environment under the NAFTA treaty, it is the best agreement drafted so far in this hemisphere. Negotiations for the other economic integration treaties in the region—the Caribbean Basin Initiative, CARICOM, MERCOSUR, the Group of Three, the Andean Pact, Amazon Pact, and the future Pact of the Americas—have all raised some environmental issues but have not incorporated protections in formal mechanisms. The General Agreement on Tariffs and Trade (GATT) is, in many ways, the worst of all treaties for environmentalism since it prohibits nations from excluding imports because of environmental considerations on how they were produced (Biggs, 1993). The GATT approach, however, answers the greatest fears of many Latin American leaders who worry that environmental restrictions on imports will become a new camouflage for protectionism of core markets (see, for example, Alsogaray, 1993; Ominami, 1993).

Finally, in discussing the environmental impact of the emergent pattern of integration of Latin America in the world-economy, it is also important to mention the potential roles of industry environmental initiatives, "green marketing," and new international quality-control standards. Though normally greeted with cynicism by environmentalists and progressives, efforts by business to incorporate environmental protection should be carefully examined and not hastily or summarily written off.

Most obviously, the new "environmental technologies" industry has grown surprisingly quickly in the past two decades: a 1994 survey by German market researchers projected global purchases of $374 billion in "green-tech" products in 1995 (Rubin, 1994).[26] "Green" firms are obviously interested in regulations and treaties that will drive the demand for their products.[27] As ex-Chilean economy minister Carlos Ominami pointedly stated, these restrictions probably will increase Latin America's technological dependency: "It is common for the same country imposing the restrictions to offer the technology or expertise necessary to satisfy them" (1993: 149).

Driven by demand for "green products" and the integration of the EEC, international quality-control standards are being developed so that industrial purchasers will know what they are buying in an increasingly global marketplace. Some of these standards are beginning to include quality control, not only for the final products, but also for the *process* by which they are produced. Standards might include worker health, some aspects of labor relations, and conformity to environmental standards, especially of emissions (Heller, 1993). An official for a major transnational chemical company, Joel Charm of Allied Signal Corporation, stated that these initiatives increase "the probability that there will be one world environmental standard," and noted that "they are likely to become law in Europe and provide a transparency for how to conduct business in the Third World" (Heller, 1993: 31). In Latin America, it appears that these standards will have the greatest initial impact on suppliers of raw materials and intermediate products such as minerals and chemicals to overseas manufacturers, especially in Europe. Small firms and the informal sector will probably continue to produce with little concern for environmental regulations. However, the linkages between informal producers and multinational export firms (Portes, Castells, and Benton, 1989) suggest that quality control and "green labeling" may force some small-scale producers to pay closer attention to environmental effects. Again, Ominami pointed out that these standards are "biased toward vertical integration" (1993). In world-system terms, consumers looking for "green labels" on products are likely to shift profits back to brand names and up the commodity chain to core distributors providing them, thus reducing markets for Latin American national brands.

CONCLUSION

This chapter's central question is whether environmental conditions in Latin America are likely to improve or erode further as nations move from strongly protected and regulated economies to ones more open to market forces. A balanced perspective must consider both positive and negative forces.

On the positive side, free-trade advocates project that if aging and inefficient ISI factories are shut down and replaced by competitive and more efficient facilities for exports, the region's air may become somewhat cleaner, while incomes will rise. For this to occur, countries will require huge infusions of (presumably foreign) capital, and decades to replace old capital equipment.

One could emphasize that global integration is bringing, albeit in fits and starts, some level of international standardization of environmental regulations. This is occurring in several ways beyond international treaties on the environment. Following side agreements in economic integration treaties such as NAFTA, the Caribbean Basin Initiative (CBI), and MERCOSUR, future trade pacts (at least those that include the United States will almost certainly incorporate environmental protection provisions into the main treaty or a side agreement.[28]

The very globalization of commerce and the demand for "green products" have forced core-based firms to create standardized quality-control guidelines, which are now spreading around the world. These guidelines, which will most affect export-oriented firms and their suppliers in Latin America, increasingly incorporate health, safety, and environmental-management systems at global levels.

Together, these elements will increase global standardization, but it is unlikely that they will reach more than 25 to 50 percent of the economy—namely, the large-scale and export sectors. National industries and the informal sector are likely to avoid increasing environmental regulations as long as possible (which could be indefinitely). This will depend largely on the growth and strength of environmental pressure from within Latin American nations.

In this regard, while external debt played a key role in the origin of environmentally destructive mega-projects between the 1960s and early 1980s, more recently, the necessity of attracting low-interest loans from multilateral sources has actually driven some Latin American countries to beef up their environmental protection efforts since 1985 (Sanderson, 1993; Roberts, 1994). Attention by these agencies to environmental issues is likely to continue only as long as the pressure on politicians and banks continues from core environmentalists who are, in turn, linked to Latin American groups. To understand the likelihood that this dynamic will continue, we need a solid understanding of both northern and southern environmental movements, and especially their class roots and public support. The internationalization of environmental and social justice NGOs strengthens the movement in the short term but might risk local support if Latin American groups must bend to international desires to the detriment of local chapters, or if core environmentalists ignore the urban, public health, and social justice–related environmental issues that inspire wider popular support in Latin America.

On the negative side, some would argue that global integration is not conducive to environmental protection because cutthroat international competition can drive nations to neglect safeguards and because austerity programs and the economic crises associated with the transition to market-centered models of accumulation create a desperation that drives poor people to unsustainable uses of their resources (Barkin, 1995; Serbin, De Lisio, and Ortiz, 1993). To correct exchange rates, control inflation, and lower tariff barriers, global integration and export orientation have been linked with drastic programs of privatization and "state shrinking" in Latin America. As the state shrinks, however, respect for the rule of law often weakens, as does confidence in environmental protection agencies.[29] Even if those agencies are well funded by outside financing, in times of austerity, many people may see them as increasingly alien and irrelevant in times of desperate hardship. Desperate times tend to favor short-term thinking, not sustainable development.

With the demise of government social programs and substantial public-sector employment, most researchers also envision greater income inequality and poverty throughout the region. An important question, then, will be whether income inequality leads to wasteful consumption with greater environmental damage without commensurate social gains (Sanderson, 1993). The direct implication of these questions is that too rapid a liberalization and "modernization" of the state risks dire environmental crisis.

Finally, if greater openness to trade brings economic growth to Latin America, it may provide the opportunity for greater spending on sanitation and urban air-pollution control. However, with economic expansion, carbon dioxide emissions and many other pollutants are almost bound to increase (from new autos, factories, mines, agrochemicals, dumping, etc.).[30] These conclusions suggest that the only force with the capacity to change the relationship between economic growth and pollution in Latin America is strong pressure brought on governments and on transnational *and* national firms through lobbying, boycotts, and direct action, all supported by cross-border links.

NOTES

Helpful comments were provided by Amy Bellone, David Barkin, Alvaro Díaz, Peter Grimes, Daniel Hilliard, Ellen Mitchell, Timothy Power, Mike Renning, Orlando San

Martín, Marc Stern, Thomas Rudel, Bill Smith, and Roberto Patricio Korzeniewicz. This research was funded by the Mellon Foundation, the Fulbright Commission, and the National Science Foundation.

1. See Grimes, Roberts, and Manale (1993), Roberts (1996), Grimes and Roberts (1995), as well as note 5 below.

2. As Orlando San Martín of the Norwegian Institute of International Affairs (NUPI) usefully pointed out, "the social costs [of ISI] that caused higher levels of income concentration [also] encouraged short-sighted approaches to resource exploitation by the rural poor" (personal communication, March 12, 1995).

3. However, subsequent empirical analyses have produced mixed results in testing whether firms are fleeing tighter environmental regulations in the core and moving to "pollution havens" in the periphery (Low and Yeats, 1992; Leonard, 1988; Pearson, 1987). Perhaps contrary to the hypothesis that firms are moving to the most unregulated locations, and contrary to my own prediction, I found in a recent analysis of global data that FDI is *positively* related to a country's likelihood to have signed international environmental treaties such as the Montreal Protocol for Ozone Protection and the endangered species treaty (Roberts, 1996). This suggests that the best "business climate" may not be found in areas of the least regulation, an idea that is supported by analyses comparing regulation and economic growth in the 50 U.S. states (Freudenberg 1990; Meyer, 1992; Hall, 1994). The causality may work in both directions, however, since the desire for positive trade relations has driven some countries to sign treaties. For the 27 Latin American nations for which there was data, levels of FDI (flows, not stocks) were not directly correlated with the environmental outcomes listed in Table 10.1.

4. This problem has been documented in Brazil, Ecuador, Peru, Bolivia, Costa Rica, and Venezuela. However, there are many cases of ISI or national integration projects also opening such corridors, and often these corridors are oriented in ways that more directly draw population from major centers.

5. By 1990, two-thirds of Latin America's exports were still fuels, minerals, metals, and other primary commodities, while only 30 percent of exports of the East and South Asian countries were (World Bank, 1992). More than their Asian counterparts, then, Latin American nations have struggled to ascend in the global system of stratification while continuing to export primary commodities, raising important questions about the viability of this route to the semiperiphery (Cicantell, 1994; Roberts, 1992). Korzeniewicz and Martin (1994) confirmed for the past few decades Wallerstein's (1974, 1979) central structural postulate: that while a few countries can move up or down in the world stratification system, the structure itself remains largely unchanged. Further, while Latin America, and the peripheral states in general, are exporting more transportation and electronics products, the relative value of their exports remains low because they continue to be excluded from the research, innovation, and marketing stages of global commodity chains. For additional discussion, see the contributions in Gereffi and Korzeniewicz (1994).

6. As Grossman and Krueger (1995) and the World Bank (1992) have pointed out, some pollutants increase in concentration with level of development (e.g., carbon dioxide, nitrogen oxides, municipal waste), while others tend to improve steadily with income levels (e.g., percent of population with basic sanitation, potable water, etc.). The relation for carbon dioxide (CO^2) emissions has been borne out with very few exceptions in world history, and as "development" proceeds, it appears that each increment in economic growth brings wider ecological impacts (Grimes and Roberts, 1995). Most interesting, perhaps, is the fact that other pollution problems tend to be worst for nations at

the middle levels of income and for both poorer and wealthier countries (e.g., problems with urban particulates, sulphur dioxide, and a series of water pollutants). Grimes, Roberts, and Manale (1993) discovered that findings forming a similar inverted-U curve also exist for the CO^2 emissions *efficiency* of nations. We explain this trend as the result of inefficient machinery and infrastructure and high deforestation in the upper peripheral and rising semiperipheral countries.

7. Its scope is comparative and regional, but my experience in Brazil means that I rely most heavily on examples from there.

8. As the cynical Brazilian saying has it, concern for the Amazon rain forest seems to be directly proportional to one's distance from it.

9. While 64 percent of São Paulo households have sewage *pipes*, about 85 percent of waste water goes untreated (Gunn, 1993).

10. Columns 1 and 2 of Table 10.1 show the percentage of households with sanitation services (World Resources Institute, 1994; Economic Commission on Latin America [ECLA] 1990, 1993). This includes pit toilets and other types of sanitation not considered by the ECLA figures.

11. This is widely cited as an underlying reason for the "Soccer War" (Durham, 1979; Faber, 1993; Green, 1991).

12. A graphic example is the fact that, fifteen years after their establishment, Brazil still has not "delimited" most of its indigenous reserves in the Amazon. Only 39 percent of these reserves had been demarcated by 1995, two years after the deadline established in Brazil's 1988 constitution (Rainforest Action Network, 1995).

13. This is especially true outside the official project's boundaries: for example the Carajás railroad and its buffer zone were carefully reseeded and protected. However, just outside that area there has been a flood of land clearing and contamination in ranches, farms, and gold mines (Becker, 1990; Roberts, 1992).

14. The environmental racism/justice movement and the NIMBY (Not in My Backyard) groups are important variants (see Dunlap and Mertig, 1992).

15. This was confirmed for the Brazilian case in interviews with environmentalists Arturo Deiges (June 19, 1993) and Beth Grimberg (June 21, 1993). For other Latin American nations, see Hochstetler (1995), Prell (1995), Price (1995), and Christen (1995).

16. See Viola (1992: 61). Political scientist Steven Sanderson (interview, November 29, 1993) made similar observations.

17. The World Values Survey found similar results for Argentina (about 50 percent). However, for their reverse-coded question, which forced pro-environment respondents to disagree with the statement that "it shouldn't cost me any money" to reduce pollution, variation was much greater. Seventy-two percent of Argentines (among the highest in the world) agreed, as did 65 percent of Brazilians, 57 percent of Chileans, and 40 percent of Mexicans.

18. Some pollsters, however, insist that *volunteered* responses of environmental concern are the best indication of the *salience* of the issue (Dunlap, 1992). Because economic and crime problems are most critical in most people's lives, only 2 to 3 percent of Uruguayans and Brazilians *volunteered* environmental problems as "the most" important problem facing their nation. However, 20 percent of Chileans and 29 percent of Mexicans did (levels far above the United States and Canada).

19. Interview, Flávio de Mattos Franco, World Wildlife Fund, June 22, 1993.

20. Marc Stern of University of California at San Diego pointed out that most envi-

ronmental loans by the World Bank since 1989 have actually been in the area of urban infrastructure, such as for water and sewage (personal communication, February 17, 1995). That the March 1995 UN Conference on Social Development in Copenhagen saw activists still pushing for social aspects of development projects to be included in decision making suggests that environmentalists have been somewhat more effective at raising their issues than were social activists.

21. Speaking to a meeting of the Amazon basin's nine nations in 1989, for example, senior Brazilian diplomat Paulo Flecha de Lima described accusations about Brazil's poor environmental record in the region as part of "a campaign to impede exploitation of natural resources in order to block [Brazil] from becoming a world power." *O Liberal* (Belém), November 14, 1989.

22. From nuclear weapons in the early 1960s to the current debate over the terms of the UN Framework Convention on Climate Change, a series of global agreements have been drafted, debated, and signed. Dietz and Kalof (1991) compiled an index of "state environmentalism" based on which of the nine treaties had been signed during the period 1963–1987 (see Table 10.1). The treaties were the Nuclear Test Ban Treaty (1963); Wetlands (Ramsar, 1971); Biological and Toxic Weapons (1972); World Cultural and Natural Heritage (1972); Ocean Dumping (1972); Endangered Species (CITES, 1973); Ship Pollution (1978); Migratory Species (1979); Law of the Sea (1982); Ozone Layer, Vienna (1985); CFC Control, Montreal (1987); and Hazardous Waste Movement (1989) (Dietz and Kalof, 1992: 355).

23. Environmental Sociologist Thomas Rudel pointed out that poorer nations are often unable to send delegates to treaty drafting sessions (personal communication, December 3, 1994). This does not prevent them from later formally agreeing to the treaty's terms.

24. This is shown in the fact that I found no statistical relationship between GDP per capita and the percentage of requirements on endangered species trade (under the CITES treaty) that the Latin American nations had met by 1990. Elsewhere I have presented a cross-sectional analysis comparing the ability of external and internal influences to predict participation in environmental treaties for a global sample (Roberts, 1996). That analysis suggested that the hierarchical world-system position (WSP) and levels of foreign investment were positive predictors of the likelihood of signing environmental treaties, while debt service, dependence on one trading partner, regime repressiveness, and military spending all had significant negative impacts. Replicating the reduced final model from that analysis for this work on Latin America, I found that only WSP was significantly tied to state environmentalism (however, the much smaller sample size was problematic).

25. This includes the Border Environmental Cooperation Commission (BECC), North American Development Bank (NADBank), the Border Ecology Project (BEP), university research centers, state government agencies, and NGO groups.

26. An earlier Organization for Economic Cooperation and Development (OECD) study estimated the market for environmental equipment and services at around U.S. $200 billion and growing at over 5 percent per year (Stevens, 1993).

27. Karliner (1994) pointed out that they often stress the cleanup rather than prevention of pollutants.

28. In cases with imbalances in regulations, it is not certain whether environmental regulations will "harmonize" at the core or peripheral levels; for example, in the case of NAFTA, Mexico is having to do the most work to "get up to speed."

29. However, through the late 1980s economic crisis, IBAMA, Brazil's environmental

protection agency continued to expand, largely through funding from the World Bank and other external sources.

30. See note 6 above.

REFERENCES

Alsogaray, María Julia. 1993. "International Trade and the Environment: A View from Argentina." In *Difficult Liaison: Trade and the Environment in the Americas*, ed. Heraldo Muñoz and Robin Rosenberg, pp. 153–158. New Brunswick, NJ: Transaction.

Amano, Hidetake. 1993. "Globalization of the Economy and the Response of the Japan Development Bank." *Japan 21st* v. 38 (December): 20–21.

Anderson, Anthony B. 1990. "Smokestacks in the Rain Forest: Industrial Development and Deforestation in the Amazon Basin." *World Development* 18: 1191–1205.

Barkin, David. 1995, March. "Wealth, Poverty, and Sustainable Development." Working Paper. Cambridge, MA: Lincoln Institute.

Becker, Bertha K. 1990. *Amazônia*. São Paulo, Brazil: Editora Ática.

Biggs, Gonzalo. 1993. "The Interrelationship between the Environment and International Trade in Latin America: The Legal and Institutional Framework." In *Difficult Liaison: Trade and the Environment in the Americas*, ed. Heraldo Muñoz and Robin Rosenberg, pp. 167–204. New Brunswick, NJ: Transaction.

Bullard, Robert D., and Beverly H. Wright. 1992. "The Quest for Environmental Equity: Mobilizing the African-American Community for Social Change." In *American Environmentalism: The U.S. Environmental Movement 1970–1990*, ed. Riley E. Dunlap and Angela G. Mertig, pp. 39–50. Philadelphia: Taylor and Francis.

Bunker, Stephen G. 1985. *Underdeveloping the Amazon: Extraction, Unequal Exchange, and the Failure of the Modern State*. Urbana: University of Illinois Press.

———. 1989. "The Eternal Conquest." *NACLA Report on the Americas* 23, 1: 27–35.

Butler, John R. 1985. "Land, Gold and Farmers: Agricultural Colonization and Frontier Expansion in the Brazilian Amazon." Ph.D. dissertation, University of Florida, Gainesville.

Cardoso, Fernando H., and Enzo Faletto. *Dependency and Development in Latin America*. Berkeley: University of California Press, 1979.

Chew, Sing C. 1995. "Environmental Transformations: Accumulation, Ecological Crisis, and Social Movements." In *A New World Order? Global Transformations in the Late Twentieth Century*, ed. David A. Smith and József Böröcz, pp. 201–215. Westport, CT: Praeger.

Christen, Catherine. 1995. "Field Scientists and Park Administrators: Environmental Conservation Initiatives in Costa Rica 1960s–1970s." Latin American Studies Association 19th international congress, September 28–30, Washington, DC.

Cicantell, Paul. 1994. "The Raw Materials Route to the Semiperiphery: Raw Materials, State Development Policies and Mobility in the Capitalist World-System." American Sociological Association annual meetings, August, Los Angeles, CA.

Dietz, Thomas, and Linda Kalof. 1992. "Environmentalism among Nation-states." *Social Indicators Research* 26: 353–366.

Dunlap, Riley E. 1992. "Trends in Public Opinion toward Environmental Issues: 1965–1990." In *American Environmentalism: The U.S. Environmental Movement*

1970–1990, ed. Riley E. Dunlap and Angela G. Mertig, pp. 89–116. Philadelphia: Taylor and Francis.

Dunlap, Riley E., George H. Gallup, Jr., and Alec M. Gallup. 1993. *Health of the Planet: Results of a 1992 International Environmental Opinion Survey of Citizens in 24 Nations.* Princeton, NJ: George H. Gallup International Institute.

Dunlap, Riley E., and Angela G. Mertig, eds. 1992. *American Environmentalism: The U.S. Environmental Movement 1970–1990.* Philadelphia: Taylor and Francis.

Durham, W. 1979. *Scarcity and Survival in Central America: The Ecological Origins of the Soccer War.* Stanford, CA: Stanford University Press.

Economic Commission on Latin America (ECLA). 1990. *Statistical Yearbook for Latin America and the Caribbean.* Santiago, Chile: ECLA.

———. 1993. *Statistical Yearbook for Latin America and the Caribbean.* Santiago, Chile: ECLA.

Faber, Daniel. 1993. *Environment under Fire: Imperialism and the Ecological Crisis in Central America.* New York: Monthly Review Press.

Freudenberg, Nicholas, and Carol Steinsapir. 1992. "Not in Our Backyards: The Grassroots Environmental Movement." In *American Environmentalism: The U.S. Environmental Movement 1970–1990*, ed. Riley E. Dunlap and Angela G. Mertig, pp. 27–38. Philadelphia: Taylor and Francis.

Freudenberg, William R. 1990. "A 'Good Business Climate' as Bad Economic News?" *Society and Natural Resources* 3: 313–331.

Gelbard, Robert. 1992. "Environment for the Americas: 'No Country Will be Able to Enjoy Economic Prosperity without Protecting the Environment That All Countries Share." *U.S. Department of State Dispatch* 3 (February 24): 142.

Gereffi, Gary, and Miguel Korzeniewicz, eds. 1994. *Commodity Chains and Global Capitalism.* Westport, CT: Praeger.

Green, Duncan. 1991. *Faces of Latin America.* London: Latin America Bureau.

Grimes, Peter E., and J. Timmons Roberts. 1995. "Oscillations in Atmospheric Carbon Dioxide and Long Cycles of Production in the World Economy, 1790–1990." American Sociological Association annual meetings, August, Washington, DC.

Grimes, Peter E., J. Timmons Roberts, and Jodie Manale. 1993. "Social Roots of Environmental Damage: A World-Systems Analysis of Global Warming." American Sociological Association annual meetings, August, Miami, FL.

Gross, Anthony. 1990. "Amazonia in the Nineties: Sustainable Development or Another Decade of Destruction?" *Third World Quarterly* 12, 3 (July): 1–24.

Grossman, Gene M., and Alan B. Krueger. 1995. "Economic Growth and the Environment." *Quarterly Journal of Economics* 110 (May): 353–377.

Gunn, Philip. 1993. "The Tietê Project." Lecture at the University of São Paulo, June 14.

Hall, Bob. 1994. "Gold and Green: Can We Have Good Jobs and a Healthy Environment?" *Southern Exposure*, Fall, pp. 4–6.

Hajek, Ernest R., ed. 1991. *La situación ambiental en América Latina: Algunos estudios de casos.* Buenos Aires, Argentina: Centro Interdisciplinario de Estudios sobre Desarrollo Latinoamericano (CIEDLA).

Hecht, Susanna, and Alexander Cockburn. 1990. *The Fate of the Forest: Developers, Destroyers and Defenders of the Amazon.* New York: Harper Perennial.

Heller, Karen. 1993. "ISO 9000: Stepping-Stone on the Road to a Global Economy:

Environmental Standards Take Center Stage." *Chemical Week*, February 10, pp. 30–32.

Hochstetler, Kathryn. 1995. "Environmental and Popular Coalitions in Local Environmental Politics in Brazil and Venezuela." Latin American Studies Association 19th international congress, September 28–30, Washington, DC.

Inglehart, Ronald. 1995. "Political Support for Environmental Protection: Objective Problems and Subjective Values in 43 Societies." *PS: Political Science and Politics* 23, 1: 57–72.

Karliner, Joshua. 1994. "The Environment Industry Profiting from Pollution." *Ecologist* 24, 2: 59–63.

Kasa, Sjur. 1993. "Environmental Reforms in Brazilian Amazonia under Collor and Sarney: Explaining some Contrasts." Working paper. Center for International Climate and Energy Research-Oslo (CICERO).

Keck, Margaret E. 1995. "Parks, People and Power: The Shifting Terrain of Environmentalism." *NACLA Report on the Americas* 28, 5: 36–41.

Korzeniewicz, Roberto P., and William Martin. 1994. "The Global Distribution of Commodity Chains." In *Commodity Chains and Global Capitalism*, ed. Gary Gereffi and Miguel Korzeniewicz, pp. 67–92. Westport, CT: Praeger.

Landim, Leilah, ed. 1992. *Sem Fins Lucrativos: As Organizações Não-Governamentais no Brasil*. Rio de Janeiro: Instituto de Estudos da Religião.

Leff, Enrique. 1986. "Notas para un análisis sociológico de los movimientos ambientalistas." In *Politica ambiental y desarrollo: Un debate para América Latina*, ed. Marta Cárdenas, pp. 115–126. Bogotá: FESCOL/INDERENA.

Leonard, H. Jeffery. 1988. *Pollution and the Struggle for the World Product: Multinational Corporations, Environment, and International Comparative Advantage*. Cambridge: Cambridge University Press.

Linden-Paramaribo, Eugene. 1995. "Chain Saws Invade Eden." *Time*, August 29.

Low, Patrick, and Alexander Yeats. 1992. "Do 'Dirty' Industries Migrate?" In *International Trade and the Environment*, ed. Patrick Low, pp. 89–104. World Bank Discussion Papers. Washington, DC: International Bank for Reconstruction and Development/World Bank.

Maguire, Andrew, and Janet Welsh Brown. 1986. *Bordering on Trouble: Resources and Politics in Latin America*. Bethesda, MD: Adler and Adler.

Meyer, Stephen M. 1992. "Environmentalism and Economic Prosperity: Testing the Environmental Impact Hypothesis." Mimeo. Massachusetts Institute of Technology Project on Environmental Politics and Policy.

Miller, Marian A. L. 1995a. "Globalization and Interdependence: The Third World in the Evolution of Environmental Regimes." International Studies Association annual meetings, February 21–26, Chicago, IL.

———. 1995b. *The Third World in Global Environmental Politics*. Boulder, CO: Lynne Rienner.

Morrison, D. E., and Riley E. Dunlap. 1986. "Environmentalism and Elitism: A Conceptual and Empirical Analysis." *Environmental Management* 10: 581–589.

Movimento Ecológico Mater Natura. 1992. *Cadastro Nacional de Instituições Ambientalistas*. Curitiba, Brazil: World Wildlife Fund/Mater Natura.

Museum of Astronomy and Related Sciences/National Council for Scientific and Technological Development (MAST/CNPq). 1992. "What Brazilians Think of Ecology." Mimeo.

Ominami, Carlos. 1993. "International Trade and the Environment: A View from Chile." In *Difficult Liaison: Trade and the Environment in the Americas*, ed. Heraldo Muñoz and Robin Rosenberg, pp. 147–151. New Brunswick, NJ: Transaction.

Pearson, Charles S. 1987. "Environmental Standards, Industrial Relocation, and Pollution Havens." In *Multinational Corporations, Environment, and the Third World: Business Matters*, ed. Charles S. Pearson, pp. 113–128. Durham, NC: Duke University Press.

Portes, Alejandro, Manuel Castells, and Lauren A. Benton, eds. 1989. *The Informal Economy: Studies in Advanced and Less Developed Countries*. Baltimore: Johns Hopkins University Press.

Prell, Renae. 1995. "Class, Education and Cultural Perspectives of Mexican and Mayan Environmentalists in the Yucatan." Latin American Studies Association 19th international congress, September 28–30, Washington, DC.

Price, Marie. 1995. "Venezuela's Environmental Voices and Actors." Latin American Studies Association 19th international congress, September 28–30, Washington, DC.

Rainforest Action Network. 1995. "Brazil Backslides on Land Demarcation." *World Rainforest Report*, July–September (electronic edition).

Roberts, J. Timmons. 1992. "Forging Development, Fragmenting Labor: Subcontracting and Local Response in an Amazon Boomtown." PhD dissertation, Johns Hopkins University.

———. 1994. "Economic Crisis and Environmental Policy [Brazil]." *Hemisphere* 6, 1: 26–30.

———. 1996. "Predicting Participation in Environmental Treaties: A World-System Analysis." *Sociological Inquiry* 66, 1: 38–57.

Rubin, Debra K. 1994. "Firms Gear up to Think Globally, Link Locally, Focus on Environment." *Engineering News-Record* 232 (February 21): 42.

Rudel, Tom, and Jil Roper. 1994. "People, Roads, and Tropical Forests: Cross-National Patterns of Tropical Deforestation, 1975–1990." Paper presented at the annual meetings of the American Sociological Association, August 5–9, Los Angeles, CA.

Sanderson, Steven E. 1993. "International Trade, Natural Resources, and Conservation of the Environment in Latin America." In *Difficult Liaison: Trade and the Environment in the Americas*, ed. Heraldo Muñoz and Robin Rosenberg, pp. 53–78. New Brunswick, NJ: Transaction.

Serbin, Andrés, Antonio De Lisio, and Eduardo Ortiz. 1993. "The Environmental Impact of International Trade and Industry: Reflections on Latin America and the Caribbean." In *Difficult Liaison: Trade and the Environment in the Americas*, ed. Heraldo Muñoz and Robin Rosenberg, pp. 127–145. New Brunswick, NJ: Transaction.

Skole, David, and Compton Tucker. 1993. "Tropical Deforestation and Habitat Fragmentation in the Amazon: Satellite Data from 1978 to 1988." *Science* 260: 1905–1910.

Smith, David A. 1993. "Uneven Development and the Environment: Toward a World-System Perspective." Paper presented at the Korean Sociological Association International Conference on Environment and Development, November, Seoul.

Stern, Paul C., Oran R. Young, and Daniel Druckman, eds. 1992. *Global Environmental*

Change: Understanding the Human Dimensions. Washington, DC: National Academy Press.

Stevens, Candice. 1993. "Organization for Economic Cooperation and Development Framework for the Discussion of Trade and Environment Concerns." In *Difficult Liaison: Trade and the Environment in the Americas*, ed. Heraldo Muñoz and Robin Rosenberg, pp. 161–166. New Brunswick, NJ: Transaction.

Viola, Eduardo J. 1992. "O Movimento Ambientalista no Brasil (1979–1991): Da Denúncia e Conscientização Pública para a Institucionalização e o Desenvolvimento Sustentável." In *Ecologia, Ciência e Política*, ed. Mirian Goldenberg, pp. 49–75. Rio de Janeiro, Brazil: Editora Revan.

Wallerstein, Immanuel. 1974. *The Modern World-System I: Capitalist Agriculture and the Origins of the European World-economy in the Sixteenth Century*. Vol. 1. New York: Academic Press.

———. 1979. *The Capitalist World-Economy*. New York: Cambridge University Press.

Wilson, E. O. 1988. "The Current State of Biological Diversity." In *Biodiversity*, ed. E. O. Wilson, pp. 3–18. Washington, DC: National Academy Press.

Wolf, Eric R., and Edward C. Hansen. 1972. *The Human Condition in Latin America*. London: Oxford University Press.

World Bank. 1992. *World Development Report 1992*. New York: Oxford University Press.

World Health Organization (WHO) and United Nations Environment Program. 1992. *Urban Air Pollution in Megacities of the World*. Oxford, UK: Blackwell Reference.

World Resources Institute (WRI). 1994. *World Resources 1994–95*. New York: Oxford University Press.

World Wildlife Fund (WWF). 1990. *Atlas of the Environment*, ed. Geoffery Lean, Don Hinrichsen, and Adam Markham. New York: Prentice Hall Press.

11

Disorderly Democracy: Redefining Public Security in Latin America

A. Douglas Kincaid and Eduardo A. Gamarra

News reports from Latin America in the mid-1990s have brought word repeatedly of soldiers in the streets. Military units have been on patrol in the major cities of Honduras and El Salvador; the Bolivian army enforces a state of siege; Brazilian troops have occupied shantytowns in Rio de Janeiro; demonstrations and riots in the Dominican Republic have been suppressed by the army; and in Venezuela, the defense ministry has presented to the president a contingency plan for the military to take control of Caracas. Unlike in past decades, however, this activity has not been accompanied by coups and dictatorships. It is all at the initiative of elected civilian presidents rather than generals.

The policy arena of public security has been largely ignored or taken for granted in debates about contemporary challenges facing the national state. This applies to both the literature on national security, which is dominated by discussions of the transformations of sovereignty and international conflict in the post–Cold War era (e.g., Mandel, 1994), and analyses of global political economy, which are concerned with state roles and constraints amid increasingly transnational economic forces (Centeno, 1993; Evans, 1995). In part, this may stem from the perception that the maintenance of internal order is a core function under even the most minimalist concept of the state, and hence is not in question, while war making and economic functions are.

It is our contention, however, that these occurrences are not isolated events but rather form part of a regional pattern of state formation and government responses to what are perceived as crises of public security. One of the principal defining characteristics of this pattern is a recourse to military intervention in support, or in place, of normal police responsibilities. Such action, in and of itself, is neither unusual from a comparative international perspective, nor necessarily nefarious with respect to democratic norms. Much depends on the circumstances and conditions under which the decisions are made and policies are implemented. Here, we focus on three specific cases—Bolivia, Brazil, and Honduras—as a means to consider some of the consequences of these actions, with respect both to public security and to the processes of democratization now underway in Latin America. In our conclusion, we argue that these actions are suggestive of a new model of public security that is emerging in Latin America in response to world-systemic, international, and domestic pressures—a model with significant and unfavorable implications for the institutions and practices of democracy.

CONCEPTS OF SECURITY AND REGIONAL PATTERNS

The backdrop for this analysis is a region where police and military institutions and missions were closely intertwined during recent decades, especially under military authoritarian rule. This relationship has been changing since the return to elected civilian governments during the 1980s, a dynamic that is a necessary point of reference in our analysis of contemporary patterns.

First, however, the discussion may be enhanced by a delineation of some basic concepts of security and their relationship to police and military forces. While *security* is an extremely broad term that varies according to the qualities it denotes and the object to which the qualities apply, we focus here on security in terms of linkages between the state, society, and citizenry. From this standpoint, we may usefully distinguish between three types of security for which modern states typically assume primary responsibility. These are national defense, public security, and citizen security.

By national defense, we refer to the upholding of the sovereignty of the national state and territory against external threats, which usually, although not exclusively, emanate from other states. Public security refers to the maintenance of public order and the enforcement of laws. Citizen security, finally, concerns the guarantees of specific rights pertaining to citizens as such, including both civil and political rights. All three types of security, along with institutional responsibilities and jurisdictions, are usually spelled out in national constitutions and elaborated within legal frameworks.

Military and police forces are examples of state institutions that are specialized to address security needs. They are not the only agencies responsible for security, of course; court systems, intelligence agencies, and a number of other state actors are likely to play significant roles as well. The military and the police are of particular interest, however, in that their ranks are trained, organized, and authorized to employ physical force in defense of security. In Max Weber's terms, they share the state's monopoly of the legitimate use of coercive force. Thus, the rules and norms governing police and military actions—as well as their interactions—are especially important, and their subordination to elected civilian authority is one of the defining features of democratic political systems.

As a general rule, military forces are given the primary responsibility for

Figure 11.1
Basic Model of Police and Military Roles in the Modern State

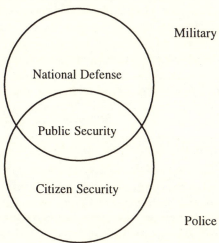

national defense, while police institutions are charged with upholding public security as well as, on a less exclusive basis, citizen security. Virtually everywhere in the world, however, the military are given some public-security functions as well—most commonly, the capacity to intervene to restore and maintain public order in case of conditions (such as large-scale riots or natural disasters) that surpass the limits of police capabilities. The typical domains of police and military institutions can thus be graphically portrayed as overlapping circles (see Figure 11.1).

Some further observations can be made concerning this division of labor. As one consequence, military and police institutions are likely to be characterized by fundamental differences of organization, doctrine, training, and deployment, among other traits. These differences bear strongly on the nature of their involvement in the realm of public security. There is an obvious potential conflict, even within the bounds of constitutionally sanctioned practices, between the maintenance of public order and the defense of citizen security. Indeed, some rights of citizens are defined as restrictions on what the state may legitimately do to them. Thus, police forces face a permanent tension in the enforcement of laws that may well represent competing collective and individual rationalities. By contrast, military forces charged with national defense and prepared for the conduct of war are necessarily centered on collective interests, and their entry into public-security functions is likely to be accompanied by the suspension or downgrading of some citizen rights.

This is an abstract portrayal of military and police institutions within modern states; in practice, there are wide variations between countries as to how these responsibilities are defined and how the boundaries of institutions are maintained (not to mention how the domains of state prerogatives and citizen rights are constitutionally provided for). As a whole, Latin America stands out in world comparisons for its history of close structural and functional linkages between the military and the police, albeit with important subregional and national variations (Bayley, 1993).

Under the authoritarian regimes that predominated in the region from the mid-1960s to the early 1980s, the reigning doctrine of national security centered on anticommunism led to more cross-national similarity than difference in these relationships. As military governments linked external defense to internal control and confrontation with domestic actors identified as enemies, police institutions and functions were increasingly subordinated to direct military control. In terms of the distinctions made in Figure 11.1, this pattern of development can be described as the militarization of the police and the recasting of public security missions as national defense, to the severe detriment of citizen security. In the wake of democratic transitions throughout the region since 1980, efforts to dislodge police institutions from military control have assumed great importance in the reform of civil-military relations (Kincaid and Gamarra, 1994). Latin American military leaders have been grudging in their acquiescence to these reforms, but the general pattern is one of substantial progress over the last decade toward the structural separation of police and military institutions.[1]

With regard to functional differentiation, however, there is a curious trend that seems to be running in the opposite direction. We can label this trend (a bit awkwardly, but symmetrically) the "policization" of the military, which involves increasing the public security functions of the armed forces. In the following sections of this chapter, we discuss three contemporary cases of military involvement in the public security arena.[2]

OPERATION RIO: THE WAR ON CRIME IN BRAZIL

On October 31, 1994, President Itamar Franco signed an emergency agreement with the governor of the state of Rio de Janeiro. The accord provided for the Brazilian military to oversee a joint command of police forces in the city of Rio de Janeiro, provide operational support to the police, and attempt to counter illegal drug and arms trafficking. This initiative was a response to increasingly vocal public frustration over what was perceived as a rising tide of crime and violence.

Murder in Rio had reached a rate of about 8,000 a year, and totaled 70,000 victims during the last decade. Illegal drug trafficking and drug-related crime seemed to be growing unchecked. The news was dominated by highly visible crimes, such as kidnappings of wealthy executives, youth gangs sweeping along the famous Rio beaches and robbing beachgoers en masse, and other gangs blockading the tunnels leading out of Rio during the afternoon rush hour and robbing commuters. Partly as a result, the city's important tourist economy suffered a disastrous drop, declining by 50 percent between 1989 and 1994, a period in which tourism revenues for Brazil as a whole were rising (Brooke, 1994).

Two aspects of the spiral of violence stood out in the dynamic leading to military intervention. One was the domination of a number of Rio's *favelas* (shantytowns) by organized criminal gangs, fueled primarily by illegal lotteries (the famous *jogo de bicho*) and, more recently and with much more nefarious consequences, narco-trafficking. The gangs increasingly were functioning as a parallel state, with local bosses (estimated to number some 300) controlling access to neighborhoods, regulating commerce, imposing curfews, and granting permission for candidates to campaign for public offices. This system rested on a combination of corruption and coercion—local police and public officials were paid off for their tolerance or active involvement, while rivalries, resistance, and disobedience were settled summarily and violently.

The other crucial element was a discredited police force, which had come to mirror the gangs in its tendencies toward corruption and violent action.[3] Brazil's police forces have long had a reputation for extralegal violence, which is in part a legacy of the military authoritarian period (Pinheiro, 1991). Brazil has two police systems that operate locally: a civilian police and a military police, both of which are organized at the state level. There is also a federal (national-level) police force, with primarily investigative responsibilities. In 1969, along with other measures to institutionalize authoritarian rule, the military police forces were placed under centralized army control and given major counterinsurgency and repressive responsibilities. Over the course of the 1970s, the military police gradually assumed a greater role in confronting common crime, evolving parallel capabilities with those of the civil police only with greater resources, and operating with the total impunity of the military justice system. By the 1980s, Brazil had become known for the application of "dirty war" practices—death squads, disappearances, and summary executions—to the control of common crime.

The adoption of a new constitution in 1988, following the return to civilian rule, marked a partial reform of police structures (Zaverucha, 1994). The military police remained part of the armed forces but were placed under the authority of civilian state governors, who also command the civil police forces. The military police's armaments, intelligence, and logistical support come from the army ministry; salaries are paid by the state governments. The civil and military police still constitute parallel organizations with overlapping functions of maintaining order, conducting investigations, serving arrest warrants, and so on.

President Franco had two options for bringing in the military to conduct police operations in Rio. One was to declare a "state of defense" (the Brazilian term for state of exception), under which the president could order a federal takeover of a state or local government for 30 days. This required the approval of the congress. The second option was to have the state governor request federal intervention for the restoration of public order, with the governor remaining in nominal control. With an election pending, and preferring not to suspend constitutional guarantees under his own responsibility, President Franco persuaded Rio's governor to request federal intervention. On November 1, Brazilian military commanders assumed responsibility for coordinating joint action among the local civil and military police, the federal police, and their own troops.[4]

Direct operations in the *favelas* began on November 19. The typical operation was for some 1,500 to 2,000 troops to cordon off a particular neighborhood, attempt to serve standing arrest warrants, search for drugs, and detain everyone who was not carrying identification. Controversy arose almost immediately, as complaints were filed with human rights groups over the soldiers' abusive treatment of those that were detained, as well as over the fact of detention itself, since carrying identification is not required under Brazilian law. Defending the actions of his forces, the army general in charge of "Operation Rio" said, "I recognize that some civil liberties have been restricted, but we are not a battalion of social workers. It is impossible to avoid excesses." A week after the operations began, a priest and a nun claimed to have witnessed soldiers torturing detainees, using electricity and near-drownings, in one *favela* operation. Following an investigation, the attorney general's office announced that it would seek prosecution of the soldiers involved ("Brazil," 1994: 2).

The operations went on periodically through December, and on January 3, 1995, newly inaugurated President Fernando Henrique Cardoso and Rio's new governor, Marcello Alencar, agreed to extend the military's authorization. The biggest operation of the entire campaign, involving 4,000 troops, was carried out during January 10–12, following an outbreak of fighting among rival gangs. When the authorization expired on February 1, the governor asked the military to withdraw but remain "on call" should further action be necessary. The call was not long in coming; in late March, following renewed violent clashes between police and gangs, Governor Alencar announced that he would be recalling the military to action at the beginning of April following consultation with President Cardoso.

"Operation Rio II" began on April 4 under the authority of the army and the state security council. Provisionally, military units were assigned to patrol major streets and points of access to the city, and to provide training for police in the use of military weapons. Raids on the shantytowns were ruled out except in backup support of police actions. On the same day the new military intervention was announced, armed gangs burned down a police station and robbed a bank.

As of mid-1995, there was little evidence that the introduction of military forces had proved an effective strategy in reducing the wave of violence in Rio. If anything, crime statistics suggested the opposite. After a temporary drop-off in November and December, the first two months of military action, Rio's homicide rate soared. The toll for the first three months of 1995 was 2,121 deaths, more than double the homicides reported for the same period in 1994 (Ellison, 1995; Latin American Newsletters, 1995). Police casualties for 1995 stood at

67 by mid-May. A few of the most wanted gang leaders were killed or captured, but drugs continued to be plentiful, and kidnappings and bank robberies also were reported on the rise.

Undaunted, Governor Alencar vowed to get tougher. In May, he appointed a retired army general, Nilton Cerqueira, as head of public security, a position giving him command of the combined Rio police forces and military backup. Cerqueira, a veteran of counterinsurgency operations who had been accused of torture by human rights groups during the military regime, ordered a new set of large-scale police incursions into the *favelas*, employing a "shoot first" policy (Ellison, 1995). Meanwhile, the governor announced plans to increase police armaments, including the acquisition of helicopter gunships. The war on crime in Rio seemed to be increasingly just that.

RECLAIMING THE STREETS: NEOLIBERAL AUSTERITY AND PUBLIC SECURITY IN BOLIVIA

Bolivia has a long and complex history of periodic attempts by the armed forces to subordinate the police under its command. These have generally been in the context of replacing or supplementing the role of the police forces in maintaining public order (Gamarra and Barrios, 1993). This pattern has taken many forms and cuts across regime types. The common feature, however, has been a recourse to states of exception (states of siege, as they are called in Bolivia), under which military units patrol city streets, carry out arrests, and generally enforce the law. Under military regimes, states of siege were declared primarily to deal with perceived threats from the left and organized labor. These actions were largely motivated by Cold War notions of national security, and the armed forces often took over all public security matters and relegated the police to a support capacity.

In the 13 years since the transition to democracy, the armed forces have been called on to break labor strikes, lift road blockades, and arrest striking union leaders. The common denominator has been worker resistance to the imposition of austerity measures. In the country's ten-year attempt to deepen structural reforms, Bolivia has become an extreme case of a society coping with the collateral effects of neoliberal adjustment.

Bolivia also stands out because of the proliferation of the coca-cocaine economy, which has led to civil unrest in the country's coca growing regions. Since the early 1980s, coca growers have organized, joined the principal labor confederation, and attempted to resist the imposition of coca-crop eradication programs. By joining forces with organized labor, peasant coca growers have also been the target of repression, especially under states of siege. While the phenomenon is primarily rural, the coca growers' marches have been defined as a public security problem when they have targeted the cities.

Significantly, every time the armed forces have been mobilized to control worker unrest, popular support for the government's actions was high among certain sectors. Two reasons account for this sentiment. First, the actions of striking workers generally disrupted life in the major cities. As strikes proliferated and the actions of workers grew more radical, popular support for them decreased, and cries for the reestablishment of order followed.

Typically, support for the measures of exception has been closely tied to social class identification. Members of the business sector, and the middle classes in general, have welcomed states of siege because they have enabled them to carry on their daily activities, while worker unrest disrupts business. In their view, striking workers constituted a public-security problem. For obvious reasons, support for strikers has generally been greater among those groups at the bottom of the socioeconomic scale, which have been most affected by the process of economic reform.

Support for austerity measures has been high because of what might be termed the *hyperinflation syndrome*.[5] This is a collective sense among the upper and middle classes that giving in to workers' demands or retreating from neoliberal programs could set off a new economic crisis. Demands for higher salaries have been characterized by successive governments as attempts to destroy the tenuous economic stability established in 1985.[6] This view has been widely accepted. In the remainder of this section we examine the dilemmas of public security and neoliberalism through one specific instance in which a democratically elected government launched a state of siege in order to deepen the process of market-oriented reform.

In April 1995, Bolivia faced a new general strike by the country's largest labor organization, the Confederación Obrera Boliviana (COB), as well as a teachers' strike over the government's educational policy, an incipient separatist movement from the southernmost department of Tarija, and a potential insurrection by coca-growing peasants in the Chapare Valley.[7] Responding to these pressures, President Gonzalo Sánchez de Lozada (the principal author of the Paz Estenssoro administration's 1985 stabilization plan) declared a state of siege on April 18, suspending all constitutional guarantees for a 90-day period. Shortly before midnight on April 18, the military and police arrested hundreds of union leaders and confined them to remote jungle and *altiplano* (highland) towns ("Estado de Sitio," 1995). These issues had paralyzed the Sánchez de Lozada government for six weeks prior to the enactment of the state of siege. Demanding that the government rescind an educational reform law that would ostensibly leave them unemployed, striking teachers erected roadblocks, threw dynamite sticks at police, and generally paralyzed life in the capital city. In the Chapare, coca growers' unions organized a movement to resist the government's attempts to enforce the coca-eradication program.[8] The COB, in turn, was in its thirteenth day of a general strike to protest low salaries and the government's refusal to give in to demands for higher levels of social spending. Finally, after staging a march with thousands of supporters, civic leaders in the city of Tarija threatened to secede from Bolivia unless the central government altered a decentralization law that would limit local government autonomy.

Throughout most of Bolivia, public opinion had little or no sympathy for the striking workers and teachers. Most Bolivians wondered if and when the government would take decisive action to end the strikes that prevented them from going to work or walking the streets without dodging tear gas, rubber bullets, and rocks. President Sánchez de Lozada's attempts at establishing a dialogue with the strikers—with the mediation of the Catholic Church—were seen mainly as a reflection of the government's weakness and indecisiveness.

On April 19, the day after the state of siege was declared, public opinion in general favored President Sánchez de Lozada's decision to mobilize the armed forces and arrest labor leaders. Media interviews with average citizens reflected a sense of relief and support for the reestablishment of order. Most did not question why the rules of exception had been implemented; instead, they wondered why the government had taken so long to react. A taxi driver captured this generalized sentiment and highlighted an all-too-common reaction throughout Latin America: "What we need is a Fujimori who will ensure, as in Peru, that authority is respected, put things in their place, and resolve the country's problems without political deals" ("Incertidumbre," 1995).

Predictably, the principal opposition political parties expressed their outrage at the imposition of a state of siege, alluding mainly to the threat to democracy and civil rights. The Catholic Church warned against human rights violations and underground union leaders announced clandestine resistance. If the past serves as a guide, then labor unions will be weakened temporarily, later to resurface to contest the process of neoliberalism that the government has promised to sustain for the rest of the century. The likelihood of greater unrest is high, however, as this is the first time that any government—military or civilian—has simultaneously targeted coca growers, unions, and civic committees. All three sectors have claims that will not disappear with repression.

President Sánchez de Lozada, in a speech at the military academy given a day after launching the measures of exception, stated that the role of the armed forces in a modern democracy was to sustain the legally constituted regime ("Incertidumbre," 1995). If this is a sign of things to come, then Bolivia can expect to require continued reliance on the military in order to enforce public security.

WHICH WAY TO THE BARRACKS? THE CASE OF HONDURAS

The evolution of police-military relations in Honduras presents an interesting counterpoint within the regional pattern (Kincaid and Juhn, 1994). On the one hand, under a lengthy period of military rule (1963–1980), police and military institutions were unified within the command structure of the armed forces. Nonetheless, after the return to civilian rule, both police and military forces exercised a more repressive role during the 1980s under civilian presidents than they had under the military regime of the preceding decade. This ambiguity of the Honduran transition process has persisted; in 1995, with civil-military relations undergoing their most fundamental reform in the last half-century, the most reform-minded of recent presidents, Carlos Roberto Reina, called the troops out to patrol the streets of Tegucigalpa and San Pedro Sula.

Following the coup that established military government in 1963, the National Police of Honduras were renamed the Special Security Corps and transferred from the Ministry of Government to the Ministry of Defense.[9] This shift reflected the military's determination to monopolize the state's coercive power and consolidate its autonomy with respect to civilian political interests. Twelve years later, in 1975, the formal subordination of the police to the military was strengthened under a new constitutive law of the Honduran military. Now called the Public Security Force (FUSEP), the police were made the fourth branch of the Honduran armed forces.

The Honduran version of the national security doctrine came late; it was implanted under a civilian president after the Honduran military had relinquished the executive office in 1980. Surrounded by the civil wars of El Salvador, Guatemala, and Nicaragua, and supported by both President Roberto Suazo Cordova and the Reagan administration, the Honduran military unleashed its own repressive model during the early 1980s. FUSEP was fully integrated into local counterinsurgency operations, despite the absence of a credible Honduran guerrilla movement. The National Directorate of Investigation (DNI), the investigative arm of the FUSEP, was responsible for more than 100 disappearances and deaths over the course of the decade. This was a small figure by Central American standards, but it was a sharp departure from prior Honduran practices.

During this period, for reasons related to the privileging of national security affairs over routine police work, public security was converted into a private commodity. Concerned over rising crime rates, a group of private-sector leaders requested that FUSEP provide their enterprises with security guard services in exchange for a payment covering the salaries of participating police agents and leaving a profit for the institution. The arrangement rapidly gained popularity and, by the 1990s, it had become a multimillion-dollar enterprise for the armed forces, into whose coffers the income went directly without passing through the national treasury. This dedication of active duty police agents to private interests has come under sharp criticism from other sectors of the population as public concern with FUSEP's inability to deal with crime has mounted.[10]

Toward the end of the 1980s, a number of civilian political leaders, supported by a variety of business, labor, and other social groups, began to call for the dissolution of the DNI and the creation of a new investigative police force, to be attached to the Ministry of Justice. With this proposal they sought two objectives. One was to strengthen the administration of justice system, which was seriously handicapped by the weak investigative capabilities of the DNI; the other was to eliminate the institution responsible for the worst abuses of citizen security during the authoritarian period.

The initial response of the military was to roundly reject any dilution of their control over the police, including the DNI. However, with peace accords putting an end to the conflicts in Nicaragua and El Salvador, and under strong pressure from the U.S. embassy (which reversed its policy of blind support during the 1980s), the Honduran military high command found itself on the defensive. In 1992, President Rafael Callejas named an ad hoc commission to study the situation of the DNI, and in March 1993, the commission reported back to the president, recommending that the DNI be immediately purged of corrupt and abusive officials and that preparations be made to turn its responsibilities over to civilian hands in the justice ministry.

In the course of this process, the attitude of the military high command shifted from open opposition to tacit acceptance—or, perhaps, tactical acceptance, as it was apparently motivated by the notion that the reform of the DNI might reduce pressure for more profound challenges to military prerogatives. In late 1993, President Callejas announced that a new cabinet-level entity, the Public Ministry, was to be created, and that it would control two new police entities, the Department of Criminal Investigations (DIC)—replacing the DNI—and the Counter-Narcotics Police, all under civilian control.

In January 1994, Carlos Roberto Reina was sworn in as president; as a candidate, he had promised to complete the restoration of civilian control over the military. With the support of the legislature, the president initiated efforts to do away with the military draft and pursue investigations to establish responsibility for the worst human rights abuses during the 1980s. In the midst of concessions that would have been virtually unthinkable only two or three years previously, the military high command acceded, in mid-1994, to the gradual separation, in principle, of FUSEP from the armed forces. In the latter decision, they may have been prodded by the idea of diverting toward civilian authorities a rising tide of public criticism over police inability to counteract increasingly violent criminal activity.

The DIC was finally inaugurated on January 23, 1995, after months of delays that seemed to indicate the lack of civilian preparedness to assume security functions previously carried out under military authority. On April 6 the Honduran legislature abolished the draft on a vote of 127 to 1; the measure was accompanied by a pay raise of 800 percent (from roughly US $5.50 to $77.00 monthly) to allow for a professional voluntary force. Later that month, the legislature began consideration of a constitutional reform bill for converting FUSEP back to a civilian-led National Police.

All this suggests substantial progress toward a more democratic model of police-military relations and public security. Against this measured pace of reform, however, the pressure to act more directly against violent crime has created a separate dynamic. In 1994, the FUSEP inaugurated a program of support for civilian "community watch" groups, with the objectives of forestalling crime and assisting the police. On April 3, 1995, one of the leading Honduran newspapers published an account of one such group in a town near San Pedro Sula. Calling themselves "Los Lobos," they wore masks, were armed with rifles and automatic weapons, and carried police communication equipment—with the mission of dispensing vigilante justice. Under pressure from the government's human rights commissioner, FUSEP commanders ordered the group disbanded, claiming that "Los Lobos" had no authorization to carry heavy weapons ("En proyecto," 1995; "FUSEP," 1995).

In February 1995, in another initiative addressed to the issue of crime, President Reina named the Archbishop of Tegucigalpa to head the nation's Ad Hoc Commission for the Prevention of Crime and Violence. In May the commission released its first report with a set of recommendations for short-term measures to confront rising crime rates ("Urge freno," 1995). Among the policy recommendations was congressional action to accelerate the separation of FUSEP from the armed forces, the creation of an externally administered emergency fund to improve FUSEP's operational capacity, and reforms to the penal code and judicial system. The commission also promised a second report that would analyze the root causes of crime and violence and propose long-term solutions.

During the same period, a different anticrime effort got underway. Prodded by the legislature, the president authorized the deployment of military forces to begin patrolling the country's major cities. In March and again in May, army troops were ordered into action on police patrol. Announcing the first deployment, the commander of the Honduran army said, "I have all the soldiers [available] in the streets and gradually they will be going out into the whole country. For each policeman, there will be five soldiers" (Reuter, 1995).

CONCLUSION

On the face of it, democracy in Latin America is a disorderly business. The demise of authoritarian military regimes and efforts to restore or create democratic political institutions have been accompanied by a widely perceived crisis of public security. One consequence of this situation has been that civilian presidents have felt compelled to assign military forces a major part in the response.

In the three cases we have described, the deployment of military forces in public security roles is of two types. One is to maintain public order under a state of constitutional exception (enacted in Bolivia and considered in Brazil), and the other is to combat crime and violence (enacted in Brazil and Honduras).[11] A first level of evaluation of these actions should be conducted in terms of intended effects.

Does the declaration of a state of exception and the deployment of troops bring about the restoration and maintenance of public order? In the short run it clearly does, in the absence of any force capable of directly challenging military force. This is a situation for which practically all states provide on an emergency basis. The question raised by the Bolivian experience (and perhaps reflected in Peru under Alberto Fujimori as well) is whether at some point, the exceptional will become the rule and the state of full constitutional guarantees will become the exception (Loveman, 1994). In such a case, the policy represents more a strategy of governance than one of emergency management.

Does assigning military units to support the police have an impact on crime and violence? The evidence here leads us to be skeptical. The deployment of military units on the streets has an obvious, immediate deterrent effect. It may also serve as a temporary arrangement to facilitate purging or reforming existing police institutions, or to create new ones. There is little evidence from the cases we have looked at, however, to suggest that the deterrence is more than temporary, and no reason to expect that military forces will be able to carry out any police functions beyond purely reactive and repressive ones. In Brazil, military intervention has failed to dismantle Rio's criminal gangs, which seem to have simply diversified their activities in adjustment to the military presence. In Honduras, where the recent wave of crime and violence has taken place while the police are still administered on a military model as a branch of the armed forces, there is even less room for optimism.

It should be emphasized that all the military interventions described in this chapter have taken place within legal, constitutional frameworks, and in response to the initiatives of elected civilian leaders. In a sense, these actions have demonstrated the achievement of the subordination of military institutions to civilian leadership, which is a key democratic tenet. In the current debates about security in the region, there is little evidence of any efforts to revive the military authoritarian models of the 1960s and 1970s.

Nonetheless, a serious threat is posed to democratic institutions by these policies. Both the recourse to states of exception and the deployment of troops to police the streets and chase criminals pose a deterioration of citizen security—of the enjoyment of basic political and civil rights. Moreover, in the characteristics of the cases we have described, we can discern the outlines of a new Latin American model of public security in the context of disorderly democracy. This model has three noteworthy features:

- a *militarization* of the provision of public security for large sectors of the population, wherein large-scale disorder is repressed but crime may well flourish, and where citizen security will be minimal;

- a simultaneous *informalization* of some public-security functions, whether provided in the form of paramilitary neighborhood groups, as have appeared in Honduras, or the "parallel state" of shantytown criminal organizations, as have sprung up in Rio; and

- a *privatization* of "public" security for those who can afford to pay for it, as a commodity to be directly purchased.[12]

To characterize these processes as a "Latin American model" is to assert both a significant generalization across a diverse array of countries and a particular causal pattern that has contributed to this outcome. We do not pretend to suggest that the militarization, informalization, and privatization of public security extend uniformly across the region, nor that all three elements will co-vary across cases.[13] We do contend, however, that these are related phenomena that are sufficiently widespread to warrant speaking of them as an emergent regional model.

There are two distinct causal explanations for the emergence of this model. One is that it represents an aspect of what Guillermo O'Donnell (1994) has called the "crisis of the state" in Latin America. By this, he referred to the contemporary interaction of neoliberal economic policies and the specific historical formations of states and political systems. From this perspective, the shrinking of the state, which is prescribed as part of the neoliberal orthodoxy by international financial institutions and embraced with varying degrees of enthusiasm by Latin American governments, undermines state capacities for extending the effectiveness of the rule of law in an equitable manner across both territory and social order. These constraints help to explain the set of government actions (and inactions) that constitute the new model of public security.

The second explanatory factor is the transnational economy of illegal drugs. This has been aptly described as a new, perverse form of integration into the world-economy for national and local economies and for social actors (Castells and Laserna, 1994). Much attention has been paid to the challenges to the state posed by the vast, unregulated flow of commodities and currencies across national boundaries. What is equally evident at this point is that the linked characteristics of illegality, high profitability, and violence create a continual political challenge as well, which is manifested in situations as diverse as those of Bolivian coca growers and Brazilian *favela* gangs.[14]

In sum, the dynamics of illegal drug trafficking interact with those of the weakened Latin American state to fuel the contemporary crisis of public security. Against this generally pessimistic scenario, some other trends and alternatives may be noted. Technical reforms, such as efforts to improve police professionalism in conformity with the rights of citizens, are underway in many countries throughout the region. These are unlikely, however, to alter the basic dynamics underlying the crisis we have described. In our view, more far-reaching changes are necessary to promote a more democratic model of public security.

One of the necessary changes will be to mitigate the popular toll exacted by neoliberal economic policies over the last decade. A number of governments have launched social emergency programs to deal with unemployment and declining standards of living. Deeper reforms to provide increased funding for social policies while maintaining adequate levels of growth may reduce unrest and minimize the deterioration of public security.[15] A second change concerns the nature of national and international law-enforcement efforts with respect to illegal drugs, and consideration of alternative options. While there are few positive trends to be cited in this regard, we would argue that policies oriented to demilitarizing efforts to cope with the transnational drug economy should be considered as a means to reducing the levels of violence associated with it.[16]

Without such bold initiatives, increasing disorder may prove the undoing of democracy in Latin America.

NOTES

This chapter draws extensively on research carried out with support from grants by the Heinz Endowment, North-South Center, Arias Foundation, and U.S. Institute of Peace, which, of course, bear no responsibility for the results. We thank Jairo Valverde for his assistance, and Bill Smith and Roberto Patricio Korzeniewicz for their helpful comments.

1. The most persistent structural ties between police and military appear to be in those countries where armed guerrilla movements remain active, as in Guatemala (Aguilera Peralta, 1993), Colombia (Leal, 1994), and Peru (Degregori and Rivera, 1993).

2. Data concerning these breaking events are drawn primarily from newspaper and wire-service reports and must be regarded with the usual caution. Our interpretations, however, are based on a regional comparative analysis grounded in a set of empirical case studies of police-military relations carried out under our direction in 1992–1993.

3. At the point when the troops were called in, military intelligence sources reported that 70 percent of the civil police and 20 percent of the military police were involved in criminal activities ("Brazil," 1994). A poll found that 58 percent of Rio residents agreed with the statement that police and criminals were the same "breed" (Harris, 1994).

4. The president's move met with widespread approval. Public opinion polls taken in Rio shortly after his decision showed more than 85 percent support for military action, and more than 50 percent in favor of direct military occupation of the *favelas* ("Brazil," 1994). The intervention was endorsed by then-presidential candidate Fernando Henrique Cardoso.

5. By *hyperinflationary syndrome* we refer to a pattern where recent memories of high levels of inflation legitimized profound structural adjustment measures despite their high social cost.

6. For an account of the 1985 stabilization program and societal responses, consult Gamarra (1994).

7. The Bolivian government faced a U.S. ultimatum that called either for the eradication of 1,750 hectares of coca leaf and the signing of an extradition treaty by June 30, 1995, or a suspension of all U.S. assistance. Using the ultimatum as an excuse, the government intensified the eradication campaign.

8. The prevailing policy that the armed forces should take a leadership role in the fight against narcotics only if the police were overrun by the traffickers was reversed by the launching of the state of siege. Under the emergency measures, troops moved into coca-growing regions and arrested the union leaders, including Evo Morales, the best known and most controversial of them.

9. Our account of police-military relations during the 1970s and 1980s is based on the work of Leticia Salomón (1994).

10. It was reported that in 1995, 6,000 police officers were being "rented" by private firms ("*Ejército*," 1995). Since this figure would encompass practically the entire national police force, it is no doubt exaggerated, but it does indicate the widespread nature of the practice.

11. We have also alluded to a third, related type of military action that concerns public

security: the military role in counter-narcotics efforts. This issue has been analyzed in more detail elsewhere; suffice it to say that the characteristics of military involvement in that sphere parallel those we have discussed here (Kincaid and Gamarra, 1994; Gamarra, forthcoming).

12. In this work we have focused almost exclusively on the first of these features, the use of military forces. Both the informalization of public security (reflecting, de facto, the absence or partial withdrawal of the state from particular zones) and privatization (in the form of private security firms mushrooming across Latin America), represent emergent phenomena that deserve serious attention.

13. It should also be obvious that we are not using the term *model* in a normative sense, as a set of behaviors to be emulated.

14. Thomson (1995) argued that undermining a state's capacity to enforce its laws constitutes a much more serious attack on the basis of national sovereignty than the reduction of the state's ability to regulate transnational economic activity.

15. For a discussion of how such programs may be implemented see Bresser, Maravall, and Przeworski (1994).

16. We have developed this argument in greater depth elsewhere (Gamarra, forthcoming). For contending views on this issue, see Bagley and Walker (1994).

REFERENCES

Aguilera Peralta, Gabriel. 1993. "Función policíaca y transición a la democracia: El Caso de Guatemala." Paper presented to the conference entitled, "Between Public Security and National Security: The Police and Civil-Military Relations in Latin America," October 21–22, Washington, DC.

Bagley, Bruce, and William O. Walker III, eds. 1994. *Drug Trafficking in the Americas.* New Brunswick, NJ: Transaction Publishers.

Bayley, David. 1993. "What's in a Uniform? A Comparative View of Police-Military Relations in Latin America." Paper presented to the conference entitled, "Between Public Security and National Security: The Police and Civil-Military Relations in Latin America," October 21–22, Washington, DC.

"Brazil: Controversy Explodes over Military Anti-Crime Operations in Rio Slums." 1994. *NotiSur: Latin American Political Affairs* (University of New Mexico), December 2.

Bresser, Luiz Carlos, José María Maravall, and Adam Przeworski. 1994. "Economic Reforms in New Democracies: A Social-Democratic Approach." In *Latin American Political Economy in the Age of Neoliberal Reform*, ed. William C. Smith, Carlos H. Acuña and Eduardo A. Gamarra, pp. 181–212. New Brunswick, NJ: Transaction Publishers.

Brooke, James. 1994. "Crime Reigns in the City Renowned for Romance." *New York Times*, October 25, p. A4.

Castells, Manuel, and Roberto Laserna. 1994. "The New Dependency: Technological Change and Socioeconomic Restructuring in Latin America." In *Comparative National Development: Society and Economy in the New Global Order*, ed. A. Douglas Kincaid and Alejandro Portes, pp. 57–83. Chapel Hill: University of North Carolina Press.

Centeno, Miguel. 1993. "The New Leviathan: The Dynamics and Limits of Technocracy." *Politics and Society* 22, 3: 307–336.

Degregori, Carlos I., and Carlos Rivera. 1993. "Peru 1980–1993: Fuerzas Armadas, subversión y democracia." Documento de Trabajo no. 53. Instituto de Estudios Peruanos, Lima, Peru.

"Ejército hondureño combate a delincuentes." 1995. *El Nuevo Herald* (Miami, FL), May 26, p. 1B.

Ellison, Katherine. 1995. "In Rio, All's Fair in Desperate War on Soaring Crime." *Miami Herald*, May 25, p. 22A.

"En proyecto: FUSEP a manos civiles." 1995. *Inforpress Centroamericana* (Guatemala), April 27, p. 15.

"Estado de Sitio: La punta de un ovillo." 1995. *Informe R.*, April 28, pp. 8–9.

Evans, Peter. 1995. *Embedded Autonomy: States and Industrial Transformation*. Princeton, NJ: Princeton University Press.

"FUSEP incapaz de controlar criminalidad." 1995. *Inforpress Centroamericana* (Guatemala), May 18, p. 13.

Gamarra, Eduardo. 1994. "Market-oriented Reforms and Democratization in Bolivia." In *A Precarious Balance: Democracy and Economic Reforms in Latin America*, ed. Joan Nelson, pp. 21–94. Washington DC: International Center for Economic Growth and Overseas Development Council.

———. Forthcoming. *Dictators, Democrats, and Drugs: A Brief History of U.S.-Bolivia Counternarcotics Policy*. Pittsburgh: University of Pittsburgh Press.

Gamarra, Eduardo, and Raúl Barrios. 1993. "Seguridad ciudadana y seguridad nacional: Relaciones policía-miltiares en Bolivia." Paper presented to the conference entitled, "Between Public Security and National Security: The Police and Civil-Military Relations in Latin America," October 21–22, Washington, DC.

Harris, Ron. 1994. "Brazil Orders Military to Combat Crime in Rio." *Los Angeles Times*, November 2, p. A1.

"Incertidumbre por estado de sitio en Bolivia." 1995. *El Nuevo Herald* (Miami, FL), April 20, p. 2B.

Kincaid, A. Douglas, and Eduardo Gamarra. 1994. "Police-Military Relations." In *Hemispheric Security in Transition: Adjusting to the Post 1995 Environment*, ed. L. Erik Kjonnerud, pp. 149–167. Washington, DC: National Defense University Press.

Kincaid, A. Douglas, and Tricia Juhn. 1994. "La seguridad pública en America Central: Perspectivas sobre las relaciones policía-militares." In *Los retos de la democracia*, ed. Leticia Salomón, pp. 33–56. Tegucigalpa Centro de Documentación de Honduras.

Latin American Newsletters. 1995. "New Security Chief Named by Alencar." *Latin American Regional Reports* (Brazil), June 8, p. 6.

Leal, Francisco. 1994. *El oficio de la guerra: La seguridad nacional en Colombia*. Bogotá: TM Editores.

Loveman, Brian. 1994. "Protected Democracies' and Military Guardianship: Political Transitions in Latin America, 1979–1993." Paper presented to the 18th international Congress of the Latin American Studies Association, March 10–12, Atlanta, GA.

Mandel, Robert. 1994. *The Changing Face of National Security: A Conceptual Analysis*. Westport, CT: Greenwood Press.

O'Donnell, Guillermo. 1994. "The State, Democratization, and Some Conceptual Problems." In *Latin American Political Economy in the Age of Neoliberal Reform:*

Theoretical and Comparative Perspectives for the 1990s, ed. William C. Smith, Carlos H. Acuña, and Eduardo A. Gamarra, pp. 157–180. New Brunswick, NJ: Transaction Publishers.

Pinheiro, Paulo Sérgio. 1991. "Police and Political Crisis: The Case of the Military Police." In *Vigilantism and the State in Modern Latin America: Essays on Extralegal Violence*, ed. Martha Huggins, pp. 167–188. New York: Praeger.

Reuter. 1995. "Honduran Troops to Combat Crime." Reuter News Service, Central and South America, March 20.

Salomón, Leticia. 1993. *Policias y militares en Honduras*. Tegucigalpa: Centro de Documentación de Honduras.

Thomson, Janice E. 1995. "State Sovereignty in International Relations: Bridging the Gap between Theory and Empirical Research." *International Studies Quarterly* 39, 2: 213–233.

"Urge freno a la violencia." 1995. *Inforpress Centroamericana* (Guatemala), June 8, pp. 4–5.

Zaverucha, Jorge. 1994. *Rumor de Sabres: Tutela Militar ou Controle Civil?* São Paulo, Brazil: Editora Atica.

## 12

Rebuilding State Capacity in Contemporary Latin America: The Politics of Taxation in Argentina and Mexico

Sergio Berensztein

During the 1980s and the early 1990s, Argentina and Mexico underwent a sweeping reformation of their public revenue systems, ultimately leading to the strengthening of both state capacity and enforcement mechanisms. The public's perceptions and attitudes toward taxation have changed dramatically. Under the previous tax system, compliance was considered foolish, and both firms and individuals tried to evade paying taxes as much as possible. In contrast, under the new system, as the tax base has been enlarged and enforcement mechanisms substantially improved, payment is now considered—at the very least—inevitable. Due to this institutional transformation, state capacity in both countries has been greatly improved.[1]

Historically, the two dominant approaches to the study of Latin American economic restructuring lead us either to encourage and embrace, or to expect and fear, the existence of a weak state. Neoliberalism asserts that since the market is the most efficient mechanism for allocating resources, economic reforms should aim to reduce state interventionism significantly and curtail most of its regulatory capabilities.[2] By the same token, excessively broad assessments of the impact of structural adjustment and/or ideologically driven, melancholic judgments opposing economic reforms argue that the reforms have been causing the destruction of the state and the dismantling of its vital institutions. Moreover, it is argued that a supposedly powerless state apparatus would not only be ineffective in checking the behavior of powerful private interests, but would also be incapable of avoiding "market failures." The new state, therefore, would ultimately provoke negative effects for economic development, social justice, and political stability.[3]

This Manichean debate surrounding neoliberalism precludes a theoretically more illuminating, empirically relevant, and politically crucial issue: *the actual institutional design of the states emerging from economic restructuring.* Such a focus allows us to move beyond this narrow debate and identify instead the specific kinds of state institutions that, in fact, are emerging in the wake of market-driven strategies of structural adjustment. Moreover, focusing on the nature and logic of institutional reforms, as well as on the emerging design of the state, clarifies the changing role of the state in an era of rapid globalization.

Many studies argue that due to the impact of financial liberalization, nation-states no longer have the state capacity or the resources to regulate their economy. Although this may indeed be the case with regard to capital flows and short-term portfolio investments, this chapter will show that the experiences of both Argentina and Mexico suggest that states still have an important role to play. They retain the ability to reform themselves and transform economic and political institutions, and therefore to affect economic and political outcomes. As always, local actors engage in the creation and refashioning of institutions in ways that change the distribution of political, symbolic, and material resources, even at times when the landscape in which these actors operate seems to be altered primarily by the shifting climate of an expanding global economy.

This chapter presents findings on the politics of taxation in Argentina and Mexico since 1982.[4] In both countries, the debt crisis triggered a long, complex, and conflictive process of deep fiscal reform regarding revenue and expenditure.[5] These reforms were implemented during the wave of stabilization and structural adjustment programs monitored by international financial institutions (IFIs) such as the International Monetary Fund (IMF) and the World Bank (International Monetary Fund, 1990; World Bank, 1991). The argument unfolds in three sections. First, I analyze the politics of taxation in both countries prior to the 1980s. Second, I focus on the emerging tax structure and analyze the material and symbolic transformations inherent in the emergent tax systems in both Argentina and Mexico. Finally, I address the spillover effects that the new tax systems may provoke and their implications for the emerging political matrices in both countries.

THE POLITICS OF TAXATION PRIOR TO THE 1980s

Before the wave of fiscal reforms that began in the 1980s, Argentina and Mexico (as well as many other Latin American countries) relied only partially on taxation as a way to extract resources from their societies; other means of collection, such as tariffs on imports and exports, foreign and domestic debt, and the inflationary tax, were considered to be politically less costly for governments than obtaining revenue through a workable, efficient tax system. Although there existed a myriad of taxes on income, sales, and property, very inefficient administrative procedures and enforcement mechanisms rendered taxation almost irrelevant. As was the case in many other sectors of the state apparatus, it became very easy for private interests to locate and take advantage of veto points through which to create and/or defend opportunities for rent seeking. Corruption was generalized, tax agencies and their personnel had extremely bad reputations, and many failed attempts to change this situation gave the impression that having a sound tax system was indeed an utopian dream.

Measures of tax collection as a proportion of GDP show the weakness of formal taxation in Argentina and Mexico (see Tables 12.1 and 12.2). However, revenue statistics tell only part of the story, as it is not only important to consider how much revenue a state can extract from its citizens and subjects, but also its methods of extraction. Indeed, the institutional framework that regulates taxation has profound consequences in terms of financial equilibrium, income redistribution, savings, investment, and economic growth (Steinmo, 1993). In Argentina and Mexico, the prevailing tax institutions operated in a vicious circle to create the wrong incentives for societal actors. The state proved to be weak, and therefore incapable of creating an efficient tax system, or even enforcing existing regulations. Thus, taxpayers found it both easy and safe to evade and/or elude their responsibilities. Although individually this was a rational act, the aggregate effect of such behaviors was suboptimal and very harmful for society, thus presenting a textbook case of a collective action problem.

Fragile public-finance structures caused macroeconomic instability and inflationary spirals, primarily in cases of external shocks. Subsequently, interest rates began to rise, making the financial cost of compliance much higher. Uncertainty and the expected drop in economic activity prompted cautious crisis-management strategies on the part of both firms and individuals. Both individuals and firms were, therefore, driven to evade their taxes in order to avoid liquidity and cash-flow problems. A lack of effective enforcement capabilities and the certainty of eventual tax "forgiveness" provided further incentives for such behavior. The only possible risk that a firm incurred was having its business inspected by revenue agents. This risk usually proved minimal, however, as corruption was rampant and businesspeople often found ways to "persuade" the tax agent to overlook the records. Since paying taxes was anything but a priority, firms and individuals allocated their money to safer, more profitable endeavors, such as the purchase of hard currency or speculation in the risky, but lucrative, domestic financial system. Bureaucrats and the rich and powerful members of society dominated this game, relegating the state and ordinary citizens to a secondary, and largely passive, role.

These complex and deficient tax systems were not merely consequences of poor implementation or faulty technical design; private actors also played a role as they found it possible to lobby in order to protect their interests in the context of "permeable" political regimes. Moreover, taxation was just one of the means through which private interests could create and perpetuate lucrative rent-seeking opportunities; other means included trade, financial, monetary, and social policies. Under the ideological umbrellas of nationalism, protectionism, infant industry arguments, and the like, both labor and capital utilized their political and economic power to mobilize public opinion as a tool to pursue their constituents' interests as well as protect their own corporatist privileges.

Problems such as improper institutional designs, administrative incapability, and poor enforcement mechanisms began to affect other areas of state involvement. As Cavarozzi (1991, 1992, 1994) has argued, since the 1980s, the more industrialized Latin American countries have been suffering a crisis of the state-centric economic and political matrix (SCM) that had emerged in the 1930s and 1940s. In this matrix, the state managed social conflicts by playing a major role as the agent of accumulation, redistribution, modernization, and incorporation of new social and political actors. A complex, and sometimes chaotic, web of economic and political institutions was established by the state and controlled by both the new and old political elites, depending on each country. The SCM remained basically unchanged under both authoritarian and democratic regimes. The matrix was able to survive as long as the state had sufficient political and economic resources to respond to domestic social demands as well as to changes in the international system (including external shocks). These resources included the capacity to finance expenditures through inflationary taxation, debt, and the improper use of public assets, funds, and savings earmarked for other purposes (e.g., the public retirement system in Argentina; oil-generated revenue in Mexico). Although the SCM began to display obvious signs of exhaustion by the mid-1970s, it was the 1982 debt crisis that delivered the final coup de grâce.[6] Until then, the SCM had proven quite resilient and resistant to change as entrenched groups and dominant actors managed to successfully reproduce their interests. In this type of inflationary environment, there was a concentration of income benefiting the wealthiest strata of the population, combined with a perverse transfer of resources away from fixed-income sectors (e.g., labor, retirees).[7]

Inflationary financing replaced taxation as a central tool for collecting revenues. Labyrinthine tax laws and inadequate enforcement mechanisms gave impetus to a vicious circle that, along with the debt crisis, eventually ended in dramatic fiscal disasters. In hindsight, not only did the state suffer the consequences of high inflation, but politicians and public-sector elites also helped to perpetuate it. As Olivera (1967) and Tanzi (1977, 1978) have demonstrated, lags in tax collection strongly influenced the level of real, inflation-adjusted levels of revenues due to the constant depreciation of the currency and the lack of sound mechanisms for indexation. In addition, the state's inability to improve tax administration was a key factor in reproducing its own weakness, especially due to the lack of effective enforcement and the ubiquity of unscrupulous inspectors. There were clear incentives for inspectors to behave in this particular manner, and for people to behave illegally, as well. Salaries were low, no one really supervised the inspectors' conduct of their duties, and consequently, the profession was altogether lacking in prestige.[8]

The state nourished this vicious circle, not only through its inflationary financing and inability to improve enforcement institutions, but also by engendering the personnel in charge of administering the perverse system: the certified public accountants (CPAs). CPAs played a crucial role in this game, which was not limited solely to the prosperous business of advising firms on the best way to evade taxes. The practice of "double-accounting" became very popular and quite sophisticated. Double-accounting meant having the administration of a business divided between "white" (or legal and taxable) activities and "black" activities, which violated the tax codes. In order to operate in this manner, a double financial system was needed, including banking accounts, stub books, receipts, and so forth.[9] In many cases, CPAs completely falsified the figures reported on tax returns.[10]

Until the 1980s, attempts to change this system failed repeatedly. Political and social actors involved in the tax process found it more convenient simply to leave the existing tax system in place, despite its inefficiency. Ruling elites, both authoritarian and democratic, seemed to prefer the inflationary tax to any other, more open and formal, revenue-collection strategy. If elites were obliged to change course and follow a different strategy, this usually meant the implementation of stabilization policies in the context of economic emergencies. These policies frequently failed, however, due to intense opposition from political and social actors. In any case, ruling elites transferred the costs of their revenue strategies to future generations, which was a logical decision in unstable political environments like the ones prevailing in Latin America. Attempts to organize a sound, efficient, and fair tax system were considered pointless, and in any case, were hardly appealing to those actors whose priorities were defined in terms of short-term goals and the pursuit of quick rewards.

Firms and individuals also preferred inflationary taxation because the alternatives were perceived to be more costly. As long as levels of inflation were not extremely high (i.e., no hyperinflation) and economic growth continued despite (and, to some extent, thanks to) inflation, there were weak or nonexistent incentives for economic agents to risk modifying their behavior. In fact, agents developed quite sophisticated strategies to deal with inflation (e.g., the indexation of contracts and other ingenious financial tricks), reducing the costs of operating in such environments. However, when inflation and macroeconomic instability spun completely out of control, all the sophisticated strategies proved to be ineffective, and the actors' preferences began to change. Until that point was reached, however, anti-inflationary policies were unpopular, preventing both democratic and authoritarian regimes from actively pursuing stabilization.

Since the onset of the debt crisis, the resulting (and unprecedented) fiscal crisis of the state completely altered the prevailing politico-economic scenarios in both Argentina and Mexico (Acuña, 1994; Heredia, 1994). During the 1980s, first in Mexico and then in Argentina, a new set of perceptions, values, options, constraints, and priorities gained momentum as inflation, for the first time in the contemporary history of both countries, came to be considered truly harmful to society.[11] Moreover, macroeconomic stability came to be recognized as a public good, and the steep social costs and political risks entailed were seen as simply the unavoidable price to be paid for achieving monetary stability. As fiscal responsibility became a crucial electoral issue, political elites, which had become separated from their previous ideological preferences, found themselves obliged to rebuild the state apparatus virtually from scratch. They started the rebuilding process by dismantling the most burdensome parts of the state apparatus (e.g., state-owned enterprises, industrial promotions schemes, and other subsidies, including, not only social spending, but also many subsidies benefiting the capitalists). This gargantuan task inevitably involved redefining—one is tempted to say "reinventing"—basic institutions such as tax agencies and the attendant tax legislation.

UNTOUCHABLES AND TERRORISTS

As a consequence of these neoliberal reforms, a very different situation now prevails in both Argentina and Mexico. A wave of tax reforms has dramatically affected people's attitudes about taxation. Former perceptions regarding the weakness of the state and, in particular, the lack of integrity of tax inspectors have quickly vanished. Changes in staff recruiting, training, wage policy and promotions have significantly bolstered inspectors' espirit de corps and modified their behavior. They have now developed a new group identity and a new loyalty to their agencies. Tax inspectors have become portrayed as crusaders of public finance, the shock troops of the modernization.[12]

Symbolic changes and mass media campaigns have helped to create a new sense of transparency and visibility for the countries' tax institutions. For instance, in Argentina the new headquarters of the national internal revenue service, the Dirección General Impositiva (DGI), is now located directly on the Plaza de Mayo, Buenos Aires's main square. (According to Spanish tradition, the headquarters of the most important institutions of society are to be located around the city's main square.) In addition to its new location, the DGI has acquired a new elite corps of inspectors and investigators that has become the special weapons and tactics (SWAT) team of tax enforcement. This group is commonly referred to as "the Untouchables," a name taken from the celebrated story about the Chicago mafia and the group of honest law enforcers led by Elliot Ness. The label itself is interesting, as it strongly suggests, not only a need for eternal vigilance, but the fact that Argentina, much like Chicago in the 1930s, is threatened by organized crime. This select group has developed a solid reputation in Argentina: it is now respected and even feared.

Tax agencies are struggling to further reduce evasion and identify the sectors of society still committing fraud and other crimes. Progress is indeed being made in both Argentina and Mexico. The traditional notions that taxation is not important, that inspectors can be easily bought, and that the tax administration is a mess have begun to disappear. As important as the increase in tax revenues generated through these changes is the fact that tax authorities and institutions are now very visible in society. The public has developed a new awareness of the tax burden, and realizing this, political parties and social actors are focusing on taxation as an electoral issue. The very idea that tax policy can become a hot electoral issue signals what may be the harbinger of an authentic revolution in the political culture of both countries.

Actual revenues generated by these reforms are of great importance. In Argentina, as Durán and Gómez Sabaini (1994) reported, tax collection increased 200 percent in real terms between the third quarter of 1991 and the fourth quarter of 1993. Table 12.1 reports that in less than three years, the deficit of the public sector (4.2 percent of GDP in 1989) turned into a surplus (0.3 percent of GDP in 1992). By 1992, total revenues reached a peak of 17.5 percent of GDP, the highest level in ten years.

Gil Díaz (1993) reported that in Mexico, the tax burden increased as much as 30 percent from 1988 to 1991, as tax revenues (excluding oil) grew from 9.3 percent of GDP in 1988 to 10.8 percent of GDP in 1991. During that period, the number of taxpayers increased 31.7 percent, primarily through the incorporation of members of the liberal professions, merchants, and service sector employees. Excluding employees and considering only these new "independent" taxpayers, the tax base grew an impressive 87.2 percent compared to the period prior to the reform (Gil Díaz, 1993).[13] Table 12.2 corroborates these findings and demonstrates that by 1991, not only was the deficit eliminated, surpluses were achieved.[14]

The omnipresence attained by the Argentine and Mexican tax agencies in recent years has been maintained primarily through media and mass-mailing campaigns, and of course, by the threat of stepped-up inspections. Tax agencies in both countries have even gone so far as to publish lists of firms and individuals that are under investigation and subject to prosecution for tax fraud. Although judicial processes are still very slow and extremely intricate, investigations have resulted in the incarceration of many tax dodgers, and numerous firms have been forced to pay their unpaid taxes. The aggressive policies of the Argentine and Mexican tax agencies have produced obvious results, although some people naturally complain that the "visible hand" of the tax collector has become too heavy and meddlesome.

Some critics argue that investigations are not carried out properly and that inspectors and tax agencies fail to correctly observe pertinent regulations. The states' "authoritative" procedures have, in many instances, become increasingly arbitrary and authoritarian in operation. There is clearly room for improvement in the new system, as numerous procedural flaws remain.[15] Despite the persistence of some degree of wrongdoing in the new system, however, the bottom line is that the strengthening of state institutions has prompted serious resistance from many of the affected sectors. For example, in 1989, following the enactment of new taxes in Mexico, powerful business associations publicly accused Francisco Gil Díaz, the civil servant then serving as the undersecretary of public finance, of "fiscal terrorism" because of his attempt to enforce the new legislation approved by Congress. Gil Díaz had drafted a new law that taxed firms' existing assets in such a way as to increase revenue, although the primary purpose was to verify the profitability of firms at a moment when many enterprises

Table 12.1
Argentina: Selected Macroeconomic Indicators

	1983	1984	1985	1986	1987	1988	1989	1990	1991	1992
% Growth of GDP	3.7	1.8	-6.6	7.3	2.3	-1.9	-6.2	0.1	8.9	8.7
Investment as % of GDP	-0.7	-3.4	-17.8	15.2	14.0	-2.0	-24.4	-9.9	25.1	30.9
% Annual inflation (CPI)	433.6	686.8	385.4	81.9	174.8	387.7	4,923.3	1,343.9	84.0	15.6
Total Revenues as % of GDP	12.1	12.2	16.8	15.6	14.7	13.1	14.0	13.4	15.4	17.5
Total Expenditures as % of GDP	22.3	18.1	20.4	19.5	20.8	17.8	16.9	15.3	17.4	19.1
Deficit as % of GDP	10.1	5.7	3.1	3.2	5.7	4.0	2.7	1.4	1.1	0.3
Tax burden as % of GDP	18.4	18.2	22.5	23.5	21.6	19.7	18.9	19.5	---	---
Tax revenue as % of total revenue	82.7	83.1	83.8	89.3	91.1	92.1	93.1	92.1	92.2	93.0
Non-tax revenue as % of total revenue	17.3	16.9	16.2	10.7	8.9	7.9	6.9	7.9	7.8	7.0
Direct taxes as % of GDP	1.3	0.9	1.4	1.6	1.7	1.8	1.2	1.0	1.1	1.5
The VAT as % of GDP	2.2	1.9	2.4	2.5	1.8	1.8	1.6	2.3	3.5	6.3

Note: VAT = value-added tax.
Sources: Inter-american Development Bank (1993); Duran and Sabaini (1994); Damill and Frenkel (1992).

Table 12.2
Mexico: Selected Macroeconomic Indicators

	1983	1984	1985	1986	1987	1988	1989	1990	1991	1992
% Growth of GDP	-4.2	3.6	2.6	-3.7	1.6	1.4	2.9	4.3	3.5	2.6
Investment as % of GDP	17.6	17.9	19.1	19.4	18.4	19.1	---	---	---	---
Annual Inflation (CPI)	80.8	59.2	63.7	105.7	159.2	51.7	19.7	30.0	19.6	10.5
Total Revenues as % of GDP	17.8	16.9	16.9	15.9	17.0	16.7	17.6	16.9	20.2	20.4
Total Expenditures as % of GDP	25.9	24.1	24.4	28.9	31.2	26.3	22.6	19.7	16.9	15.9
Deficit as % of GDP	8.2	7.2	7.6	13.0	14.2	9.6	5.0	2.8	-3.3	-4.5
Tax burden as % of GDP	20.1	19.1	19.1	17.5	17.8	21.5	---	---	---	---
Tax revenue as % of total revenue	57.4	61.0	60.5	70.4	62.9	72.2	67.5	67.2	57.5	58.9
Non-tax revenue as % of total revenue	42.6	39.0	39.5	29.6	37.1	27.8	32.5	32.8	42.5	41.1
Direct taxes as % of GDP	4.2	4.2	4.1	4.3	3.9	4.8	---	---	---	---
VAT as % of GDP	2.8	2.7	2.8	2.7	2.8	3.0	3.0	---	---	---

Sources: Inter-american Development Bank (1993); Carciofi et al. (1992).

were filing tax returns claiming bankruptcy. If a terrorist is defined as "one who favors or uses terror-inspiring methods of governing" (*The Concise Oxford Dictionary of Current English*, 1959: 1316), then it is understandable that business associations regarded the new legislation as "terror-inspiring." Gil Díaz was certainly breaking an accepted code that had been in place in Mexico for decades. More important, such "odd behavior" by a state functionary had obvious material consequences for those who were now obliged to honor their responsibility to pay taxes.

There is evidence that the informal "black" economy has shrunk significantly as enforcement capabilities have expanded, although informality and the resulting tax evasion still remain a significant problem in many large urban areas. The role of the CPA has also changed as a result of the new regulations. CPAs are now the key link between the state and the taxpayers, and are responsible for the communication of pertinent client information to the various tax agencies. In both Argentina and Mexico, taxpayer information must now be delivered on computer-readable forms, thus facilitating more rapid and accurate scrutiny. Moreover, in both countries, CPAs are now held legally responsible for the truthfulness of the information provided to authorities on behalf of their clients and could be forced to forfeit their licenses (or even be incarcerated) if fraud were to be proven.

In short, tax reform on the revenue side has generated new institutional arrangements by changing tax laws and enforcement mechanisms, enhancing revenue-collection agencies, and improving administrative procedures. Consequently, tax reforms must be understood as a part of an overall, and very ambitious, strategy aimed at the elimination of direct and indirect subsidies that have grossly protected large sectors of the economy. Though by no means through a smooth, linear process, successive tax reforms in both Argentina and Mexico ultimately led to: (1) the broadening of the tax base, thus incorporating large sectors that had previously been able to avoid paying taxes; (2) the reduction of the nominal tax burden for income taxes, the elimination of ineffective taxes, and the overall simplification (in relative terms, as it is claimed that the regulations can be further simplified) of administrative procedures for taxpayers; (3) the increased reliance on indirect taxation, namely, the value-added tax (VAT), as a crucial policy tool; and (4) the tightening of tax regulations, as well as improvement in the agencies in charge of collecting and overseeing taxation through the incorporation of up-to-date technology and new personnel, thus bringing about a substantial improvement of efficiency and capabilities in tax collection.

There are broader consequences of these reforms. First, tax reforms have helped achieve macroeconomic stability. They have drastically changed the allocation of the tax burden by incorporating people that have been traditionally out of the system, especially the middle-class sectors, professionals, and the self-employed. Second, by increasing revenues and reducing fiscal imbalances, these reforms have made a modest contribution toward greater equity by curbing the regressive distributional impact of the so-called "inflation tax."[16]

Third, taxation is currently an important electoral issue, and thus there is a novel concern regarding the allocation of resources by governments. There is not yet a "party of taxpayers" in Argentina and Mexico. The new awareness of fiscal questions may, however, prompt further changes in the electoral agenda and programmatic platforms of the political parties.[17] Finally, strengthening state capabilities in the area of taxation may eventually produce long-term "spillover" effects in upgrading state capacity in other important policy arenas (e.g., alleviating poverty, combating environmental degradation, promoting competition and antitrust regulation in the context of the privatization of public enterprises, etc.).[18]

TAX REFORM AND INSTITUTIONAL DESIGN

How was it possible to undertake such drastic reform of the tax institutions in Argentina and Mexico? Who was in charge of designing and implementing these significant policy changes? What were the roles of opposing groups and affected sectors? The findings reported in this chapter indicate that success in the implementation of the new tax strategies was an outcome of the prevailing structural economic crisis and the resulting transformation of societal preferences and strategies.

The economic crisis of the 1980s dramatically changed people's social preferences as macroeconomic stability became the major priority, even if this meant sacrificing (at least temporarily) well-entrenched symbols and ideological discourses concerning social justice, economic sovereignty, and political independence. The concomitant crisis of the SCM impeded the social and political actors associated with that matrix from articulating a sound and feasible alternative to neoliberalism. This was due to the impossibility of maintaining the state as a mobilizing mechanism and to the fact that atomized, individual strategies were substituted for collective ones as the legitimacy of those actors associated with the SCM was drastically reduced.[19] In addition to these factors, the debt crisis, the fiscal crisis of the state, and the need to bargain with private lenders all served to strengthen the role of the international financial institutions (IFIs) in Latin American societies. The new tax strategies in both Argentina and Mexico were very similar to the strategy advocated by the International Monetary Fund, the World Bank, and the Inter-American Development Bank. As the financial situations of both Argentina and Mexico continued to deteriorate, the international financial institutions capitalized on this opportunity to strongly influence domestic policy choices. The capacity of the IFIs to influence domestic economic policy has increased since 1982 due to crisis of the SCM and the myriad of societal and political changes that the crisis brought about. In sum, the change in domestic coalitions, societal preferences, state elites' strategies and capabilities, and the role of IFIs (all of which are closely related to the debt crisis and its aftermath) have combined to facilitate the transformation of tax institutions in Argentina and Mexico.[20]

However, the key players in reforming tax institutions have been state actors. Although the international financial institutions and other domestic actors have also been involved, a new breed of so-called "technopols"—comprised of the leading members of the "economic teams" and other new recruits to key posts in the executive branch—have largely displaced more traditional technocrats, who were affiliated with entrepreneurial interests or the political parties, and assumed a preeminent role in articulating the ideological discourse that attempts to legitimate the neoliberal revolution to citizens who are increasingly afflicted by plummeting living standards.[21] In evaluating the role of these technocrats, of course, it is important to consider that the presidency has been substantially reinforced under both Carlos Menem in Argentina and Carlos Salinas in Mexico. These stronger presidencies have facilitated the effective implementation of economic-restructuring policies, and particularly tax reform.[22]

Claiming that state capacity in Argentina and Mexico has increased is contradictory to both the neoclassical and the (more-or-less radical) neostructuralist paradigms.[23] Both these paradigms, their theoretical and normative differences notwithstanding, generally assert that the state should be, or will be, weakened in the process of neoliberal reform, and that there will be a tendency for markets to assume a more dominant role in the allocation of resources. However, due to tax reforms, in both Argentina and Mexico the state has increased its capacity and ability to extract and distribute resources. In addition, asserting that state actors have been the key players in reforming tax institutions challenges the argument that stabilization and structural reform packages (including tax reforms) were imposed by international financial agencies and creditors and that local actors lacked the capacity to decide how, when, and what to reform. Even though it is impossible to ignore the role of international actors, it is nevertheless the case that local actors, coalitions, and political processes (in other words, the political mechanisms behind economic reforms) are the dominant actors in the reform process.

As part of the policies of economic restructuring, a contingent coalition formed by incumbents, technocrats, private actors, and representatives of the international financial institutions both design, and participate in, the implementation of the tax reforms. This coalition may eventually experience internal struggle over particular issues, leading reformers to strengthen the tools that can dissuade real or potential adversaries and prevent less-than-enthusiastic members of the reform coalition from straying. For instance, the use of decrees, executive orders, and the threat of veto power of the executive can discipline the behavior of both supporters and opponents of reform. The core of the coalition ("the reformers") may also eventually employ some informal tools to secure compliance among its members.[24]

The tax reforms themselves can be used as a tool to encourage support for the larger neoliberal reform strategy, particularly among those sectors that had borne much of the tax burden under the previous revenue structure (i.e., high-income individuals, big local conglomerates, etc.). These sectors could conceivably have been targeted to increase the direct taxation of corporations and wealthy individuals. However, while direct taxes affecting these interests have risen slightly, current reforms have emphasized indirect taxation as the primary means to increase revenues. Moreover, by increasing the number of taxpayers and reducing the nominal burden, the reformers discouraged the development of opposing coalitions.

The experience of both Argentina and Mexico suggests that when dealing with potential opponents, reforming coalitions can also: (1) enlarge the tax base for both direct and indirect taxes; (2) expand the relative and absolute importance of the value-added tax; and (3) attempt to compensate the losers of the new scheme through enacting appropriate compensatory social policies directed toward the victims of reform or by hailing the positive consequences for the overall welfare of the citizenry of such general policy outcomes as price stability.[25] Consequently, even though specific private interests may eventually oppose particular policies (according to the particular actor's interests and relative political and economic resources), such partial opposition would not be likely to jeopardize the continuation of economic reforms. Finally, the particular dynamic of economic restructuring (i.e., its complexity, scope, and the lack of information about actual or probable consequences) helps to frustrate the emergence of coalitions espousing rival strategies.

The preceding explanation of reforming coalitions challenges a series of partial (and generally accepted) interpretations regarding particular aspects of economic restructuring. First, it is usually argued that uncertainty generates defensive strategies. However, my argument is that uncertainty, coupled with the positive initial results of restructuring policies, can help prevent defensive behaviors. Second, it is generally assumed that the reforming coalition is coherent and harmonious because its members share common interests in pursuing economic restructuring. My argument, however, is that the internal dynamics of the reforming coalition are seldom as melodious as is usually assumed. This is especially true for the so-called technocrats, a group that plays a crucial role in creating (and reinventing) incentives for the principal actors to help them persevere in their support of economic restructuring. In this sense, fiscal and monetary policies can also be interpreted as tools for reformers to use to keep the coalition together. In sum, the political engineering behind economic reforms is as important as the content itself of some policies and their apparent coherence (or lack thereof) vis-à-vis the overall economic strategy.[26]

CONCLUSION

How permanent are the recent policy and institutional reforms, including those affecting taxation, wrought by neoliberal restructuring in Latin America? Have the macroeconomic and political conditions that reduce uncertainty and allow actors to lengthen their time horizons become firmly institutionalized? At the macroeconomic level, if the permanence of recent transformations is not assured, speculative movements of internationally mobile capital in so-called emerging markets can challenge the efforts of states and international financial institutions, resulting in recessions and unstable political and economic scenarios. At a rather more microeconomic level, a rise of domestic or international interest rates could motivate a new surge of tax evasions.[27] After all, for taxpayers to continue complying with the law, their payoffs must not only exceed the costs of compliance, there must be certainty that in the medium to long term, no backsliding or return to the previous situation of free-riders and pervasive rent seekers will take place. Furthermore, given the fragility of the party systems in Latin America, the logic of electoral competition could eventually initiate a bidding war for taxpayer support; incumbents seeking reelection could find it electorally costly to attempt to sanction noncompliance behavior.[28]

Various ''routes to the past'' are possible, with predictably disastrous economic consequences and troubling implications for the consolidation and deepening of democratic institutions and practices. The story of tax reform remains open-ended; the course of future economic policy in both countries is also quite indeterminate. Moreover, it still remains to be seen whether the process of reconstructing state capacity will broaden beyond taxation to include other significant arenas of state policy. It is always logical—even imperative—to think of the possibility of a future tax reform, perhaps with a quite different orientation. These caveats notwithstanding, the transformations in Argentina and Mexico that were highlighted in this analysis lead to one certain conclusion: the script and the leading protagonists of the drama have changed. The Untouchables are now in town—and they are here to stay.

NOTES

1. By state capacity, I mean the state's ability to implement its own goals (including the creation and restructuring of political and social institutions) in the face of opposing societal actors and adverse macroeconomic conditions (Nordlinger, 1981; Skocpol, 1979; Knight, 1992).

2. Constrast Williamson's (1990) first statement of the ''Washington Consensus'' with his more recent position (1994), which is characterized by a greater recognition of the importance of state regulation and the strengthening of civil society.

3. As Acuña and Smith (1994) have maintained, this approach is certainly much less homogeneous. The main point that critics have in common is the rejection of neoclassical economic principles; principally, the idea that market mechanisms, by themselves, in the present international context are capable of promoting economic growth and development without state intervention (Borón, 1991; Evans, 1992; Fanelli et al., 1990; O'Donnell, 1992; Sunkel, 1993).

4. Haggard and Kaufman (1994) also recognized the strengthening of state capacity as a result of tax reform in the context of the instrumentation of neoliberal economic policies.

5. To have a more thorough understanding of this issue, considerations about the expenditure side must also be included. However, for the purpose of this chapter, I focus solely on the revenue side of fiscal reform, stressing especially those institutional and policy changes that led to the strengthening, thus leaving out other important problems such as the distributional and power consequences for different sectors (see the comments on this issue in note 23 below). For a further understanding of the politics of economic reform, see Haggard and Kaufman (1992), and Smith, Acuña, and Gamarra (1994a, 1994b). On taxation and tax reform, see Bird (1992); Carciofi et al. (1992); Durán and Gómez Sabaini (1994); Elizondo (1994, 1995); Gil Díaz (1993); Gillis (1989); and World Bank (1991).

6. See McCoy and Smith (1995) for an extension of Cavarozzi's discussion of the SCM to incorporate Venezuela's petro-state model of rentier capitalism.

7. Unions usually tried to get raises by renegotiating salaries after the official figure of inflation was released. However, it proved difficult for labor to get increases sufficient enough to counterbalance inflation. Moreover, the consumer price index (CPI) included a number of goods and services that did not necessarily correspond to what an average household actually consumed.

8. The social status of inspectors was as low as any other ordinary state employee for whom citizens had little respect. Working for the state was perceived to be synonymous with laziness and incompetence. Though this was a prejudice, people's daily experience justified this perception: any simple transaction at a public (not just a tax) agency or state enterprise required interminable waits in seemingly endless lines. Complicated procedures, proliferating regulations, and irrational instructions often turned objectively uncomplicated issues into inordinately time-consuming endeavors.

9. For instance, employees would receive part of their salaries "in white" (i.e., the minimum stipulated by the law) and part of them "in black" (i.e., a complementary and nontaxable amount). Therefore, contributions to social security would be calculated taking into consideration only the "white" part of the salary. Under this system, employees would get more money than they would if the system was just "white." Since the pension system was also mismanaged, workers had no incentive whatsoever to give more money to the pension system.

10. The regular procedure consisted of finding out how much money the owner of the firm (since they were primarily family businesses), or the financial manager, was willing to pay. Then, the equation was inverted. CPAs had to do their job in such a way as (a) to satisfy owners' greed (as they were ultimately the bosses) and/or make things compatible with the firm's overall double system and financial constraints; and (b) to avoid calling the attention of the tax collector by reporting tiny profits or figures inconsistent with previous years.

11. Before the 1980s, some efforts to modernize the tax structure were attempted in both Argentina and Mexico (as well as elsewhere in Latin America and other developing countries). However, as the core of the SCM remained very solid, achievements were only partial and generally proved ephemeral.

12. The notion of crusaders is not just allegorical. Carlos Tacchi, the current undersecretary of public revenue and the major actor involved in the new tax policy in Argentina, very recently stated in a celebrated TV show:

I owe God three very important things. I owe Him my own existence. He saved my son when he suffered a terrible accident riding a horse. And, third, He allowed me to continue living even though

I have cancer. For those reasons, I promise God just one thing: I'm going to exterminate people who evade taxes. I'm going to screw them all. ("Tiempo Nuevo," April 12, 1995)

13. For a further discussion of fiscal reform in Mexico, see Aspe Armella (1993); Bazdresch et al. (1993); López (1994); and Lustig (1992).

14. The financial collapse of late 1994 has, of course, seriously undermined macroeconomic stability and will make it difficult for the Zedillo government to sustain the progress of previous years.

15. For instance, since the wages of inspectors are partially related to the fines they collect, minor mistakes or technical violations might be used as an excuse to levy fines. Moreover, the complexity of the tax laws and other regulations may lead to misunderstandings as taxpayers and their CPAs, as well as inspectors, commit accidental mistakes. The only way to resolve these problems is by further simplifying regulations. In both countries, there is an emergent consensus in this regard.

16. Similarly, although indirect taxes have actually increased, effective enforcement mechanisms helped to eliminate another source of inequality: the transfer of resources from consumers to the owners of firms. Under the previous system, final prices included the value-added tax (VAT), so consumers did not have the opportunity to evade payment; in contrast, firms (especially smaller firms) commonly were able to evade payment of the VAT tax. Moreover, the evasion of the VAT (and the "black" economy in general), created further inequalities within sectors by helping inefficient firms to compete. In turn, this situation (in a closed economy) discouraged investment, technological innovation, and so forth. Finally, broad sectors of the upper-middle class in both Argentina and Mexico, and especially the "liberal professions" (physicians, lawyers, CPAs, dentists, etc.), which were previously beyond the reach of the tax collector, now pay taxes. In short, although indirect taxes (which impact workers and salaried employees disproportionately) have actually increased, the overall operation of the reformed tax systems have complex consequences that are ill-captured by such linear notions as "progressive" or "regressive."

17. The recent economic crisis in Mexico also allows us to evaluate how much taxation has changed in both countries. Thus, in the context of ambitious stabilization policies, both governments have relied heavily on the VAT as a tool to increase revenue. Mexico increased the VAT by 50 percent (from 10 percent to 15 percent), while Argentina increased it by 11.7 percent (from 18 percent to 21 percent). Had tax reforms in both countries not occurred, it would have been unthinkable for the governments to even consider the VAT as a useful instrument. The Chilean experience in the 1990s also suggests that the state could assume a reformulated, but still vital, role in social policy, and that taxation could become an appropriate tool, not only for funding new social programs, but also for achieving macroeconomic stability (i.e., as a tool for applying restrictive fiscal policies if inflationary trends are detected). See Berensztein (1994) for further analysis of these questions.

18. Although the process of state reform clearly still has a long way to go, some positive signs are already visible. Thus, in Mexico, migration agencies are learning from tax agencies' experience on how to improve administration, incorporate computer systems, train personnel, and so forth. In Argentina, the DGI is now in charge of the pension system, leading to a notable improvement in collection and operational efficiency.

19. The impacts of the collapse of the SCM on labor and capital are different, however. Indeed, the consequences of structural reforms within sectors are perhaps as im-

portant as those between them. In particular, the main divide seems to be between tradable and nontradable goods. Among the producers of nontradable goods, some sectors can better resist economic liberalization due to their capacity to obtain special protectionist policies (e.g., the auto industry). However, as a general rule, it could be argued that even though the emerging matrix seems to offer few opportunities for the exercise of veto powers compared to the SCM, capital obviously retains its ability to exercise market power, and particularly the capacity to determine the level of investment. Moreover, market power, and particularly control over the level of investment, is currently much more important than during the SCM era, as the public sector has been forced by the exigencies of fiscal equilibrium into a relatively passive role regarding investment.

20. For general arguments relating the role of external constraints and actors such as the IFIs to a shift in the direction of market-oriented strategies, see Stallings (1992) and Acuña and Smith (1994).

21. For an articulate defense of the "technopols," see the essays in Williamson (1994).

22. In both countries, strong executives have been a major attribute of their political systems, and democratic traditions have been fragile in Argentina and notoriously weak in Mexico. Therefore, although it is apparent that the concentration of power in the executive has had detrimental consequences for democracy, this should be interpreted as a continuity of prevailing features of their political systems and relations between the state and civil society, rather than as peculiarities specifically associated with recent neoliberal reforms. What is new, however, is the kind of tax policy that is being implemented. State actors are now strengthening tax institutions, which is indeed a sign of fundamental change.

23. It is worth noting that although some important contributions have already underscored the need to go beyond these simple notions (e.g., Acuña and Smith, 1994, and the other chapters in this volume), these paradigms still have a notable popularity.

24. For example, these measures can be used to threaten local producers with a further reduction of trade barriers, should prices increase, or to threaten local banks with tightened banking regulations, should administrative costs not be reduced.

25. Distributive considerations have prevented reformers from increasing the relative importance of the VAT as much (and as quickly) as they really wanted.

26. See Acuña and Smith (1994) for general arguments about "Hobbesian" strategies and the incentives shaping the response of different actors during the process of neoliberal restructuring.

27. In fact, the recent Mexican crisis and the "Tequila effect" in Argentina seem to corroborate this speculation, as tax collection has declined in nominal and real terms in both countries since December 20, 1994.

28. It is worth noting that in the long run, both Argentina and Mexico may have to reduce the tax burden, mainly for business. The rigidity of the current monetary policy in Argentina, for example, may make the level of taxation the only modifiable cost (at least in the short term) able to promote domestic activity and exports. In Mexico, as Reyes Heroles (1991) correctly argued, the current tax burden for business is very high if public goods obtained as a result of paying taxes are considered. As security, infrastructure, labor skills, and the like are very deficient, firms must provide those goods and services by themselves, thus increasing transaction costs. Finally, the wave of market-oriented reforms undergone by numerous other countries with so-called emergent markets may also influence the level of taxation in Argentina and Mexico. Thus, in an increasingly

competitive international environment, where both countries badly need inflows of foreign investment, the tax burden could become a variable that is adjusted in order to encourage direct foreign investment.

REFERENCES

Acuña, Carlos H. 1994. "Politics and Economics in the Argentina of the Nineties (Or Why the Future No Longer Is What It Used To Be)." In *Democracy, Markets, and Structural Reform in Latin America: Argentina, Bolivia, Brazil, Chile, and Mexico*, edited by William C. Smith, Carlos H. Acuña, and Eduardo A. Gamarra, pp. 31–74. New Brunswick, NJ: Transaction.

Acuña, Carlos H., and William C. Smith. 1994. "The Political Economy of Structural Adjustment: The Logic of Support and Opposition to Neoliberal Reform." In *Latin American Political Economy in the Age of Neoliberal Reform: Theoretical and Comparative Perspectives for the 1990s*, ed. William C. Smith, Carlos H. Acuña, and Eduardo A. Gamarra, pp. 17–66. New Brunswick, NJ: Transaction.

Aspe Armella, Pedro. 1993. *El camino mexicano de la transformación económica*. México, D.F.: Fondo de Cultura Económica.

Bazdresch, Carlos, et al. 1993. *Mexico: Auge, crisis y ajuste*. México, D.F.: El Trimestre Económico.

Berensztein, Sergio. 1994. "Política, economía y transición a la democracia en Chile." *Revista Internacional de Sociología* 7: 145–179.

Bird, Richard. 1992. "Tax Reform in Latin America: A Review of Some Recent Experiences." *Latin American Research Review* 27, 1: 7–36.

Borón, Atilio. 1991. *Memorias del capitalismo salvaje*. Buenos Aires: Imago Mundi.

Carciofi, Ricardo, et al. 1992. *"Reformas tributarias en América Latina: Revisión de algunas experiencias de la década del ochenta."* Buenos Aires: Comisión Económica para América Latina.

Cavarozzi, Marcelo. 1991. "Más allá de las transiciones a la democracia en América Latina." *Revista de Estudios Políticos* 74: 85–111.

———. 1992. "Paths of Democratization and State-Shrinking in South America." Overseas Development Council, Washington, DC. Mimeo.

———. 1994. "Politics: A Key for the Long Term in South America." In *Latin American Political Economy in the Age of Neoliberal Reform: Theoretical and Comparative Perspectives*, ed. William C. Smith, Carlos H. Acuña, and Eduardo A. Gamarra, pp. 127–156. New Brunswick, NJ: Transaction.

The Concise Oxford Dictionary of Current English. 1959. London: Oxford University Press.

Damill, José María, and Roberto Frenkel. 1992. "Reestructuración democrática y política económica: Argentina, 1984–1991." Centro de Estudios de Estado y Sociedad, Buenos Aires, Argentina. Mimeo.

Durán, Viviana, and Juan Carlos Gómez Sabaini. 1994. *Lecciones sobre reformas fiscales en Argentina 1990–1993*. Buenos Aires, Argentina: Organización de los Estados Americanos, Centro Interamericano de Tributación y Administración Financiera.

Elizondo, Carlos. 1994. "In Search of Revenue: Tax Reform in Mexico under the Administrations of Echeverría and Salinas." *Journal of Latin American Studies* 26, 1: 159–190.

————. 1995. "The Politics of Tax Reform in Latin America." México, D.F.: Centro de Investigación y Docencia Económicas. Mimeo.

Evans, Peter. 1992. "The State as Problem and Solution: Predation, Embedded Autonomy, and Structural Change." In *The Politics of Economic Adjustment: International Constraints, Distributive Conflicts, and the State*, ed. Stephan Haggard and Robert Kaufman, pp. 139–181. Princeton, NJ: Princeton University Press.

Evans, Peter, Dietrich Reuschemeyer, and Theda Skocpol, eds. 1985. *Bringing the State Back In*. Cambridge: Cambridge University Press.

Fanelli, José et al. 1990. *Growth and Structural Reform in Latin America. Where We Stand*. Documento CEDES 57. Buenos Aires: Centro de Estudios de Estado y Sociedad.

Gil Díaz, Francisco. 1993. *Análisis y evaluación de las reformas tributarias en México: 1980–1992*. Santiago: Comisión Económica para América Latina.

Gillis, Malcolm, ed. 1989. *Tax Reform in Developing Countries*. Durham, NC: Duke University Press.

Haggard, Stephan, and Robert Kaufman, eds. 1992. *The Politics of Economic Adjustment: International Constraints, Distributive Conflicts, and the State*. Princeton, NJ: Princeton University Press.

————. 1994. "The Challenges of Consolidation." *Journal of Democracy* 5, 4: 5–16.

Heredia, Blanca. 1994. "Making Economic Reform Politically Viable: The Mexican Experience." In *Democracy, Markets, and Structural Reform in Latin America: Argentina, Bolivia, Brazil, Chile, and Mexico*, ed. William C. Smith, Carlos H. Acuña, and Eduardo A. Gamarra, pp. 265–296. New Brunswick, NJ: Transaction.

Inter-American Development Bank (IDB). 1993. *Progreso económico y social en América Latina*. Washington, DC: Inter-American Development Bank.

International Monetary Fund (IMF). 1990. *"The IMF and Tax Reform."* Washington, DC: IMF, Fiscal Affairs Department.

Knight, Alan. 1992. *Institutions and Social Conflict*. Cambridge: Cambridge University Press.

López, Julio, ed. 1994. *México: La nueva macroeconomía*. México, D.F.: CEPNA and Nuevo Horizonte.

Lustig, Nora. 1992. *Mexico: The Remaking of an Economy*. Washington, DC: Brookings Institution.

McCoy, Jennifer, and William C. Smith. 1995. "The Challenge of Democratic Reequilibration in Venezuela: Theoretical and Comparative Perspectives." In *Venezuelan Democracy under Pressure*, ed. Jennifer McCoy, William C. Smith, Andrés Serbin, and Andrés Stambouli, pp. 237–284. New Brunswick, NJ: Transaction.

Nordlinger, Eric. 1981. *On the Autonomy of the Democratic State*: Cambridge: Harvard University Press.

O'Donnell, Guillermo. 1994. "The State, Democratization, and Some Conceptual Problems (A Latin American View with Glances at Some Post-Communist Countries)." In *Latin American Political Economy in the Age of Neoliberal Reform: Theoretical and Comparative Perspectives for the 1990s*, ed. William C. Smith, Carlos H. Acuña, and Eduardo A. Gamarra, pp. 157–180. New Brunswick, NJ: Transaction.

Olivera, Julio. 1967. "Money, Prices and Fiscal Lags: A Note on the Dynamics of Inflation." *Banca Nazionale del Lavoro Quarterly Review* 20: 258–267.

Reyes Heroles, José. 1991. "El sistema fiscal como determinante de la competitividad en el contexto del tratado trilateral de libre comercio." Paper presented to the conference entitled, "Integración Económica y Tributación." September 26, Guadalajara, Mexico.

Skocpol, Theda. 1979. *States and Social Revolutions: A Comparative Analysis of France, Russia, and China.* Cambridge: Cambridge University Press.

Smith, William C., Carlos H. Acuña, and Eduardo A. Gamarra, eds. 1994a. *Democracy, Markets, and Structural Reform in Latin America: Argentina, Bolivia, Brazil, Chile, and Mexico.* New Brunswick, NJ: Transaction.

————. 1994b. *Latin American Political Economy in the Age of Neoliberal Reform: Theoretical and Comparative Perspectives for the 1990s.* New Brunswick, NJ: Transaction.

Stallings, Barbara. 1992. "International Influence on Economic Policy: Debt, Stabilization, and Structural Reform." In *The Politics of Economic Adjustment: International Constraints, Distributive Conflicts, and the State,* ed. Stephan Haggard and Robert R. Kaufman, pp. 41–88. Princeton, NJ: Princeton University Press.

Steinmo, Sven. 1992. *Taxation and Democracy: Swedish, British and American Approaches to Financing in the Modern State.* New Haven, CT: Yale University Press.

Sunkel, Osvaldo, ed. 1993. *Development from Within: Toward a Neo-Structuralist Approach for Latin America.* Boulder, CO: Westview.

Tanzi, Vito. 1977. "Inflation, Lags in Collection, and the Real Value of Tax Revenue." International Monetary Fund (IMF) Staff Papers, vol. 24.

————. 1978. "Inflation, Real Tax Revenue and the Case for Inflationary Finance: Theory with an Application to Argentina." International Monetary Fund (IMF) Staff Papers, vol. 25.

Williamson, John, ed. 1990. *Latin American Adjustment. How Much Has Happened?* Washington, DC: Institute for International Economics.

————. 1994. *The Political Economy of Policy Reform.* Washington, DC: Institute for International Economics.

World Bank. 1991. *Lessons from Tax Reform: An Overview.* Washington, DC: World Bank.

## 13

Economic Dynamism and Institutional Rigidity in Chile: Risks and Opportunities at the Turn of the Twentieth Century

Alvaro Díaz

Shortly before the inauguration of the Frei administration (1964–1970), a distinguished Economic Commission on Latin America (ECLA) economist, Aníbal Pinto, pointed out that "the Chilean case has shown for quite a while relatively advanced forms of social organization and institutional forms that contrast with a relative absence of changes in its economic structure, a dissociation that has become wider during the last two decades" (1975: 246). From 1964 to 1990, that disparity compelled governments of the right, center, and left to implement radical political and structural reforms.

These reforms have managed to modify, from above, the fundamental contours of the nation. During the last twenty years, Chile's economy has experienced dramatic and profound transformations that irreversibly modified, not only its own structure, but also that of the country's fundamental underlying institutions. Indeed, the nature of private companies and economic groups, of markets, and of attendant networks in which business activities are coordinated, as well as the role of the state in the promotion of development, in regulation, in the field of social welfare, and in the provision of productive infrastructure, are all substantially different from twenty years ago (see, among others, Silva, 1992, 1993; Vergara, 1985; Valenzuela and Valenzuela, 1986).

Thirty years later, Chile is beginning to experience the inversion of Pinto's old asymmetry. With protectionist anti-oligarchic barriers out of the way, the Chilean economy is growing healthily within a context of considerable macroeconomic stability. Today, however, Chilean institutions that were shaped by almost two decades of authoritarian rule and preserved through the first half of the 1990s by virtue of a pacted transition exhibit signs of obsolescence, not only as pertains to democracy, but also in the prevalent socioeconomic institutional context (cf. Garretón and Espinoza, 1992; Garretón, 1994). In a country characterized by expanding opportunity, such an institutional rigidity is alarming. If not seriously tackled within the next five years, this rigidity may threaten Chile's economic development, and could even culminate in a new sociopolitical crisis.

Revisiting Pinto's argument from the early 1960s, the central hypothesis analyzed in this chapter is that there is a growing disparity between the liberalization of the Chilean economy and the continued rigidity of its socioeconomic and political institutions. This asymmetry is gradually generating persistent and worsening difficulties, that not only threaten economic expansion as the country has thus far experienced it, but also prevent the construction of a more democratic sociopolitical order capable of offering a better life for all Chileans. Within this context, I will discuss three models that permit a more sophisticated and generalizable analysis of the challenges posed by the globalization of the world-economy and internationalization of Latin American economies: an Asian Pacific model, a model of neoliberal restructuring, and a balanced model of export-oriented insertion in the world-economy.[1] Hence, although this chapter deals with the specific experience of Chile, its purpose is to use the Chilean experience to engage a larger debate on future development paths in Latin America.

ECONOMIC EXPANSION AND INSTITUTIONAL RIGIDITY

After a decade of continuous growth, it is important to assess the degree of development achieved by Chile's economy, since this constitutes the point of departure for determining the potential effects of the internationalization of trade and regional integration schemes, as well as the possibility of Chile's entrance into the North American Free Trade Area (NAFTA) or even broader free trade agreements. As Table 13.1 demonstrates, Chilean development has moved into a *second exporting phase* (SEP), characterized by five basic tendencies: (1) the diversification of a core nucleus of enterprises oriented toward exports (a core that is no longer merely confined to copper but now includes a greater variety of products and destination markets); (2) the growth of an industry of "industrially processed raw materials" (IPRMs), which are experiencing a notable technological improvement; (3) the unexpected growth of manufacturing exports (not based on national IPRMs), which increased seven-fold between 1987 and 1994; (4) the rise of service exports, which grew by twenty times over during the last decade; and (5) the significant increase of direct Chilean investment in neighboring countries (surpassing U.S. $2 billion in the case of Argentina).[2]

The "real" SEP is, in fact, much broader than was depicted by theorists in the late 1980s. It is not merely limited to the manufacturing area, nor does it imply a complete rupture with the traditional phase of export-led growth. On the one hand, it is clear that Chile will not cease to be an exporter of raw materials such as minerals and forestry products. On the other hand, the SEP favors the growth of nontraditional exports, including goods, services, and capital. It therefore makes more sense to compare Chile with Sweden, Finland,

Table 13.1
Chilean Goods and Service Exports, 1987–1994 (Millions of Dollars FOB)

Exports	1987	1990	1994	% variation 1987-1994
Raw Materials % Participation in X_t	$3,614 57%	$5,587 54%	$6,422 44%	8.6%
Processed Raw Materials % Participation in X_t	$1,410 22%	$2,167 21%	$3,815 26%	15.3%
Manufactures % Participation in X_t	$200 3%	$569 6%	$1,410 10%	32.2%
Services % Participation in X_t	$1,085 17%	$2,001 19%	$2,860 20%	14.9%
Total	$6,309	$10,323	$14,507	12.8%

FOB: Free on Board (Port of Shipment price).

X_t: Exports for year in question.

Source: Raw Data from Banco Central (Chile). Estimates for 1994 are preliminary. Methanol is included as an industrial commodity.

Denmark, and New Zealand—countries with intensive export capacity in regard to processed raw materials—than with Taiwan and South Korea. What is peculiar about Chile, however, is its highly segmented mode of international insertion: although exports of processed raw materials generally flow toward Asia, Europe, and the United States, manufactured goods and a large share of services are oriented toward other Latin American markets.

The consolidation of the SEP faces three major problems: the so-called Dutch syndrome, asymmetrical income distribution, and politico-institutional rigidity.

The *Dutch syndrome* entails a drop of real exchange rates—at least in the middle term—that results from the success of primary exports and influx of foreign investment (which in Chile's case is channeled chiefly into the mining sector). In addition, real salaries persistently tend to rise due to the tension created by a labor market that is segmented into tradable and nontradable sectors.[3] When combined, these tendencies may adversely affect the gains made by

Table 13.2
Household Participation in Income Distribution in Chile

	Lowest 40%	Middle 40%	Top 10%	Equity Lowest 40% Top 10%
Chile				
1968	13.7	35.4	34.4	0.40
1978 (a)	14.5	34.5	35.0	0.41
1988	13.4	30.8	41.9	0.32
1990	14.5	29.6	42.2	0.34
1993	15.1	31.0	40.0	0.38
Sweden	21.2	41.9	20.8	1.02
Japan	21.9	40.6	22.4	0.98
Germany	19.5	41.9	23.4	0.83
Spain	19.4	40.5	24.5	0.79
U.S.	15.7	42.4	25.0	0.63
Hong Kong	16.2	36.8	31.3	0.52
Singapore	15.0	36.0	33.5	0.45
Malaysia	13.9	35.5	34.8	0.40
Venezuela	14.3	36.3	33.2	0.43
Mexico	12.7	33.1	38.1	0.33
Brazil	7.0	25.7	51.3	0.14

Sources: All calculations by the author. Chilean data provided by the Instituto Nacional de Estadística. For other countries, see World Bank (1975–1993).

the manufacturing sector and the growth of spinoff industries and other production linkages. This has not yet occurred, which underscores the considerable amount of competitive resources enjoyed by this sector. However, it is far from clear whether it could withstand prolonged exposure to these tendencies. This vulnerability, coupled with the possible obsolescence of the system of promotion of nontraditional exports and the lack of effective safeguards against disloyal competition, suggests the possibility of a future involution of the SEP and a return to a more traditional export model based on primary products. This would, in turn, provoke a new wave of defensive rationalizations on the part of the industrial sector, a rise in unemployment, and the loss of previously accumulated exporting experience.

Asymmetrical income distribution is another problem of the SEP. Despite obvious improvements in the standard of living of its population, the data in Table 13.2 reveal that, in comparison with other countries, Chile has not experienced changes in its highly skewed income distribution between 1968 and 1993. Although income distribution improved slightly between 1988 and 1993, it is even more skewed than it was in 1968, when it was already significantly asymmetrical.[4] Indeed, Chile is far from attaining the income equity levels found in developed countries, even lagging behind the "Asian Tigers" (e.g., South Korea, Singapore, Hong Kong). Among late-developing economies, only Mexico and Brazil have more uneven income distribution structures.[5]

A cursory comparative reading of data from 1988 and 1993 could suggest that there is increasing income equity in Chile, with progress being slowed and conditioned by the economy's capacity to sustain high growth rates with low inflation. However, the evidence does not yet support this claim. For example, the Gini coefficient was 0.46 in 1991, 0.49 in 1992, and 0.47 in 1993, showing no clear tendency. Moreover, Chile's integration into global markets could stimulate combined expansion/decline cycles, which in the industrial and agricultural sectors would manifest themselves through a stagnation of employment levels, new rationalizations of firms, and even increased disparity between productivity and salaries.

There are institutional and structural variables that explain the persistence of a highly uneven income distribution. Institutional variables include the specific nature of factory regimes and the organization of work along Taylorist lines, the existence of unregulated labor markets, and the absence of "safety net" mechanisms designed to protect the temporarily unemployed. Most important, structural variables include a high degree of economic concentration (70 percent of exports are concentrated among eighteen large companies and trading firms).[6] Uneven income distribution is only one manifestation of the large power asymmetries present throughout Chilean society.

A final difficulty associated with the SEP involves *politico-institutional rigidity*. The politico-institutional model that emerged under the authoritarian aegis between 1975 and 1985 has not been significantly altered. Furthermore, there currently are no social and political conflicts on the horizon that might be capable of initiating an overhaul of existing institutional arrangements. A specific political regime, with a certain institutional configuration and specific compliance mechanisms, has taken root. Within this matrix, the rightist opposition defends the status quo and seeks to preserve a particular modernizing strategy, while the center-left political forces controlling the central government aim at modifying the existing order and instituting a different strategy. The center-left coalition government has the support of most of the population, although with the disadvantage that Chilean civil society is still largely silent and disorganized, expressing itself through relatively few public actors. Thus, the government has as its main reference the world of "public opinion," which is chiefly voiced through mass communications media that are almost overwhelmingly controlled by economic elites and conservative forces.

All attempts at reforming socioeconomic regulatory mechanisms invariably collide with a conservative senate in which the rightist opposition is over-represented as a result of a system designed in part during the previous military regime (including the appointment of "designated," nonelected senators and a cameral electoral scheme). As a consequence of these electoral arrangements, the postauthoritarian democratic governments have found it difficult to propose significant reforms and instead tend to move toward the adoption of policies that are "administrative" in nature, appearing resigned to operate within the context of a "frozen" political system whose features cannot be revamped.

There is thus a growing asymmetry in Chile between two great forces that are reshaping the country: on the one hand, internationalization and democratic transition, and on the other, the rigidity and obsolescence of the political and economic institutions inherited from the previous authoritarian regime and its neoliberal economic policies. This constitutes an inversion from the dissociation that characterized the country prior to 1973. That disparity led to radical attempts at transforming and modernizing the economic structure between 1964 and 1990, transformations that were carried out by governments of the center (Eduardo Frei Montalva from 1964 to 1970), the left (Salvador Allende between 1970 and 1973), and the right (the neoliberal dictatorship of General Augusto Pinochet from 1973 to 1990).

The contemporary asymmetry is very different, however. The Chilean economy is undoubtedly growing by leaps and bounds. This vertiginous growth is rapidly modifying the economic structure of the country. However, this growth contrasts with a noticeable lag in the evolution of socioeconomic institutions. If this rigidity continues unchanged, the Chilean state may be left powerless to confront the important challenges of the future.[7]

THE (APPARENT) SILENCE OF CIVIL SOCIETY

Chile is notable for the apparent silence and docility of its civil society, in stark contrast with countries such as Mexico, Brazil, and Argentina (Tironi and Lagos, 1991; Acuña and Smith, 1994; Smith and Acuña, 1994). True, Chile has clearly experienced greater improvements in the standard of living of millions of its citizens. Even though income concentration has not changed, the number living in poverty has declined. Salaries have risen, and formal employment has expanded. Chileans today consume much more than at any point in the past. Nevertheless, there remain considerable insecurity and dissatisfaction with working and living conditions. In this sense, the "silence" of civil society might seem a mere appearance, as civil society expresses itself in many ways, sometimes openly and at other times in a more veiled manner. However, regardless of the modes of these expressions, the current situation is in clear contrast with the first half of the 1980s, when large public protests against the dictatorship were commonplace. The current silence is not simply felt in the streets; it has also taken root at a cultural level. Chile has not become a more open society. Instead, it seems that conservative tendencies, and even an authoritarian culture, have become stronger and more deeply embedded.

Table 13.3
Social Destructuring and Restructuring in Chile, 1972–1992

Transformations in Occupational Structure (% of economically active population).	Year		
	1972	**1982**	**1992**
Unemployment	4.3%	19.6%	4.4%
Wage Earners	60.2%	39.2%	60.4%
Service Workers	50.9%	61.8%	51.5%
Informalization	22.9%	22.7%	25.1%
Emergency Employment	0.0%	11.0%	0.0%
Public Employment	12.0%	8.0%	6.0%

Source: Calculated by author using data supplied by the Ministerio de Planificación y Cooperación (MIDEPLAN).

The explanation for this silence can only be found in the analysis of the events of the last two decades. From 1972 to 1982, Chilean society was characterized by the disarticulation of the old social structure, the chief manifestations of which were a rise of unemployment, wage loss, growth of informal urban labor, an increase of spurious tertiary employment, and general impoverishment. Subsequently, from 1983 to 1993, a new social structure, which was distinguished by a rapid decrease of unemployment levels, wage increases, relative shrinkage of the informal sector, a decline of spurious tertiary employment coupled with the emergence of a new tertiary labor sector, and a general reduction of poverty levels (especially between 1988 and 1992), began to emerge. The changes have been well documented (Díaz, 1991); they are summarized on Table 13.3, which depicts the relevant peaks of the 1972–1982 period.

In 1982, at least 50 percent of Chilean workers were unemployed, subscribed to emergency employment programs, or were part of the informal sector. This proportion changed drastically ten years later, when only three out of ten Chilean workers operated under the same conditions. In short, the labor force grew from 3.8 million in 1982 to 4.8 million in 1992, but the number of unemployed or underemployed workers declined from 2 million to 1.5 million. In addition, salaries rose and informal unemployment rates fell, indicating the emergence of a new social structure.

The data in Table 13.3 can be interpreted in terms of a superimposed sequence of three distinct social cycles.[8] The first cycle was characterized by the erosion of the social structure associated with the import-substitution industrialization model, with an attendant increase in the social costs of authoritarian repression. During the second cycle, the social structure associated with neoliberal reform took form only to subsequently enter into a process of decomposition, leading to mass protests and the emergence of antisystemic social movements. Finally, the third cycle, which is now emerging, entails the consolidation of new social structures linked to the expansion of an export-based economy and is characterized by the ascendancy of systemic social actors that are more fully incorporated into production, the market, and institutionalized forms of political participation.

What is interesting about the Chilean case is that, in contrast with other Latin American cases (such as Mexico), it included two *successive* phases of social disarticulation and rearticulation.[9] Chileans suffered massively during the 1973–1983 period, but they also enjoyed the benefits of the post-1984 recovery, particularly after 1990. This entailed the transformation and recomposition of the social bases that gave rise to the urban protest movement of the first half of the 1980s. New social actors, which are still in process of constitutive maturation, emerged during this period of social transformation.

The combination of destructuring and restructuring features is a phenomenon that has only been clearly discernable since the early 1990s, when certain production areas (e.g., coal, textiles, and some others) underwent processes of reconversion. In Chile, however, there are sharp sectoral and regional inverse relationships linking the degree of social activism to the level of economic growth. Industries affected by recession or decline (and the geographic regions in which they are based) have better-organized social actors. In contrast, those sectors of production that are in a process of expansion have inchoate collective social actors that are still in process of formation.[10]

This asymmetry is common to a number of Latin American societies. It is a by-product of a style of capitalist modernization characterized by strong private appropriation of benefits coupled with a socialization of losses and other negative effects. One of the most serious consequences of this asymmetry is that it poses major obstacles to dialogue between progressive, center-left political elites that subscribe to a modernizing view of society, and the popular sectors, who feel the most negative effects of that type of modernization. The result is a cleavage that alienates political parties (especially those concerned with governing) from the representatives of the subaltern strata of civil society.

THE CHALLENGE OF INTERNATIONALIZATION

The Chilean government has frequently reiterated its goal of inserting the country into a variety of trade blocs as a strategy designed to consolidate the level of diversification and international insertion thus far achieved. This strategic goal is congruent with the features of Chile's already-diversified international trade structure. It is for this reason that, having abandoned unilateral liberalization, the Chilean government has placed its bets on free-trade agreements rather than customs unions. It is for the same reason that, having made considerable inroads in the area of bilateral treaties, it also bets simultaneously on the North American Free Trade Agreement (NAFTA) and MERCOSUR, the Common Market of the Southern Cone, without losing sight of the potential represented by the Asian Pacific Economic Community (APEC) and agreements with the European Union.

This free-trade discourse is not mere rhetoric. It reflects significant efforts made by various cabinet ministries (finance, foreign relations, and economy) along many trade fronts, with a clear emphasis of the ministry of finance on NAFTA, and of the ministry of foreign relations on MERCOSUR. This represents a shift from the 1990–1993 period, when all efforts centered on achieving Chile's entrance into NAFTA, to the detriment of trade agreements with neighboring countries. The current strategy aims at correcting the strategic error of underestimating the dynamism of MERCOSUR, a policy error that underscores the perils of institutional rigidity. The Chilean leadership simply did not have sufficient margins of flexibility at the time when MERCOSUR was created, which precluded Chile's alignment with that bloc at its inception.

Many analysts overestimate the advantages of the "strategic anchor" that membership in NAFTA presumably will provide, while ignoring the fact that South America is an important market for a large part of Chile's industry and important segments of its agricultural and service sectors. It is important to ensure that Chile does not blindly follow the model implemented by the former Spanish Prime Minister Felipe González, who was the first to devise a "strategic anchor" policy that relied on membership in the European Economic Community (EEC) as the key to the consolidation of Spain's democracy and the modernization of its market economy.

However, a harmonious integration of Chile into NAFTA and MERCOSUR (as well as other trade blocs) constitutes a strategy that can only succeed if and when either (1) the entire world-economy becomes fully integrated, or (2) the Americas become a free-trade area. Neither of these scenarios is likely in the immediate future. This has a number of consequences. First, it is important to acknowledge that there is strong tension between the NAFTA and MERCOSUR options, as the concessions that Chile could offer within the context of NAFTA are not the same it could offer to MERCOSUR.[11] Second, the Chilean government faces uncertainties that will be difficult to overcome, regardless of political will. It cannot prematurely place all its bets in favor of one treaty to the detriment of the other, because *both* strategic options offer advantages, and also because events are largely beyond its control. Third, the government faces negotiations along two fronts: one with international trade blocs, and the other with domestic actors and pressure groups that present increasingly insistent demands of a corporatist nature. Finally, the government risks becoming trapped between the pressure exerted by state institutions (given the sensitivity of the various cabinet ministries to sectoral pressures) and the fissures produced by the division of labor among the cabinet ministries (reflected by the preference of the Ministry of foreign relations for MERCOSUR and the Ministry of Finance for NAFTA, for example). Thus far, these pressures have not exceeded certain bounds. However, as the negotiations progress (or stagnate), new uncertainties and difficulties will render the elaboration of a coherent strategy increasingly problematic.

What will be the consequences of this next phase of economic restructuring? Several propositions can be advanced. First, every process of integration generates benefits and costs that inevitably are unevenly distributed geographically and by area of occupation. Second, although trade agreements focus on commercial exchanges, a synergy occurs with the integration of financial markets, which are much more integrated and difficult to regulate.[12] Third, all integration agreements have social consequences.

Taking these propositions into consideration, integration is likely to bring along changes that will be massive and traumatic. Even though Chile probably will be able to maintain an annual GDP growth rate of between 5 and 6 percent, the expansion of some economic areas will be counterbalanced by the deterioration of other industries, geographic regions, and social actors. We already have seen many examples of this. For example, while the telecommunications industry thrives, coal production declines and textile and shoe production are in a difficult process of reconversion. Such complex scenarios probably will become much more commonplace during the next few years. Likewise, following integration into NAFTA, MERCOSUR, and the new General Agreement on Tariffs and Trade (GATT) regime, it will be difficult for Chile to sustain the levels of economic growth and social welfare of the 1990–1994 period in the absence of significant institutional changes, including, for example, the establishment of unemployment insurance and a better worker-training system.[13] Finally, contemporary processes of economic integration tend to induce an export-oriented dynamic favoring large-scale industrial endeavors. Despite its immediate benefits, this dynamic will exacerbate environmental pollution and require significant investment and regulation to promote the recycling of industrial waste and protect the environment, while ensuring the quality of life of the population.

In sum, internationalization will further stimulate Chile's economy, but it will also generate new economic and social disequilibria. If the benefits of globalization are regressive and very unevenly distributed, globalization will exert a destabilizing influence. The presence of both winners and losers will not neutralize the ensuing conflicts, as some observers might erroneously imagine. To the contrary, social tensions may rise in direct proportion to the deepening of social differences associated with sequential phases of economic restructuring.

Compounding these problems, governability might become increasingly problematic. Several analysts have noted that, regardless of intent, trade policy is being built as a substitute for an industrial policy that is oriented to the promotion of specific sectors of production. Such an avenue appears attractive, as policy makers face many obstacles in attempting to design a development strategy but few in negotiating a free-trade accord. However, herein lies one of the most serious flaws of the current strategy. Trade negotiations will not emerge from a strategic plan designed and agreed on by domestic sectors. Rather, trade deals will result from an uncertain and complex bargaining process. Domestic and external pressures, as well as a combination of forces among blocs, may produce a relatively disorderly opening to the world-economy, increasing in the future the difficulties of governing.

One of the sources of consistency in any trade strategy is the transparency of the general development model, which should not be a rigid blueprint, but rather a flexible strategy that takes aim at clearly established objectives. Chile's development strategy is unclear and has not been designed consensually. Moreover, there are no signs that any relevant dialogue will take place anytime soon. If these trends continue, the current drive for integration increasingly runs the risk of undermining the benefits that have been thus far achieved.

THREE MODELS OF DEVELOPMENT AND INTERNATIONAL INSERTION

In view of the known positions espoused by Chilean political and intellectual elites, one can identify three alternative models to the SEP. Although many of their main components remain largely implicit, these models reflect current debates on the issues at hand. As depicted in Table 13.4, these models reflect different social interests, are expressed through divergent economic policies, and entail different state configurations.

The *Asian Route* (Model I) has as its point of reference the East Asian paradigm (Japan, South Korea, and Taiwan). It seeks to mobilize surpluses from the primary and tertiary sectors to assemble a large-scale export industry. This requires the presence of an active state with a "market-friendly" industrial policy promoting exports of relatively high technological content.

Even leaving aside cultural differences, it is debatable whether this model could be applied to Chile. First, the country is endowed with resources of a different nature. It has a small population and vast natural resources (the opposite is true in Japan and South Korea). Second, the powerful Asian states of the 1950s emerged from a historical reality quite different from that of Chile,

Table 13.4
Three Strategies to "Deepen" the Second Exporting Phase

Model	I: Asian Route	II: Neoliberal Route	III: Balanced Development
Principal Sectors	Secondary exporting sector transferring surpluses from the primary and tertiary sectors	Primary and tertiary, with adjustments to the manufacturing and agricultural sectors	Even development of the three sectors
Type of State	"Developmentalist" state of the East Asian variety	Neoliberal	New state geared to an export-led economy
Type of Economic Strategy	Industrial policy results in macro- and micro-level over-regulation	Increasing "self-regulation" of financial markets and trade liberalization	Macro- and micro-level regulation, with technological, infrastructure, education, and human development policies

where the postwar climate favored national unity and a strong state–private sector partnership. Finally, the present global and domestic historical context does not favor export-promotion policies, which require a powerful protectionist state.

The *Neoliberal Route* (Model II) seeks to maintain the growth of the primary exporting sector while favoring the service industry. In Chile, its advocates assume that the agricultural and secondary sectors are not competitive internationally because they require excessive subsidies from the state. They also assert that primary exports will regain importance in view of the volume of investment flowing toward the mining and forestry sectors. However, this analysis neglects the fact that agricultural and fishing exports are not going to grow at the rate of the 1980s. In addition, it assumes that the Dutch syndrome will not be a problem because it reduces the cost of imports and thus favors the consumer, thus overlooking its destructive effects on the industrial and agricultural sectors.

Last, but not least, the neoliberal model assumes—without proving it—that the Chilean financial sector will have sufficient competitive advantages to constitute a financial-services platform. Simply asserting that Chile can become another Switzerland or Panama is a risky venture, since there are no certainties, but only flexible specialization in some industrial and agricultural areas in international financial markets.

The neoliberal model considers NAFTA, APEC, and an accord with the European Union as the only reliable path of successful international insertion. It ascribes no importance to MERCOSUR. Since Chile has already entered the second exporting phase, however, the result could well be an involution of the secondary exporting sector and the return to primary sector specialization in exports. This could unleash a new wave of defensive industrial rationalizations, foster unemployment, and destroy accumulated exporting experience. The result would be an even more skewed pattern of income distribution.

The third option involves a *Balanced Model of Development* (Model III), which asserts that export-led development can be maintained by diversifying exports among the primary, secondary, and tertiary sectors.[14] This is the best path for achieving a more equitable and sustainable income distribution, while promoting the modernization of the country in a context of global integration. The goal is also feasible, since the second exporting phase has already been successful in inducing a relatively balanced development among the three exporting sectors thanks to economic policies that prevented rigid and excessive overspecialization.

To accomplish balanced, export-led development, envisioning the type of foreign trade that will be dominant during the next decade, it is necessary to replace the conventional concept of *intersectoral* export specialization for a greater emphasis on *intrasectoral* specialization. Chile's future does not lie in the exploitation of its primary-sector comparative advantages and the relegation of the rest of its economy under the headings "nontradable" or "import substitutes." The achievements of the 1990–1994 period suggest that Chile's future hinges instead on its ability to take advantage of comparative advantages that will vary across sectors and industries.[15]

A balanced development of Chilean exports of goods, services, and investment precludes either a pursuit of an "Asian route" (for example, efforts to increase manufactures until they reach 30 percent of all exports) or a return to a model of primary-sector export specialization. The alternative model would consolidate the level of primary exports that has already been achieved (between 10 and 15 percent), so as to ensure a growth rate similar to that enjoyed by the total of exports. This would facilitate the modernization of the industrial sector and encourage innovative efforts to capture competitive export niches.

CONCLUSION: BEYOND NEOLIBERAL RESTRUCTURING

Structural adjustment took place within neoliberal parameters in Mexico, Argentina, Chile, Colombia, and other Latin American countries. The relative strength and cohesion of the state was one of the most significant factors responsible for the degree of success achieved by neoliberal reform projects. The Chilean case offers important lessons in this respect. The experience of 1983–

1990 and the subsequent transformations show that the Chilean state had, and still has, a significant interventionist capacity. In fact, it is by virtue of this capability that the state was able to reorganize its economy during the authoritarian period. Perhaps never before had a Chilean state been so powerful in its reach. Far from a "minimalist" state, what existed during the 1973–1990 dictatorship was a strong, neoliberal interventionist state whose industrial and social policies were quite regressive but whose policies in the financial-fiscal sphere were very activist in seeking to control the most important macroeconomic variables. Even now, after most of the neoliberal project has been implemented, the state has by no means been dismantled, as it clearly continues to enjoy relatively wide margins of action.

Neoliberalism-as-discourse continues to be largely hegemonic in Chilean society. However, neoliberalism is largely spent as a force for transforming the society, economy, and polity, and it does not constitute a long-term option. The neoliberal model *has* been applied in its entirety, but Chile now is moving into a post-neoliberal phase, as the old model progressively recedes before the advance of the democratic transition and the emergence of new challenges that call for the opening of the national economy. This transformation is not unique to Chile; it is common throughout the hemisphere. The neoliberal phase is coming to an end in all of Latin America. Shortly, there will be no more state enterprises to privatize; unilateral economic liberalization has given way to negotiated arrangements. Moreover, deregulation and the dismantling of old legislation restricting markets and limiting the options of both management and labor are already nearing completion.

Chile, Mexico, and Argentina have already moved into the post-neoliberal period, albeit at different tempos and with varying consequences.[16] The most important privatizations have been completed, as has the deregulation of old market-control mechanisms. The most important factors now affecting these economies involve integration into the regional and global economies, which are processes that require new forms of action on the part of the state. The post-neoliberal state will need to be more proficient in the management of macroeconomic variables, since commercial integration exacerbates the financial and monetary exchange difficulties inherent in internationalization. New conditions also will demand more "market-friendly" industrial and technological policies that, nonetheless, will still entail a significant component of subsidies to firms and workers. What will be increasingly required is a state that is actively involved in the allocation of resources and performs a vital catalytic role in the economy. In fact, new forms of industrial policy are currently being designed and implemented, signaling an irreversible erosion of the old neoliberal orthodoxy and the imperative of combining growth with equity in the context of more democratic societies.

The neoliberal model of the past is proving increasingly inadequate to face the challenges of the future. The challenges imposed by the internationalization of the economy in the context of a democratic transition call for the creation of a new developmental state. This new state should be oriented toward developing markets and private enterprises, but it must also be capably engaged on educating, training, fostering technological advancement, regulating, and developing the country's infrastructure. A new basis of bargaining and compromise must be found between workers and entrepreneurs, as well as between peripheral regions and the core of the country. Moreover, a new welfare state must be constructed, which is circumscribed by current levels of fiscal discipline and firmly anchored on decentralized structures. This new system would at once stimulate private initiative and possess the effective regulatory capacity needed to ensure a reasonable level of flexibility in the productive sector without jeopardizing employment.

Modernization entails transformation. In the context of the increasing globalization of the world-economy and the dawning of a period of great changes, the strategic design of an open, export-led economy will not be viable except for a modern state geared toward achieving development, building domestic consensus in a climate of partnership and cooperation, and ensuring the welfare of the citizenry in a manner congruent with the realities of the new age. Ultimately, a modern, export-led economy cannot be sustained without a free civil society and a more representative and democratic political system.

NOTES

The author would like to thank Erick Bridoux for translating this chapter from Spanish, and Bill Smith and Roberto P. Korzeniewicz for their useful comments and editorial suggestions.

1. By *globalization* I refer to the sum of financial, commercial, cultural, and social processes that link Chile to ongoing transformations in the world-economy. By *internationalization* I mean the sum of decisions and strategic actions undertaken by governing elites to effect and regulate the economic liberalization. Although both terms seem to be synonymous, they operate in entirely different realms. Globalization is initially an exogenous and, later, endogenous process that accelerates, at various levels, certain changes that have been taking place for a number of centuries. Internationalization, for its part, is an endogenous process related to the actions of actors in a small, peripheral country such as Chile. These actors—state elites, national economic groups, transnational enterprises, and others—seek to channel the benefits of globalization, mitigate its more destructive and centrifugal effects, and obtain a more convenient place in the new international order.

2. It is interesting to note that this type of investment emerged entirely as a result of an industrial logic. It makes more sense for some Chilean companies to purchase and modernize Argentine companies than to attempt to double their capacity within Chile. The significance of these investments may *not* appear evident in examining Chile's trade balance but will be reflected in the capital ledger, and perhaps also in the balance of services (see Table 13.1).

3. Moreover, there is a possibility that countries such as Argentina and Brazil will attempt to resolve their balance-of-payments problems through currency devaluations (as in Mexico) or by erecting tariff or nontariff barriers. This would not affect the level of

raw material or industrial commodity exports but would alter the volume of manufactured exports to Latin America.

4. It is important to point out that the poorest 30 percent of the population increased its share of national income from 7.5 percent to 9.2 percent between 1988 and 1993. Nevertheless, this change is practically marginal and does not substantially modify the situation.

5. Of course, we are dealing with economies that are still undergoing structural adjustment, with considerable economic expansion a strong possibility.

6. These companies produce commodities in continuous- and semicontinuous-processing plants (celluloid, paper, fish meal, refined copper, etc.) that have high capital- and labor-intensive configurations. The economic viability of these ventures rests on the construction of "mega-projects," which can only be made possible through multinational enterprises, large domestic economic groups, or joint ventures capable of mobilizing resources and investments often exceeding a hundred million dollars.

7. Indeed, in less than a decade, certain export-promotion mechanisms (such as the system of simplified tax incentives for exports) will cease to exist in their present form and will have to be replaced by a new set of instruments to stimulate production and the diffusion of new technologies. The same is true for regulatory mechanisms (such as "antidumping" regulations), which will have to be adjusted to new GATT norms. Unless a new system of export promotion (based more on technology than direct subsidies) is crafted, Chile may be trapped in an institutional vacuum that will impede its ability to take advantage of opportunities and adequately face the challenges posed by increased integration into the global economy.

8. How are these structural changes related to transformations in collective social action? The hypothesis I advanced in a previous work is that the relative dynamism and/ or acquiescence of social actors between 1972 and 1992 can best be understood, at least in the first instance, from factors found in the sociopolitical sphere. However, the structural transformations *consolidated* a process that began as a radical project emerging from the sociopolitical arena. For example, the nature of resistance to the Pinochet dictatorship would have been different if it had proved possible to maintain employment in the key industrial sector at the same high levels characteristic of the previous decades of ISI. This did not occur, of course. The drastic decline of industrial employment between 1975 and 1980 shows that the cooptation of the labor movement was the result, not only of government repression, but also of something that went much deeper. The neoliberal reform and structural adjustment processes destroyed the social bases that had sustained the power of the labor unions and political parties of the left during the 1960s. Ten years later, in the same vein, the antigovernment resistance of 1985 would have been quite different had the economic crisis continued unabated, pushing unemployment upward and enhancing the importance of the informal sector—that is to say, propping up the social actors that were the main protagonists of the antiregime events. This, too, failed to take place. The economic recovery and resumption of growth slowly altered the social structure and diluted the social and cultural bases that had catalyzed the great mobilizations of 1983–1986.

9. See Díaz (1996) for a more complete theoretical elaboration of this argument. Torre's (1996) comments comparing the Mexican and Chilean cases argue in a similar vein.

10. For example, this situation contrasts with the case of the "new unionism" in the late 1970s in the São Paulo region, where this asymmetry was not present.

11. This is true especially as pertains to some agricultural and industrial sectors. This is precisely what Brazilian and Argentine negotiators protest, even though they agree to Chile's status as only an associate member (and therefore recognize that it should not be obligated to raise its tariffs, which are lower than those mandated by MERCOSUR rules).

12. Hence, judging by the recent Mexican financial collapse and its so-called "tequila effect" on the other regional economies, the problem is not merely one of exchange rate instability but also one of great sensitivity to short-term capital movement.

13. See Vergara (1990, 1994) for critiques of the limitations of labor market, social welfare, and human capital formation policies, which stress the element of continuity under democracy with the practices inherited from the Pinochet dictatorship.

14. This development strategy can ameliorate the effects of some tendencies (for example, declining exchange rates) without nullifying them in the long term.

15. The textile sector is an example of this. Between 1991 and 1994, textiles experienced a continuous process of industrial adjustment that reduced the number of firms and contracted employment. In fact, this sector no longer encompasses the entire production chain but rather now concentrates on segments such as commercialization, services, and the final assembly of knitted products. This translates into a significant increase of Chilean goods being exported, as well as of Chilean investment flowing to neighboring countries. The textile industry is by no means dying; it is simply adjusting and specializing in niche exports.

16. See Acuña and Smith (1994) and Smith and Acuña (1994) for a theorization of possible alternative future politico-economic scenarios envisioning different combinations of market-oriented reform, disarticulation and rearticulation of collective actors, and various modes of democratic consolidation. Chile, in their analysis, stands out as the most successful case of neoliberal reform, although its democratic transition is characterized as "incomplete" due to the authoritarian enclaves and institutional arrangements put in place under the previous military regime.

REFERENCES

Acuña, Carlos H., and William C. Smith. 1994. "The Political Economy of Structural Adjustment: The Logic of Support and Opposition to Neoliberal Reform." In *Latin American Political Economy in the Age of Neoliberal Reform: Theoretical and Comparative Perspectives for the 1990s*, ed. William C. Smith, Carlos H. Acuña, and Eduardo A. Gamarra, pp. 17–66. New Brunswick, NJ: Transaction.

Díaz, Alvaro. 1991. "Nuevas tendencias en la estructura social chilena (asalarización informal y pobreza en los ochenta." *Revista Proposiciones* 20 (August).

———. 1996. "New Tendencies toward Social and Economic Restructuring in Latin America." In *The Politics of Social Change and Economic Restructuring in Latin America*, ed. William C. Smith and Roberto P. Korzeniewicz. Boulder, CO, and London: Lynne Rienner.

Garretón, Manuel Antonio. 1994. "The Political Dimensions of Processes of Transformation in Chile." In *Democracy, Markets, and Structural Reform in Latin America: Argentina, Bolivia, Brazil, Chile, and Mexico*, ed. William C. Smith, Carlos H. Acuña, and Eduardo A. Gamarra, pp. 217–236. New Brunswick, NJ: Transaction.

Garretón, Manuel Antonio, and Malva Espinoza. 1992. "Reforma del Estado o cambio de la matriz socio-política?" *Estudios Sociales* 74.

Pinto, Aníbal. 1975. "Desarrollo económico y relaciones sociales en Chile." In *Inflación: Raíces estructurales.* México, D.F.: Fondo de Cultura Económica.

Silva, Eduardo. 1992. "The Political Economy of Chile's Transition to Democracy." In *The Struggle for Democracy in Chile, 1982–88,* ed. Paul Drake and Iván Jaksic. Lincoln: University of Nebraska Press.

———. 1993. "Capitalist Coalitions, the State, and Neoliberal Economic Restructuring in Chile, 1973–1988." *World Politics* 45, 4: 526–559.

Smith, William C., and Carlos H. Acuña. 1994. "Future Politico-Economic Scenarios for Latin America." In *Democracy, Markets, and Structural Reform in Latin America: Argentina, Bolivia, Brazil, Chile, and Mexico,* ed. William C. Smith, Carlos H. Acuña, and Eduardo A. Gamarra, pp. 1–28. New Brunswick, NJ: Transaction.

Tironi, Eugenio, and Ricardo Lagos. "Actores sociales y ajuste estructural." *Revista de la Cepal* 44 (November).

Torre, Juan Carlos. 1996. "The Politics of Transformation in Historical Perspective." In *The Politics of Social Change and Economic Restructuring in Latin America,* ed. William C. Smith and Roberto P. Korzeniewicz. Boulder, CO, and London: Lynne Rienner.

Valenzuela, Arturo, and Samuel Valenzuela, eds. 1986. *Military Rule in Chile: Dictatorship and Oppositions.* Baltimore, MD: Johns Hopkins University Press.

Vergara, Pilar. 1985. *Auge y caída del neoliberalismo en Chile.* Santiago: Facultad Latinoamericana de Ciencias Sociales.

———. 1990. *Políticas hacia la extrema pobreza en Chile.* Santiago: Facultad Latinoamericana de Ciencias Sociales.

———. 1994. "Market Economy, Social Welfare, and Democratization in Chile." In *Democracy, Markets, and Structural Reform in Latin America: Argentina, Bolivia, Brazil, Chile, and Mexico,* ed. William C. Smith, Carlos H. Acuña, and Eduardo A. Gamarra, pp. 237–262. New Brunswick, NJ: Transaction.

World Bank. Various years. *World Development Report.* Baltimore: Johns Hopkins University Press.

Zermeño, Sergio. 1991. "Desidentidad y desorden: México en la economía global y en el libre comercio." *Revista Mexicana de Sociología* 53, 2.

———. 1996. "State and Society in the Crisis of Dependent Neoliberalism: The Case of Mexico." In *The Politics of Social Change and Economic Restructuring in Latin America,* ed. William C. Smith and Roberto P. Korzeniewicz. Boulder, CO, and London: Lynne Rienner.

INDEX

About the Contributors

AMY E. BELLONE is a Ph.D. candidate in the interdisciplinary Latin American Studies program at Tulane University. Her major field of study is sociology, with minor fields in economics and political science. The main focus of her research is comparative urban development. Her dissertation fieldwork examines the impact of national policies, urban planning efforts, and trends in the world economy on individual households in Santa Cruz de la Sierra, Bolivia.

SERGIO BERENSZTEIN is a Ph.D. candidate in Political Science at the University of North Carolina, Chapel Hill. He is currently a Research Fellow at Centro de Investigación y Docencia Económicas (CIDE) in Mexico City. He has published articles on taxation and tax reform in Latin America in *Política y Gobierno* and *Revista Internacional de Sociología*.

ALVARO DÍAZ is a sociologist and economist. His professional and academic experience has been in Latin America (Chile, Costa Rica, Nicaragua, Argentina, and Brazil). He is currently Senior Research Associate at the Centro de Estudios Sociales SUR, Professor of Economic Sociology at the Universidad de Chile, and a consultant to the Economic Commission of Latin America and the Caribbean (ECLAC). Since 1991 he has been an advisor in the Chilean Ministry of Economics and is currently the executive director of the Program in Technological Development and Innovation coordinated by the Ministry of Economics.

EDUARDO A. GAMARRA is Associate Professor of Political Science and Acting Director of the Latin American and Caribbean Center at Florida International University. He is the author of *Dictators, Democrats, and Drugs: A Brief History of U.S.-Bolivian Counternarcotics Policy* (forthcoming), the coauthor of *Revo-*

lution and Reaction: Bolivia, 1964–1985 (1989), and the coeditor of *Latin American Political Economy in the Age of Neoliberal Reform* (1994) and *Democracy, Markets, and Structural Reform in Latin America* (1994). His current research interests focus on civil-military relations, legislatures and political parties, narcotics trafficking, and U.S.–Latin American relations.

JOSÉ ITZIGSOHN is Assistant Professor of Sociology at Brown University. He has recently published papers on remittances and development, grass-roots political participation, and urbanization in the Caribbean in *Social Forces, International Journal of Urban and Regional Research*, and *Latin American Research Review*. His current research focuses on the rise of ethnic economies in the United States and the informal economy in Latin America.

SUSANNE JONAS teaches Latin American and Latino Studies at the University of California, Santa Cruz. She is currently engaged in a major collaborative project on Salvadoran and Guatemalan immigrant/refugee communities in the Los Angeles and San Francisco Bay areas. Among her research interests and writing focuses are issues of structural change, immigration, and refugee policies of the United States and Mexico, and reconceptualizations of citizenship in the Americas. Her most recent books are *The Battle for Guatemala* (1991) and an edited volume, *Latin America Faces the 21st Century* (1994). She has published a recent article on peace negotiations in Guatemala in *Foreign Policy*.

A. DOUGLAS KINCAID is Associate Professor of Sociology and Research Director of the Latin American and Caribbean Center at Florida International University. He is the coeditor of several volumes, including *Americas: An Anthology* (1992) and *Comparative National Development: Society and Economy in the New Global Order* (1995). His articles on development theory, civil-military relations, and rural politics in Central America have appeared in several anthologies and in journals such as *Sociological Forum* and *Comparative Studies in Society and History*.

MIGUEL E. KORZENIEWICZ is Assistant Professor of Sociology at the University of New Mexico. He has published on emerging forms of economic organization in Latin America in several edited volumes and sociological journals. He is the coeditor of *Commodity Chains and Global Capitalism* (1994). His current research interests include postindustrial exports and corporate social responsibility on a global scale.

ROBERTO PATRICIO KORZENIEWICZ is Assistant Professor of Sociology at the University of Maryland in College Park. He is the coeditor of *The Politics of Social Change and Economic Restructuring in Latin America* (forthcoming), and his publications have appeared in *Sociological Forum, Latin American Research Review, Hispanic American Historical Review, Revista Mexicana de So-*

ciología, and the *Bulletin of Latin American Studies*. He is currently completing a book on labor, gender, and political identity in Argentina, 1886–1946.

LINDA MILLER MATTHEI is Assistant Professor of Sociology and Anthropology at East Texas State University, Commerce, Texas. Her research interests focus on gender and international labor migration, the political economy of the English-speaking Caribbean, and migration as a process of constructing transnational network building. Her article on gender and migration will appear in an upcoming issue of *Social Justice*.

BRUCE M. PODOBNIK is a Ph.D. candidate in Sociology at Johns Hopkins University. In addition to his continuing research on radical political movements in the periphery, he is working on a dissertation analyzing the energy foundations of the modern world-economy.

ALEJANDRO PORTES is Chair of Sociology and John Dewey Professor of Sociology and International Relations at Johns Hopkins University. His recent books include *Labor, Class, and the International System* (1981), *Latin Journey: Cuban and Mexican Immigrants in the United States* (1985), *Immigrant America: A Portrait* (1990), *City on the Edge: The Transformation of Miami* (1993), and several edited volumes, including *The Informal Economy: Studies in Advanced and Less Developed Countries* (1989) and *Comparative National Development: Society and Economy in the New Global Order* (1995).

J. TIMMONS ROBERTS is Assistant Professor of Sociology and Latin American Studies at Tulane University. His current research examines questions such as the value of world-system approaches in elucidating the social roots of environmental damage, the psychosocial effects of hazardous work, and the environmental initiatives of chemical industries in Latin America. His recent articles have appeared in *Sociological Inquiry, World Development, Economic Development and Cultural Change*, and *Social Problems*.

DAVID A. SMITH is Associate Professor of Sociology at the University of California, Irvine. He recently has published a series of articles on comparative urbanization and development, technology in the world-system, and network analysis of the global economy in *Urban Affairs Quarterly; Science, Technology, and Human Values*; and *Social Forces*. Among his ongoing research interests are studies mapping the world city system, tracing raw-material commodity chains, and examining Los Angeles as a global city.

WILLIAM C. SMITH is Professor of Political Science at the Graduate School of International Studies of University of Miami. He is the author of *Authoritarianism and the Crisis of the Argentine Political Economy* (1989) and the coeditor of several volumes, including *Latin American Political Economy in the Age of*

Neoliberal Reform (1994), *Democracy, Markets, and Structural Reform in Latin America* (1994), and *The Politics of Social Change and Economic Restructuring in Latin America* (forthcoming). His articles have appeared in journals such as *Revista Mexicana de Sociología, Desarrollo Económico, Dados, Journal of Interamerican Studies and World Affairs, Studies in Comparative International Development,* and *Political Power and Social Theory.*

DAVID SPENER is a postdoctoral research fellow with the Program in Border and Migration Studies of the Population Research Center of the University of Texas. As a sociologist, his main research interests include economic sociology, Latinos in the United States, and comparative international development. He is currently helping to direct a binational study of the effects of U.S.-Mexican economic integration on small businesses and labor markets in the Texas-Mexico transborder region. His doctoral dissertation, "Entrepreneurship and Small-Scale Enterprise in the Texas Border Region: A Sociocultural Perspective," was completed at the University of Texas in 1995.

Studies in the Political Economy of the World-System
(Formerly published as Political Economy of the World-System Annuals)

States versus Markets in the World-System
edited by Peter Evans, Dietrich Rueschemeyer, and Evelyne Huber Stephens

Crises in the Caribbean Basin: Past and Present
edited by Richard Tardanico

Rethinking the Nineteenth Century: Contradictions and Movements
edited by Francisco O. Ramirez

Racism, Sexism, and the World-System
edited by Joan Smith, Jane Collins, Terence K. Hopkins, and Akbar Muhammad

Revolution in the World-System
edited by Terry Boswell

War in the World-System
edited by Robert K. Schaeffer

Semiperipheral States in the World-Economy
edited by William G. Martin

Cities in the World-System
edited by Resat Kasaba

Pacific-Asia and the Future of the World-System
edited by Ravi Arvind Palat

Commodity Chains and Global Capitalism
edited by Gary Gereffi and Miguel Korzeniewicz

Food and Agrarian Orders in the World-Economy
edited by Philip McMichael

A New World Order?: Global Transformations in the Late Twentieth Century
edited by David A. Smith and József Böröcz

ISBN 0-313-29814-9

90000>

EAN

9 780313 298141

HARDCOVER BAR CODE